GOD'S PROPHETIC BLUEPRINT IN DANIEL & REVELATION

RON RHODES

HARVEST PROPHECY
AN IMPRINT OF HARVEST HOUSE PUBLISHERS

Other Scripture versions used are listed at the back of the book.

Italicized emphasis in Scripture quotations is added by the author.

Cover design by Bryce Williamson

Cover images © Cristian Mircea Balate, pamela_d_mcadams, freedom007, vicnt, CURAphotography, coka-coka, MAKSYM MALCEV, dima_zel, releon8211 / Getty Images; Jason Busa, Infinity T29 / Shutterstock; Allistair / People Images

Interior design by KUHN Design Group

For bulk, special sales, or ministry purchases, please call 1-800-547-8979.
Email: CustomerService@hhpbooks.com

God's Prophetic Blueprint in Daniel and Revelation
The content of this book is taken from *40 Days Through Daniel* and *40 Days Through Revelation* with updates and revisions.

Published by Harvest House Publishers
Eugene, Oregon 97408
www.harvesthousepublishers.com

ISBN 978-0-7369-9164-3 (pbk)
ISBN 978-0-7369-9165-0 (eBook)

Library of Congress Control Number: 2025936294

Printed in the United States of America

25 26 27 28 29 30 31 32 33 / LB / 10 9 8 7 6 5 4 3 2 1

To my beloved wife, Kerri

ACKNOWLEDGMENTS

After I became a Christian, I read one prophecy book after another. I could not get enough.

At the time, I seemed to gravitate toward prophecy books written by professors at Dallas Theological Seminary—especially John F. Walvoord, J. Dwight Pentecost, and Charles Ryrie. I found their books to be intelligently and persuasively written. Their words about the prophetic future, based on the Bible, resonated with me.

Little did I know then that in the not-too-distant future, I would actually enroll at Dallas Theological Seminary and take courses under these men, obtaining both a master of theology degree and a doctor of theology degree. As I now write about the prophetic books of Daniel and Revelation, I want to acknowledge my personal indebtedness to these godly teachers of the Word. Their work continues to bear fruit in my life.

I also want to offer continued praise and thanksgiving to God for the wonderful family He has blessed me with—my wife, Kerri, and my two grown children, David and Kylie. With each year that passes (*much too quickly!*), I grow in affection and appreciation for these three.

Thank You, Lord! I am grateful.

CONTENTS

40 DAYS THROUGH REVELATION

INTRODUCTION

THE PROPHETIC CONNECTION BETWEEN DANIEL AND REVELATION

The books of Daniel and Revelation occupy a distinctive place in the Bible as apocalyptic books. Both are filled with prophetic imagery and visions that offer profound insights into God's sovereign plan for humankind and the ultimate victory of good over evil.

Written during a time of great turmoil for the Jewish people, Daniel offered hope and guidance in the midst of their captivity in Babylon. Revelation, written by the apostle John, speaks to the early Christian communities under Roman oppression, offering a vision of hope and ultimate triumph. Although separated by centuries, these two books echo similar themes of divine sovereignty, judgment, and redemption.

Bible scholars have long recognized the value of studying these two books together. Each illuminates aspects of the other, deepening our understanding of the end times. Together, they offer a comprehensive and unified vision of what lies ahead.

It is no surprise that these books align because both are inspired by God, who does not contradict Himself (2 Peter 1:21). Jesus plays a central role in the prophecies of both books. Revelation is described as "the revelation of Jesus Christ" and concerns "things that must soon take place" (Revelation 1:1). Similarly, Jesus is central to the prophecies of Daniel (and the other biblical prophets). As noted in 1 Peter 1:10-11, "the prophets who prophesied" conveyed messages from "the Spirit of Christ in them."

Many, including myself, interpret 1 Peter 1:11 as a reference to Jesus Christ, while others understand "the Spirit of Christ" as the Holy Spirit. Both interpretations are valid. If "the Spirit of Christ" refers to the Holy Spirit, it's important to remember that the role of the Holy Spirit is to uphold and expound the teachings of Jesus Christ (John 14:26). Therefore, whether "the Spirit of Christ" refers to Jesus Himself or to the Holy Spirit, the prophetic messages given to Daniel and other prophets are fundamentally rooted in the teachings of Jesus, whether delivered directly by Him or through the Holy Spirit.

The prophecies of Jesus are trustworthy because He is omniscient—He knows everything. The apostle John observed that Jesus didn't need anyone to tell Him about people because He already knew their innermost thoughts (John 2:25). The disciples acknowledged, "Now we know that you know all things" (John 16:30). After His resurrection, when Jesus asked Peter three times if he loved Him, Peter replied, "Lord, you know everything; you know that I love you" (John 21:17). Jesus demonstrated His omniscience by knowing the exact location of fish in the water (Luke 5:4-6; John 21:6-11) and identifying the specific fish with a coin in its mouth (Matthew 17:27). He also has intimate knowledge of the Father, just as the Father knows Him (Matthew 11:27; John 7:29; 8:55; 10:15; 17:25). Because of Jesus' complete knowledge, we can have confidence in the prophecies that come from Him.

THE PERSPECTIVE OF CHURCH HISTORY

Since the early centuries of Christianity, the connection between Daniel and Revelation has captivated biblical interpreters. Here is a sampling of key historical figures who explored this relationship:[1]

- **Irenaeus (AD 130–202)**, in *Against Heresies*, drew parallels between the visions of Daniel and Revelation, especially concerning the antichrist and the end times.
- **Hippolytus (AD 170–235)**, in his *Commentary on Daniel* and *Treatise on Christ and the Antichrist*, was among the first to link these two books explicitly. He emphasized their complementary messages about the end times, linking the beasts and kingdoms of Daniel with the apocalyptic imagery of Revelation.

- **Jerome (AD 342–420)** wrote extensive biblical commentaries that reflected a deep engagement with Daniel and Revelation, using one to illuminate the other.
- In his commentary on Revelation, **Victorinus of Pettau (died AD 303)** frequently referred to Daniel, highlighting the intertwined nature of these prophetic visions.
- **Augustine (AD 354–430)**, in his magnum opus *The City of God*, took a more allegorical approach, interpreting Daniel and Revelation as depictions of the spiritual struggle between good and evil.
- In his commentary on Revelation, **Bede the Venerable (AD 672–735)** incorporated Daniel's insights and demonstrated their thematic connections.
- **Joachim of Fiore (AD 1135–1202)**, a medieval theologian, developed a theory of history heavily influenced by the apocalyptic visions of Daniel and Revelation, predicting an age of spiritual renewal.
- **Martin Luther (AD 1483–1546)**, a key figure in the Reformation, viewed Daniel and Revelation as prophetic critiques of the Roman Catholic Church, identifying the papacy as the antichrist.
- **Philip Melanchthon (AD 1497–1560)**, a close associate of Luther, explored Daniel and Revelation in his theological works, seeing them as offering insights into the church's struggle and eventual triumph over its adversaries.
- **John Knox (AD 1514–1572)**, a Scottish reformer, believed that Daniel and Revelation contained prophecies about the church's struggle with the antichrist, which he identified with the Roman Catholic papacy.
- **Jonathan Edwards (AD 1703–1758)**, an American theologian, wrote extensively, including on eschatology. He referred to Daniel and Revelation to discuss the end times and the second coming of Christ.

The tradition of studying Daniel and Revelation in parallel spans the history of the church. As countless scholars and theologians have discovered, studying these two scriptural books together offers profound spiritual insights. We, too, can expect great rewards as we explore their intertwined messages.

YOU CAN TRUST DANIEL AND JOHN

You can trust Daniel and John (the author of Revelation) because Jesus Himself validated both. In Matthew 24:15-16, Jesus spoke prophetically to His disciples: "When you see the abomination of desolation spoken of by the prophet Daniel, standing in the holy place (let the reader understand), then let those who are in Judea flee to the mountains." Here, Jesus confirms Daniel as a true and trustworthy prophet.

Similarly, Revelation 1:1-2 states: "The revelation of Jesus Christ, which God gave him to show to his servants the things that must soon take place. He made it known by sending his angel to his servant John, who bore witness to the word of God and to the testimony of Jesus Christ, even to all that he saw." In this passage, Jesus recognizes John as a faithful and reliable witness to the truth.

A SURVEY OF PARALLELS BETWEEN DANIEL AND REVELATION

Because Daniel and Revelation are the only apocalyptic books in the Bible, it is natural to expect numerous similarities between them. And indeed, the parallels abound! Here's a look at some of these striking connections:

- Both Daniel and Revelation present apocalyptic visions that reveal future events and God's ultimate plan for humanity.
- Scrolls and books appear in both Daniel and Revelation. Daniel 12:4 mentions a sealed book to be kept until the end times. Similarly, in Revelation 5, John sees a scroll with seven seals, which only the Lamb (Jesus) is worthy to open, revealing the events of the end times.
- God's complete and supreme authority over the universe is evident in both Daniel (chapters 3 and 6) and Revelation (1:5; 19:6).
- Daniel 7:9-10 depicts the Ancient of Days (God) seated on a throne,

accompanied by a host of angels. Likewise, in Revelation 4–5, John is transported to heaven, where he witnesses God's throne surrounded by living creatures and elders in worship.

- The theme of repentance is central in Daniel (for example, 4:27) and is echoed in Revelation (2:5, 16, 21, 22; 3:3, 19; 9:20-21; 16:9, 11).
- God's discipline of His children is a recurring theme. According to Daniel, Israel faces severe punishment when the Jews are taken into captivity in Babylon (1:1-2). Similarly, Revelation shows the Lord disciplining those He loves (3:19).
- The archangel Michael plays a pivotal role in God's prophetic plan, as seen in Daniel 10:13 and Revelation 12:7.
- Angels are instrumental in delivering God's end-time revelations to humankind in both Daniel (8:15-27) and Revelation (1:1).
- A cosmic struggle between good and evil angels for control of the nations is portrayed in Daniel 10:13, 20 and Revelation 12:7; 20:3.
- God's power to protect His people from danger is displayed in Daniel 3:19-25; 6:18-23 and Revelation 3:7.
- The tribulation will be a time of unprecedented trouble, as described in Daniel 12:1 and Revelation 3:10; 6; 8–9; 16.
- Daniel saw a vision of four beasts coming up out of the sea, representing successive world empires (Daniel 7:1-8). John saw one beast coming out of the sea and another out of the earth, symbolizing the rise of the antichrist and the false prophet (Revelation 13:1-5, 11-18).
- In the end times, a Roman Empire will arise with ten principal rulers (Daniel 7:7, 20, 24; Revelation 13:1-2).
- The antichrist will lead the Roman Empire, as described in Daniel 7:8, 20 and Revelation 13:1-10.
- The antichrist is characterized by arrogance and conceit (Daniel 7:8, 25; Revelation 13:5-6).

- The antichrist will speak against God, exalting himself above all gods and blaspheming the Supreme God (Daniel 11:36; Revelation 13:5-8).
- The antichrist will wage war against the saints and prevail over them (Daniel 7:21, 25; Revelation 13:7).
- The antichrist's reign will bring great destruction upon the earth during the tribulation period (Daniel 7:23; Revelation 4–18).
- God humbles the rulers of the world, as seen in Daniel 4:28-33 and Revelation 18:9-20.
- Jesus will return in glory, fulfilling the prophetic visions of Daniel 7:13 and Revelation 19:11-16.
- God's everlasting kingdom will triumph (Daniel 2:34-35, 44-45; 4:34-35; Revelation 20:1-6; 21–22).
- Good will ultimately prevail over evil (Daniel 2:44-45; Revelation 19:20; 20:11-15; 21:1).
- God's people will enter Christ's millennial kingdom (Daniel 7:27; Revelation 20:4-5; 21:1-4).
- Jesus Christ, the divine Messiah, will reign forever (Daniel 7:14; Revelation 19:16; 20:4, 6).
- Some will be resurrected to eternal life, while others will rise to shame and everlasting contempt (Daniel 12:2; Revelation 20:5-6).

Such parallels reveal the deep interconnectedness of Daniel and Revelation, with both books offering a complementary prophetic vision of the culmination of God's plan for the world.

THE WISDOM OF STUDYING DANIEL AND REVELATION TOGETHER

It is wise to study the books of Daniel and Revelation together. Here's why:

- *Two Apocalyptic Books.* Daniel and Revelation are the only apocalyptic texts in the Bible, and both are rich in end-times prophecy. Studying them side by side makes perfect sense.

- *Comprehensive Understanding.* Studying these books together provides a more complete understanding of Bible prophecy. Daniel's visions lay a foundation that Revelation expands upon, offering detailed insights into world empires, the rise of the antichrist, and the last days.
- *Same Source.* Although written 500 years apart, Daniel and Revelation share parallel teachings, underscoring their divine origin in God (or Jesus Christ).
- *Enhanced Understanding of Prophetic Imagery.* Both books employ similar symbols and imagery. By comparing these elements, readers can more accurately interpret the prophetic messages they contain.
- *Scripture Interprets Scripture.* Analyzing these texts together conforms to the timeless principle that "Scripture interprets Scripture," providing deeper clarity.
- *Chronological Sequence.* Studying Daniel and Revelation together helps clarify the sequence of end-time events. For instance, both books affirm that God's everlasting kingdom will triumph after the fall of the antichrist's kingdom (Daniel 2:34-35, 44-45; 4:34-35; Revelation 20:1-6; 21–22).
- *Key Prophetic Themes.* Together, Daniel and Revelation clarify the major components of prophecy—the tribulation period, the person and work of the antichrist, and the persecution of the saints, to name a few.
- *A Core Framework.* The combined study of these books provides a core framework for understanding end-time prophecies found in other books of the Bible (for example, in Matthew, John, 1 and 2 Corinthians, and 1 and 2 Thessalonians).
- *Strengthened Faith.* Daniel's stories of unwavering faith—such as Daniel in the lion's den and Shadrach, Meshach, and Abednego in

the fiery furnace—combined with Revelation's promises to those who persevere, inspire faith and commitment in believers of all ages.

- *Deepening Confidence in God's Sovereignty*. Daniel highlights God's control over history, empires, and their leaders, while Revelation reveals His ultimate victory over evil and His sovereign rule over all creation. Together, these books strengthen our confidence in God's sovereign plan.
- *Increased Awareness of Spiritual Warfare*. Daniel highlights the conflict between God's people and demonic powers (Daniel 10:13-14). Revelation describes the cosmic battle between good and evil, including the efforts of Satan and demons against believers (Revelation 11:7; 12:17; 20:8-9). Therefore, a study of Daniel and Revelation helps to increase our awareness of the spiritual battles we may face and the assurance of God's triumph over all evil.
- *Increased Devotion*. Daniel's example of prayer and fasting (Daniel 9) and Revelation's portrayal of heavenly worship (Revelation 4–5) inspire deeper personal devotion to Christ.
- *Call to Holiness*. Daniel models holy living in a corrupt world (Daniel 1:8-21), and Revelation calls believers to purity and readiness for Christ's return (Revelation 2–3; 19:7-8). Studying these texts together encourages a life of holiness and sanctification.
- *Longing for the Kingdom*. Daniel foretells the establishment of God's everlasting kingdom (Daniel 2:44), while Revelation describes its ultimate fulfillment with the new heaven and new earth (Revelation 21–22). Together, these books deepen our longing for God's kingdom.

In conclusion, the combined study of Daniel and Revelation is wise because it provides a rich and rewarding experience that deepens our understanding of Bible prophecy, strengthens our faith, and provides practical insights for daily living.

HOW TO READ THIS TWO-IN-ONE BOOK

I recommend starting with *40 Days Through Daniel* while making a few detours into key verses in Revelation along the way. Throughout *40 Days Through Daniel,* I provide some key cross-references that show important parallels between Daniel and Revelation. Throughout *40 Days Through Revelation*, I provide helpful Scripture quotes from Daniel. Be sure to consider these references.

Once you've finished Daniel, continue with *40 Days Through Revelation.* You will find that Daniel provides a prophetic foundation, and Revelation expands on that foundation.

Between the two books, you'll find a chapter entitled "Bridging Daniel and Revelation." This chapter offers additional insights into studying these prophetic books together.

Whether you are studying Daniel or Revelation, be sure to pray:

> *Lord, open my eyes to see the wonderful spiritual truths in the prophetic Scriptures. And please transform my life through this study of Your Word.*

40 DAYS THROUGH DANIEL

40 DAYS STUDYING DANIEL

Thank you for joining me in this exciting journey through the book of Daniel. You are in for a spiritually uplifting time! My hope and prayer is that as you read *40 Days Through Daniel*, you will experience several significant blessings:

- an awareness that God is a personal being who personally interacts with His people
- a conviction that God blesses righteous living
- an understanding of the need for God's people to maintain faith in Him regardless of the outward circumstances
- an understanding of God's sovereignty and control over the events of human history, including not only kings and nations but also the specifics of each of our individual lives
- an awareness that God will one day providentially cause good to triumph over evil
- an awareness that God is now providentially guiding human history toward its prophetic culmination
- an exalted view of the true majesty and glory of Jesus Christ, the divine Messiah
- an increased conviction of the trustworthiness of the Bible in general and the prophecies in the Bible in particular

As we begin our journey together, I want to address a few things that will lay a foundation for better understanding the book of Daniel. In this introduction, I will briefly look at the big picture. Then, in the chapters that follow, I will zero in on the details.

THE PROPHET DANIEL

Daniel was born into a royal family (Daniel 1:3, 6) and was apparently physically attractive (1:4). He became one of the major prophets of the Old Testament. His name means "God is my judge." He was uncompromising in his faithfulness to God. His contemporaries acknowledged both his righteousness and his wisdom (see Ezekiel 14:14, 20; 28:3).

Daniel was taken captive as a youth to Babylon by King Nebuchadnezzar in 605 BC. He was likely 15 or 16 years old when this happened. As providence had it, he spent the rest of his life there—perhaps 85 years or more. He was assigned to be a governmental official in charge of assisting with the imported Jews.

There were actually three deportations involved in Babylon's victory over Judah. The first took place in 605 BC and included Daniel and his friends. The second took place in 597 BC and included Ezekiel. The third took place in 586 BC, when the Babylonians destroyed Jerusalem and the temple.

Daniel wrote the biblical book that bears his name (see Daniel 8:15, 27; 9:2; 10:2, 7; 12:4-5). His book was titled Daniel not only because he was one of the chief characters in the book but also because it was customary in Bible times to affix the author's name to the book he wrote. In the New Testament, Jesus Himself identified Daniel as a prophet of God (Matthew 24:15; Mark 13:14).

CAPTIVITY AND EXILE

In the book of Deuteronomy, God, through Moses, promised great blessings if the nation lived in obedience to the Sinai covenant. God also warned that if the nation disobeyed His commands, it would experience the punishments listed in the covenant—including exile from the land (Deuteronomy 28:15-68).

Old Testament history is replete with illustrations of Israel's unfaithfulness to the covenant. The two most significant periods of exile for the Jewish people began with the fall of Israel to the Assyrians in 722 BC and the collapse of Judah to the Babylonians in 605 BC. Just as God promised, disobedience brought exile for God's people.

As a backdrop, it is interesting to observe that the first chapter of Isaiah takes the form of a lawsuit against Judah. Judah was indicted by the Lord (through Isaiah) because of Judah's "breach of contract" in breaking the Sinai covenant, which had been given to the nation at the time of the Exodus from Egypt. In this courtroom scene, the Lord called on heaven and earth to act as witnesses as He leveled accusations against the nation (Isaiah 1:2). The whole universe was to bear witness that God's judgments are just.

The Lord indicted Judah for rebelling against Him. It is noteworthy that the Hebrew word translated "rebelled" in Isaiah 1:2 often referred to a subordinate state's violation of a treaty with a sovereign nation. In Isaiah 1, the word points to Judah's blatant violation of God's covenant. Therefore, Judah went into captivity.

The Babylonian captivity was God's means of chastening Judah. This punishment, of course, was intended as a corrective. Both the Old and New Testaments demonstrate that just as an earthly father disciplines his children, so God the Father disciplines His children. His goal is to purify, train, and educate them (Hebrews 12:1-5; see also Job 5:17; 33:19; Psalm 118:18; Proverbs 3:11-12). The prophet Daniel indicates that God yet has a future for His people.

DANIEL'S BOOK

The book of Daniel is categorized as apocalyptic literature. It was written in about 537 BC and contains history as well as prophecy of the end times.

Scholars tell us that apocalyptic literature is a special kind of writing that arose among the Jews and Christians to reveal certain mysteries about heaven and earth, especially regarding the world to come. This type of literature is often characterized by visions—and there are plenty in the book of Daniel. Certain themes are common to apocalyptic literature:

- a growing sense of hopelessness as wicked powers grow in strength
- the promise that the sovereign God will intervene
- visions with a heavenly perspective that help the faithful endure present suffering

- God's intervention in overcoming and destroying evil
- the call to believers to live righteously
- the call to persevere under trial
- God's final deliverance and restoration, with the promise to dwell with His people

We see all of this in the book of Daniel.

AN OUTLINE OF THE BOOK OF DANIEL

Daniel's Personal History (1)

Daniel was deported with other young men and placed in a training program in Nebuchadnezzar's court in Babylon. Their names were changed, as were their diets. Daniel, however, refused to eat food dedicated to idols, and the Lord rewarded him for his faithfulness.

God's Prophetic Plan for the Gentiles (2–7)

Daniel was able to interpret Nebuchadnezzar's disturbing dream of a great statue (2). By God's power, Daniel revealed that the dream indicated that God would raise up and then bring down four Gentile empires—the fourth being a revived Roman Empire over which the antichrist would rule. The times of the Gentiles would finally end at the second coming of Jesus Christ.

Nebuchadnezzar set up a golden image and decreed that all bow to it (3:1-7). Shadrach, Meshach, and Abednego (Daniel's three Hebrew friends) refused and were subsequently tossed into a fiery furnace as punishment. (Daniel was engaged in official business at the time, but had he been there, he too would have refused!) God delivered the three Hebrew youths, after which they were all promoted (3:8-30).

The self-inflated, prideful Nebuchadnezzar then had a dream indicating that God was going to bring him down and humiliate him for a time, causing him to dwell with animals. Nebuchadnezzar was eventually restored and afterward offered praises to God (4).

We then read of Belshazzar, the next Babylonian king mentioned in Scripture. He arrogantly defied God. Soon enough, he saw handwriting on the wall signifying that his kingdom had been numbered, weighed, and divided. That very night, the kingdom of the Babylonians fell to Darius and the Medes (5).

While Darius was king, he banned prayer to any god other than himself. Daniel ignored the decree and was thrown into a den of lions overnight. But God delivered Daniel, and Daniel was further exalted (6).

Daniel then had a vision of four strange beasts, representing four kingdoms that play an important role in biblical prophecy. These were Babylon, Medo-Persia, Greece under Alexander the Great, and a revived Roman Empire, which is yet future (7). It is over this latter empire that the antichrist will rule during the future tribulation period.

God's Prophetic Plan for Israel (8–12)

God yet has a plan for Israel. Daniel spoke of 70 weeks of years that constitute a prophetic timetable for Israel (9). Israel's timetable was divided into 70 groups of 7 years, totaling 490 years. The first 69 groups of 7 years, or 483 years, counted the years from the issuing of a decree to restore and rebuild Jerusalem until Jesus the Messiah came (Daniel 9:25). After that, God's prophetic clock stopped. Daniel said there would be a gap between these years and the final 7 years of Israel's prophetic timetable.

The final "week" of 7 years will begin for Israel when the antichrist confirms a covenant for 7 years (Daniel 9:27). The signing of this peace pact will signal the beginning of the tribulation period. Daniel became frightened at this momentous vision. He prayed to the Lord for strength, and an angel eventually arrived in answer to the prayer. The angel promised to show Daniel further things to come in the prophetic future (10).

Daniel revealed that the antichrist will emerge in the end times and will "go out with great fury to destroy and devote many to destruction" (11:44). The tribulation period "shall be a time of trouble, such as never has been since there was a nation till that time" (12:1). Daniel was instructed to "shut up the words and seal the book, until the time of the end. Many shall run to and fro, and knowledge shall increase" (12:4).

HOW TO USE THIS BOOK

As you begin each chapter, consider using this prayer:

Lord, I ask You to open my eyes and enhance my understanding so I can grasp what You want me to learn today [Psalm 119:18]. *I also ask You to enable me, by Your Spirit, to apply the truths I learn to my daily life and to be guided moment by moment by Your Word* [Psalm 119:105; 2 Timothy 3:15-17]. *I thank You in Jesus' name. Amen.*

Following this short prayer, you can read the assigned section of the book of Daniel using your favorite Bible. With your Bible still in hand, you can then work your way through the insights, where I provide some fascinating contextual background information. I suggest you go verse by verse through your Bible again, but this time, after reading each verse, also read the appropriate notes in the book.

After the insights on each verse in the passage, I provide four brief summaries:

- *Major Themes.* These topical summaries will help you learn how to think theologically as you study the Bible.
- *Digging Deeper with Cross-References.* These will help you discover relevant insights from other books of the Bible.
- *Life Lessons.* This is where you learn to apply what you have read to your everyday life. You will discover that the book of Daniel is rich in transforming truths!
- *Questions for Reflection and Discussion.* Use these for your personal journaling or for lively group interactions.

Lord, by the power of Your Spirit, please enable my readers to understand and apply truth from the book of Daniel. Please excite them with Your Word and instill in them a sense of awe for You—our wondrous and majestic God. I thank You in Jesus' name. Amen.

DAY 1

DANIEL'S HISTORICAL CIRCUMSTANCES

DANIEL 1:1-7

SCRIPTURE READING AND INSIGHTS

Begin by reading Daniel 1:1-7 in your favorite Bible. Read with the anticipation that the Holy Spirit has something important to teach you today (see Psalm 119:105).

In today's lesson, we will focus our attention on the historical circumstances of Daniel and his friends. With your Bible still accessible, consider the following insights on the biblical text, verse by verse.

Daniel 1:1-2

Third year (1:1): This would have been 605 BC.

Jehoiakim (1:1): See Major Themes.

Judah (1:1): Judah was one of the 12 sons of Jacob. (His mother was Leah.) The tribes of Judah and Benjamin formed the southern kingdom, also known as Judah (see Genesis 29:35; 37:26; 44:14; 49:8-10; Numbers 1:27; Judges 1:8; 2 Samuel 2:4; 1 Kings 12:20, 23).

Nebuchadnezzar (1:1): See Major Themes.

Babylon (1:1): Babylon was situated on the banks of the Euphrates River, a little more than 50 miles south of modern Baghdad. Because of its ideal location, Babylon was an important commercial and trade center in the ancient world. The nation was also brimming with paganism.

Jerusalem (1:1): This city rests in the Judean hills at about 2,640 feet above sea level. King David of Israel captured the city in the tenth century BC and built his palace there. His son Solomon eventually became king and built a magnificent temple, making Jerusalem the center of Israel's religious life. Jerusalem would later become famous worldwide because it was the scene of Jesus' arrest, trial, crucifixion, and resurrection.

The Lord gave Jehoiakim king of Judah into his hand (1:2): The Lord used the Babylonians as His whipping rod to chastise the people of Judah for their unrepentant sins (see Jeremiah 25:9; 27:6).

Vessels of the house of God (1:2): The house of God was the Jewish temple built by Solomon in Jerusalem. The temple was rectangular, running east and west, and was about 87 feet long, 30 feet wide, and 43 feet high. The walls of the temple were made of cedar, and carved into the wood were cherubim (angels), flowers, and palm trees. The walls were overlaid with gold. The floor was made of cypress.

Solomon's temple had a Holy Place and a Most Holy Place. The Holy Place (the main outer room) housed the golden incense altar, the table of showbread, and five pairs of lampstands, as well as utensils used for sacrifice. Double doors led into the Most Holy Place, where the Ark of the Covenant was placed. The ark rested between two wooden cherubim, each standing ten feet tall. God manifested Himself in the Most Holy Place in a cloud of glory (1 Kings 8:10-11). This temple—the heart and center of Jewish worship for the kingdom of Judah—was destroyed by Nebuchadnezzar and the Babylonians.

The "vessels" were sacred objects in the temple. The Babylonians seized these sacred objects as spoils, believing this represented the victory of Babylon's gods over the God of Israel. Little did the Babylonians know that it was actually the one true God of Judah who handed His own people over to the Babylonians for chastisement (see Deuteronomy 28:64; Jeremiah 25:8-14).

In any event, the sacred objects of the temple would have included "the golden altar, the golden table for the bread of the Presence, the lampstands of pure gold...the lamps, and the tongs, of gold; the cups, snuffers, basins, dishes for incense, and fire pans, of pure gold; and the sockets of gold, for the doors of the innermost part of the house" (1 Kings 7:48-51).

Shinar (1:2): Another term for Babylon.

House of his god...treasury of his god (1:2): Like other pagan nations of the Ancient Near East, the Babylonians believed in many false gods and goddesses. These gods were thought to control the entire world of nature, so being successful in life required placating the gods. The Babylonians also believed that their military victories indicated that their gods were more powerful than any other nation's gods. However, in the Babylonian religious system, the gods' behavior was considered unpredictable at best.

Each city in Babylon had a patron god with an accompanying temple. Several small shrines were also scattered about each city, and people often met there to worship various other deities. The chief of the Babylonian gods was Anu, considered the king of heaven, and the patron god of Babylon was Marduk. "His god" (1:2) is likely a reference to Marduk.

Daniel 1:3-5

Chief eunuch (1:3): This term does not necessarily refer to a man who was castrated. The Hebrew term *saris* can simply refer to a government official (see 2 Kings 8:6).

Bring some of the people of Israel (1:3): In one section of the Mosaic Law, recorded in Leviticus 26:33, 39, God threatened His people with exile if they chose to be unfaithful to the terms of the covenant established at Mount Sinai (see also Deuteronomy 4:27; 28:64). As it happened, the people of Judah disobeyed the Lord for an extended time. The resulting exile did not occur all at once. Initially, only "some of the people of Israel" were brought to Babylon, including Daniel and his friends. This would have been in 605 BC. The exile came to full fruition in 597 BC when Babylon destroyed both Jerusalem and its temple, and at that time countless Jews were exiled to Babylon.

Youths (1:4): Young teenagers—probably between 14 and 17 years old.

Teach them (1:4): The Babylonian literature they were required to study probably included writings on agriculture, architecture, astrology, astronomy, law, mathematics, and the difficult Akkadian language. (One recalls that Moses was likewise trained in Egyptian literature—Acts 7:22.) Nebuchadnezzar wanted these young men to be enculturated and assimilated into Babylonian society (see Major Themes). As we will see throughout the rest of the book, however, Babylon influenced Daniel and his friends very little. Instead, they greatly influenced Babylon by remaining faithful to the one true God.

Food...wine (1:5): That the king allowed the youths the food and wine he partook of was likely designed to foster dependence, gratitude, and loyalty to the king.

Educated (1:5): The youths were educated for three years, not quite as long as it would take a person to get a college degree today.

Daniel 1:6-7

Daniel (1:6): In the ancient world, a name was not a mere label, as it is today. A name was equivalent to whomever or whatever bore it. A person's name could indicate his or her character, personality, or allegiance. Knowing a person's name therefore amounted to knowing a great deal about him or her.

We see this illustrated in the names of major Bible characters. The name Abraham, for instance, means "father of a multitude," which was fitting because Abraham was the father of the Jewish nation. The name David means "beloved," and of course, David was a king specially loved by God. The name Solomon comes from a word meaning "peace"—and Solomon's reign was characterized by peace. In each case, we learn something about the individual from his name.

The same is true regarding the names given to the four Hebrew youths mentioned in Daniel 1:6: Daniel, Hananiah, Mishael, and Azariah. Daniel's name, for example, means "God has judged," or perhaps "God is my Judge." Note that the ending of Daniel's name, *el*, is a Hebrew term for God. Daniel's parents were apparently God-fearing people.

Hananiah (1:6): This name means "Yahweh has been gracious." Note that the *iah* ending (or *yah*) is an abbreviation for God's name, Yahweh.

Mishael (1:6): This name means "Who is what God is?" Again we see the *el* ending, a Hebrew name for God.

Azariah (1:6): Azariah's name means "Yahweh has helped." Again, the *iah* ending (or *yah*) is an abbreviation for God's name, Yahweh.

Tribe of Judah (1:6): The Israelites were divided into 12 tribes, each descended from one of the 12 sons of Jacob: Reuben, Gad, Manasseh, Asher, Naphtali, Zebulon, Issachar, Ephraim, Benjamin, Judah, Simeon, and Dan. The tribe of Judah is particularly significant, for Genesis 49:10 prophesied that the Messiah would come from the tribe of Judah and reign as King. Judah is therefore a royal tribe.

Belteshazzar (1:7): Daniel and his friends all had Hebrew names that honored the one true God of Israel. The Babylonians believed their gods were superior to the God of Israel. The young men's names were therefore changed to honor Babylonian deities instead of the God of Israel. Daniel was renamed Belteshazzar, meaning "Bel, protect his life," or "Bel, protect the king's life." (Bel was a Babylonian deity.)

Shadrach (1:7): Hananiah's name was changed to Shadrach, apparently meaning "Command of Aku." (Aku was another Babylonian deity.)

Meshach (1:7): Mishael's name was changed to Meshach, meaning "Who is Aku?"

Abednego (1:7): Azariah's name was changed to Abednego, meaning "Servant of Nebo." (Nebo, also known as Nabu, was yet another Babylonian deity.)

MAJOR THEMES

1. *King Nebuchadnezzar of Babylon.* Nebuchadnezzar's name means "Nabu has protected my inheritance." Nebuchadnezzar was the most powerful of the Babylonian kings. He is famous for taking multitudes of Jews into captivity from 605 to 597 BC, among whom were Daniel and his companions (Jeremiah 27:19; 40:1; Daniel 1:1-7). After Daniel's companions were thrown into the fiery furnace and miraculously delivered (Daniel 3), the king became afflicted with a strange mental disease as a punishment for his pride and vanity. He was eventually restored.

2. *King Jehoiakim of Judah.* Jehoiakim was the second son of Josiah and became the eighteenth king of Judah (2 Kings 23:33-34; 2 Chronicles 36:6-7). He was born about 633 BC. He was a vicious, cruel, selfish, rebellious, and irreligious man who encouraged idolatry (see Jeremiah 19). He flaunted his impiety when he destroyed a prophetic scroll written by the prophet Jeremiah. He died a violent death (2 Kings 24:3-4; Jeremiah 22:18-19; 36:30).

3. *The enculturation of exiles.* Daniel and his Jewish friends were enculturated in Babylon. They were trained in Babylonian language and literature and

instructed to eat Babylonian food (though Daniel was able to make other arrangements). They were given Babylonian names that honored Babylonian gods. The idea was to make them suitable for service in the king's palace.

DIGGING DEEPER WITH CROSS-REFERENCES

Exile as the consequence of disobedience—Genesis 15:13-14; Exodus 1:11-14; Deuteronomy 28:36; Judges 2:14; 2 Kings 17:6-7; Isaiah 39:6; Amos 5:27

Sacred objects of the temple—Exodus 25:29; 37:16; 40:9; 1 Kings 7:51; 2 Kings 14:14; 24:13; 25:14; 2 Chronicles 36:18; Ezra 1:7; 5:14; Jeremiah 28:3

LIFE LESSONS

1. *A failure to repent brings God's discipline.* A failure to repent of sin always brings God's discipline in the life of a believer. Recall that this is what happened to David following his sin with Bathsheba (Psalms 32:3-5; 51). This can happen to us today too (Hebrews 12:5-11). Never forget, "If we would examine ourselves, we would not be judged by God in this way" (1 Corinthians 11:31 NLT).

2. *God is sovereign over human affairs.* Daniel 1:2 reveals that God sovereignly allowed Judah's captivity. Scripture reveals that God is absolutely sovereign—He rules the universe, controls all things, and is Lord over all. He may utilize various means to accomplish His ends, but He is always in control. You might want to meditate for a few minutes on Psalms 50:1; 66:7; Proverbs 16:9; 19:21; 21:30; Isaiah 14:24; 40:15, 17; 46:10.

QUESTIONS FOR REFLECTION AND DISCUSSION

1. What does the reality of God's sovereignty mean to you personally? Does this doctrine comfort you, frighten you, or maybe a little of both?

2. If you were forced to live in a part of the world brimming with paganism, do you think you'd still be able to effectively serve God with a good attitude?

3. Has God ever moved you outside of your comfort zone? If so, how did you adapt?

DAY 2

DANIEL'S FAITHFULNESS

DANIEL 1:8-16

SCRIPTURE READING AND INSIGHTS

Begin by reading Daniel 1:8-16 in your favorite Bible. As you read, remember that the Word of God is alive and working in you (Hebrews 4:12).

In the previous lesson, we studied the historical circumstances of Daniel and his friends, newly exiled in Babylon. In today's lesson, we zero in on Daniel's faithfulness to God while living in a pagan society. With your Bible still accessible, consider the following insights on the biblical text, verse by verse.

Daniel 1:8

Daniel resolved (1:8): The word "resolved" carries the idea, "Daniel purposed in his heart," or "Daniel determined in his heart," or "Daniel set upon his heart." He was a man of strong convictions, and he consistently acted on them.

King's food...wine (1:8): Why didn't Daniel and his friends want to eat the king's food? Here are four possible explanations.

- The food was prepared by Gentiles, so it was "unclean" according to the requirements of the Mosaic Law. Also, the fare probably included foods that were forbidden by the Mosaic Law (see Leviticus 11:1-23; Deuteronomy 14:1-21).
- Pagan nations often devoted food to pagan deities before eating it. If Daniel and his friends had eaten what they were served, they

would have defiled themselves by rendering honor to false gods (see Exodus 34:15).

- Daniel and his friends might have been rejecting the luxurious lifestyle—including the extravagant food—offered to those in the king's court. Perhaps they reasoned that such materialism might defile them or lure them away from complete commitment to God.
- Jewish people drank wine diluted with water (see Major Themes). The Babylonians did not dilute their wine, and "strong drink" was unacceptable to the Jews (see Proverbs 20:1). Moreover, the Babylonians poured their wine on pagan altars in the worship of their deities. Daniel and his friends would have wanted no part of this.

Ultimately, Daniel resolved that even though he lived in a land that did not honor God's Law, he himself would nevertheless do everything possible to continue obeying the Lord's commands. Walking in faithfulness to God was harder in Babylon than in Judah, but God rewarded Daniel's faithfulness.

Therefore he asked (1:8): James 2:17 tells us, "Faith by itself, if it does not have works, is dead." Daniel didn't just make a resolution in his heart ("faith") but also acted on that resolution ("works"). He took immediate steps to make other arrangements for food.

Daniel 1:9-10

God gave Daniel favor and compassion (1:9): God has the power to turn the hearts of unbelieving leaders so that they are favorable to God's people (see Exodus 11:3). He also honors those who first honor Him (1 Samuel 2:30; 2 Chronicles 16:9). Proverbs 16:7 tells us, "When a man's ways please the LORD, he makes even his enemies to be at peace with him." (See Life Lessons.)

I fear my lord the king (1:10): The chief eunuch was charged with overseeing the physical and mental development of Daniel and his friends. If the king was not pleased with this development, that would reflect badly on the chief eunuch, and he could be punished or even lose his life.

Worse condition (1:10): Evidenced by looking worse.

Endanger my head (1:10): Disappointing the king could result in execution.

Daniel 1:11-14

Daniel said (1:11): Notice that Daniel did not rebel. He did not use harsh language, raise his voice, or get into a heated argument. Instead, he used good judgment by courteously offering a reasonable alternative to the steward. He came up with a creative solution that avoided offense and enabled him and his friends to remain faithful to God in the process.

Steward (1:11): Daniel surmised from the chief eunuch's words that his request for a special diet had been denied. Daniel thus approached the steward who had been placed in charge of the four youths. Daniel requested a ten-day period in which they would be fed only vegetables and water. He implied that he and his friends would have a better appearance in ten days than those eating the king's food. The steward had no authority on his own, so he likely okayed this with the chief eunuch before proceeding. The God who brings favor in the eyes of others was clearly at work behind the scenes here.

Vegetables (1:12): The Old Testament word translated "vegetables" means "things grown from seeds." The word could refer either to fresh vegetables or even to wheat or barley grain. Vegetables—things grown from seeds—were a safe choice, for the Mosaic Law did not categorize any vegetables as unclean. Therefore, no matter what vegetables were brought to Daniel and his friends, they would not be defiled.

Some Bible expositors have suggested the possibility that in addition to avoiding defilement, Daniel avoided meat and other foods in order to engage in a kind of fast as an expression of their mourning, having been exiled. One must note, however, that their attitudes before the Babylonians were always upbeat and positive.

So he listened (1:14): Daniel's suggestion was okayed and put into practice.

Daniel 1:15-16

Better in appearance and fatter in flesh (1:15): To be better in appearance and fatter in flesh was taken as evidence that they were healthier than those who ate the king's diet. This was precisely the opposite of what Ashpenaz, the chief eunuch, had feared.

Some scholars have been careful to point out that this verse cannot be taken as a biblical endorsement of vegetarianism. After all, it was ultimately

God who made them healthy and gave them the outer appearance of health. The youths had honored God, and now God honored them by keeping them healthy. Though vegetables are definitely healthy, God ultimately blessed them because they obeyed His will, not simply because they ate vegetables instead of other foods.

Scripture stands against legalists who, for religious reasons, "require abstinence from foods that God created to be received with thanksgiving by those who believe and know the truth. For everything created by God is good, and nothing is to be rejected if it is received with thanksgiving, for it is made holy by the word of God and prayer" (1 Timothy 4:3-5). Acceptable foods certainly include meat (Genesis 9:3).

In Old Testament times, the Jews believed—based on divine revelation—that health came from pleasing God, while sickness and disease came from displeasing Him. God Himself affirmed in Exodus 15:26, "If you will diligently listen to the voice of the Lord your God, and do that which is right in his eyes, and give ear to his commandments and keep all his statutes, I will put none of the diseases on you that I put on the Egyptians, for I am the Lord, your healer." God commanded, "You shall serve the Lord your God, and he will bless your bread and your water, and I will take sickness away from among you" (Exodus 23:25). Scripture promises that if you "fear the Lord, and turn away from evil...it will be healing to your flesh and refreshment to your bones" (Proverbs 3:7-8).

So the steward took away (1:16): As a result of the ten-day experiment, a permanent diet of vegetables and water was allowed for Daniel and his friends.

MAJOR THEMES

1. *Avoiding defilement.* The ancient Jews believed that a number of things could render a person unclean. For example, a woman was rendered ceremonially unclean during menstruation and following childbirth (Leviticus 12:2-5; Ezekiel 16:4). Touching a dead animal rendered one unclean (Leviticus 11:24-40), as did touching any dead body (Numbers 19:11). A person with a skin infection was considered unclean (Leviticus 13:3). Sexual discharges rendered one unclean (Leviticus 15:2). The Samaritans of New Testament times were considered unclean because they were of mixed ancestry (Israelite

and Assyrian—see John 4:9). Likewise, eating certain prohibited foods rendered one unclean or defiled (Leviticus 11:46-47; Ezekiel 4:13-14; Hosea 9:3-4). This is what Daniel was seeking to avoid (Daniel 1:8).

2. *Drinking wine.* In day-to-day meals in biblical times, wine was often mixed with water as a means of purifying it. A popular beverage of ancient times was a mixture of twenty parts water mixed with one part wine. It was essentially wine-flavored water. In other cases, one part wine might be mixed with one part water (or no water at all), and this was considered strong wine. Drinking wine in moderation is permissible for Christians (John 2:9; 1 Timothy 3:3, 8; but also see Romans 14:21; 1 Corinthians 6:12; 10:31). Drunkenness is prohibited (Ephesians 5:18).

3. *A good conscience.* Daniel and his friends were concerned not only about moral purity but also about ceremonial purity. They wanted to avoid *any* kind of defilement. They may have been forced to move to Babylon, but it was important to them to maintain a good conscience in all things. This is a thread that runs all through Daniel. We are reminded of the apostle Paul's instruction in 1 Timothy 1:19 for young Timothy to keep a strong faith as well as a good conscience (see also 1 Peter 3:16). Daniel is a good example of the kind of man Paul wanted Timothy to be.

DIGGING DEEPER WITH CROSS-REFERENCES

Unclean foods the Israelites were to avoid—Leviticus 11:46-47; Ezekiel 4:13-14; Hosea 9:3-4; 1 Corinthians 8

Health promised for obedience—Exodus 15:26; 23:25; Deuteronomy 7:15; 2 Kings 20:5; Psalms 30:2; 91:5-6; 103:3; Proverbs 3:7-8; 4:20-22; James 5:14-15; 3 John 2

LIFE LESSONS

1. *Be faithful to God.* Daniel and his companions were faithful to God. You and I are likewise called to be faithful to God (meditate on Proverbs 3:3; Matthew 25:23; Romans 12:12; and Revelation 2:10). Scripture reveals that as we walk in dependence on the Holy Spirit, faithfulness is part of

the fruit of the Spirit that will be produced in our lives (Galatians 5:16, 22). It makes good sense to therefore depend on the Holy Spirit every day of our lives!

2. *God gives favor.* Scripture often displays God giving His people favor in the eyes of others. For example, when Joseph was in prison, God gave him favor in the eyes of the prison warden (Genesis 39:21). God likewise gave Daniel favor in the eyes of the chief eunuch (Daniel 1:9). God can cause people to look upon us favorably as well (see Exodus 3:21; 11:3; 12:36). Why not incorporate this into your prayers? "Lord, please grant me favor in the eyes of…"

3. *Be a person of integrity.* Daniel was clearly a man of integrity. The Bible speaks a great deal about what it means to be a man of integrity.

   - "Better is a poor man who walks in his integrity than a rich man who is crooked in his ways" (Proverbs 28:6).
   - "Better is a poor person who walks in his integrity than one who is crooked in speech and is a fool" (Proverbs 19:1).
   - "The integrity of the upright guides them" (Proverbs 11:3).
   - "The righteous who walks in his integrity—blessed are his children after him!" (Proverbs 20:7).
   - Daniel was certainly right in line with Paul's words in 2 Corinthians 8:21: "We aim at what is honorable not only in the Lord's sight but also in the sight of man." In other words, we aim at integrity both before the Lord and before human beings. Here are some helpful verses worthy of meditation: Psalms 25:21; 26:1; Micah 6:8; Acts 24:16; Titus 2:1-14; Hebrews 13:18; James 1:22-25.

QUESTIONS FOR REFLECTION AND DISCUSSION

1. Does Daniel's resolution in verse 8 motivate you to follow his lead and make your own resolution?

2. What do you learn about God's sovereignty in verse 9 in regard to authority figures in your life? (Contemplate how Proverbs 21:1 might relate to this.)

3. What impresses you most about how Daniel handled himself in his circumstances?

DAY 3

DANIEL RISES IN FAVOR BEFORE THE KING

DANIEL 1:17-21

SCRIPTURE READING AND INSIGHTS

Begin by reading Daniel 1:17-21 in your favorite Bible. As you read, remember that those who obey the Word of God are truly blessed (Psalm 119:2; Luke 11:28; Revelation 1:3).

In yesterday's lesson, we considered Daniel's faithfulness to God while living in a pagan society. Today we'll see Daniel's providential rise in favor with the king. With your Bible still accessible, consider the following insights on the biblical text, verse by verse.

Daniel 1:17

God gave them learning and skill (1:17): As a result of God's special gifting, the four Hebrew youths were equipped with reasoning skills that enabled them to think clearly and logically. They gained a heightened discernment that enabled them to interpret events and circumstances in their true light.

Wisdom (1:17): The Hebrew word for wisdom is *hokmah*. This word was commonly used for the skill of craftsmen, sailors, singers, administrators, and counselors. *Hokmah* pointed to the experience and efficiency of these various workers in using their skills. Similarly, a person who possesses *hokmah* in his spiritual life and relationship to God is both knowledgeable and experienced in following God's way. Biblical wisdom involves skill in the art of godly living. This broad wisdom makes for skilled living and empowers people to be successful at home, at work, in human relationships, in finances, in eternal issues, and much more. Daniel and his friends received *hokmah* from God.

We might note in passing that God has not stopped giving His people wisdom when they need it. In James 1:5 we are promised, "If any of you lacks wisdom, let him ask God, who gives generously to all without reproach, and it will be given him." Also, God often uses people with excellent educational backgrounds. This was certainly true of Moses (Acts 7:22), Daniel and his friends, and the apostle Paul (Acts 22:3).

Understanding in all visions and dreams (1:17): Daniel had a gift that set him apart from all others in Babylon. He was given a special ability to understand visions and dreams. Others in Babylon may have known as much about literature as Daniel did, but no one else had his special, God-given ability to interpret dreams. How could they? The false gods of Babylon (who were not really gods at all) could not help the magicians or enchanters understand dreams. Only the one true God knows the meaning of dreams, and as we will see, God conveyed those meanings to Daniel (see Daniel 2:2-11; 4:6-7).

Of course, when God gives His people learning and skill, He doesn't intend for those gifts to lie stagnant in their lives. Rather, He gives His people these qualities so they can be used. We will see throughout the rest of the book of Daniel that these four youths put to excellent use the gifts of learning and skill God gave them.

Daniel 1:18-19

At the end of the time (1:18): This refers back to verse 5—"They were to be educated for three years, and at the end of that time they were to stand before the king." Now the time had come.

Brought them in (1:18): Ashpenaz, the chief eunuch, now displayed his students of three years before Nebuchadnezzar for their final examination. Though Ashpenaz was no doubt confident in his abilities as a trainer, he nevertheless likely experienced some anxiety, knowing that a failure to please Nebuchadnezzar could lead to punishment or even death.

The king spoke with them (1:19): The king gave an oral examination to all those present, likely covering topics that were most important to him and his agenda.

Among all of them (1:19): Recall from verses 5 and 6 that these four youths were among a larger group of youths that the king commanded to be trained. Apparently, the entire group of youths now stood before the king.

None was found like (1:19): Daniel and his three friends were the cream of the crop among all those trained. As a result of the special abilities God gave them, they were clearly superior to all others. At this time, they would have been about 20 years old—about the age of a modern college student.

Therefore they stood before the king (1:19): One is reminded of Proverbs 22:29: "Do you see a man skillful in his work? He will stand before kings."

Daniel 1:20-21

In every matter of wisdom and understanding (1:20): The final examination was comprehensive. It covered a wide spectrum of topics and issues. The four youths didn't excel in only a few of these topics but rather in "every matter" that was brought up.

Ten times better (1:20): This phrase signifies completeness or fullness. The four youths were completely superior to the others around them. They outshone everyone else. They stood heads and shoulders above the others.

This again brings to mind Joseph, to whom God also gave special abilities. Pharaoh "sent and called for all the magicians of Egypt and all its wise men. Pharaoh told them his dreams, but there was none who could interpret them to Pharaoh" (Genesis 41:8). With God's help, Joseph succeeded where all others had failed. "Then Pharaoh said to Joseph, 'Since God has shown you all this, there is none so discerning and wise as you are'" (Genesis 41:39).

Magicians and enchanters (1:20): These individuals typically used divination, astrological charts, and soothsaying to ascertain their answers. They were occultists, and as occultists they were energized by demonic spirits, though they claimed to be spokesmen for Babylon's pagan gods.

One must not miss the religious significance of what is going on here. The contest between the four youths and the magicians and enchanters is very much a contest between the one true God and the many false gods of Babylon.

The four youths stood out because the one true God was the source of their wisdom and skills. All others dimmed in their presence because they derived their power from false gods, which were, in fact, nonexistent. The false gods were no competition with the one true God of Israel.

We witness a similar contest between the true God and false gods in Moses' ongoing confrontation with Pharaoh over the Jews' slavery. Moses expressed God's absolute incomparability in two ways. The most common was negation—"There is no one like the Lord our God" (Exodus 8:10). The other way was by rhetorical questions, such as "Who is like you, O Lord, among the gods?" (Exodus 15:11). The implied answer is, "No one in all the universe." This was particularly significant in view of Moses' experience in Egypt, which was brimming with false gods.

God used ten plagues to openly demonstrate His superiority over the gods of Egypt. For example, the first plague, which turned the Nile's water into blood (Exodus 7:14-25), was a judgment against one of Egypt's most prominent gods. The Nile itself was worshiped as a god, and as its water was virtually the lifeblood of Egypt, this blow was devastating. The Exodus account reveals that Nilus, the Egyptian river god, was impotent in the face of the true God of Scripture.

The ninth plague brought darkness to the whole land (Exodus 10:21-29). This was a judgment against the Egyptian sun god, Re. The sun god was regarded as the creator, father, and king of the gods. He was considered the most distinguished god in the pantheon and was praised as stronger, mightier, and more divine than the other gods. But Re was nowhere to be found when the true God of Scripture darkened the land.

Babylon was now learning the same lesson the Egyptians had learned much earlier. But in the present case, the true God's victory over Babylon's false gods was evident in the four youths' superiority over all the magicians and enchanters of Babylon.

Until the first year of King Cyrus (1:21): Daniel's ministry in the royal court of Babylon continued until the overthrow of the Babylonian Empire by Cyrus in 539 BC. Daniel was one of the first captives exiled to Babylon, but he lived to see the first exiles return to Jerusalem in 538 BC under Cyrus's decree.

MAJOR THEMES

1. *Dreams in Bible times.* In Old Testament times, God often communicated with believers as well as unbelievers through dreams. Here are a few examples:

Abimelech (Genesis 20:3-7)	Pharaoh's butler and baker (Genesis 40:5)
Jacob (Genesis 28:12; 31:10)	Pharaoh himself (Genesis 41:1-8)
Laban (Genesis 31:24)	a Midianite (Judges 7:13-14)
Joseph (Genesis 37:9-11)	Nebuchadnezzar (Daniel 2:1)

   Such revelatory dreams continued in New Testament times, such as Joseph's dream about Mary's pregnancy by the Holy Spirit (Matthew 1:20; see also 2:12-13, 19). Today, we have the Bible as God's primary means of revelation (2 Timothy 3:15-17). Interestingly, however, Acts 2:17 tells us, "In the last days it shall be, God declares, that I will pour out my Spirit on all flesh, and your sons and your daughters shall prophesy, and your young men shall see visions, and your old men shall dream dreams."

2. *Magicians and enchanters.* The king of Babylon often consulted with occultists (magicians and enchanters) for wisdom. It was thought that such individuals had supernatural insights. God, of course, condemns all forms of occultism, including magic (Exodus 22:18; Leviticus 19:31; Deuteronomy 18:9-13; Ezekiel 13:18; Acts 19:19-20; Galatians 5:20; Revelation 9:21; 21:8). The magicians were influenced by demons, while Daniel was influenced by God. No wonder Daniel could provide answers when the magicians could not (Daniel 1:20).

DIGGING DEEPER WITH CROSS-REFERENCES

The interpretation of dreams—Genesis 40:8, 12, 18; 41:12, 25; Daniel 1:17; 2:4, 28, 36, 45; 4:20, 24

God's people exalted—Genesis 41:41; Exodus 7:1; 11:3; Joshua 3:7; 4:14; 1 Samuel 2:8; Job 5:11; Psalms 27:6; 37:34; 113:7; 145:14; 148:14; Isaiah

40:31; Habakkuk 3:19; Matthew 23:12; 25:21; Luke 13:30; 14:11; Romans 8:18; 1 Corinthians 6:2; 1 Peter 5:6

LIFE LESSONS

1. *God gives special abilities.* Daniel 1:17 tells us that God gave Daniel and his friends special abilities that enabled them to serve well. In fact, Scripture often reveals God giving special abilities to people. Christians today are equipped with the gifts of the Holy Spirit, which are to be used in serving the body of Christ (see Romans 12:6; 1 Corinthians 12:4; Ephesians 4:11). The gifts God gives one believer are often different from the gifts He gives another. But we all serve the same body.

2. *Adapting to new circumstances.* Sometimes God allows us to experience circumstances that are outside our comfort zone. When that happens, it is best to adapt to our new circumstances and find ways to serve God. Daniel and his friends excelled in their assigned tasks in Babylon (Daniel 1:20). Likewise, after Joseph was betrayed by his brothers, he served God faithfully in every new circumstance that befell him (for example, see Genesis 39:4-6, 21-23). When the apostle Paul was thrown in jail, he didn't wallow in self-pity but was used by God in writing some of the New Testament books (Ephesians, Philippians, Colossians, and Philemon). The lesson we learn is simple: Be ready and willing to serve God in every situation!

QUESTIONS FOR REFLECTION AND DISCUSSION

1. Can you think of another person in Scripture who received great learning and wisdom from God? (See 1 Kings 3:12, 28.) What does God's gift of such learning say about His sovereignty? What does it say about His grace?

2. Do you think Daniel and his friends were living examples of the truth found in Proverbs 4:23? How so?

3. Do you know what your spiritual gifts are? (Not sure? The best way to find out is to get involved in ministry at your local church. Spiritual gifts typically surface in the context of ministry.)

DAY 4

NEBUCHADNEZZAR'S DREAMS

DANIEL 2:1-6

SCRIPTURE READING AND INSIGHTS

Begin by reading Daniel 2:1-6 in your favorite Bible. As you read, keep in mind that just as we eat food for physical nourishment, so we need the Word of God for spiritual nourishment (1 Corinthians 3:2; Hebrews 5:12; 1 Peter 2:2). Seek to feed upon God's Word today.

Yesterday we focused attention on Daniel's rise in favor with the king. Now let's shift our attention to Nebuchadnezzar's dreams. With your Bible still accessible, consider the following insights on the biblical text, verse by verse.

Daniel 2:1

The second year of the reign of Nebuchadnezzar (2:1): In Babylonian reckoning, Nebuchadnezzar's accession year would have been the first year of the four youths' training (605–604 BC). Nebuchadnezzar's first full year of reigning would have been the second year of the youths' training (604–603 BC). His second full year of reigning would have been their third year of training (603–602 BC). So Nebuchadnezzar must have had the dreams immediately following the youths' third year of training, toward the end of his second full year of reigning (602 BC).

Nebuchadnezzar had dreams (2:1): The plural reference to dreams apparently means that Nebuchadnezzar was experiencing a recurring dream night after night. This must have been the case since Daniel recalled and interpreted only one dream, not several different dreams (Daniel 2:24-26).

His spirit was troubled (2:1): Nebuchadnezzar's troubled heart is an indication that he considered the dream and its meaning significant. He couldn't rest until he found out what it meant.

His sleep left him (2:1): Sleep often eludes people with troubled hearts.

Daniel 2:2-3

The king commanded (2:2): The appearance of the various occultists before the king was not a mere invitation. They were given a direct order to appear before Nebuchadnezzar.

The magicians, the enchanters, the sorcerers, and the Chaldeans (2:2): The Babylonians believed that dreams were messages from the gods. The various occultists in Babylon were expected to be able to interpret them. If one group of occultists couldn't accomplish the task, perhaps another group could. In the present case, they were all summoned to appear before Nebuchadnezzar because the king wanted answers!

The Chaldeans mentioned in this verse were priests who served as astrologers or soothsayers.

Summoned to tell the king his dreams (2:2): Here is where the problem begins for these occultists. If the king told them his dream, they could take a stab at interpreting it. But here Nebuchadnezzar instructs them to tell him his dream before giving him the interpretation. This would prove to be an impossible task for these occultists because God was the One who gave this dream to Nebuchadnezzar. Only a man of God would be able to reveal it and interpret it. The false gods of Babylon would prove impotent in this task.

I had a dream (2:3): Nebuchadnezzar's statement, "I had a dream" (singular), qualifies the statement in verse 1, "Nebuchadnezzar had dreams." As noted previously, the king must have had a single dream that recurred over a number of nights. The recurrence of the dream demonstrated its importance.

My spirit is troubled to know the dream (2:3): Nebuchadnezzar may have been troubled that the dream somehow indicated that he would fall from power as king. He wondered, *What does this dream say about me and my future?*

Daniel 2:4

Aramaic (2:4): Daniel's narrative switches from Hebrew to Aramaic in this verse and continues through chapter 7, where the narrative then switches back to Hebrew. Aramaic was a common language among the Babylonians, Assyrians, and Persians. The language was often used in diplomacy, commerce, and trade. Aramaic was truly an international language in that part of the world.

One might wonder why the Chaldeans chose to speak in Aramaic. The answer is that the various occultists who appeared before the king came from different provinces and used various dialects, but they all understood Aramaic.

In addition, Daniel 1:1–2:4a and 8:1–12:13 were written in Hebrew, likely because the scriptural text deals with Hebrew issues. In contrast, Daniel 2:4b–7:28 was written in Aramaic, apparently because the scriptural text deals with issues of interest to the Gentile nations.

O king, live forever! (2:4): The Chaldeans were quite eager to please King Nebuchadnezzar. They accordingly addressed the king with an expression of common courtesy in that part of the world. We see this courtesy elsewhere in Scripture. For example, recall that "Bathsheba bowed with her face to the ground and paid homage to the king and said, 'May my lord King David live forever'" (1 Kings 1:31; see also Nehemiah 2:3; Daniel 3:9; 5:10; 6:21).

Tell your servants the dream (2:4): Notice that no one said, "Tell me the dream." No one wanted to try to interpret the dream alone. Rather, they were confident that with their combined efforts they'd be able to come up with something that would satisfy the king.

Daniel 2:5-6

The word from me is firm (2:5): Negotiation was not an option. Things would be done the king's way, or people would lose their lives. The king was resolved to ensure that the interpretation of his dream would be without deception.

Some have asked whether the king may have forgotten his dream. After all, people today have dreams that are disturbing, but upon awakening, they sometimes forget their dreams. Moreover, some have tried to argue that the clause "the word from me is firm" could be translated "the thing is gone from me," implying that the king forgot the dream.

The latter translation seems foreign to the context in the present case. After all, if the king had forgotten the dream, the occultists could simply make up a dream and reveal it to him. The king wouldn't know any better, and the occultists' lives would be spared. Contrary to such an idea, the context seems to indicate that the king is putting the occultists to a test that goes something like this: "I know what I've dreamed night after night, and if you can't tell me the details of this recurring dream, you're all dead men." So Nebuchadnezzar withheld the facts of the dream before those present, not because he forgot them but because he wanted to test his "wise men."

Let's not forget that in the Bible, when God gave someone a dream, no one ever forgot the details of it. (See "Notable Dreams" in Digging Deeper with Cross-References.) Daniel 2:1 indicates that Nebuchadnezzar awoke because the dream was so troubling, and he wasn't able to go back to sleep precisely because he remembered it.

If you do not make known to me (2:5): In the past, the king had likely had other dreams and received satisfactory interpretations from his occultic advisors. Apparently, however, this dream was so important to the king that he imposed extremely stringent requirements on his occultic advisors. The king seemed to reason that if he was going to trust their interpretation of the future based on his dream, they ought also to be able to reveal the past—that is, they ought to be able to tell the king his dream. If they botched up the past, they would be likely to botch up the future.

Some Bible expositors have pointed out that Nebuchadnezzar was a young king, while these advisors were quite old, having served Nebuchadnezzar's father. Nebuchadnezzar may have thought that these aged men might be trying to pull the wool over his eyes, thinking he was a naive young man. He therefore may have doubted their loyalty to him. Nebuchadnezzar's test may have been engineered to sift out the bad with a view to bringing in people he could really trust.

Torn limb from limb...houses...laid in ruins (2:5): The consequences for failure would be severe: Death and destruction of personal property. These words were probably more severe than these aged men had ever heard from Nebuchadnezzar's father.

Gifts and rewards and great honor (2:6): On the other hand, the reward for success would be great. The stakes were very high.

Therefore show me the dream and its interpretation (2:6): The occultists had their backs against the wall, and they knew it. This was an either-or crisis.

Either they get it right and get rewarded, or they get it wrong and die. There was no middle option.

MAJOR THEMES

1. *Sorcerers.* Sorcery in ancient times sometimes involved conjuring spells (Deuteronomy 18:11). Other times it might involve interpreting omens (Genesis 30:27; 44:5). Still other times it might involve practicing soothsaying by, for example, examining the liver of a dead animal that had been used for sacrifice. If there were any abnormalities in the liver, they would try to interpret those abnormalities as a possible indication of some aspect of the will of the gods. The Bible condemns all forms of sorcery (Exodus 22:18; Leviticus 19:26, 31; 20:27).

2. *Astrologers.* Astrology can be traced back to the religious practices of ancient Mesopotamia, Assyria, Babylon, and Egypt. It is a form of divination—an attempt to seek paranormal counsel or knowledge by occultic means. It was believed that the study of the arrangement and movement of the stars could enable one to foretell events and determine whether they would be good or bad (see Daniel 2:10, 27; 4:7; 5:7). As well, in Babylon the stars were viewed as being connected to the pagan gods (Daniel 5:11). Astrology is strictly off-limits for Christians (Deuteronomy 18:9-12; Isaiah 47:13-15).

DIGGING DEEPER WITH CROSS-REFERENCES

Notable dreams—Genesis 28:12; 37:5, 9; 40:5, 16; 41:1; Judges 7:13; 1 Kings 3:5, 15; Matthew 1:20; 2:12-13, 19, 22; 27:19

Magicians—Genesis 41:8; Exodus 7:11, 22; 8:7, 19; Daniel 1:20; 2:2, 10, 27; 4:7; 5:7

LIFE LESSONS

1. *Sleeplessness versus sound sleep.* We read about sleeplessness not only in the book of Daniel (2:1; 6:18-19), but elsewhere in Scripture as well (Esther 6:1; Job 7:4-5; 30:17; Psalm 77:4; Ecclesiastes 2:23). Scripture also speaks of those who enjoy good sleep (Psalms 3:5; 4:8; 127:2; Proverbs 3:21-24;

6:20-22). Do you want to sleep soundly? Scripture urges us to always trust God, obey God, and fill our minds with God's Word.

2. *Dealing with threats.* In Daniel 2:5, the various occultists were threatened with death if they didn't tell the king what he wanted to hear. God's people, too, are often threatened. For example, in Acts 4:17-21 the Jewish Sanhedrin threatened the apostles to keep silent about Jesus. The apostles responded by praying, "And now, Lord, look upon their threats and grant to your servants to continue to speak your word with all boldness" (verse 29). We can adopt this prayer as our own as we encounter threats in our increasingly anti-Christian culture.

QUESTIONS FOR REFLECTION AND DISCUSSION

1. Can you think of any popular modern occultists who claim to have answers to the mysteries of life? Why might they be so popular?

2. What do the polar opposite consequences in Daniel 2:5-6 reveal about the king's character?

3. We will soon see Daniel clearly explaining that the power to interpret dreams is from God. What source empowered the magicians, the enchanters, and the sorcerers? What does Scripture elsewhere reveal about this source? (See John 8:44; 2 Corinthians 4:4; 11:14; 1 Peter 5:8.)

DAY 5

NEBUCHADNEZZAR DEMANDS AN INTERPRETATION

DANIEL 2:7-16

SCRIPTURE READING AND INSIGHTS

Begin by reading Daniel 2:7-16 in your favorite Bible. As you read, remember that storing God's Word in your heart can help you to avoid sinning (Psalm 119:9, 11).

Yesterday we focused on Nebuchadnezzar's recurring dream and his demand for an interpretation. Today we will see him prepare to carry out his threats against his "wise men." With your Bible still accessible, consider the following insights on the biblical text, verse by verse.

Daniel 2:7

Let the king tell his servants the dream (2:7): The occultists knew their backs were against the wall. They therefore implored the king again to reveal the dream to them so they could offer him an interpretation.

As is so often the case in the Bible, the occultists were unable to deliver. The same thing had happened twice in the Egyptian pharaoh's court—once with Joseph (Genesis 41:1-8) and again with Moses (Exodus 8:16-19). The contest between the one true God and the powers of darkness (who energized these occultists) turns out to be no real contest at all.

Daniel 2:8-9

You are trying to gain time (2:8): The king took the second plea from the occultists as an attempt to stall for time. Perhaps they thought that if they could stall long enough, the king would simply acquiesce and not pursue the matter any further. They hoped their stall tactics would provide sufficient time for the king to cool down and forget about the incident.

The word from me is firm (2:8): The king would not bend. His mind was made up. He seemed intent on exposing their hypocrisy. The occultists claimed to be wise men, but how wise were they really? The king suspected they were bogus—all talk and no substance. Their stall tactics were leading them toward an early grave.

As we have seen, these men had worked for Nebuchadnezzar's father. They may have thought the new king was inexperienced, immature, and naive. Perhaps they thought that given enough time, he might grow up and act more kingly, like his father. If so, this was a gross miscalculation on their part, for they were all close to losing their lives.

There is but one sentence for you (2:9): The king reiterates the penalty for failure in order to emphasize the gravity of the occultists' situation. They would either reveal the dream or forfeit their lives (see verse 5).

Tell me the dream (2:9): The king was convinced he could trust the occultists' interpretation of the dream only if they first revealed the dream to him. If they couldn't do that, the king must conclude they conspired against him and "agreed to speak lying and corrupt words...till the times change."

The truth is that only a person with supernatural insight could meet the king's demands. The failure of the so-called "wise men" sets the stage for Daniel's impressive intervention.

Daniel 2:10-11

There is not a man on earth (2:10): In an attempt to save their lives, the occultists pleaded with the king—he was making an impossible and unreasonable request that no one was capable of fulfilling. Of course, they were correct. No man, not even Daniel, has the intrinsic ability to tell another human being his or her dreams.

No great and powerful king (2:10): No other potentate had ever asked wise men to do what Nebuchadnezzar was now asking.

No one can show it to the king except the gods (2:11): Notice the contrast we see in verses 10 and 11 between the earthly and the non-earthly. No one on earth could meet the king's demand (verse 10), only the gods, "whose dwelling is not with flesh" (verse 11). In other words, these gods do not dwell on earth with mere mortals. The truth, of course, is that these gods don't live anywhere, for they don't even exist (see 1 Corinthians 8:4-6).

There is another thing worth noting here. When the occultists said that no one but the gods could reveal the dream to the king, they admitted that their previous interpretations of dreams were bogus, since only the gods can give such information. We might paraphrase the point this way: "Even though we've given many interpretations of dreams in the past, the truth is (*ahem*) that only the gods can do it."

Only the one true God in heaven could answer the king's request. God would soon do this through his beloved servant Daniel (Daniel 4). We are again reminded of the Egyptian magicians in Joseph's time who were unable to interpret Pharaoh's dream. With God's help, Joseph did so. Pharaoh said to Joseph, "Since God has shown you all this, there is none so discerning and wise as you are" (Genesis 41:39). Daniel and Joseph were seemingly cut from the same cloth!

Daniel 2:12-13

The king was angry (2:12): The king became angry for several reasons. The occultic "wise men" were in fact not wise because they could not tell the king his dream. They claimed to be in contact with the divine, but obviously they were not. Instead of immediately granting the king's request, they stalled for time, hoping the incident would be forgotten. The king concluded these men were deceivers who considered him gullible enough to fall for their lies.

To make matters worse, the wise men implied that the king's request was inappropriate and, in fact, impossible. The king was to be viewed as divine, and the wise men were to be his servants, so they were out of line saying such a thing to a god.

The decree went out (2:13): The king had had enough and ordered the execution of all the wise men in his kingdom. Biblical scholars have noted several examples of ancient potentates executing an entire class of servants or workers (compare 1 Samuel 22:13-19).

The wise men were about to be killed (2:13): Daniel and his friends were in the class of "wise men" in Babylon even though they were completely unlike any of the occultists. Therefore the king's instruction to kill all the wise men in the kingdom included them.

Daniel 2:14-16

Daniel replied (2:14): Confronted by the captain of the king's guard about the death sentence imposed on all wise men, Daniel again showed his wisdom, prudence, and discretion (see Proverbs 15:1).

Why…so urgent? (2:15): Instead of responding in a reactionary way, Daniel simply inquired why the king had made this urgent decree. Arioch then informed Daniel of all that had transpired.

Requested the king to appoint him a time (2:16): Notice three things about this verse. First, notice that Daniel had direct access to the king. This indicates that Daniel was held in high regard. No ordinary person would be granted an urgent appointment with the king.

Second, notice how bold Daniel was. The wise men had previously stalled and delayed in answering the king. Now Daniel asked the king to "appoint him a time"—which, in fact, would also involve a delay. Perhaps the king granted Daniel's request because Daniel had proved himself trustworthy in the past.

Third, notice Daniel's faith. He made an appointment to reveal and interpret the dream for the king even though God had not yet revealed the dream to Daniel. He knew that God would come through for him.

MAJOR THEMES

1. *The error of believing in many gods.* The Chaldeans told the king that no one could tell the king his dream "except the gods" (Daniel 2:11). Daniel consistently pointed to the one true God in contrast to the many false gods of Babylon. Scripture consistently testifies that only one true God exists. God himself positively affirmed through Isaiah the prophet, "I am the first and I am the last; besides me there is no god" (Isaiah 44:6; see also 37:20; 43:10; 45:14, 21-22). He asserted, "I am the Lord, and there is no other, besides me there is no God" (Isaiah 45:5). He later affirmed, "I am God, and there is no other; I am God, and there is none like me" (46:9;

see also Deuteronomy 6:4; 32:39; 2 Samuel 7:22). The New Testament also emphasizes the oneness of God (John 5:44; 17:3; Romans 3:29-30; 16:27; Galatians 3:20; Ephesians 4:6; 1 Thessalonians 1:9; 1 Timothy 1:17; 2:5; 1 John 5:20; Jude 25). Belief in one God is known as monotheism. Belief in many gods is called polytheism.

2. *Royal decrees.* Daniel 2:13 informs us, "The decree went out, and the wise men were about to be killed." The decree came from Nebuchadnezzar. A decree is essentially an order, declaration, or edict from a person in high authority that has the force of law. Royal decrees were common in biblical times (for example, see Esther 1:19-22; Acts 17:7). Most often, such decrees were first spoken aloud by a person in high authority and then committed to writing. To disobey the decree amounted to disobeying the one who issued it. In Daniel 2, Arioch, the captain of the king's guard, knew that if he didn't obey the decree, he would likely lose his life.

DIGGING DEEPER WITH CROSS-REFERENCES

The limits of human understanding—Genesis 41:8; Job 8:9; Proverbs 20:24; 27:1; 30:3; Ecclesiastes 3:22; 8:7; 9:12; Daniel 2:10, 27; 4:7, 18; 5:8, 15; 12:8; Matthew 11:25; 1 Corinthians 13:9; James 1:5

The use of time—Ephesians 5:16; Colossians 4:5

The true God outshines the powers of darkness—Exodus 7–11; 1 Kings 18; Jeremiah 28; Acts 13:1-12

LIFE LESSONS

1. *The Christian and prudence.* God desires that His followers be prudent, like Daniel (Daniel 2:14). The prudent person always looks ahead to see what is coming (Proverbs 14:8) and foresees danger (Proverbs 22:3; 27:12). The prudent person always carefully considers his steps (Proverbs 14:15). He is consistently cautious (Proverbs 14:16). He consistently saves money for the future (Proverbs 6:6-11) and guards his mouth and his tongue (Psalm 39:1; Proverbs 21:23). Moreover, he is aware that consulting many counselors is one key to success (Proverbs 15:22). One great way to

increase prudence is to focus studied attention on the book of Proverbs (see Proverbs 1:1-6).

2. *Beware of the deception of occultists.* John 8:44 tells us that Satan is the father of lies. It therefore makes sense that magicians, enchanters, and sorcerers—all of whom are energized by Satan—would be deceptive as well. Satan deceives in many ways. He has his own church—the "synagogue of Satan" (Revelation 2:9). He has his own ministers of darkness who bring false sermons (2 Corinthians 11:4-5). He has formulated his own system of theology, called "teachings of demons" (1 Timothy 4:1; see also Revelation 2:24). His ministers proclaim his gospel—"a gospel contrary to the one we preached to you" (Galatians 1:7-8). He has his own throne (Revelation 13:2) and his own worshipers (Revelation 13:4). He inspires false Christs (Matthew 24:4-5) and employs false teachers who bring in "destructive heresies" (2 Peter 2:1). He sends out false prophets (Matthew 24:11) and sponsors false apostles who imitate the true (2 Corinthians 11:13). Christians beware!

QUESTIONS FOR REFLECTION AND DISCUSSION

1. Daniel made an appointment to tell the king the interpretation of the dream (Daniel 2:16) *before* the interpretation had been revealed to him by God (verse 19). What does this show us about Daniel's faith?

2. In today's world, where the tyranny of the urgent rules and distractions confront us at every corner, do you find it difficult to keep God at the forefront of your thinking the way Daniel did? If so, do you want to make any changes today?

3. What are some ways that modern occultists, such as psychics, engage in deception?

DAY 6

GOD REVEALS THE MEANING OF THE DREAM TO DANIEL

DANIEL 2:17-23

SCRIPTURE READING AND INSIGHTS

Begin by reading Daniel 2:17-23 in your favorite Bible. As you read, remember that the Word of God teaches us, trains us, and corrects us (2 Timothy 3:15-17).

In yesterday's reading, Nebuchadnezzar demanded an interpretation of his dream. In today's lesson, God reveals the dream and its meaning to Daniel. With your Bible still accessible, consider the following insights on the biblical text, verse by verse.

Daniel 2:17-18

Daniel went to his house (2:17): Daniel was deliberately calm in this crisis. Though his life and his companions' lives were at stake, he remained tranquil and steady as he trusted in God.

Told them to seek mercy from the God of heaven (2:18): Upon arriving home, Daniel immediately asked his friends to pray to God for mercy. Notice that in this context of intercessory prayer to God, Daniel's associates were addressed not by their Babylonian names but by their Hebrew names—Hananiah, Mishael, and Azariah. They were praying not to the false gods of Babylon but to the God of the Hebrews—the true God.

Daniel knew that their only hope rested with God and His mercy. If God did not intervene, they would all be dead men. Daniel knew that in himself he was just as ignorant of the dream and its meaning as the occultists were. From Daniel's perspective, God *had* to intervene. Notice that in their prayer, Daniel and his friends were trusting God to give them a definite answer within definite time parameters. They were stepping out on a limb, and if God did not intervene, they were history.

We again note the contrast between earth and heaven. Earlier in Daniel 2, the occultists informed the king that no man on *earth* could reveal the dream (verse 10). They were right about that. Now, we find Daniel appealing to the God of *heaven* for answers. The ascription "God of heaven" is used four times in this chapter (verses 18-19, 37, 44). "Lord of heaven" is used in 5:23, and we read, "There is a God in heaven" in 2:28.

Throughout this entire ordeal, we see no sense of panic in Daniel or his associates. They prayed to God, they trusted in God, and they were at peace. One is reminded of the apostle Paul's teaching on prayer in Philippians 4:6-7: "Do not be anxious about anything, but in everything by prayer and supplication with thanksgiving let your requests be made known to God. And the peace of God, which surpasses all understanding, will guard your hearts and your minds in Christ Jesus" (see also Isaiah 26:3).

Concerning this mystery (2:18): Daniel and his friends asked God to enable them to unravel the mystery. In the Bible, a mystery is a truth that cannot be discerned simply by human investigation but requires special revelation from God. They desperately needed a special revelation from God regarding Nebuchadnezzar's dream and its meaning.

Daniel 2:19

The mystery was revealed (2:19): God answered their prayers. He showed them the mercy they requested.

Vision of the night (2:19): On the very night that Daniel and his friends prayed, God communicated Nebuchadnezzar's dream to Daniel in a vision (compare Numbers 12:6; 2 Kings 6:8-12; Job 33:15-16). What was hidden from Babylon's occultists was now revealed to Daniel. The former were impotent to accomplish their task, but God showed Himself strong on Daniel's behalf, thereby rescuing him and his associates from execution.

Daniel 2:20-23

Blessed be the name of God forever and ever (2:20): Notice that Daniel did not immediately rush off to Arioch to tell him the good news. Daniel's highest priority was God. The first thing he did after receiving the vision was to give thanks and praise to God for His mighty deliverance. God, not Daniel, was to get all the credit in this episode. Daniel was truly grateful to God!

This opening statement is significant. God's name represents all that He is (see Major Themes). To bless someone is to pronounce goodness or favor upon them.

Examples of God blessing people abound in Scripture (for example, Genesis 1:22, 28; 12:2; 22:17; 24:35; 32:29; Exodus 20:24; Job 42:12; Psalm 45:2). Examples of people blessing people are well illustrated in several famous biblical personalities, including Isaac (Genesis 27:26-40), Jacob (Genesis 49:1-27), Moses (Deuteronomy 33), Joshua (Joshua 22:6-7), and Jesus (Luke 24:50). Scripture indicates that human beings bless God when they recognize and give thanks to Him for His wonderful acts of mercy and grace in their lives (see Psalms 63:4; 104:1; 145:1-2). This is what Daniel was doing in our present context.

Daniel's blessing of God brings to mind Psalm 103:1-2: "Bless the Lord, O my soul, and all that is within me, bless his holy name! Bless the Lord, O my soul, and forget not all his benefits." Daniel was definitely a Psalm 103 kind of person.

To whom belong wisdom and might (2:20): Daniel recognized that God was both wise and mighty, for only a wise and mighty God could have intervened in his life through a vision to rescue Daniel and his friends from certain death.

He changes times and seasons; he removes kings and sets up kings (2:21): In verses 21-22, Daniel provides illustrations of God's wisdom and might. For example, God is so mighty that He can control history (changing times and seasons) and determine the destiny of nations (removing kings and setting up kings). This means Nebuchadnezzar was king of Babylon for only one reason—God sovereignly determined to use him for His providential purposes.

He gives wisdom to the wise (2:21): As the God of wisdom, God is the source of wisdom for those who follow Him (see Proverbs 1:2-5). Daniel and his friends acted wisely in Babylon because God gave them wisdom. Daniel

1:17 says of the four youths, "God gave them learning and skill in all literature and wisdom, and Daniel had understanding in all visions and dreams."

He reveals deep and hidden things (2:22): This includes Nebuchadnezzar's dream.

He knows what is in the darkness (2:22): God is both all-knowing (omniscient) and everywhere-present (omnipresent). This means that nothing escapes His notice, even in the darkest places in the universe. Even a person's dreams cannot escape His notice. Nebuchadnezzar's dream was "darkness" to him, but God's light revealed the meaning of it to Daniel.

The light dwells with him (2:22): In context, this carries the idea that even though people may be in the dark about things (just as Daniel had no knowledge of Nebuchadnezzar's dream), all things are clear to God. Psalm 36:9 says of God, "In your light do we see light." Job 12:22 tells us, "He uncovers the deeps out of darkness and brings deep darkness to light." Psalm 139:12 says of God, "Even the darkness is not dark to you; the night is bright as the day, for darkness is as light with you." In Jeremiah 23:24 God Himself affirms, "Can a man hide himself in secret places so that I cannot see him? declares the Lord. Do I not fill heaven and earth? declares the Lord."

God of my fathers (2:23): This is the God of Abraham, Isaac, Jacob, and the other patriarchs (see, for example, Genesis 31:42). He is the one true God of the universe.

I give thanks and praise (2:23): Through the vision God gave Daniel, Daniel and his friends obtained the knowledge that would save their lives. Daniel's appropriate response was thanksgiving and praise to God. Like Daniel, we should always have praise for God on our lips (see Psalm 34:1). We should praise God in the depths of our hearts (Psalm 103:1-5, 20-22) and continually "offer up a sacrifice of praise to God" (Hebrews 13:15). One means of praising God is through spiritual songs (Psalm 69:30).

You have...made known to me what we asked of you (2:23): Daniel and his friends made a specific request of God in prayer. God gave a specific answer. They asked for wisdom, and God gave it (see James 1:5). The Babylonian wise men were unaware of it at the time, but the true wise men—the four Hebrew youths—would bring about even their deliverance.

Through it all, Daniel and his friends discovered the truth of Psalm 50:15, where God said, "Call upon me in the day of trouble; I will deliver you, and you shall glorify me."

MAJOR THEMES

1. *The name of God.* Daniel praised God by saying, "Blessed be the name of God forever and ever." In the ancient world, a name was not a mere label as it is today. A name was considered equivalent to whoever or whatever bore it. The sum total of a person's being and his internal and external pattern of behavior was gathered up into his name. Indeed, knowing a person's name amounted to knowing his essence (see 1 Samuel 25:25). So when Daniel praised God's name, he was praising everything about God.

2. *God is omnipotent.* Daniel affirmed that God controls the course of world events (Daniel 2:21). Scripture more broadly reveals that God is omnipotent, or all-powerful (Genesis 18:14; Jeremiah 32:17, 27; Matthew 19:26; Mark 10:27; Luke 1:37). He is abundant in strength (Psalm 147:5) and has incomparably great power (2 Chronicles 20:6; Ephesians 1:19-21). No one can hold back His hand (Daniel 4:35), and no one can thwart Him (Isaiah 14:27). Therefore, He is able to control the course of world events, as Daniel said. The next time life throws you a punch, trust in the all-powerful God of the Bible.

DIGGING DEEPER WITH CROSS-REFERENCES

Seeking God's mercy—Psalms 6:2; 9:13; 25:7, 16; 27:7; 30:10; 31:9; 33:22; 40:11; 41:10; 51:1; 57:1; 85:7; 86:3; 119:58, 77; 123:3

God as light—Matthew 4:16; John 1:9; 8:12; 12:45-46; Ephesians 5:14; James 1:17; 1 Peter 2:9; 1 John 1:5; Revelation 21:23

LIFE LESSONS

1. *Mercy.* The term points to compassion and kindness shown to another. In the New Testament, God shows mercy on the basis of the work of Christ on the cross (Ephesians 2:4-5). Theologically, grace and mercy are closely related. The word "grace" means "unmerited favor." The word

"mercy," as related to our salvation, carries the idea of withholding deserved punishment. Because of what Jesus did for us at the cross, we not only receive God's unmerited favor (grace) with a wondrous salvation, we also escape the judgment we deserve for our sins (mercy). What a wonder is our Jesus! (See 1 Peter 2:10; 2 John 3; Jude 21.)

2. *Intercessory prayer.* Intercession is a common feature of the prayers of God's people in the Bible. Jesus urged His followers, "Pray for those who persecute you" (Matthew 5:44). He informed Peter, "I have prayed for you that your faith may not fail" (Luke 22:32). Speaking of those who crucified Him, Jesus prayed, "Father, forgive them, for they know not what they do" (Luke 23:34). Sometime later, the apostle Paul spoke of the importance of "making supplication for all the saints" (Ephesians 6:18). He said, "I urge that supplications, prayers, intercessions, and thanksgivings be made for all people" (1 Timothy 2:1). Paul urged the Corinthian believers, "Help us by prayer" (2 Corinthians 1:11). James speaks of intercessory prayer for the sick: "Is anyone among you sick? Let him call for the elders of the church, and let them pray over him" (James 5:14; see also Acts 7:60; Philippians 1:19). Praying for others ought to be our regular practice.

QUESTIONS FOR REFLECTION AND DISCUSSION

1. What do you learn about the attributes of God in Daniel 2:20-23? Why does Daniel see these attributes as praiseworthy?

2. Whom can you intercede for in prayer this week?

3. Do you sufficiently engage in thanksgiving and praise to God? We could probably all do better. Why not make Hebrews 13:15 one of your theme verses?

DAY 7

DANIEL INFORMS NEBUCHADNEZZAR THAT GOD HAS REVEALED THE MEANING

DANIEL 2:24-30

SCRIPTURE READING AND INSIGHTS

Begin by reading Daniel 2:24-30 in your favorite Bible. As you read, never forget that you can trust everything recorded in the Word of God (Matthew 5:18; John 10:35).

In the previous lesson, God revealed the meaning of Nebuchadnezzar's dream to Daniel. In today's lesson, Daniel reports to Nebuchadnezzar that God told him about the dream and its meaning. With your Bible still accessible, consider the following insights on the biblical text, verse by verse.

Daniel 2:24-25

Daniel went in to Arioch (2:24): Daniel immediately went to see Arioch because the stakes were so high in quickly meeting the king's demands. One should not miss the fact that Daniel not only had easy access to Arioch but also enjoyed some level of influence with him. This indicates the high respect that Arioch and others in the royal service had for Daniel. Daniel had a good reputation.

Do not destroy the wise men of Babylon (2:24): Daniel sought to prevent any further executions of Babylon's wise men. Here again we find Daniel manifesting a godly attitude, focusing on the safety of others. Much later in history, the apostle Paul would describe this attitude in Philippians 2:4: "Let each of you look not only to his own interests, but also to the interests of others." Recall that Jesus Himself taught, "You shall love your neighbor as yourself" (Matthew 22:39). Daniel loved and cared for the other wise men even though they were occultists.

Bring me in before the king (2:24): Daniel requested that Arioch take him immediately to see the king, for he now knew the dream and its interpretation. Notice that Daniel had no hesitation in sharing this news with Arioch. He was not unsure of himself. He did not say, "I *think* I know the dream and its interpretation." Nor did he say, "I have a *good idea* what the dream is and its interpretation." Daniel was absolutely sure that God had accurately revealed the dream and its meaning to him. He was completely confident in God.

Arioch brought in Daniel before the king in haste (2:25): Just as Daniel had quickly gone to see Arioch, so now Arioch quickly took Daniel to see the king. Perhaps Arioch thought that if he brought good news to the king, the king might reciprocate by looking upon him more favorably. Perhaps the king might even reward him. Time was of the essence. The sooner he got to the king, the better he would look.

I have found among the exiles from Judah (2:25): Notice how Arioch distorted what really happened. Daniel had come to Arioch, but Arioch boasts that he went out and found Daniel, as if he were busily trying to solve the king's dilemma. Daniel, a man of integrity, did not seek to correct Arioch on this.

Notice that Arioch introduced Daniel as one from "among the exiles from Judah." It is interesting to observe how often God has used a Jewish person to bring deliverance to others. Recall that when a number of kings joined in a coalition to overthrow Sodom and Gomorrah, Lot and many others were taken captive. Abraham, the father of the Jewish race, delivered them from bondage (Genesis 14). God used Joseph to deliver many Egyptians (and others) from the great famine that came upon the land (Genesis 37–50). God used a resistant Jonah to bring a message of repentance to Nineveh, after which they all repented, and God withheld His punishment of the nation (Jonah 1–3). And who can forget the wondrous salvation that has come through the divine Messiah, Himself a Jewish man (Matthew 1:1; John 3:16).

Daniel 2:26

Are you able to make known to me the dream...and its interpretation? (2:26): The king—perhaps a bit cynical after the failure of all the other wise men in Babylon—got right to the point with Daniel. Notice again that the interpretation of the dream would not be enough to satisfy the king. Daniel must first reveal the dream itself and then give the interpretation. Daniel was subjected to the same test of truth that the other wise men experienced.

Recall that the other wise men informed the king, "The thing that the king asks is difficult, and no one can show it to the king except the gods, whose dwelling is not with flesh" (Daniel 2:11). Thus Daniel's claim to know the dream and its message must have seemed extraordinary to Nebuchadnezzar. However, his knowledge of the dream was not from "the gods" but rather from the one true God.

Daniel 2:27

No wise men (2:27): Daniel's main point in Daniel 2:27-28 is that no one could possibly satisfy the king's request on his own. Daniel's reference to "wise men" referred not only to the occultists who failed to reveal the dream but also to himself. Daniel freely admitted that left to his own abilities, he could not tell the king his dream or its meaning. The good news, however, is that God in heaven does have this ability, and Daniel received revelation from God through a vision.

Daniel 2:28-30

God in heaven (2:28): The phrase "God in heaven" distinguishes Daniel's God from the multiple local deities of Babylon. Daniel was careful to emphasize that he knew the dream and its meaning only because the God of heaven had revealed it to him (compare with Genesis 41:16). Unlike Arioch, Daniel had no interest in promoting himself, but rather sought to honor and glorify God.

Who reveals mysteries (2:28): This God in heaven is the One who reveals mysteries. In the present case, the mystery involved Nebuchadnezzar's dream and its meaning. In the Bible, a mystery is a truth that cannot be discerned simply by human investigation, but requires special revelation from God. The God of heaven gave special revelation to Daniel about Nebuchadnezzar's dream.

He has made known to King Nebuchadnezzar (2:28): The moment had now arrived. Daniel was about to pass on to Nebuchadnezzar what God Himself had passed on to him.

He who reveals mysteries made known (2:29): Daniel informed Nebuchadnezzar that God was revealing the prophetic future to Nebuchadnezzar.

The Old Testament use of the term "last days" (and similar terms) typically refers to the time leading up to the second coming of the Messiah to set up His millennial kingdom on earth. More specifically, the Old Testament usage of such terms as "latter days," "last days," "latter years," "end of time," and "end of the age" all refer to Israel's time of tribulation, which leads to the second coming of the Messiah.

We will investigate the specifics of this prophetic dream in the next chapter. We will see that Nebuchadnezzar's dream spanned Gentile history and dominion, including the kingdom of his day and the kingdoms that followed, up to the days preceding the coming of Israel's Messiah in the prophetic future. The dream focuses heavily on what Jesus called "the times of the Gentiles" (Luke 21:24). The future sequence of Gentile kingdoms would one day climax with the appearance of God's eternal kingdom.

As for me (2:30): Daniel again took the path of humility. He took no credit for the dream or its interpretation, nor did he claim to be superior to the other wise men in Babylon. The mystery was revealed to him by the God of heaven. Despite Daniel's personal humility on the matter, one must recall that Nebuchadnezzar himself had earlier found Daniel and his friends to be "ten times better than all the magicians and enchanters that were in all his kingdom" (Daniel 1:20).

Take a moment to ponder some of the rich spiritual truths about God we have uncovered in today's biblical text:

- He is the only true God and is infinitely greater than all.
- He is sovereign over all kings and nations and is guiding human history.

- He is omniscient and knows the distant future.
- He answers prayer, gives revelation to human beings, and providentially protects His people.

Our God is an awesome God!

MAJOR THEMES

1. *God is omniscient.* Daniel knew that God is omniscient, so he boldly informed the king, "There is a God in heaven who reveals mysteries, and he has made known to King Nebuchadnezzar what will be in the latter days" (Daniel 2:28). Scripture reveals that God knows all things, both actual and possible (Matthew 11:21-23). He knows all things past (Isaiah 41:22), present (Hebrews 4:13), and future (Isaiah 46:10). And because He knows all things, His knowledge can neither increase nor decrease. Psalm 147:5 affirms that God's understanding is beyond measure. God's knowledge is infinite (Psalms 33:13-15; 139:11-12; Proverbs 15:3; Isaiah 40:14; 46:10). Thus, God could easily reveal to Daniel the king's dream and its meaning.

2. *God alone knows the future.* Closely related to God's omniscience is the biblical teaching that the one true God can foretell the future: "Fear not, nor be afraid; have I not told you from of old and declared it?" (Isaiah 44:8). "Who told this long ago? Who declared it of old? Was it not I, the LORD?" (45:21). "I declared them to you from of old, before they came to pass I announced them to you" (48:5). You and I may not know what the future holds for us or for anyone else. But we do know the One who knows the future—our all-knowing God.

DIGGING DEEPER WITH CROSS-REFERENCES

God's foreknowledge—Exodus 3:19; Deuteronomy 31:16; Isaiah 42:9; 44:7; 46:9-10; 48:3; Matthew 21:2; 24:36; Acts 2:23; 3:18; Romans 8:29; 1 Peter 1:2

Looking out for the interests of others—Daniel 2:24; Romans 12:10; Ephesians 4:2; 5:21; Philippians 2:3-4; 1 Peter 5:5

LIFE LESSONS

1. *God reveals the prophetic future to human beings.* Someone has rightly said that God *moved* and the prophet *mouthed* prophetic truths. God *revealed* and man *recorded* His words about the future (see 2 Timothy 3:16; 2 Peter 1:21; see also Jeremiah 1:9; Zechariah 7:12; Acts 1:16; 4:24-25). If there's one thing we learn from this, it is that we ought to place our trust not in human psychics, who make many mistakes and who are involved in occultism, but rather in the one true God, who knows the future.

2. *Following Daniel's example of humility.* Daniel was a humble man who pointed away from his own abilities and pointed to God instead (Daniel 2:27-28). The Scriptures tell us that those who would please God must walk in humility. Not only that, but God exalts the humble: "Humble yourselves before the Lord, and he will exalt you" (James 4:10; see also Luke 1:52). Daniel humbled himself all throughout the book of Daniel, and God subsequently exalted him. Scripture exhorts us to clothe ourselves with humility (1 Peter 5:5).

QUESTIONS FOR REFLECTION AND DISCUSSION

1. Can you think of another Old Testament personality who was challenged to interpret a dream for a high government official? (Hint: The answer is in the book of Genesis.) Try to think of at least five ways these two are alike.

2. What leadership qualities do you see in Daniel in today's Scripture reading?

3. Do a little self-inventory. Ask yourself, *Am I more interested in building others up or in building myself up in the eyes of others?* What have you learned in this lesson that might help you seek the kind of humility Daniel displayed?

DAY 8

DANIEL REVEALS THE MEANING OF THE DREAM TO NEBUCHADNEZZAR

DANIEL 2:31-49

SCRIPTURE READING AND INSIGHTS

Begin by reading Daniel 2:31-49 in your favorite Bible. As you read, trust God to open your eyes so you can discover wondrous things in His Word (Psalm 119:18).

In yesterday's lesson, Daniel reported to Nebuchadnezzar that God had provided the meaning of the dream to him. Now Daniel reveals the dream and its meaning to the king. With your Bible still accessible, consider the following insights on the biblical text, verse by verse.

Daniel 2:31-35

A great image (2:31): As a backdrop, apocalyptic literature is a special kind of writing that arose among the Jews and Christians in Bible times to reveal certain mysteries about the end times and the world to come. This type of literature is often characterized by visions, exhortations to make ethical and moral decisions or changes as a result of such visions, and a pervasive use of symbols and imagery. Daniel is an apocalyptic book, so we are not surprised to find kingdoms described as a statue made of gold, silver, bronze, iron, and clay (Daniel 2:32-35).

Its appearance was frightening (2:31): The size and appearance of the image must have been staggering, especially considering the metals from which it was constructed. With a head of gold on top and fragile feet at the bottom, this image seemed likely to topple.

Head...chest and arms...middle and thighs...legs...feet (2:32-33): The various metals and clay make this an interesting image. The head was made of gold, the chest and arms of silver, the stomach area and thighs of bronze, the legs of iron, and the feet a mix of iron and clay. Nebuchadnezzar probably considered this mix to be the most confusing element of the dream. Simply eyeballing the image gave no clue about its meaning. That would require revelation from God.

A stone was cut out (2:34): With a head of gold and fragile feet, the top-heavy image seemed prone to topple, but Nebuchadnezzar's dream revealed that a stone would aid the process by striking the image.

PARALLELS

Daniel 2:34—Christ crushes the antichrist's kingdom.

Revelation 3:21; 5:5; 17:14—Christ is Conqueror.

All together were broken in pieces, and became like the chaff (2:35): First the feet and then the rest of the body shattered, and the remaining particles were blown away in the wind like chaff. ("Chaff" refers to the worthless husks that are separated from grain during the process of threshing.) Not a trace of the image could thereafter be found.

The stone that struck the image (2:35): The stone then became a great mountain that filled the whole earth. Nebuchadnezzar must have been baffled by this dream—no wonder it unnerved him.

Daniel 2:36-45

The dream...its interpretation (2:36): Daniel had informed Nebuchadnezzar of his dream. Part two of the process would now begin—the interpretation of the image. We will see that as Daniel explains the image, he is actually referring to the Gentile nations that would rule over Palestine and the people of Israel.

You, O king, the king of kings…you are the head of gold (2:37-38): Daniel first revealed that Nebuchadnezzar—the "king of kings" whom God put into power, not only over human beings but over the animal kingdom as well—is the head of gold. The reference to animals brings to mind Genesis 1:26, where God affirmed after creating human beings, "Let them have dominion over the fish of the sea and over the birds of the heavens and over the livestock and over all the earth and over every creeping thing that creeps on the earth."

Another kingdom (2:39): Nebuchadnezzar was a finite being. He would not live forever, so another kingdom would arise after his. This next kingdom relates to the "chest and arms of silver" we read about in verse 32. The two arms of silver represent the rise of the Medes and Persians, who would conquer Babylon in 539 BC. Though the Medo-Persian Empire was strong and would last more than 200 years, it was nevertheless inferior to the kingdom of Babylon, just as silver is inferior to gold.

A third kingdom (2:39): Yet another kingdom would arise after the Medo-Persian Empire. This relates to the "middle and thighs of bronze" mentioned in verse 32. The word "middle" refers to the stomach area of the image. This refers to the Greek Empire, which conquered the Medo-Persian Empire between 334 and 330 BC under the leadership of Alexander the Great.

A fourth kingdom (2:40): A fourth kingdom would arise after the Greek Empire. This relates to the "legs of iron" mentioned in verse 32. This refers to the Roman Empire, which conquered the Greeks in 63 BC. Just as iron is the strongest among metals, so this empire would be stronger than all the previous empires. So strong was Rome that it was able to conquer many peoples and subdue any rebellion.

Feet and toes, partly of potter's clay and partly of iron (2:41): Scholars have debated this verse and those that follow, some ascribing the verses to the Roman Empire of old, and others ascribing the verses to the revived Roman Empire in the end times, over which the antichrist will rule. There are several reasons that make the latter view preferable.

First, the ten toes in Daniel 2:41 and the ten horns in Daniel 7 seem to represent the same ten kings. These revelations belong together. These kings will exercise rule in the revived Roman Empire in the end times.

Second, prophecy scholars have noted that the ten toes of Nebuchadnezzar's image have not yet corresponded to anything in history and therefore must relate to the prophetic future. As prophecy scholar John F. Walvoord put it, "According to Daniel's prophecy, the kingdoms represented by the ten toes existed side by side and were destroyed by one sudden catastrophic blow. Nothing like this has yet occurred in history."[1] But this *will* occur in history as the final revived Roman Empire is shattered at the second coming of Jesus Christ in glory.

Third, Old Testament prophecies commonly gloss over long periods of time. For example, some Old Testament prophecies lump together predictions concerning the first and second comings of Christ without mentioning the extended time between the two. Consequently, the legs of Nebuchadnezzar's image can easily refer to the Roman Empire of old, and the toes can refer to the revived Roman Empire in the end times.

Thus we can say that this latter-day Roman Empire will not attain true unity or cohesiveness, but will be like a mixture of iron and clay. It will be as strong as iron but will be characterized by divisions.

The God of heaven will set up a kingdom (2:44): Daniel now speaks of the overthrow of all earthly kingdoms, including the revived Roman Empire of the end times. Nebuchadnezzar had witnessed a rock smashing into the image (verse 34). The term "rock" is often used in reference to the divine Messiah, Jesus Christ (see Psalm 118:22; Isaiah 8:14; 28:16; 1 Peter 2:6-8). Christ will not only overthrow earthly kingdoms but will—following the second coming—set up His own millennial kingdom that will last 1,000 years on earth (Revelation 11:15; 19:11-20; 20:4). Following the millennial kingdom, Christ will continue His reign forever and ever.

PARALLELS

Daniel 2:44—God's kingdom stands eternal.

Revelation 11:17; 12:10; 19:6—God Almighty reigns supreme.

The dream is certain (2:45): The interpretation of the dream is certain, for the source of the interpretation is God Himself, the Revealer of mysteries (see verses 19, 23, 28, 30).

Daniel 2:46-47

Nebuchadnezzar fell upon his face (2:46): Nebuchadnezzar was "blown away" by Daniel's account of God's interpretation of the dream. He fell down and paid homage to Daniel and commanded that an offering and incense be offered up to him—actions traditionally reserved for the worship of Babylon's deities.

Your God is God of gods and Lord of kings (2:47): Daniel already knew that his God was superior to the gods of Babylon (which actually didn't exist). Now Nebuchadnezzar was forced to admit the superiority of Daniel's God.

PARALLELS

Daniel 2:47—God unveils mysteries.

Revelation 1:1; 4:1; 17:7; 22:6, 16—God reveals mysteries and foretells the future.

Daniel 2:48-49

High honors...great gifts...ruler...chief prefect (2:48): Daniel was rewarded with incredible material wealth as well as greatly increased authority in Babylon.

Daniel made a request (2:49): Daniel did not forget his friends. Through his influence, he was able to secure promotions for them as well. They became administrators under Daniel's authority. Of course, Nebuchadnezzar's promotion of Daniel and his friends was the providential work of the sovereign God.

MAJOR THEMES

1. *The supremacy of the one true God.* From the very beginning of the Old Testament, the one true God (Yahweh) is portrayed as incomparable to false, pagan gods. Moses said, "There is no one like the Lord our God" (Exodus 8:10). Rhetorical questions emphasized this same truth: "Who is like you,

O Lord, among the gods?" (Exodus 15:11). The implied answer is, no one in the entire universe. God is supreme and incomparable. Nebuchadnezzar came to realize this, and the book of Daniel continually emphasizes it.

2. *Nebuchadnezzar paid Daniel homage.* Following Daniel's revelation of the dream and its meaning, the king greatly honored both Daniel and Daniel's God. We should not miss the fact that if Daniel had taken all the credit for himself, the king would have honored only Daniel. But because Daniel gave glory to God in this episode, the king said, "Truly, your God is God of gods and Lord of kings" (Daniel 2:47). Pay special attention to the word "kings," which includes Nebuchadnezzar himself. Because of Daniel's witness, Nebuchadnezzar acknowledged that the true God was supreme even over him. That's quite an admission for a pagan king who claimed to be divine.

DIGGING DEEPER WITH CROSS-REFERENCES

God's eternal kingdom—2 Samuel 7:16; Psalms 145:13; 146:10; Isaiah 9:7; Micah 4:7; Luke 1:32-33; Hebrews 12:28; 2 Peter 1:11; Revelation 11:15

The exaltation of the true God—Exodus 15:2; 1 Chronicles 29:11; Nehemiah 9:5; Job 22:12; Psalms 21:13; 46:10; 57:11; 92:8; 97:9; 108:5; Isaiah 2:11; 6:1; 25:1; Ezekiel 38:23

LIFE LESSONS

1. *The humble are exalted.* This theme is repeated over and over again in Daniel. God providentially exalted Daniel in Babylon because he was consistently humble. As 1 Peter 5:6 puts it, "Humble yourselves, therefore, under the mighty hand of God so that at the proper time he may exalt you" (see also James 4:10). Proverbs reminds us, "Humility comes before honor" (15:33), "The reward for humility and fear of the Lord is riches and honor and life" (22:4), and "One's pride will bring him low, but he who is lowly in spirit will obtain honor" (29:23).

2. *True believers.* Daniel and his Jewish colleagues were the "real deal." They not only talked the talk but also walked the walk (see James 2:14-26).

Some have said that many today are secret-agent Christians who have never blown their cover. In other words, it's hard to recognize that some people are Christians by their words or actions, for they don't seem very "Christian." But Daniel and his friends lived out their faith for all to see, regardless of the consequences. What a great example they set for each of us!

QUESTIONS FOR REFLECTION AND DISCUSSION

1. Daniel explained, "The God of heaven will set up a kingdom that shall never be destroyed...it shall stand forever" (Daniel 2:44). What do you learn in this passage about the prominence of God's kingdom over the finite kingdoms of the earth? Does that give you a sense of security?
2. What attributes of God do you see highlighted in today's lesson?
3. If somebody accused you of being a Christian, would there be enough evidence to convict you?

DAY 9

NEBUCHADNEZZAR MAKES A GOLDEN IMAGE TO BE WORSHIPED

DANIEL 3:1-7

SCRIPTURE READING AND INSIGHTS

Begin by reading Daniel 3:1-7 in your favorite Bible. As you read, ask God to help you understand His Word (Psalm 119:73).

In yesterday's reading, Daniel revealed the dream and its meaning to Nebuchadnezzar. In today's lesson, Nebuchadnezzar constructs a golden image to be worshiped by all the people in his kingdom. With your Bible still accessible, consider the following insights on the biblical text, verse by verse.

Daniel 3:1

Image of gold (3:1): Having been identified as the head of gold in the image in his dream (Daniel 2:38), Nebuchadnezzar in his megalomania erected a full golden image of himself—gold from head to toe—to put an exclamation point on his greatness. Some Bible expositors suggest that Nebuchadnezzar may have also been trying to bring greater unity to his kingdom by affirming his authority as king and by centralizing worship. As we will see shortly, there were many varying ranks of government officials in Babylon, but this image portrays Nebuchadnezzar as the one who is over all. No one else in the kingdom would have such an image.

The image was ninety feet high but only nine feet wide. If the image were in the form of a human being, this ten-to-one ratio would make him appear to be very skinny. (The ratio of a normal human being is more like five to one.) It may be that the image pictured a more normal-looking human figure elevated on some type of massive base that made him appear high and exalted.

The construction of this golden image shows Nebuchadnezzar's true colors. Recall from Daniel 2:47 that following Daniel's revelation of the meaning of Nebuchadnezzar's dream, Nebuchadnezzar had exulted to Daniel, "Truly, your God is God of gods and Lord of kings." Apparently, his high thoughts of Daniel's God were short-lived, for he now had only high thoughts of himself.

In any event, because of its height and the gold appearance, the image was no doubt an imposing symbol of Nebuchadnezzar's majesty and authority. Because it was to be worshiped, it is properly categorized as an idol. (See Major Themes.)

Plain of Dura (3:1): "Dura" comes from an Akkadian word meaning "walled," "walled area," or "walled enclosure." Therefore, the plain of Dura may have been a plain surrounded either by walls or perhaps by mountains or hills. Archeologists have uncovered a site that may be where the golden image stood, but there is no certainty on this as of yet.

Daniel 3:2-3

Satraps (3:2): These were the chief representatives of the king over specific regions. Note that the seven positions listed in verse 2 are apparently in descending rank.

Prefects (3:2): These were military chiefs or commanders of armies.

Governors (3:2): These were the civil administrators, lieutenants, or viceroys.

Counselors (3:2): These were legal experts or lawyers. They may have assisted the king in the formation of new laws. Or they may have been counselors to those in various levels of governmental authority.

Treasurers (3:2): These were in charge of Babylon's treasure houses and administered the funds of the kingdom.

Justices (3:2): These were the government's arbiters and administrators of the law.

Magistrates (3:2): These were judges who passed judgment in keeping with the law.

And all the officials (3:2): These were all other types of civil leaders in Babylon.

The dedication of the image (3:2): All seven classes of government officials would be required to bow in worship of the image to show their full and unqualified allegiance to Nebuchadnezzar. Note that Daniel would not have been present with this group because he remained in the capital city "at the king's court" (Daniel 2:49). Daniel's three friends—Shadrach, Meshach, and Abednego—were called to Dura to show their loyalty. As we will see, they refused to bow down, just as Daniel would have refused had he been there.

They stood before the image (3:3): In obedience to Nebuchadnezzar, the seven classes of government officials all showed up for the dedication and demonstrated their respect by standing before the image. They were required to bow down and worship the image, so it had both religious and political significance. Bowing to the image acknowledged not only acceptance of Nebuchadnezzar's divine status, but also submission to his political power and authority. This would unify the kingdom religiously and politically.

Daniel 3:4-5

The herald proclaimed (3:4): Heralds publicly announced the king's decrees on various matters. In the present case, the heralds indicated to all seven classes of government officials that by their act of bowing before the image, they would recognize Nebuchadnezzar's political and religious power and authority. Bowing would be an open act of submission.

When you hear (3:5): Music was used for a variety of purposes in biblical times (see Major Themes). In the present case, music was a cue to bow down and worship the golden image.

Horn (3:5): There were various kinds of horns in biblical days. The *geren* was a form of trumpet, made from the horn of an animal (see Leviticus 25:9; Joshua 6:4). A trumpet made from a ram's horn was called a *shofar* and was used for special occasions during the Jewish year, particularly on the Hebrew New Year's Day and the Day of Atonement. The horn used in Babylon was no doubt something similar.

Pipe (3:5): The pipe was a wind instrument. An example of this type of instrument was the *halil*, which was basically a hollow pipe made of cane or wood that utilized a reed to make a musical sound.

Lyre (3:5): The lyre was a stringed instrument with a wooden frame (see Genesis 4:21; 2 Samuel 6:5; 1 Kings 10:12). David, the shepherd king of Israel, was apparently able to play both the lyre and the harp and often used such musical instruments to soothe the nerves of King Saul (1 Samuel 16:16, 23).

Trigon (3:5): This was a small harp with smaller strings and higher tones.

Harp (3:5): Similar to the lyre, the harp was a musical instrument made from a wooden frame that had strings on it. Again, David was a gifted harpist, with the ability to play several different kinds of harps (see 1 Samuel 16:18-23). David was also a proficient poet, as evidenced in the psalms he wrote, many of which were accompanied by music. He was known as the "sweet psalmist of Israel" (2 Samuel 23:1).

Bagpipe (3:5): Unlike the modern bagpipe, Babylon's bagpipe was apparently some type of percussion instrument.

Fall down and worship (3:5): The sound of the music would be the cue to worship the idolatrous image. (See Major Themes.)

Daniel 3:6-7

Whoever does not fall down and worship...a burning fiery furnace (3:6): The penalty for refusing to bow down and worship the image was incineration in what was apparently an industrial-sized oven used for smelting metals and baking bricks. This was a punishment Nebuchadnezzar had elsewhere used on two Judean false prophets, Zedekiah and Ahab (Jeremiah 29:22). The Code of Hammurabi (sections 25, 110, and 157) indicates that this may have been a common Babylonian means of execution.

As soon as all the peoples heard (3:7): An awesome and formidable image stood before the people. The king had given the command. Now the music started. On cue, all the government officials showed their submission by bowing before the image in worship. Nebuchadnezzar thereby achieved what he wanted—an open display of leaders vowing political and religious submission.

PARALLELS

Daniel 3:7—Many worship idols.

Revelation 13:4—Satan and the antichrist are worshiped.

MAJOR THEMES

1. *The making of idols.* Daniel had told Nebuchadnezzar that the head of gold in his dream represented him (Daniel 2:38). It must have gone to his head! Now the king had a 90-foot-high gold image of himself constructed—not just a head, but apparently the entire body—to reflect his greatness, glory, and self-proclaimed deity. This image was likely not made of solid gold but rather featured a gold overlay, similar to other objects discovered in the ruins of Babylon (see Isaiah 40:19). An image that large made of solid gold would have been entirely too difficult to handle because of its incredible weight. Regardless of how glorious it appeared, Daniel's friends refused to bow down and worship it. The New Testament consistently urges Christians to avoid all forms of idolatry (1 Corinthians 5:11; 2 Corinthians 6:16; Galatians 5:19-21; Colossians 3:5; 1 John 5:21). (More on this in the next lesson.)

2. *Musical instruments in biblical times.* Music was used for a variety of purposes in Bible times. Music was played for the homecoming party of the prodigal son (Luke 15:25). It was also used at banquets and feasts (Isaiah 5:12; 24:8-9) as well as for laments (Matthew 9:23). Music was performed at the coronation of kings (2 Chronicles 23:11-13) as well as at temple ceremonies (1 Chronicles 16:4-6; 2 Chronicles 29:25). Music was often performed during pilgrimages (2 Samuel 6:5). Sometimes music was used to enable a prophet to enter into a trance so he could receive divine oracles (see 2 Kings 3:15). Music was also used to celebrate military victories (Exodus 15:1; 2 Chronicles 20:27-28). In the present case, music was used as a signal to bow down and worship a pagan idol (Daniel 3:10).

DIGGING DEEPER WITH CROSS-REFERENCES

Execution by burning—Genesis 38:24-25; Leviticus 20:14; 21:9; Daniel 3:6, 21

Idolatrous images of gold—Exodus 20:23; 32:2-4; Deuteronomy 7:25; 1 Kings 12:28; Psalms 115:4-8; 135:15; Isaiah 2:20; 30:22

LIFE LESSONS

1. *Worship is reserved for the one true God.* Worship involves reverencing God, adoring Him, praising Him, venerating Him, and paying homage to Him, not only externally (with words, songs, and rituals) but also in our hearts (Isaiah 29:13; see also 1 Samuel 15:22-23). The Hebrew word for worship, *shaha*, means "to bow down" or "to prostrate oneself" (see Genesis 22:5; 42:6). Likewise, the New Testament word for worship, *proskuneo*, means "to prostrate oneself" (see Matthew 2:2, 8, 11). In Old English, "worship" was rendered "worthship," pointing to the worthiness of the object that was worshiped. Such worship is the proper response of a creature to the divine Creator (Psalm 95:6). Worship can be congregational (1 Corinthians 11–14) or individual (see Romans 12:1). Worship does not stop on earth but continues in heaven when believers enter into glory (see Revelation 4–5). Some have said that true worship is the missing jewel in the modern church. Let's resolve to recover that jewel!

2. *False objects of faith.* It has been well said that everybody has faith in something. Even members of cults and false religions can have a strong faith, but their faith is misdirected to a false object of faith. The people commanded to bow down and worship Nebuchadnezzar's golden image had no hesitation in doing so, not only because they were accustomed to worshiping pagan gods but also because of the death penalty for refusing. Daniel's friends—Shadrach, Meshach, and Abednego—were present at this ceremony. They had faith in the one true God, and their faith was unwavering in the face of persecution and even the threat of death (compare Psalm 118:8; Proverbs 3:5; Jeremiah 17:7; 2 Corinthians 5:7; 1 Peter 1:7). In the next chapter, we will see that their faith in God and their faithfulness to God landed them in a fiery furnace (Daniel 3:20-21).

QUESTIONS FOR REFLECTION AND DISCUSSION

1. Daniel and his friends did not obey the command to worship the golden image. Do you think peaceful civil disobedience is ever justified? If so, under what circumstances? (See Acts 5:29.)

2. Can you say without hesitation that God is your foremost object of faith? Are you sometimes tempted to trust other things in place of Him?

3. Why might music have been used in this worship ceremony? In what ways can music affect people?

DAY 10

SHADRACH, MESHACH, AND ABEDNEGO ARE ACCUSED

DANIEL 3:8-12

SCRIPTURE READING AND INSIGHTS

Begin by reading Daniel 3:8-12 in your favorite Bible. As you read, remember that reading Scripture can strengthen your faith in God (Romans 10:17).

Yesterday we saw Nebuchadnezzar construct a golden image to be worshiped. Now let's watch as Shadrach, Meshach, and Abednego get into life-threatening trouble for refusing to worship the image. With your Bible still accessible, consider the following insights on the biblical text, verse by verse.

Daniel 3:8

Chaldeans (3:8): The word "Chaldeans" can be used in different senses in Scripture. It can function simply as a general ethnic term for the Babylonian people. In the present case, however, the term is used more narrowly in reference to priests who functioned as astrologers, soothsayers, and wise men in Nebuchadnezzar's government.

Maliciously accused the Jews (3:8): The phrase "maliciously accused" translates a rather vulgar expression that means, "devour the pieces of flesh torn off a person's body." It came to connote doing injury to another person through malicious slander. The Chaldeans were making a serious accusation against Shadrach, Meshach, and Abednego in order to destroy them.

PARALLELS

Daniel 3:8—Pagans persecute the Jews.

Revelation 12:13—Satan targets the Jews.

The motivation of the Chaldeans for maliciously accusing the Jews was probably threefold. First is the issue of racism, for many Babylonians hated the Jews. We see this same type of hatred elsewhere in Scripture. Esther 3:5-6 tells us, "When Haman [a Persian] saw that Mordecai [a Jew] did not bow down or pay homage to him, Haman was filled with fury. But he disdained to lay hands on Mordecai alone. So, as they had made known to him the people of Mordecai, Haman sought to destroy all the Jews, the people of Mordecai, throughout the whole kingdom of Ahasuerus." The psalmist laments to God of the attempted genocide against the Jews: "For behold, your enemies make an uproar; those who hate you have raised their heads. They lay crafty plans against your people; they consult together against your treasured ones. They say, 'Come, let us wipe them out as a nation; let the name of Israel be remembered no more!'" (Psalm 83:2-4). Many Babylonians would have been happy to completely do away with the Jews.

Second, aside from hatred of the Jews, there was also the issue of jealousy. When one nation took the people of another nation into captivity, the captives were generally assigned positions of servitude in the conquering nation. They were not typically elevated to positions of authority, but Daniel and his friends had become governing officials in the kingdom. Nebuchadnezzar himself had previously spoken of them with high praise: "In every matter of wisdom and understanding about which the king inquired of them, he found them ten times better than all the magicians and enchanters that were in all his kingdom" (Daniel 1:20). The Chaldeans no doubt bitterly resented this praise and their high appointments. We recall from Daniel 2:49 that Daniel himself "made a request of the king, and he appointed Shadrach, Meshach, and Abednego over the affairs of the province of Babylon. But Daniel remained at the king's court." The Chaldeans referred to the king's appointment of these Jews during their accusation of them: "There are certain Jews *whom you have appointed* over the affairs of the province of Babylon: Shadrach, Meshach, and Abednego" (Daniel 3:12). One can almost see the jealousy dripping from their lips.

Third, their accusation was ultimately self-serving. The Chaldeans had bowed before the golden image, whereas Shadrach, Meshach, and Abednego had not. Perhaps they were trying to make themselves look good at the expense of Shadrach, Meshach, and Abednego. Perhaps they were seeking personal favor from the king.

Notice that Daniel was not among the accused. Daniel would not have been present with this group because he remained in the capital city "at the king's court" (Daniel 2:49). Besides, these Chaldeans may have considered it risky to say anything negative about Daniel, who was a higher official and was highly regarded. Let us be clear, however, that Daniel would have refused to bow before the image with as much fervor as Shadrach, Meshach, and Abednego had he been there.

Daniel 3:9-11

O king, live forever (3:9): Before launching their verbal attack against Shadrach, Meshach, and Abednego, the Chaldeans said, "O king, live forever." This was apparently a common show of respect when beginning a conversation with the king. Later in the book of Daniel, when the high officials and satraps appeared before another king with the intention of entrapping Daniel, they began their conversation, "O King Darius, live forever" (Daniel 6:6). Daniel ended up in the lions' den as a result of their entrapment. But the next morning, the king rushed down to the den to see if Daniel was okay. Daniel answered, "O king, live forever! My God sent his angel and shut the lions' mouths" (6:21-22).

You, O king, have made a decree (3:10): The unscrupulous Chaldeans reminded the king of his decree that the penalty for not bowing before the golden image was death by incineration.

Every man who hears (3:10): The cue for bowing before the image was to be the sound of musical instruments playing. As the music played, however, Shadrach, Meshach, and Abednego didn't budge. They continued to stand upright.

Whoever does not (3:11): The word "whoever" communicates the idea that there were to be no exceptions. Any person who failed to bow before the image was to experience capital punishment by burning.

Cast into a burning fiery furnace (3:11): A form of capital punishment that was not only effective but also terribly painful.

Daniel 3:12

Certain Jews...Shadrach, Meshach, and Abednego (3:12): Notice the subtle insinuation that the king made a mistake in assigning foreigners high positions of leadership. One can almost see the finger pointing: "There are certain Jews whom *you* have appointed over the affairs of the province of Babylon."

Pay no attention to you; they do not serve your gods or worship the golden image (3:12): Shadrach, Meshach, and Abednego were acting under clear instructions from God's Law.

> You shall have no other gods before me. You shall not make for yourself a carved image, or any likeness of anything that is in heaven above, or that is in the earth beneath, or that is in the water under the earth. You shall not bow down to them or serve them, for I the LORD your God am a jealous God (Exodus 20:3-5).

Shadrach, Meshach, and Abednego had to choose between King Nebuchadnezzar and the one true God, who is the King of kings. They chose wisely!

The three Hebrew youths likely recalled some of God's promises. Here's an example:

> Fear not, for I have redeemed you; I have called you by name, you are mine. When you pass through the waters, I will be with you; and through the rivers, they shall not overwhelm you; when you walk through fire you shall not be burned, and the flame shall not consume you (Isaiah 43:1-2).

Based on their faith in the God of promises, Shadrach, Meshach, and Abednego stood tall when all other leaders bowed low.

This brings up a controversial question: Are God's people ever justified in disobeying civil authorities? Many Christians have concluded that they must obey the government *unless* the government explicitly commands them to go against one or more of God's commands found in Scripture. In such a case, believers must obey God rather than the government.

The New Testament illustrates this principle. After being commanded by the Sanhedrin (the Jewish government) not to preach any further, "Peter and the apostles answered, 'We must obey God rather than men'" (Acts 5:29). God commanded Peter and the others to preach; the Jewish government commanded them not to preach. So they chose to obey God rather than human government.

Shadrach, Meshach, and Abednego likewise chose to obey God instead of men. Sometime later, Daniel righteously disobeyed when the government commanded him to go against God's revealed will (Daniel 6).

Of course, believers must guard against abusing this principle, for Scripture elsewhere instructs them to obey government (Romans 13:1). So, for example, believers would certainly *not* be justified in disobeying the government in cases where they simply disagreed with its policies.

MAJOR THEMES

1. *Nebuchadnezzar's golden image.* The large image constructed by Nebuchadnezzar was not unique to him. Archeologists have discovered other large statues from the Babylonian, Persian, and Greek Empires. Herodotus, a Greek historian who lived in the fifth century BC, speaks of an 18-foot golden image of a man in a Babylonian temple. Diodorus Siculus, a Greek historian who wrote *Bibliotheca Historica* (*Universal History*) between 60 and 30 BC, mentions a 40-foot image of Zeus atop a Bel temple. Nebuchadnezzar's golden image was 90 feet tall, thus pointing to the highly exalted view he had of himself.

2. *Death by burning.* History reveals that Assyria, Babylon, Persia, and Greece all used burning as a method of capital punishment. In a sixth-century BC Mesopotamian record, a king instructs that a corrupt priest be burned in an oven. Nebuchadnezzar burned two Judean false prophets to death, Zedekiah and Ahab (Jeremiah 29:22). Burning as a form of execution was sanctioned in the Hammurabi Code. The oven was likely not originally

constructed for capital punishment but rather to cast and smelt metal and to bake bricks and pottery.

DIGGING DEEPER WITH CROSS-REFERENCES

The decrees of kings—Ezra 5:13; 7:21; Esther 1:20; 2:1; 4:8; 8:14; Daniel 2:13; 3:4, 10, 22, 29; 6:9, 26; Jonah 3:7; Luke 2:1

Troublemakers—Proverbs 6:16-19; 16:28-30; Matthew 5:44; Romans 12:18; 16:17; Titus 3:10

LIFE LESSONS

1. *Obey God no matter what.* Daniel and his friends were committed to obeying God no matter what. Daniel and his friends remind us that obeying God may often entail sacrifice, but it also has many benefits. For example, obedience brings great blessing (Luke 11:28), long life (1 Kings 3:14; John 8:51), happiness (Psalms 112:1; 119:56), peace (Proverbs 1:33), and a state of well-being (Jeremiah 7:23; see also Exodus 19:5; Leviticus 26:3-4; Deuteronomy 4:40; 12:28; 28:1; Joshua 1:8; 1 Chronicles 22:13; Isaiah 1:19). Never get discouraged in your obedience to God.

2. *Enduring despite pressure.* Daniel and his friends patiently endured whatever they faced in Babylon—including persecution for refusing to worship an idol. You and I are also called to patiently endure whatever comes our way. Hebrews 12:1-2 exhorts believers, "Let us also lay aside every weight, and sin which clings so closely, and let us run with endurance the race that is set before us, looking to Jesus, the founder and perfecter of our faith." Jesus described Christian commitment this way: "If anyone would come after me, let him deny himself and take up his cross and follow me. For whoever would save his life will lose it, but whoever loses his life for my sake will find it" (Matthew 16:24-25). Let's not forget, "Blessed is the man who remains steadfast under trial, for when he has stood the test he will receive the crown of life, which God has promised to those who love him" (James 1:12).

QUESTIONS FOR REFLECTION AND DISCUSSION

1. Have you ever been maliciously accused by someone who sought to get you in trouble? Were you able to forgive that person?
2. Do you think you'd have the courage to obey God in a circumstance that might lead to your death?
3. Can you think of any modern-day examples of Christians standing strong in their faith and losing their lives for it?

DAY 11

SHADRACH, MESHACH, AND ABEDNEGO REMAIN FAITHFUL TO GOD

DANIEL 3:13-18

SCRIPTURE READING AND INSIGHTS

Begin by reading Daniel 3:13-18 in your favorite Bible. As you read, allow the Word of God to bring revival to your soul (Psalm 119:25, 93, 107).

In yesterday's reading, the Chaldeans accused Shadrach, Meshach, and Abednego of not bowing before Nebuchadnezzar's golden image. Today we'll see the three Hebrews remain unbendingly faithful to God in the face of accusation. With your Bible still accessible, consider the following insights on the biblical text, verse by verse.

Daniel 3:13

Nebuchadnezzar in furious rage (3:13): It would have been one thing for Shadrach, Meshach, and Abednego to privately refuse to bow before the golden image. But the three youths publicly refused to bow before the image and worship it. To Nebuchadnezzar, this represented a public defiance of his religious and political authority. He was therefore enraged. He immediately ordered that these three be brought before him.

Nebuchadnezzar had previously held these three youths in high esteem (Daniel 1:20), but that did not exempt them from submitting to his decree regarding the golden image. They now had to answer for their defiance.

We note in passing the growing evidence that Nebuchadnezzar may have had an anger problem. Recall that when the wise men could not tell the king his dream, "the king was angry and very furious" (Daniel 2:12). Now, when he heard that Shadrach, Meshach, and Abednego refused to bow down to the golden image, he was "in furious rage" (3:13). Later, when the three youths definitively stated to the king that they would not worship the image, he was "filled with fury" (3:19). He seemed to *react* far more often than he *responded.*

Notice again that Daniel is not part of this group. This is only because Daniel was not at the dedication ceremony. Had he been there, he too would have refused to worship the golden image, and he too would have found himself being dragged before Nebuchadnezzar.

Daniel 3:14-15

Is it true, O Shadrach, Meshach, and Abednego (3:14): It appears that by the time Shadrach, Meshach, and Abednego arrived before Nebuchadnezzar, he had gained a bit more control of his emotions. Instead of passing immediate judgment on the three, he asked them if the Chaldeans' accusation was true. If it turned out that the accusation was false, he would drop the matter.

If you are ready…well and good (3:15): Nebuchadnezzar gave the three lads a second chance—perhaps due to his former high esteem of them. He informed them that if they would bow before the image upon hearing the music, then all would be forgiven. They would escape punishment, and life would go back to normal.

If you do not worship (3:15): If the three lads refused to bow before the image, they would be cast into a fiery furnace. That is the consequence for defying the king's authority.

Who is the god who will deliver you out of my hands? (3:15): Nebuchadnezzar's question no doubt stimulated the three lads' faithfulness to the one true God. This reminds us of Pharaoh's defiant statement to Moses: "Who is the Lord, that I should obey his voice and let Israel go?" (Exodus 5:2).

Nebuchadnezzar apparently considered himself to be higher than all other gods, for no other god could turn back his hand. No other god could circumvent his authority. Nebuchadnezzar was here claiming for himself what is ultimately true only of the one true God. Indeed, God affirms, "My counsel shall stand, and I will accomplish all my purpose…I have spoken, and I will bring it to pass; I have purposed, and I will do it" (Isaiah 46:10-11). He asserts, "For the Lord of hosts has purposed, and who will annul it? His hand is stretched out, and who will turn it back?" (14:27).

Nebuchadnezzar would soon learn that he would lose any contest with Yahweh. Nebuchadnezzar asked, "Who is the god who will deliver you out of my hands?" Yahweh would soon indicate, "That would be Me" (see 3:25-29).

Daniel 3:16-18

O king, we have no need to answer (3:16): The three youths may initially appear to be disrespecting the king with an in-your-face attitude. This is not the case, however. Their point was that their commitment to Yahweh was so firm and so rock-solid that they would not consider doing anything to offend Him. They knew Him to be the true and living God, so they had "no need to answer" because they could take no other course of action. They would remain forever faithful to God.

Our God whom we serve is able to deliver us (3:17): The same God who delivered the Israelites from the hand of the Egyptian pharaoh (Exodus 18:10) could deliver the three youths from the hand of the Babylonian king. These three men may have been employed by Nebuchadnezzar (Daniel 2:49), but they did not serve the false gods of Babylon. They served only the one true God. And they had confidence that this one true God could deliver them.

We are again reminded of the First and Second Commandments, which were pivotal to the thinking of these Hebrew youths: "You shall have no other gods before me. You shall not make for yourself a carved image, or any likeness of anything that is in heaven above, or that is in the earth beneath, or that is in the water under the earth. You shall not bow down to them or serve them, for I the Lord your God am a jealous God" (Exodus 20:3-5).

Moreover, the three youths were fully aware that God not only has the power to deliver His people but also has promised to do so. We again recall what God said in Isaiah 43:1-2: "Fear not, for I have redeemed you; I have called you by name, you are mine. When you pass through the waters, I will be with you; and through the rivers, they shall not overwhelm you; when you walk through fire you shall not be burned, and the flame shall not consume you."

But if not, be it known to you (3:18): The Hebrew youths affirmed that God's deliverance was possible and even likely. They also recognized that martyrdom was possible. But one outcome was impossible from their perspective—come what may, they would never worship false gods. Regardless of the outcome, their commitment was to do God's will in all things. On that, they would not bend. They firmly believed that God would deliver them, and they would trust Him even if He didn't.

One is reminded of Joshua's attitude when he said to the Israelites, "Choose this day whom you will serve, whether the gods your fathers served in the region beyond the River, or the gods of the Amorites in whose land you dwell. But as for me and my house, we will serve the Lord" (Joshua 24:15). Like Joshua, the three Hebrew youths chose to follow and serve God alone.

The three Hebrew youths remind us of an important lesson—we should maintain faith in God even when our circumstances remain difficult. We are reminded of this truth in Habakkuk 3:17-19: "Though the fig tree should not blossom, nor fruit be on the vines, the produce of the olive fail and the fields yield no food, the flock be cut off from the fold and there be no herd in the stalls, yet I will rejoice in the Lord; I will take joy in the God of my salvation. God, the Lord, is my strength; he makes my feet like the deer's; he makes me tread on my high places."

MAJOR THEMES

1. *Belief in false gods*. Daniel and his associates knew that in reality the gods of Babylon were not true gods at all. Scripture consistently affirms that there is only one true God. God Himself affirmed, "Before me no god was formed, nor shall there be any after me" (Isaiah 43:10). He said, "I am the Lord, and there is no other, besides me there is no God" (Isaiah 45:5). That there is only one God is the consistent testimony of Scripture (John 5:44; 17:3; Romans 3:29-30; 16:27; 1 Corinthians 8:4; Galatians 3:20; Ephesians 4:6; 1 Thessalonians 1:9; 1 Timothy 1:17; 2:5; James 2:19; 1 John 5:20-21; Jude 25). God understandably commands, "You shall have no other gods before me" (Exodus 20:3).

2. *Human arrogance*. Nebuchadnezzar is a sad example of unrestrained human

arrogance—a character trait that God hates. Scripture reveals, "Pride and arrogance and the way of evil and perverted speech I hate" (Proverbs 8:13). God promises, "I will put an end to the pomp of the arrogant, and lay low the pompous pride of the ruthless" (Isaiah 13:11; see also 1 Samuel 2:3). Jeremiah 50:32 affirms, "The proud one shall stumble and fall, with none to raise him up." God promises, "The haughtiness of man shall be humbled, and the lofty pride of men shall be brought low, and the LORD alone will be exalted in that day" (Isaiah 2:17).

DIGGING DEEPER WITH CROSS-REFERENCES

Human boasting—1 Samuel 17:10, 44; Psalms 73:9; 75:4; Ezekiel 35:13; Daniel 3:15; Matthew 26:33, 35; Acts 8:9; Romans 1:30; 1 Corinthians 4:7; 2 Timothy 3:2; James 3:5; 4:16; Jude 16; Revelation 13:5

Divine deliverance—Judges 8:34; 11:21; 1 Samuel 14:12; 17:37, 46; 24:15; 2 Samuel 18:28; 22:2, 18, 49; 2 Kings 17:39; 19:19; 2 Chronicles 16:8; Psalms 18:2, 17, 43; 34:4, 17; 54:7; 56:13; 68:20; 109:31; Jeremiah 1:8; Matthew 6:13; Luke 22:42; 2 Corinthians 1:10; 2 Timothy 3:11; 4:18; Hebrews 2:15

LIFE LESSONS

1. *Courageous believers.* The three Hebrew youths were unbendingly courageous in the face of Nebuchadnezzar's threats. You and I can be bold and courageous as well. The early believers in the book of Acts prayed, "And now, Lord, look upon their threats and grant to your servants to continue to speak your word with all boldness" (Acts 4:29). We are then told that "they were all filled with the Holy Spirit and continued to speak the word of God with boldness" (verse 31). We can be bold in the power of the Holy Spirit, just as the early believers were (see Psalm 138:3; 2 Corinthians 3:12; 1 Thessalonians 5:14; 2 Timothy 1:12). Deuteronomy 31:6 exhorts us, "Be strong and courageous...it is the LORD your God who goes with you. He will not leave you or forsake you." Stand strong for the Lord!

2. *Confidence in God.* Daniel and his friends were courageous because of their strong confidence in God. They seemed to have had the same confidence in God as portrayed in the psalms. The psalmist said, "The LORD is my

light and my salvation; whom shall I fear? The LORD is the stronghold of my life; of whom shall I be afraid?" (Psalm 27:1). The psalmist goes on to say, "Though an army encamp against me, my heart shall not fear; though war arise against me, yet I will be confident" (verse 3). He affirms, "The LORD is a stronghold for the oppressed, a stronghold in times of trouble" (Psalm 9:9). He says to God, "My times are in your hand; rescue me from the hand of my enemies and from my persecutors!" (Psalm 31:15). God promises us, "I will never leave you nor forsake you" (Hebrews 13:5). You can be confident in God!

QUESTIONS FOR REFLECTION AND DISCUSSION

1. What stands out to you about Nebuchadnezzar's character in Daniel 3:13-15?

2. What inspires you most about the three Hebrew youths' response to the king in Daniel 3:16-18?

3. When was the last time you felt pressured to compromise your faith? How did you respond?

DAY 12

GOD RESCUES SHADRACH, MESHACH, AND ABEDNEGO FROM THE FIERY FURNACE

DANIEL 3:19-30

SCRIPTURE READING AND INSIGHTS

Begin by reading Daniel 3:19-30 in your favorite Bible. As you read, never forget that God urges you to quickly obey His Word in all things (Psalm 119:60).

Yesterday we watched as Shadrach, Meshach, and Abednego remained unbendingly faithful to God by refusing to worship the golden image. Today we will witness God's glorious rescue of the three youths. With your Bible still accessible, consider the following insights on the biblical text, verse by verse.

Daniel 3:19-20

Filled with fury (3:19): Nebuchadnezzar had previously held these three youths in high regard (Daniel 1:20). But they had publicly defied his authority, and their continued defiance now brought public consequences. Burning them alive would provide a public example to anyone thinking about defying his authority in the future.

The expression of his face (3:19): So angry was the king that his countenance changed.

He ordered the furnace heated (3:19): So angry was the king that he ordered that the fiery furnace be heated as much as humanly possible ("seven times more"). He wanted the furnace to be intensely hot as an expression of his intense wrath. (See Major Themes.)

The mighty men of his army (3:20): As a show of his own personal strength, the king ordered that his strongest soldiers bind the youths and cast them into the furnace.

To cast them into the burning fiery furnace (3:20): Nebuchadnezzar's industrial-size oven had doors on top as well as a door on the side that allowed for ventilation. The king's strong men would cast the Hebrew youths into the fire through the top door, and the victims would be observed through the side door.

Daniel 3:21-23

Bound in their cloaks (3:21): Normally a person would be stripped naked before being cast into the flames of a furnace. In the present case, however, the three Hebrew youths remained fully clothed because the king had commanded an immediate execution.

The flame of the fire killed (3:22): A furnace burning at a lower temperature causes the victim to suffer more as he or she takes longer to die. But in a furnace that is heated "seven times more," the temperature is so hot that victims are instantly incinerated. Nebuchadnezzar may not have anticipated that anyone near the top door of the superheated furnace would be incinerated as the hot flames burst up through the opening.

Fell bound into the burning fiery furnace (3:23): Apparently, once the top door of the furnace was opened, the explosive heat instantly killed the king's strong men, and the three Hebrew youths fell directly into the flames.

Daniel 3:24-25

Nebuchadnezzar was astonished (3:24): Though the main door was atop the furnace, there was also a secondary door on the side of the furnace, likely intended to provide ventilation for effective burning. Because of what he saw through this opening, Nebuchadnezzar "was astonished and rose up in haste," and asked those with him, "Did we not cast three men bound into the fire?" And they said, "True, O king."

PARALLELS

Daniel 3:24-27—God rescues Daniel's friends from danger.

Revelation 12:13-14—God rescues the Jewish remnant from peril.

I see four men unbound...the appearance of the fourth is like a son of the gods (3:25): The king now verbalized what astonished him. This fourth person was likely a preincarnate appearance of Jesus Christ (see Major Themes). Though Nebuchadnezzar had no personal knowledge of the Son of God (Jesus Christ), he witnessed what appeared to be a supernatural person or heavenly being who was saving the other three. The thing that must have stood out to Nebuchadnezzar as he witnessed all this was that none of Babylon's gods could have accomplished such a feat. He had earlier said to the three youths, "Who is the god who will deliver you out of my hands?" (verse 15). The answer was now clear. The God of Shadrach, Meshach, and Abednego had delivered them out of his hands.

Recall the New Testament teaching that the entire universe was created by Jesus Christ. John 1:3 says of Him, "All things were made through him, and without him was not any thing made that was made." Colossians 1:16 likewise says of Him, "For by him all things were created, in heaven and on earth, visible and invisible, whether thrones or dominions or rulers or authorities—all things were created through him and for him." Now, the same One who created the universe maintains absolute control over the elements in the universe, including fire. If Christ indeed made a preincarnate appearance in the burning furnace, His control of the effects of the fire would have been in perfect keeping with His divine power.

GOD AND HIS ACTIVITIES		
TOPIC	**DANIEL**	**REVELATION**
The Living God	Daniel 6:20, 26	Revelation 7:2
God Is Righteous and Just	Daniel 9:14	Revelation 15:3; 16:5; 19:2
Revelations from God	Daniel 2:47	Revelation 1:1; 4:1; 17:7; 22:6, 16
Prophetic Revelations	Daniel 8:17	Revelation 1:1; 4:1; 17:7; 22:6, 16
Writing Down God's Revelations	Daniel 7:1	Revelation 1:19
Divine Deliverance	Daniel 3:24-27	Revelation 12:13-14
God Shields from Harm	Daniel 6:23	Revelation 7:3; 11:5
Lamb's Book of Life	Daniel 12:1	Revelation 3:5; 13:8; 17:8; 20:12
Divine Balances	Daniel 5:27	Revelation 6:5

Daniel 3:26-28

Servants of the Most High God, come out, and come here (3:26): Earlier the Hebrew youths had informed the king, "Be it known to you, O king, that we will not serve your gods" (verse 18). Now the king looks into the furnace and recognizes that Shadrach, Meshach, and Abednego are servants of the Most High God, who was quite obviously more powerful than any of the gods Babylon offered. Earlier the king had referred to the youth's God as the "God of gods and Lord of kings" (2:47). Now he calls Him "the Most High God." This represented a major paradigm shift for Nebuchadnezzar. He had previously thought that Babylon's gods—and especially he himself—were more powerful than all other gods. Witnessing what transpired in the furnace was a game changer.

Nebuchadnezzar likely recalled the words of the Hebrew youths: "Our God whom we serve is able to deliver us from the burning fiery furnace, and he will deliver us out of your hand, O king" (verse 17). As requested, the three Hebrew youths exited the furnace—apparently through the side door—and came out to Nebuchadnezzar.

The fire had not had any power over the bodies (3:27): Nebuchadnezzar had ordered the furnace to be heated "seven times more," and yet their bodies were not burned, their hair was not singed, their clothes were not harmed, and no smell of fire was upon them. Nebuchadnezzar was not alone in witnessing this. Other government officials witnessed it as well. As Hebrews 11:34 describes it, in this miraculous act, God "quenched the power of fire."

Blessed be the God of Shadrach, Meshach, and Abednego (3:28): This carries the sense, "May the God of these three Hebrew youths be honored."

Who has sent his angel and delivered his servants (3:28): This was likely the "Angel of the Lord," or "Angel of Yahweh"—a preincarnate appearance of Christ. One is reminded of Psalm 34:7: "The angel of the LORD encamps around those who fear him, and delivers them."

Who trusted in him (3:28): Proverbs 3:5-6 affirms, "Trust in the LORD with all your heart, and do not lean on your own understanding. In all your ways acknowledge him, and he will make straight your paths"—including a straight path right out of the furnace.

And set aside the king's command (3:28): Nebuchadnezzar was apparently impressed that the three youths were so committed to their God that they were willing to yield up their bodies rather than serve and worship any god except their own God.

Daniel 3:29-30

I make a decree (3:29): Don't misunderstand Nebuchadnezzar. He was not here committing to following the Hebrew God alone. He was still a polytheist who believed in many gods. The king essentially added Yahweh to a large pantheon of deities. The purpose of his edict was to prevent anyone from criticizing the God of the Hebrews.

Nebuchadnezzar had still not learned his lesson. Recognizing Yahweh as part of a pantheon of deities was grossly misguided. Nebuchadnezzar would soon learn that Yahweh is not one among many, but is rather the unique and singular God.

Torn limb from limb (3:29): Anyone who disobeyed this edict was to be dismembered and suffer utter ruination.

There is no other god who is able to rescue in this way (3:29): Even though Nebuchadnezzar still believed in many gods, he became convinced that no god could bring miraculous deliverance the way the Hebrews' God did.

The king promoted Shadrach, Meshach, and Abednego (3:30): Nebuchadnezzar not only honored the one true God but also honored Shadrach, Meshach, and Abednego by giving them a promotion.

MAJOR THEMES

1. *Heated seven times more.* Bible scholars have noted that the number seven in the Bible often indicates completeness or perfection (see Leviticus 26:18-28; Proverbs 6:31; 24:16). To heat the furnace "seven times more" than normal may just be a metaphorical way of saying, "as hot as it can get," or "intensely." Notice that the more hotheaded the king became, the hotter he ordered the furnace to be heated.

2. *God's angel.* The one described as "a son of the gods" may have been the Angel of the Lord, an appearance of the preincarnate Christ. Scripture reveals that the Angel of the Lord—or more accurately, the Angel of Yahweh—*is* in fact Yahweh (Exodus 3:2-6). But the angel of Yahweh was also *sent by* Yahweh to minister to God's people (Judges 13:8-9), just as the Father sent Jesus in New Testament times. We begin to detect Trinitarian distinctions here. The Angel of Yahweh is often seen functioning as Sustainer and Rescuer of His people in Old Testament times (Genesis 16:10-13; 22:15-18; Exodus 23:21; Joshua 5:14; Zechariah 1:12-17).

DIGGING DEEPER WITH CROSS-REFERENCES

The testing of faith—Genesis 22:2; Matthew 9:28; 14:30; Mark 4:38; Luke 1:18; 5:5; John 4:50; Hebrews 11:8, 17; James 1:3; 1 Peter 1:7

Divine preservation—Genesis 7:23; 45:7; Deuteronomy 6:24; 8:4; Joshua 24:17; Nehemiah 9:6, 21; Job 10:12; Isaiah 43:2; Jeremiah 39:18; Jonah 1:17; Acts 17:28; Colossians 1:17; Hebrews 1:3

LIFE LESSONS

1. *Obedience to the point of death.* Daniel and his friends were obedient to God to the point of death—that is, they were willing to die rather than disobey God (Daniel 3:16-18). In the New Testament, Stephen was stoned to death because of his faithful testimony of Christ (Acts 7:54-60). Revelation 6:9 refers to those who were martyred because of their faithful witness to Christ. The apostle Paul was stoned and left for dead (Acts 14:19), though he survived. We do well to keep in mind the words of Jesus Christ: "Whoever would save his life will lose it, but whoever loses his life for my sake will find it" (Matthew 16:25). Those who die for Christ have eternal life waiting for them in heaven (see John 10:28; 2 Corinthians 5:8; Philippians 3:21; Revelation 2:10).

2. *The incomparability of God.* Nebuchadnezzar said of God, "There is no other god who is able to rescue in this way." I have noted previously that the Old Testament portrays God as being incomparably great. This is typically communicated with the declaration, "There is none like God," as well as the rhetorical question, "Who is like God?" The ancient Egyptians had earlier discovered this reality. Indeed, the Egyptian sun god (Ra) could not stop Yahweh from covering the land with darkness. Nor could the Egyptian river god (Nilus) prevent Yahweh from turning the Nile—the lifeblood of Egypt—into real blood. Our God truly is incomparable (see Exodus 15:11; Numbers 33:4). Regardless of the mountain you are facing, our incomparably great God can always help you.

QUESTIONS FOR REFLECTION AND DISCUSSION

1. How does Psalm 25:2 reflect the attitude of the three youths in this passage?

2. How does Proverbs 19:21 relate to Nebuchadnezzar's intentions in this passage?

3. Is your faith presently being tested? What have you learned in this lesson that might help you?

DAY 13

NEBUCHADNEZZAR PRAISES GOD AND HAS A SECOND DREAM

DANIEL 4:1-7

SCRIPTURE READING AND INSIGHTS

Begin by reading Daniel 4:1-7 in your favorite Bible. As you read, keep in mind that God desires for you not only to hear His Word but also to do it (James 1:22).

Yesterday we watched as God miraculously rescued Shadrach, Meshach, and Abednego from the fiery furnace. Today we will listen in as Nebuchadnezzar praises God for His awesomeness, and we will also touch on Nebuchadnezzar's second dream. With your Bible still accessible, consider the following insights on the biblical text, verse by verse.

Daniel 4:1

To all peoples (4:1): The events we read about in Daniel 4 took place some years after the episode of the three youths in the fiery furnace. Notice that Daniel 4 begins (verses 1-3) and ends (verses 34-37) with Nebuchadnezzar offering praise to God. In between, Nebuchadnezzar narrates how God allowed him to suffer great humiliation to further teach him about God's greatness. This is the structure of the chapter:

1. I praise God for His greatness because

2. God put me through some humbling circumstances that thoroughly taught me about His greatness, and so, again,
3. I praise God for His greatness.

Nebuchadnezzar's praise of God is especially noteworthy in view of his earlier highly exalted view of his own greatness (see Daniel 3:1-7). Now Nebuchadnezzar understood that God is truly the Great One.

Nebuchadnezzar addressed his proclamation of God's greatness "to all peoples, nations, and languages, that dwell in all the earth." This form of opening was common in royal inscriptions (on a stela) as well as letters in ancient Persia and Babylon. It was also common in such inscriptions and letters to include a wish for well-being—a salutation. In the present case, Nebuchadnezzar says, "Peace be multiplied to you!" (compare with 1 Peter 1:2; 2 Peter 1:2).

Of course, not all "peoples, nations, and languages, that dwell in all the earth" even knew who Nebuchadnezzar was at the time. So in its initial context, the text is probably better understood as referring to all peoples, nations, and languages that were under the rule of Nebuchadnezzar. The proclamation was regional, not global.

There is another context, however, in which Nebuchadnezzar's words were, in fact, to "*all* peoples, nations, and languages, that dwell in all the earth." After all, Nebuchadnezzar's words are recorded in the Bible, and the Bible has global distribution.

Daniel 4:2-3

Show the signs and wonders (4:2): Nebuchadnezzar describes what he has witnessed of God as "signs and wonders." The word "sign" often carries the idea of a miracle with a message, whereas "wonder" refers to a miracle that evokes amazement (see Major Themes). As we will see, God's humbling of Nebuchadnezzar would be a miracle with a message (the message being that God is awesomely powerful and great), and the whole episode—including Nebuchadnezzar's restoration—would be amazing (see Deuteronomy 6:22; 7:19; 13:1-2; 26:8; Nehemiah 9:10; Isaiah 8:18).

Most High God (4:2): Notice again that Nebuchadnezzar refers to Yahweh as the Most High God. The one true God has no real competition, for all other alleged deities are false deities—that is, they are not deities at all.

How great are his signs (4:3): In Daniel 3, God gave Nebuchadnezzar a revelation of His awesome power by delivering the three Hebrew youths from the power of the burning flames in the fiery furnace. But God was not finished giving revelation to Nebuchadnezzar. He would give further revelation to the king by allowing him to go through some humbling circumstances for a period of time, after which he would recover. The new revelation Nebuchadnezzar learned through his experience was that God's signs are great, His wonders are mighty, His kingdom is eternal, and He reigns from generation to generation.

When Nebuchadnezzar said "great are his signs," it was with the recognition that signs always signal something. ("Sign" and "signal" come from the same root.) In this case, God performed miracles (signs) that signaled His identity as the only true God.

How mighty his wonders (4:3): God's miracles are "wonders" because they are amazing, astonishing, and unparalleled. Similar language was used to refer to God's great deliverance of the Jews from the Egyptian pharaoh. Following this deliverance, Moses spoke to the people:

> Has any god ever attempted to go and take a nation for himself from the midst of another nation, by trials, by signs, by wonders, and by war, by a mighty hand and an outstretched arm, and by great deeds of terror, all of which the Lord your God did for you in Egypt before your eyes? To you it was shown, that you might know that the Lord is God; there is no other besides him (Deuteronomy 4:34-35).

As was the case in God's deliverance of the Jews from Egypt, God performed these signs and wonders in Babylon to demonstrate that "there is no other besides him."

An everlasting kingdom (4:3): Nebuchadnezzar realized that human kings can rise and fall. His experience of going mad and dwelling with animals, which he would recount in detail later in Daniel 4, is an example of a human king falling—though God would later restore him. So Nebuchadnezzar speaks from firsthand experience when he affirms that in contrast to temporal human kingdoms, God's kingdom is everlasting (see Daniel 2:44).

His dominion endures (4:3): Again, Nebuchadnezzar speaks from firsthand experience in affirming that in contrast to human kings, whose dominion lasts only as long as they are alive (and in their right minds, in Nebuchadnezzar's case), God—who Himself is eternal—has everlasting dominion as King of kings. Moreover, no human ruler possesses any authority except by God's permission. Human kings' authority is *derived* from God Himself. As Romans 13:1-2 puts it, "Let every person be subject to the governing authorities. For there is no authority except from God, and those that exist have been instituted by God."

Daniel 4:4-5

At ease in my house (4:4): Nebuchadnezzar now narrates the circumstances that led to his high praise of Yahweh. It all began with a dream. At the time of the dream, Nebuchadnezzar was prospering. All seemed to be going well. His earlier years had involved a lot of military conquest, but his vast domains now rested in security. Wars were over, and he was enjoying the spoils of his conquests. As he was in this peaceful state, the dream seemed to come out of nowhere.

A dream that made me afraid (4:5): Nebuchadnezzar's sense of ease and prosperity was interrupted by a dream that frightened him. He had visions in his head that alarmed him. God was not about to allow him to remain at peace while his kingdom was filled with injustice and oppression (Daniel 4:27) and he remained full of pride (4:30). The serenity of the king's misguided life came to an abrupt halt.

Daniel 4:6-7

The wise men…brought before me (4:6): It was probably with a sense of dread that Nebuchadnezzar decreed that the wise men of Babylon be brought before him to interpret the dream. They failed miserably at their previous attempt. Perhaps the king thought that given another chance, they might be able to redeem themselves. Besides, because the king was afraid, he wanted any input he could get on the dream and its meaning.

They could not make known (4:7): This time Nebuchadnezzar revealed the dream to the wise men. Still, the magicians, the enchanters, the Chaldeans, and the astrologers were unable to interpret it (see Daniel 2:27). Daniel to the rescue (in the next lesson).

MAJOR THEMES

1. *God's signs and wonders*. In the Bible, the word "sign" often carries the idea of a miracle with a message. A sign is a miracle that attests to something (see Deuteronomy 6:22; 7:19; 13:1-2; 26:8; Nehemiah 9:10; Isaiah 8:18). We will see that King Nebuchadnezzar was greatly humbled for a period of time and then fully restored. He saw this as a sign that attested to the awesome power of God. This is the unspoken assumption: Where miracles are, deity is present. The miracle is also a wonder in the sense that it evokes astonishment or amazement in the beholder. In the New Testament, Jesus' miracles were signs and wonders that attested to His deity (John 2:11; 4:54; 6:2; 12:18).

2. *God's eternal kingdom*. Nebuchadnezzar affirmed that God's kingdom "is an everlasting kingdom, and his dominion endures from generation to generation" (Daniel 4:3). This is in contrast to human kingdoms, which rise and fall according to God's sovereign will (see Daniel 2; 7; Revelation 17:12-13). The central emphasis in the New Testament is on the Ruler of the eternal kingdom. The New Testament says of Jesus, "Of his kingdom there will be no end" (Luke 1:33). Indeed, "He shall reign forever and ever" (Revelation 11:15). Because the kingdom is eternal, nothing can injure or destroy it. We are therefore urged, "Let us be grateful for receiving a kingdom that cannot be shaken" (Hebrews 12:28).

DIGGING DEEPER WITH CROSS-REFERENCES

God as the Most High—Genesis 14:22; Deuteronomy 32:8; 2 Samuel 22:14; Psalms 7:17; 9:2; 47:2; 57:2; 73:11; 83:18; 91:9; Acts 7:48

Blessing of peace—Genesis 43:23; Judges 6:23; 19:20; 1 Samuel 25:6; 1 Chronicles 12:18; Ezra 5:7; Luke 10:5; 24:36; John 20:21; Romans 1:7

LIFE LESSONS

1. *God sovereignly reigns from heaven.* One lesson we encounter repeatedly in the book of Daniel is that God sovereignly reigns from heaven. In fact, this theological thread runs through the entire Bible from Genesis to Revelation. God Himself affirmed, "My counsel shall stand, and I will accomplish all my purpose" (Isaiah 46:10). The psalmist tells us that "his kingdom rules over all" (Psalm 103:19). Our God is "a great king over all the earth" (Psalm 47:2). First Chronicles 29:12-13 affirms of God, "You rule over all. In your hand are power and might, and in your hand it is to make great and to give strength to all. And now we thank you, our God, and praise your glorious name." We, too, should be thankful to God and praise Him for His sovereign oversight of our lives.

2. *Ruling and overruling.* God's desire is that human beings respond to His sovereign rule from heaven. When human beings choose not to respond to His rule, He often *overrules* them. By the time we get to Daniel 4, Nebuchadnezzar has seen plenty of evidence that Yahweh is the one true God, including the deliverance of the three Hebrew youths from the fiery furnace (Daniel 3). But Nebuchadnezzar remained a polytheist, acknowledging Yahweh as a powerful god in a pantheon of deities. Nebuchadnezzar should have responded to God's obvious rule from heaven. As we will see in the next two lessons, God will overrule Nebuchadnezzar's reign and severely humble him so that he recognizes God's true greatness. Sometimes, God even has to overrule His own people. After all, God's people sometimes fail to respond to His rule, they go astray, and they fail to repent. In such cases, God overrules by bringing discipline—sometimes severe discipline—so His people will be motivated to return to the right path (Job 5:17; 33:19; Psalms 94:12; 118:18; 119:75; Proverbs 3:11-12). The best policy is to consistently submit to God's rule so He doesn't have to overrule us in our stubbornness.

QUESTIONS FOR REFLECTION AND DISCUSSION

1. Nebuchadnezzar was about to learn his lesson the hard way. Can you think of a time when God had to teach you a lesson the hard way?

2. Do you think God still does "signs and wonders" today? Why or why not?

3. What does it mean to you personally that God is the Most High God?

DAY 14

NEBUCHADNEZZAR REVEALS HIS SECOND DREAM TO DANIEL

DANIEL 4:8-18

SCRIPTURE READING AND INSIGHTS

Begin by reading Daniel 4:8-18 in your favorite Bible. As you read, stop and meditate on any verses that speak to your heart (Joshua 1:8; Psalm 1:1-3).

In yesterday's reading, Nebuchadnezzar praised God for His awesome signs and wonders, and he summoned the Babylonian wise men to interpret a second, more troubling dream. In today's lesson, Nebuchadnezzar reveals this dream to Daniel. With your Bible still accessible, consider the following insights on the biblical text, verse by verse.

Daniel 4:8-9

Belteshazzar (4:8): When the king originally invited the wise men to interpret the second dream, Daniel was not among them. By now, Daniel was in a position of significant governmental authority. He had risen far above the wise men of Babylon.

Daniel's assigned Babylonian name was Belteshazzar. This name means "Bel, protect his life," or "Bel, protect the king's life." Apparently, Bel had been Nebuchadnezzar's favorite Babylonian deity, because he referred to this deity as "my god." Nebuchadnezzar's continued use of this name indicates that despite Yahweh's open display of miracles, Nebuchadnezzar was still somehow a polytheist.

One wonders why Nebuchadnezzar did not summon Daniel at first. The other wise men of Babylon had a dismal track record. Perhaps the king was hoping to avoid hearing something from Daniel he did not want to hear. He may have expected the wise men to offer a more positive interpretation of the dream. Or perhaps, if the meaning was negative, they would soften it a bit rather than declare the hard truth, as Daniel would likely do.

In any event, our text tells us, "At last Daniel came in." One can almost hear Nebuchadnezzar breathing a sigh of relief. Whether the interpretation was positive or negative, at least the king would now know the meaning of the dream.

In whom is the spirit of the holy gods (4:8): Nebuchadnezzar was not affirming a belief that Daniel was filled with the Holy Spirit, the third person of the Trinity. He knew nothing of the Trinity. Rather, based on his earlier encounters with Daniel, Nebuchadnezzar appears to be acknowledging that the true God worked within Daniel, which made him capable of unraveling mysteries.

One must keep in mind that Nebuchadnezzar had recently been chastised in the fiery furnace episode (Daniel 3:24-30), and he affirmed that only Daniel's God was "a revealer of mysteries" (2:47). This being so, it is probably better to translate Daniel 4:8, "the Spirit of the holy God" instead of "the spirit of the holy gods." Some scholars argue against the plural (gods) because no pagans believed their deities were holy. This is something true only of the singular God of Daniel.

Chief of the magicians (4:9): Daniel did not call himself the "chief of the magicians." This was apparently a title ascribed to him by the pagans in Babylon (compare Daniel 2:48).

Another possibility is that Daniel was called "chief of the magicians" not because he was in authority over them but rather because he was wiser and more discerning than any other wise man in Babylon. In the same way, many have referred to Benjamin Warfield as "prince of theologians." Warfield had authority over no one, but he was a powerful theologian. Likewise, Daniel was a deeply insightful wise man.

No mystery is too difficult for you (4:9): Of course, Nebuchadnezzar got it wrong here. The truth of the matter is that no mystery is too difficult for *God.* God communicated the meaning of these mysteries to Daniel.

Daniel 4:10-12

A tree in the midst of the earth, and its height was great (4:10): We will focus our attention on Daniel's interpretation of this dream in the next lesson. For now, we simply wish to investigate the details of the dream itself.

Nebuchadnezzar sees a tree of great height. The Bible often describes kingdoms or the realms of kings as trees. For example, we read of Assyria, "Behold, Assyria was a cedar in Lebanon, with beautiful branches and forest shade, and of towering height, its top among the clouds" (Ezekiel 31:3; see also 17:1-10, 22-24; 2 Kings 14:9; Psalms 1:3; 37:35; 52:8; 92:12). (See Major Themes.)

Grew and became strong (4:11): The tree grew powerful, sturdy, and abounding in strength.

Its top reached to heaven (4:11): This is a hyperbole, a purposeful exaggeration to make a point. This tree grew so tall that its top metaphorically reached into heaven. This same type of language was used to describe the Tower of Babel: "Come, let us build ourselves a city and a tower with its top in the heavens, and let us make a name for ourselves, lest we be dispersed over the face of the whole earth" (Genesis 11:4).

Visible to the end of the whole earth (4:11): This was another hyperbole, intended to make the point that the tree was so tall that it could be seen from far away.

Food…shade (4:12): The tree not only grew large and powerful but also provided food and shelter for beasts and birds. It had abundant foliage and plenty of fruit.

Daniel 4:13-18

A watcher, a holy one (4:13): This is an angel from heaven, commissioned by God to watch and observe. (See Major Themes.) One of the primary purposes of angels has always been to deliver messages to human beings on earth. The word translated "angel" means "messenger." This angel appears and issues instructions about what is to be done to the tree. The angel's message clearly points to an impending judgment.

Chop down the tree (4:14): The angel instructed that the tree be cut down, its branches lopped off, its leaves stripped, and its fruit scattered. The beasts and the birds were to flee.

Leave the stump of its roots (4:15): The stump of the tree was to be left, with its roots still in the earth. This indicates that the tree, though stripped of its size and its greatness, is still alive and would one day be revived.

A band of iron and bronze (4:15): This protects the stump to ensure the tree's survival. The tree's "portion" would now be "with the beasts in the grass of the earth."

Let his mind be changed (4:16): The metaphorical nature of the tree now becomes clear. The tree is a man who will lose his sanity. His mental ability will not exceed that of an animal. Some scholars have suggested that Nebuchadnezzar's judgment involved the disease boanthropy, which causes a person to believe he or she is a bovine and to act accordingly.

Let seven periods of time pass over him (4:16): This state of being was to last for "seven periods," or seven years. Note that in the Bible seven is the number of completeness. Nebuchadnezzar would suffer a complete and thorough chastening from God through this experience.

The sentence is by the decree (4:17): Though the judgment is by the decree of the angels, one must not forget that the angels are here as representatives or ambassadors of God, who alone is the sovereign King.

That the living may know (4:17): The purpose of this judgment on Nebuchadnezzar is stated plainly: "That the living may know that the Most High rules the kingdom of men and gives it to whom he will and sets over it the lowliest of men." More to the point, Nebuchadnezzar is finite and weak—the lowliest of creatures when compared to the unfathomable greatness of God. God can raise kings up. God can bring kings down.

Tell me the interpretation (4:18): Nebuchadnezzar no doubt suspected bad news, but he was bold enough to ask.

MAJOR THEMES

1. *Watcher angels*. Daniel 4:13 refers to angels who are called "watchers." Apparently these are angels who have been sent by God specifically to observe what is transpiring on the earth. The term suggests that these angels are especially vigilant. (The Aramaic word translated "watcher" communicates the idea of making sleepless watch.) We might consider the watchers to be God's reconnaissance agents. The watchers may relate

to certain angels said to have many eyes. The cherubim, for example, are "full of eyes all around" (Ezekiel 1:18). The angels in Revelation 4:6 are "full of eyes in front and behind," and "full of eyes all around and within" (verse 8).

2. *Large, cosmic trees.* The idea of a large, cosmic tree at the center of the earth was common in ancient times.

> In the Myth of Erra and Ishum, Marduk speaks of the meshu tree, whose roots reach down through the great subterranean ocean to the underworld and whose top rises above the heavens. A sacred tree appears in various forms of Assyrian art. [1]

The Bible refers to a great tree in Ezekiel 17, 31, and Daniel 4. In the next lesson, we will see that trees can also represent evil people. As we have seen, apocalyptic literature—including the books of Daniel and Revelation—often contains dreams, visions, and symbolic imagery.

DIGGING DEEPER WITH CROSS-REFERENCES

General appearances of angels—Genesis 18:2; 22:11; Exodus 3:2; Daniel 8:15; 10:5; 12:5; Matthew 1:20; 2:13; 28:2; Luke 16:22; 22:43; Acts 5:19; 12:7; Hebrews 1:14; 13:2

Angels specifically coming down from heaven—Genesis 28:12; Zechariah 14:5; Matthew 25:31; Jude 14; Revelation 19:14

LIFE LESSONS

1. *The indwelling spirit.* Nebuchadnezzar referred to Daniel as one "in whom is the spirit of the holy gods" (Daniel 4:8). Though Nebuchadnezzar was not referring to the New Testament doctrine of the filling of the Holy Spirit, this is a doctrine we need to be aware of. Ephesians 5:18 instructs us, "Be filled with the Spirit." The word "filled" here is a present tense imperative verb. The present tense indicates continuing action. Moment by moment, you and I as Christians are to be filled with the Spirit. The imperative means it is a command from God. Being filled with the Spirit is

not merely optional. As we are filled with the Holy Spirit, we will manifest the fruit of the Holy Spirit (Galatians 5:22-23).

2. *God deals with prideful leaders.* God knows what is in the human heart: "I the Lord search the heart and test the mind" (Jeremiah 17:10). "I am he who searches mind and heart" (Revelation 2:23). God "will bring to light the things now hidden in darkness and will disclose the purposes of the heart" (1 Corinthians 4:5). Looking into Nebuchadnezzar's heart, God saw unrestrained pride. The king could issue as many decrees as he wanted to (Daniel 2:13, 15; 3:10, 29; 6:7-13, 15, 26), but what really matters are heaven's decrees (Daniel 4:17, 24; 9:24-27). Nebuchadnezzar was about to be humbled by the Almighty (see Psalm 103:19). God humbles you and me, too, if we maintain an attitude of pride (James 4:6).

QUESTIONS FOR REFLECTION AND DISCUSSION

1. Daniel was named Belteshazzar—a tribute to Nebuchadnezzar's favorite god, Bel. You and I are called Christians, which means "belonging to Christ." Is it obvious to other people that you belong to Christ?

2. Do you have a healthy relationship with the Holy Spirit? Is it your goal to be controlled by the Holy Spirit in your day-to-day living?

3. Daniel 4:17 tells us that God "rules the kingdom of men." Are there any areas of your life right now that you are not submitting to God's rule?

DAY 15

DANIEL INTERPRETS THE SECOND DREAM

DANIEL 4:19-27

SCRIPTURE READING AND INSIGHTS

Begin by reading Daniel 4:19-27 in your favorite Bible. As you read, remember that God's Word is the true source of hope (Psalm 119:81).

In the previous lesson, Nebuchadnezzar revealed his second dream to Daniel. In today's lesson, Daniel interprets this second dream. With your Bible still accessible, consider the following insights on the biblical text, verse by verse.

Daniel 4:19

Daniel...was dismayed (4:19): Daniel did not get upset while interpreting Nebuchadnezzar's first dream (2:27-45). After all, in that dream, Nebuchadnezzar was portrayed as a head of gold. But this second dream was far different. It indicated that Nebuchadnezzar was to be greatly humiliated for an extended time as a form of divine discipline. Daniel became dismayed, perhaps because he had grown somewhat fond of the king—a surprising development because Nebuchadnezzar was the one who brought Daniel into captivity. Or perhaps Daniel was dismayed because bringing bad news to the king could result in his fall from the king's favor. At any rate, breaking this bad news to the king was difficult for Daniel.

Let not the dream...alarm you (4:19): The king could tell from Daniel's countenance that the news was not good. He nevertheless instructed Daniel not to be alarmed but to go ahead and share the meaning of the dream. Nebuchadnezzar's words might be paraphrased this way: "Speak out, and let the event be what it will."

May the dream be for those who hate you (4:19): Daniel prepared the king by confirming that the meaning of the dream was not good.

Daniel 4:20-22

The tree you saw…it is you, O king (4:20-22): Daniel got straight to the point. After repeating the description of the great tree, Daniel informed Nebuchadnezzar that the tree represented him. Daniel began tactfully, indicating that just as the tree had become great and strong, so Nebuchadnezzar's kingdom had also become great and strong. "Your greatness has grown and reaches to heaven, and your dominion to the ends of the earth" (verse 22).

Some Bible expositors have suggested that ancient Near Eastern kings were sometimes identified with the tree of life because they protected and sustained their people. If the king acted wickedly, however, the tree of life could become a tree of death, for protection and sustenance would vanish.

Daniel 4:23-25

It is a decree of the Most High (4:24): The judgment that was to fall on Nebuchadnezzar was a decree from the Most High God, who had rescued the three Hebrew youths from the fiery furnace. This decree was communicated through watcher angels.

You shall be driven from among men (4:25): Nebuchadnezzar was now to be removed from his position of authority in his own kingdom. He would no longer live in the palace, but would dwell among the wild animals and even act like one. As we saw in the previous chapter, some scholars have suggested that Nebuchadnezzar suffered from boanthropy, which causes a person to think he or she is a bovine and act accordingly.

Seven periods of time shall pass over you (4:25): This judgment—a decree from the Most High God—was to last for seven years, a significant portion of Nebuchadnezzar's life. For seven years, Nebuchadnezzar would live in a demented state like a wild animal. (Note that the word "times" is used again in Daniel 7:25, where it also refers to years.)

Till you know (4:25): The purpose of the judgment is now revealed. For years Nebuchadnezzar had been full of pride, acting like a god before the subjects of his kingdom. He apparently thought of himself as divine. Now Nebuchadnezzar must be shown the truth. The cutting down of the tree represents the breaking down of Nebuchadnezzar's pride. Nebuchadnezzar was to experience severe humiliation for an extended time in order to teach him "that the Most High rules the kingdom of men and gives it to whom he will." Indeed, it is God, not Nebuchadnezzar, who is the Lord of all the nations. No matter how powerful human beings may become, they are puny when measured against the infinite power and greatness of the Most High God.

Psalm 107:40 speaks of God's judgment on self-exalted rulers: "He pours contempt on princes and makes them wander in trackless wastes." The psalmist also tells us, "It is God who executes judgment, putting down one and lifting up another" (Psalm 75:7). God affirms, "It is I who by my great power and my outstretched arm have made the earth, with the men and animals that are on the earth, and I give it to whomever it seems right to me" (Jeremiah 27:5).

Daniel 4:26-27

Leave the stump of the roots of the tree (4:26): Despite the horror of such news, there was still hope for Nebuchadnezzar. The fact that the stump was left in the ground indicates that after his time of chastisement, Nebuchadnezzar would one day be restored to the throne. But that restoration to the throne would not take place until Nebuchadnezzar humbly acknowledged that God alone is the true Sovereign over humanity.

From the time that you know that Heaven rules (4:26): Daniel indicated that before Nebuchadnezzar came out of chastisement, he must come to understand that "Heaven rules." This phrase is a Jewish way of saying, "God rules," just as "kingdom of heaven" and "kingdom of God" are equated in the New Testament (see Matthew 5:3; Luke 6:20).

Break off your sins by practicing righteousness (4:27): With the hope of perhaps warding off such an extended punishment, Daniel urged the king to break off sin and pursue righteousness. God typically withholds promised judgment when He sees repentance. The repentance of the Ninevites in the book of Jonah is a powerful example of this truth. When Daniel said, "Break off your sins by practicing righteousness," he was probably speaking of Nebuchadnezzar's prideful and self-exalted behavior. A key means of practicing righteousness is to live humbly before God. If Nebuchadnezzar did this one thing, it would affect everything else he did during his reign. Had Nebuchadnezzar been able to do this, he may have averted seven years of chastisement, and his kingdom would have been much better off. "Righteousness exalts a nation, but sin is a reproach to any people" (Proverbs 14:34).

Mercy to the oppressed (4:27): This is another aspect of practicing righteousness. Nebuchadnezzar's reign had been spent building a grand city that would be a monument to his greatness, and in the process, the poor were oppressed and uncared for. This must stop, Daniel said. God's Word speaks a great deal about the proper attitude toward the poor. Referring to the poor, God commanded His people, "You shall give to him freely, and your heart shall not be grudging when you give to him, because for this the LORD your God will bless you in all your work and in all that you undertake. For there will never cease to be poor in the land. Therefore I command you, 'You shall open wide your hand to your brother, to the needy and to the poor, in your land'" (Deuteronomy 15:10-11). Proverbs 29:14 exhorts, "If a king faithfully judges the poor, his throne will be established forever." Likewise, "Open your mouth, judge righteously, defend the rights of the poor and needy" (Proverbs 31:9).

A lengthening of your prosperity (4:27): By following Daniel's good advice, Nebuchadnezzar could have continued his prosperity. But being a prideful and thick-headed ruler, he refused and paid the consequences for it. In a test of wills, God will always win.

MAJOR THEMES

1. *Trees are representative of evil people.* It is interesting to observe that evil people are sometimes metaphorically represented as trees. The psalmist affirmed, "I have seen a wicked, ruthless man, spreading himself like a green laurel tree" (Psalm 37:35). God raises some kings and brings down others: "All the trees of the field shall know that I am the LORD; I bring low the high tree, and make high the low tree, dry up the green tree, and make the dry tree flourish. I am the LORD; I have spoken, and I will do it" (Ezekiel 17:24). In the New Testament, Jesus urged, "Even now the

axe is laid to the root of the trees. Every tree therefore that does not bear good fruit is cut down and thrown into the fire" (Matthew 3:10; see also Luke 3:9).

2. *Seeking God to relent.* Daniel urged Nebuchadnezzar to repent of evil and turn to righteousness "that there may perhaps be a lengthening of your prosperity" (Daniel 4:27). Perhaps Daniel thought God might relent if Nebuchadnezzar repented. There is scriptural precedent for such an idea. The Ninevites repented at Jonah's preaching. "When God saw what they did, how they turned from their evil way, God relented of the disaster that he had said he would do to them, and he did not do it" (Jonah 3:10). This is in keeping with God's promise in Jeremiah 18:7-8: "If at any time I declare concerning a nation or a kingdom, that I will pluck up and break down and destroy it, and if that nation, concerning which I have spoken, turns from its evil, I will relent of the disaster that I intended to do to it" (compare with Acts 8:22).

DIGGING DEEPER WITH CROSS-REFERENCES

God the sovereign King—Exodus 15:18; 1 Chronicles 16:31; 2 Chronicles 20:6; Psalms 22:28; 47:7; 93:1; 95:3; Isaiah 6:5; 44:6, 10; Romans 14:11; 1 Corinthians 15:23-28; Ephesians 1:11; 1 Timothy 1:17; Revelation 19:6

Examples of wise counsel—Genesis 41:35; Exodus 10:7; Numbers 13:30; Job 29:21; Proverbs 1:5; Ecclesiastes 9:17; Daniel 2:14; 4:27; Acts 5:35; Revelation 3:18

LIFE LESSONS

1. *God brings down the proud.* God sovereignly decrees to bring low the mighty King Nebuchadnezzar (Daniel 4:25). Corrie ten Boom offered a good word about pride. She said she was once asked if it was difficult for her to remain humble amid all the attention she was getting. She simply replied, "When Jesus rode into Jerusalem on Palm Sunday on the back of a donkey, and everyone was waving palm branches and throwing garments on the road, and singing praises, do you think that for one moment it ever entered the head of that donkey that any of that was for him?" Her point

was, "If I can be the donkey on which Jesus Christ rides in His glory, I give Him all the praise and all the honor."[1] As we've affirmed previously in this book, Scripture says God not only exalts the humble (Luke 1:52; James 4:10) but also humbles the proud (Isaiah 13:11; James 4:6; 1 Peter 5:5).

2. *Stop sinning and do what is right.* Daniel urged the king, "Break off your sins by practicing righteousness" (Daniel 4:27). Daniel's comment was motivated by two spiritual realities: First, sin leads to destruction and death (Acts 5:1-11; 1 Corinthians 5:5; 11:29-32; 1 John 5:16). Second, righteousness leads to blessing and long life (Deuteronomy 4:40; 2 Kings 20:1-6; Proverbs 10:27; Ephesians 6:2-3). Daniel knew it was in the king's best interest to turn from sin and pursue righteousness. The same thing is true of you and me. God fervently desires to bless us. But before that can happen, we must become "blessable" by turning from evil and pursuing righteousness (Exodus 19:5; Deuteronomy 4:40; Joshua 1:8; 1 Kings 2:3; Matthew 5:2-12).

QUESTIONS FOR REFLECTION AND DISCUSSION

1. Do you think you are presently a blessable person? If not, what changes do you need to make in your life?
2. Are you content to be a donkey on which Jesus rides in glory?
3. What impressed you most about today's Scripture reading?

DAY 16

NEBUCHADNEZZAR IS HUMILIATED AND LATER RESTORED

DANIEL 4:28-37

SCRIPTURE READING AND INSIGHTS

Begin by reading Daniel 4:28-37 in your favorite Bible. As you read, remember that great spiritual wisdom comes from studying God's Word (Psalm 119:98-104).

In yesterday's lesson, Daniel interpreted Nebuchadnezzar's second dream. Today we'll see this dream come to pass in Nebuchadnezzar's humiliation and restoration. With your Bible still accessible, consider the following insights on the biblical text, verse by verse.

Daniel 4:28-30

All this (4:28): Our text affirms plainly and simply, "All this came upon King Nebuchadnezzar." Everything God said would happen, did in fact happen. We recall Numbers 23:19: "God is not man, that he should lie." God made good on His word.

At the end of twelve months (4:29): It is significant that 12 months had passed since Daniel had given his exhortation to repent to Nebuchadnezzar. This was apparently a period of grace during which God gave Nebuchadnezzar the chance to repent. We are reminded of 2 Peter 3:9: "The Lord is not slow to fulfill his promise as some count slowness, but is patient toward you, not wishing that any should perish, but that all should reach repentance." God desired repentance, not suffering, for Nebuchadnezzar. But Nebuchadnezzar would not bend.

Had Nebuchadnezzar heeded Daniel's advice and repented (verse 27), he could have averted the chastisement of God. But during this 12-month period, he proved he had no real interest in changing his self-exalting attitude. Apparently, he completely ignored Daniel's advice. By the end of the 12 months, he was ripe for judgment.

Walking on the roof of the royal palace (4:29): Nebuchadnezzar had three palaces in Babylon. Some have suggested that he may have been walking on the top terrace of the famous hanging gardens at his main palace, considered one of the seven wonders of the ancient world.

My mighty power...the glory of my majesty (4:30): Nebuchadnezzar considered the glory of Babylon as a reflection of his own glory and majesty. The Aramaic phrase translated "which I have built" is more literally "which I myself have built." No credit is given to God as the Giver of all good gifts (see James 1:17). One recalls the words that the apostle Paul once spoke to the immature Corinthian believers: "What do you have that you did not receive? If then you received it, why do you boast as if you did not receive it?" (1 Corinthians 4:7). The same question could legitimately be asked of Nebuchadnezzar.

Daniel 4:31-32

While the words were still in the king's mouth (4:31): Nebuchadnezzar was given a 12-month grace period to repent. He failed to repent, however, and there would now be no further delay in judgment. As the king was speaking his prideful words, judgment fell decisively and suddenly.

One is reminded of Jesus' warning in His parable of the rich fool. This fool said to himself, "Soul, you have ample goods laid up for many years; relax, eat, drink, be merry." But God said to him, "Fool! This night your soul is required of you, and the things you have prepared, whose will they be?" (Luke 12:19-20). Nebuchadnezzar, another rich fool, was unprepared for God's sudden chastisement, even though he had been warned.

A voice from heaven (4:31): The source of the judgment was the Most High God (see Daniel 4:24).

To you it is spoken (4:31): This message of judgment was not communicated to Nebuchadnezzar through Daniel the prophet. Rather, God spoke directly to Nebuchadnezzar.

The kingdom has departed from you (4:31): The Babylonian kingdom—which Nebuchadnezzar had just been pridefully gazing on—was immediately taken from him. What he had thought was a reflection of his own majesty and glory would now be a reminder of what he had lost.

Driven from among men...with the beasts of the field (4:32): Nebuchadnezzar had ruled over the people of Babylon for many years, and he had exalted himself over them. Now he was no longer fit to live among them. He would live as a beast among other beasts.

Seven periods of time (4:32): This period of chastisement would last seven years. How ironic that the Babylonian king who had taken Israel into exile for seventy years now found himself in exile for seven years. Just as the seventy years of exile had a purifying effect on Israel, so this seven-year exile would have a purifying effect on Nebuchadnezzar.

Until you know that the Most High rules (4:32): Nebuchadnezzar was to remain in his beastly condition until he learned "that the Most High rules the kingdom of men and gives it to whom he will." God had communicated this truth to Nebuchadnezzar earlier in his life, but he wouldn't listen. Now Nebuchadnezzar would learn the lesson the hard way.

Daniel 4:33

Immediately the word was fulfilled (4:33): How suddenly and unexpectedly a judgment can fall! One minute the wicked can walk freely, feeling secure. The next minute—*bam!* Judgment falls.

During the time of Nebuchadnezzar's affliction, his counselors apparently carried out the administrative duties of the kingdom. Daniel would likely have played a critical role (see Daniel 2:48-49).

His body was wet...his hair grew...his nails were like birds' claws (4:33): Nebuchadnezzar apparently suffered from boanthropy, a disease in which a person believes he or she is a bovine. This disease can result in the patient growing long, matted hair and thickened fingernails.

Like other beasts of the field, Nebuchadnezzar was unconcerned about bodily appearance. No longer was he groomed like a king. Instead of a royal appearance, he now had a barnyard appearance. Some have suggested that the king may have spent his time of insanity as a beast in one of the royal parks.

Daniel 4:34-35

At the end of the days (4:34): As stipulated by God, the chastisement ended after seven years.

My reason returned to me (4:34): No longer was Nebuchadnezzar insane. His reasoning ability returned to him.

I blessed the Most High (4:34): Nebuchadnezzar learned his lesson well. The first thing he did after his reason returned to him was to bless the Most High God.

Praised and honored him (4:34): Nebuchadnezzar praised and honored God as the one true God who manifested Himself in His mighty deeds. Notice that the king who had previously sought praise and honor for himself was now praising and honoring God. Notice also that the tenses of the verbs used here point to continued or habitual action. Nebuchadnezzar continued to praise and honor God.

His dominion...his kingdom (4:34): Nebuchadnezzar acknowledged that contrary to the temporal rule of finite earthly kings, God's dominion is everlasting, just as His kingdom is everlasting. Nebuchadnezzar also knew from firsthand experience how quickly a finite, earthly king could fall from power.

Inhabitants of the earth (4:35): Nebuchadnezzar conceded that when compared to the Most High God, "all the inhabitants of the earth are accounted as nothing." Again, Nebuchadnezzar was speaking from firsthand experience. He knew that he himself, when compared to God, was as nothing.

He does according to his will (4:35): God accomplishes His sovereign will both in heaven and on earth. Nebuchadnezzar's seven-year chastisement and subsequent restoration was a manifestation of God's will on earth. Nebuchadnezzar was now a believer in God's authority and sovereignty.

None can stay his hand (4:35): Nebuchadnezzar reasoned that if he, the king of Babylon, could not stay God's hand, no one could. The Most High God truly is Almighty.

Or say to him, "What have you done?" (4:35): One is reminded of Isaiah

29:16: "You turn things upside down! Shall the potter be regarded as the clay, that the thing made should say of its maker, 'He did not make me'; or the thing formed say of him who formed it, 'He has no understanding'?" (see also Isaiah 45:9).

Daniel 4:36-37

Reason returned to me...splendor returned to me (4:36): God sovereignly restored Nebuchadnezzar's reason and his kingdom. God can exalt a person as easily as He can humble a person.

All his works are right and his ways are just (4:37): God's chastisement of Nebuchadnezzar was right and just.

Those who walk in pride he is able to humble (4:37): Nebuchadnezzar learned this lesson the hard way.

MAJOR THEMES

1. *God's sure word.* Things happened to Nebuchadnezzar just as God indicated they would. God's word is sure and trustworthy (see Genesis 21:1; 41:54; Exodus 7:13). No wonder we read of God, "Has he said, and will he not do it? Or has he spoken, and will he not fulfill it?" (Numbers 23:19). God said, "I will not...alter the word that went forth from my lips" (Psalm 89:34). God Himself proclaimed, "So shall my word be that goes out from my mouth; it shall not return to me empty, but it shall accomplish that which I purpose, and shall succeed in the thing for which I sent it" (Isaiah 55:11). He asserted, "I have spoken, and I will bring it to pass; I have purposed, and I will do it" (Isaiah 46:11). "The mouth of the Lord has spoken" (Isaiah 58:14).

2. *Judgment from God.* God is a God of judgment in the face of unrepentant sin. Judgment fell on Nebuchadnezzar because of his relentless self-exaltation (Daniel 4:31-33). Judgment likewise fell on Adam and Eve because of their disobedience to God (Genesis 3). Judgment fell on the Jews for rejecting Christ (Matthew 21:42-44), on Ananias and Sapphira for lying to God (Acts 5), on Herod for self-exalting pride (Acts 12:21-23), and on Christians in Corinth for irreverence regarding the Lord's Supper (1 Corinthians

11:29-32). Christians will one day stand before the judgment seat of Christ (1 Corinthians 3:12-15; 2 Corinthians 5:10). Unbelievers will be judged at the great white throne judgment (Revelation 20:11-15).

DIGGING DEEPER WITH CROSS-REFERENCES

Sudden reversals—Psalms 75:7; 147:6; Isaiah 22:25; 26:5; 40:23; Ezekiel 21:26; Daniel 4:31; Matthew 19:30; 20:16; Luke 1:52; 6:25; 16:25

God's voice—Genesis 3:8-9; 8:15-16; 9:8-11; Exodus 3:4; 19:19; Leviticus 1:1-2; Numbers 7:89; Deuteronomy 4:12, 33, 36; 5:22; 13:18; 26:14; 28:1; 1 Samuel 3:4; 2 Samuel 22:14; Job 37:2; Psalm 29:4; Isaiah 6:8; Ezekiel 10:5; Matthew 17:5

LIFE LESSONS

1. *No one can hold back God's hand.* When Nebuchadnezzar recovered from his affliction, he extolled God by saying, "None can stay his hand" (Daniel 4:35). We likewise read in Isaiah 14:27, "The LORD of hosts has purposed, and who will annul it? His hand is stretched out, and who will turn it back?" Job asks, "Who can turn him back?" (Job 9:12). Proverbs 21:30 assures us, "No wisdom, no understanding, no counsel can avail against the LORD." You can trust that God will surely do all that He has planned and promised to do!

2. *God can bring restoration.* God ultimately restored Nebuchadnezzar's sanity and his kingdom (Daniel 4:36). Scripture reveals that God can restore people in many different ways. God can restore people spiritually: "The LORD is my shepherd; I shall not want. He makes me lie down in green pastures. He leads me beside still waters. He restores my soul" (Psalm 23:1-3). He can restore the joy of salvation: "Restore to me the joy of your salvation" (Psalm 51:12). God can restore us after we've experienced trials: "After you have suffered a little while, the God of all grace, who has called you to his eternal glory in Christ, will himself restore, confirm, strengthen, and establish you" (1 Peter 5:10; see also Psalm 71:20). If you are in need of restoration, turn to God without delay!

QUESTIONS FOR REFLECTION AND DISCUSSION

1. What is most striking to you about the fulfillment of Nebuchadnezzar's dream (Daniel 4:28-33)?

2. Do you think Nebuchadnezzar (a pagan king) became a part of God's family? Why or why not?

3. Do you sense any need for spiritual restoration? If so, what have you learned in this lesson that might help you?

DAY 17

BELSHAZZAR PARTIES IT UP AND SEES HANDWRITING ON THE WALL

DANIEL 5:1-9

SCRIPTURE READING AND INSIGHTS

Begin by reading Daniel 5:1-9 in your favorite Bible. As you read, notice how the Word of God is purifying your life (John 17:17-18).

In the previous lesson, God humiliated Nebuchadnezzar for seven years and then restored him. In today's lesson, Belshazzar, another king, is partying it up when he suddenly sees handwriting on the wall. With your Bible still accessible, consider the following insights on the biblical text, verse by verse.

Daniel 5:1

King Belshazzar (5:1): The time span between Daniel 4:37 and Daniel 5:1 was about 23 years. After Nebuchadnezzar's death in 562 BC, a number of obscure kings reigned in Babylon until Nabonidus took the throne in 556 BC. Nabonidus then placed his son Belshazzar on the throne as coregent in about 553 BC. Belshazzar was in charge of the city while his father was reopening trade routes that Cyrus and the Persians had taken.

Belshazzar's name means "Bel protects [the king]" (Bel was a Babylonian deity). The name was a sign of wishful thinking because Babylon was now under siege by the Medo-Persian army, and a sense of doom permeated the city.

A great feast (5:1): Belshazzar may have sponsored this feast to allay the fears and boost the morale of the people of Babylon in the face of impending defeat at the hands of the Medo-Persian army. It is noteworthy that two ancient Greek historians, Herodotus and Xenophon, document the all-night festivities and partying that transpired as Babylon was being taken over by the Medo-Persian army.

A thousand of his lords (5:1): Archeologists have uncovered a royal room in ancient Babylon large enough to accommodate this group.

Daniel 5:2-4

Vessels of gold and of silver (5:2): These items were taken from Solomon's temple when Babylon overran Jerusalem and its temple. They were considered precious, holy instruments.

Nebuchadnezzar his father (5:2): While Belshazzar was the "son" of Nebuchadnezzar, the Aramaic term for a son could also refer to a grandson, descendant, or successor. Belshazzar was not the literal son of Nebuchadnezzar, but was rather a descendant or royal successor of Nebuchadnezzar. In keeping with this, the Aramaic word for a father can refer to an ancestor or a predecessor.

The temple in Jerusalem (5:2): This was Solomon's temple. (See Major Themes.)

His wives, and his concubines (5:2): Belshazzar had many wives and concubines, though we are unsure how many. Bible expositors suggest this feast may have been like an orgy.

We should note in passing that monogamy has always been God's will for human beings. From the very beginning, God set the pattern by creating a monogamous marital relationship between one man and one woman, Adam and Eve (Genesis 1:27; 2:21-25). This God-established example of one woman for one man was the general practice of the human race (Genesis 4:1) until interrupted by sin (Genesis 4:23). The Law of Moses clearly commands that the king "shall not acquire many wives" (Deuteronomy 17:17). Our Lord affirmed God's original intention for one male and one female to be joined in marriage (Matthew 19:4). The New Testament stresses that "each man should have his own wife and each woman her own husband" (1 Corinthians 7:2). Belshazzar was clearly outside of God's will in his countless wives and concubines.

Drink from them...drank from them (5:2-3): Nebuchadnezzar had honored the true God toward the end of his life, but Belshazzar chose to show contempt for God by defiling these holy vessels. Instead of using them to honor the true God, he used them to dishonor the true God and to honor the false gods of Babylon (see verse 4). Belshazzar was apparently trying to undo Nebuchadnezzar's influence and undermine his positive words about the God of Israel. Though Belshazzar was unaware of it at the time, God's judgment on him would be swift and devastating. Belshazzar was about to lose his life.

Praised the gods of gold and silver, bronze, iron, wood, and stone (5:4): Perhaps the act of drinking wine from these holy vessels and then praising the gods of Babylon was a desperate attempt to invoke Babylon's deities to rescue them from impending doom at the hands of the Medo-Persians.

Daniel 5:5-6

The fingers of a human hand appeared and wrote (5:5): As Belshazzar was partying it up, things took an abrupt turn for the worse. Fingers of a human hand suddenly appeared and began writing on the plastered wall. The king witnessed it with his own eyes and was stunned. This was not a mystical vision that Belshazzar alone experienced. The handwriting was visible to everyone.

Notice the irony taking place here. At Belshazzar's command, Babylonian hands had taken hold of God's holy vessels, defiling and polluting them at a pagan feast, thereby showing utter contempt for God. Now the sovereign hand of the Most High God responds by writing words of judgment on the wall.

The king's color changed (5:6): The king was terrified when the divine hand began writing God's message on the wall. A doomsday pallor came to his face. His legs weakened and his knees shook. The party was over.

Daniel 5:7-9

Bring in the enchanters, the Chaldeans, and the astrologers (5:7): Belshazzar had no idea what the handwriting on the wall meant. He immediately summoned his occultists to help him decipher the meaning of the words. He promised that any who could interpret the strange words on the wall would be given splendid purple attire—*royal* attire. The successful interpreter would also become the third ruler in the kingdom, after Nabonidus and Belshazzar.

The fact that Belshazzar promised such a great reward is an indication of the great fear in his heart.

We recall that Pharaoh similarly rewarded Joseph. "Then Pharaoh took his signet ring from his hand and put it on Joseph's hand, and clothed him in garments of fine linen and put a gold chain about his neck. And he made him ride in his second chariot. And they called out before him, 'Bow the knee!' Thus he set him over all the land of Egypt" (Genesis 41:42-44). Such rewards seem to have been common among kings who lived in ancient times.

They could not read the writing (5:8): The Babylonian deities were impotent in helping these occultists, which is understandable because these deities did not really exist (see Daniel 2:4-11; 4:7; 5:15). Only Daniel, who depended on the one true God, would be able to help the king understand the mysterious words.

Greatly alarmed (5:9): "King Belshazzar was greatly alarmed, and his color changed, and his lords were perplexed." Though the king had no idea about the meaning of the words, he surmised that they did not bring good news.

MAJOR THEMES

1. *Solomon's temple.* Daniel 5:2 tells us that when the Jewish people went into Babylonian captivity, Nebuchadnezzar took precious items out of Solomon's temple in Jerusalem. This temple was rectangular, running east and west, and measured about 87 feet long, 30 feet wide, and 43 feet high. The walls of the temple were made of cedar wood, and carved into the wood were cherubim angels, flowers, and palm trees. The walls were overlaid with gold. The floor was made of cypress. This temple had a Holy Place and a Most Holy Place. The Holy Place (the main outer room) housed the golden incense altar, the table of showbread, five pairs of lampstands, and utensils used for sacrifice. Double doors led into the Holy of Holies, where the Ark of the Covenant sat. This temple—the heart and center of Jewish worship—was destroyed by Nebuchadnezzar and the Babylonians in 587 BC.

2. *The finger of God.* The finger of God often symbolizes God's interaction with His creation in some way. When the Egyptian magicians could not

mimic one of Moses' miracles, they acknowledged, "This is the finger of God" (Exodus 8:19). The two stone tablets containing God's Law that He gave to Moses were "written with the finger of God" (Exodus 31:18). Indeed, "The tablets were the work of God, and the writing was the writing of God, engraved on the tablets" (Exodus 32:16; see also Deuteronomy 9:10). When the psalmist looked up at the stars at night, he asked, "When I look at your heavens, the work of your fingers, the moon and the stars, which you have set in place, what is man that you are mindful of him?" (Psalm 8:3-4). The miraculous writing on the wall was also a manifestation of the finger of God, appearing as a human hand.

DIGGING DEEPER WITH CROSS-REFERENCES

Feasts in the Bible—Leviticus 23:5-8, 34-44; Exodus 5:1; 23:16; Deuteronomy 12:5-14; John 7:37-39; 1 Corinthians 11:23-26

Concubines—Genesis 16:1-4; 21:9-14; 25:6; 30:4; 35:22; 2 Samuel 3:7; 5:13; 1 Kings 11:1-4; 2 Chronicles 11:21; Daniel 5:3, 23

Terror—Genesis 35:5; Leviticus 26:16; Job 9:34; 24:17; Psalm 91:5; Ezekiel 21:12; Luke 21:9; 24:37; Hebrews 12:21; 1 Peter 3:14

LIFE LESSONS

1. *Rich apparel.* People often pay great attention to what they wear. Nothing is wrong with wearing nice clothes, but one must be on guard against impure motives. Jesus, for example, warned, "Beware of the scribes, who like to walk around in long robes and like greetings in the marketplaces" (Mark 12:38). In this case, fine clothing was a manifestation of arrogance and pride. James warned of the sin of showing favoritism toward those who dress better than others (James 2:3-4). We glean an important insight from the Lord's words in 1 Samuel 16:7. Israel was seeking a king to lead the people, but God told Samuel, "Do not look on his appearance or on the height of his stature...The LORD sees not as man sees: man looks on the outward appearance, but the LORD looks on the heart." In other words, God cares more about our hearts than our clothing. With this in mind, Paul exhorted Christians to "put on the Lord Jesus Christ" (Romans 13:14)

and to "put on...compassionate hearts, kindness, humility, meekness, and patience" (Colossians 3:12).

2. *Turn from idolatry.* The guests at Belshazzar's feast "praised the gods of gold and silver, bronze, iron, wood, and stone" (Daniel 5:4). This is idolatry—the worship of other things in the place of the one true God. Pagan nations like Babylon typically believed in a plethora of gods who were often represented as statues of humans or animals. People would then worship these images. Some scholars have suggested that by promoting the idolatrous gods of Babylon, Belshazzar was attempting to undo any influence of Nebuchadnezzar's earlier honoring of the God of Israel (recall Daniel 4:34-35). The New Testament consistently urges Christians to avoid all forms of idolatry (1 Corinthians 5:11; 2 Corinthians 6:16; Galatians 5:19-21; Colossians 3:5; 1 John 5:21).
3. *The fear of the Lord.* Belshazzar was terrified at this communication from God, and he had good reason to be. Thankfully, you and I need not feel terror in our relationship with God. But we are nevertheless called to live in reverent fear of Him (1 Samuel 12:14, 24; 2 Chronicles 19:9; Acts 10:35; 1 Peter 1:17; 2:17). Fear (or reverence) of the Lord motivates obedience to God: "Fear God and keep his commandments, for this is the whole duty of man" (Ecclesiastes 12:13; see also Deuteronomy 5:29). It also fuels our desire to serve Him (Deuteronomy 6:13). In that sense, fearing God is a good thing.

QUESTIONS FOR REFLECTION AND DISCUSSION

1. Why might God have chosen to use visible fingers as a means of communicating His message to Belshazzar?
2. What can you conclude about the character of Belshazzar in Daniel 5:2-4?
3. How do you assess your heart's attitude regarding external appearances versus inner beauty?

DAY 18

BELSHAZZAR REQUESTS DANIEL TO INTERPRET THE HANDWRITING

DANIEL 5:10-16

SCRIPTURE READING AND INSIGHTS

Begin by reading Daniel 5:10-16 in your favorite Bible. As you read, keep in mind that the Word of God brings spiritual maturity (1 Corinthians 3:1-2; Hebrews 5:12-14).

In yesterday's lesson, Belshazzar was partying it up when suddenly he saw fingers writing on the wall. In today's reading, Belshazzar asks Daniel to interpret the handwriting. With your Bible still accessible, consider the following insights on the biblical text, verse by verse.

Daniel 5:10-12

The queen (5:10): This was apparently the queen mother. All the wives of the king were present at the feast. However, this woman had easy access to the king as only a queen mother could. (See Major Themes.)

Because of the words of the king and his lords (5:10): The queen mother was on top of things. She was aware of the crisis facing the king. She heard the king and those under him strategizing on what to do next.

Came into the banqueting hall (5:10): Because of what she heard taking place, she decided to get involved. She had a solution to the king's problem and would now share it.

O king, live forever (5:10): As we have seen, this was apparently a common greeting of courtesy to kings in ancient times. The Chaldeans had earlier addressed Nebuchadnezzar in this way (Daniel 2:4; see also 3:9; 6:6). Bathsheba used a similar phrase when addressing King David: "Bathsheba bowed with her face to the ground and paid homage to the king and said, 'May my lord King David live forever'" (1 Kings 1:31; see also Nehemiah 2:3; Daniel 3:9; 5:10; 6:21).

Let not your thoughts alarm you or your color change (5:10): The queen mother spoke to the king in motherly terms. In modern vernacular, she said something like this: "You're looking pale. Don't worry. Things will work out."

A man...in whom is the spirit of the holy gods (5:11): The queen mother described Daniel in terms similar to how he'd been described throughout his captivity in Babylon (Daniel 4:8-9, 18). Some take this to be a claim that in some sense the gods of Babylon communicated their wisdom through Daniel. The phrase can also be translated, "the Spirit of the holy God," in which case it could refer to the one true God of Israel working in Daniel.

In the days of your father (5:11): Nebuchadnezzar died in 562 BC. The year was now 539 BC, more than 20 years later. By now, Daniel was about 80 years old. Perhaps as an old man he had retired. With the change in kings, Daniel might have faded in importance. Or perhaps the present administration simply distanced itself from both Daniel and Nebuchadnezzar because they both praised the one true God of Israel, and the present administration wanted to exalt Babylon's gods. In any event, the queen mother now indicated to the king that Daniel was the right man to solve the king's crisis.

Light and understanding and wisdom (5:11): Daniel's "light and understanding and wisdom" had enabled him to interpret Nebuchadnezzar's strange dreams. That being so, surely he would also be able to interpret the handwriting on the wall. The queen mother seemed to reason that a mystery is a mystery. Whatever form the mystery may take, Daniel would be able to figure it out.

Nebuchadnezzar...made him chief (5:11): To add a stamp of authority to Daniel, the queen mother reminded Belshazzar that Nebuchadnezzar had appointed Daniel to be "chief of the magicians, enchanters, Chaldeans, and astrologers." Daniel could thus succeed where the other wise men failed.

An excellent spirit, knowledge, and understanding (5:12): The queen mother continued to sing Daniel's praises. She said he had "an excellent spirit, knowledge, and understanding to interpret dreams, explain riddles, and solve problems." This was in dire contrast to Babylon's wise men, who were completely unable to solve such mysteries during Nebuchadnezzar's reign and now in Belshazzar's reign.

Daniel...Belteshazzar (5:12): It is interesting that the queen mother first referred to Daniel using his proper Hebrew name, but also mentioned his Chaldean name. Belteshazzar means "Bel, protect his life," or "Bel, protect the king's life." (Bel was a Babylonian deity.)

He will show the interpretation (5:12): The queen mother urged the king to call for Daniel. There is a sense of immediacy to her words.

Daniel 5:13-14

You are that Daniel (5:13): The king took the queen mother's advice and summoned Daniel to appear before him. As soon as he arrived, the king said to him: "You are that Daniel, one of the exiles of Judah, whom the king my father brought from Judah." The king was seeking Daniel's help, but he was also putting Daniel in his place. Belshazzar is the king, whereas Daniel is a mere captive.

I have heard of you (5:14): The king said to Daniel, "I have heard of you that the spirit of the gods is in you, and that light and understanding and excellent wisdom are found in you." The king was issuing a challenge: "I've heard you're good at interpreting mysteries. Well, let's see how good you really are."

Daniel 5:15-16

The wise men...could not show the interpretation (5:15): Maintaining this sense of challenge, the king informed Daniel that Babylon's wise men had been brought in to interpret the handwriting on the wall, but they were unable to do so. He was implying, "Let's see if you can succeed where the others have failed."

Notice that the failure of the wise men has now become a recognizable pattern in the book of Daniel. They claimed to be empowered by Babylon's gods, but they consistently failed to interpret mysteries. Daniel, a worshiper of the one true God, consistently succeeded in revealing the meaning of mysteries.

I have heard that you can give interpretations (5:16): We must not forget that Daniel consistently indicated that he had no special gift in himself. Rather, the one true God enabled him to decipher mysteries. Daniel 1:17 tells us, "God gave them [Daniel and his Hebrew buddies] learning and skill in all literature and wisdom, and Daniel had understanding in all visions and dreams." Daniel boasted of God, "He reveals deep and hidden things; he knows what is in the darkness, and the light dwells with him" (2:22). In keeping with this, Daniel informed Nebuchadnezzar, "There is a God in heaven who reveals mysteries" (2:28).

If you can read the writing (5:16): The king informed Daniel what would happen if he provided the proper interpretation of the words on the wall. "You shall be clothed with purple and have a chain of gold around your neck and shall be the third ruler in the kingdom." This is the same thing that had been earlier promised to Babylon's wise men if they were able to interpret the words. Purple attire is royal attire. A chain of gold held great monetary value. Becoming the third ruler in the kingdom would place Daniel right after Nabonidus and Belshazzar. This is similar to the type of reward Pharaoh gave Joseph (Genesis 41:42-44).

One cannot help but notice that Belshazzar's offer to Daniel would soon be absolutely worthless. Babylon was now under siege by the Medo-Persians. That very night Babylon would fall, so being given royal attire and being made "third ruler" in the kingdom would essentially amount to being third ruler over nothing.

MAJOR THEMES

1. *Divine communication through writing*. In today's Scripture passage, God used fingers writing on a wall to communicate revelation about impending judgment. This may seem a rather bizarre episode, but it reminds us that over and over again in the Bible, God instructs that His revelation be written down and preserved for coming generations. "Moses wrote down all the words of the Lord" (Exodus 24:4). Joshua "wrote these words in the Book of the Law of God" (Joshua 24:25-26). Samuel "told the people the rights and duties of the kingship, and he wrote them in a book and laid it up before the Lord" (1 Samuel 10:25). God instructed Isaiah, "Take

a large tablet and write on it in common characters" (Isaiah 8:1). Isaiah was told, "And now, go, write it before them on a tablet and inscribe it in a book, that it may be for the time to come as a witness forever" (Isaiah 30:8). Belshazzar was frightened (with good cause) by the fingers and their written message, but you and I should be thankful to God for going to such pains for us to have the written Word (the Bible).

2. *The queen.* The reference to the queen in our biblical text was the queen mother. Four reasons are offered in support of this view:

    - She seems to be distinct from Belshazzar's many wives mentioned in Daniel 5:2-3.
    - The queen freely and without restriction entered the king's presence as easily as a mother would enter to see her son—something none of the common wives would dare do (5:10).
    - Her personal knowledge that Daniel had been active "in the days of your father" (5:11) must mean she'd been around for a while and was therefore older than the common wives.
    - She was influential—the king acted on her advice.

DIGGING DEEPER WITH CROSS-REFERENCES

Men with wisdom—Deuteronomy 1:13; 1 Kings 3:12, 28; 4:29; 5:12; 10:3, 24; 2 Chronicles 9:22; Proverbs 28:2; Daniel 1:4, 20; Acts 6:3

Spiritual discernment—Job 12:11; Psalms 82:5; 92:5-6; 119:125; Acts 17:11; Romans 3:11; 1 Corinthians 2:14-16; 1 John 4:1-6; Revelation 2:2

LIFE LESSONS

1. *An earthly perspective versus a divine perspective.* The queen mother, speaking from an earthly perspective, said to the king, "O king, live forever" (Daniel 5:10). But Daniel, who spoke for God, would soon inform the king that he was doomed. The king actually died that night (we'll address this in detail in the next lesson).

    You and I as Christians are called to maintain an eternal perspective, for we do not know how long we will live. In Colossians 3:1-2, we read, "If then you have been raised with Christ, seek the things that are above, where Christ is, seated at the right hand of God. Set your minds on things that are above, not on things that are on earth." The original Greek of this passage is intense, carrying the idea: "Diligently, actively, and single-mindedly pursue the things above." It is also a present tense, carrying the idea, "*Perpetually* keep on seeking the things above. Make it an ongoing process." Christians who maintain an eternal perspective are highly motivated to serve God.

2. *The importance of a good reputation.* Daniel had a stellar reputation, dating back to the reign of Nebuchadnezzar, who first took him into captivity. His good reputation not only brought him before kings but also brought him great honor throughout life. This reminds us of Proverbs 22:29: "Do you see a man skillful in his work? He will stand before kings" (see also Genesis 41:46). As Christians, we too ought to pursue a reputation of honesty and integrity, of being honorable, wise, and self-giving, like Daniel (see Proverbs 22:1; Ecclesiastes 7:1).

QUESTIONS FOR REFLECTION AND DISCUSSION

1. Do you have a good reputation before others, or could you stand to improve in this area? What steps might you take to improve?
2. Someone claimed that some Christians think about heaven so much that they are of no earthly good. Do you agree with that statement, or do you think the opposite may be true?
3. Would you say you are very wise, somewhat wise, not too wise, or unwise? How might you become more wise? (See Proverbs 1:1-7.)

DAY 19

DANIEL INTERPRETS THE WORDS OF DOOM

DANIEL 5:17-31

SCRIPTURE READING AND INSIGHTS

Begin by reading Daniel 5:17-31 in your favorite Bible. Read with the anticipation that the Holy Spirit has something important to teach you today (see Psalm 119:105).

Yesterday we saw Belshazzar ask Daniel to interpret the handwriting on the wall. In today's reading, Daniel interprets the words of impending doom. With your Bible still accessible, consider the following insights on the biblical text, verse by verse.

Daniel 5:17

Daniel answered and said before the king (5:17): King Belshazzar offered Daniel a reward for providing the interpretation of the handwriting on the wall: "You shall be clothed with purple and have a chain of gold around your neck and shall be the third ruler in the kingdom" (verse 16). Daniel responded, however, by asking the king to keep the gifts for himself and to give the rewards to another. Abram responded the same way to the king of Sodom: "Abram said to the king of Sodom, 'I have lifted my hand to the LORD, God Most High, Possessor of heaven and earth, that I would not take a thread or a sandal strap or anything that is yours, lest you should say, "I have made Abram rich"'" (Genesis 14:22-23).

It is not wise to receive gifts from unworthy leaders for services rendered to them (see 2 Kings 5:15-16). Besides, Daniel had never been motivated by or impressed by material rewards. He was more interested in doing what was right. He was not trying to be disrespectful, but he had to remain true to his principles. Further, Daniel knew that the rewards and gifts—mostly pertaining to increased authority in Babylon—would soon be worth nothing, for Babylon was under siege from the Medo-Persians.

I will read the writing (5:17): Despite declining the gifts and rewards, Daniel nevertheless assured the king, "I will make known...the interpretation."

Daniel 5:18-21

The Most High God gave Nebuchadnezzar (5:18): Daniel first informed King Belshazzar of what God had given Nebuchadnezzar. By referring to God as "Most High God," Daniel was explicitly elevating Yahweh over all the false gods of Babylon, which Belshazzar worshiped (see Psalms 7:17; 9:2; 47:2; 57:2; 73:11; 83:18; 91:9). And by affirming that it was God who made Nebuchadnezzar great, glorious, and majestic, Daniel was pointing to God's sovereignty over human leaders. Daniel had earlier affirmed that God "removes kings and sets up kings" (Daniel 2:21). The psalmist likewise observed, "It is God who executes judgment, putting down one and lifting up another" (Psalm 75:7).

Because of the greatness that he gave him (5:19): Because of God's blessing on Nebuchadnezzar, people came to fear him and tremble before him. A single word from him could keep people alive or put them to death.

When his heart was lifted up (5:20): Daniel pointed to Nebuchadnezzar's life as a demonstration of the danger of pride and arrogance. Nebuchadnezzar remained prideful and did not humble himself before the true God, so God brought him down so he would be forced to learn humility.

He was driven from among the children of mankind (5:21): Nebuchadnezzar was removed from his throne, his glory was stripped from him, he was driven from among humans to live among animals, and he acted like an animal for seven years.

Until he knew that the Most High God rules (5:21): Nebuchadnezzar was forced to live this kind of existence until he recognized God's sovereignty. Belshazzar failed to absorb this lesson from Nebuchadnezzar's experience.

Daniel 5:22-23

You...Belshazzar, have not humbled your heart (5:22): Belshazzar should have learned from Nebuchadnezzar's experience. He should have humbled himself before God, knowing the judgment that had fallen on Nebuchadnezzar. He failed to grasp the critical lesson that "whoever exalts himself will be humbled, and whoever humbles himself will be exalted" (Matthew 23:12).

You have lifted up yourself against the Lord of heaven (5:23): Instead of humbling himself, Belshazzar lifted himself up against God by defiantly using the holy vessels from the Jewish temple—the very house of God—for a wild, orgy-like feast.

You have praised the gods of silver and gold, of bronze, iron, wood, and stone (5:23): Instead of submitting to the one true God, Belshazzar worshiped idols, "which do not see or hear or know" (compare Jeremiah 10:5, 15; 14:22: 50:38; 51:17).

But the God in whose hand is your breath (5:23): Belshazzar worshiped gods that had no true life in themselves, ignoring the God on whom his own life depended. Belshazzar had entrusted his life to dead idols—the height of folly.

Daniel 5:24-28

From his presence the hand was sent (5:24): Daniel informed the king that the one true God—the God who had severely chastened Nebuchadnezzar for his pride and arrogance—sent the hand to write on the wall. Daniel, of course, knew that those words brought judgment. But rather than softening the stern message of God's judgment when speaking to Belshazzar, he told the truth.

This is the writing that was inscribed (5:25): The writing on the wall was a direct message from God: "Mene, Mene, Tekel, and Parsin."

Mene *(5:26)*: This Aramaic word means "numbered" or "counted." It is doubled in the present context to bring emphasis. Because of Belshazzar's pride and wickedness, God had numbered his days and his kingdom. The invading Medo-Persian force would soon bring the kingdom to its demise.

Tekel *(5:27)*: This Aramaic word means "weighed" or "assessed." God is the one who weighs a person's actions and motives (see 1 Samuel 2:3; Psalm 62:9). He evaluates people as the divine Judge. Belshazzar had been weighed, and he and his kingdom were found to be ripe for judgment.

Peres *(5:28)*: This Aramaic word means "divided." Babylon was soon to be destroyed and taken over by the Medo-Persian Empire.

In short, God's message to Belshazzar was this: "You have grievously sinned. You have been defiant. You have not repented. You are terminated."

Daniel 5:29-31

Then Belshazzar gave the command (5:29): One might think that after hearing such words of judgment, Belshazzar might have put Daniel to death. Instead, the king gave the command to give Daniel the gifts and rewards he had promised. Again, however, the rewards were essentially useless because Babylon was about to fall to the Medo-Persian army.

That very night (5:30): That very night, King Belshazzar—who had pridefully and arrogantly exalted himself—forfeited his life through divine judgment at the hands of the invading Medo-Persian forces.

PARALLELS

Daniel 5:30—Judgment struck Belshazzar suddenly and swiftly.

Revelation 18:10, 19—Judgment struck Babylon suddenly and swiftly.

We are reminded of the scriptural teaching that death often comes suddenly. We read in Ecclesiastes 9:12 that "man does not know his time. Like fish that are taken in an evil net, and like birds that are caught in a snare, so the children of man are snared at an evil time, when it suddenly falls upon them." In Proverbs 27:1, the wise man urged, "Do not boast about tomorrow, for you do not know what a day may bring." Each new day may bring the prospect of death. For this reason, the wise person—unlike Belshazzar—maintains a consistent awareness of his mortality so he will make good use of the time God has given. The psalmist therefore prayed, "O Lord, make me know my end and what is the measure of my days; let me know how fleeting I am" (Psalm 39:4). Those who maintain such an awareness live with great appreciation for each new day.

Darius the Mede (5:31): Darius was a popular name among Persian kings. The name is used most famously in reference to Darius the Mede. There has been much debate regarding Darius's actual identity. Three possibilities have been suggested:

- Darius could be an honored title for Cyrus.
- Darius could have been appointed by Cyrus to rule over Babylon.
- Darius may have been a son of Cyrus.

I believe the second option is probably best.

MAJOR THEMES

1. *Pride is predominant among human leaders.* Human leaders seem especially prone to pride and arrogance. Exodus 5:2 tells us that "Pharaoh said, 'Who is the LORD, that I should obey his voice and let Israel go? I do not know the LORD, and moreover, I will not let Israel go.'" Second Chronicles 26:16 says of Uzziah, "When he was strong, he grew proud, to his destruction. For he was unfaithful to the LORD his God." In the New Testament, Herod gave a speech, and the people shouted out, "The voice of a god, and not of a man!" Immediately following this, "an angel of the Lord struck him down, because he did not give God the glory, and he was eaten by worms and breathed his last" (Acts 12:22-23). Godly leaders, by contrast, are humble (see Luke 22:26).

2. *The vanity of worshiping idols.* Worshiping idols is the ultimate futility. This is a common theme in the book of Daniel. Daniel 5:23 reveals the obvious: The false gods of Babylon "do not see or hear or know." Jeremiah 10:5 likewise tells us, "Their idols are like scarecrows in a cucumber field, and they cannot speak; they have to be carried, for they cannot walk." Jeremiah 51:17 affirms that "every goldsmith is put to shame by his idols, for his images are false, and there is no breath in them." Habakkuk 2:18 warns, "What profit is an idol when its maker has shaped it, a metal image...Its maker trusts in his own creation when he makes speechless idols!" No wonder the apostle Paul declared, "An idol has no real existence" (1 Corinthians 8:4). Idolatry is sheer futility.

DIGGING DEEPER WITH CROSS-REFERENCES

Sudden destruction—Genesis 19:24, 28; Numbers 16:31-33; Deuteronomy 32:35; Psalm 35:8; Proverbs 6:14-15; Ecclesiastes 9:12; Isaiah 47:11; Jeremiah 15:8; Daniel 5:30; Luke 17:27; 1 Thessalonians 5:3

Death as a penalty for sin—Genesis 6:5-7; 1 Chronicles 10:13; Job 27:8; Proverbs 2:22; 10:27; Luke 12:20-21; Acts 5:1-10; Romans 5:12; 6:23

LIFE LESSONS

1. *Don't be enticed by what the world has to offer.* Notice that Daniel couldn't have cared less about the gifts the king offered. We should follow Daniel's lead. You and I must perpetually guard against the lure of what this world has to offer. "For all that is in the world—the desires of the flesh and the desires of the eyes and pride of life—is not from the Father but is from the world. And the world is passing away along with its desires, but whoever does the will of God abides forever" (1 John 2:16-17).

2. *The humble are often exalted at the hands of others.* We have already talked in this book about how God humbles the proud and exalts the humble. But notice that when God chooses to exalt one of His servants, He often does so by means of another powerful person. For example, in Egypt, Joseph was elevated to a position of great authority by the pharaoh (Genesis 41:37-43). Daniel was exalted to a position of great authority by several kings (for example, Daniel 5:29). God can do the same today. God may use a president, a governor, a mayor, the president of a company, or some other person in authority to exalt one of His servants.

QUESTIONS FOR REFLECTION AND DISCUSSION

1. What does today's Scripture reading reveal about Daniel's character?

2. How would you characterize King Belshazzar's response to Daniel's words of impending judgment?

3. What is the most important spiritual lesson you learned from today's study?

DAY 20

A PLOT IS LAUNCHED AGAINST DANIEL

DANIEL 6:1-9

SCRIPTURE READING AND INSIGHTS

Begin by reading Daniel 6:1-9 in your favorite Bible. As you read, remember that the Word of God is alive and working in you (Hebrews 4:12).

In yesterday's reading, Daniel interpreted the words of doom written on the wall. King Belshazzar was killed, and King Darius came into power. In today's lesson, a devious plot is launched against Daniel. With your Bible still accessible, consider the following insights on the biblical text, verse by verse.

Daniel 6:1-2

120 satraps (6:1): Darius divided his kingdom into 120 provinces, each one governed by a single satrap (a lieutenant or viceroy). The territory of each satrap was called a satrapy.

Three high officials, of whom Daniel was one (6:2): These 120 satraps were under the oversight of three administrators, perhaps with 40 satraps under each administrator. The key character trait required of these three administrators was trustworthiness. Daniel was an obvious fit for this position. This system of government greatly aided Darius in his administrative responsibilities.

That the king might suffer no loss (6:2): The 120 satraps were responsible for the security of their provinces and for collecting the proper tributes. The three administrators were then responsible for ensuring that the satraps didn't embezzle any money and that the tributes reached the king's treasury.

Daniel 6:3

Daniel became distinguished (6:3): Daniel was now more than 80 years old. He was working with people who were much younger than he was and had more vitality than he did, but they were not believers in the one true God who guided Daniel and gave him strength. Despite the age advantage of his younger workers, Daniel—with God's favor and blessing—proved himself much more capable than the others. For that reason, the king came to greatly respect him.

An excellent spirit was in him (6:3): This was one reason for Daniel's rise to prominence in Babylon. Recall from Daniel 1:17 that Daniel and his associates had "learning and skill in all literature and wisdom, and Daniel had understanding in all visions and dreams." As well, "an excellent spirit, knowledge, and understanding to interpret dreams, explain riddles, and solve problems were found in this Daniel" (5:12).

Bible expositors have taken the reference to "an excellent spirit" in various ways. Some take it as referring to the Babylonians' belief that their deities worked through Daniel. Others, however, say the phrase likely means that Daniel had a good character. He was a man of integrity. He was honest and faithful. He always accomplished his assigned task with a good attitude.

The king planned to set him over the whole kingdom (6:3): This would have made Daniel much like a prime minister. As noted previously in this book, when God exalts one of His own faithful children, He often does so through a powerful leader.

Daniel 6:4-5

A ground for complaint against Daniel (6:4): The satraps and other government officials in Babylon were apparently jealous and envious of Daniel's exaltation. They resented the king's favor toward him. They may have especially resented this favor being shown to Daniel since he was a Jew.

We learn elsewhere in Scripture that jealousy and envy are extremely dangerous. Jesus taught that negative emotions emerge from within the human heart: "What comes out of a person is what defiles him. For from within, out of the heart of man, come evil thoughts...coveting, wickedness, deceit...envy, slander, pride, foolishness" (Mark 7:20-22). James indicates that such negative attitudes are earthly and unspiritual: "If you have bitter jealousy and selfish ambition in your hearts...This is not the wisdom that comes down from above, but is earthly, unspiritual, demonic" (James 3:14-16; see also Galatians 5:19-21). The better policy, of course, is to ignore self-honor and seek God's honor in all things. But such thinking was entirely foreign to the officials who plotted against Daniel.

He was faithful (6:4): Daniel diligently accomplished every task assigned to him. No one could impugn his faithfulness. Perhaps the best way to describe Daniel is that he persevered in faithfulness.

No error or fault (6:4): In terms of Daniel's work habits, he was faultless. He didn't arrive to work late or leave early, he didn't sleep on the job, he didn't waste time, he never daydreamed, he never settled for mediocrity...rather, his intent was to show excellence in accomplishing all his tasks.

The law of his God (6:5): These officials concluded, "We shall not find any ground for complaint against this Daniel unless we find it in connection with the law of his God." Their intent was to undermine Daniel based on his religious practices.

Don't miss the fact that Daniel's commitment to the one true God was well known among the pagans in Babylon. Daniel was not a secret-agent believer. He followed God openly and served Him regardless of the consequences.

Daniel 6:6-9

These high officials and satraps came by agreement (6:6): The plot was launched. These unscrupulous men appeared before Darius the king with evil intent. They began by buttering him up with words of respect: "O King Darius, live forever!" (recall Daniel 2:4; 3:9; 5:10).

All the high officials of the kingdom...are agreed (6:7): The officials who appeared before Darius lied. Not *everyone* agreed to their agenda—Daniel, one of the top three leaders, was certainly not consulted. All this was kept from Daniel, for the instigators knew that Daniel would not have agreed with this course of action. If a man of Daniel's high respect had warned the king against this ordinance, the king probably would have declined. So the government officials kept all this hush-hush to ensure Daniel would not find out about it until it was too late.

The king should establish an ordinance (6:7): The government officials played on the king's ego: "Whoever makes petition to any god or man for thirty days, except to you, O king, shall be cast into the den of lions." Ancient kings were often worshiped as gods. The Egyptian pharaoh was himself considered a god—the son of the sun god, Re. Likewise, emperor worship in Rome became common in New Testament times. Recall that Nebuchadnezzar had once spoken of himself in divine terms (see Daniel 3:1-7). Darius was no doubt greatly flattered by this course of action, and he consented.

The law of the Medes and the Persians (6:8): Medo-Persian custom dictated that once an injunction was signed into law by the king, it could not be undone, even by the king himself. The leaders emphasized that an ordinance "cannot be changed, according to the law of the Medes and the Persians, which cannot be revoked." We also see this in Esther 1:19, where a royal order was "written among the laws of the Persians and the Medes so that it may not be repealed." To put it in modern vernacular, the injunction was set in concrete (see also Esther 8:8).

King Darius signed the document (6:9): The flattered king signed the document. By appealing to Darius's pride and vanity, the government officials were able to manipulate him into signing an irrevocable law that would put Daniel's life in jeopardy. The government officials knew Daniel would never compromise his commitment to God by praying to Darius, so he would be thrown into the lions' den. Government officials reasoned that they would finally be rid of Daniel.

MAJOR THEMES

1. *Human conspiracies*. Human conspiracies are common in the Bible. Joseph's brothers, in their jealousy and envy, conspired against him and sold him into slavery (Genesis 37:18-20). Korah and his associates engaged in a conspiracy against Moses (Numbers 16:1-35). Delilah and several Philistine leaders conspired against the mighty Samson (Judges 16:4-21). Jewish leaders conspired against the apostle Paul (Acts 23:12-15). And of

Jesus we read, "The Pharisees went out and conspired against him, how to destroy him" (Matthew 12:14). The Jewish leaders "plotted together in order to arrest Jesus by stealth and kill him" (Matthew 26:4). Daniel thus finds himself in good company.

2. *People who lay snares.* Closely related to engaging in conspiracies is the laying of snares to entrap others—also common in Scripture. The psalmist lamented, "For without cause they hid their net for me; without cause they dug a pit for my life" (Psalm 35:7), and "The insolent have dug pitfalls for me; they do not live according to your law" (Psalm 119:85). "The arrogant have hidden a trap for me, and with cords they have spread a net; beside the way they have set snares for me" (Psalm 140:5). When one encounters such snares, the wisest policy is to obey God no matter what: "The wicked have laid a snare for me, but I do not stray from your precepts" (Psalm 119:110). One must maintain faith in God, for "He Himself will deliver you from the hunter's net...His faithfulness will be a protective shield" (Psalm 91:3-4 HCSB). One is also wise to pray to God, "Keep me from the trap that they have laid for me and from the snares of evildoers!" (Psalm 141:9).

DIGGING DEEPER WITH CROSS-REFERENCES

Honor and promotion in the book of Daniel—Daniel 2:48-49; 3:30; 5:29

Examples of evil counsel—Numbers 31:16; 2 Samuel 16:21; 1 Kings 22:52; 2 Chronicles 22:3; Job 2:9; Psalms 1:1; 2:2; Proverbs 12:5; Jeremiah 9:14; Nahum 1:11

Prayer should be to God alone—2 Chronicles 7:14; Daniel 6:10; Matthew 6:5-15; Philippians 4:6-7

LIFE LESSONS

1. *Good stewardship*. Daniel was consistently a good steward. He had proved this earlier during the reign of Nebuchadnezzar, and now it was obvious to Darius. You and I are called to be consistent good stewards as well. As Colossians 3:23 puts it, "Whatever you do, work heartily, as for the Lord

and not for men." Related to this, Jesus asked, "Who then is the faithful and wise servant, whom his master has set over his household?" (Matthew 24:45). The context reveals that the faithful servant conscientiously fulfills his responsibilities and obligations while his master is away. He honors the stewardship entrusted to him. He pays careful attention to the details of his assigned tasks and avoids living carelessly and becoming lax in service. He governs his life so that he is prepared whenever his master returns. You and I are called to be good stewards, or good servants of the Lord, until His coming (see 1 Peter 4:10).

2. *Faultless living.* God blessed Daniel because he lived faultlessly before God and before other human beings (Daniel 6:4). Faultless living is described for us in Psalm 119. The psalmist boasted, "Blessed are those whose way is blameless" (verse 1). God blesses those who "seek him with their whole heart, who also do no wrong" (verses 2-3). The psalmist acknowledged to God, "You have commanded your precepts to be kept diligently" (verse 4). The psalmist then yearned, "Oh that my ways may be steadfast in keeping your statutes! Then I shall not be put to shame, having my eyes fixed on all your commandments" (verses 5-6). None of us is perfect, but we should all seek to be "Psalm 119" Christians.

QUESTIONS FOR REFLECTION AND DISCUSSION

1. Have you ever been victimized by others? If so, do you think God taught you any spiritual lessons in the experience?

2. Do you think Daniel exemplified Jesus' words in Matthew 5:11-12?

3. Have you ever thought of your Christian life as a stewardship involving service to Christ? If not, would you like to begin now?

DAY 21

DANIEL IS THROWN INTO THE LIONS' DEN

DANIEL 6:10-17

SCRIPTURE READING AND INSIGHTS

Begin by reading Daniel 6:10-17 in your favorite Bible. As you read, remember that those who obey the Word of God are truly blessed (Psalm 119:2; Luke 11:28; Revelation 1:3).

In the previous lesson, a devious plot was launched against Daniel by some unscrupulous government officials. In today's lesson, we see the result of that plot—Daniel is thrown into the lions' den. With your Bible still accessible, consider the following insights on the biblical text, verse by verse.

Daniel 6:10-11

When Daniel knew (6:10): The injunction signed by the king became public knowledge. As soon as Daniel became aware of it, he did what he normally did when facing a crisis: He prayed to God. He knew that God is always the believer's first line of defense.

Toward Jerusalem (6:10): The windows in Daniel's upper chamber faced Jerusalem. The temple in Jerusalem was considered God's dwelling place. Exiled Jews often prayed toward Jerusalem. (See Major Themes.)

On his knees three times a day (6:10): Jewish people commonly prayed three times a day (see Psalm 55:16-17). Daniel consistently followed this tradition. Despite the threat of death in a lions' den, Daniel would not cease praying to the one true God. Notice that Daniel's intention was not to disobey the king but rather to obey the King of kings—the one true God. Daniel was obeying a higher authority (compare Acts 5:29).

Gave thanks (6:10): Instead of complaining about the bad circumstances he now faced—circumstances that could lead to his death—Daniel began his prayer with thanksgiving. We are reminded of Psalm 95:2: "Let us come into his presence with thanksgiving." Psalm 100:4 also comes to mind: "Enter his gates with thanksgiving." Despite the present crisis, Daniel was thankful for God's continued goodness to him.

These men came by agreement (6:11): The conspiracy against Daniel continued to unfold. The group collectively sought to catch Daniel violating the king's injunction. One is reminded of Psalm 37:32-33: "The wicked watches for the righteous and seeks to put him to death. The LORD will not abandon him to his power or let him be condemned when he is brought to trial."

Found Daniel making petition and plea (6:11): Though Daniel began his prayer with thanksgiving, he also made "petition and plea" to God for help and guidance in the present situation. The conspirators now had the evidence they needed against Daniel to ensure his destiny in the lions' den.

Daniel 6:12-13

Did you not sign an injunction (6:12): Like adolescent tattletales, the conspirators rushed to the king and said, "O king! Did you not sign an injunction, that anyone who makes petition to any god or man within thirty days except to you, O king, shall be cast into the den of lions?" Because King Darius's injunction was according to the custom of the Medes and Persians, it was irrevocable, and the king could not negotiate on Daniel's behalf.

Daniel...pays no attention to you...or the injunction...but makes his petition (6:13): The conspirators' spin on the situation made Daniel look bad. The gist of their accusation was this: "Daniel is so defiant of you that he has disobeyed you not once, but thrice." Notice two things here. First, Daniel most certainly did pay attention to the king. But on a higher level, he paid greater attention to the Most High King of kings. Second, Daniel never had any intention of doing wrong to the king. In verse 22, he affirms, "Before you, O king, I have done no harm."

Daniel 6:14

The king...was much distressed (6:14): The king "set his mind to deliver Daniel." He stayed up all night trying to think of a way to rescue Daniel. But it was to no avail.

Some Bible expositors suggest that the king's distress may have been twofold. Primarily, he was distressed that Daniel would end up in the den of lions. Beyond that, however, he may have been distressed at the sudden recognition that he had fallen prey to a plot against Daniel by the devious government officials.

Of course, had the king exercised foresight, he wouldn't have gotten himself into this dilemma in the first place. More specifically, had he remembered that Daniel was faithful to his God, he never would have gone along with this request from the satraps and other governmental officials. We learn an important lesson here. Before making decisions, we should always take the long look and evaluate the possible consequences. Proverbs warns against choosing too quickly: "Do you see a man who is hasty in his words? There is more hope for a fool than for him" (Proverbs 29:20; see also 19:2; 21:5).

Daniel 6:15-17

It is a law of the Medes and Persians (6:15): The devious government officials were not going to let the king off the hook. They reminded him that his injunction was irrevocable. Darius himself was bound by the very law he made.

Daniel was brought and cast into the den of lions (6:16): The king had no choice. He issued the command, and Daniel was cast into the den of lions. This brutal form of execution was one of several that were common among the Persians.

PARALLELS

Daniel 6:16—Daniel faced persecution.

Revelation 12:13; 17:6—The "martyrs of Jesus" will face persecution and death.

The Aramaic word translated "den" carries the idea, "to dig." Dens were therefore underground pits. Such pits often had two entrances. There was an opening at the top for feeding the animals. People could also be lowered through this opening, if necessary. The lions would have entered through a second door, which likely was located on the side of a hill and led into the underground pit. Daniel was apparently lowered into the pit from above.

The king declared to Daniel (6:16): He said, "May your God, whom you serve continually, deliver you!" Notice the irony here. Daniel's commitment to the Most High God got him thrown into the lions' den as a result of the king's injunction. Now the king expresses his desire that the Most High God would rescue Daniel. The king's recognition that Daniel served God continually brings to mind the exhortation in 1 Corinthians 15:58: "Therefore, my beloved brothers, be steadfast, immovable, always abounding in the work of the Lord."

A stone was brought (6:17): A stone was "laid on the mouth of the den" so that Daniel could not escape.

The king sealed it with his own signet (6:17): A signet was typically worn on a chain around the neck and was engraved with the owner's name as well as a unique and distinct symbol. Anything imprinted with this signet carried the authority of the person who owned it. A modern counterpart might be a signature on a contract. The king's signet indicated that the door into the lions' den and the stone atop it were not to be tampered with.

Sometimes kings gave their signet rings to high officials who acted on their behalf, just as the Egyptian pharaoh gave his signet ring to Joseph (Genesis 41:42).

That nothing might be changed concerning Daniel (6:17): The seal guaranteed that no one would tamper with the lions' den—not even the king himself.

MAJOR THEMES

1. *Facing Jerusalem in prayer*. There is no command in Scripture for Jews to face Jerusalem during their prayers. However, it became common for the Jews in Bible times to face Jerusalem during prayer when they were away from Jerusalem. After all, it is the holy city, and in this holy city was the Jewish temple, the dwelling place of God. Facing Jerusalem amounted to

facing God in prayer (see 1 Kings 8:29-45; 2 Chronicles 6:20-40). Even when the Jews went into captivity in Babylon, and Jerusalem and the temple were destroyed, the practice remained. Daniel's prayers toward Jerusalem were therefore in keeping with the Jewish practices of the day.

2. *Praying three times a day.* This was another common practice among the Jews in Bible times. For example, in Psalm 55:17 the psalmist affirms, "Evening and morning and at noon I utter my complaint and moan, and he hears my voice." Scripture also makes individual references to morning prayers (Psalms 5:3; 88:13; 92:2), noontime prayers (Acts 10:9), and evening prayers (Psalm 141:2; Acts 3:1). In the New Testament we are instructed to "pray without ceasing" (1 Thessalonians 5:17). This means that believers can bring their prayers and petitions to God throughout the day as the need arises.

DIGGING DEEPER WITH CROSS-REFERENCES

Thankfulness to God—1 Chronicles 23:30; Psalms 30:12; 35:18; 69:30; 95:2; 100:4; 116:17; Matthew 11:25; John 6:11; Ephesians 5:20; Philippians 4:6; Colossians 2:7; 3:15; 4:2; 1 Thessalonians 5:18; 1 Timothy 4:4

Kneeling and bowing before God—Exodus 4:31; 12:27; 34:8; 1 Kings 8:54; Ezra 9:5; Psalm 95:6; Isaiah 45:23; Acts 7:60; Ephesians 3:14

Slander—1 Samuel 24:9; Job 1:11; Psalm 50:20; Jeremiah 18:18; Luke 7:33; Romans 3:8; 2 Timothy 3:3

Malice—Leviticus 19:18; Psalms 38:19; 69:4; Proverbs 6:14, 18-19; 21:10; Zechariah 8:17; John 8:44; Ephesians 4:31; Colossians 3:8; 1 Peter 2:1

LIFE LESSONS

1. *Components of prayer.* Daniel prayed consistently and regularly. He sets a great example for each of us. As we peruse Scripture, we find that prayer should involve at least five key components.

    - thanksgiving (Psalms 95:2; 100:4; Ephesians 5:20; Colossians 3:15)
    - praise (Psalms 34:1; 103:1-5, 20-22; Hebrews 13:15)

- worship (Exodus 20:3-5; Deuteronomy 5:7; Psalm 95:6; Hebrews 12:28; Revelation 14:7)
- confession (Proverbs 28:13; 1 John 1:9)
- requests to God for specific things (Matthew 6:11; Philippians 4:6-7)

Let's resolve to pray consistently and regularly, just as Daniel did.

2. *How to engage in effective prayer.* Scripture provides a number of principles for effective praying. Here are six of the most important:

   - All our prayers are subject to the sovereign will of God (1 John 5:14).
   - Prayer should be continual (1 Thessalonians 5:17).
   - Sin is a hindrance to answered prayer (Psalm 66:18).
   - Living righteously, by contrast, is a great benefit to prayer being answered (Proverbs 15:29).
   - We should pray in faith (Mark 11:22-24).
   - We should pray in Jesus' name (John 14:13-14).

3. *Trust in God even when things look their bleakest.* Sometimes our problems may be so severe and our future outlook so bleak that we feel like withdrawing and hiding from our difficulties. But God calls us to trust Him: "Call upon me in the day of trouble; I will deliver you, and you shall glorify me" (Psalm 50:15). "Trust in him at all times…God is a refuge for us" (Psalm 62:8). "It is better to take refuge in the LORD than to trust in man" (Psalm 118:8). "Trust in the LORD with all your heart, and do not lean on your own understanding. In all your ways acknowledge him, and he will make straight your paths" (Proverbs 3:5-6). Remember, we may not know every single detail of what our future holds, but we do know the One who knows every single detail of our future. So let's make a daily habit of trusting Him!

QUESTIONS FOR REFLECTION AND DISCUSSION

1. What is the most significant thing you learned about prayer in today's lesson?
2. What is the most significant thing you learned about trusting God in this lesson?
3. Did Daniel have a good reason to trust in God's deliverance, based on his past experiences with God? How so?

DAY 22

GOD PROTECTS DANIEL

DANIEL 6:18-23

SCRIPTURE READING AND INSIGHTS

Begin by reading Daniel 6:18-23 in your favorite Bible. As you read, keep in mind that just as we eat food for physical nourishment, so we need the Word of God for spiritual nourishment (1 Corinthians 3:2; Hebrews 5:12-14; 1 Peter 2:2).

In yesterday's lesson, Daniel was thrown into the lions' den. In today's reading, God protects Daniel throughout the night while he is in the lions' den. With your Bible still accessible, consider the following insights on the biblical text, verse by verse.

Daniel 6:18

The king went to his palace (6:18): We noted in the previous lesson that the king was troubled and upset on several levels. First, he was upset that Daniel would likely lose his life. This was especially irksome because the king knew that Daniel was an innocent and noble man. Second, he was upset that he had been duped by his own government officials. How dare they entrap him by his own law! They had pretended to seek his exaltation. In reality, their only interest was to injure Daniel and prevent the king from doing anything about it. The result was that the king couldn't sleep or eat.

Daniel 6:19-20

At break of day (6:19): So anxious was the king that at daybreak—the earliest allowable time—he got up and rushed immediately to the lions' den. He couldn't stand the anguish any further. He hoped against hope that Daniel was still alive, and accordingly made haste to the den.

At this juncture, one cannot help but remember the words spoken by Daniel's three Hebrew friends to Nebuchadnezzar when threatened with being thrown into the fiery furnace: "Our God whom we serve is able to deliver us from the burning fiery furnace, and he will deliver us out of your hand, O king" (Daniel 3:17). The same God who can deliver from fire can also deliver from lions.

Cried out in a tone of anguish (6:20): One can easily imagine the king panting and his heart racing. In modern vernacular, he was a bundle of nerves.

O Daniel (6:20): The king shouted out, "O Daniel, servant of the living God, has your God, whom you serve continually, been able to deliver you from the lions?" Notice that the king was well aware of Daniel's faithful service to God. The king likely reasoned that if Daniel's God did not deliver him, it was not because his God was displeased with Daniel, but rather because He was simply unable to help Daniel. That is why Darius asked if God had been able to rescue Daniel. Perhaps Darius's hopes were high because he had heard about what God had done for Daniel and his friends during the reigns of Nebuchadnezzar and Belshazzar.

PARALLELS

Daniel 6:20, 26—The "living God."

Revelation 7:2—The "living God."

Notice also that Darius referred to Daniel's God as "the living God." The term "living God" distinguishes Daniel's God from the lifeless idols and false gods of Babylon (see Deuteronomy 5:26; Joshua 3:10; Isaiah 37:17-18).

Daniel 6:21-22

My God sent his angel (6:22): Daniel immediately responded, "My God sent his angel and shut the lions' mouths, and they have not harmed me." This was probably another appearance of the "Angel of the Lord"—the preincarnate Christ—who rescued Daniel's three friends in the fiery furnace (Daniel 3:25; see also Psalm 91:11; Hebrews 1:14). Recall Psalm 34:7: "The angel of the LORD encamps around those who fear him, and delivers them."

It is important to understand that God could have simply decreed that the lions' mouths would remain shut and not harm Daniel. Instead, he sent the Angel of the LORD. Daniel was rescued, and apparently the preincarnate Christ kept him company throughout the night, just as He remained with the three Hebrew youths during their fiery ordeal (Daniel 3:24-25).

Daniel was always quick to give God all the glory: "My God sent his angel..." We see this not only in our present passage but also in previous chapters in the book of Daniel (see, for example, Daniel 2:27-28). Daniel was consistently a God-exalting man.

What a relief Daniel's deliverance was to Darius. Despite the best efforts of the devious governmental leaders who sought Daniel's destruction, their plans were thwarted by God's intervention on Daniel's behalf. The king's back had been against the wall as a result of the law of the Medes and Persians, but the King of kings was watching out for Daniel. The king's law may have been irrevocable on earth, but it held no sway in heaven. Indeed, heaven overruled earth in this case.

One is immediately reminded of the truth spoken by the apostle Paul in the book of Romans: "If God is for us, who can be against us?" (8:31). We are also reminded of Proverbs 19:21: "Many are the plans in the mind of a man, but it is the purpose of the LORD that will stand."

I was found blameless (6:22): Daniel now gives the reasons that God chose to rescue him. Primarily, Daniel "was found blameless before him." Scholars have debated what this means. Some believe it refers to Daniel's flawless lifestyle. He avoided sin and did good works. Others believe that "found blameless" refers more narrowly to Daniel's deliberate trust in the Most High God while facing this singular dire situation. In this latter view, God saved Daniel not because of any good works but rather because of his strong faith in God.

Perhaps both views are correct—God rescued Daniel because he was righteous *and* because he trusted in God. One is reminded that James in the New Testament not only spoke about the importance of strong faith (James

2:14-26) but also said, "The prayer of a righteous person has great power as it is working" (5:16).

And also before you, O king (6:22): Daniel then noted a secondary reason God had rescued him—he had "done no harm" before the king. The devious and conspiratorial government officials had harmed the king; Daniel had not.

Daniel 6:23

Exceedingly glad (6:23): King Darius was elated. He had sweat bullets all night and hadn't slept a wink. Now he was able to rest comfortably, knowing that God had indeed rescued Daniel. Daniel was immediately "taken up out of the den." Recall that the Aramaic word translated "den" carries the idea, "to dig." The den was likely an underground pit with an opening at the top for feeding the animals. It was through this top opening that Daniel was lifted out of the den.

Interestingly, this event—along with the rescue of Daniel's three friends from the fiery furnace—made it into faith's hall of fame in the New Testament. In Hebrews 11:33-34, we read about those "who through faith conquered kingdoms, enforced justice, obtained promises, stopped the mouths of lions, quenched the power of fire..."

No kind of harm (6:23): It would have been one thing for Daniel to have survived the night with scars all over his body. But our text tells us that "no kind of harm was found on him, because he had trusted in his God." This reminds us of how the three Hebrew youths were unharmed by the fiery furnace: "The fire had not had any power over the bodies of those men. The hair of their heads was not singed, their cloaks were not harmed, and no smell of fire had come upon them" (Daniel 3:27).

PARALLELS

Daniel 6:23—God shielded Daniel from harm.

Revelation 11:5—God will shield the two prophetic witnesses from harm.

Bible expositors are careful to point out that while God completely delivered the three Hebrew youths in the fiery furnace and Daniel in the lions' den, there are other occasions in the Bible where God allowed His servants to suffer and even become martyrs. Such individuals are described for us in Hebrews 11:36-40 (see also Revelation 6:9-11). We must remain faithful and maintain our faith in God—even if our desired deliverance may not seem to be coming. Recall that the three Hebrew youths informed the king that even if God did not deliver them from the fiery furnace, they would not bow down to an idol (Daniel 3:18).

MAJOR THEMES

1. *Fasting.* The king was worried sick for Daniel's survival and spent the entire night fasting (Daniel 6:18). The word "fast" is rooted in a Hebrew word that means "cover the mouth"—thus indicating abstinence from food and/or drink. Ideally, fast days were to be a time of self-denial and repentance from sin. During fasts, people were to humble their souls before God while abstaining from food. They were also to reflect on their relationship with God and the need to fully obey His commandments. King Darius, on the other hand, apparently fasted because he was simply too worried to eat.

2. *Trials of ordeal in the ancient Near East.* It is interesting to observe that in the ancient Near East, "trials of ordeal" determined people's guilt or innocence by exposing them to dangerous situations. If they survived the jeopardy, it was assumed that their deity had intervened, and the person was deemed innocent. If the person did not survive the jeopardy, it was assumed that the deity purposefully chose not to intervene, and guilt was assumed. Some Bible expositors believe that Daniel's night in the lions' den illustrates this type of trial.

DIGGING DEEPER WITH CROSS-REFERENCES

The protective ministry of angels—Genesis 18:22; 2 Kings 6:17; Psalm 91:11; Matthew 18:10; Acts 5:18-19

God is our shield in dangerous circumstances—Genesis 15:1; Deuteronomy 33:29; Psalms 33:20; 84:11; 115:9; Proverbs 30:5

LIFE LESSONS

1. *Servants of God.* Darius addresses Daniel as "servant of the living God" (Daniel 6:20). Many servants of God are mentioned in Scripture. Abraham was a servant of God (Psalm 105:6, 42), as were Moses (Deuteronomy 34:5; Joshua 1:1, 13, 15; Psalm 105:26) and Joshua (Joshua 24:29; Judges 2:8). The prophets were God's servants (Ezra 9:11; Jeremiah 7:25; Daniel 9:6; Amos 3:7). The apostles and their fellow workers were bondservants of God (Romans 1:1; Colossians 4:12; Titus 1:1; James 1:1; 2 Peter 1:1; Jude 1; Revelation 1:1). Even Nebuchadnezzar, whom God used as His whipping rod to chastise Israel, was called God's servant (Jeremiah 27:6; 43:10). You and I are called to be servants of God as well (1 Peter 2:16).

2. *Trusting God.* Our text says of Daniel, "No kind of harm was found on him, because he had trusted in his God" (Daniel 6:23). Trusting God is a common theme in Scripture. A great verse that applies to Daniel's situation is Proverbs 3:5-6: "Trust in the LORD with all your heart, and do not lean on your own understanding. In all your ways acknowledge him, and he will make straight your paths." According to his own understanding, Daniel could not possibly have survived a night in the lions' den. But Daniel didn't lean on his own understanding. He trusted God with all his heart, and God gave him a "path" right out of the lions' den. In keeping with this, Psalm 37:5 affirms, "Commit your way to the LORD; trust in him, and he will act." Daniel trusted God, and God acted (see also Psalms 40:4; 50:15; 62:8; 118:8; John 14:1; Hebrews 10:35).

QUESTIONS FOR REFLECTION AND DISCUSSION

1. Are you facing any crises right now in which you need to trust *not* in your own understanding but rather in the Lord?

2. Daniel's name literally means "God is my judge." How is this name illustrated in today's passage of Scripture?

3. Who rested more comfortably throughout the night—King Darius or Daniel? Why?

DAY 23

THE GOD OF DANIEL IS EXALTED

DANIEL 6:24-28

SCRIPTURE READING AND INSIGHTS

Begin by reading Daniel 6:24-28 in your favorite Bible. As you read, remember that storing God's Word in your heart can help you to avoid sinning (Psalm 119:9, 11).

In yesterday's reading, God protected Daniel while he was in the lions' den. Today we'll see the king exalt God as a result of this miraculous deliverance. With your Bible still accessible, consider the following insights on the biblical text, verse by verse.

Daniel 6:24

Those men who had maliciously accused Daniel (6:24): Now that Daniel was safe, it was time to mete out justice to the unscrupulous governmental leaders who had launched this deadly scheme against Daniel. The wicked destiny they had planned for Daniel would now become their own destiny. (See "Justice" in Major Themes.)

PARALLELS

Daniel 6:24—Judgment falls on the wicked.

Revelation 20:11-15—Judgment will fall on the wicked.

They, their children, and their wives (6:24): The wives and children of these wicked men were also thrown into the lions' den. This reminds us of Hosea 8:7: "They sow the wind, and they shall reap the whirlwind." These men had committed a great evil but would now suffer a catastrophically greater evil in that both they and their families would pay the ultimate price. Greek historian Herodotus indicates that executing an entire family for a single family member's crime was a common practice among the Persians (*Histories*, 3.119). This was intended as a deterrent against criminal acts. Of course, one must keep in mind that the Bible records many events that it does not condone.

The lions overpowered them (6:24): Death came quickly. Unlike our modern justice system, ancient rulers often rendered justice with extreme rapidity.

Daniel 6:25-27

King Darius wrote to all the peoples (6:25): Darius testified of God's greatness. We recall what Nebuchadnezzar said earlier: "I make a decree: Any people, nation, or language that speaks anything against the God of Shadrach, Meshach, and Abednego shall be torn limb from limb, and their houses laid in ruins, for there is no other god who is able to rescue in this way" (Daniel 3:29; see also 4:34-37). Daniel lived such a godly and uncompromising lifestyle and had exhibited such open trust in God that two kings were impacted with the truth.

I make a decree (6:26): A decree was an order or a declaration from a person in high authority. Royal decrees were common in biblical times (see, for example, Ezra 4:19, 21; 5:3, 9, 13).

Tremble and fear (6:26): Darius instructed that throughout his entire kingdom, people were to tremble and fear before the God of Daniel. Darius's words reflect the sentiment in a number of psalms: "Serve the Lord with fear, and rejoice with trembling" (2:11). "Let all the earth fear the Lord; let all the inhabitants of the world stand in awe of him!" (33:8). "The Lord reigns; let the peoples tremble! He sits enthroned upon the cherubim; let the earth quake! The Lord is great in Zion; he is exalted over all the peoples. Let them praise your great and awesome name!" (99:1-3). "My flesh trembles for fear of you, and I am afraid of your judgments" (119:120).

The living God (6:26): Darius discovered a pivotal truth that is emphasized throughout the book of Daniel. The God of Daniel truly is the "living God," unlike the many inanimate idols of Babylon. The living God is portrayed in Scripture as continually being among His people, and this is certainly true in the lives of Daniel and his three Hebrew friends. (See Life Lessons.)

Enduring forever (6:26): Darius acknowledged that Daniel's God endures forever. This is in contrast to the temporal, false deities of Babylon and other pagan cultures. The Bible often recognizes God as eternal. He has always existed and is beyond time altogether. He is the King eternal (1 Timothy 1:17) who alone is immortal (6:16). The psalmist affirmed, "From everlasting to everlasting you are God" (Psalm 90:2).

His kingdom shall never be destroyed (6:26): We recall that Nebuchadnezzar had earlier said that God's kingdom "is an everlasting kingdom, and his dominion endures from generation to generation" (Daniel 4:3). This is in contrast to human kingdoms, which rise and fall (see Daniel 2:1-49; 7:1-28; Revelation 17:12-13).

His dominion shall be to the end (6:26): We learn elsewhere in Scripture of Christ's central role in exercising dominion forever and ever. The New Testament says of Jesus, "Of his kingdom there will be no end" (Luke 1:33). Indeed, "he shall reign forever and ever" (Revelation 11:15). Because the kingdom is eternal, nothing can injure or destroy it. We are therefore urged, "Let us be grateful for receiving a kingdom that cannot be shaken" (Hebrews 12:28).

He delivers and rescues (6:27): The book of Daniel offers undeniable empirical evidence for this fact. God had earlier delivered and rescued the three Hebrew youths from the fiery furnace (Daniel 3:8-30). Now God had delivered and rescued Daniel from the lions' den (6:16-23). The implication is that if God can rescue His people from these dire circumstances, He can rescue His people in any situation.

Signs and wonders (6:27): We have noted that in the Bible, the word "sign" often carries the idea of a miracle with a message. It attests to something (see Deuteronomy 6:22; 7:19; 13:1-2; 26:8; Nehemiah 9:10; Isaiah 8:18). In the present context, God attested that He is the one true, living God by delivering Daniel from the jaws of death in the lions' den. The word "wonder" is appropriate because God's miracles often have a jaw-dropping effect on people. Recall that Nebuchadnezzar had earlier said, "It has seemed good to me to show the signs and wonders that the Most High God has done for me" (Daniel 4:2).

Who has saved Daniel from the power of the lions (6:27): Darius here memorialized God's deliverance of Daniel. Everyone throughout his kingdom would now become aware of it.

Daniel 6:28

Daniel prospered (6:28): This section closes with a recognition of Daniel's prosperity during the reigns of Darius and Cyrus. God prospers those who are committed and obedient to Him. Daniel was definitely a Psalm 1 kind of man: "Blessed is the man who walks not in the counsel of the wicked, nor stands in the way of sinners, nor sits in the seat of scoffers; but his delight is in the law of the LORD, and on his law he meditates day and night. He is like a tree planted by streams of water that yields its fruit in its season, and its leaf does not wither. In all that he does, he prospers."

We witness parallels between Daniel and Joseph, who was another Psalm 1 kind of man: "The LORD was with Joseph, and he became a successful man" (Genesis 39:2). When Joseph was unjustly thrown in prison, "the LORD was with Joseph and showed him steadfast love and gave him favor in the sight of the keeper of the prison" (verse 21). "Whatever he did, the LORD made it succeed" (verse 23). As it was with Joseph, so it was with Daniel. God prospered Daniel because, like Joseph, he was a faithful and obedient servant of God.

MAJOR THEMES

1. *God is eternal.* Darius recognized that Daniel's God endures forever (Daniel 6:26). The eternal nature of God is a common theme in the Bible. Indeed, Scripture teaches that God transcends time altogether. As an eternal being, He has always existed. God is the King eternal (1 Timothy 1:17), who alone is immortal (6:16). God is the "Alpha and the Omega" (Revelation 1:8), who affirms, "I am the first and I am the last" (Isaiah 44:6; 48:12). God exists "from everlasting to everlasting" (Psalms 41:13; 90:2) and lives forever (Psalm 102:12, 27; Isaiah 57:15).

2. *Justice.* The king was aware that unscrupulous governmental officials had

wronged Daniel and himself. He therefore brought about justice by having them executed. Indeed, they suffered the same fate they had intended for Daniel. This brings to mind Proverbs 11:8: "The righteous is delivered from trouble, and the wicked walks into it instead." We also recall Proverbs 26:27: "Whoever digs a pit will fall into it." We see this type of thing quite often in Scripture. Recall that Pharaoh had ordered the death of the Hebrew male babies, but ultimately the Egyptian firstborn died. He gave the order for Jewish newborns to be drowned in the Nile, but later his own army drowned in the Red Sea (Exodus 14–15). The evil Haman was hanged on the very gallows he had made to execute the righteous Mordecai (Esther 7:9-10; 9:25).

DIGGING DEEPER WITH CROSS-REFERENCES

God's awesome signs and wonders—Deuteronomy 6:22; Nehemiah 9:10; Psalms 105:26-36; 135:9; Jeremiah 32:20-21; Daniel 3:28-29; 4:3; 6:27

Justice—Psalms 99:4; 106:3; 112:5; Proverbs 29:4; Leviticus 19:15; Isaiah 9:7; 61:8; Luke 18:7-8; Acts 17:31; Revelation 19:11

LIFE LESSONS

1. *The living God.* Darius referred to Daniel's God as "the living God" (Daniel 6:26). This is a common ascription used of God throughout Scripture (see Deuteronomy 5:26; 1 Samuel 17:26-36; Psalm 84:2). The living God is "among" His people (Joshua 3:10). This is certainly illustrated in the life of Daniel, for God was with both Daniel and his three friends in their times of trouble. The term "living God" is often used in contexts that contrast the Lord with lifeless idols (see Deuteronomy 5:26; Joshua 3:10; Isaiah 37:17-18). In his wonderful book *The Living God*, Bible scholar R.T. France explains how the ancients viewed God as living.

> Watch the hand of this living God intervening, in answer to His people's prayers, working miracles, converting thousands, opening prison doors, and raising the dead, guiding His messengers to people and places they had never thought of, supervising the whole operation and every figure in it so as to work out His purpose in

> the end. Is it any wonder they prayed, constantly, not in vague generalities, but in daring specific requests? To them, God was real; to them He was the living God.[1]

You and I have the privilege of interacting with the living God.

2. *Salvation.* The king affirmed that God "saved Daniel from the power of the lions" (Daniel 6:27). This illustrates for us that there are different nuances of the words "saved" and "salvation." We most often think of being saved as it pertains to our eternal salvation in heaven (see John 3:14-17; 5:24; 6:29, 47; Ephesians 2:8-9). Our text in Daniel, however, indicates that God can also temporally save a person from earthly danger. A person can also be saved from sickness (James 5:15-16). Salvation can refer to God delivering His people from oppressors (Exodus 14:13) and rescuing a person from trouble (Exodus 15:2; Psalm 62:2). Salvation can also take place as a local church works out its internal problems (Philippians 2:12). Let us never forget that God can save in many different ways.

QUESTIONS FOR REFLECTION AND DISCUSSION

1. List at least five reasons you are thankful that God is a living God.

2. Are you facing any tough circumstances right now in which you need the salvation of the Lord (Exodus 14:13; 2 Chronicles 20:17; Lamentations 3:26)? What have you learned in today's lesson that can give you confidence in this regard?

3. What impacted you most in Darius's words about God after Daniel's deliverance?

DAY 24

DANIEL'S FIRST VISION, PART 1

DANIEL 7:1-8

SCRIPTURE READING AND INSIGHTS

Begin by reading Daniel 7:1-8 in your favorite Bible. As you read, trust God to open your eyes so you can discover wondrous things from His Word (Psalm 119:18).

In yesterday's reading, King Darius exalted God following Daniel's mighty deliverance in the lions' den. In today's lesson, Daniel receives his first vision from God. With your Bible still accessible, consider the following insights on the biblical text, verse by verse.

Daniel 7:1-3

The first year of Belshazzar king of Babylon (7:1): We've been talking about King Darius, who reigned after Belshazzar, so this must represent a flashback to 14 years prior to the fall of Babylon (about 553 BC). This means that the events described in Daniel 7 actually predate those described in Daniel 5–6. Daniel must therefore have had this vision when he was about 68 years old.

Daniel saw a dream (7:1): In Bible times, many people had visions during their waking hours. Daniel, however, had this vision while he was asleep.

Daniel had helped kings solve mysteries, whether they related to dreams or to handwriting on the wall. Now, however, Daniel himself had a prophetic dream and visions.

PARALLELS

Daniel 7:1—Daniel "wrote down" God's revelations.

Revelation 1:19—John was commanded to "write" God's revelations.

The four winds of heaven (7:2): This phrase (or something similar) is sometimes used of God's providential acts among human beings or their nations (see Jeremiah 23:19; 49:36; 51:16; Zechariah 6:1-6; 7:14; Revelation 7:1-3). The word "sea" often represents nations and peoples (compare Isaiah 17:12-13; 57:20). So Daniel's vision focuses on God's providential actions among the Gentile nations.

Four great beasts (7:3): These four beasts represent the four kingdoms that play an important role in the unfolding of biblical prophecy. Notice that these nations were previously identified in Nebuchadnezzar's dream (Daniel 2:31-35) and that they are increasingly violent.

PARALLELS

Daniel 7:3—Beasts "came up out of the sea."

Revelation 13:1—A beast was "rising out of the sea."

Daniel 7:4

The first was like a lion and had eagles' wings (7:4): However, Daniel said, "its wings were plucked off." This imagery apparently represents Babylon, its lionlike quality indicating power and strength. It is interesting to observe that winged lions guarded the gates of Babylon's royal palaces (see Jeremiah 4:7, 13). Also, some biblical passages represent Nebuchadnezzar as a lion (see Jeremiah 4:7; 49:19; 50:17, 44). The wings on the lion indicate rapid mobility, while the plucking of the wings indicates a removal of mobility—perhaps a reference to Nebuchadnezzar's insanity or to Babylon's deterioration following his death.

Daniel 7:5

Behold, another beast, a second one, like a bear (7:5): This animal of great strength represents the kingdom of Medo-Persia. The fact that the bear was "raised up on one side" indicates that the Persians maintained the higher status in the Medo-Persian alliance. The bear "had three ribs in its mouth between its teeth; and it was told, 'Arise, devour much flesh.'" The ribs were the vanquished nations—apparently Lydia (conquered 546 BC), Babylon (conquered 539 BC), and Egypt (conquered 525 BC). Medo-Persia was well known for its strength and fierceness in battle (see Isaiah 13:17-18).

Daniel 7:6

Another, like a leopard (7:6): The third beast had "four wings of a bird on its back. And the beast had four heads, and dominion was given to it" (Daniel 7:6). The leopard is known for its swiftness, cunning, and agility. This imagery represents Greece under Alexander the Great (born in 356 BC). The four heads are the four generals who divided the kingdom following Alexander's death, ruling Macedonia, Asia Minor, Syria, and Egypt.

Daniel 7:7

A fourth beast, terrifying and dreadful and exceedingly strong (7:7): The fourth beast was more powerful than the three preceding beasts. The wild imagery refers to the Roman Empire, which existed in biblical times but fell apart in the fifth century AD.

It had ten horns (7:7): This empire will be revived in the end times. It will apparently be comprised of ten nations ruled by ten kings (ten horns). It is noteworthy that Rome never consisted of a ten-nation confederacy with ten co-rulers. If it hasn't happened yet, this means this prophecy must deal with the future. (See Major Themes.)

PARALLELS

Daniel 7:7—The beast had "ten horns."

Revelation 13:1—The beast had "ten horns."

Daniel 7:8

Another horn, a little one (7:8): Speaking of the prophetic future, Daniel now refers to an eleventh horn—a little horn (the antichrist) who seems insignificant at first but grows powerful enough to uproot three of the existing horns (kings). The antichrist will emerge from apparent obscurity. With his profound diplomatic skills, however, he will win the admiration of the political world and compel others to follow his lead. Though he will begin his political career as just a "little horn," his brilliant statesmanship will catapult him into global fame and power. He will quickly ascend to the topmost rung of the political world. Once he gains ascendancy, no one will challenge his political power. His political domain will eventually be global. All other political leaders will be pawns in his hands.

The antichrist, of course, will be energized by none other than Satan, who is pictured in Revelation 12:3 as a "great red dragon." The color red may imply bloodshed, which would be expected because Satan has always been a murderer (John 8:44). This dragon (Satan) is pictured with "seven heads and ten horns, and on his heads seven diadems." From similar descriptions in Daniel 7:7-8, 24 and Revelation 13:1, we infer that this terminology points to Satan's control over world empires during the tribulation period, apparently through the antichrist.

The ten horns apparently represent the ten kings of Daniel 7:7 and Revelation 13:1, over whom the antichrist—empowered by Satan—will gain authority. The ten countries headed by the ten kings will form the nucleus of the antichrist's (and thus Satan's) empire. The seven heads and seven crowns apparently refer to the principal rulers of the empire.

The eyes of a man (7:8): This idiom refers to intelligence, shrewdness, or powers of observation. This intelligence and shrewdness will enable the antichrist to come into world dominion in the end times.

A mouth speaking great things (7:8): The antichrist will apparently be an oratorical genius—a master of the spoken word (see also verse 20). He has "a lion's mouth" (Revelation 13:2), which Bible interpreters believe means that his oratorical skills will be majestic and awe-inspiring. Most world dictators have been persuasive speakers, able to motivate the masses to support their political agenda. The antichrist will mesmerize the world through his words.

Most Bible expositors believe that the "great things" spoken by the antichrist will include self-exalting things. Revelation 13:5 tells us, "The beast [antichrist] was given a mouth uttering haughty and blasphemous words." Indeed, "it opened its mouth to utter blasphemies against God, blaspheming his name and his dwelling, that is, those who dwell in heaven" (verse 6). The antichrist's blasphemous words are in keeping with his blasphemous nature (see 2 Thessalonians 2:3-11). The root meaning of the Greek and Hebrew words for blasphemy carries the idea of injuring the reputation of another. This can range from a lack of reverence to utter contempt for God (Leviticus 24:16; Matthew 26:65; Mark 2:7). It can also involve making claims of divinity for oneself, as the antichrist will do (compare Mark 14:64; John 10:33).

MAJOR THEMES

1. *Horns.* Animals use horns as weapons. For this reason, the horn came to be seen as a symbol of power and might. As an extension of this symbol, horns in biblical times were sometimes used as emblems of dominion, representing kingdoms and kings, as is the case in the books of Daniel and Revelation (see Daniel 7–8; Revelation 12:13; 13:1, 11; 17:3-16).

2. *The connection between Daniel 2 and Daniel 7.* According to Daniel 7, in the end times, the antichrist will come into absolute power and dominance over a revived Roman Empire. This will likely occur about the midpoint of the future tribulation period.

   In Daniel 2 we read of Nebuchadnezzar's prophetic dream, in which this end-times Roman Empire was pictured as a mixture of iron and clay (see verses 41-43). Daniel, the great dream interpreter, saw this as meaning that just as iron is strong, so this latter-day Roman Empire would be strong. But just as iron and clay do not naturally mix with each other, so this latter-day Roman Empire would have some divisions. There would not be complete internal cohesion in the empire.

3. *Identifying this end-times Roman Empire.* Many modern biblical interpreters see the present European Union as the primary prospect for the ultimate fulfillment of this prophecy. This confederacy is currently characterized by

both unity and some division. It appears that the stage is even now being set for the fulfillment of Daniel 2 and 7. Once the antichrist emerges into power in a revived Rome, it is only a matter of time before he comes into complete global domination.

DIGGING DEEPER WITH CROSS-REFERENCES

Visions—Genesis 46:2; Numbers 12:6; Psalm 89:19; Daniel 2:19; 4:5, 13; 10:7; Hosea 12:10; Joel 2:28; Luke 1:22; Acts 2:17; 10:3; 11:5; 16:9; 18:9; 2 Corinthians 12:1

The four winds of heaven—Daniel 8:8; 11:4; Jeremiah 49:36; Ezekiel 37:9; Zechariah 2:6; Revelation 7:1

Ten horns—Daniel 7:20; Revelation 12:3; 13:1; 17:12

LIFE LESSONS

1. *The primacy of Scripture.* When interpreting biblical prophecy, we must always be cautious to maintain the primacy of Scripture. Be careful not to use current events to interpret the Scriptures. Rather, use Scriptures to interpret current events. In other words, we must never force current events into biblical prophecy. The better policy is to first learn what the prophetic Scriptures teach and then observe the world to watch for any legitimate correlations between world events and biblical prophecy. We are not to be sensationalistic in studying prophecy. Rather, as 1 Peter 4:7 puts it, "The end of all things is at hand; therefore be self-controlled and sober-minded."

2. *God's sovereignty and human fear.* The description of this final earthly kingdom sounds a bit scary. But when we remember that God is sovereign over the nations, Christians never need to be afraid. In the book of Job we read, "He makes nations great, and he destroys them; he enlarges nations, and leads them away" (Job 12:23). We are told that "from one man he created all the nations throughout the whole earth. He decided beforehand when they should rise and fall, and he determined their boundaries" (Acts 17:26 NLT). Daniel 2:21 tells us that "it is He who changes the times and the

epochs; He removes kings and establishes kings" (NASB). So regardless of what happens in earthly kingdoms, we can rest in the comfort of knowing that God is in absolute control.

QUESTIONS FOR REFLECTION AND DISCUSSION

1. Are you ever fearful of world events—especially those that are related to terrorism? What have you learned in this lesson that comforts you?

2. Do you think we are living in the end times? Why or why not?

3. Has your study of biblical prophecy bolstered your faith in God and your confidence in the Bible? If so, how?

DAY 25

DANIEL'S FIRST VISION, PART 2

DANIEL 7:9-14

SCRIPTURE READING AND INSIGHTS

Begin by reading Daniel 7:9-14 in your favorite Bible. As you read, allow the Word of God to bring revival to your soul (Psalm 119:25, 93, 107).

In the previous lesson, we were introduced to Daniel's first vision. In today's lesson, we continue to explore it. With your Bible still accessible, consider the following insights on the biblical text, verse by verse.

Daniel 7:9

Thrones were placed (7:9): One of these would be occupied by the Ancient of Days—the Most High God.

Ancient of Days (7:9): God's names in the Bible reveal something about His nature. God's name *Yahweh*, for example, indicates that He is eternally self-existing and that He is the faithful covenant-keeping God of His people. The name *Elohim* indicates that God is a mighty God. The ascription *Adonai* indicates that God is Lord and is sovereign over all things in the universe. Many biblical scholars believe the descriptive phrase "Ancient of Days" indicates that God is an eternal being. Others believe it points to God as the divine Judge. If this latter view is correct, the idea is that the Most High God not only assigns power to the kingdoms of humankind but will also judge those kingdoms in the end. (See Major Themes.)

His clothing was white as snow, and the hair of his head like pure wool (7:9): This apparently points to the infinite wisdom, holiness, and purity of the Most High God (compare Psalm 51:7; Revelation 1:14).

His throne was fiery flames (7:9): This affirmation reflects God's incredible glory and purity. Revelation 4:5 says of God's throne, "From the throne came flashes of lightning." We are elsewhere told that God "dwells in unapproachable light" (1 Timothy 6:16). The psalmist says of God, "You are clothed with splendor and majesty, covering yourself with light as with a garment" (Psalm 104:2).

PARALLELS

Daniel 7:9—The glory of the "Ancient of Days" is described.

Revelation 1:14—The glory of Jesus Christ is described.

Interestingly, in Isaiah 6:1-6 we read of seraphim (angels) surrounding the throne of God and constantly affirming, "Holy, holy, holy is the Lord of hosts." These seraphim had six wings each. With two of these wings they cover their faces. This seems to communicate that even the holy angels cannot look at the full, unveiled glory of God on His glorious throne.

Its wheels were burning fire (7:9): This apparently pictures God as sitting on a chariot-like throne from which He issues His sovereign decrees. This recalls God's fiery throne-chariot with wheels in Ezekiel 10:2-6.

Daniel 7:10

A stream of fire (7:10): From the burning bush that Moses saw at Horeb (Exodus 3:3) to the pillar of fire that guided the Israelites through the wilderness (Exodus 13:21), fire often represents the presence of God. Fire is also pictured as going before God as a preparation for His coming: "Our God comes...before him is a devouring fire" (Psalm 50:3). Indeed, "fire goes before him" (Psalm 97:3).

A thousand thousands served him (7:10): This is a reference to the countless angels who render service to God. We have seen that God's angels are countless. Luke 2:13 refers to "a multitude of the heavenly host" (see Psalm 68:17). Their number is elsewhere described as "myriads of myriads and thousands of thousands" (Revelation 5:11).

PARALLELS

Daniel 7:10—Countless angels serve God.

Revelation 1:1; 5:11—"Myriads of myriads and thousands of thousands" of angels serve God.

Ten thousand times ten thousand stood before him (7:10): While the "thousand thousands" serving God are His countless angels, the "ten thousand times ten thousand" standing before Him are apparently those being judged in God's divine court. Daniel witnessed God judging virtually millions who were standing before Him.

The court sat in judgment, and the books were opened (7:10): This is similar to the language of judgment in Revelation 20:12: "I saw the dead, great and small, standing before the throne, and books were opened. Then another book was opened, which is the book of life. And the dead were judged by what was written in the books, according to what they had done." These books point to the reality that God keeps accurate records and will use these as a basis for future judgment (compare Exodus 32:32; Psalms 69:28; 139:16; Malachi 3:16; Philippians 4:3; Revelation 20:12, 15; 21:27).

PARALLELS

Daniel 7:10—Books were opened in judgment.

Revelation 20:12—Books will be opened in judgment.

Of course, all people will one day stand in judgment before God. Unbelievers will face Christ at the great white throne judgment, after which they will be cast into the lake of fire (Revelation 20:11-15). Christians will not appear at this judgment, for their salvation is already secure. Rather, they will receive or lose rewards at a separate judgment—the judgment seat of Christ (Romans 14:8-10; 1 Corinthians 3:11-15)—and spend eternity with Christ.

Daniel 7:11-12 (Meanwhile, on earth...)

The great words that the horn was speaking (7:11): The "little horn"—the antichrist—was boasting and speaking blasphemous words against God (compare with verse 8; see also 2 Thessalonians 2:4).

The beast was killed (7:11): The fourth beast—referring to the Roman Empire, revived in the end times and led by the antichrist—would be "killed," or destroyed, not by another nation, but rather as a result of divine judgment (compare Luke 21:24-27; Revelation 19:20). The empire and its wicked leader, the antichrist, will be divinely terminated. The antichrist will be destroyed at Christ's second coming (see Revelation 19:20; 20:10; compare with Daniel 2:35, 45).

PARALLELS

Daniel 7:11—"The beast was killed."

Revelation 19:20—"The beast was captured" and thrown into the lake of fire.

This event will put an end to what is called "the times of the Gentiles" (Luke 21:24, 27). This phrase refers to the Gentile domination of Jerusalem. This period began with the Babylonian captivity that started in 606 BC. This time will last all the way through the seven-year future tribulation period (Revelation 11:2), finally ending with the second coming of Jesus Christ.

The rest of the beasts (7:12): The remaining three kingdoms (or some part of their cultures) would remain in some form—but only as faint reflections of their former prominence and power—until Christ's messianic kingdom is initiated. No longer would these three kingdoms have any kind of dominance.

Daniel 7:13-14 (Back in heaven...)

There came one like a son of man (7:13): While "the Ancient of Days" is a reference to the Father, the first person of the Trinity, "a son of man" is a messianic title for Jesus Christ, the second person of the Trinity (see Matthew 24:30; 25:31; 26:24; Mark 13:26; Luke 21:27; John 12:34). The "clouds of heaven" that accompany His appearance apparently refer to divine glory (see Exodus 16:10; 40:34-35; Numbers 16:42; 1 Kings 8:10-11; Isaiah 6:4).

He came to the Ancient of Days (7:13): The second person of the Trinity appears before the first person of the Trinity. Jesus, the divine Messiah, appears before the heavenly Father. Scripture consistently portrays Jesus as in submission to the heavenly Father: "I have come down from heaven, not to do my own will but the will of him who sent me" (John 6:38; see also John 4:34; 5:19; 14:31; 16:28).

PARALLELS

Daniel 7:13-14—The Messiah receives "dominion and glory and a kingdom."

Revelation 19:11-16—Christ will return to reign over His kingdom.

To him was given dominion (7:14): The four beasts (or four earthly kingdoms headed up by powerful human leaders) had sought dominion over the earth. They are now destroyed, and Jesus the Messiah is given global dominion. All the authority, glory, and sovereign power that had been sought by the earthly rulers is at last conferred on Christ so that He is sovereign over "all peoples, nations, and languages." This represents a fulfillment of the promise the Father had earlier made to the Son: "I have set my King on Zion, my holy hill...I will make the nations your heritage, and the ends of the earth your possession" (Psalm 2:6-8). This will take place at the second coming of Jesus Christ (see Matthew 24:30; 25:31; Revelation 11:15).

PARALLELS

Daniel 7:14—Christ's "dominion is an everlasting dominion."

Revelation 11:15—Christ "shall reign forever and ever."

Everlasting dominion (7:14): Christ's kingdom will be everlasting. It will never be conquered by another. This reign will be established in the future millennial kingdom (Revelation 20:1-6). Following that, Christ's reign continues forever in the eternal state (1 Corinthians 15:24-28).

MAJOR THEMES

1. *The Son of Man.* In his vision, Daniel witnessed "one like a son of man" (Daniel 7:13). The term "son of man" is an important messianic title. We see the term not only in Daniel but also in the Gospels (see Matthew 8:20; 20:18; 24:30). The title is often used in the context of Christ's deity. For example, the Bible says that only God can forgive sins (Isaiah 43:25; Mark 2:7). But as the Son of Man, Jesus had the power to forgive sins (Mark 2:10). Likewise, after the tribulation period, "then will appear in heaven the sign of the Son of Man, and then all the tribes of the earth will mourn, and they will see the Son of Man coming on the clouds of heaven with power and great glory" (Matthew 24:30).

2. *The Ancient of Days.* Daniel in his vision witnessed the Ancient of Days. This is a reference to Yahweh, the God and divine Judge of the universe (Daniel 7:9, 13, 22). The portrayal of the Ancient of Days is awesome and majestic, for "his clothing was white as snow, and the hair of his head like pure wool; his throne was fiery flames" (verse 9). Indeed, "a stream of fire issued and came out from before him; a thousand thousands served him" (verse 10). The great age of this majestic individual is not intended to communicate that God actually ages. Rather, it is a symbolic representation of God's eternal nature (see Exodus 3:6, 14; Isaiah 9:7). This is in obvious contrast to the temporal, finite rulers of earth.

DIGGING DEEPER WITH CROSS-REFERENCES

Throne of God—Psalms 45:6; 103:19; Isaiah 66:1; Revelation 20:11

Messianic prophecies—Genesis 3:15; 12:3; 49:10; Deuteronomy 18:15; Psalms 2:2; 69:21; 110:1; 118:22; 132:11; Isaiah 7:14; 9:6-7; 11:10; 25:8; 61:1; Jeremiah 23:5; Daniel 7:13; Micah 5:2; Zechariah 11:12; 12:10

LIFE LESSONS

1. *God's countless angels.* Daniel 7:10 says that "a thousand thousands" served God. Scripture elsewhere refers to "a multitude of the heavenly host" (Luke 2:13). Their number is also described as "myriads of myriads and thousands of thousands" (Revelation 5:11). The word "myriad" means "vast number" or "innumerable." Job 25:3 understandably asks, "Is there any number to his armies?" Scripture never specifies for us the exact number of God's angels. But one thing is certain: There are more than enough angels to serve as "ministering spirits" to Christians (Hebrews 1:14).

2. *God's books.* Our passage tells us that "the books were opened" (Daniel 7:10). The opening of God's books implies that God keeps an accurate record, which He will use as the basis for His future judgment of humankind. Recall that Moses interceded in prayer on behalf of the Israelites and asked that they be forgiven. If not, he said, "Please blot me out of your book that you have written" (Exodus 32:32). The psalmist urged that the wicked "be blotted out of the book of the living" (Psalm 69:28). The psalmist conceded that his entire life was recorded in God's book: "In your book were written, every one of them, the days that were formed for me, when as yet there was none of them" (Psalm 139:16). The apostle Paul spoke of his coworkers, "whose names are in the book of life" (Philippians 4:3). At the future judgment, God's books will be opened (Revelation 20:12, 15; 21:27). You and I ought to rejoice that our names are recorded in the book of life!

QUESTIONS FOR REFLECTION AND DISCUSSION

1. What strikes you most regarding the description of God as the Ancient of Days?

2. What do you learn from Matthew 24:30 about the Son of Man, who is coming "on the clouds of heaven"? What about Matthew 26:24? Mark 13:26? Acts 1:9-11?

3. Does the reality that your name is in God's book impact the way you live? Do you want to make any midcourse corrections in your life?

DAY 26

DANIEL'S VISION INTERPRETED, PART 1

DANIEL 7:15-22

SCRIPTURE READING AND INSIGHTS

Begin by reading Daniel 7:15-22 in your favorite Bible. As you read, never forget that God urges you to quickly obey His Word in all things (Psalm 119:60).

In the previous two lessons, we were introduced to Daniel's first vision. Now let's zero in on the interpretation of this vision. With your Bible still accessible, consider the following insights on the biblical text, verse by verse.

Daniel 7:15

My spirit within me was anxious (7:15): Daniel was troubled. He indicated this in two ways: His spirit was anxious, and the visions alarmed him. He understood that judgment was coming on his people as a result of sin, and this made him sad. A little later, after Daniel understands the full meaning of his dream, we read, "As for me, Daniel, my thoughts greatly alarmed me, and my color changed" (verse 28).

A pattern we see emerging in the book of Daniel is that dreams cause alarm. We recall that when Nebuchadnezzar had a dream, "his spirit was troubled, and his sleep left him" (Daniel 2:1). Sometime later, we read that when Daniel became aware of Nebuchadnezzar's second dream, "Daniel, whose name was Belteshazzar, was dismayed for a while, and his thoughts alarmed him" (4:19).

Daniel 7:16

I approached one of those who stood there (7:16): On previous occasions, Daniel had interpreted other people's dreams and the handwriting on the wall. With God's empowerment, Daniel was gifted at deciphering mysteries. Presently, however, Daniel's interpretive abilities escaped him. He did not know what his own dream and visions meant.

For this reason, Daniel "approached one of those who stood there and asked him the truth concerning all this." This may well have been the angel Gabriel. After all, in Daniel 8:16, Gabriel is instructed, "Gabriel, make this man understand the vision." A bit later, Daniel said, "While I was speaking in prayer, the man Gabriel, whom I had seen in the vision at the first, came to me in swift flight at the time of the evening sacrifice" (9:21).

One is reminded that God used Gabriel to bring other important revelations to humankind. For example, in the New Testament—some 500 years after the time of Daniel—Gabriel told Zechariah about the birth of John the Baptist, and he also announced the birth of Jesus to the Virgin Mary (Luke 1:11-17, 26-38).

Daniel 7:17-18

Four great beasts (7:17): Gabriel explained to Daniel, "These four great beasts are four kings who shall arise out of the earth." We have already noted the identity of the four kingdoms. The nation that was "like a lion and had eagles' wings" (verse 4) was Babylon. The nation "like a bear" (verse 5) was Medo-Persia. The nation "like a leopard" (verse 6) was Greece. The nation that was "terrifying and dreadful and exceedingly strong" (verse 7) was the Roman Empire. The "kings" of these kingdoms were, respectively, the four most notable leaders: Nebuchadnezzar, Cyrus, Alexander the Great, and the so-called "little horn" (the antichrist).

The saints of the Most High (7:18): Gabriel then revealed that "the saints of the Most High shall receive the kingdom and possess the kingdom forever, forever and ever." The word "saints" means "holy people." These people are not intrinsically holy, but rather are made holy as a result of trusting in Christ's work of salvation on the cross (compare Romans 1:7; 12:2; 1 Corinthians 14:33; 2 Corinthians 5:17; Hebrews 12:1; Revelation 5:8; 8:3; 14:12).

Christians debate over what group of people is meant by the term "saints." Some say it refers to all of God's people throughout all ages. Others say it refers specifically to the church. Still others say it refers to believing Jews. Because Daniel's book deals only with the Jews, and the church is not created until New Testament times (see Matthew 16:18), it seems likely that Daniel is indeed referring to Jews—more specifically, to the Jews who are redeemed in the end times.

Armageddon seems to be the historical context in which Israel is finally converted (Zechariah 12:2–13:1). In terms of chronology, Israel's restoration will include the confession of Israel's national sin (Leviticus 26:40-42; Jeremiah 3:11-18; Hosea 5:15), and then the remnant of the Jews will be saved, thereby fulfilling Paul's prophecy of Israel in Romans 11:25-27. In dire threat from the antichrist at Armageddon, Israel will plead for their newly found Messiah to return and deliver them (they will "mourn for him, as one mourns for an only child"—Zechariah 12:10; see also Isaiah 53:1-9; Matthew 23:37-39), at which point their deliverance will surely come (see Romans 10:13-14). Israel's leaders will finally realize the reason that the tribulation has fallen on them—perhaps due to the Holy Spirit's enlightenment of their understanding of Scripture, or the testimony of the 144,000 Jewish evangelists, or perhaps the testimony of the two (Jewish) prophetic witnesses. These redeemed Jews will enter into Christ's millennial kingdom, where the land promises of the Abrahamic covenant (Genesis 12:1-3; 15:18-21) and the throne promises of the Davidic covenant (2 Samuel 7:12-13) will finally be fulfilled.

Of course, the fact that the Jews will "possess the kingdom" doesn't rule out the church's role in the millennial kingdom. Christ will rule from the throne of David, and previously raptured believers will reign with Christ. Revelation 5:10 reveals that believers have been made "a kingdom and priests to our God, and they shall reign on the earth." Likewise, Revelation 20:6 affirms, "Blessed and holy is the one who shares in the first resurrection! Over such the second death has no power, but they will be priests of God and of Christ, and they will reign with him for a thousand years."

Daniel 7:19-22

The truth about the fourth beast (7:19): Daniel seemed to have understood what he needed to know about the first three kingdoms—Babylon,

Medo-Persia, and Greece. But he wanted to know more about the Roman Empire. He especially wanted to know more about "its teeth of iron and claws of bronze," and how it "devoured and broke in pieces and stamped what was left with its feet," and "the ten horns that were on its head," and "the other horn...that had eyes and a mouth that spoke great things" (Daniel 7:19-20). Gabriel would shortly tell Daniel all he needed to know about the Roman Empire (7:23-27).

Made war with the saints (7:21): At this juncture, Gabriel simply informed Daniel that the little horn "made war with the saints and prevailed over them." As noted previously, this little horn is none other than the antichrist, who will rise to power during the future seven-year tribulation period. He seems to emerge from insignificance to absolute control and dominance over a revived Roman Empire. As a ruler, he starts out small but eventually becomes the greatest of all (compare 2 Thessalonians 2:3-10; Revelation 13:1-10).

PARALLELS

Daniel 7:21—The antichrist will prevail over the saints.

Revelation 13:7—The antichrist will conquer the saints.

As in verse 18, the "saints" in verse 21 are apparently the nation of Israel. The antichrist will launch a great persecution against the Jewish people during the tribulation period (compare with Matthew 24:15-22; 2 Thessalonians 2:4). In the next lesson, we will see that Daniel 7:25 affirms that the antichrist "shall wear out the saints of the Most High...and they shall be given into his hand for a time, times, and half a time." "A time" is a year, "times" is two years, and "half a time" is half a year. This comes to three and a half years—the second half of the tribulation period (see also Matthew 24:16-31; Revelation 12:4-6).

Until the Ancient of Days came (7:22): The Ancient of Days is the indescribably glorious heavenly Father, who, through the Mediator Jesus Christ, overrules the agenda of the antichrist. At His second coming, Christ rescues the newly reborn Jewish remnant, and the antichrist is defeated and thrown into the lake of fire. The saved Jews then enter into Christ's millennial kingdom—the messianic kingdom promised in the Abrahamic and Davidic covenants (see Genesis 12:1-3; 15:18-21; 2 Samuel 7:12-13). God is a promise keeper, and the Jews will finally be in possession of all that God promised so long ago.

PARALLELS

Daniel 7:22—The saints will inherit God's kingdom.

Revelation 1:6—Believers enter God's kingdom.

MAJOR THEMES

1. *Human kingdoms versus God's kingdom.* Our passage describes four human kings and their kingdoms that will rise and fall. These kingdoms are Babylon, Medo-Persia, Greece, and a future revived Roman Empire that will rise under the leadership of the antichrist but then fall by God's judgment. In contrast to these temporal human kingdoms, God's kingdom is eternal. This is good news for God's saints. We are told, "The saints of the Most High shall receive the kingdom and possess the kingdom forever, forever and ever" (Daniel 7:18). The Most High's "kingdom shall be an everlasting kingdom, and all dominions shall serve and obey him" (verse 27).

2. *God is the Most High.* In our passage God is referred to as the Most High (Daniel 7:18, 22). The title is also used elsewhere in Scripture (Genesis 14:18; Numbers 24:16; Deuteronomy 32:8-9; Psalm 73:11; Isaiah 14:14). The term carries several nuances of meaning. Foundationally it indicates God's universal authority over all things. The confession of God as the Most High by a pagan, such as Nebuchadnezzar (Daniel 3:26), carries the idea that Yahweh is absolutely supreme over all other gods (Daniel 4:2, 17, 34). To a Jew, the title means that Yahweh is the only true God, and all other acclaimed gods are false gods (see Daniel 4:24-32; 5:18, 21; 7:18-27).

DIGGING DEEPER WITH CROSS-REFERENCES

The antichrist—Matthew 24:4-5; 2 Thessalonians 2:1-11; 1 John 2:18, 22; 4:3; 2 John 1:7-11; Revelation 13:1-10; 19:20

God's saints exalted in the book of Revelation (which parallels some of Daniel's prophecies)—Revelation 2:26; 3:9, 21; 4:4; 5:10; 11:12; 20:4

LIFE LESSONS

1. *Trusting God's control over the prophetic future.* One of the purposes of Bible prophecy is to bring comfort to God's people. The book of Revelation is a good example. The recipients of the book of Revelation were suffering persecution, and some of them were even being killed (Revelation 2:13). John therefore wrote this book to give his readers strong hope that would help them patiently endure amid relentless suffering (see Revelation 21–22). The same is true of the book of Daniel. The Jewish captivity in Babylon was not the end of the story. As we noted in the introduction, common themes in apocalyptic literature (such as Daniel) include the promise that our sovereign God will intervene and overcome all evil. God's people are therefore called to live righteously and to patiently endure their trials, knowing that restoration will soon come. Today, in the midst of a world that often seems out of control, we too can trust that God will intervene, overcome evil, and deliver us.

2. *Casualties of war.* In Daniel's dream about the future tribulation period, the antichrist "made war with the saints and prevailed over them" (Daniel 7:21). Many of these will be martyred for their faith (see Revelation 6:9-11). Scripture seems to teach that Christians will be raptured before the tribulation begins (1 Thessalonians 1:9-10; 5:9; Revelation 3:10) and therefore will escape encounters with the antichrist. But they may still encounter persecution, and some may even forfeit their lives (Galatians 3:4; 1 Thessalonians 3:4; 2 Timothy 3:12; Hebrews 10:32; 1 Peter 3:14; 4:12; 3 John 1:10). Even today, Christians in various parts of the world suffer martyrdom (compare Matthew 10:21, 39). Let us therefore never forget the words of Jesus: "Do not fear what you are about to suffer...Be faithful unto death, and I will give you the crown of life" (Revelation 2:10).

QUESTIONS FOR REFLECTION AND DISCUSSION

1. Do you think war is being made on the saints in our own day? How so?
2. Have you ever been persecuted for your faith in Christ? How did you handle it?
3. What does it mean to you personally that you will one day possess God's kingdom "forever, forever and ever" (Daniel 7:18)?

DAY 27

DANIEL'S VISION INTERPRETED, PART 2

DANIEL 7:23-28

SCRIPTURE READING AND INSIGHTS

Begin by reading Daniel 7:23-28 in your favorite Bible. As you read, ask God to help you understand His Word (Psalm 119:73).

Yesterday we began our study of the interpretation of Daniel's visions. Now let's further explore the interpretation of these visions. With your Bible still accessible, consider the following insights on the biblical text, verse by verse.

Daniel 7:23

Different from all the kingdoms (7:23): This last of the four kingdoms will be different in two key ways. First, it will be different in its leadership, for the leader will expressly be against (anti) Christ and will be energized by Satan (2 Thessalonians 2:9). Second, it will be different in its scope, not embracing a single geographical territory but rather engulfing the entire world.

Shall devour the whole earth (7:23): The antichrist, who will rule over this kingdom, will "devour the whole earth, and trample it down, and break it to pieces." The antichrist will be an unparalleled military ruler. Revelation 6:2 tells us that the antichrist will come out "conquering, and to conquer." People living during that time will say, "Who is like the beast, and who can fight against it?" (Revelation 13:4). His military exploits will not be regional, but global.

Daniel 7:24

The ten horns (7:24): Previously in the book I noted that because animals use horns as weapons, the horn is a symbol of power and might. As an extension of this symbol, horns in biblical times were sometimes used as emblems of dominion, representing kingdoms and kings. The ten horns of verse 24 indicate that the revived Roman Empire will be comprised of ten nations ruled by ten kings.

PARALLELS

Daniel 7:24—The ten horns represent ten kings ruling their kingdoms.

Revelation 12:3—The ten horns symbolize ten kingdoms.

Another shall arise after them (7:24): An eleventh horn—a little horn (the antichrist)—seems to emerge from insignificance to absolute control and dominance over this revived empire. As a ruler, he starts out small but becomes the greatest of all (see 2 Thessalonians 2:3-10; Revelation 13:1-10).

Shall put down three kings (7:24): The antichrist starts out in an insignificant way, but he nevertheless grows powerful enough to uproot (defeat) three of the existing horns (or rulers) who resist his rise to power. He eventually rises to total dominion over the entire revived Roman Empire.

Daniel 7:25

Shall speak words against the Most High (7:25): The antichrist will be an oratorical genius—a master of the spoken word. Verse 8 reveals that he will have "a mouth speaking great things" (see also verse 20). He has "a lion's mouth" (Revelation 13:2), which Bible interpreters believe means that his oratorical skills will be majestic and awe-inspiring.

Much that comes from the mouth of the antichrist will be blasphemous. As we have seen, the root meaning of the Greek and Hebrew words for blasphemy carries the idea of injuring the reputation of another. Biblically, the meaning can range from a lack of reverence for God to extreme contempt for

God or a sacred object (see Leviticus 24:16; Matthew 26:65; Mark 2:7). It can involve speaking evil against God (Psalm 74:18; Isaiah 52:5; Romans 2:24; Revelation 13:1, 6; 16:9, 11, 21). It can also involve showing contempt for the true God by making claims of divinity for oneself (see Mark 14:64; John 10:33).

The most heinous blasphemy found in the pages of Scripture relates to the antichrist. The apostle John tells us, "I saw a beast rising out of the sea, with ten horns and seven heads, with ten diadems on its horns and blasphemous names on its heads" (Revelation 13:1). The antichrist "was given a mouth uttering haughty and blasphemous words, and it was allowed to exercise authority for forty-two months. It opened its mouth to utter blasphemies against God, blaspheming his name and his dwelling, that is, those who dwell in heaven" (verses 5-6; see also 17:3). The antichrist's blasphemous words are in keeping with his blasphemous nature (see 2 Thessalonians 2:3-11).

Shall wear out the saints (7:25): The antichrist will persecute, oppress, and even kill the Jewish people. As one who is against (anti) Christ, he is certainly against the race that gave birth to the Christ.

PARALLELS

Daniel 7:25—The antichrist will wear out the saints.

Revelation 13:7—The antichrist will "make war on the saints and...conquer them."

Shall think to change the times and the law (7:25): The antichrist will set up laws in keeping with his own evil agenda instead of God's agenda.

Shall be given into his hand for a time, times, and half a time (7:25): A comparison with other prophetic verses indicates that this is the last three and a half years of the tribulation. We know, for example, that the antichrist's persecution of the saints begins at the midpoint of the tribulation (verse 21; Revelation 13:7-10). This persecution will continue for "a time, times, and half a time"—three and a half years—until the "time came when the saints possessed the kingdom"—that is, until Christ's millennial kingdom begins, following the second coming of Jesus Christ (see Zechariah 14:1-9; Revelation 19:11–20:6).

We should note that the last three and a half years of the tribulation period is called the *great* tribulation because it is especially intense. Some have claimed there is a contradiction between saying that the second half of the tribulation is three and a half years long and Jesus' end-times affirmation recorded in Matthew 24:21-22: "Then there will be great tribulation, such as has not been from the beginning of the world until now, no, and never will be. And *if those days had not been cut short*, no human being would be saved. But for the sake of the elect *those days will be cut short.*"

Was Jesus saying He would make the great tribulation shorter than three and a half years, or was He saying that He would shorten it to three and a half years?

To answer this question, we turn to the parallel verse in Mark 13:20: "And if the Lord had not cut short the days, no human being would be saved. But for the sake of the elect, whom he chose, he shortened the days." Greek scholars note that the two verbs in this verse—"cut short" and "shortened"—express action that was *taken by God in the past.* In this view, God in eternity past sovereignly decreed a limitation on the length of the great tribulation. In other words, God in the past already shortened the great tribulation. He did so in the sense that in the past He sovereignly decreed to cut it off at a specific time rather than let it continue indefinitely. In His omniscience, God knew that if the great tribulation were to continue indefinitely, all of humanity would perish. To prevent that from happening, God in eternity past sovereignly set a specific time for the great tribulation to end—that is, when it had run its course for three and a half years.

PARALLELS

Daniel 7:25-27—Christ will overthrow the antichrist's kingdom.

Revelation 17:14—"The Lamb will conquer them."

Daniel 7:26-28

The court shall sit in judgment (7:26): The one true God, the divine Judge, will judge the antichrist and take away his power. The antichrist will be utterly destroyed at Christ's second coming. As we read in 2 Thessalonians 2:8, "The lawless one will be revealed, whom the Lord Jesus will kill with the breath of his mouth and bring to nothing by the appearance of his coming." In Revelation 19:20 we read of the antichrist's end: "The beast was captured, and with it the false prophet who in its presence had done the signs by which he deceived those who had received the mark of the beast and those who worshiped its image. These two were thrown alive into the lake of fire that burns with sulfur."

PARALLELS

Daniel 7:26—The antichrist's "dominion shall be taken away."

Revelation 19:20—The antichrist will be captured and cast into the lake of fire.

The kingdom and the dominion (7:27): At the second coming of Jesus Christ, the armies gathered against God will be destroyed (Revelation 19:17, 21), the beast (antichrist) and the false prophet will be cast into the lake of fire (19:20), and Satan will be bound (20:1-3). Christ will then set up His millennial kingdom, and at long last, God's covenant promises to Israel will be fulfilled (Genesis 12:1-3; 15:18-21; 2 Samuel 7:12-13).

PARALLELS

Daniel 7:27—Christ's kingdom "shall be an everlasting kingdom."

Revelation 11:15—Christ will "reign forever and ever."

My thoughts greatly alarmed me (7:28): All of this was a phenomenal amount to take in. The prophecies of Israel in the tribulation period were particularly burdensome to Daniel.

MAJOR THEMES

1. *The earth.* Daniel 7:23 and the verses that follow speak of the earth as the arena of an end-times conflict between evil and good. In view of the sheer vastness of the stellar universe, it is truly amazing that God sovereignly chose our tiny planet as the center of divine activity. Relatively speaking, the earth is but an astronomical atom among the whirling constellations, only a tiny grain of sand among the ocean of stars and planets in the universe. To the naturalistic astronomer, the earth is but one of many planets in our small solar system, all of which are in orbit around the sun. But the earth is nevertheless the center of God's work of salvation in the universe. On this little planet, God made unconditional covenants, God's Son became incarnate, and God's Son died on the cross. To this earth God's Son will one day return. The centrality of the earth is also evident in the creation account, for God created the earth before He created the rest of the planets and stars.

2. *God the Judge.* Many verses in the Bible refer to God as the divine Judge. Psalm 50:6 affirms, "God himself is judge." In Genesis 18:25 Abraham asks, "Shall not the Judge of all the earth do what is just?" (This points to God as the perfectly fair Judge.) In Psalm 96:13 we are told, "He comes to judge the earth. He will judge the world in righteousness." Such verses indicate that God's judgment of the antichrist will be just (compare John 5:22; 2 Corinthians 5:10; 2 Timothy 4:1).

DIGGING DEEPER WITH CROSS-REFERENCES

Blasphemy against God—Exodus 20:7; Leviticus 19:12; 22:32; Deuteronomy 5:11; 2 Chronicles 32:17; Psalm 73:9; Matthew 12:31-32; 2 Thessalonians 2:4

God's universal kingship—Numbers 14:21; Psalms 47:7; 59:13; 65:5; 67:7;

68:31; 72:8, 11; 82:8; 102:22; 103:19; 108:9; Isaiah 54:5; Jeremiah 3:17; Micah 5:4; Zechariah 9:10; 14:9

LIFE LESSONS

1. *Patiently enduring persecution.* God calls His people to patiently endure in the midst of their trials and tribulations. The book of James emphasizes this: "Blessed is the man who remains steadfast under trial, for when he has stood the test he will receive the crown of life, which God has promised to those who love him" (James 1:12). We are urged, "Be patient, therefore, brothers, until the coming of the Lord...Be patient. Establish your hearts, for the coming of the Lord is at hand...The Judge is standing at the door" (James 5:7-9; see also 1 Peter 1:6-7).

2. *God's control of time.* Our passage makes reference to "a time, times, and half a time" (Daniel 7:25). Scripture says a lot about time. Regardless of what comes our way in life, our times are in God's hands (Psalm 31:15). Therefore we are to "trust in him at all times" (Psalm 62:8). We are urged to make "the most of every opportunity, because the days are evil" (Ephesians 5:16 NIV). We are to "walk in wisdom toward outsiders, making the best use of the time" (Colossians 4:5). And because God is in sovereign control of the universe, we must ever be mindful that our use of time tomorrow is subject to God's will (James 4:13-17). Our goal should be to constantly be about the business of doing what is right, day in and day out (Psalm 106:3).

QUESTIONS FOR REFLECTION AND DISCUSSION

1. Why might Daniel have kept the matter in his heart?

2. Have you ever thought about God's gift of time to each of us? Do you think you are a good steward of time?

3. What impacted you most about this lesson?

DAY 28

DANIEL HAS ANOTHER VISION

DANIEL 8:1-14

SCRIPTURE READING AND INSIGHTS

Begin by reading Daniel 8:1-14 in your favorite Bible. As you read, never forget that you can trust everything that is recorded in the Word of God (Matthew 5:18; John 10:35).

Yesterday we completed our study of the interpretation of Daniel's first vision in a dream. In today's lesson and the lesson that follows, we will investigate an entirely different vision that provides Daniel (and us) details on the rise of Antiochus Epiphanes, the cruel persecutor of the Jews and diabolical forerunner of the antichrist. With your Bible still accessible, consider the following insights on the biblical text, verse by verse.

Daniel 8:1-2

The third year of the reign of King Belshazzar (8:1): This would have been about 551 BC, some two years after the dream and visions in Daniel 7 but before Babylon's fall in 539 BC. At this time Daniel would have been close to 70 years old.

Daniel no doubt included this material here because these latter chapters in Daniel focus exclusively on Israel during the times of the Gentiles. Accordingly, the text changes from Aramaic back to Hebrew. Recall that the phrase "times of the Gentiles" refers to the extended time of Gentile domination over Jerusalem. This period began in 606 BC with the Babylonian captivity and will not end until the second coming of Jesus Christ.

I was in Susa the citadel (8:2): In the vision, Daniel saw himself in Susa, the chief city of the Medo-Persian Empire, some 250 miles east of Babylon. (See Major Themes.) The Ulai canal was apparently a man-made canal.

Daniel 8:3-4

A ram standing on the bank of the canal...two horns (8:3): As in previous visions in the book of Daniel, the animals in this vision represent world kingdoms. Daniel first saw a ram, which represented the Medo-Persian Empire. (This becomes clear in the next section of Daniel, which we will explore in the next lesson.) The two horns on the ram represent the Medes and the Persians respectively. One of the horns was longer than the other, even though it came up after the other horn. This larger horn represents Persia, which was originally the weaker of the two nations but eventually became dominant.

Charging westward and northward and southward (8:4): Daniel said, "No beast could stand before him, and there was no one who could rescue from his power. He did as he pleased and became great." This indicates that the Medo-Persian Empire dominated all the territory it moved against. No nation could withstand it. The empire became great, and its dominion was irresistible, regardless of which direction the empire expanded.

Daniel 8:5-7

A male goat came from the west...a conspicuous horn (8:5): This goat represents the Greek Empire, and the conspicuous horn represents Alexander the Great. Its movement across the earth without touching the ground represents Alexander's speedy conquest of Asia Minor, Syria, Egypt, and Mesopotamia in a mere three years (334–331 BC). History reveals that Alexander had an army of 35,000 soldiers.

Came to the ram (8:6): The goat, full of wrath, ran against the ram with two horns. This means that Alexander the Great's Greek army attacked the Medo-Persian Empire.

Struck the ram (8:7): The Medo-Persian Empire was powerless in the face of Alexander's massive onslaught. The ram's two horns—the Medes and the Persians—broke. Alexander "trampled" the Medes and the Persians. Previously no nation could withstand the Medo-Persian Empire. Now, even the Medo-Persian Empire could not withstand the Greek Empire.

Daniel 8:8-12

The goat became exceedingly great (8:8): The Greek Empire became exceedingly great and powerful as a result of the conquests of Alexander the Great.

Great horn was broken...four conspicuous horns (8:8): The Greek Empire was seemingly invincible. But then Alexander the Great died in 323 BC at the young age of 32 and at the height of his power, perhaps from malaria or typhoid fever. His empire was then divided among four of Alexander's prominent generals. These four generals are pictured as "four conspicuous horns." Cassander took over Macedonia and Greece. Lysimachus governed Thrace and Asia Minor. Seleucus ruled Syria and Babylon. Ptolemy reigned in Egypt.

A little horn (8:9): This little horn is not the little horn of Daniel 7:8. The context is entirely different. In Daniel 7, the little horn is the antichrist and emerges in a future revived Roman Empire. The little horn in Daniel 8:9 emerged out of Greece and refers to Antiochus Epiphanes. Our text tells us that Antiochus "grew exceedingly great toward the south, toward the east, and toward the glorious land." This means that he conquered territories to the south and the east, but also dominated the glorious land of Israel.

It grew great (8:10): Antiochus ruled the Seleucid Empire from 175 BC until his death in 164 BC. History reveals that Antiochus opposed the worship of Yahweh, defiled the Jewish temple by slaughtering a pig in the Most Holy Place, set up a graven image of himself, and treated the Jews cruelly.

Some of the host and some of the stars (8:10): Antiochus Epiphanes threw these to the ground and trampled on them. There is no small amount of controversy among Bible expositors as to what this terminology means. However, a consensus has emerged among many that the terms "host" and "stars" likely refer to the Jewish people, so this metaphorical language apparently describes Antiochus's relentless persecution of the Jewish people. Keep in mind that "stars" often refer to the Jewish people. For example, recall Joseph's dream: "Behold, I have dreamed another dream. Behold, the sun, the moon, and eleven stars were bowing down to me" (Genesis 37:9). In this dream, the sun (Joseph's father), the moon (Joseph's mother), and the 11 stars (Joseph's

11 brothers) would one day bow before him. These astronomical terms refer to the whole clan of Israel. Likewise, in Revelation 12:1 we encounter a metaphorical description of Israel as a woman with a "crown of twelve stars." The 12 stars represent the 12 tribes of Israel. We conclude, then, that Antiochus's trampling of the "host" and the "stars" refers to his trampling of the Jewish people. History reveals that Antiochus brutally persecuted the Jewish people from 170 to 164 BC.

As great as the Prince of the host (8:11): Our text tells us that Antiochus "became great, even as great as the Prince of the host." In other words, he set himself up as being great as the Most High God. This, of course, is not the first time in Daniel that a human leader imagined himself to be God. Recall how Nebuchadnezzar spoke of himself in divine terms (Daniel 2:1-7). Darius, too, was prayed to as a god for a time (6:6-9).

The regular burnt offering was taken away (8:11): Antiochus stopped the daily sacrifices in the Jewish temple, thereby halting Israel's religious practices, and also defiled the temple by slaughtering a pig in the Most Holy Place. He was apparently seeking to destroy the Jewish faith.

A host will be given over to it (8:12): This verse is difficult to interpret. The opening clause seems to indicate that Antiochus's activities against God and His people were divinely permitted by the Most High God—but only for a time (see verse 14). His rebellious stand against God and His people included prohibiting the daily sacrifices in the Jewish temple, apparently substituting some form of paganized worship, thus bringing great transgression against God.

It will throw truth to the ground (8:12): Antiochus trashed the Law of Moses, which was communicated to Moses by God. This act essentially amounted to trashing God. Speaking of Antiochus, 1 Maccabees 1:56-57 informs us, "The books of the law which they found they tore in pieces and burned with fire. Where the book of the covenant was found in the possession of anyone, or if anyone adhered to the law, the decree of the king condemned them to death."

It will act and prosper (8:12): Antiochus prospered in all his plans—but only for a time, according to the divine timetable (verse 14).

How long (8:13-14): One of God's angels—a "holy one"—announced that Antiochus's defiling of Israel and her temple would last only 2,300 evenings and mornings—from 171 BC to 165 BC. In 164 BC, the temple would be rededicated by Judas Maccabeus.

MAJOR THEMES

1. *Susa.* Susa was a strategic, diplomatic, and administrative city in the Medo-Persian Empire, about 250 miles east of Babylon (Nehemiah 1:1; Esther 2:8; 3:15). The city's name comes from the word *shushan* ("lily") and refers to the abundance of lilies in the area. Ancient Susa was located in modern Iran. It was a well-developed city with a fortress. In the vision, Daniel saw himself in this city even though he wasn't there physically (just as Ezekiel had a vision of Jerusalem's temple even though he wasn't there physically—Ezekiel 8–11). Susa is the site where the Code of Hammurabi, an ancient law code, was discovered.

2. *The heavenly host.* One might initially be inclined to interpret the host of heaven as the realm of angels, for elsewhere in Scripture the angels are called the heavenly host (2 Chronicles 18:18; Psalm 148:2; Luke 2:13). In the present context, however, the host of heaven refers to God's people, the Jews, who were being horribly persecuted by Antiochus (see Genesis 15:5; Daniel 12:3). The stars being thrown to the ground metaphorically represents the fall of God's people under persecution. This attack against God's people (the host of heaven) amounts to an attack against heaven itself.

DIGGING DEEPER WITH CROSS-REFERENCES

The wicked resist the truth—Isaiah 59:4; Jeremiah 9:5; 2 Thessalonians 2:10; 1 Timothy 6:5; 2 Timothy 3:8

Rebellion—Deuteronomy 9:24; Psalm 32:1-2; 1 Samuel 15:23; 2 Thessalonians 2:3

LIFE LESSONS

1. *Prolonged trials.* God's people sometimes go through sustained trials. This reality is especially reflected in the psalms: "My soul also is greatly troubled. But you, O Lord—how long?" (Psalm 6:3). "How long, O Lord? Will

you forget me forever? How long will you hide your face from me?" (13:1). "How long, O Lord, will you look on? Rescue me from their destruction, my precious life from the lions!" (35:17; see also 74:10; 79:5; 80:4; 89:46; 90:13; 94:3; 119:84). The solution is for believers to patiently endure in the midst of the trials regardless of how long they last, knowing that even in our suffering, God is working good in our lives. Meditate on Deuteronomy 8:2, 16; Psalms 66:10; 119:71; Isaiah 1:25; Ezekiel 14:11; John 15:2; 2 Corinthians 4:17; 12:7; Hebrews 12:5; 1 Peter 1:7.

2. *God's Word endures forever.* Daniel 8:12 tells us that one of Antiochus's transgressions was that truth was thrown to the ground, meaning that Antiochus destroyed some copies of Scripture—more specifically, scrolls of the Torah (see 1 Maccabees 1:56-57). (The Torah refers to the first five books of the Old Testament, all written by Moses.) Regardless of such acts, the Word of God cannot be destroyed. "The grass withers, the flower fades, but the word of our God will stand forever" (Isaiah 40:8). "The word of the Lord remains forever" (1 Peter 1:25). Jesus affirmed, "Heaven and earth will pass away, but my words will not pass away" (Matthew 24:35). Aren't you thankful that God's Word is always with us?

QUESTIONS FOR REFLECTION AND DISCUSSION

1. What might be the reason God gave people visions that featured animals?

2. In what way do people "throw truth to the ground" today (Daniel 8:12)?

3. Why is God's absolute truth so important?

DAY 29

DETAILS OF DANIEL'S VISION

DANIEL 8:15-27

SCRIPTURE READING AND INSIGHTS

Begin by reading Daniel 8:15-27 in your favorite Bible. As you read, notice how the Word of God is purifying your life (John 17:17-18).

Yesterday we considered some basic details of Daniel's vision relating to the rise of Antiochus Epiphanes. Today we will learn more about this disconcerting vision, which Daniel received during the third year of the reign of King Belshazzar. With your Bible still accessible, consider the following insights on the biblical text, verse by verse.

Daniel 8:15-16

I sought to understand it (8:15): In earlier years, Daniel had been the one to interpret the mysteries of God to others. He interpreted two dreams for Nebuchadnezzar (Daniel 2:31-45; 4:19-27) and the handwriting on the wall for Belshazzar (5:13-31). But Daniel needed help interpreting his own dreams and visions.

One having the appearance of a man (8:15): Gabriel appeared to Daniel in the form of a man. This reminds us of Hebrews 13:2: "Do not neglect to show hospitality to strangers, for thereby some have entertained angels unawares." Angels can appear so realistically as human beings that they may be taken for human beings.

Gabriel (8:16): The angel Gabriel helped Daniel understand the vision. Gabriel is portrayed in Scripture as one who brings revelation to the people of God regarding God's purpose and program (Daniel 9:21; Luke 1:11-19, 26-38).

PARALLELS

Daniel 8:16—Daniel heard a voice speaking to him.

Revelation 1:12—John heard a voice speaking to him.

Daniel 8:17-19

The vision is for the time of the end (8:17): "The time of the end" cannot refer only to the last days, when the antichrist emerges during the tribulation period. The vision also relates more immediately to Antiochus Epiphanes. This has led many Bible expositors to conclude that "the time of the end" has both a near and a far fulfillment—near as it pertains to Antiochus Epiphanes, but far as it pertains to the antichrist and the last days.

PARALLELS

Daniel 8:17—Daniel's vision was "for the time of the end."

Revelation 1:10, 19—John, "in the Spirit on the Lord's day," was told: "Write therefore the things that you have seen, those that are and those that are to take place after this."

I fell into a deep sleep (8:18): Daniel became weak in the presence of Gabriel—a common occurrence during heavenly visitations. (See Major Themes.)

He touched me (8:18): When Daniel became weak in Gabriel's presence, Gabriel touched him and made him stand up. One of the ministries of angels is to strengthen humans when there is a need. Psalm 91:11-12 promises that God's angels "will bear you up." Jesus experienced this in the Garden of Gethsemane, when He struggled under the tremendous weight of what was ahead of Him at the cross. After He prayed to the Father, an angel appeared from heaven and strengthened Him (Luke 22:43).

The appointed time of the end (8:19): God's plan for the ages unfolds according to a divine timetable (see, for example, Psalm 31:15; Ecclesiastes 3:1; John 7:6; Galatians 4:4).

Daniel 8:20-22

The ram...with the two horns (8:20): This is the Medo-Persian Empire. Recall from the previous lesson that one of the horns was longer than the other even though it came up after the other horn. This larger horn represents Persia, originally the weaker of the two nations but eventually the more dominant (see verse 3). Note that this is the same empire represented by the bear raised up on one side (7:5).

The goat (8:21): The goat represents Greece. (See notes on Daniel 8:5-7.)

The great horn (8:21): The large horn on the goat is the first king of Greece—Alexander the Great, who rapidly conquered the Medo-Persians and many others.

The horn that was broken, in place of which four others arose (8:22): Following Alexander's death, the Greek Empire was divided among four of Alexander's prominent generals. After some 22 years of fighting, Cassander ruled in Macedonia and Greece, Lysimachus reigned in Thrace and Asia Minor, Seleucus governed Syria and Babylon, and Ptolemy took over Egypt.

Daniel 8:23-25

A king of bold face (8:23): A bold and fierce Antiochus took the throne through deceit and guile. Note that some Bible expositors believe Antiochus was a *type* of the coming antichrist. A type is an Old Testament institution, event, person, object, or ceremony that has reality and purpose in biblical history but also by divine design foreshadows something yet to be revealed. Antiochus set himself up as God and defiled the Jewish temple, and the antichrist will do the same in the future tribulation period (see 2 Thessalonians 2:4). Antiochus was a fierce persecutor of the Jews, just as the antichrist will be.

His power shall be great (8:24): Antiochus's power was manifest in his conquests and subjugation of others.

But not by his own power (8:24): This comes through loud and clear in our passage: God is sovereign over and controls the nations of the world and their leaders. Psalm 113:4 tells us, "The Lord is high above all nations." "Kingship belongs to the Lord, and he rules over the nations" (Psalm 22:28). In Job 12:23 we read, "He makes nations great, and he destroys them; he enlarges nations, and leads them away." Jehoshaphat affirmed to God, "In your hand are power and might, so that none is able to withstand you" (2 Chronicles 20:6; see also Jeremiah 27:5-6). God, for His own sovereign purposes, allowed Antiochus to rise to power. God would also bring him down.

PARALLELS

Daniel 8:24—The antichrist's "power shall be great," bringing "fearful destruction."

Revelation 17:13, 17—The antichrist is given "power and authority," which he destructively abuses.

He shall cause fearful destruction (8:24): Antiochus intended to destroy not only the Jewish religion but also the Jews themselves.

He shall make deceit prosper (8:25): Antiochus was deceitful, cunning, full of guile, treacherous, and unscrupulous.

He shall destroy many (8:25): Many of those destroyed were Jewish people. In this way, Antiochus foreshadows the future antichrist.

He shall even rise up against the Prince of princes (8:25): As a pagan king who claimed divinity, Antiochus raised himself up against Israel's king, the Most High God, the Ruler of heaven and earth.

He shall be broken—but by no human hand (8:25): Just as Antiochus came into power according to God's divine providence, so he would be destroyed by God's hand. God is sovereign over the day a person dies. Job said to God, "[Man's] days are determined, and the number of his months is with you, and you have appointed his limits that he cannot pass" (Job 14:5; see also Psalm 139:16; Acts 17:26). Scripture also reveals that God sometimes inflicts premature death as a judgment (see Acts 5:1-10; 12:23; 1 Corinthians 11:30; 1 John 5:16).

Daniel 8:26-27

The evenings and the mornings (8:26): Antiochus would defile Israel and her temple for 2,300 evenings and mornings—from 171 to 165 BC. In 164 BC, the temple would be rededicated by Judas Maccabeus.

Seal up the vision (8:26): Why did God tell Daniel, "Seal up the vision, for it refers to many days from now"? Some interpret this as meaning that Daniel shouldn't share the vision during Belshazzar's reign because some people might accuse Daniel of treason or insurrection. Others believe it means to "put away for safekeeping" (for future generations). Others say it means, "Keep the vision confidential for now because it pertains to the distant future and has little relevance for the present moment." Still others say the word simply means, "Conclude the vision."

I, Daniel, was overcome (8:27): Daniel said, "I was appalled by the vision and did not understand it." Daniel was sickened because he loved his fellow Jews, and he was saddened to become aware of the future that awaited them.

MAJOR THEMES

1. *Fainting with fear during heavenly encounters.* When Gabriel came near to Daniel, Daniel said, "I was frightened and fell on my face...I fell into a deep sleep with my face to the ground" (Daniel 8:17-18). We often witness men of God becoming weak-kneed and falling down in the presence of heavenly beings. It happened to Abram (Genesis 17:3), to Moses and Aaron (Numbers 16:22), to Ezekiel (Ezekiel 1:28), to John (Revelation 1:17), and to the apostle Paul (Acts 9:4).

2. *The prosperity of the wicked.* Scripture reveals that the evil Antiochus will seem to prosper for a time. This brings to mind the words of the psalmist: "I saw the prosperity of the wicked...They are not in trouble as others are; they are not stricken like the rest of mankind. Therefore pride is their necklace...They set their mouths against the heavens" (Psalm 73:3-9). If this were the end of the story, then all would be vanity. But the truth is, the wicked fall hard in the end. The psalmist affirmed to God, "You make them fall to ruin. How they are destroyed in a moment, swept away utterly by terrors" (verses 18-19). Antiochus may have prospered for a time, but he fell hard and permanently.

DIGGING DEEPER WITH CROSS-REFERENCES

The time of the end—1 Timothy 4:1; 2 Timothy 3:1–4:5; James 5:3; 2 Peter 3:3; Jude 18

Self-exaltation—Proverbs 3:34; 8:13; 16:5, 18-19; 18:12; 21:4; Isaiah 13:11; Ezekiel 28:2; Daniel 4:37; Matthew 23:12; Luke 18:11; 20:46; Romans 12:16; Philippians 2:3; 2 Timothy 3:2; James 4:6; 1 Peter 5:5

The persecution of the saints—Proverbs 29:27; Matthew 5:10, 44; 10:21; Luke 6:22-23; Acts 8:1-4; 11:19; 2 Corinthians 6:5; 11:23; 1 Thessalonians 2:14-15; 2 Timothy 1:12; 2:9; 3:12; 1 Peter 3:17; 1 John 3:13; Revelation 2:10

LIFE LESSONS

1. *The full measure of sin.* Daniel 8:23 refers to transgressors who "have reached their limit." This reminds us of the scriptural teaching that once the fullness of sin has come about in a person or a nation, God takes action. In Genesis 15:16, God explained why He did not judge the Amorites immediately: "The iniquity of the Amorites is not yet complete." First Peter 3:20 reveals that before the worldwide flood, the wicked "did not obey, when God's patience waited in the days of Noah." God's patience lasted only so long, and then He acted. In Revelation 2:21 we read Christ's assessment of Jezebel: "I gave her time to repent, but she refuses to repent of her sexual immorality." As Christians, we all ought to repent and confess sin as soon as we become aware of it in our lives (Psalm 32:1-5; 1 John 1:9).

2. *God's purpose for futuristic prophecy.* Out of the 23,210 verses in the Old Testament, 6,641 (28.5 percent) are prophetic. The New Testament contains 7,914 verses, and 1,711 (21.5 percent) are prophetic. Merging the Old and New Testaments together, 8,352 of the Bible's 31,124 verses are prophetic. That comes to 27 percent of the Bible—more than one-fourth—being prophecy. God did not give us all this prophecy so we'd have mere head knowledge of what the future holds. Rather, there are underlying themes in prophecy that are life-changing. For example, prophecy demonstrates that God is sovereign over human history. It assures us that God will triumph over evil. Prophecy causes us to yearn for the soon coming of Jesus Christ. It gives us a powerful hope for reuniting with our Christian loved ones in heaven. It gives us an exalted view of Jesus Christ. Prophecy gives us a strong sense of the trustworthiness of the Bible.

QUESTIONS FOR REFLECTION AND DISCUSSION

1. What do you learn about God's awesome sovereignty from our passage?
2. What have you learned about God's patience toward human sin in this lesson?
3. Can you relate to how Daniel reacted to the vision?

DAY 30

DANIEL PRAYS FOR HIS PEOPLE, PART 1

DANIEL 9:1-7

SCRIPTURE READING AND INSIGHTS

Begin by reading Daniel 9:1-7 in your favorite Bible. As you read, remember that God's Word is the true source of hope (Psalm 119:81).

Yesterday we concluded our study of Daniel's second vision, which indicated hard times were ahead for the Jewish people. In today's reading, Daniel prays for his people. With your Bible still accessible, consider the following insights on the biblical text, verse by verse.

Daniel 9:1-2

In the first year of Darius the son of Ahasuerus (9:1): This was the first year of the reign of Darius the Mede, which would have been about 538 BC. This was about 67 years after Daniel had been taken captive in Babylon along with his three Hebrew friends. Daniel would have been more than 80 years old at this time.

I, Daniel, perceived in the books (9:2): Daniel is referring specifically to the book of Jeremiah, completed about a generation prior to the events described in Daniel 9. The prophet Daniel recognized from Jeremiah 25:11-13 and 29:10 that Jerusalem's desolation was to last only 70 years. The first wave of Jews was taken captive in 605 BC, and it was now 538 BC, so the 70-year period was almost over. The Jews in Babylon would soon be free.

We can make an interesting observation here. The book of Jeremiah had not been written for very long, but Daniel already considered it to be Scripture. This goes against the modern liberal allegation that the books of Scripture were not determined until much later by various councils.

Daniel 9:3

Prayer and pleas (9:3): Because his people were about to be released from captivity, Daniel sought the Lord "by prayer and pleas for mercy." After all, Daniel wanted his people not only to be released from bondage to Babylon but also to be fully restored to God. He wanted his people to make a fresh start with God, which would necessarily include repentance of sin. No doubt recalling the Law of Moses, Daniel knew that obedience to God brings blessing from God, whereas disobedience to God brings discipline from God (compare with Deuteronomy 28:48-57, 64-68). Daniel desired to see an end to the present discipline from God.

Daniel's prayer was accompanied by fasting, sackcloth, and ashes—Hebrew means of expressing grief and contrition for the sins of his people (see Genesis 37:34; Nehemiah 9:1-2; Job 2:12-13). We will see that throughout the prayer, Daniel did not separate himself from his people, but rather included himself in the prayer of confession.

Daniel 9:4-5

Made confession (9:4): The first step in restoration to God is the confession of sin. Though the Jews had rebelled against God and had consequently landed themselves in captivity as a divine discipline, God has a long track record of showing mercy to those who confess their sins. Proverbs 28:13 tells us, "Whoever conceals his transgressions will not prosper, but he who confesses and forsakes them will obtain mercy." Deuteronomy 4:31 reminds us, "The LORD your God is a merciful God." As we discover in Lamentations 3:22-23, "The steadfast love of the LORD never ceases; his mercies never come to an end; they are new every morning." Following a great sin, David prayed, "Have mercy on me, O God, according to your steadfast love; according to your abundant mercy blot out my transgressions" (Psalm 51:1).

O Lord, the great and awesome God (9:4): God had repeatedly demonstrated just how awesome He was among the Jews in captivity. Highlights included God's rescue of the three Hebrew youths from the fiery furnace (Daniel 3:23-26) and His rescue of Daniel in the lions' den (6:16-28).

God, who keeps covenant and steadfast love (9:4): The Old Testament consistently emphasizes that God, in His faithful covenant love, will ultimately restore and bless His wayward people. He will eventually turn away His anger and shower love upon them. His people had been unfaithful, but God Himself is always faithful.

Those who love him and keep his commandments (9:4): Notice the strong connection between love for God and obedience to Him. In Exodus 20:5-6 God said, "I the Lord your God am a jealous God...showing steadfast love to thousands of those who love me and keep my commandments." In Deuteronomy 7:9 God affirmed, "Know therefore that the Lord your God is God, the faithful God who keeps covenant and steadfast love with those who love him and keep his commandments, to a thousand generations." He also affirmed to His people, "Because you listen to these rules and keep and do them, the Lord your God will keep with you the covenant and the steadfast love that he swore to your fathers" (Deuteronomy 7:12). Nehemiah referred to God as "the great and awesome God who keeps covenant and steadfast love with those who love him and keep his commandments" (Nehemiah 1:5). (See Life Lessons.)

PARALLELS

Daniel 9:4—Those who love God keep His commandments.

Revelation 2:4-5—Those who love God will show it by their works.

We have sinned (9:5): Notice two things here. First, as noted previously, Daniel included himself in the confession of sin even though his personal behavior had been praiseworthy. Daniel was identifying with his people in order to more effectively intercede on their behalf before God. Second, notice the comprehensive description of the Jews' wrongdoing: "We have sinned and done wrong and acted wickedly and rebelled, turning aside from your commandments and rules."

The word "sin" carries the idea of "missing the mark." The target was God's Law contained in God's Word, but the Jews had consistently missed the mark by a wide margin. The phrase "done wrong" carries the idea of committing a bent or twisted act. Instead of walking the straight and narrow path, they had deviated from God's requirements. The phrase "turning aside from your commandments and rules" carries the idea of scorning God's commandments and rules. In short, the Jewish people had woefully rebelled against God (compare Psalm 106:6; Isaiah 53:6).

Daniel 9:6

We have not listened (9:6): Daniel conceded that his people had not listened to the prophets, who were God's servants. We are reminded of Jeremiah 7:25-26, where God lamented, "From the day that your fathers came out of the land of Egypt to this day, I have persistently sent all my servants the prophets to them, day after day. Yet they did not listen to me or incline their ear, but stiffened their neck." God's lament is also recorded for us in Psalm 81:13: "Oh, that my people would listen to me, that Israel would walk in my ways."

The word "prophet"—from the Hebrew word *nabi*—refers to a spokesman for God who either declares God's message regarding a contemporary situation to humankind, or foretells God's actions based on divine revelation. The predictive role is often stressed, but the Bible equally emphasizes the teaching function. Both aspects require communication from God to the prophet (see 2 Samuel 7:27; Jeremiah 23:18). In the present context, God's prophets call Israel to repentance as well as prophesy about her future.

Daniel 9:7

To you, O Lord, belongs righteousness (9:7): Righteousness is among the most important attributes of God. The Scriptures portray God as singularly righteous, with no hint of unrighteousness. We read, "Righteous are you, O LORD" (Jeremiah 12:1). "The LORD is righteous; he loves righteous deeds" (Psalm 11:7). "He loves righteousness and justice" (Psalm 33:5). "Righteousness and justice are the foundation of your throne" (Psalm 89:14). Daniel acknowledged to God that He had been perfectly righteous and just in disciplining the Jews, for the Jews had been utterly rebellious against God. Daniel knew that his people got just what they deserved.

But to us open shame (9:7): This carries the idea of public shame of face—that is, one is so shamed by something that one has a look of embarrassment and humiliation on one's face, a shame that others witness firsthand. We might translate it "public shame." The New Living Translation puts it nicely: "Our faces are covered with shame."

The lands to which you have driven them (9:7): The Lord had earlier warned His people that if they turned from His law and rebelled against Him, "The Lord will bring you and your king whom you set over you to a nation that neither you nor your fathers have known...You shall father sons and daughters, but they shall not be yours, for they shall go into captivity...because you did not obey the voice of the Lord your God, to keep his commandments and his statutes that he commanded you" (Deuteronomy 28:36-45; see also verses 49-68). God had given them plenty of time to repent, but they remained hard-hearted against Him.

Treachery (9:7): This word carries the idea of disloyalty. God had previously called His people to be loyal to His covenant. Instead, they were disloyal and therefore treacherous.

MAJOR THEMES

1. *Expressions of mourning.* Daniel's "sackcloth and ashes" were expressions of intense mourning (Daniel 9:3). Mourners often wore sackcloth and put ashes on their heads (see Genesis 37:34; Nehemiah 9:1; Esther 4:1, 3; Isaiah 58:5; Jeremiah 49:3; Ezekiel 7:18; Joel 1:8; Matthew 11:21). Daniel's mourning was rooted in the sins of his people. He knew these sins had brought judgment from God.

2. *God is a promise keeper.* This is a thread that runs through this passage and, in fact, all of Scripture. Numbers 23:19 asserts, "God is not a man, that he should lie, or a son of man, that he should change his mind. Has he said, and will he not do it? Or has he spoken, and will he not fulfill it?"

Prior to his death, an aged Joshua declared, "Now I am about to go the way of all the earth, and you know in your hearts and souls, all of you, that not one word has failed of all the good things that the Lord your God promised concerning you. All have come to pass for you; not one of them has failed" (Joshua 23:14). Solomon later proclaimed, "Blessed be the Lord who has given rest to his people Israel, according to all that he promised. Not one word has failed of all his good promise, which he spoke by Moses his servant" (1 Kings 8:56; see Joshua 21:45).

DIGGING DEEPER WITH CROSS-REFERENCES

The importance of searching God's Word—Deuteronomy 17:19; Isaiah 34:16; Matthew 19:4; 22:31; Luke 10:26; John 5:39; Acts 8:28; 17:11; Romans 15:4; 1 Timothy 4:13; Revelation 22:19

The shame of sin—Genesis 3:7, 10; Ezra 9:6; Job 8:22; Psalm 44:15; Proverbs 13:18; Jeremiah 3:25; Ezekiel 7:18; Luke 15:19

Confession of sin—Psalms 32:3, 5; 38:18; 51:4; Proverbs 28:13; 1 John 1:9

LIFE LESSONS

1. *Prayer and fasting.* Previously in the book I noted that the word "fast" is rooted in a Hebrew word that means "cover the mouth," thus indicating abstinence from food and/or drink. During fasts, people were to humble their souls before God while abstaining from food. Fasting goes hand in hand with fervent prayer. This was the case with Daniel (Daniel 9:3). He so wanted to intercede on his people's behalf that he denied himself food. You and I, too, can engage in prayer and fasting on occasion, especially when facing a major crisis (see Exodus 34:28; 1 Samuel 7:6; 2 Samuel 3:35; Matthew 4:2; 6:16).

2. *Love and obedience.* Daniel refers to those "who love him and keep his commandments" (Daniel 9:4). Scripture often draws a connection between love for God and obedience to Him. In the New Testament, Jesus informed His followers, "If you love me, you will keep my commandments... Whoever has my commandments and keeps them, he it is who loves me" (John

14:15, 21). Closely related to this, 1 John 2:3 tells us, "By this we know that we have come to know him, if we keep his commandments" (compare with John 15:10).

QUESTIONS FOR REFLECTION AND DISCUSSION

1. Do you make a habit of expressing your love to God by obeying Him?
2. Have you ever fasted during a crisis? If so, did you find it fruitful?
3. Did today's lesson motivate you to deal with any sin that may yet linger in your life?

DAY 31

DANIEL PRAYS FOR HIS PEOPLE, PART 2

DANIEL 9:8-19

SCRIPTURE READING AND INSIGHTS

Begin by reading Daniel 9:8-19 in your favorite Bible. As you read, remember that great spiritual wisdom comes from studying God's Word (Psalm 119:98-104).

In yesterday's reading, we were introduced to Daniel's prayer for his people. In today's lesson, we continue our study of Daniel's prayer. With your Bible still accessible, consider the following insights on the biblical text, verse by verse.

Daniel 9:8

Open shame (9:8): When something is repeated in consecutive verses in the Bible, the author is strongly emphasizing a point. Recall that in the previous verse, Daniel said to God, "To you, O Lord, belongs righteousness, but to us open shame." He repeats himself in verse 8: "To us, O Lord, belongs open shame." The repetition indicates that Daniel was lamenting and grieving over the dire state of his people.

To our kings, to our princes, and to our fathers (9:8): No one is exempt from condemnation. Guilt for sin ranges from the top leadership down to the common person. All are liable before God. There is none righteous. (See Major Themes.)

Daniel 9:9-10

Mercy and forgiveness (9:9): When used of God, the term "mercy" indicates God's compassion and kindness. This includes the withholding of deserved punishment. Daniel knew his people were guilty of gross sin, so he appealed to God to withhold the judgment they deserved. He appealed to God's mercy.

Mercy is closely connected to forgiveness. Again, Daniel knew his people were guilty. This is why they were subjected to captivity in Babylon. Now that the captivity was coming to an end, Daniel appealed to God to forgive the Jews. Daniel desired for his people to begin anew with a clean slate from God.

Have not obeyed the voice of the LORD (9:10): How were God's voice and His laws communicated? Through God's prophets, who were His mouthpieces in Old Testament times. But the Jews predominantly ignored the warnings of the prophets.

> The LORD warned Israel and Judah by every prophet and every seer, saying, "Turn from your evil ways and keep my commandments and my statutes, in accordance with all the Law that I commanded your fathers, and that I sent to you by my servants the prophets." But they would not listen, but were stubborn, as their fathers had been, who did not believe in the LORD their God. They despised his statutes and his covenant that he made with their fathers and the warnings that he gave them (2 Kings 17:13-15).

Daniel 9:11-15

All Israel has transgressed (9:11): When Daniel said, "All Israel has transgressed your law and turned aside," we are reminded of what Daniel said just previously: "To us, O LORD, belongs open shame, to our kings, to our princes, and to our fathers" (verse 8). All Israel—from the top of the social ladder to the bottom—had sinned against God.

The curse and oath (9:11): As a result of their unrepentant sin, the Jews suffered the "curse and oath that are written in the Law of Moses" (see Leviticus 26:21-42; Deuteronomy 28:15-68). The Jews had the choice of obedience or disobedience. Their continued disobedience caused them to suffer the curse. Had they rendered obedience to God, they would have experienced great blessings (see Leviticus 26:3-13; Deuteronomy 28:1-14). This illustrates the age-old maxim that choices have consequences—sometimes severe consequences.

We should note that God offered grace even in the midst of His chastisement of the Jews. If His people would only repent, He would bring upon them renewed blessing (Leviticus 26:40-42).

We should also be mindful that the purpose of God's chastising of His people was never to get even. Rather, it was to cause His people to repent and turn back to Him. God's chastisement is like a divine form of parental discipline.

He has confirmed his words (9:12): God had promised His people that if they sinned against Him and refused to repent, they would experience captivity at the hands of foreign nations as well as other manifestations of the curse (Leviticus 26:21-39; Deuteronomy 28:15-68). God "confirmed his words" by sending His people into captivity in Babylon.

A great calamity (9:12): Daniel lamented, "Under the whole heaven there has not been done anything like what has been done against Jerusalem." God's disciplinary act of using the Babylonians as His whipping rod against Israel during the captivity was unique in all of history. God dealt with the Jews as no other people had ever been dealt with.

As it is written in the Law of Moses (9:13): The main point here is that Israel had been warned. God, through the Law of Moses, had instructed His people about the connection between behavior and consequences: Obey God and be blessed, or disobey God and be cursed. Despite God's clear instructions and warnings, the Jews chose not to remain faithful to God and fell into gross sin.

Yet we have not entreated the favor of the Lord our God (9:13): To add insult to injury—that is, to add to their earlier sins—Israel had now failed to turn to God in prayer. Despite God's chastising judgment, there had been no repentance, no revival, and no restoration to God. The people simply persisted in their evil ways. Daniel recognized that because the people had spurned the mercy of God, God had no other recourse but to bring discipline upon Israel. This is why, in the verses that follow, Daniel pled for mercy and forgiveness for his people.

The Lord has kept ready the calamity (9:14): God's disciplinary hand has always been at the ready to deal with His rebellious child, Israel.

The Lord our God is righteous (9:14): Daniel repeated the contrast between

God's righteousness and Israel's disobedience. God dealt with Israel with justice. There had been no unfair treatment.

PARALLELS

Daniel 9:14—"The Lord our God is righteous."

Revelation 19:2—God's "judgments are true and just."

Who brought your people out of the land of Egypt (9:15): Recall from verses 4-5 that Daniel had spoken of "the great and awesome God" and then acknowledged the great sin of His people Israel. Daniel now essentially repeats all this, affirming that God delivered His people from Egyptian bondage with a mighty hand and admitting, "We have sinned, we have done wickedly." God is great, but we have sinned! The idea is this: "God, you have honored Yourself by delivering us from Egypt, but now we have dishonored You by our sin."

Daniel 9:16-19

Let your anger and your wrath turn away (9:16): Daniel appealed to God's faithful mercies to turn away from His displeasure with Israel because of her sins. After all, the neighboring nations were mocking and laughing at Israel's suffering under her load of guilt. These nations were also apparently mocking Israel's God, claiming He was impotent, utterly unable to deliver the Jews from Babylonian bondage. Daniel appealed to God to forgive Israel and to vindicate Himself in the eyes of neighboring nations.

Listen to the prayer of your servant (9:17): There is a strong sense of urgency in Daniel's prayer here and in the following verses. "Incline your ear and hear" (verse 18). "O Lord, hear; O Lord, forgive. O Lord, pay attention and act" (verse 19). Don't miss the passion in Daniel's voice. He is crying out to the Lord on behalf of his people.

For your own sake, O Lord (9:17): This carries the idea, "Renew Your honor in the eyes of neighboring pagan nations, who think of You as weak and unable to help us."

Open your eyes and see (9:18): In other words, "Open Your eyes with a view to moving Your mighty hand on our behalf."

Your great mercy (9:18): Daniel's appeal is not based on Israel being deserving of God's response. Rather, it's based entirely on God's mercy and compassion (compare Exodus 34:6; Jonah 4:1-3; Micah 6:8).

Pay attention and act. Delay not (9:19): By God's providence, it was not long after this that King Cyrus issued a decree allowing the Jewish people to return to Judea (see Ezra 1:1-4). A new temple was built, completed by 515 BC. God answered Daniel's prayer on behalf of his people.

MAJOR THEMES

1. *Universal sin.* In Daniel's confession, he says to God, "All Israel has transgressed your law and turned aside" (Daniel 9:11). Scripture consistently teaches the universality of sin. "All we like sheep have gone astray; we have turned—every one—to his own way" (Isaiah 53:6). "Surely there is not a righteous man on earth who does good and never sins" (Ecclesiastes 7:20). "If we say we have no sin, we deceive ourselves, and the truth is not in us" (1 John 1:8). This obviously includes you and me.

2. *Just retribution.* In the context of God punishing Israel for her sins, Daniel affirmed, "The Lord our God is righteous in all the works that he has done, and we have not obeyed his voice" (Daniel 9:14). God brought just retribution on the sinful Jewish people. God's just retribution is a common theme in Scripture. In Isaiah 42:24 we read, "Who gave up Jacob to the looter, and Israel to the plunderers? Was it not the LORD, against whom we have sinned, in whose ways they would not walk, and whose law they would not obey?" God had promised, "Thus says the Lord GOD: I will deal with you as you have done" (Ezekiel 16:59). God also says, "I the LORD search the heart and test the mind, to give every man according to his ways, according to the fruit of his deeds" (Jeremiah 17:10).

DIGGING DEEPER WITH CROSS-REFERENCES

Impenitence—1 Samuel 15:23; Psalms 52:7; 78:8; 81:11-12; 95:8; 106:25;

Proverbs 1:24; Isaiah 48:4, 8; Jeremiah 5:21; 7:13; 16:12; 44:10; Hosea 4:17; Acts 7:51; Hebrews 3:8

God's delays according to the psalms—Psalms 6:3; 13:1; 40:17; 69:3; 70:5; 119:82

LIFE LESSONS

1. *God's forgiveness.* A popular Old Testament passage on the forgiveness of sins is Psalm 103:11-12: "For as high as the heavens are above the earth, so great is his steadfast love toward those who fear him; as far as the east is from the west, so far does he remove our transgressions from us." There is a definite point that is north and another that is south—the North and South Poles. But there are no such points for east and west. Regardless of how far one goes to the east, one will never arrive where east begins because by definition east is the opposite of west. The two never meet. They will never meet and never could meet because they are defined as opposites. To remove sins "as far as the east is from the west" is by definition to put them where no one can ever find them. This is the kind of forgiveness that Daniel sought for his people Israel.

2. *Urgency in prayer.* Notice the sense of urgency in Daniel's prayer. "Now therefore, O our God, listen to the prayer of your servant and to his pleas...incline your ear and hear...pay attention and act. Delay not" (verses 17-19). This brings to mind James 5:16: "The urgent request of a righteous person is very powerful in its effect" (HCSB). The word "urgent" in this verse carries the idea of "earnest" or "heartfelt." You and I, too, ought always to offer up earnest and heartfelt prayers to God.

QUESTIONS FOR REFLECTION AND DISCUSSION

1. What did you learn about prayer that most impacted you from today's lesson?

2. Does God's just retribution scare you or comfort you?

3. Do you intellectually agree that God has forgiven you? Do you *feel* forgiven? What did you learn from Psalm 103:11-12 that could help you connect your understanding and your emotions?

DAY 32

DANIEL PROPHESIES ABOUT THE 70 WEEKS

DANIEL 9:20-27

SCRIPTURE READING AND INSIGHTS

Begin by reading Daniel 9:20-27 in your favorite Bible. As you read, remember that reading Scripture can strengthen your faith in God (Romans 10:17).

In the previous lesson, we finished our study of Daniel's intercessory prayer for his people. In today's lesson, we zero in on Daniel's prophecy of the 70 weeks. With your Bible still accessible, consider the following insights on the biblical text, verse by verse.

Daniel 9:20-21

While I was speaking and praying...the man Gabriel...came to me in swift flight (9:20-21): The amazing thing about this text is how quickly Daniel's prayer was answered. Daniel was still praying—confessing Israel's sins and petitioning God for the restoration of his people—when the angel Gabriel suddenly appeared. Of course, Daniel had just requested God, "Delay not" (verse 19). And now Gabriel arrives "in swift flight."

We are reminded of what God said in Isaiah 65:24: "Before they call I will answer; while they are yet speaking I will hear." God likewise affirmed in Isaiah 58:9, "Then you shall call, and the Lord will answer; you shall cry, and he will say, 'Here I am.'"

Notice that the angel Gabriel is called a man in this text because he took on the appearance of a man (compare Daniel 8:16; Hebrews 13:2).

The holy hill of my God (9:20): This refers to Jerusalem. Recall God's words in Psalm 2:6: "As for me, I have set my King on Zion, my holy hill." Jerusalem's temple rested on a hill. Because the temple itself was holy, the hill was therefore considered holy as well.

At the time of the evening sacrifice (9:21): The Mosaic Law required both a morning and an evening sacrifice (Exodus 29:39-40; Numbers 28:3-4). The Jewish temple had been destroyed, making these sacrifices impossible. Daniel nevertheless reserved this time for prayer to God, thereby indicating his reverence for God. This was likely one of the three times Daniel prayed each day (see Daniel 6:10).

Daniel 9:22-23

I have now come out to give you insight and understanding (9:22): Gabriel came to inform Daniel what lay ahead in the immediate and distant future for his people. Recall that Gabriel is often portrayed in Scripture as bringing revelation to God's people regarding God's purpose and program. This is the second time he appeared to Daniel (see 8:16). Five hundred years later, he told Zechariah about the upcoming birth of John the Baptist, and soon after that, he announced the birth of Jesus to the Virgin Mary (Luke 1:11-17, 26-38).

At the beginning of your pleas (9:23): Gabriel informed Daniel, "At the beginning of your pleas for mercy a word went out, and I have come to tell it to you." Bible expositors have suggested two possibilities as to what this word was. The word may have related to God's sovereign decree to end Israel's exile and allow the Jews to return to Jerusalem. Or the word may simply have been God's instruction to Gabriel to appear to Daniel and explain the future to him. The latter view seems to best fit the context.

You are greatly loved (9:23): The phrase "greatly loved" is rich in the original Hebrew. The Holman Christian Standard Bible translates it, "You are treasured by God." The New Living Translation renders it, "You are very precious to God." The Amplified Bible renders it, "You are greatly beloved."

Daniel 9:24

Seventy weeks are decreed about your people and your holy city (9:24): Gabriel gave a real mouthful of revelation to Daniel in this verse. He provided Daniel with a prophetic timetable for the nation of Israel. It was divided into 70 groups of 7 years, totaling 490 years. At the end of these 490 years, six things will occur.

1. Israel's apostasy will end at the second coming of Jesus Christ, when she repents of her rejection of Jesus Christ as the divine Messiah.
2. Israel's sin will be removed, now having trusted in Jesus Christ (see Ezekiel 37:23; Romans 11:20-27).
3. When Israel repents of her rejection of Jesus Christ at the second coming, the atonement He wrought at the cross will bring salvation to the Jews.
4. Christ will bring about perfect righteousness in His covenant people in the millennial kingdom (see Isaiah 60:21; Jeremiah 23:5-6).
5. All the covenant promises to Israel in the Old Testament will be "sealed"—that is, fully realized in the millennial kingdom. (In this context, an "unsealed" prophecy is an unfulfilled prophecy.)
6. The Most Holy Place in the millennial kingdom will be consecrated (see Ezekiel 41–46).

Daniel 9:25-26

Seven weeks...sixty-two weeks (9:25-26): Gabriel provided some rather complex details about both the immediate future and the more distant end-times future. Here is the gist of what is important to grasp: Gabriel informed Daniel about 70 weeks of years. A week of years is 7 years, so 70 weeks of years comes to a total of 490 years.

Gabriel spoke of 7 weeks of years followed by 62 weeks of years. Seven weeks plus 62 weeks adds up to 69 weeks of years. And what is 69 weeks of years? It comes to 483 years (69 multiplied by 7). Here is the important point: Gabriel indicated that there was to be a 483-year period from the issuing of a decree to rebuild Jerusalem to the time the Messiah comes (that is, the first coming of Jesus Christ, not the second coming). The day Jesus rode into Jerusalem on a donkey to proclaim Himself Israel's Messiah was 483 years to the day after the command to restore and rebuild Jerusalem had been given.

After the sixty-two weeks (9:26): At the coming of the Messiah, God's prophetic clock was to stop. Daniel described a gap between these 483 years and the final 7 years of Israel's prophetic timetable.

Several events were to take place during this gap, according to Daniel 9:26:

1. The Messiah would be killed (or "cut off").

2. The city of Jerusalem and its temple would be destroyed (which occurred in AD 70).

3. The Jews would encounter difficulty and hardship from that time on.

Daniel 9:27

He shall make a strong covenant (9:27): The final week of seven years will begin for Israel in the end-times future when the antichrist confirms a covenant for seven years. When this peace pact is signed, the tribulation period will begin. This signature marks the beginning of a seven-year countdown to the second coming of Christ, which follows the tribulation period.

For half of the week he shall put an end to sacrifice and offering (9:27): Scripture reveals that the Jews will rebuild their temple during the first part of the seven-year tribulation period (Daniel 9:27; 12:11; Matthew 24:15-16). The Jewish sacrificial system will be reinstated. But in the middle of the tribulation period, the antichrist will put a stop to Jewish sacrifices. From then on, no one on earth will be permitted to worship anyone but the antichrist. The antichrist will set himself up as a deity and demand worship from all on earth (see 2 Thessalonians 2:4). In this way, the antichrist will take on the character of Satan, who energizes him (see Isaiah 14:12-17; Ezekiel 28:11-19; 2 Thessalonians 2:9).

One who makes desolate (9:27): Later, in Daniel 11:31, we read of the antichrist, "Forces from him shall appear and profane the temple and fortress, and shall take away the regular burnt offering. And they shall set up the abomination that makes desolate." We find further clarity on this "abomination that makes desolate" in the New Testament. It will take place at the midpoint of the future tribulation period when the antichrist—the "man of lawlessness" (2 Thessalonians 2:3)—sets up an image of himself inside the Jewish temple (see Matthew 24:15). This amounts to the antichrist enthroning himself in the place of deity, displaying himself as God (compare Isaiah 14:13-14; Ezekiel 28:2-9). This blasphemous act will utterly desecrate the temple, making it abominable and therefore desolate. The antichrist—the world dictator—will then demand that the world worship and pay idolatrous homage to him. Any who refuse will be persecuted, and many will be martyred.

MAJOR THEMES

1. *Strong covenant.* Daniel 9:24-27 contains an important prophecy in reference to the future seven-year tribulation period. This period begins when the antichrist signs a covenant with Israel: "He shall make a strong covenant with many for one week" (verse 27). Crucial to our present study is the fact that the seven years (the "one week") that follow the signing of this agreement will be the seven worst years in human history (see Isaiah 24:1-4, 20-21; 26:20-21; Jeremiah 30:7; Joel 1:15; Amos 5:18; Zephaniah 1:15, 18; Revelation 14:7). This means that in the end times, the antichrist will seem to have solved the Middle East problem—but only for a time. At the midpoint of the tribulation, he will double-cross the Jews, who will be forced to flee for their lives out of Jerusalem (Matthew 24:16-20).

2. *The abomination of desolation.* In the book of Daniel, the term "abomination of desolation" conveys the outrage and horror of a barbaric act of idolatry inside God's holy temple (Daniel 9:27; 11:31; 12:11). This abomination will apparently take place at the midpoint of the future tribulation period when the antichrist—the "man of lawlessness" (2 Thessalonians 2:3)—sets up an image of himself inside the Jewish temple (Daniel 9:27; Matthew 24:15). Such an abomination took place once before in Israel's history. Antiochus Epiphanes desecrated the Jewish temple by erecting an altar to Zeus in it and then sacrificing a pig—an unclean animal—on it.

DIGGING DEEPER WITH CROSS-REFERENCES

Prayers answered—Genesis 17:20; 19:21; 25:21; 30:22; Exodus 8:31; 32:7-14;

33:17; Judges 3:9; 13:9; 1 Samuel 1:20, 27; 1 Kings 9:3; 17:22; 1 Chronicles 4:10; Ezra 8:23; Psalms 21:2; 118:5; Luke 1:13

Names and titles of Christ—Isaiah 7:14; 9:6; Matthew 1:1, 23; 16:20; Mark 14:61; Luke 9:20; 23:2; John 1:29, 41; 6:48; 8:12; 10:11; 15:1; Ephesians 2:20; 5:23; Colossians 1:18; 1 Timothy 2:5; Titus 2:13; Hebrews 4:14; 6:20; 13:20; 1 Peter 2:4; 2 Peter 1:1; Revelation 1:8, 17; 3:14; 5:5; 19:11, 16; 22:13

LIFE LESSONS

1. *Gabriel.* The name Gabriel literally means "mighty one of God." It speaks of Gabriel's incredible power as endowed by God. His high rank in the angelic realm is obvious from both his name and his continuous standing in the presence of God (Luke 1:19). When carrying out God's bidding, Gabriel apparently has the ability to fly swiftly—perhaps faster than the other angels (Daniel 9:21). Scripture portrays Gabriel as the deliverer of revelation to God's people regarding God's purpose and program (Daniel 8:16-17; 9:21; Luke 1:11-17, 26-38).

2. *The Anointed One—Jesus the Messiah.* The word "Messiah" comes from the Hebrew term *masiah*, which means "the anointed one." The Greek parallel to this term is "Christ" (*christos*). That the terms are equated is clear from John 1:41: "[Andrew] found his own brother Simon and said to him, 'We have found the Messiah' (which means Christ)." Hundreds of Old Testament messianic prophecies point to the coming of the Messiah, Jesus Christ (for example, Isaiah 7:14; 9:1-7; 11:2-5; 52:13–53:12). Jesus made His identity as the Christ the primary issue of faith (Matthew 16:13-20; John 11:25-27). He warned that others would come falsely claiming to be the Christ (Matthew 24:4-5, 23-24).

QUESTIONS FOR REFLECTION AND DISCUSSION

1. Why is it important for us to confess our sins to God, as Daniel did (Daniel 9:20)? What insight does 1 John 1:9 give you?

2. Do you think an angel has ever intervened in your life? Why or why not?

3. What impacts you most from the cross-references on answered prayer?

DAY 33

DANIEL IS VISITED BY AN ANGEL

DANIEL 10:1-9

SCRIPTURE READING AND INSIGHTS

Begin by reading Daniel 10:1-9 in your favorite Bible. As you read, keep in mind that God desires for you not only to hear His Word but also to do it (James 1:22).

In yesterday's lesson, we considered Daniel's prophecy of the 70 weeks. Now let's look at a preliminary introduction to Daniel's special visitation from an angel, which we'll continue to study in the next lesson. With your Bible still accessible, consider the following insights on the biblical text, verse by verse.

Daniel 10:1

The third year of Cyrus king of Persia (10:1): This would be 536 BC. Daniel's prayer to God had been answered. The Jewish exile in Babylon was over. By this time, two years had elapsed since the first decree to allow the Jews to go back to Jerusalem (see Ezra 1:1–2:1; 2:64–3:1). A remnant of Jews returned to Judea under Zerubbabel and Jeshua's leadership. These Jews were now laying the foundations of the second temple (see Ezra 3).

Meanwhile, Daniel remained in Babylon, perhaps because he was less mobile at 84 years old. While still in Babylon, he received a "word" and a "vision" about Israel's future.

Who was named Belteshazzar (10:1): Recall from chapter 1 that Daniel and his friends all had Jewish names that honored the one true God of Israel.

Daniel's name, for example, means "God has judged," or perhaps "God is my Judge." (The ending of Daniel's name, *el*, is a Hebrew term for God.) The Babylonians believed their gods were superior to Israel's God, so Daniel and his friends were given Babylonian names to honor Babylonian deities. Daniel was renamed Belteshazzar, meaning "Bel, protect his life," or "Bel, protect the king's life." (Bel was a Babylonian deity.)

The word was true (10:1): "The word" Daniel received was quite obviously true because it was a revelation from God. In syllogism form: God is true; revelation is from God; therefore revelation is true.

It was a great conflict (10:1): Daniel had earlier been prophetically made aware of the end-times conflicts that awaited his people (Daniel 7:21, 25; 8:24-25; 9:27). He knew of the significant persecution that would fall on them at the hands of the "little horn," who is the antichrist (8:10-14). Now the new word given to Daniel was also "a great conflict." The phrase "great conflict" can be translated "great warfare" or "great suffering." Daniel was distressed to hear that pain and suffering lay ahead for the Jews of Israel. Details of this particular suffering are found in Daniel 11:2–12:3, which we will examine in a later lesson.

He understood the word and had understanding of the vision (10:1): This is in noted contrast to Daniel's visions recorded in Daniel 7–8, which Daniel needed help to understand.

Daniel 10:2-3

Mourning for three weeks (10:2): Bible expositors offer various explanations as to why Daniel mourned. Some say he mourned as a result of the visions he had about the future of his people. Others suggest that he mourned because of the extremely poor condition of the captives returning to Judea. They encountered great difficulty in resettling in the land. Still others suggest he may have mourned because the reconstruction of the temple had stalled due to resistance from the Samaritans (see Ezra 4:5, 24). This would have been extremely disconcerting to Daniel, for his greatest desire was the full restoration of Jerusalem and its temple.

Ate no delicacies (10:3): Daniel said, "No meat or wine entered my mouth, nor did I anoint myself at all, for the full three weeks." He engaged in a partial fast in order to commit himself fully to prayer. He limited himself to basic nourishment. One recalls the commitment of a much younger Daniel: "Daniel resolved that he would not defile himself with the king's food, or with the wine that he drank" (Daniel 1:8).

Daniel 10:4-6

Standing on the bank of the great river (10:4): Daniel was standing on the bank of the Tigris on the twenty-fourth day of the first month. This provides positive proof that Daniel did not go back to Judea with the other exiles, for the Tigris River is only about 20 miles from Babylon. The Tigris is a major river in Mesopotamia with a number of significant cities along its banks. Nineveh was one of the most famous.

A man clothed in linen (10:5): Some have taken this as an appearance of the preincarnate Christ, for he is described in similar terms to Christ (see Revelation 1:13-14; see also Daniel 7:9). However, it is more likely that this is one of God's glorious angels (compare Daniel 10:16, 18; 12:6-7). Some believe it may have been Gabriel, who had previously appeared to Daniel (8:16). (See Major Themes.)

As was true previously in Daniel, the angel is called a man simply because he took on the appearance of a man. This is often the case in the Bible. When three angels appeared to Abraham, he "lifted up his eyes and looked, and behold, three men were standing in front of him" (Genesis 18:2). Angels can appear as human beings so realistically that Hebrews 13:2 exhorts us, "Do not neglect to show hospitality to strangers, for thereby some have entertained angels unawares."

Body...face...eyes...arms and legs...sound of his words (10:6): This verse contains the language of analogy. Notice the repetition of the word "like." This is an attempt to use finite human language to describe the indescribable glory of one of God's angels. Even our Lord used analogical language, for He often said "the kingdom of heaven is like..." (Matthew 13:31, 33, 44-45, 47, 52).

PARALLELS

Daniel 10:6—A glorious angel is described.

Revelation 10:1—A glorious angel is described.

Daniel 10:7

I, Daniel, alone saw the vision (10:7): Those who were present with Daniel sensed a terrifying presence, but they saw nothing. One is reminded of Saul's vision of the risen Christ on the road to Damascus. "The men who were traveling with him stood speechless, hearing the voice but seeing no one" (Acts 9:7). Paul described the account in Acts 22:9: "Now those who were with me saw the light but did not understand the voice of the one who was speaking to me." One also recalls that when the Father spoke audibly to His Son, "the crowd that stood there and heard it said that it had thundered" (John 12:29). This is a curious phenomenon. Somehow, when a person experiences a supernatural encounter, those nearby may sense something without seeing everything the person sees.

Daniel 10:8-9

No strength was left in me...I retained no strength...I fell on my face in deep sleep (10:8-9): We recall that when Joshua saw the Lord, "Joshua fell on his face to the earth and worshiped and said to him, 'What does my lord say to his servant?'" (Joshua 5:14). When Abraham beheld the Almighty, he "fell on his face" (Genesis 17:3). When Manoah and his wife saw the Angel of the Lord (an appearance of the preincarnate Christ), they "fell on their faces to the ground" (Judges 13:20). Ezekiel saw the glory of God and said, "I fell on my face" (Ezekiel 3:23; 43:3; 44:4). Leviticus 9:24 tells us, "Fire came out from before the Lord and consumed the burnt offering and the pieces of fat on the altar, and when all the people saw it, they shouted and fell on their faces." First Chronicles 21:16 tells us, "David lifted his eyes and saw the angel of the Lord standing between earth and heaven, and in his hand a drawn sword stretched out over Jerusalem. Then David and the elders, clothed in sackcloth, fell upon their faces." The apostle John, upon seeing Christ in His glory, "fell at his feet as though dead" (Revelation 1:17; see also Isaiah 6:5). Daniel's response to this supernatural encounter put him in good company.

MAJOR THEMES

1. *King Cyrus of Persia.* Cyrus, king of Persia, engaged in conquests with lightning-like rapidity. His empire became vast. Babylon was among the

many nations he conquered. He ultimately issued a decree for the liberation of the Jews, allowing them to return to Jerusalem and rebuild their temple (Ezra 1:1-2; Isaiah 44:28; 45:1-2). Daniel's encounter with the angel took place in the third year after Cyrus's conquest of Babylon in 539 BC (see Daniel 10:1). Cyrus died less than a decade later in 530 BC.

2. *The man clothed in linen.* Daniel's description of the "man clothed in linen" has been taken by some expositors to be an appearance of the preincarnate Christ. After all, his face was like lightning, his eyes were like torches, and his voice was like the sound of a multitude (Daniel 10:6). This is similar to the description of the resurrected and glorified Christ in Revelation 1:13-14. The problem with this view, however, is that this (apparently) same "man" said, "The prince of the kingdom of Persia withstood me twenty-one days, but Michael, one of the chief princes, came to help me" (Daniel 10:13). If this were truly the preincarnate Christ, he would be all-powerful, and no one could withstand him. Jesus, of course, exercises power and authority over the devil (Matthew 16:23). In view of this one pivotal fact, it seems best to take the "man clothed in linen" as a glorious angel, and not the preincarnate Christ.

DIGGING DEEPER WITH CROSS-REFERENCES

Appearances of the preincarnate Christ—Genesis 5:22; 16:7-13; Exodus 3:6-8, 14; Judges 6:11-23; 13:1-21; 1 Kings 19:4-8; Psalm 34:7; Zechariah 1:12-13; 3:1-2; Daniel 3:15-20; 6:16-25

Mourning—Genesis 50:10; 1 Samuel 15:35; 25:1; Ezra 9:4-7; Job 2:5-8; Psalms 30:11; 42:9; Jeremiah 31:13; Joel 1:9-10; Matthew 5:4; Revelation 18:11

LIFE LESSONS

1. *The Word is true.* Daniel acknowledged that the heavenly message he had received was true (Daniel 10:1). This brings to mind the reality that God's Word is truth. Proverbs 30:5 tells us, "Every word of God proves true." This is similar to Psalm 18:30: "The word of the Lord proves true." Psalm 19:8 likewise affirms, "The precepts of the Lord are right." Psalm

33:4 states, "The word of the LORD is upright." In the New Testament, Colossians 1:5 refers to God's Word as "the word of the truth." John 17:17 likewise affirms, "Your word is truth." We would expect God's Word to be true, for everything God says is true. "I the LORD speak the truth; I declare what is right" (Isaiah 45:19).

2. *Abstinence.* Various kinds of abstinence are found in the Bible. Manoah's wife abstained from wine, strong drink, and unclean foods (Judges 13:3-4, 7). Samson abstained from using a razor (Judges 16:17). Hannah abstained from wine and strong drink (1 Samuel 1:15). Daniel abstained from the king's food and wine (Daniel 1:8). He later abstained from delicacies, meat, and wine, and from anointing himself (Daniel 10:3). John the Baptist abstained from wine and strong drink (Luke 1:13-15). Husbands and wives sometimes abstain from sexual relations for a time (1 Corinthians 7:5). Generally speaking, believers sometimes abstain from certain things for a season so they can focus their attention on the Lord.

QUESTIONS FOR REFLECTION AND DISCUSSION

1. Have you ever engaged in any form of abstinence for spiritual reasons? Was it a positive spiritual experience?

2. Do you believe the Bible is absolutely true in all its parts? In other words, do you believe in an inspired and inerrant Bible?

3. In view of the great glory of the angels (see Daniel 10:6), is it more understandable to you that some humans were initially inclined to worship them (see Revelation 19:10)?

DAY 34

THE ANGEL EXPLAINS THE FUTURE TO DANIEL

DANIEL 10:10–11:1

SCRIPTURE READING AND INSIGHTS

Begin by reading Daniel 10:10–11:1 in your favorite Bible. As you read, stop and meditate on any verses that speak to your heart (Joshua 1:8; Psalm 1:1-3).

Yesterday we focused on a preliminary introduction to Daniel's special visitation from an angel. Now let's find out how the angel strengthened Daniel so he could receive revelation about Israel's future. With your Bible still accessible, consider the following insights on the biblical text, verse by verse.

Daniel 10:10-12

A hand touched me (10:10): Our previous lesson concluded with Daniel falling asleep: "I fell on my face in deep sleep with my face to the ground" (Daniel 10:9). Today's lesson begins with an angel touching Daniel to awaken him so he could receive new revelation about Israel's future. Upon awakening, Daniel was so frightened, he trembled on his hands and knees.

Man greatly loved (10:11): The way the angel addressed Daniel may indicate that the angel was Gabriel, for just earlier, Gabriel had informed Daniel, "You are greatly loved" (9:23). This carries the idea, "You are very precious to God."

Understand the words (10:11): The angel then instructed Daniel to "understand the words that I speak to you, and stand upright" (compare with Daniel 1:17). Daniel stood trembling, apparently still frightened.

Fear not, Daniel (10:12): The angel recognized Daniel's anxiety and tried to calm him. The angel's explanation that followed would help alleviate all his fears.

From the first day (10:12): The angel informed Daniel, "From the first day that you set your heart to understand and humbled yourself before your God, your words have been heard." Daniel may have been concerned about the apparent delay in God's answer to his prayer (compare with Daniel 10:2-3). We now learn that the prayer was actually answered from day one. This was no doubt a great encouragement to Daniel.

I have come because of your words (10:12): Here is a clear example of God sending an angel to earth in response to the prayers of a human being.

Daniel 10:13-14

The prince of the kingdom of Persia withstood me (10:13): This is why the answer to Daniel's prayer was delayed for three weeks. There are different ranks among God's holy angels as well as the fallen angels (Ephesians 6:12; Colossians 1:16). Michael and Gabriel are preeminent among the holy angels. If the angel who was assigned by God to go to Daniel was Gabriel, then the "prince of Persia" must have been an extremely high-ranking fallen angel, working under Satan's command. This demonic spirit was called the "prince of the kingdom of Persia" apparently because he was assigned by Satan to try to influence the kings of Persia to stand against God's people Israel and thus oppose God's plan.

Michael, one of the chief princes (10:13): Michael the archangel—presumably heaven's most powerful angel—came to help the angel who had been assigned to visit Daniel.

Your people in the latter days...days yet to come (10:14): The angel then revealed to Daniel that his mission was to help Daniel understand what was to happen to his people in the "latter days...days yet to come." The Old Testament use of the term "latter days" (and similar terms) typically points to the future tribulation period, leading up to the coming of the Messiah to set up His millennial kingdom on earth. The angel informed Daniel that his people will go through the tribulation period.

Daniel 10:15-17

Turned my face toward the ground and was mute (10:15): Daniel's reaction was likely due to several factors. He was likely still weak from being in the presence of a glorious angel (see Genesis 17:3; Judges 13:20; Ezekiel 3:23; 43:3; 44:4). He may also have been stunned to discover the level of spiritual warfare that had erupted in response to his prayer. Most important, he was apparently greatly saddened to discover what awaited his people in the "latter days"—the future tribulation period.

PARALLELS

Daniel 10:15—Daniel turned his face "toward the ground" in reverence and humility.

Revelation 4:10; 7:11; 11:16—God's servants "fall down before him" in reverence and humility.

Touched my lips (10:16): Responding to Daniel's muteness, an angel (in the appearance of a man—see Hebrews 13:2) touched his lips (compare with Isaiah 6:7; Jeremiah 1:9).

Pains have come upon me (10:16): This verse is better translated by the Holman Christian Standard Bible: "My lord, because of the vision, anguish overwhelms me and I am powerless."

No strength remains in me (10:17): Daniel was still weak. Some Bible expositors suggest that he may have felt unworthy to speak to the angelic messenger, not only because the angel was so glorious (see Revelation 19:10; 22:9) but also because Daniel was continuing to identify with his people, who had grievously sinned against the Lord (see Daniel 9). Daniel's anxiety caused a physiological response of weakness and breathlessness.

Daniel 10:18–11:1

Touched me and strengthened me (10:18): Angels often did this in biblical times (compare with Psalm 91:12; Luke 4:11; 22:43).

Fear not...be strong and of good courage (10:19): Daniel was indeed strengthened, and then he asked the angel to continue his message about the future (compare Joshua 1:6-9; Judges 6:23; Isaiah 35:4; 43:1).

Do you know why I have come to you? (10:20): The angel apparently asked Daniel this because Daniel had been so weak and needed to refocus his attention on the vision of the future.

Fight against the prince of Persia (10:20): The angel informed Daniel that he would need to resume his battle against the demonic spirit that was influencing the human leadership of Persia. Persia must not be allowed to thwart God's purposes for Israel.

Prince of Greece (10:20): This is apparently a demonic spirit assigned by Satan to influence the government of Greece. It is noteworthy that the angel mentions both Persia and Greece, since these empires have been a heavy focus in the book of Daniel (see chapters 2, 7, 8, and 10).

The book of truth (10:21): There is some debate among Bible expositors as to what this refers to. It may be a divine book that contains God's plans for human beings and the nations in which they live (see Daniel 12:1). It may be a book that contains God's sovereign decrees. We recall from Isaiah 46:9-11, "Remember the former things of old; for I am God, and there is no other; I am God, and there is none like me, declaring the end from the beginning and from ancient times things not yet done, saying, 'My counsel shall stand, and I will accomplish all my purpose.'" In any event, we find a number of references in Scripture to God's books (see, for example, Exodus 32:32; Psalms 69:28; 139:16).

Michael, your prince (10:21): The angel then informed Daniel, "There is none who contends by my side against these except Michael, your prince." Apparently, the angel speaking to Daniel (Gabriel?) would soon engage the demonic spirits of Persia and Greece with the archangel Michael by his side. Michael is called "your prince" because he guards Israel (Daniel 12:1).

And as for me (11:1): This verse closes Daniel 10 instead of beginning Daniel 11. The angel said, "And as for me, in the first year of Darius the Mede, I stood up to confirm and strengthen him." We are not given the context or any interpretive clues as to what this means. Some Bible expositors suggest that the angel somehow encouraged and protected Darius at the beginning of his reign. This indicates that God is active in the political affairs of the world.

MAJOR THEMES

1. *Spiritual warfare.* Spiritual warfare is evident in our passage. We learn most of what we know about spiritual warfare from the New Testament—particularly regarding the Christian's defense against the powers of darkness. First and foremost, the Lord Jesus prays for us (Romans 8:34; Hebrews 7:25). As well, God has provided us with spiritual armor for our defense (Ephesians 6:11-18). Effective use of the Word of God is especially important for spiritual victory (see Matthew 4). Each believer must be informed and thereby alert to the attacks of Satan (2 Corinthians 2:11; 1 Peter 5:8). We are instructed to take a decisive stand against Satan (James 4:7). We must "give no opportunity to the devil" by going to bed angry (Ephesians 4:26-27). We are instructed to rely on the indwelling Spirit of God, remembering that "he who is in you is greater than he who is in the world" (1 John 4:4).

2. *Michael the archangel.* The angel Michael is mentioned in Daniel 10:21. He is the only archangel mentioned in the Bible. The word "archangel" implies a rank first among angels. Apparently Michael is in authority over all the other angels, including the thrones, dominions, rulers, and authorities mentioned in Colossians 1:16. The term "archangel" occurs only twice in the New Testament (1 Thessalonians 4:16; Jude 9), and in both instances it is used in the singular. Some scholars conclude from this that the term is restricted to a single archangel—Michael, who is called "one of the chief princes" (Daniel 10:13) and "the great prince" (12:1).

DIGGING DEEPER WITH CROSS-REFERENCES

Jesus' divine touch—Matthew 8:3, 15; 9:29-30; 17:7; 20:34; Mark 7:33, 35; 10:13, 16; Luke 22:51

The humility of God's servants—Numbers 12:3; 2 Samuel 22:28; 2 Chronicles 7:14; Psalm 25:9; Proverbs 3:34; 18:12; Isaiah 13:11; Daniel 4:37; Zephaniah 2:3; Matthew 11:29; Ephesians 4:2; Philippians 2:3; Colossians 2:23; 3:12; Titus 3:1-2; James 4:6, 10; 1 Peter 3:8, 5:5-6

LIFE LESSONS

1. *Reverence for God.* We are not to fear God in the sense of being frightened of Him, but we are called to fear Him in the sense of living in reverence of Him (1 Peter 1:17; 2:17; 1 Samuel 12:14, 24; 2 Chronicles 19:9; Acts 10:35). Fear of the Lord motivates obedience to God (Deuteronomy 5:29; Ecclesiastes 12:13) and service to God (Deuteronomy 6:13). Fear of the Lord motivates one to avoid evil (Proverbs 3:7; 8:13; 16:6). Fear of the Lord is true wisdom (Job 28:28; Psalm 111:10) and the beginning of knowledge (Proverbs 1:7). God blesses those who fear Him (Psalm 115:13). Fear of the Lord leads to riches, honor, and long life (Proverbs 22:4). God shows mercy to those who fear Him (Luke 1:50).

2. *Delays in answered prayer.* God sometimes dispatches angels to take care of our prayer requests (Acts 12:6-19). Fallen angels sometimes oppose them. This happened when the prophet Daniel prayed. Daniel 10:13 reveals that an angel that had been sent by God to take care of Daniel's prayer request was detained by a more powerful fallen angel. Only when the archangel Michael showed up to render aid was the lesser angel free to carry out his task. Here, then, is an important thing to remember: We must be fervent in our prayers and not think that God is not listening simply because His answer is delayed. You never know what's going on behind the scenes in the spiritual world.

QUESTIONS FOR REFLECTION AND DISCUSSION

1. Daniel 10:21 indicates that Michael the archangel is involved in spiritual warfare. What more do you learn about Michael's role in spiritual warfare from Jude 9 and Revelation 12:7-8?

2. What have you learned about spiritual warfare in this lesson that will help you in your Christian life?

3. Do a little self-examination. Does your life manifest a proper reverence for God?

DAY 35

PROPHECIES CONCERNING KEY NATIONS

DANIEL 11:2-19

SCRIPTURE READING AND INSIGHTS

Begin by reading Daniel 11:2-19 in your favorite Bible. As you read, keep in mind that the Word of God brings spiritual maturity (1 Corinthians 3:1-2; Hebrews 5:12-14).

In yesterday's reading, an angel gave Daniel strength to receive revelation about the prophetic future. In today's lesson, we will focus on specific prophetic revelations concerning the southern and northern nations. With your Bible still accessible, consider the following insights on the biblical text, verse by verse.

Daniel 11:2-4

Now I will show you the truth (11:2): This truth is apparently "what is inscribed in the book of truth" (Daniel 10:21).

Three more kings shall arise in Persia (11:2): The angel told Daniel that Persia's present leadership would be succeeded by four more rulers. The first three kings mentioned would be Cambyses (530–522 BC), Pseudo-Smerdis (522), and Darius I Hystaspes (522–486).

A fourth shall be far richer...become strong (11:2): The fourth king—far richer, far more influential, and far more powerful than the others—would be Xerxes (486–465 BC), also known as Ahasuerus in the book of Esther.

A mighty king shall arise (11:3): The angel affirmed that this king "shall rule with great dominion and do as he wills." This mighty king of Greece was none other than Alexander the Great (336–323 BC), who conquered the Medo-Persian Empire, Asia Minor, Syria, and Egypt, thereby building a massive empire in a little more than a decade (compare with Daniel 8:5, 8). History reveals that Alexander's army featured 35,000 soldiers.

His kingdom shall be broken and divided (11:4): In 323 BC, Alexander the Great succumbed to illness and died at the young age of 32 and the height of his power. The Greek Empire was then divided among four of Alexander's prominent generals. Cassander reigned over Macedon and Greece. Lysimachus ruled Thrace and Asia Minor. Seleucus governed Syria and Babylon. Ptolemy led Egypt. Alexander the Great was anticipated earlier in the book of Daniel in the vision of the goat with the conspicuous horn, which then broke into four conspicuous horns (see Daniel 8:5-8).

Daniel 11:5-6

King of the south (11:5): In the verses that follow, we encounter a somewhat tedious account of the rise and fall of various leaders of the north and south, with plenty of battles along the way. This is unquestionably the most complicated part of the book of Daniel. I encourage you not to get bogged down in the details. There are still good spiritual lessons to learn here.

The angel first revealed to Daniel that the king of the south will be strong. This was Ptolemy I Soter. Formerly a general who served under Alexander the Great, he governed Egypt from 323 to 285 BC. The Ptolemaic dynasty controlled the Holy Land from 323 to 198 BC. The term "south" is to be understood as "south of Palestine." (North, south, west, and east in the Bible are always understood in relation to Palestine.) Egypt is actually to the south-southwest of Palestine.

We are then told that one of Ptolemy I Soter's "princes shall be stronger than he and shall rule, and his authority shall be a great authority." This prince was Seleucus I Nicator (born 311 BC), also a general under Alexander. Seleucus I Nicator abandoned Ptolemy I Soter and became the ruler of a Seleucid kingdom in Syria and Babylon that was more powerful and more extensive than Ptolemy's Egypt in the south.

They shall make an alliance (11:6): Later, the king of the south, now Ptolemy

II Philadelphus (285–246 BC), entered into an alliance with the king of the north, now Antiochus II Theos (261–246 BC). In sealing treaties in ancient days, it was customary for a lesser king to give his daughter in marriage to the greater king. This was considered a token of friendship and sealed the relationship between the two kings. In the present case, the daughter of Ptolemy II Philadelphus, princess Berenice, was sent as a wife to Antiochus II Theos. Antiochus divorced his wife at the time, Laodice, in order to marry Berenice. However, Princess Berenice was unable to retain her power. Laodice (the spurned former wife) murdered Antiochus, Berenice, and their child. Laodice's own son, Seleucus II Callinicus, then became king of the north.

Daniel 11:7-9

From a branch from her roots one shall arise in his place...He shall also carry off to Egypt (11:7-8): The brother of the now-deceased Berenice, Ptolemy III Euergetes of Egypt (246–221 BC), stood in place of his father and became king of the south. He invaded Syria (in the north) and avenged the death of his sister by executing Laodice. He seized all the treasures of Syria, returning south to Egypt with many spoils.

The latter shall come into the realm of the king of the south (11:9): Later, the king of Syria ("the north"), now Seleucus II, attacked the king of Egypt ("the south"), now Ptolemy IV. Seleucus II was soundly beaten and retreated back north (about 240 BC).

Daniel 11:10-13

His sons shall wage war (11:10): In Daniel 11:9-13 we read of a continuous conflict between the Ptolemies in the south (Egypt) and the Seleucids in the north (Syria). During this time, the land of Israel was invaded first by one power and then by the other. They were continually vying for control of the strategically located land of Palestine, which lay between these two military powers. It was not a good time for Israel.

In Daniel 11:10 we are informed that Seleucus's sons (successors) in the north—that is, Seleucus III Ceraunus (226–223 BC) and Antiochus III (223–187 BC)—continued to wage war against the king of the south. The conflict seemed never-ending.

The king of the south...shall come out and fight (11:11): Sometime later, the king of the south, now Ptolemy IV Philopator (222–203 BC), fought against the king of the north, now Antiochus III the Great (223–187 BC). He enjoyed victory, but any sense of superiority would be short-lived.

His heart shall be exalted (11:12): Ptolemy IV Philopator (in the south), in great arrogance, slaughtered tens of thousands of the northern Seleucid troops. However, he would not be able to prevail.

The king of the north shall again raise a multitude (11:13): Meanwhile, Antiochus III the Great (king of the north) had been busy conquering other lands. Thirteen years later, he had accumulated a vast, new army with plenty of military supplies.

Daniel 11:14-19

The violent among your own people (11:14): Some Jews chose to join forces with Antiochus, king of the north. These Jews had hoped to gain independence from both Egypt (in the south) *and* Syria (in the north) by participating in the conflict. But it was all in vain. Their hopes were not realized.

The forces of the south shall not stand (11:15): Antiochus III's newly enlarged northern army won a resounding victory over the south, even capturing the well-fortified city of Sidon.

He shall stand in the glorious land (11:16): Antiochus III of the north took dominion over the glorious land—that is, over Israel.

Shall bring terms of an agreement (11:17): Antiochus III (of the north) forced a peace treaty on the Ptolemies (of the south). He even gave his daughter Cleopatra as a wife to Ptolemy V Epiphanes (about 192 BC), hoping to control the Ptolemies through her influence (and her spying). Antiochus's plan backfired, however, because Cleopatra ended up supporting her Ptolemaic husband.

He shall turn his face to the coastlands (11:18): Antiochus III, from the north, now sought to conquer Greece, along the Mediterranean coastlands. But Rome didn't like this and opposed him. Roman commander Lucius Cornelius Scipio defeated Antiochus III at Magnesia in Asia Minor in 190 BC. Antiochus's expansionism was stopped dead in its tracks.

He shall stumble and fall (11:19): This forced Antiochus to retreat back to his own land in the north. He was assassinated a year later while attempting to plunder a temple in the province of Elymais.

MAJOR THEMES

1. *Self-will versus God's will.* In Daniel 11:3 we read of a mighty king who will "do as he wills." Self-will lies at the very heart of how the Bible views sin. In the earliest recorded instance of such self-will, Lucifer rebelled against God: "I will set my throne on high...I will make myself like the Most High" (Isaiah 14:13-14). After he fell into sin and suffered God's judgment, he tempted Eve in the Garden of Eden, and Eve by self-will ate the forbidden fruit instead of obeying God's will (Genesis 3:6). The truth is, human beings are prone to self-importance (Galatians 6:5), self-pity (Psalm 37), self-righteousness (Luke 18:9), self-seeking (1 Corinthians 13:5), self-confidence (Matthew 26:35), self-will (Acts 7:51), and self-confident boasting (2 Corinthians 11:17). Dangerous stuff!

2. *The truth.* The angel said to Daniel, "And now I will show you the truth" (Daniel 11:2). The absolute nature of truth is assumed throughout the book of Daniel. We observe that Christianity rests on a foundation of absolute truth (1 Kings 17:24; Psalm 25:5; John 8:44; 2 Corinthians 6:7; Ephesians 4:15; 2 Timothy 2:15; 1 John 3:19), and that foundation is as sturdy as a rock. Biblical Christians believe that moral absolutes are grounded in the absolutely moral God of Scripture (Matthew 5:48). God stands against the moral relativist whose behavior is based on whatever is right in his own eyes (Deuteronomy 12:8; Judges 17:6; 21:25). And since the absolutely moral Creator-God (Isaiah 44:24) has communicated precisely what He expects of us in terms of moral behavior (Exodus 20:1-17), we as His creatures are responsible to render obedience (Deuteronomy 11:13, 27-28).

DIGGING DEEPER WITH CROSS-REFERENCES

Being uprooted—Deuteronomy 29:28-29; Amos 9:15; Zephaniah 2:4; Luke 17:6; Jude 12

Fortresses can be strong, but they can also fall—Judges 9:51; 2 Samuel 5:9; Isaiah 17:3; 25:12; Ezekiel 33:27; Hosea 10:14

Powerless in the face of a strong army—Deuteronomy 1:44; 28:32; Joshua 7:5, 12; Judges 6:2; Isaiah 21:15

LIFE LESSONS

1. *The cause of war.* James 4:1-2 affirms, "What causes quarrels and what causes fights among you? Is it not this, that your passions are at war within you? You desire and do not have, so you murder. You covet and cannot obtain, so you fight and quarrel." As someone once said, wars may be fought on the battlefield, but they are first waged in the human heart.

2. *Earthly riches can be lost.* Earthly riches can quickly be lost (see Daniel 11:8). It is wiser to build up heavenly riches. Jesus instructed, "Do not lay up for yourselves treasures on earth, where moth and rust destroy and where thieves break in and steal, but lay up for yourselves treasures in heaven, where neither moth nor rust destroys and where thieves do not break in and steal" (Matthew 6:19-20). The apostle Paul adds, "We brought nothing into the world, and we cannot take anything out of the world" (1 Timothy 6:7). Therefore, Paul says the rich should not "set their hopes on the uncertainty of riches, but on God" (verse 17).

3. *Human leaders come and go.* Human leaders may become great for a short time, but they all eventually pass away. Job said that "man who is born of a woman is few of days" (Job 14:1). The psalmist used bold hyperbole: "Behold, you have made my days a few handbreadths, and my lifetime is as nothing before you" (Psalm 39:5). We ought to place our faith not in finite, temporal human leaders but rather in the infinite and eternal Ruler of the universe, God Himself.

QUESTIONS FOR REFLECTION AND DISCUSSION

1. Do you sometimes find it difficult to replace self-will with obedience to God's will?

2. What is your attitude toward money and material things? Are you focused on building up heavenly treasures?

3. Think about all the wars and conflicts in the world today. What do you see that confirms the truth of James 4:1-2?

DAY 36

PROPHECIES CONCERNING ANTIOCHUS EPIPHANES

DANIEL 11:20-35

SCRIPTURE READING AND INSIGHTS

Begin by reading Daniel 11:20-35 in your favorite Bible. As you read, remember that the Word of God can help you be spiritually fruitful (Psalm 1:1-3).

In the previous lesson, we studied prophecies concerning the southern and northern nations, Egypt and Syria. In today's lesson, we zero in on the prophecies concerning Antiochus Epiphanes. With your Bible still accessible, consider the following insights on the biblical text, verse by verse.

Daniel 11:20-21

Then shall arise in his place (11:20): Seleucus IV Philopator (187–176 BC) was the son of Antiochus III of the north. His tax collector, Heliodorus, collected massive amounts of money from the populace with which to pay tribute to Rome. After reigning for a short seven years, Seleucus was poisoned to death by Heliodorus.

A contemptible person (11:21): Seleucus IV Philopator was succeeded by his brother, Antiochus IV Epiphanes (175–164 BC). The throne was not rightfully his. Antiochus seized power when Seleucus's very young son—Demetrius I Soter, the rightful heir—was being held hostage in Rome. Antiochus turned out to be a contemptible, cruel, and idolatrous king. In his arrogance, he christened himself Epiphanes, meaning "the Illustrious One." Some who knew of his character assigned him the nickname "Epimanes"—a name meaning "madman."

Antiochus hated the Jewish people. During his reign he declared the Jewish Mosaic ceremonies illegal and attempted to destroy Judaism.

Daniel 11:22-23

Armies shall be utterly swept away (11:22): Antiochus's northern forces "swept away" the Ptolemaic (Egyptian) armies of the south like a raging flood. Antiochus was militarily ruthless.

The "prince of the covenant" may have been the Jewish high priest Onias III, who was assassinated by his defecting brother Menelaus in 170 BC at the request of Antiochus.

An alliance...he shall act deceitfully (11:23): During a volatile time when several Egyptian leaders were vying for supremacy on Egypt's throne, Antiochus took sides and entered into an alliance with Ptolemy VI Philometor over his rival Ptolemy VII Euergetes II. He thereby deceitfully sought to secure greater power and influence throughout Egypt. With a small force, Antiochus was also able to conquer a territory in Egypt.

Daniel 11:24-25

He shall come into the richest parts of the province (11:24): Some Bible expositors believe this means that Antiochus, under the guise of friendship, entered Egypt with some of his soldiers, seized wealth from some of the richest sections of Egypt, and then distributed his battle spoils among his followers to gain favor with them. His ultimate goal was to take over Egypt.

Other Bible expositors say that Antiochus, without warning, came into Jerusalem and seized the riches of the Jewish temple, exacted large tributes from the Jews living in Jerusalem, killed many Jews, and stationed his troops there. In this view, Antiochus may have spread the spoils of victory among his soldiers to motivate loyalty to him.

He shall do what neither his fathers nor his fathers' fathers have done, scattering among them plunder, spoil, and goods (11:24): Antiochus's strategy was unlike that of his father, who acquired spoils to increase his own personal wealth. Antiochus, by contrast, acquired wealth to buy favor from others.

Against the king of the south (11:25): The king of the south (in Egypt) was now Ptolemy VI Philometor (181–146 BC). Antiochus IV Epiphanes launched two attacks against Egypt between 170 BC and 168 BC. Though Egypt's army was strong, it was not strong enough.

"Plots" were "devised against" Ptolemy VI Philometor as trusted supporters double-crossed him and soon became captives to Antiochus.

Daniel 11:26-28

His army shall be swept away (11:26): Egyptian counselors who sat at the table with Ptolemy VI Philometor conspired against him, thereby ensuring his defeat. The Egyptian army was eventually "swept away" by the flood-like army of Antiochus.

As for the two kings (11:27): With Egypt's army devastated, Antiochus IV Epiphanes and Ptolemy VI Philometor—the victor and the vanquished—sat at the same table together. Both feigned the goal of a peaceful coexistence with each other, but both were deceptive. Ptolemy VI Philometor no doubt sought reinstatement to his throne. Antiochus IV Epiphanes sought control of all of Egypt, not just select territories he had previously moved against. With their perpetual lies to each other, neither had a satisfactory outcome.

Ptolemy VI Philometor was in a much weaker position than he previously enjoyed, now having to share rulership with another Egyptian ruler. Antiochus IV Epiphanes was likewise frustrated because he had desired total sovereign control of Egypt but did not obtain it.

Neither of them realized that Antiochus was actually fulfilling prophecy according to God's divine timetable.

His heart shall be set against the holy covenant (11:28): Returning from Egypt with great riches and spoils, Antiochus's hatred of the Jews intensified as never before. History reveals that on the way back to his homeland, he attacked Israel with a vengeance, executing some 80,000 Jewish men, women, and children and taking 40,000 prisoners as slaves. He also plundered the riches from the Jewish temple (about 169 BC). This is what is meant when our text says, "He shall work his will and return to his own land." His angry devastation of the Jews was likely caused in part by the frustrated outcome of the roundtable meeting in Egypt.

Daniel 11:29-30

He shall return and come into the south (11:29): Antiochus moved against the Egyptians in the south two years later (168 BC). This was his third attack on the south, this time against the joint rulership of Egypt. However, this campaign would be much less successful.

Ships of Kittim shall come against him (11:30): The reason for Antiochus's lesser success was that the "ships of Kittim"—that is, a Roman fleet led by Gaius Popilius Laenas—forced his withdrawal in humiliation. The Roman general drew a circle in the sand, made Antiochus stand inside it, and forced him to concede defeat before stepping outside of the circle. Antiochus had to submit or prepare for war with Rome.

Take action against the holy covenant (11:30): Antiochus again attacked and plundered Jerusalem. He killed many and took many as slaves. He also instructed that all copies of the Mosaic Law be burned.

Daniel 11:31-32

Profane the temple and fortress (11:31): Antiochus grossly desecrated the Jewish temple by erecting an altar to Zeus in it and sacrificing a pig—an unclean animal—on it. This was an "abomination that makes desolate." He also prohibited Jewish sacrifices from that point forward.

This typologically points forward to another "abomination that makes desolate" during the future tribulation period. The antichrist—the "man of lawlessness" (2 Thessalonians 2:3-4)—will set up an image of himself inside the Jewish temple. This amounts to the antichrist enthroning himself in the place of deity, displaying himself as God (compare Isaiah 14:13-14; Ezekiel 28:2-9). This blasphemous act will utterly desecrate the temple, making it abominable and therefore desolate. And like Antiochus, the antichrist will cause the Jewish sacrifices during the tribulation period to cease.

He shall seduce with flattery (11:32): In the interest of self-preservation, some Jews became compromisers. Convinced by Antiochus's flattery, they sided with him and thereby became corrupted. They became violators of the covenant. Other Jews, however, remained loyal to God and refused to compromise. These were the Hasidean Jews, who chose death rather than submitting to such a compromise (compare 1 Maccabees 1:62-63). There were many Jewish martyrs during this time (compare with Micah 5:7-9; Zechariah 9:13-16; 10:3-6).

Daniel 11:33-35

The wise among the people shall make many understand (11:33): Those godly Jews who understood and believed the truth as contained in the Scriptures would teach others while continuing to suffer persecution and die under Antiochus. Some Bible expositors relate Hebrews 11:36-38 in the Hebrews Hall of Fame to what happened under Antiochus:

> Others suffered mocking and flogging, and even chains and imprisonment. They were stoned, they were sawn in two, they were killed with the sword. They went about in skins of sheep and goats, destitute, afflicted, mistreated—of whom the world was not worthy—wandering about in deserts and mountains, and in dens and caves of the earth.

They shall receive a little help (11:34): This "little help" refers to the Maccabees, who instigated a national revolt—a Jewish "guerrilla uprising"—which Antiochus, who was presently occupied elsewhere, was unable to squash. Three years after Antiochus had desecrated the Jewish temple, the Maccabeans recaptured Jerusalem, removed the desecrating objects from the temple, cleansed the altar, and restored the Jewish sacrifices.

Refined, purified, and made white (11:35): Many of the faithful died as martyrs. The persecution under Antiochus had a purifying effect on the remnant who survived. Such trials refine the faith of the godly.

Bible expositors have interpreted "the time of the end" in various ways. Some say this refers to the end of Antiochus's oppression of the Jewish people, and not to the end of days. Others say it refers to the final tribulation period when the antichrist—foreshadowed by Antiochus Epiphanes—will be in power, and will continue persecution against the Jews.

Whichever is the case, we will focus on the antichrist in the next lesson.

MAJOR THEMES

1. *The people of the holy covenant.* In Daniel 11:28 we read that Antiochus Epiphanes "shall return to his land with great wealth, but his heart shall be set against the holy covenant." This holy covenant relates to God's institution of the Law and sacrificial worship for His people's temple—that is, the Jewish temple. Our passage points to how Antiochus profaned the Jewish sacrificial system, plundered the temple in Jerusalem, and massacred some 80,000 men, women, and children in the city (see 1 Maccabees 1:20-28). This was a first-century holocaust.

2. *Plunder.* In Daniel 11 we read of a "contemptible person"—Antiochus Epiphanes—who came into power and scattered to his followers the plunder obtained from the peoples he conquered. In ancient days, when a powerful nation overthrew a weaker nation, the more powerful nation would take possession of cattle, sheep, camels, donkeys, clothing, armor, jewelry, and money. As well, if any items of value were in a temple—such as silver, gold, or brass items—they, too, would be taken (see Exodus 3:22; Numbers 31:32; Mark 3:27; 1 Samuel 17:53).

DIGGING DEEPER WITH CROSS-REFERENCES

Covenant breakers—Genesis 17:14; Deuteronomy 31:16, 20; Joshua 7:11, 15; 23:16; 1 Kings 11:11; 2 Kings 17:15; Psalm 78:10; Jeremiah 11:10

The wicked ensnared—Exodus 14:23-25; Esther 7:9-10; Job 5:13; 18:8; Psalms 7:15; 9:15; 10:2; 35:8; 57:6; 69:22; 141:10; Proverbs 26:27; 28:10

LIFE LESSONS

1. *Flattery.* Some people try to get their way by using flattery, as we see in our passage (Daniel 11:21). Solomon, the wisest man who ever lived, points out the dangers of flattery. He affirmed, "A lying tongue hates its victims, and a flattering mouth works ruin" (Proverbs 26:28). As well, "A man who flatters his neighbor spreads a net for his feet" (Proverbs 29:5). Proverbs also warns of "smooth words" (Proverbs 7:5) and "seductive speech" (Proverbs 7:21).

2. *Treachery*. In our passage we witness leaders engaging in treachery, making "deceitful promises" (Daniel 11:23 NLT). There are many examples of treachery in the Bible. The sons of Jacob used treachery to destroy the evil inhabitants of Shechem (Genesis 34:25). Treachery was used against Samson (Judges 16:9, 19). Saul engaged in treacherous activities toward David (1 Samuel 19:11). David was treacherous against Uriah the Hittite (2 Samuel 11:15). Haman was treacherous against the Jews (Esther 3:8). Judas, of course, was treacherous toward Christ (Matthew 26:16, 23, 49).

QUESTIONS FOR REFLECTION AND DISCUSSION

1. Has anyone ever tried to take advantage of you by using flattering words? How did it make you feel? How did you respond?

2. Have you ever been tempted to engage in treacherous actions against another person?

3. What personally impacted you most in this lesson?

DAY 37

PROPHECIES CONCERNING THE ANTICHRIST

DANIEL 11:36-45

SCRIPTURE READING AND INSIGHTS

Begin by reading Daniel 11:36-45 in your favorite Bible. Read with the anticipation that the Holy Spirit has something important to teach you today (see Psalm 119:105).

In yesterday's lesson, we considered prophecies concerning Antiochus Epiphanes. Now let's learn about the prophecies of the antichrist. With your Bible still accessible, consider the following insights on the biblical text, verse by verse.

Daniel 11:36-37

Shall do as he wills (11:36): As a preface, note that from here to the end of chapter 11, the antichrist is in view. The details of this section do not fit what we know to be historically true of Antiochus Epiphanes. Bible scholars believe that Daniel 11:1-35 deals with the past, whereas Daniel 11:36-45 deals with the future.

We can make two observations about the scriptural assertion that the antichrist "shall do as he wills": (1) Instead of seeking God's will, the antichrist will be self-willed. (2) As a qualification, however, Scripture also seems to indicate that the antichrist will do as Satan wills. Second Thessalonians 2:9 tells us that "the coming of the lawless one is by the activity of Satan." Of course, Satan himself is self-willed, so it is not surprising that the antichrist will be as well.

He shall exalt himself and magnify himself (11:36): Notice that just as the antichrist will exalt himself as God and seek to be worshiped (2 Thessalonians 2:4; Revelation 13:5-8), Scripture reveals that Satan earlier sought to exalt himself to deity (Isaiah 14:12-17; Ezekiel 28:11-19).

PARALLELS

Daniel 11:36—The antichrist will magnify himself with a view to being worshiped.

Revelation 13:8—The antichrist will be worshiped.

And shall speak astonishing things against the God of gods (11:36): This is in keeping with what we read of the antichrist in Revelation 13:5-6: "The beast was given a mouth uttering haughty and blasphemous words, and it was allowed to exercise authority for forty-two months. It opened its mouth to utter blasphemies against God, blaspheming his name and his dwelling, that is, those who dwell in heaven." There is no greater blasphemy than this. The antichrist truly is *anti*-Christ, even putting himself in Christ's place (see Revelation 13:7-8). We are also told that the antichrist—the world dictator—will demand that the world worship him and pay idolatrous homage to him. Those who refuse will be persecuted and even martyred.

PARALLELS

Daniel 11:36—The antichrist "shall speak astonishing things against the God of gods."

Revelation 13:6—The antichrist "opened its mouth to utter blasphemies against God."

What is decreed shall be done (11:36): In other words, the duration of the antichrist's rule has been sovereignly predetermined by God. God elsewhere affirmed, "My counsel shall stand, and I will accomplish all my purpose" (Isaiah 46:10).

Pay no attention to the gods of his fathers (11:37): The antichrist will pay no attention to the pagan gods of his forerunners, such as Antiochus Epiphanes and other pagan leaders who worshiped false deities. The antichrist will have no respect for any such gods, especially since he will set himself up as God during the tribulation period (2 Thessalonians 2:4; Revelation 13:5-8).

The one beloved by women (11:37): This is apparently a reference to Jesus, the divine Messiah. During New Testament times, it was the desire of Jewish women everywhere to be blessed with the privilege of being the mother of the Jewish Messiah. Therefore the Messiah was "the one beloved by women." This verse thus indicates that the antichrist will pay no attention to Jesus Christ.

He shall magnify himself above all (11:37): The antichrist will not only utter blasphemies against the one true God (Revelation 13:5-6) but also exalt himself to a preeminent divine status during the tribulation period (2 Thessalonians 2:4; Revelation 13:5-8).

Daniel 11:38-39

The god of fortresses (11:38): The "god of fortresses" is a metaphorical way of describing the antichrist's unquenchable thirst and quest for power. In other words, power will be the antichrist's god. He won't be satisfied until he attains world dominion. He will use the incredible material wealth at his disposal (gold, silver, precious stones) to build up his military arsenal.

A foreign god (11:39): This "foreign god" is apparently the same god mentioned in verse 38—that is, the god of power and military might, a god foreign to most religious people's thinking.

Those who acknowledge him (11:39): Just as Antiochus Epiphanes did so long ago, the antichrist will reward those who show loyalty to him. He will bestow honors on loyalists and grant them positions in his administration.

Daniel 11:40-43

At the time of the end (11:40): Our text tells us, "The king of the south shall attack him, but the king of the north shall rush upon him like a whirlwind, with chariots and horsemen, and with many ships." Recall that Jesus prophesied of the end times, "You will hear of wars and rumors of wars" (Matthew 24:6). Among the wars that will break out in the tribulation period is one involving two military powers—one from the south and one from the north—who engage in a pincer movement against the antichrist. This attack will apparently take place sometime after the midpoint of the seven-year tribulation period.

He shall come into the glorious land (11:41): The threat of these armies launching an attack will cause the antichrist to return to Palestine, making his headquarters between Jerusalem and the Mediterranean (compare verse 45).

He shall stretch out his hand against the countries...Egypt...Libyans... Cushites (11:42-43): As war continues to unfold, the forces of the antichrist will destroy Egypt, Libya, and Sudan.

Daniel 11:44-45

News from the east and the north (11:44): Sometime following the antichrist's relocation, he is made aware that armies from the east and the north are deploying, getting ready to attack. This infuriates him, for his plans for world dominion seem to be quickly falling apart all around him. He therefore lashes out "with great fury to destroy and devote many to destruction."

Pitch his palatial tents (11:45): The antichrist will relocate to the area between Jerusalem and the Mediterranean (compare Zechariah 12:2-3; 14:2-3; Revelation 19:17-21). Though the antichrist will attempt to position himself in place of Christ reigning from Jerusalem, he will soon come to his end, for only the one true Christ belongs on the throne of David in Jerusalem (2 Samuel 7:12-13).

He shall come to his end (11:45): It would appear that the antichrist meets his end in connection with Israel's conversion to Christ at the end of the tribulation period (Zechariah 12:2–13:1). Scripture reveals that Israel will confess its national sin (Leviticus 26:40-42; Jeremiah 3:11-18; Hosea 5:15) and be saved, thereby fulfilling Paul's prophecy in Romans 11:25-27. In dire threat at Armageddon, as the antichrist's forces are closing in on the Jewish remnant, Israel will plead for their newly found Messiah to return and deliver them (they will "mourn for him, as one mourns for an only child"—Zechariah 12:10; Matthew 23:37-39; see also Isaiah 53:1-9), at which point their deliverance will surely come (see Romans 10:13-14). Israel's leaders will finally realize the reason that the tribulation has fallen on them—perhaps due to the

Holy Spirit's enlightenment of their understanding of Scripture, or the testimony of the 144,000 Jewish evangelists, or perhaps the testimony of the two prophetic witnesses. We are told that at the Lord's second coming, "the beast [antichrist] was captured, and with it the false prophet...These two were thrown alive into the lake of fire that burns with sulfur" (Revelation 19:20).

THE ANTICHRIST		
TOPIC	**DANIEL**	**REVELATION**
Out of the Sea	Daniel 7:3	Revelation 13:1
Ten Horns	Daniel 7:7, 24	Revelation 12:3; 13:1
Blasphemy of the Antichrist	Daniel 11:36	Revelation 13:1, 5; 16:11, 21
War on the Saints	Daniel 7:21	Revelation 11:7; 13:7
Antichrist Overcomes the Saints	Daniel 7:25	Revelation 13:7
The Antichrist's Power	Daniel 8:24	Revelation 17:13, 17
Christ Defeats Antichrist	Daniel 7:25	Revelation 17:14
Antichrist's Power Removed	Daniel 7:26	Revelation 19:20
The Beast Is Judged	Daniel 7:11	Revelation 19:20; 20:10

MAJOR THEMES

1. *Prophecy and the law of double reference.* According to the law of double reference, a prophetic passage of Scripture may seemingly blend two unique events or two persons into one picture. These events or persons may be separated by a significant time period. This means that a single prophecy might have two fulfillments, one dealing with the immediate future and one dealing with the distant future. Many scholars believe this is what we encounter in Daniel 11, where we read of both Antiochus Epiphanes and the future antichrist.

2. *The rise of the antichrist.* The apostle Paul warned of a future "man of lawlessness"—the antichrist (2 Thessalonians 2:3, 8-9). This individual will perform counterfeit signs and wonders and deceive many people during the future tribulation period (2 Thessalonians 2:9-10). The apostle John describes him as "the beast" (Revelation 13:1-10), a satanically energized individual who will rise to prominence during the tribulation period. He will make a peace treaty with Israel (Daniel 9:27). But he will then seek to dominate the world, double-cross the Jews and then seek to destroy them, persecute believers, and set up his own kingdom (Revelation 13). He will glorify himself with arrogant and boastful words (2 Thessalonians 2:4). His assistant, the false prophet, will entice the world to worship him (Revelation 13:11-12). He will force people around the world to receive his mark, without which they cannot buy or sell, giving him control of the global economy (Revelation 13:16-17). The antichrist will eventually rule the whole world (Revelation 13:7) with his headquarters in a revived Roman Empire (Revelation 17:8-9). This beast will be defeated and destroyed by Jesus at His second coming (Revelation 19:11-20).

DIGGING DEEPER WITH CROSS-REFERENCES

The God of gods—Deuteronomy 10:17; Psalm 136:2; Daniel 2:47; 11:36

Challenges to the God of gods—2 Thessalonians 2:3-4; Revelation 13:5-6

Utterly godless—2 Kings 17:34; Job 21:15; Psalms 10:4; 36:1; 52:7; 86:14; Jeremiah 44:10; Romans 1:28-30; 3:11, 18

LIFE LESSONS

1. *Prophetic signs of the times.* No one can know the day or the hour of end-time events (Matthew 24:36; Acts 1:7). Yet in the parable of the fig tree (Matthew 24:33), the Lord Jesus indicated that we can know the general season of His coming. The term "signs of the times" describes specific characteristics and/or conditions that will exist in the end times. When we witness these signs, we can deduce that we are in the season of the end times. For example, Jesus warned of the rise of false Christs, nations rising against nations, famines, earthquakes, an increase in lawlessness,

and more (Matthew 24:4-14). Likewise, in 2 Timothy 3:1-5 the apostle Paul gave this warning:

> In the last days there will come times of difficulty. For people will be lovers of self, lovers of money, proud, arrogant, abusive, disobedient to their parents, ungrateful, unholy, heartless, unappeasable, slanderous, without self-control, brutal, not loving good, treacherous, reckless, swollen with conceit, lovers of pleasure rather than lovers of God, having the appearance of godliness, but denying its power (see also 1 Timothy 4:1).

2. *God is sovereign over all human history.* If there is one thing that biblical prophecy teaches us—and this is emphasized repeatedly in the book of Daniel—it is that God is absolutely sovereign over human affairs. God rules the universe, controls all things, and is Lord over all (see Ephesians 1). All forms of existence are within the scope of His absolute dominion. God asserts, "My counsel shall stand, and I will accomplish all my purpose" (Isaiah 46:10). God assures us, "As I have planned, so shall it be, and as I have purposed, so shall it stand" (Isaiah 14:24). God is also absolutely sovereign over the affairs of individual nations in the world. In the book of Job we read, "He makes nations great, and he destroys them; he enlarges nations, and leads them away" (Job 12:23; see also Daniel 2:20-21).

QUESTIONS FOR REFLECTION AND DISCUSSION

1. What prophetic "signs of the times" indicate that we may be in the season of the Lord's return?

2. With some of the horrible things that go on in the world, do you ever struggle to believe that God is absolutely sovereign? How do you personally reconcile God's sovereignty with the bad things that sometimes happen around the world?

3. Does the teaching of the apostle Paul in Colossians 3:1-2 help you in regard to the evil things that transpire on earth?

DAY 38

PROPHECIES CONCERNING THE TIME OF THE END

DANIEL 12:1-4

SCRIPTURE READING AND INSIGHTS

Begin by reading Daniel 12:1-4 in your favorite Bible. As you read, remember that the Word of God is alive and working in you (Hebrews 4:12).

Yesterday we focused attention on prophecies about the future antichrist during the tribulation period. Now let's zero in on more prophecies of the time of the end. With your Bible still accessible, consider the following insights on the biblical text, verse by verse.

Daniel 12:1

At that time (12:1): This phrase refers to the same time frame as the latter part of Daniel 11—the future seven-year tribulation period.

Michael, the great prince who has charge of your people (12:1): The phrase "your people" refers to Daniel's people, the Jews. Clearly God has assigned Michael the role of "guardian of Israel" during the future tribulation period (compare with Psalm 91:11-12).

Recall from Daniel 10:13 that Michael was one of the angels doing battle with the "prince of the kingdom of Persia," a demonic spirit no doubt seeking to influence Persia's leadership to move against Israel. Even then, Michael was watching out for Israel's interests (see also Revelation 12:7). (See Major Themes.)

There shall be a time of trouble (12:1): This is the tribulation period. The word "tribulation" literally means "to press" (as grapes), "to press together," "to press hard upon," and it refers to times of oppression, affliction, and distress. We learn more about the tribulation period in the New Testament. As a backdrop, the New Testament Greek word (*thlipsis*) is translated variously as "tribulation," "affliction," "anguish," "persecution," "trouble," and "burden." The word has been used in relation to:

- those "hard pressed" by the calamities of war (Matthew 24:21)
- a woman giving birth to a child (John 16:21)
- the afflictions of Christ (Colossians 1:24)
- those pressed by poverty and lack (Philippians 4:14)
- great anxiety and burden of heart (2 Corinthians 2:4)
- a period in the end times that will bring unparalleled tribulation (Revelation 7:14)

It is critical that general tribulation be distinguished from the tribulation period in the end times. All Christians may expect a certain amount of general tribulation in their lives. Jesus Himself said to the disciples, "In the world you will have tribulation" (John 16:33). Paul and Barnabas also warned that "through many tribulations we must enter the kingdom of God" (Acts 14:22).

The following facts demonstrate that such general tribulation is to be distinguished from the tribulation period:

- Scripture refers to a definite period of time at the end of the age (Matthew 24:29-35).
- It will be so severe that no period in history past or future will equal it (Matthew 24:21).
- It will be shortened for the elect's sake (Matthew 24:22). Otherwise, no flesh could survive it.

- It is called the time of Jacob's trouble, for it is a judgment on Messiah-rejecting Israel (Jeremiah 30:7; Daniel 12:1-4).
- The nations will also be judged for their sin and rejection of Christ (Isaiah 26:21; Revelation 6:15-17).
- This tribulation period will last seven years (Daniel 9:24, 27).
- It will be so bad that people will want to hide and even die (Revelation 6:16).

The horror of this period cannot be overstated. This period will be characterized by wrath (Zephaniah 1:15, 18), judgment (Revelation 14:7), indignation (Isaiah 26:20-21), trial (Revelation 3:10), trouble (Jeremiah 30:7), destruction (Joel 1:15), darkness (Amos 5:18), desolation (Daniel 9:27), overturning (Isaiah 24:1-4), and punishment (Isaiah 24:20-21). Simply put, no passage of Scripture alleviates to any degree whatsoever the severity of this time.

PARALLELS

Daniel 12:1—"There shall be a time of trouble, such as never has been since there was a nation till that time."

Revelation 16:18—"There were flashes of lightning, rumblings, peals of thunder, and a great earthquake such as there had never been since man was on the earth."

Scripture reveals that this tribulation will come upon the whole world. Revelation 3:10 describes it as "the hour of trial that is coming on the whole world." Isaiah 24:1 likewise speaks of this tribulation: "Behold, the Lord will empty the earth and make it desolate, and he will twist its surface and scatter its inhabitants." He continues along the same lines in verse 17: "Terror and the pit and the snare are upon you, O inhabitant of the earth!"

At that time your people shall be delivered (12:1): Even in the midst of such dark circumstances, there is yet hope. Indeed, due in no small part to Michael's protective ministry, the Jewish people are told, "Your people shall be delivered, everyone whose name shall be found written in the book." This means a remnant of Jews will survive the tribulation period. "The book" apparently records the names of all the saved (see Revelation 13:8; 17:8; 20:12, 15; 21:27; see also Philippians 4:3).

PARALLELS

Daniel 12:1—The names of God's people are "found written in the book" (book of life).

Revelation 21:27—The new Jerusalem is for "only those who are written in the Lamb's book of life."

It is critically important that this remnant survive, for this remnant will convert to Christ at the end of the tribulation period. The forces of the antichrist will be in the process of moving against this remnant when Israel suddenly experiences a national spiritual awakening (see Joel 2:28-29). In dire threat at Armageddon, Israel will plead for their newly found Messiah to return and deliver them (Zechariah 12:10; Matthew 23:37-39; see also Isaiah 53:1-9), at which point their deliverance will surely come (see Romans 10:13-14). The apostle Paul's prophecy about Israel will then have come to pass (Romans 11:25-27).

Daniel 12:2

Many of those who sleep...shall awake (12:2): Our text adds, "Some to everlasting life, and some to shame and everlasting contempt." This is speaking of the resurrection of believers as well as the resurrection of unbelievers. Many people will die during the tribulation period, but the good news for God's people is that death is not final. Conversely, the bad news for unbelievers is that death is not final. Both groups will be resurrected, but they have different eternal destinies—heaven or hell. (See Life Lessons.)

PARALLELS

Daniel 12:2—"Many of those who sleep in the dust of the earth shall awake, some to everlasting life, and some to shame and everlasting contempt."

Revelation 20:5-6—There is a "first resurrection" (of believers) and a "second resurrection" (of unbelievers).

Note that the reference to "sleep" in this context does not mean that people are unconscious after they die. The believer's soul in the afterlife is fully awake and consciously active in the presence of God (Revelation 6:9-11; see also Philippians 1:21-23; 2 Corinthians 5:8). The unbeliever's soul is fully conscious in a place of great suffering (Luke 16:19-31). The word "sleep" is used only of the body, which takes on the appearance of sleep at death.

Daniel 12:3-4

Those who are wise (12:3): The wise are those who know the true God, see through the antichrist's deception, and turn in faith to Jesus, the divine Messiah. They lead others to the truth. Such individuals metaphorically shine in their witness and their example before others.

Shut up the words and seal the book (12:4): The "time of the end" is the tribulation period. The words of the prophecy were to be kept safe and preserved for future generations—especially for those living during the future tribulation days.

Many shall run to and fro, and knowledge shall increase (12:4): This apparently means that during the tribulation, as people are trying to understand what has come upon the world, Daniel's preserved revelation from God will provide the information they need.

MAJOR THEMES

1. *Michael, the guardian of Israel.* In Daniel 12:1 we read, "At that time shall arise Michael, the great prince who has charge of your people." The phrase "your people" refers to Daniel's people, the Jews. Apparently, Michael has

a special role as the guardian of Israel. Theologian Louis Berkhof, in his *Systematic Theology*, says that in Michael we see a "valiant warrior fighting the battles of Jehovah against the enemies of Israel and against the evil powers in the spirit-world."[1] The question is, does this protective ministry take place throughout human history or just during the tribulation period? Our passage refers only to the tribulation period, for "that time" points back to Daniel 11:36-45, which focuses specifically on the tribulation period. This ministry of Michael will be especially important for Israel during the tribulation period because the antichrist will attempt to destroy the Jews (Revelation 12:17).

2. *The resurrection of Christ—the basis of our resurrection*. There is massive evidence for the resurrection of Jesus Christ, so we can rest assured that we, too, will be resurrected, as promised in Daniel 12:2.

    - The circumstances at the tomb reveal a missing body. And the Roman guards had fled their guard duty—an act that carried the death penalty.
    - The biblical account has Jesus appearing first to a woman, Mary Magdalene (John 20:1, 11-17), an indicator of the authenticity of the resurrection account. In ancient Jewish culture, no one would make up a resurrection account in this way, for a woman's testimony was considered weightless.
    - After the crucifixion, the disciples were fearful and full of doubt. Suddenly they became witness-warriors, willing to die for their claims. Only the resurrection explains the change.
    - Only the resurrection could explain the conversion of hardcore skeptics—including the apostle Paul (Acts 9); James, the half-brother of Jesus (John 7:1-5; Acts 1:14; 1 Corinthians 15:7); and doubting Thomas (John 20:25-28).
    - Only the resurrection of Jesus could explain the exponential growth and survival of the Christian church, especially considering the Roman persecution of Christians.

- There were too many appearances over too many days to too many people for the resurrection to be easily dismissed (Acts 1:3).
- Jesus on one occasion appeared to 500 people at one time. Many of these were still living and could have disputed resurrection claims if Paul had uttered any falsehoods (1 Corinthians 15:6). They did not do this, however, because the resurrection appearances of Christ were well attested.

DIGGING DEEPER WITH CROSS-REFERENCES

God's book of life—Exodus 32:32-33; Psalm 69:28; Luke 10:20; Philippians 4:3; Revelation 3:5; 20:15

Eternal life—Psalm 23:6; John 3:14-16, 36; 4:14; 5:24; 6:51, 54, 58; 10:28; 17:3; Romans 6:23; 2 Corinthians 4:17–5:1; 1 Timothy 6:12; 1 John 5:11-13, 20

Everlasting disgrace and punishment—Matthew 25:41, 46; Hebrews 6:2; Revelation 14:11; 20:10

LIFE LESSONS

1. *The first and second resurrections.* The Scriptures indicate that there are two types of resurrection (Daniel 12:2). The first is appropriately called the "first resurrection" (Revelation 20:5), also called the "resurrection of life" (John 5:29), the "resurrection of the just" (Luke 14:14), and the "better resurrection" (Hebrews 11:35). This is the resurrection of believers. The second resurrection is the last resurrection (Revelation 20:5; see also verses 6, 11-15), and is appropriately called the resurrection of condemnation (John 5:29; see also Daniel 12:2; Acts 24:15). This is the resurrection of the wicked. As noted previously, our resurrection is based on Christ's resurrection from the dead.

2. *Everlasting life versus everlasting contempt.* Daniel 12:2 tells us that "many of those who sleep in the dust of the earth shall awake, some to everlasting life, and some to shame and everlasting contempt." Believers will rise to eternal life in heaven (1 Corinthians 15; 2 Corinthians 5:1-10). Unbelievers will be

raised to eternal punishment in hell (see Matthew 25:46; 2 Thessalonians 1:5-10; Jude 7, 13; Revelation 14:9-11). Notice that the punishment of the wicked in hell is just as enduring as the eternal blessedness of believers in heaven. Both are called "everlasting." In the New Testament, Romans 16:26 refers to the *eternal* God, Hebrews 9:14 refers to the *eternal* Spirit, and Matthew 25:46 uses the same adjective when referring to the *eternal* punishment of the wicked.

QUESTIONS FOR REFLECTION AND DISCUSSION

1. Do you think our present world is nearing the "time of trouble, such as never has been since there was a nation till that time" (Daniel 12:1)?

2. Do you fear death? How does your belief in the resurrection affect your daily mindset on death and dying?

3. Has today's lesson motivated you in any way to pursue righteousness before God?

DAY 39

THE WORDS OF THE PROPHECY ARE SEALED

DANIEL 12:5-13

SCRIPTURE READING AND INSIGHTS

Begin by reading Daniel 12:5-13 in your favorite Bible. As you read, notice how the Word of God is purifying your life (John 17:17-18).

In the previous lesson, we studied prophecies of Israel in the future tribulation period. In today's lesson, we learn more about how Daniel's words of prophecy are sealed until the end times. With your Bible still accessible, consider the following insights on the biblical text, verse by verse.

Daniel 12:5-6

Two others stood (12:5): Daniel beheld two angels on the banks of the Tigris River. The number two is significant, for Scripture reveals that two is the minimum number of witnesses (Deuteronomy 17:6; 19:15) required to confirm the oath that the linen-clad angel (Daniel 10:5) is about to utter.

How long shall it be till the end of these wonders? (12:6): This question is apparently from one of the witnessing angels. The word "wonders" refers to the prophetic events described in Daniel 11:36-45.

PARALLELS

Daniel 12:6—An angel is "clothed in linen."

Revelation 15:6—An angel is "clothed in linen."

Daniel 12:7

The man clothed in linen...swore by him who lives forever (12:7): The linen-clad angel then uttered an oath. He "raised his right hand and his left hand toward heaven and swore by him who lives forever that it would be for a time, times, and half a time."

The raising of the hands indicates that truth is about to be uttered. "Him who lives forever" is a reference to our eternal God (see Deuteronomy 33:27; Psalm 90:2; Isaiah 44:6; 48:12; Revelation 1:8).

The word "time" refers to a year, "times" is two years, and "half a time" is half a year, totaling three and a half years—the second half of the tribulation period. So when the angel asks how long it would be until the prophetic events of Daniel 11:36-45 are completed, the answer is, after the last three and a half years of the tribulation period.

PARALLELS

Daniel 12:7—The second half of the tribulation lasts for "a time, times, and half a time" (three and a half years).

Revelation 12:14—God protects the Jewish remnant for "a time, and times, and half a time."

The angel then clarified, "When the shattering of the power of the holy people comes to an end all these things would be finished." At the very end of the tribulation period, the holy people (Israel) will be shattered as the forces of the antichrist move toward them in the wilderness during Armageddon. They have no chance of surviving the coming onslaught. This causes them to turn in faith to their long-rejected Messiah, Jesus. In dire threat at Armageddon, Israel will plead for their newly found Messiah to return and deliver them (Zechariah 12:10; Matthew 23:37-39; see also Isaiah 53:1-9). Then the second coming occurs, and the divine Messiah delivers them (see Romans 10:13-14). This brings "to an end all these things"—that is, the prophecies for Israel are fulfilled.

Daniel 12:8-10

What shall be the outcome of these things? (12:8): Daniel heard what the angel said but didn't feel he had a firm grasp on things. The word "lord" here does not mean the angel is God. In biblical times, "lord" was often used as a term of respect, much like the modern word "sir."

We might paraphrase Daniel's words to this angel this way: "Sir, I heard what you said. But please clarify for me what God's program for Israel will be following this future tribulation period."

The words are shut up and sealed until the time of the end (12:9): As noted previously in the book, the fact that the words were to be "shut up and sealed until the time of the end" means they were to be kept safe and preserved for future generations—especially for those who may be alive during the future tribulation days.

PARALLELS

Daniel 12:9—"The words are shut up and sealed until the time of the end."

Revelation 10:4; 19:12—"Seal up what the seven thunders have said, and do not write it down."

Many shall purify themselves (12:10): In verses 10 through 13, the angel provided a few final clarifying comments to Daniel. In verse 10, he indicated that many Jews who come to salvation during the tribulation period would have their faith refined by the trials they endure. The apostle Paul, himself a Jew who came to faith in Christ, summarized how trials benefit believers: "We rejoice in our sufferings, knowing that suffering produces endurance, and endurance produces character, and character produces hope, and hope does not put us to shame, because God's love has been poured into our hearts through the Holy Spirit who has been given to us" (Romans 5:3-5).

The wicked shall act wickedly (12:10): Meanwhile, the wicked would continue in their wicked ways. These would continue to ignore God and succumb to following the antichrist's leadership.

Those who are wise shall understand (12:10): These people are wise in the sense that they have insight into God's ways, based on God's Word, and live their lives accordingly, despite their persecution in the tribulation period.

Daniel 12:11-13

From the time...there shall be 1,290 days (12:11): The abomination of desolation will take place at the midpoint of the tribulation period when the antichrist—the "man of lawlessness" (2 Thessalonians 2:3)—sets up an image of himself inside the Jewish temple (Daniel 9:27; Matthew 24:15). This amounts to the antichrist enthroning himself in the place of deity, displaying himself as God (compare Isaiah 14:13-14; Ezekiel 28:2-9). This blasphemous act will utterly desecrate the temple, making it abominable and therefore desolate.

From the time this happens at the midpoint of the tribulation, there would be 1,290 days. The three and a half years of the second half of the tribulation period is actually only 1,260 days. The extra 30 days allow for Christ's judgment of the nations (Matthew 25:31-46) prior to the beginning of the millennial kingdom.

Blessed is he who waits and arrives at the 1,335 days (12:12): The 1,335-day period from the midpoint of the tribulation includes not only the 30 additional days for the judgment of the nations (Matthew 25:31-46) but also an additional 45 days. Many Bible expositors believe that Christ will establish His millennial government during this month and a half. People are "blessed" in reaching this time because they are about to enter into Christ's 1,000-year kingdom on earth.

You shall rest and shall stand in your allotted place (12:13): We might paraphrase the angel's words this way: "Go your way and live in faith for the rest of your earthly life. Following death, your soul will enter heavenly rest. At the appointed time, you will be physically resurrected, with your soul rejoining an eternal resurrection body. You will stand, and you will receive your eternal inheritance."

MAJOR THEMES

1. *The divine timetable*. A witnessing angel asked, "How long shall it be till the end of these wonders?" (Daniel 12:6). It appears that God has a divine

timetable for the fulfillment of prophesied events in human history. A number of phrases found in Daniel testify to this: "Behold, I will make known to you what shall be at the latter end of the indignation, for it refers to the appointed time of the end" (8:19). "The end is yet to be at the time appointed" (11:27). "At the time appointed he shall return and come into the south" (11:29). "Some of the wise shall stumble, so that they may be refined, purified, and made white, until the time of the end, for it still awaits the appointed time" (11:35). God truly is sovereign over all things (see Isaiah 46:10; 1 Corinthians 15:23-28; Ephesians 1:11).

2. *The swearing of oaths.* In our passage, the man clothed in linen "raised his right hand and his left hand toward heaven and swore by him who lives forever" (Daniel 12:7). Some well-meaning Christians have taken a stand against oaths altogether by appealing to the words of Jesus in Matthew 5:33-37. The problem Jesus was addressing in that passage, however, was that oaths had become so common in biblical times that people had started to assume that when you did not take an oath, perhaps you were not being truthful. To counter such an idea, Jesus instructed His followers that they should have no duplicity in their words, that their "yes should be yes" and their "no should be no." In certain contexts, however, oaths are just fine. A number of legitimate oaths are mentioned in the Old Testament (Exodus 20:7; Leviticus 5:1; 19:12; Numbers 30:2-15; Deuteronomy 23:21-23). Some are mentioned in the New Testament as well (Acts 2:30; Hebrews 6:16-18; 7:20-22). Even the apostle Paul said, "I call God to witness..." (2 Corinthians 1:23).

3. *Blessing in biblical prophecy.* Our text tells us, "Blessed is he who waits and arrives at the 1,335 days" (Daniel 12:12), referring to the days just prior to the beginning of Christ's glorious millennial kingdom. Blessing is attached to another prophetic book closely connected to Daniel—the book of Revelation. There we read, "Blessed is the one who reads aloud the words of this prophecy, and blessed are those who hear, and who keep what is written in it, for the time is near" (Revelation 1:3). At the end of Revelation, we are reminded, "Blessed is the one who keeps the words of the prophecy of this book" (Revelation 22:7). Here we see an obvious

connection between obedience to God and blessing. We recall James's instruction that we should not just be hearers of God's Word, but doers of it (James 1:22-25).

DIGGING DEEPER WITH CROSS-REFERENCES

God's eternality (Daniel 12:7)—Psalms 9:7; 41:13; 45:6; 55:19; 90:2; 92:8; 93:2; 102:12, 24; 111:3; 135:13; 145:13; 146:10

Human ignorance in the book of Daniel (Daniel 12:8)—Daniel 2:10, 27; 4:7, 18; 5:8, 15; 12:8

The last days—Genesis 49:1; Isaiah 2:2; Daniel 2:28; 10:14; 12:9; Hosea 3:5; Micah 4:1; John 11:24; Acts 2:17; 1 Timothy 4:1; 2 Timothy 3:1; James 5:3; 2 Peter 3:3; 1 John 2:18

LIFE LESSONS

1. *Resting in heaven.* The angel informs Daniel, "You shall rest" (Daniel 12:13). This refers to resting in death—that is, in the afterlife. Christians in the intermediate state enjoy a sense of serene rest in the presence of Christ. They have no tedious labors to attend to. All is tranquil. The apostle John said, "I heard a voice from heaven saying, 'Write this: Blessed are the dead who die in the Lord from now on.' 'Blessed indeed,' says the Spirit, 'that they may rest from their labors'" (Revelation 14:13). This rest will be comprehensive, including rest from all toil of the body, from all laborious work, from all the diseases and frailties of the body, from all outward sorrows, from all inward troubles, from the temptations and afflictions of Satan, and from all doubts and fears. How blessed will be that rest!

2. *God's holy people.* Daniel 12:7 refers to "the holy people." This verse refers to Israel during the tribulation period, but the truth is that holiness is an important doctrine for all of us. Hebrews 12:14 tells us that without holiness, no one can see God. On our own, we are unfit for God's presence, for we have no intrinsic righteousness. But 2 Corinthians 5:21 tells us, "For our sake he made him to be sin who knew no sin, so that in him we might become the righteousness of God." Because of Jesus, we are made fit for

God's presence, for Christ's righteousness and holiness are imputed to us, just as our sin was imputed to Him at the cross. There has been a great exchange. As the great Reformer Martin Luther said, "Lord Jesus, You are my righteousness; I am Your sin. You have taken upon Yourself what is mine and given me what is Yours. You have become what You were not so that I might become what I was not."

QUESTIONS FOR REFLECTION AND DISCUSSION

1. Are you inquisitive, like Daniel, about when certain end-time events will occur?

2. What reasons can you suggest for avoiding the tendency to predict the dates of end-time events? (See Matthew 24:36; Acts 1:7.)

3. What impacted you most about today's Scripture reading?

DAY 40

IMITATING DANIEL

Here we are on day 40—and what an eye-opening study this has been! As we bring our time here to a close, let's review some of the more important spiritual lessons sprinkled throughout the book of Daniel. I've listed these lessons in the form of resolutions. I hope you'll join me in making these resolutions. Let's resolve to imitate Daniel!

Like Daniel, let's resolve to maintain a holy fear of, or reverence for, the one true God.

After witnessing God's great power in delivering Daniel from the lions' den, King Darius decreed that "people are to tremble and fear before the God of Daniel" (Daniel 6:26). Of course, no one had to tell Daniel and his Hebrew friends that, for they consistently lived their lives in the fear of God and in reverence for Him. This led to their consistent obedience to God even in the face of death.

The theme of fearing God or revering God is found not only in Daniel but throughout the whole of Scripture. Take a few moments to meditate on 1 Samuel 12:14, 24; 2 Chronicles 19:9; Acts 10:35; and 1 Peter 1:17; 2:17.

Fear of the Lord motivates one to be obedient to God (Deuteronomy 5:29; Ecclesiastes 12:13) and serve Him (Deuteronomy 6:13). Fear of the Lord motivates one to avoid evil (Proverbs 3:7; 8:13; 16:6). Fear of the Lord is true wisdom (Job 28:28; Psalm 111:10) and the beginning of knowledge (Proverbs 1:7). God blesses those who fear Him (Psalm 115:13). Fear of the Lord leads to riches, honor, and long life (Proverbs 22:4). God shows mercy to those who fear Him (Luke 1:50). Clearly, it is in our best interest to follow Daniel's example in reverencing God.

Like Daniel, let's resolve to be consistently obedient to God.

Daniel and his Hebrew friends obeyed God regardless of what they faced. When King Darius banned prayer to any god but himself for 30 days, Daniel responded by going home and praying to the one true God, just as he had always done. Daniel simply would not disobey God. For that, he was thrown into the lions' den. God, of course, honored Daniel's obedience by rescuing him from the lions (Daniel 6).

Nebuchadnezzar commanded Daniel's three Hebrew friends to bow down and worship his golden image. But they would not disobey the one true God in this matter. They told the king, "Our God whom we serve is able to deliver us from the burning fiery furnace, and he will deliver us out of your hand, O king. But if not, be it known to you, O king, that we will not serve your gods or worship the golden image that you have set up." God honored their obedience by rescuing them from the fiery furnace (Daniel 3). Daniel and his friends obeyed God no matter what!

As we examine the rest of Scripture, we discover that it is always in our best interest to be obedient to God. After all, such obedience brings…

- blessing (Luke 11:28)
- long life (1 Kings 3:14; John 8:51)
- happiness (Psalm 112:1; 119:56)
- peace (Proverbs 1:33)
- well-being (Jeremiah 7:23; see also Exodus 19:5; Leviticus 26:3-4; Deuteronomy 4:40; 12:28; 28:1; Joshua 1:8; 1 Chronicles 22:13; Isaiah 1:19)

Daniel and his friends enjoyed these realities. So can you and I!

Like Daniel, let's resolve to show our love for God by our obedience to Him.

Closely related to the previous resolution, Daniel makes the critically important point that our love for God is displayed in our obedience to Him. In his prayer to God, Daniel acknowledged that God "keeps covenant and steadfast love with those who love him and keep his commandments" (9:4). This reminds us of Exodus 20:5-6: "I the LORD your God am a jealous God...showing steadfast love to thousands of those who love me and keep my commandments." Deuteronomy 7:9 likewise refers to "the faithful God who keeps covenant and steadfast love with those who love him and keep his commandments." Nehemiah the prophet referred to God as "the great and awesome God who keeps covenant and steadfast love with those who love him and keep his commandments" (Nehemiah 1:5). This Old Testament backdrop sheds light on Jesus' instruction to His followers: "If you love me, you will keep my commandments...Whoever has my commandments and keeps them, he it is who loves me" (John 14:15, 21).

Like Daniel, let's resolve to recognize and respond to God's work of discipline in our lives.

Daniel 1:1-2 tells us, "In the third year of the reign of Jehoiakim king of Judah, Nebuchadnezzar king of Babylon came to Jerusalem and besieged it. And the Lord gave Jehoiakim king of Judah into his hand." God was disciplining Israel for its disobedience.

As this Scripture demonstrates, when those of us who believe don't repent of our sin, God responds by disciplining us. We recall that following David's sin with Bathsheba, the Lord disciplined him for an extended time (Psalm 32:3-5; 51). God also disciplines us when we go astray: "My son, do not regard lightly the discipline of the Lord, nor be weary when reproved by him. For the Lord disciplines the one he loves, and chastises every son whom he receives" (Hebrews 12:5-6). Scripture also reminds us, "If we would examine ourselves, we would not be judged by God in this way" (1 Corinthians 11:31 NLT).

Like Daniel, let's resolve to always walk by faith and not by sight.

Even when things seem at their most hopeless, the God of miracles can come through in ways we would never have fathomed. We've seen this repeatedly in the book of Daniel. Daniel was tossed into a lions' den, which from a human perspective is about as bad as things can get. From a "walking by sight" perspective, death was certain. But Daniel walked by faith and not by sight. God rewarded that faith by rescuing him from the lions (Daniel 6).

The same is true of Daniel's three Hebrew friends. From a human perspective, being thrown into a fiery furnace is unimaginable. From a "walking by sight" perspective, they too had received a death sentence. But they were walking by faith and not by sight. They knew that the unseen God could deliver them from the fire (Daniel 3).

This same truth is illustrated numerous times throughout both the Old and New Testaments. From a human perspective, David stood no chance against the giant Goliath. But the invisible God empowered David to slay the giant (1 Samuel 17). David walked by faith and not by sight. In the New Testament, walking by sight tells us that dead people stay dead, but walking by faith recognizes that God can resurrect people from the dead (see Matthew 9:25; Luke 7:13-15; John 11:43-44; Acts 9:36-42).

Regardless of what we encounter, let's resolve to walk by faith and not by sight (2 Corinthians 5:7). Let's keep our faith strong (Psalms 40:4; 118:8; Proverbs 3:5; Jeremiah 17:7; Matthew 15:28; 21:21-22; Luke 17:5-6; Romans 10:17; 2 Corinthians 5:7; 1 Timothy 1:19; Hebrews 10:35; 11:1; 1 Peter 1:7).

Like Daniel, let's resolve to pray consistently, thankfully, specifically, and urgently.

Daniel 6:10 tells us that Daniel "got down on his knees three times a day and prayed and gave thanks before his God, as he had done previously." Notice that Daniel began his prayers with thanksgiving. We are reminded of Psalm 95:2: "Let us come into his presence with thanksgiving." Psalm 100:4 also comes to mind: "Enter his gates with thanksgiving."

After giving thanks, Daniel brought "petition and plea" before God, making specific requests of God. One is reminded of the apostle Paul's teaching on prayer in Philippians 4:6-7: "Do not be anxious about anything, but in everything by prayer and supplication with thanksgiving let your requests be made known to God. And the peace of God, which surpasses all understanding, will guard your hearts and your minds in Christ Jesus."

Daniel was certainly a believer in intercessory prayer—that is, praying for other people and not only for himself (Daniel 2:17-18). He also believed in confessing sin during prayer when appropriate (Daniel 9:8-15; see also Proverbs 28:13; 1 John 1:9). Still further, we notice that Daniel prayed with a great sense of urgency (Daniel 9:16-19). We are reminded of James 5:16: "The urgent request of a righteous person is very powerful in its effect" (HCSB). The word "urgent" in this verse carries the idea of "earnest" or "heartfelt." Let's resolve to imitate Daniel in his prayer life.

Like Daniel, let's resolve to always be mindful of God's sovereign control over all things.

In the book of Daniel, we repeatedly see that God sovereignly reigns from heaven. God was sovereign over the captivity of Israel, the fiery furnace, the lions' den, the rise and fall of kings and nations, and much more.

God's sovereignty is a theological thread running through the entire Bible, from Genesis to Revelation. God Himself affirmed, "My counsel shall stand, and I will accomplish all my purpose" (Isaiah 46:10). He assures us, "As I have planned, so shall it be, and as I have purposed, so shall it stand" (Isaiah 14:24). The psalmist tells us that "his kingdom rules over all" (Psalm 103:19). Our God is "a great king over all the earth" (Psalm 47:2). First Chronicles 29:12-13 affirms of God, "You rule over all. In your hand are power and might, and in your hand it is to make great and to give strength to all. And now we thank you, our God, and praise your glorious name." You and I, too, should be thankful to God and praise Him for His sovereign oversight of our lives.

Like Daniel, let's resolve to trust that God can restore our lives.

In Daniel 9, Daniel earnestly prayed that his people Israel would be restored to God and to the Promised Land. Daniel sought this with all his heart. In the chapters that follow, God revealed to Daniel that He yet has a future for Israel. God would one day restore Israel.

God restores our individual lives as well. God can restore people spiritually: "The LORD is my shepherd; I shall not want. He makes me lie down in green pastures. He leads me beside still waters. He restores my soul" (Psalm 23:1-3). God can restore the joy of salvation: "Restore to me the joy of your salvation" (Psalm 51:12). God can restore us after we've experienced trials: "After you have suffered a little while, the God of all grace, who has called you to his eternal glory in Christ, will himself restore, confirm, strengthen, and establish you" (1 Peter 5:10; see also Psalm 71:20). Let us always remember, as Daniel did, that our God is a God of restoration.

Like Daniel, let's resolve to maintain a good reputation.

Daniel's stellar reputation began in the first year of his captivity and lasted all the way to his death. His good reputation not only brought him before kings but also brought him great honor and exaltation throughout life. Scripture provides examples of people with good reputations (1 Samuel 2:1-5; 29:3; Psalms 86:2; 87:3; 109:4; Proverbs 22:1; Acts 17:11) and bad reputations (2 Samuel 20:1; Proverbs 24:8; Acts 15:37-38). As Christians, we should always pursue a good reputation (see Proverbs 22:1; Ecclesiastes 7:1).

Like Daniel, let's resolve to always be people of integrity.

Daniel was consistently a man of integrity, and this integrity was evident to all who encountered him. Daniel would have agreed with Paul's words in 2 Corinthians 8:21: "For we aim at what is honorable not only in the Lord's sight but also in the sight of man."

The Bible speaks a great deal about being a person of integrity: "Better is a poor man who walks in his integrity than a rich man who is crooked in his ways" (Proverbs 28:6). "Better is a poor person who walks in his integrity than one who is crooked in speech and is a fool" (Proverbs 19:1). "The integrity of the upright guides them" (Proverbs 11:3). "The righteous who walks in his integrity—blessed are his children after him!" (Proverbs 20:7). Good verses on which to meditate include Psalms 25:21; 26:1; Micah 6:8; Acts 24:16; Titus 2:1-14; Hebrews 13:18; and James 1:22-25.

Like Daniel, let's resolve to walk in humility.

Daniel was a humble man who consistently pointed away from his own abilities and pointed rather to God (Daniel 2:27-28). He had the same humble attitude as John the Baptist, who said of Jesus, "He must increase, but I must decrease" (John 3:30).

The Scriptures tell us that those who want to please God must walk in humility. Not only that, but God exalts the humble: "Humble yourselves before the Lord, and he will exalt you" (James 4:10; see also Proverbs 15:33;

22:4; 29:23; Luke 1:52; 1 Peter 5:5-6). Daniel humbled himself throughout his life, and God consistently exalted him.

Like Daniel, let's resolve to be people of prudence.

Daniel 2:14 tells us that Daniel spoke with prudence and discretion. We should do likewise. The prudent person always looks ahead to see what is coming (Proverbs 14:8) and foresees danger (Proverbs 22:3; 27:12). The prudent person always carefully considers his steps (Proverbs 14:15) and is consistently cautious (Proverbs 14:16). He consistently saves for the future (Proverbs 6:6-11) and consistently guards his mouth and his tongue (Psalm 39:1; Proverbs 21:23). Moreover, he is aware that consulting many counselors is one key to success (Proverbs 15:22). It is always in our best interest to maintain prudence, just as Daniel did.

Like Daniel, let's resolve to live for God now.

Daniel never delayed to live for God. For him, living as a believer was a present-tense proposition. Let's imitate Daniel and resolve not to wait one more minute in totally committing ourselves to God and living for Him. Let's begin now, with no further delay.

Join me. Let's do it.

BRIDGING DANIEL AND REVELATION

Congratulations! You've reached the halfway point of our journey. Having completed *40 Days Through Daniel*, you are now ready to begin *40 Days Through Revelation.*

As you continue, you will notice that each chapter is organized in the same way as *40 Days Through Daniel.* A summary of this structure is provided in the next chapter.

The book of Daniel has provided a solid prophetic foundation for our exploration of Revelation. Let's take a moment to review the critical elements of that foundation.

A REVIVED ROMAN EMPIRE

Daniel 7:7 reveals that a revived Roman Empire will emerge in the last days. This empire, composed of ten nations, each with its own king, will be unified under the rule of the antichrist. However, the empire would not be completely united, for it will experience some internal divisions (2:41).

THE ANTICHRIST WILL RISE TO POWER

The antichrist is prophesied to emerge from obscurity and rise to absolute power over a coalition or empire of ten nations, each ruled by a king (Daniel 7:24). Although the antichrist begins with little influence, he will quickly rise to become the empire's most dominant figure. Initially dismissed as a minor player, he quickly rises to a position of immense authority, quelling the opposition of three kings and securing total control over the alliance.

With exceptional diplomatic skills, the antichrist will win the admiration and support of the global political community, forcing others to follow his lead. His masterful statesmanship would catapult him to international fame and unparalleled power. His authority will remain unchallenged as he reaches the pinnacle of political influence. His dominion will eventually span the globe, reducing all other political leaders to mere pawns under his command.

THE TRIBULATION PERIOD IS THE SEVENTIETH WEEK OF DANIEL

Daniel 12:1 warns of a time of unprecedented trouble: "There shall be a time of trouble, such as never has been since there was a nation till that time." This verse points to the tribulation period, often called the "seventieth week of Daniel" (Daniel 9:24-26). In this context, the term "week" represents seven years, indicating that the tribulation will last seven years. Just as the first 69 "weeks" were centered on Israel, the seventieth week is also primarily centered on Israel, as emphasized in Daniel 9:24: "Seventy weeks are decreed about your [Daniel's] people" (insertion added for clarity).

THE ANTICHRIST'S SIGNING OF A COVENANT WILL BEGIN THE TRIBULATION PERIOD

The final seven-year period, known as the tribulation, will begin when the antichrist signs a seven-year covenant with Israel, as foretold in Daniel 9:27. This event will set in motion a seven-year countdown culminating in the second coming of Christ, which follows the tribulation.

During the first half of the tribulation, the Jewish people will restore the sacrificial system in a newly rebuilt temple. However, three and a half years into this period, the antichrist will abruptly stop these sacrifices (Daniel 9:27). From that point on, he will demand exclusive worship and forbid the worship of any other deity worldwide.

Daniel 9:27 also reveals that the antichrist will desecrate the rebuilt Jewish temple. As described in Daniel 11:31, he will "profane the temple...and shall take away the regular burnt offering" and will "set up the abomination that makes desolate." The New Testament sheds more light on this "abomination of desolation," indicating that the antichrist will set up an image of himself in the temple (Matthew 24:15). This act of self-deification will defile the temple, making it abominable and therefore desolate.

THE ANTICHRIST WILL POSSESS POWERFUL ORATORICAL SKILLS

Daniel 7:8 characterizes the antichrist as having "a mouth speaking great things." Many scholars interpret this as a sign of his exceptional oratorical skills. Throughout history, powerful dictators have often been persuasive speakers, able to rally the masses to their cause. The antichrist, too, will captivate the world with his eloquence.

THE ANTICHRIST WILL SPEAK AGAINST GOD

Daniel 7:25 prophesies that the antichrist will "speak words against the Most High." These blasphemous words will be aimed at tarnishing God's reputation and showing utter disrespect to Him.

This theme is echoed in Daniel 11:36, which affirms that the antichrist will make shocking statements against the God of gods. The Hebrew language used here is rich in meaning. The Amplified Bible renders it as saying that the antichrist "will speak astounding and disgusting things against the God of gods." The Common English Bible puts it, "He will say unbelievable things against the God of gods." The NASB says the antichrist "will speak monstrous things against the God of gods," while the NIV states he "will say unheard-of things against the God of gods."

THE ANTICHRIST WILL PERSECUTE GOD'S PEOPLE

Daniel 7:21 tells us that the antichrist will "make war with the saints." Here, "the saints" likely refers to the Jews living during the tribulation. The antichrist will unleash severe persecution against them and gain the upper hand. As the ultimate adversary of Christ, he naturally opposes the people who brought Christ into the world. Verse 25 says that the antichrist "shall wear out the saints of the Most High." It is no wonder that this tribulation period is also called "a time of distress for Jacob" (or Israel, as described in Jeremiah 30:7).

THE ANTICHRIST WILL DO AS HE WILLS

The antichrist will act according to his own desires (Daniel 11:36). Instead of following God's will, he will be driven entirely by self-interest. Notably, Scripture also reveals that the antichrist will pursue the desires of Satan (2 Thessalonians 2:9). Because Satan is self-centered by nature, it's no surprise that the antichrist will mirror this trait.

THE ANTICHRIST WILL EXALT HIMSELF

Daniel 11:36 says the antichrist "shall exalt himself and magnify himself." We can infer that the antichrist will be influenced by Satan, who, earlier in history, sought to exalt and magnify himself (Isaiah 14:12-17; Ezekiel 28:11-19).

THE SECOND HALF OF THE TRIBULATION WILL BE ESPECIALLY BAD

The Jewish people will suffer greatly under the antichrist during the second half of the tribulation. As Daniel 7:25 states, "They shall be given into his hand for a time, times, and half a time," marking the final three-and-a-half years of the seven-year tribulation. This intense period of tribulation ultimately prepares the way for the Jewish remnant to turn to Christ at the end of the tribulation.

CHRIST WILL SET UP HIS MILLENNIAL KINGDOM

The prophecies in the book of Daniel often focus on the future millennial reign of Christ, a period spanning 1,000 years. Daniel 2:44-45 predicts that God will overthrow every earthly kingdom (including that of the antichrist) and establish His own eternal kingdom: "The God of heaven will set up a kingdom that shall never be destroyed...It shall break in pieces all these kingdoms and bring them to an end, and it shall stand forever."

Daniel 7:14 describes the reign of the Son of Man: "To Him was given dominion and glory and a kingdom, that all peoples, nations, and languages should serve Him; His dominion is an everlasting dominion, which shall not pass away, and His kingdom one that shall not be destroyed." This everlasting kingdom is prophesied to begin immediately after Christ's return.

THERE WILL BE A FUTURE RESURRECTION

The prophecies in the book of Daniel foresee not only the future glorification of Jesus Christ but also the resurrection of humankind: "Many of those who sleep in the dust of the earth shall awake, some to everlasting life, and some to shame and everlasting contempt" (Daniel 12:2). This passage speaks to the resurrection of both believers and nonbelievers. While many will perish during the tribulation, the comforting message for God's people is that death is not the end. But the stark reality for unbelievers is that death is not the end for them either. Both groups will be resurrected, but they will face very different eternal destinies—either heaven or hell.

To sum up—as we now delve into the book of Revelation, be sure to focus on what it reveals about these key prophetic themes found in Daniel:

- the tribulation period, especially its latter half
- the rise, character, and works of the antichrist
- the second coming of Christ
- Christ's triumph over the antichrist and his dark kingdom
- the establishment of the millennial reign of Christ
- the future resurrection of all people

SCRIPTURE INTERPRETS SCRIPTURE

I often remind Bible students that *Scripture interprets Scripture.* No verse stands alone; each one fits into a larger context. That context includes all of Scripture. Professor Bernard Ramm affirmed that "the entire Holy Scripture is the context and guide for understanding the particular passages of Scripture."[1] The interpretation of a particular passage must not contradict the overall teaching of Scripture on any point. Individual verses are not isolated fragments but parts of a whole. Therefore, the exposition of these verses must include setting them in proper relation to the whole and to each other.

In our present study, this means that the exposition of verses found in the book of Daniel must be exhibited in proper relation to similar verses found in the book of Revelation, and vice versa. By following this interpretive policy, we can gain a fuller and more accurate understanding of what is to come.

Practically speaking, this means you should compare what Daniel and Revelation say about the revived Roman Empire, the antichrist, the tribulation period, Jewish persecution, the second coming, the millennial kingdom of Christ, and other prophetic topics.

In addition, it's essential to explore the cross-references between Daniel and Revelation. You're off to a good start if your Bible has good cross-references. If not, I've included some of the most important ones in this book. You might also consider obtaining *The New Treasury of Scripture Knowledge*, which is packed with good cross-references. The 2023 edition I use has a large, easy-to-read typeface that's easy on the eyes.

Here are some of the best cross-references from Daniel and Revelation on a range of prophetic topics. Feel free to refer to this list as you make your way through *40 Days Through Revelation*. They are listed in the order in which they occur in the book of Daniel.

Christ the Conqueror—Daniel 2:34; Revelation 3:21; 5:5; 17:14

God's Reign and Kingdom—Daniel 2:44; Revelation 11:17; 12:10; 19:6

Revelations from God—Daniel 2:47; Revelation 1:1; 4:1; 17:7; 22:6, 16

Idolatry—Daniel 3:7; Revelation 13:4

Jewish Persecution—Daniel 3:8; Revelation 12:13

Divine Deliverance—Daniel 3:24-27; Revelation 12:13-14

Divine Balances—Daniel 5:27; Revelation 6:5

Sudden Destruction—Daniel 5:30; Revelation 18:10, 19

Persecution—Daniel 6:16; Revelation 12:13; 17:6

The Living God—Daniel 6:20, 26; Revelation 7:2

God Shields from Harm—Daniel 6:23; Revelation 7:3; 11:5

Judgment and Retribution—Daniel 6:24; Revelation 20:11-15

Writing Down God's Revelations—Daniel 7:1; Revelation 1:19

Out of the Sea—Daniel 7:3; Revelation 13:1

Ten Horns—Daniel 7:7; Revelation 13:1

Glorious Appearance—Daniel 7:9; Revelation 1:14

Ministry of Angels—Daniel 7:10; Revelation 1:1; 5:11

Beast Judged—Daniel 7:11; Revelation 19:20; 20:10

Second Coming—Daniel 7:13; Revelation 19:11-16

Christ's Dominion—Daniel 7:14; Revelation 11:15

War on the Saints—Daniel 7:21; Revelation 11:7; 13:7

Possessing the Kingdom—Daniel 7:22; Revelation 1:6; 3:21

Ten Horns—Daniel 7:24; Revelation 12:3

Antichrist Overcomes Saints—Daniel 7:25; Revelation 13:7

Christ Defeats Antichrist—Daniel 7:25; Revelation 17:14

Antichrist's Power Removed—Daniel 7:26; Revelation 19:20

Christ's Kingdom Established—Daniel 7:27; Revelation 11:15

Hearing a Voice—Daniel 8:16; Revelation 1:12

Prophetic Revelations—Daniel 8:17; Revelation 1:1; 4:1; 17:7; 22:6, 16

The Antichrist's Power—Daniel 8:24; Revelation 17:13, 17

God Is Righteous and Just—Daniel 9:14; Revelation 15:3; 16:5; 19:2

Face Shining—Daniel 10:6; Revelation 1:16; 10:1

Godly Reverence—Daniel 10:15; Revelation 4:10; 7:11; 11:16

Blasphemy of the Antichrist—Daniel 11:36; Revelation 13:1, 5; 16:11, 21

Time of Trouble—Daniel 12:1; Revelation 16:18

Book of Life—Daniel 12:1; Revelation 3:5; 13:8; 17:8; 20:12; 21:27; 22:19

Resurrection—Daniel 12:2; Revelation 20:12-13

Clothed in Linen—Daniel 12:6; Revelation 15:6

Time, Times, and Half a Time—Daniel 12:7; Revelation 12:14

Knowledge Withheld—Daniel 12:9; Revelation 5:3; 10:4; 19:12

Blessed Ones—Daniel 12:12; Revelation 1:3; 14:13; 19:9; 20:6; 22:7, 14

REMINDER—MAINTAIN THE DISTINCTION BETWEEN ISRAEL AND THE CHURCH

Because Daniel is an Old Testament book and Revelation is a New Testament book, it is natural that Daniel does not address the church as Revelation does. Briefly, the primary concern I want to address is the idea that the church is the "new Israel" and that all the prophetic promises made to Israel in the Old Testament are fulfilled in the New Testament church.

Contrary to such an idea, Israel and the church are always portrayed as distinct in the New Testament. In 1 Corinthians 10:32, the apostle Paul clearly distinguishes between the two. In the book of Acts, "Israel" appears 20 times, while "church" is mentioned 19 times—something that would not be the case if the church were the "new Israel."

Paul assured the Jews that God still had a prophetic plan for them (Romans 9–11). As a Jew himself, Paul was convinced that Israel would ultimately fulfill God's ancient covenant promises. Thus, the church does not replace Israel in fulfilling these prophetic promises. In the study of prophecy, *Israel remains Israel*, and *the church remains the church*. Keep this in mind as you study Revelation.

THE SYMBOLS IN REVELATION

Like the book of Daniel, the book of Revelation is rich with symbolism. Yet, like Daniel, every symbol in Revelation points to a literal reality.

Often, these symbols are defined within the text itself:

- The "seven stars" in Christ's right hand symbolize "the angels of the seven churches" (Revelation 1:20).
- The "seven gold lampstands" stand for "the seven churches" (1:20).
- The "golden bowls full of incense" represent "the prayers of the saints" (5:8).
- "The waters" signify "peoples and multitudes and nations and languages" (17:15).

Each symbol conveys something literal. Additional insight into these symbols can often be found in the book of Revelation or elsewhere in the Bible—especially in the Old Testament. As my Dallas Seminary professor, J. Dwight Pentecost, once advised: If you have six months to study Revelation, devote at least the first month to the Old Testament. Many of the symbols of Revelation are found there.

THE DIVINE MESSIAH

Since prophecy is Christocentric—centered on Jesus Christ—let Him be your focus as you journey through *40 Days Through Revelation*. The book of Daniel lays the foundation by revealing Jesus as the Son of Man who will one day reign (Daniel 7:13-14). Revelation builds on this, offering a deeper exploration of Jesus as the divine Messiah and revealing many other names and titles.

As you study Revelation, I encourage you to pay special attention to these names and titles ascribed to Jesus. These include "the faithful witness," "the firstborn of the dead," "the ruler of kings on earth," "the son of man," "the Lamb," "Faithful and True," "King of kings and Lord of lords," and many more. Each name reveals a facet of His character, so reflect on what you learn about Jesus through these powerful titles.

Lord, I pray that You guide my reader in studying Scripture. Grant each one an understanding of Daniel and Revelation that brings a sense of excitement about the Word of God and motivates them to share these wonderful truths with others. Thank you, Lord, for Your Word.

40 DAYS THROUGH REVELATION

40 DAYS STUDYING REVELATION

Thank you for joining me on this exciting journey through the book of Revelation. You are in for a spiritually uplifting time! My hope and prayer is that as you read *40 Days Through Revelation*, you will attain…

- a thorough understanding of God's sovereignty and control over human history,
- an assurance that God will one day providentially cause good to triumph over evil,
- a yearning for the soon coming of Jesus Christ at the rapture,
- a joyful anticipation of our future in heaven, where we will not only be reunited with Christian loved ones but also dwell face to face with God Himself,
- an exalted view of the true majesty and glory of Jesus Christ,
- a deep appreciation for the wondrous salvation we have in Jesus Christ,
- and an increased conviction of the trustworthiness of the Bible in general and the prophecies in the Bible in particular.

The book of Revelation is the only book in the Bible that promises a special blessing to those who read it and obey its message: "Blessed is the one who reads aloud the words of this prophecy, and blessed are those who hear, and who keep what is written in it, for the time is near" (Revelation 1:3). "Blessed is the one who keeps the words of the prophecy of this book" (Revelation 22:7). So be encouraged. Blessings await you as you study this fascinating prophetic book.

As we begin our journey together, I want to address a few things that will lay a foundation for better understanding the book of Revelation. Let's look at the big picture first, and then we'll zoom in on the details in subsequent chapters.

THE AUTHOR AND RECIPIENTS OF REVELATION

The author of the book of Revelation is the apostle John (see Revelation 1:1, 4, 9; 22:8). This is confirmed by second-century witnesses such as Justin Martyr, Irenaeus, Clement of Alexandria, and Tertullian.

John was imprisoned on the island of Patmos, in the Aegean Sea, for the crime of sharing the message of Jesus Christ (Revelation 1:9). This island is where John received the revelation. The book was apparently written around AD 95.

The original recipients of the book were Christians who lived some 65 years after Jesus had been crucified and resurrected from the dead. Many of these were second-generation Christians, and the challenges they faced were great. Their lives had become increasingly difficult because of Roman hostilities toward Christianity.

The recipients of the book were suffering persecution, and some of them were even being killed (Revelation 2:13). Unfortunately, things were about to get even worse. John therefore wrote this book to give his readers a strong hope that would help them patiently endure amid relentless suffering.

At the time, evil seemed to be prevailing at every level. However, Revelation indicates that evil will one day come to an end. Sin, Satan, and suffering will be forever banished. Believers will no longer know sorrow or death, and fellowship with God will be perpetual and uninterrupted. This was good news for the suffering church in John's day.

A CONTEXTUAL OUTLINE OF REVELATION

John provides a contextual outline of his prophetic book in Revelation 1:19: "Write therefore the things that you have seen, those that are and those that are to take place after this."

- The "things that you have seen" is a reference to Revelation 1, where we find a description of Jesus in His present majestic glory and an introduction to the book of Revelation.
- "Those that are" relates to the then-present circumstances of the seven churches of Asia Minor recorded in Revelation 2–3. John directed his book to these seven churches.
- "Those that are to take place after this" refers to the futuristic prophecies of the tribulation period, the second coming, the millennial kingdom, the great white throne judgment, and the eternal state, which are described in Revelation 4–22.

The book closes by informing God's people that they will enjoy His presence forever in a new heaven and a new earth (Revelation 21:1). Jesus promises, "I am coming soon" (22:20). Such wonderful promises regarding the future empower suffering believers to patiently endure the present.

APPROACHES TO THE BOOK OF REVELATION

Scholars throughout the ages have taken four primary interpretive approaches in studying the book of Revelation.

1. The historicist view. This approach to Revelation holds that the book supplies a prophetic panorama of church history from the first century to the second coming of Christ. This approach emerged in the fourth century when some interpreters saw parallels between current events and biblical prophecy. Later, Joachim of Fiore (AD 1135–1202) developed the approach by dividing history into three ages. The Reformers were attracted to historicism and viewed the pope as the antichrist.

But a comparison of Revelation with other prophetic Scriptures (for example, Daniel 9:25-27; Matthew 24–25, 2 Thessalonians 2:1-12; Titus 2:13-14) reveals that these prophecies point to the future tribulation period, antichrist, second coming, millennial kingdom, great white throne judgment, and eternal state.

2. The idealist view. This view holds that the book of Revelation is primarily a symbolic description of the ongoing battle between God and the devil, between good and evil. However, it is hard to see how the idealist approach to Revelation could bring any genuine comfort to the original recipients of the book, who were undergoing great persecution.

Moreover, this view ignores the specific time markers within the book. For example, it refers to 42 months in Revelation 11:2 and 1,260 days in Revelation 12:6. Furthermore, the many symbols in the book of Revelation point to real people and real events in the future tribulation period—the antichrist, Christ's second coming, Christ's millennial kingdom, the great white throne judgment, and the eternal state.

3. The preterist view. This approach holds that the prophecies of Revelation were fulfilled in AD 70 when Titus and his Roman army overran Jerusalem and destroyed the Jewish temple. So in this scheme, the book of Revelation does not deal with the future.

A primary problem with this view is that Revelation claims to be prophecy (see Revelation 1:3; 22:7, 10, 18-19). Further, multiple events described in Revelation bear no resemblance to the events of AD 70. For example, a third of mankind was not killed, as was predicted in Revelation 9:18.

Moreover, substantive evidence indicates that the book of Revelation was written about AD 95, far after the destruction of Jerusalem. Writing in the second century, Irenaeus declared that Revelation had been written toward the end of the reign of Domitian (AD 81–96). Later writers, such as Clement of Alexandria, Origen, Victorinus, Eusebius, and Jerome affirm the Domitian date. This being the case, the book of Revelation must refer to events that had not yet happened.

4. The futurist view. The futurist approach to interpreting the book of Revelation—the view we will follow in this book—holds that most of the events described in the book will take place in the end times, just prior to the second coming of Jesus Christ. This view honors the book's claim to be prophecy. It also recognizes that just as the Old Testament prophecies of the first coming of Christ were fulfilled literally (more than 100 of them!), so the prophecies of the second coming and the events that will lead up to it will be fulfilled literally.

The early church took a futurist view of the book, seeing the tribulation, second coming, and millennium as yet-future events. Later writers who took a futurist approach included Francisco Ribera (1537–1591) and John Nelson Darby (1800–1882). As we examine specific prophecies throughout Revelation, we will see that a futurist approach makes very good sense.

HOW TO USE THIS BOOK

As you begin each chapter, pray something like this:

> *Lord, I ask You to open my eyes and enhance my understanding so that I can grasp what You want me to learn today* [Psalm 119:18]. *I also ask You to enable me, by Your Spirit, to apply the truths I learn to my daily life, and to be guided moment by moment by Your Word* [Psalm 119:105; 2 Timothy 3:15-17]. *I thank You in Jesus' name. Amen.*

Following this short prayer, read the assigned section of the book of Revelation using your favorite Bible. With your Bible still in hand, you can then go verse by verse through your Bible again, but this time, after reading each verse, also read the appropriate notes in this book.

You'll notice that some of the biblical phrases I comment on are in quote marks and some aren't. Whenever John is speaking, quote marks are not used. Whenever someone else is speaking (such as Jesus or an angel), quotation marks are used.

After the insights on each verse in the passage, I provide four brief summaries:

- *Major Themes.* These topical summaries will help you learn to think theologically as you study the Bible.
- *Digging Deeper with Cross-References.* These will help you discover relevant insights from other books of the Bible.
- *Life Lessons.* This is where you learn to apply what you have read to your daily life. You will find that the book of Revelation will transform you!
- *Questions for Reflection and Discussion.* Use these for your own journaling or for lively group interactions.

> *Lord, by the power of Your Spirit, please enable my reader to understand and apply truth from the book of Revelation. Please excite him or her with Your Word and instill a sense of awe for the person of our Lord Jesus Christ. I thank You in Jesus' name. Amen.*

DAY 1

JOHN'S INTRODUCTORY PROLOGUE

REVELATION 1:1-8

SCRIPTURE READING AND INSIGHTS

Begin by reading Revelation 1:1-8 in your favorite Bible. Read with the anticipation that the Holy Spirit has something important to teach you today (see Psalm 119:105).

In the introduction, we noted the outline of Revelation in 1:19: "Write therefore the things that you have seen, those that are and those that are to take place after this." In this chapter, we will begin to examine "the things that you [John] have seen." With your Bible still accessible, consider the following insights on Revelation 1:1-8, verse by verse.

Revelation 1:1-3

The revelation of Jesus Christ (1:1): The word "revelation" carries the idea of "uncovering" or "revealing." The book of Revelation uncovers and reveals prophetic truth. "Revelation *of* Jesus Christ" can mean either revelation that comes from Christ or revelation that is about Him. Both senses are probably intended in this verse.

Which God gave him (1:1): The Father gave this revelation to Jesus Christ.

> God "reveals deep and hidden things...There is a God in heaven who reveals mysteries" (Daniel 2:22, 28).

Things that must soon take place (1:1): This should not be taken to mean that the events described in Revelation would all take place within a few years of the time John saw them. John recorded Revelation in Greek, and the Greek word translated "soon" can mean "quickly, swiftly, speedily, at a rapid rate" (see Luke 18:8). In Revelation 1:1, the term indicates that when the predicted events first start to occur in the end times, they will then progress rapidly.

He made it known by sending his angel (1:1): God the Father gave this revelation to Jesus Christ, and Christ then communicated it to John using an angel as an intermediary. The specific angel is not mentioned by name, but some speculate that it might be Gabriel, who delivered notable revelations from God to Daniel, Mary, and Zechariah (Daniel 8:16; 9:21-22; Luke 1:18-19, 26-31).

To his servant John (1:1): The angel was an intermediary between Christ and John. Elsewhere in Revelation John receives communications directly from Christ (Revelation 1:10-16), from an elder (7:13), and from a voice in heaven (10:4). John was commissioned to pass this revelation on to the seven churches of Asia Minor (2–3).

Witness (1:2): John faithfully testifies to and vouches for all he witnessed in this divine revelation of Jesus Christ.

Blessed (1:3): The word "blessed" means "spiritually happy." This is the first of seven pronouncements of blessing in the book of Revelation (see 14:13; 16:15; 19:9; 20:6; 22:7, 14).

The one who reads aloud (1:3): Revelation is the only book in the Bible that promises a blessing to the person who reads it aloud and the person who listens to it, responding in obedience. John's contemporaries did not own copies of Scripture. They had to go to church, where they listened to Scripture being read aloud.

Blessed are those who hear, and who keep what is written in it (1:3): Obedience brings blessing. We should not just be hearers of God's Word, but doers of it (James 1:22-25).

For the time is near (1:3): This should not be taken to mean that the events in this book will necessarily happen soon. After all, Scripture elsewhere indicates that there will be enough of a delay in the second coming that some people will begin to wonder if it will ever occur (see Matthew 24:36-39; 2 Peter

3:3-4). "Near" communicates imminence. The next event in God's prophetic calendar—the rapture of the church—could occur at any time.

Revelation 1:4-6

John to the seven churches that are in Asia (1:4): These seven churches were experiencing severe persecution. They were called to shine as lights in the midst of the darkness (see Matthew 5:14-16; Philippians 2:15). Revelation 2–3 reveals that five of these seven churches needed to make some internal corrections. One reason the book of Revelation was written was to encourage and motivate these suffering believers.

Grace to you and peace (1:4): "Grace" refers to God's unmerited favor to those who believe in Jesus. "Peace" refers to the believer's standing and experience in relation to God. It is rooted in Christ's work of salvation on the cross.

From him who is and who was and who is to come (1:4): This is the eternal Father.

Seven spirits (1:4): In the Bible, the number seven is often associated with completion, fulfillment, and perfection (see, for example, Genesis 2:2; Exodus 20:10; Leviticus 14:7; Acts 6:3). The number seven occurs often in the book of Revelation. In addition to the seven spirits, we find seven...

- churches (1:4)
- lampstands (1:12)
- stars (1:16)
- torches before the throne (4:5)
- seals on the scroll (5:1)
- horns and eyes of the Lamb (5:6)
- spirits of God (4:5; 5:6)
- angels and trumpets (8:2)
- thunders (10:3)
- heads of the dragon (12:3)
- heads of the beast (13:1)

- golden bowls (15:7)
- kings (17:10)

Some scholars suggest that the seven spirits are seven angels that are before the throne of God in heaven. Others suggest the seven spirits are the seven angels mentioned in conjunction with the seven churches of Revelation 2–3.

Still others understand the seven spirits to be a metaphorical reference to the Holy Spirit in His fullness. If this is correct, a possible cross-reference is Isaiah 11:2, which speaks of the sevenfold ministry of the Holy Spirit as related to the divine Messiah: "The Spirit of the LORD shall rest upon him, the Spirit of wisdom and understanding, the Spirit of counsel and might, the Spirit of knowledge and the fear of the LORD."

From him who is and who was and who is to come...the seven spirits...Jesus Christ (1:4-5): If the seven spirits represent the Holy Spirit, we witness each person of the Trinity in verses 4-5.

Jesus Christ the faithful witness (1:5): Jesus is a faithful and reliable source of the revelation being communicated to John. John could thus trust what he was being told.

The firstborn of the dead (1:5): This could mean that Christ was the first to be permanently raised from the dead. More likely, however, the term indicates that Christ is the supreme or preeminent One among those who have been or will be raised from the dead (see Psalm 89:27; Colossians 1:15).

The ruler of kings on earth (1:5): Christ is absolutely sovereign. He rules over all. He is the King of kings and Lord of lords (Revelation 19:16). Though Christ is the absolute ruler of the kings of the earth, He will not fully exercise this authority until His second coming, when He sets up His millennial kingdom (Revelation 19–20).

Freed us from our sins (1:5): Jesus saves His people from sin, as His name proclaims. "Jesus" means "Yahweh saves" or "Yahweh is salvation."

Made us a kingdom, priests to his God and Father (1:6): All Christians become a part of God's kingdom and submit to Christ's rule. As priests, Christians have the privilege of entering God's presence and serving Him forever.

To him be glory and dominion forever and ever (1:6): This is the yearning and utterance of praise of Christians of all generations who recognize that our God is an awesome God.

Revelation 1:7

He is coming with the clouds (1:7): Clouds are often used in association with God's visible glory (Exodus 16:10; 40:34-35; 1 Kings 8:10-11; Matthew 17:5). Just as Christ was received by a cloud in His ascension (Acts 1:9), so He will return again in the clouds of heaven (Matthew 24:30; 26:64; Mark 13:26; 14:62; Luke 21:27). Just as Jesus left with this visible manifestation of the glory of God, so He will return at the second coming with the same visible manifestation of the glory of God. (Note that the second coming is different from the rapture. I'll address this when I discuss Revelation 3:10.)

Every eye will see him (1:7): The second coming of Christ may not be an instantaneous event. It may be visible for a full day or more so that as the earth rotates, every eye on earth can witness the coming of Christ with the armies of heaven. Of course, television broadcasts and the Internet will likely play a role.

Even those who pierced him (1:7): This is a reference to Christ's crucifixion (John 19:34) and to the Jews living on the earth at the time of the second coming (see Zechariah 12:10). These Jews will represent those who crucified Christ in the first century (see Acts 2:22-23; 3:14-15).

All tribes of the earth will wail on account of him (1:7): They will wail and mourn for fear of punishment from the divine Messiah, the Judge of humankind (Revelation 20:4; see also Matthew 24:30).

Revelation 1:8

"I am the Alpha and the Omega" (1:8): This is a powerful confirmation of Jesus' divine identity (compare with Revelation 22:13). "Alpha and Omega" is used exclusively of God in the Old Testament (Isaiah 44:6; 48:12-13). The title expresses eternality and omnipotence. Jesus is the all-powerful One of eternity past and eternity future. He is the eternal God who has always existed in the past and who will always exist in the future.

"Who is and who was and who is to come" (1:8): Christ, as God, is an eternal being.

"The Almighty" (1:8): This depicts absolute deity. Christ is supreme and sovereign over all things, including the unfolding of events in the book of Revelation (see Revelation 4:8; 11:17; 15:3; 16:7, 14; 19:15; 21:22).

MAJOR THEMES

1. *God is a revealer.* God takes the initiative in revealing Himself and His will (Hebrews 1:1-2). The ultimate revelation came in the person of Jesus Christ (John 1:18).
2. *God is a Trinity.* The doctrine of the Trinity is based on three lines of evidence:
   - There is only one true God (Isaiah 44:6; 46:9; John 5:44; 17:3; Romans 3:29-30; 16:27; 1 Corinthians 8:4; Galatians 3:20; Ephesians 4:6; 1 Timothy 2:5; James 2:19).
   - Three persons are recognized as God—the Father (1 Peter 1:2), Jesus (John 20:28; Hebrews 1:8), and the Holy Spirit (Acts 5:3-4).
   - There is a three-in-one-ness within the one God (Matthew 28:19; 2 Corinthians 13:14).

DIGGING DEEPER WITH CROSS-REFERENCES

Angels—2 Kings 6:17; Psalm 91:11; Matthew 25:31; Luke 15:7-10; Colossians 1:16; Hebrews 1:14; 13:2

God is Almighty—Genesis 17:1; Psalm 91:1; 2 Corinthians 6:18; see also Matthew 19:26; Mark 10:27

LIFE LESSONS

1. *You can trust the Bible.* The Bible is God's revelation to you. It is God's voice to you. It is God speaking to you (see Psalm 119; 2 Timothy 3:15-17).
2. *Obedience brings blessing.* Obedience to God brings blessing (Luke 11:28), long life (1 Kings 3:14), happiness (Psalms 112:1; 119:56), peace (Proverbs 1:33), and a state of well-being (Jeremiah 7:23; see also Exodus 19:5; Deuteronomy 4:40; 12:28; 28:1-14; Joshua 1:8; 1 Chronicles 22:13; Isaiah 1:19).

QUESTIONS FOR REFLECTION AND DISCUSSION

1. Christ is the Alpha and the Omega. What difference does that make in the way you live your daily life?
2. Christ is coming again. What difference does that make in the way you live your daily life?
3. You have been freed from your sins. Does that motivate you to live for Christ? How?
4. Revelation 1:3 promises that obedient Christians will be blessed. Does this motivate you to obey God's Word? How?

DAY 2

JOHN'S AWESOME VISION

REVELATION 1:9-20

SCRIPTURE READING AND INSIGHTS

Begin by reading Revelation 1:9-20 in your favorite Bible. Read with the anticipation that the Holy Spirit has something important to teach you today (see Psalm 119:105).

In yesterday's reading, Christ was described as the Alpha and the Omega and as the One who is and who was and who is to come. In this chapter we will focus on John's description of the glorified Christ in heaven and on Jesus' intimate familiarity with churches on earth. With your Bible still accessible, consider the following insights on the biblical text, verse by verse.

Revelation 1:9-11

I, John, your brother and partner in the tribulation (1:9): John and his readers were persecuted by Roman authorities for their faith in Christ. Jesus had affirmed, "In the world you will have tribulation" (John 16:33). The apostle Paul taught the same (Acts 14:22).

Patient endurance (1:9): The trials John and his readers faced called for patient endurance amid conflict. The prophecies in the book of Revelation were intended to empower them to patiently endure, for God assured them of victory in the end.

That are in Jesus (1:9): Jesus gives us His strength and peace in the midst of the storm. Recall what He had told His followers: "Peace I leave with you;

my peace I give to you. Not as the world gives do I give to you. Let not your hearts be troubled, neither let them be afraid" (John 14:27).

On the island called Patmos (1:9): Patmos is a mountainous and rocky desert island on the Aegean Sea with an area of about 60 square miles. It lies off the southwest coast of Asia Minor—modern Turkey. People were banished and exiled to this desolate and barren island for crimes committed on the mainland of Rome and were usually forced to engage in hard labor in mines. Patmos was a Roman penal colony.

The testimony of Jesus (1:9): John gave relentless testimony for and about Jesus. This is why he was persecuted by Rome.

I was in the Spirit (1:10): This refers to the state of spiritual ecstasy in which John received a vision containing a revelation from the Lord. The Lord supernaturally "pulled back the veil" so John could see things to come (see Acts 10:10-11).

On the Lord's day (1:10): Some scholars take this as Sunday, the first day of the week, on which Christians gathered to worship and celebrate the Lord's Supper (1 Corinthians 11:20). This may be the case, or John may have been saying, "I was in the Spirit on a Lord-glorifying and Lord-manifesting day."

I heard behind me a loud voice like a trumpet (1:10): John had probably not heard the voice of his beloved Savior for more than 60 years. Now he hears it again, this time "like a trumpet"—loud, majestic, and otherworldly.

"Write what you see in a book" (1:11): "Book" indicates a scroll made of parchment. God often directed people to write down His revelations for future generations (Exodus 24:4; Joshua 24:25-26; 1 Samuel 10:25; Isaiah 8:1).

"Send it to the seven churches" (1:11): These churches are addressed in Revelation 2–3. The order of mention of these seven churches forms a geographical half-moon, beginning with Ephesus, going north to Smyrna and Pergamum, and moving east and south to Thyatira, Sardis, Philadelphia, and Laodicea. John had apparently been like a spiritual father to these churches.

Revelation 1:12-16

I saw seven golden lampstands (1:12): Jesus reveals in Revelation 1:20 that "the seven lampstands are the seven churches"—that is, the ones addressed in Revelation 2–3. The churches are symbolized as lampstands because they bear God's light in a dark world (see Matthew 5:16).

A son of man, clothed with a long robe and with a golden sash around his chest (1:13): "Son of man" is a messianic title derived from Daniel 7:13. It was Jesus' favorite title during His three-year ministry (it occurs 81 times in the Gospels).

Jesus, the Son of Man, is in the midst of the churches—that is, He is intimately acquainted with all that is going on in each of them. Revelation 2:1 tells us that Jesus walks among the churches. The long robe and sash designate Christ as a priest (see Exodus 28:4; Leviticus 16:1-4; Hebrews 2:17).

The hairs of his head were white, like white wool, like snow (1:14): This points to the infinite wisdom and purity of Christ, the divine Messiah. The white hair may also symbolize eternity, much like "Ancient of Days" (Daniel 7:9, 13, 22).

His eyes were like a flame of fire (1:14): This description points not only to Christ's absolute holiness but also to His penetrating scrutiny in seeing all things as they truly are. For example, He accurately diagnoses the strengths and weaknesses of the seven churches in Revelation 2–3. Christ's eyes of scrutiny will also play a key role at the future judgment (see 1 Corinthians 3:13).

His feet were like burnished bronze, refined in a furnace (1:15): The polished brass feet may symbolize divine judgment. Fire consumed sin offerings on the bronze altar. Seen in this light, Christ the divine Judge moves among the seven churches to judge what is right and what is wrong.

His voice was like the roar of many waters (1:15): No one would dare challenge One with such a voice!

In his right hand (1:16): Scripture always portrays the right hand as a place of honor and distinction (see Ephesians 1:20).

He held seven stars (1:16): Revelation 1:20 reveals that the seven stars are the angels of the seven churches. This could indicate that each church has a guardian angel assigned to it. Or "angels" could refer to the pastors of each of the seven churches, because the Greek term for "angel" literally means "messenger" (see Luke 9:52; James 2:25). If this is correct, then the fact that Christ holds the stars in His hand demonstrates Christ's providential control over each church and its leaders.

From his mouth came a sharp two-edged sword (1:16): This is apparently a reference to the Word of God. Ephesians 6:17 refers to "the sword of the Spirit, which is the word of God." Hebrews 4:12 tells us that "the word of God is living and active, sharper than any two-edged sword." Christ stands against His enemies with the sword of His Word (see Revelation 2:16; 19:19-21).

His face was like the sun shining in full strength (1:16): Christ's bright white appearance here is similar to Christ's appearance on the Mount of Transfiguration, where "his face shone like the sun, and his clothes became white as light" (Matthew 17:2). Christ is the God of glory (see John 17:5).

Revelation 1:17-18

I fell at his feet as though dead (1:17): Falling before the Lord was a common response among those who saw the Lord in Bible times (Genesis 17:3; Numbers 16:22; Ezekiel 1:28; Acts 9:4). This too reminds us of the Mount of Transfiguration, where the disciples "fell on their faces and were terrified" (Matthew 17:6).

"Fear not" (1:17): The Lord comforted and reassured John by touching him and speaking to him. Just as Christ had exhorted His followers not to fear during His three-year ministry (Matthew 10:31; Luke 8:50; 12:7, 32), so He encouraged John.

"I am the first and the last" (1:17): The phrase "the first and the last" is used of Almighty God in the Old Testament (Isaiah 44:6). Christ's use of this title here (and Revelation 2:8; 22:13) demonstrates His equality with God.

"The living one" (1:18): Christ was crucified, and then He defeated death by rising from the dead (John 2:19; Revelation 1:5).

"I have the keys of Death and Hades" (1:18): In the New Testament, a key implies authority to open a door and give entrance to a place or realm. Jesus' words here imply that as God, He has the authority to grant entrance and exit from the realms of death and Hades (John 5:21-26; 1 Corinthians 15:54-57; Hebrews 2:14; Revelation 20:12-14). Jesus sovereignly decides who lives, who dies, and when.

Revelation 1:19

"Write therefore…" (1:19): Here we find a three-part outline of the book of Revelation. "The things that you have seen" points to the things John saw and recorded in chapter 1. "Those that are" points to the current state of the seven churches (chapters 2–3). "Those that are to take place after this" points to future events (chapters 4–22).

Revelation 1:20

"As for the mystery" (1:20): A biblical mystery is a truth that cannot be discerned simply by human investigation and that requires special revelation from God. Generally, this word refers to a truth that was unknown to people living in Old Testament times but explained in the New Testament (Matthew 13:17; Colossians 1:26).

"The seven stars...the seven golden lampstands" (1:20): Jesus is apparently referring to the seven pastors of the seven churches.

MAJOR THEMES

1. *Names and titles.* In the ancient world, names and titles were not mere labels as they are today. A name revealed important characteristics about a person. That is why we learn much about Jesus Christ in Revelation 1.

2. *The glory of God and Jesus.* God's glory is the luminous manifestation of His person. Brilliant light consistently accompanies His glory (Matthew 17:2-3; 1 Timothy 6:16). The word "glory" is often linked with verbs of seeing (Exodus 16:7; 33:18; Deuteronomy 5:24; Isaiah 40:5) and appearing (Exodus 16:10).

3. *The kingdom.* Scripture uses the word "kingdom" in two primary senses. Presently, God spiritually rules over His people from heaven (Colossians 1:13; see also 1 Corinthians 4:20). In the future, after His second coming, Christ will reign on earth in the millennium (Revelation 20:1-6; see also Isaiah 65:17–66:24; Jeremiah 32:36-44; Zechariah 14:9-17).

DIGGING DEEPER WITH CROSS-REFERENCES

Fear—Psalms 27:1; 56:11; Proverbs 3:25; Isaiah 51:12; John 14:27; Romans 8:31; 2 Timothy 1:7; 1 John 4:18

Death—Psalms 23:4; 116:15; Ecclesiastes 3:1-2; 7:2; 8:8; Isaiah 25:8; Ezekiel 33:11; Romans 14:8; 1 Corinthians 15:26; Philippians 1:21; Hebrews 9:27; Revelation 21:3-4

Being a witness of Christ—Acts 2:32; 3:15; 4:18-20; 10:39-40; 2 Peter 1:16; 1 John 1:1

LIFE LESSONS

1. *Strength from other Christians.* Each of us is a "brother and partner" for every other Christian (Revelation 1:9). Remember that "a threefold cord is not quickly broken" (Ecclesiastes 4:12). We gain strength from each other, especially during trials.

2. *Trusting God with the future.* We may not know every single detail of what the future holds, but we do know the One who does. Let's trust Him (Psalm 37:5; Proverbs 3:5-6).

3. *A worshipful attitude toward Jesus.* Though Jesus is our Savior and Friend, let's not forget that He is also our glorious and majestic Lord and sovereign God who deserves our utmost reverence (Revelation 1:17; see also Exodus 3:5).

QUESTIONS FOR REFLECTION AND DISCUSSION

1. What evidence do you see in Revelation 1 that Revelation is a Christ-centered book? Be specific. What implications might this have for your own life being Christ-centered?

2. John refers to "patient endurance" in Revelation 1:9. What does James teach us about this (James 1:2-4)?

Day 3

THE CHURCHES AT EPHESUS AND SMYRNA

REVELATION 2:1-11

SCRIPTURE READING AND INSIGHTS

Begin by reading Revelation 2:1-11 in your favorite Bible. As you read, remember that the Word of God is alive and working in you (Hebrews 4:12).

In yesterday's reading, we were introduced to seven churches and their pastors in Asia Minor. John was apparently their general overseer. In today's lesson, we will focus our attention on the strengths and weaknesses of two of these churches—those in Ephesus and Smyrna. With your Bible still accessible, consider the following insights on the biblical text, verse by verse.

Revelation 2:1-3

"To the angel of the church" (2:1): This could be either an angel assigned to protect the church in Ephesus or, more likely, the pastor (literally, "messenger") of the church.

"In Ephesus" (2:1): Ephesus was well known for its temple of the Roman goddess Diana (in Greek, Artemis). Many pagans lived here. During his third missionary tour, the apostle Paul spent about three years in Ephesus building up the church (Acts 19). When he left, Paul's young associate Timothy pastored there for another year (1 Timothy 1:3). Paul later wrote his epistle to the Ephesians while a prisoner in Rome in AD 61.

"'The words of him who holds the seven stars in his right hand'" (2:1): That Christ

holds the stars (apparently the pastors of the churches) in His hand symbolizes His sovereign and providential control over each church and its leaders.

"'Who walks among the seven golden lampstands'" (2:1): Jesus was intimately acquainted with all that was going on in each of the churches. He walks among them, observing what is right and what is wrong in each.

"'I know your works, your toil and your patient endurance'" (2:2): In Revelation 2–3, Jesus reveals that the churches are often in need of correction. Still, He commends them if they have done something commendable.

"'You cannot bear with those who are evil'" (2:2): The believers in Ephesus refused to compromise by participating with pagans, whose immoral acts indicated they had no fear of God.

"'Have tested those who call themselves apostles and are not, and found them to be false'" (2:2): These Ephesian believers tested false apostles against the clear teachings of Scripture (compare with Acts 17:11; 1 Thessalonians 5:21). Decades before Revelation was written, the apostle Paul warned the Ephesian elders that false teachers would seek to lead them astray (Acts 20:28-31; see also 2 Corinthians 11:13). The discerning believers at Ephesus remembered this and rejected the teachings of the false apostles.

"'You are enduring patiently'" (2:3): At the time of the writing of Revelation, the church at Ephesus had patiently remained faithful to the Lord for some 40 years.

"'Bearing up for my name's sake'" (2:3): It was for the sake of the Savior that these Ephesians were willing to suffer. They took up their cross and followed Christ (Matthew 16:24).

"'You have not grown weary'" (2:3): These believers had not given up. Their commitment to Christ kept them unbendingly faithful, even amid great suffering.

Revelation 2:4-5

"'I have this against you'" (2:4): Despite their faithfulness and commitment to sound doctrine, they were still in need of correction.

"'You have abandoned the love you had at first'" (2:4): Thirty years earlier, the church at Ephesus had been commended for the love it had shown to others and to the Lord (Ephesians 1:15-16). Their love had since waned. They needed to renew their love (Matthew 22:37-38; John 14:21, 23; 1 Corinthians 16:22).

"'Remember therefore from where you have fallen'" (2:5): The Greek word translated "remember" literally means "keep on remembering." They were never to forget from where they had fallen.

"'Repent, and do the works you did at first'" (2:5): To repent is to change one's thinking and behavior (Matthew 4:17; Luke 24:47; Acts 3:19). These believers in Ephesus were to change by increasing their love for Christ.

"'If not, I will come to you and remove your lampstand from its place'" (2:5): This may mean that the Lord would remove the church from its place of service and usefulness. Or it may mean that God would bring an end to the church.

Revelation 2:6-7

"'Yet this you have'" (2:6): Despite their lack of love, something was still very much in their favor.

"'You hate the works of the Nicolaitans'" (2:6): The Nicolaitans condoned license in Christian conduct, ate food sacrificed to idols, and engaged in idolatry. Christians at Ephesus were commended for their stand against the Nicolaitans.

"'He who has an ear, let him hear'" (2:7): In Bible times, hearing often implied obedience.

"'What the Spirit says to the churches'" (2:7): Ultimately, the Holy Spirit inspires all Scripture (2 Timothy 3:15-17; 2 Peter 1:21). The Holy Spirit is God (Acts 5:3-4) and the Spirit of truth (John 15:26; 16:13), so this Scripture containing prophecy is trustworthy (John 10:35).

"'The one who conquers'" (2:7): Jesus promised a blessing for conquering or overcoming Christians (Revelation 2:11, 17, 26; 3:5, 12, 21). "Conquering" and "overcoming" are essentially synonyms for "faithfulness" and "obedience." Christians who fail to conquer (those who are unfaithful and disobedient) suffer a loss of rewards but not a loss of salvation (Romans 14:10-12; 1 Corinthians 3:10-15; 2 Corinthians 5:10).

"'Eat of the tree of life'" (2:7): The tree of life is first seen in Eden. It bestows continuing life (Genesis 2:9, 17; 3:1-24). It will appear again in the eternal city of heaven, the new Jerusalem (Revelation 22:2).

"'In the paradise of God'" (2:7): The word "paradise" literally means "garden of pleasure" or "garden of delight." It refers to heaven in 2 Corinthians 12:3.

Revelation 2:8-9

"To the angel of the church" (2:8): This is likely the pastor of the church.

"In Smyrna" (2:8): Smyrna was located about 35 miles north of Ephesus and was a prosperous commercial center. The Roman imperial cult severely persecuted Christians in this city who refused to say, "Caesar is Lord."

"'The first and the last'" (2:8): Christ indicates He is eternal God, who has always existed and who always will.

"'Who died and came to life'" (2:8): Christ was crucified (John 19:17-42) but was gloriously resurrected (Matthew 28:9-10, 16-20; Luke 24:13-43; John 20:11-18, 26-29; 1 Corinthians 15:3-6).

"'I know your tribulation and your poverty'" (2:9): Christ sees everything (Revelation 1:14), so He is aware of all circumstances of all believers (Matthew 11:27; John 2:25; 21:17; Acts 1:24; Hebrews 4:13). He was fully aware of the suffering of the Christians in Smyrna.

"'But you are rich'" (2:9): These believers actually had a large storehouse of eternal riches awaiting them in heaven (see Matthew 6:19-20).

"'The slander of those who say that they are Jews and are not'" (2:9): Because the apostate Jews in this city hated Christ, they also hated all who followed Christ. They slandered Christians, just as the devil does. They were Jews by physical lineage but did not hold to the religion of their Jewish ancestors, such as Abraham. They had become paganized in a pagan culture.

"'Synagogue of Satan'" (2:9): Because these apostate Jews were engaged in false religion, they were instruments of the devil, and the synagogue they attended was in reality a habitat of Satan.

Revelation 2:10-11

"'Do not fear what you are about to suffer'" (2:10): "Do not fear" in Greek is literally "stop having fear." The believers in Smyrna were already experiencing fear. God knows in advance the sufferings His people will encounter (see Genesis 15:13; Acts 9:16). Christ knows in advance the suffering about to be experienced by the Christians in Smyrna. He thus exhorts them not to be fearful.

"'The devil'" (2:10): The devil is a fallen angel who is aligned against God and His purposes. The word "devil" carries the idea of "adversary" (1 Peter 5:8).

"'Is about to throw some of you into prison'" (2:10): It is not stated whether

apostate Jews or pagans will accomplish this. But the devil will be the instigator behind it.

"'That you may be tested'" (2:10): The testing will show where their true loyalty lies.

"'For ten days you will have tribulation'" (2:10): This may refer to ten literal days of particularly intense persecution yet to come, or it may refer to ten short outbreaks of persecution under ten Roman emperors: Nero, Domitian, Trajan, Hadrian, Septimus Severus, Maximin, Decius, Valerian, Aurelian, and Diocletian.

"'Be faithful unto death, and I will give you the crown of life'" (2:10): In the second century, the pastor of the church in Smyrna, Polycarp (a pupil of the apostle John), was burned alive for refusing to worship Caesar.

All believers must face the judgment seat of Christ (Romans 14:8-10; 1 Corinthians 3:1-10; 2 Corinthians 5:10). Believers will either receive or forfeit rewards, such as the crown of life. The crown of life is given to those who persevere under trial and especially to those who suffer to the point of death (James 1:12).

"'He who has an ear, let him hear'" (2:11): Hearing implies obedience to that which was heard.

"'What the Spirit says to the churches'" (2:11): The Holy Spirit is ultimately behind these prophetic revelations (2 Timothy 3:15-17; 2 Peter 1:21).

"'The one who conquers'" (2:11): This refers to faithful and obedient Christians.

"'Will not be hurt by the second death'" (2:11): The "first death" is physical death, the separation of the spirit or soul from the body (as in Genesis 35:18). Virtually all people (except Christians who are raptured) will experience the first death. The second death is for unbelievers only and refers to eternal separation from God in the lake of fire, or eternal hell.

In this figure of speech, a positive idea is emphasized by negating its opposite. For example, "I am not amused" means "I am annoyed." The Lord's point is that faithful believers may eagerly anticipate a wonderful eternal life.

MAJOR THEMES

1. *True apostles.* The apostles were chosen messengers of Christ, handpicked by the Lord or the Holy Spirit (Matthew 10:1-4; Acts 1:26). They were

the special recipients of God's self-revelation (1 Corinthians 2:13). They recognized their special divine authority (1 Corinthians 7:10; 11:23) and were authenticated by miracles (Acts 2:43; 3:3-11; 5:12-16; 9:32-42; 19:11-17).

2. *The resurrection of Christ (Revelation 2:8).* The resurrection of Christ is the foundation stone of the Christian faith. Paul wrote, "If Christ has not been raised, your faith is futile" (1 Corinthians 15:17). Jesus made many appearances to many people over many days to prove that He had been resurrected (see Acts 1:3; 1 Corinthians 15:6).

DIGGING DEEPER WITH CROSS-REFERENCES

Love for God—Matthew 22:37; Mark 12:30; Luke 10:27; John 14:15, 21, 23; 21:15-17; James 2:5; 1 Peter 1:8

Spiritual riches—Matthew 6:19-21; 19:21; Luke 12:13-21; Hebrews 10:34; 11:26; James 2:5; 1 Peter 1:3-4

Satanic persecution—John 8:44; Acts 16:16-18; Revelation 2:10, 13; 12:4, 12

LIFE LESSONS

1. *Take up your cross.* Living as a committed Christian can be costly. As we continue to near the end times, the persecution of Christians will continue to increase. Regardless of what the world throws at us, however, our destiny is secure, and a glorious inheritance awaits us in heaven (Romans 8:18; 1 Peter 1:4). Never hesitate to take up your cross and follow Jesus on a daily basis (Matthew 16:24).

2. *Repentance.* True repentance shows itself in the way one lives. John the Baptist urged Jewish leaders to "bear fruit in keeping with repentance" (Matthew 3:8). People are urged to "repent and turn to God, performing deeds in keeping with their repentance" (Acts 26:20).

QUESTIONS FOR REFLECTION AND DISCUSSION

1. Do you test all religious teachings against the Scriptures, whether you hear them at church, on the radio, or on TV? (Meditate on Acts 17:11 and 1 Thessalonians 5:21.)

2. Is your love for the Lord as fervent as it was when you first became a Christian?

3. Do you pay more attention to building up eternal riches than accumulating material riches?

DAY 4

THE CHURCHES AT PERGAMUM AND THYATIRA

REVELATION 2:12-29

SCRIPTURE READING AND INSIGHTS

Begin by reading Revelation 2:12-29 in your favorite Bible. As you read, remember that the Word of God is alive and working in you (Hebrews 4:12).

In the previous lesson, we studied the messages to the churches in Ephesus and Smyrna. In today's lesson, we focus attention on the strengths and weaknesses of the churches in Pergamum and Thyatira. With your Bible still accessible, consider the following insights on the biblical text, verse by verse.

Revelation 2:12-13

"To the angel of the church" (2:12): This is likely the pastor of the church.

"In Pergamum" (2:12): Pergamum is in northwest Asia Minor. It featured large buildings and a library with more than 200,000 items. At one time, Pergamum was the capital city of the Roman province of Asia.

"'The sharp two-edged sword'" (2:12): This is apparently a reference to the Word of God (see Ephesians 6:17; Hebrews 4:12; Revelation 19:19-21).

"'I know where you dwell, where Satan's throne is'" (2:13): Satan is not omnipresent (only God is), so he can be in only one place at a time. Perhaps at the time Christ spoke these words, Satan was localized in Pergamum.

Pergamum was the official center of emperor worship in Asia. It also featured a temple of Asclepius, a pagan god whose symbol was a serpent (like

Satan—see Genesis 3:1; 2 Corinthians 11:3). A giant altar of Zeus overlooked the city. With this abundance of false religion, it is not surprising that Satan has a throne there.

"'You hold fast my name'" (2:13): Citizens of Pergamum were expected to participate in the civil and pagan religion of emperor worship. Failure to comply was interpreted as disloyalty to the state. The Christians in Pergamum refused to participate.

"'You did not deny my faith even in the days of Antipas my faithful witness, who was killed among you'" (2:13): Antipas—perhaps a church leader—was a faithful defender of the truth who was burned to death inside a brass bull positioned over burning flames.

"'Where Satan dwells'" (2:13): As a bastion of anti-Christian false religion, this area would have made Satan feel right at home.

Revelation 2:14-15

"'I have a few things against you'" (2:14): Despite these believers' commitment to Christ, they were not faultless. Corrective action was required.

"'The teaching of Balaam'" (2:14): In Old Testament times, Balaam was hired by Balak, the king of Moab, to lure the hearts of the Israelites away from the Lord God by having Moabite women seduce Israelite men into intermarriage (Numbers 22–25; 31). The Israelites succumbed to fornication and idolatrous feasts.

"'The teaching of the Nicolaitans'" (2:15): The Nicolaitans were open to license in Christian conduct; they ate food sacrificed to idols, and they engaged in idolatry.

Revelation 2:16-17

"'Therefore repent'" (2:16): Repentance involves a change in one's thinking that yields changed behavior (see Matthew 4:17; Luke 24:47; Acts 3:19). Members of the church were called to repent of their openness to false teachings.

"'I will come to you soon'" (2:16): This is not the second coming, but rather a coming in judgment. These church members would not be permitted to continue in sin.

"'War against them with the sword of my mouth'" (2:16): Antipas had died

by the Roman sword, but some members of this church would encounter Christ's "sword" if they did not repent.

"'He who has an ear, let him hear'" (2:17): Hearing implies obedience to the message.

"'What the Spirit says to the churches'" (2:17): The Holy Spirit inspires all Scripture, including prophetic Scripture (2 Timothy 3:15-17; 2 Peter 1:21).

"'The one who conquers'" (2:17): This describes the Christian who is faithful and obedient. He will be rewarded at the judgment seat of Christ.

"'Hidden manna'" (2:17): Just as manna sustained the Hebrews during the wilderness sojourn (Exodus 16:32-36; Hebrews 9:4), so Christ Himself, the bread of life, sustains believers (see John 6:33, 35, 48, 51). Believers who refused to eat food sacrificed to idols would enjoy a much better banquet in heaven—the hidden manna, Jesus Christ Himself.

"'A white stone'" (2:17): There are several viable interpretations of the significance of the white stone. Winning athletes in biblical times were given white stones that served as admission passes to a winners' celebration. The faithful believer's white stone may point to admittance into the ultimate winners' celebration: eternal life in heaven.

Roman gladiators who became favorites were granted retirement from life-endangering combat. A white stone was given to them to symbolize this retirement. Perhaps believers who are engaged in battle against sin and an ungodly world will be granted "retirement" to heaven, where they enjoy eternal rest (see Revelation 14:13).

Judges in Bible times indicated defendants' innocence by placing a white stone in a vessel. Perhaps the white stone represents the believer's assurance of being acquitted before God (see Romans 8:1).

"'With a new name written on the stone'" (2:17): In the Old Testament, the high priest wore 12 stones on his breastplate that were inscribed with the names of the 12 tribes (God's chosen people). A new name on a stone may point to believers being included in God's chosen people.

Revelation 2:18-19

"To the angel of the church" (2:18): Apparently the pastor of the church.

"In Thyatira" (2:18): Thyatira was located about halfway between Pergamum

and Sardis and had been under Roman rule for centuries. The city was a thriving commercial center. Its primary industries were wool and dye (see Acts 16:14).

"'The Son of God'" (2:18): This is a title of deity. Whenever Jesus claimed to be the Son of God, His Jewish contemporaries fully understood that He was making an unqualified claim to be God (see John 5:18; 19:7).

"'Eyes like a flame of fire'" (2:18): Christ has penetrating scrutiny and sees all things as they truly are—something He will demonstrate at the future judgment (see 1 Corinthians 3:13).

"'Whose feet are like burnished bronze'" (2:18): The polished brass feet may symbolize divine judgment. Fire consumed sin offerings on the bronze altar.

"'I know your works, your love and faith and service and patient endurance'" (2:19): Christ with His eyes "like a flame of fire" (Revelation 1:14) is aware of all the good things that characterize members of this church.

Revelation 2:20-23

"'I have this against you'" (2:20): Despite the love, faith, and patient endurance these believers had, they were nevertheless in need of corrective action.

"'You tolerate that woman Jezebel'" (2:20): This brings to mind the idolatrous queen who enticed Israel to engage in Baal worship (1 Kings 16–19). The evil woman of Revelation 2:20 may have been named Jezebel. Or Jezebel may have been her pseudonym or simply Christ's description of her—a Jezebel-like woman.

"'Seducing my servants to practice sexual immorality'" (2:20): This woman promoted the idea that people could engage in sins of the outer body (such as sexual immorality) without injuring the inner spirit (see Acts 15:19-29).

"'I gave her time to repent'" (2:21): God always provides people with ample time to repent (Genesis 15:16; Isaiah 48:9; Romans 2:4-5). Recall that He gave the Ninevites 40 days to repent, which they did, thus averting judgment (Jonah 3:4; see also Jeremiah 18:7-10).

"'She refuses to repent'" (2:21): Many people harden their hearts against God, refusing to repent (see 2 Kings 17:14; 2 Chronicles 28:22; 33:23; Nehemiah 9:29; Jeremiah 6:15; Daniel 9:13; Luke 16:31; Revelation 9:21). The false prophetess Jezebel was hardened against God.

"'I will throw her onto a sickbed'" (2:22): Notice the irony. This woman promoted sexual immorality, a sin committed on a bed. In judgment, she would be thrown on a sickbed.

"'I will throw into great tribulation'" (2:22): The Greek is literally, "throw into great distress." Severe judgment was imminent.

"'Unless they repent'" (2:22): Only repentance can avert judgment (Jeremiah 18:7-10).

"'I will strike her children dead'" (2:23): These are not literal offspring but rather her followers.

"'I am he who searches mind and heart'" (2:23): Nothing escapes God's (Christ's) notice. He has perfect knowledge of what transpires in every human heart (see Psalm 7:9; Proverbs 24:12).

"'I will give to each of you according to your works'" (2:23): God's (Christ's) judgment is just, commensurate with one's deeds (Matthew 16:27; Romans 2:6; Revelation 20:12).

Revelation 2:24-29

"'The rest of you'" (2:24): Not everyone in the church had been unfaithful to the Lord, and He provides a special word for them.

"'The deep things of Satan'" (2:24): This apparently refers to the seductive false teachings that led to eating food sacrificed to idols and sexual immorality. (Contrast this with the deep things of God—1 Corinthians 2:10.)

"'I do not lay on you any other burden'" (2:24): Christ did not wish to make their already difficult lives any more difficult.

"'Hold fast what you have'" (2:25): Jesus urges these faithful believers not to give up in resisting evil.

"'Until I come'" (2:25): Believers are to remain faithful until Christ's second coming, at which time He will reward all of them for their faithfulness (Revelation 3:3; 16:15; 22:7, 17, 20).

"'The one who conquers'" (2:26): The Christian who is faithful and obedient.

"'Who keeps my works until the end'" (2:26): God's people are to perpetually remain faithful.

"'I will give authority over the nations'" (2:26): Faithful believers will reign with Christ during His future millennial kingdom (Revelation 20:6; see also

1 Corinthians 6:2-3; 2 Timothy 2:12; Revelation 3:21). Believers who do not remain faithful apparently forfeit participation in this reign.

"'He will rule them with a rod of iron'" (2:27): Christ will rule in the millennial kingdom with unbending and relentless righteousness, justice, and equity (see Psalm 2:9).

"'Even as I myself have received authority from my Father'" (2:27): Christ received His authority from His Father (see John 5:22). Faithful believers will have authority under Christ.

"'I will give him the morning star'" (2:28): Christ Himself is the morning star (see Revelation 22:16). Though the morning star has already dawned in the hearts of believers (2 Peter 1:19), they will one day encounter Him directly and in fullness.

"'He who has an ear, let him hear'" (2:29): Hearing implies obedience to the message.

"'What the Spirit says'" (2:29): The Holy Spirit inspires all Scripture, including prophetic Scripture (2 Timothy 3:15-17; 2 Peter 1:21).

MAJOR THEMES

1. *Satan.* Satan is called the ruler of this world (John 12:31) and the god of this world (2 Corinthians 4:4). He deceives the whole world (Revelation 12:9; 20:3). He has power in government (Matthew 4:8-9), health (Luke 13:11, 16; Acts 10:38), spiritual forces (Jude 9; Ephesians 6:11-12), and religion (Revelation 2:9; 3:9).

2. *God doesn't want people to perish.* God typically delays judgment to give people time to repent and thus not perish. Second Peter 3:9 affirms, "The Lord is not slow to fulfill his promise as some count slowness, but is patient toward you, not wishing that any should perish, but that all should reach repentance."

DIGGING DEEPER WITH CROSS-REFERENCES

Martyrdom—Matthew 10:39; 16:25; 24:9; Mark 13:12; Luke 9:24; Revelation 6:9; 11:7; 16:6

Spiritual adultery—Hosea 3:1; Matthew 12:39; 16:4; James 4:4; 1 John 2:15-16

Importance of correct doctrine—Romans 16:17; Ephesians 4:14; 1 Timothy 1:10; 4:1; 6:3; 2 Timothy 4:3-4; Titus 1:9; 2:1

LIFE LESSONS

1. *A failure to repent brings discipline.* A failure to repent of sin always brings God's discipline to believers (Psalms 32:3-5; 51; Hebrews 12:5-11). Developing a lifestyle of repentance before God therefore makes good sense. First Corinthians 11:31 affirms, "If we judged ourselves truly, we would not be judged."

2. *Avoid sexual immorality.* Christians are commanded to abstain from fornication (Acts 15:20). People should flee fornication (1 Corinthians 6:13, 18). Fornication should not be named among Christians (Ephesians 5:3).

QUESTIONS FOR REFLECTION AND DISCUSSION

1. Is sexual purity a high priority in your life?

2. A failure to repent of sin can bring discipline from God. It is therefore wise to periodically examine yourself. Reflect for a few moments and consider whether there might be any sin in your life, and experience the freeing power of repentance.

3. Does false doctrine bother you? Do you ever feel tempted to turn a blind eye toward false doctrine in order to avoid conflict with others?

DAY 5

THE CHURCHES AT SARDIS AND PHILADELPHIA

REVELATION 3:1-13

SCRIPTURE READING AND INSIGHTS

Begin by reading Revelation 3:1-13 in your favorite Bible. As you read, remember that those who hear and obey the Word of God are truly blessed (Psalm 119:2; Luke 11:28; Revelation 1:3).

In yesterday's reading, we studied Jesus' message to the churches in Pergamum and Thyatira. In today's lesson, we focus attention on the strengths and weaknesses of the churches in Sardis and Philadelphia. With your Bible still accessible, consider the following insights on the biblical text, verse by verse.

Revelation 3:1

"To the angel of the church" (3:1): Apparently the pastor of the church.

"In Sardis" (3:1): Sardis is located about 30 miles southeast of Thyatira, at the foot of Mount Tmolus, on the river Pactolus. The primary business of this industrial city was harvesting wool, dyeing it, and making garments from it. This city featured extensive pagan worship.

"'The words of him who has the seven spirits of God'" (3:1): The seven spirits are apparently a metaphorical reference to the Holy Spirit in His fullness (seven is a number of completeness or fullness). Perhaps the Holy Spirit is mentioned because the Holy Spirit is the One who can bring new life to this lifeless church (see Galatians 5:22-23).

"'And the seven stars'" *(3:1)*: The seven stars are "the angels of the seven churches" (see Revelation 1:20). This likely refers to the pastors of the seven churches.

"'I know your works'" *(3:1)*: Christ, who has eyes "like a flame of fire" (Revelation 1:14), knows all the works of church members in Sardis.

"'You have the reputation of being alive, but you are dead'" *(3:1)*: This church had no spiritual vitality even though it still had a few genuine believers (verse 4). The church members were similar to the Pharisees: Outwardly they appeared spiritual, but they were actually spiritually dead (Matthew 23:27-28).

Revelation 3:2-3

"'Wake up, and strengthen what remains and is about to die'" *(3:2)*: Church members needed to awaken from their spiritual slumber and fan into a flame their dying embers of spiritual commitment (see Romans 13:11).

"'I have not found your works complete in the sight of my God'" *(3:2)*: The works of these believers fell short of what God required of them.

"'Remember, then, what you received and heard'" *(3:3)*: "Remember" is literally "keep in mind." They were to keep in mind their rich spiritual heritage and return to the attitudes and activities their teachers had taught them earlier.

"'Keep it, and repent'" *(3:3)*: Repentance involves a change in thinking with a subsequent change in behavior (see Matthew 4:17; Luke 24:47; Acts 3:19). Christ required immediate repentance.

> "Break off your sins by practicing righteousness" (Daniel 4:27).

"'If you will not wake up, I will come like a thief, and you will not know at what hour I will come against you'" *(3:3)*: If church members failed to rectify things, Christ would bring swift judgment at a time when they would least expect it.

Revelation 3:4-6

"'Yet you have still a few names in Sardis, people who have not soiled their garments'" *(3:4)*: Garments in the Bible often metaphorically refer to a person's

character. Soiled garments indicate a polluted character. This verse thus indicates that some people in the church had remained spiritually unstained (see Jude 23).

"'They will walk with me in white, for they are worthy'" (3:4): The redeemed will be dressed in white (Revelation 6:11; 7:9, 13; 19:8, 14), indicating their imputed righteousness and purity.

"'Will be clothed thus in white garments'" (3:5): This promise would have been especially meaningful to people who lived in a city where woolen garments were manufactured.

"'I will never blot his name out of the book of life'" (3:5): The book of life is a heavenly record of the names of the redeemed who will inherit heaven (Revelation 3:5; 13:8; 17:8; 20:12, 15; 21:27; see also Luke 10:20; Philippians 4:3). Believers will not have their names blotted out. This is a Hebrew literary device in which a positive truth is taught by negating its opposite.

"'I will confess his name before my Father and before his angels'" (3:5): In the Gospels Christ promised, "Everyone who acknowledges me before men, I also will acknowledge before my Father who is in heaven" (Matthew 10:32).

"'He who has an ear, let him hear what the Spirit says'" (3:6): Believers must hear and obey this prophetic Scripture inspired by the Holy Spirit (2 Timothy 3:15-17; 2 Peter 1:21).

Revelation 3:7-8

"To the angel of the church" (3:7): Apparently the pastor of the church.

"In Philadelphia" (3:7): Philadelphia was a city in Lydia, located in western Asia Minor, about 28 miles from Sardis. Its major industry was wine. Its chief deity was the god of wine, Dionysus.

"'The words of the holy one'" (3:7): Only God is holy (Isaiah 6:3), and Jesus is "the holy one" (compare Mark 1:24; Luke 4:34; John 6:69), so Jesus is here portrayed as God.

"'The true one'" (3:7): Jesus is also called true. Unlike the false gods of paganism, Jesus was genuinely God.

"'Who has the key of David'" (3:7): The key of David represents the authority to open and shut the door that leads to the Davidic kingdom—Christ's future millennial kingdom (see Isaiah 22:22; Matthew 1:1).

"'Who opens and no one will shut, who shuts and no one opens'" (3:7): An open door is an opportunity for ministry (see Acts 14:27; 1 Corinthians 16:9; 2 Corinthians 2:12; Colossians 4:3).

"'I know your works'" (3:8): Christ, who has eyes "like a flame of fire" (Revelation 1:14), knows all the works of church members in Philadelphia.

"'I have set before you an open door, which no one is able to shut'" (3:8): Jesus sovereignly gave the church in Philadelphia an opportunity to serve in ministry, and no one can thwart this opportunity (see Acts 16:6-10).

"'I know that you have but little power'" (3:8): God's strength is more than able to make up for human weakness (see 2 Corinthians 12:9).

"'You have kept my word and have not denied my name'" (3:8): The Jews who rejected Jesus Christ probably tried to force church members to deny Christ's name. But these believers stood firm.

Revelation 3:9-11

"'I will make those of the synagogue of Satan who say that they are Jews and are not, but lie'" (3:9): These were Jews by lineage, descendants of Abraham. Having rejected Jesus Christ (see John 8:31-59), however, they became tools of Satan.

"'I will make them come and bow down before your feet'" (3:9): Eventually these Jewish antagonists would be forced to admit their error. This may take place at the great white throne judgment (Revelation 20:11-15).

"'They will learn that I have loved you'" (3:9): Contrary to Jewish exclusivism, everyone will see that God has loved these Gentile believers who were faithful to Jesus.

"'You have kept my word about patient endurance'" (3:10): Church members kept Christ's word—that is, they were obedient to it and patiently endured all the trials and persecutions they encountered.

"'I will keep you from the hour of trial that is coming on the whole world, to try those who dwell on the earth'" (3:10): Many Bible expositors believe this verse looks beyond Philadelphia and is a promise to deliver the entire church from the tribulation period by means of the rapture. Notice the definite article—"*the* hour." The church would be kept from the actual hour of testing, not just the testing itself.

The Greek preposition (*ek*) translated "from" carries the idea of separation from something. Believers will be kept *from* the hour of testing in the sense that they will be completely separated from it by being raptured before the period even begins. This makes sense because the church is not appointed to wrath (Romans 5:9; 1 Thessalonians 1:9-10; 5:9).

"'I am coming soon'" (3:11): We do not know when this will occur, so we must always be ready, living in righteousness and purity (Titus 2:13-14).

"'Hold fast what you have'" (3:11): Christ encouraged the believers to stand strong and not to give up or weaken in their resolve.

"'So that no one may seize your crown'" (3:11): The rewards Christians will receive from Jesus at the judgment seat of Christ are often described as crowns (1 Corinthians 9:25; 2 Timothy 4:8; James 1:12; 1 Peter 5:4). Christ exhorts these believers not to act in such a way as to forfeit their reward at the judgment seat of Christ.

Revelation 3:12-13

"'The one who conquers'" (3:12): Christians conquer by being faithful and obedient.

"'I will make him a pillar in the temple of my God'" (3:12): Magistrates were honored in Philadelphia by having a pillar placed in a temple in their name. Jesus indicated that faithful believers would be honored (see Revelation 21:22).

"'Never shall he go out of it'" (3:12): In contrast to earthly temples, in which pillars eventually decay and fall over, believers will continue forever in the temple in heaven—the new Jerusalem.

"'I will write on him the name of my God'" (3:12): In Bible times, imprinting a name indicated ownership. God writes His name on Christians to show that they belong to Him, they are His redeemed property, and they are in His eternal family.

"'The name of the city of my God, the new Jerusalem'" (3:12): The new Jerusalem is the heavenly city in which the saints of all ages will eternally dwell (see John 14:1-3; Hebrews 11:10).

"'Which comes down from my God out of heaven'" (3:12): After God creates the new heavens and new earth, the new Jerusalem—the eternal city where

believers will dwell forever—will come down out of heaven and rest on the renewed earth (see Revelation 21:2, 10).

"'My own new name'" (3:12): A person's name in the Bible often points to his or her character, so Christ's new name may indicate that believers in heaven will have the opportunity to behold the full wonder of Christ's glorious character.

"'He who has an ear, let him hear what the Spirit says to the churches'" (3:13): Believers must hear and obey this prophetic Scripture inspired by the Holy Spirit (2 Timothy 3:15-17; 2 Peter 1:21).

MAJOR THEMES

1. *The rapture (Revelation 3:10).* The rapture is that glorious event in which the dead in Christ will be resurrected, living Christians will be instantly translated into their glorified bodies, and both groups will be caught up to meet Christ in the air and taken back to heaven (John 14:1-3; 1 Corinthians 15:51-54; 1 Thessalonians 4:13-17).

2. *Character and clothing.* Scripture often relates character to clothing (as in Revelation 3:4). For example, 1 Peter 5:5 exhorts, "Clothe yourselves, all of you, with humility toward one another." Colossians 3:12 exhorts, "Put on…compassionate hearts, kindness, humility, meekness, and patience" (see also Romans 13:14).

DIGGING DEEPER WITH CROSS-REFERENCES

The rapture—John 14:1-3; Romans 8:19; 1 Corinthians 1:7-8; 15:51-53; 16:22; Philippians 3:20-21; 4:5; Colossians 3:4; 1 Thessalonians 1:10; 2:19; 4:13-18; 5:9, 23; 2 Thessalonians 2:1, 3; 1 Timothy 6:14; 2 Timothy 4:1, 8; Titus 2:13; Hebrews 9:28; James 5:7-9; 1 Peter 1:7, 13; 5:4; 1 John 2:28–3:2; Jude 21

The second coming—Daniel 7:9-14; 12:1-3; Zechariah 12:10; 14:1-15; Matthew 13:41; 24:15-31; 26:64; Mark 13:14-27; 14:62; Luke 21:25-28; Acts 1:9-11; 3:19-21; 1 Thessalonians 3:13; 2 Thessalonians 1:6-10; 2:8; 1 Peter 4:12-13; 2 Peter 3:1-14; Jude 14-15; Revelation 1:7; 19:11–20:6; 22:7, 12, 20

LIFE LESSONS

1. *The imminence of the rapture.* "Imminent" literally means "ready to take place" or "impending." The rapture is imminent—that is, no more prophecies must be fulfilled before the rapture can occur (1 Corinthians 1:7; 16:22; Philippians 3:20; 4:5; 1 Thessalonians 1:10; Titus 2:13; Hebrews 9:28; James 5:7-9; 1 Peter 1:13; Jude 21). This reality ought to motivate us to live in purity (Romans 13:11-14; 2 Peter 3:10-14; 1 John 3:2-3).

2. *Avoid hypocrisy.* Hypocrisy is the pretense of having a virtuous character, religious beliefs, or moral principles that one does not really possess (see Revelation 3:1). Jesus spoke sternly against the religious hypocrisy of His day (Matthew 23:28; Mark 12:15; Luke 12:1).

QUESTIONS FOR REFLECTION AND DISCUSSION

1. Is there any discrepancy between who you are on the inside and how you appear to others externally (Revelation 3:1)?

2. Does the fact that you will one day appear before the judgment seat of Christ motivate you in your spiritual life?

3. Just as Christ knows all that goes on in the churches, so He knows all that goes on in each of our lives. Does that reality please you or scare you? Why?

DAY 6

THE CHURCH AT LAODICEA

REVELATION 3:14-22

SCRIPTURE READING AND INSIGHTS

Begin by reading Revelation 3:14-22 in your favorite Bible. As you read, remember that those who hear and obey the Word of God are truly blessed (Psalm 119:2; Luke 11:28; Revelation 1:3).

In yesterday's lesson, we looked at the letters to the churches in Sardis and Philadelphia. In today's lesson, we focus our attention on the strengths and weaknesses of the church in Laodicea. With your Bible still accessible, consider the following insights on the biblical text, verse by verse.

Revelation 3:14

"To the angel of the church" (3:14): Apparently the pastor of the church.

"In Laodicea" (3:14): Laodicea was a wealthy and commercially successful city that was east of Ephesus, west of Colossae. It had three primary industries: banking, wool, and medicine. Because of an inadequate water supply in the city, an underground aqueduct was built that carried water from hot springs into the city.

"'The words of the Amen'" (3:14): Isaiah 65:16 refers to "the God of truth," which in Hebrew is "the God of amen." This was a title of God in the Old Testament. The title is applied to Jesus here, for Christ is the God of truth. He is now about to tell the truth about the condition of the church of Laodicea. Honesty is the first step in correcting a problem.

"'The faithful and true witness'" (3:14): He is the reliable source of the revelation being communicated to John (see John 14:6). John could thus trust what he was being told.

"'The beginning of God's creation'" (3:14): The Greek word *arche* has a wide range of meanings. Here it is translated "beginning," but the word also carries the important meaning of "one who begins," "origin," "source," "creator," or "first cause." This is the intended meaning of the word in this verse. Jesus is the Creator, the first cause of creation. The English word "architect" is derived from *arche*. We might say that Jesus is the architect of all creation (see John 1:3; Colossians 1:16; Hebrews 1:2).

Greek scholars note that another possible meaning of *arche* is "ruler" or "magistrate." They observe that when *arche* is used of a person in Scripture, it is almost always used of a ruler (see Romans 8:38; Ephesians 3:10; Colossians 2:15). The English word "archbishop" is related to this sense of the Greek word *arche*. An archbishop is one who is in authority over other bishops. If "ruler" is the correct meaning for *arche* in Revelation 3:14, then it means that Christ has authority over all creation.

It may be that in the case of Christ, both senses are intended. Scripture portrays Christ as both the Creator (Hebrews 1:2) and Ruler (Revelation 19:16) of all things.

Revelation 3:15-17

"'I know your works'" (3:15): Christ has eyes "like a flame of fire" (Revelation 1:14). He sees all. Nothing escapes His all-knowing gaze. He knows all the works of church members at Laodicea.

"'You are neither cold nor hot. Would that you were either cold or hot!'" (3:15): This is an allusion to the underground aqueduct, in which water became lukewarm in transit to Laodicea. This contrasted with the hot springs in nearby Hieropolis and the pure, cold water in nearby Colossae.

Just as a resident of Laodicea recognized that the water that was piped in was neither cold nor hot, so Christ recognized that church members were neither cold nor hot. The church at Laodicea was not spiritually dead, but neither was it filled with spiritual zeal. Church members were neutral and even compromising. This needed to be rectified.

"'Because you are lukewarm, and neither hot nor cold, I will spit you out of my mouth'" (3:16): Just as a person might be tempted to spit out the dirty, tepid water of Laodicea, so Christ wanted to spit out lukewarm church members. A neutral or compromising attitude of church members was unacceptable to the Lord. He calls for complete obedience and commitment. Partial obedience will not suffice. Spitting out is apparently a graphic metaphor representing divine discipline.

"'You say, I am rich, I have prospered, and I need nothing'" (3:17): The three primary industries of the city—gold, clothing, and eye salve—made this a wealthy city. The residents had nice homes, nice clothes, and plenty of affluence. This outward wealth led the church to a state of spiritual complacency.

"'Not realizing that you are wretched, pitiable, poor, blind, and naked'" (3:17): Church members were so enamored with material things that they were blind to their true condition. Words like "wretched" and "pitiable" paint a horrible picture of the spiritual state of this church.

Revelation 3:18-20

"'Buy from me gold refined by fire...white garments...salve'" (3:18): The Lord alludes to the city's three main sources of income: banking, the production of wool cloth, and medicine. Jesus draws a powerful contrast in terms they understand. The Laodiceans' gold blinded them to their spiritual poverty. Their expensive garments hid their spiritual nakedness. They produced eye salve but were unaware of their spiritual blindness. Christ calls the church to repentance.

"'Those whom I love'" (3:19): Despite the fact that these believers have some staggering problems to rectify—problems that were offensive to Christ—Christ nevertheless affirms His relentless love for them.

"'I reprove and discipline'" (3:19): If the children of God sin and refuse to repent, God brings discipline (sometimes very severe) into their lives to bring them to repentance (Proverbs 3:11-12; Hebrews 12:4-11). Christians will respond either to God's light or to His heat.

"'Be zealous and repent'" (3:19): "Be zealous" is a present imperative in the Greek. The imperative indicates that this is a command and not a mere option. The present tense indicates that the action is to be ongoing and

perpetual. We might paraphrase this, "Keep on being zealous, moment by moment, day by day."

"Repent" is more literally from the Greek, "repent at once." The word "repent" means to change one's thinking with a subsequent change in behavior (see Matthew 4:17; Luke 24:47; Acts 3:19). These church members needed to immediately turn from their wrong thinking and behavior.

"'I stand at the door and knock'" (3:20): Sometimes this verse is applied to evangelism. The idea is that Christ is knocking at the door of the unbeliever's heart and wants to come in. In context, however, these words were directed at a church, not unbelievers. Amazingly, Christ had to speak these words to a church because it was excluding Him. Christ reveals to them that He seeks intimate fellowship with them, and He takes the initiative by knocking at their hearts.

"'If anyone hears my voice and opens the door'" (3:20): Notice that the Lord here speaks not to the church as a whole but rather to the individual. If more individuals develop a close relationship with Christ, the entire church will benefit.

Revelation 3:21-22

"'The one who conquers'" (3:21): This refers to a Christian who is faithful and obedient.

"'I will grant him to sit with me on my throne'" (3:21): Scripture promises that Christ will gloriously reign from the Davidic throne (2 Samuel 7:12-13). But Scripture also promises that the saints will reign with Christ. In 2 Timothy 2:12, for example, the apostle Paul explains, "If we endure, we will also reign with him." Those who faithfully endure trials will one day rule with Christ in His future kingdom.

This presents an interesting parallel between Jesus Christ and Christians. Christ Himself endured and will one day reign (1 Corinthians 15:25). In the same way—though obviously to a much lesser degree, and under the lordship of Christ—believers must endure and will one day reign with Him.

The idea of reigning with Christ is compatible with what we learn elsewhere in the book of Revelation. For example, Revelation 5:10 reveals that believers have been made "a kingdom and priests to our God, and they shall reign on the earth." Revelation 20:6 makes a similar affirmation: "Blessed and holy is the one who shares in the first resurrection! Over such the second death has no power, but they will be priests of God and of Christ, and they will reign with him for a thousand years."

This privilege of reigning with Christ continues beyond the millennial kingdom. Revelation 22:5 describes the eternal state that follows the millennial kingdom: "Night will be no more. They will need no light of lamp or sun, for the Lord God will be their light, and they will reign forever and ever." What an awesome privilege and blessing!

"'He who has an ear, let him hear what the Spirit says to the churches'" (3:22): The Holy Spirit inspires all Scripture (2 Timothy 3:15-17; 2 Peter 1:21). The entire book of Revelation constitutes "what the Spirit says to the churches." The Holy Spirit is God (Acts 5:3-4), and He is the "Spirit of truth" (John 15:26; 16:13), so this Scripture can be utterly trusted (see John 10:35). Every Christian is therefore called to hear these words and obey what is written.

MAJOR THEMES

1. *The Trinity and creation.* The Old Testament attributes the act of creation to God (Genesis 1:1; Psalms 96:5; 102:25; Isaiah 37:16; 44:24; 45:12; Jeremiah 10:11-12), sometimes through His Spirit (Job 26:13; 33:4; Psalm 104:30). The New Testament also attributes the act of creation to the Father in a broad, general sense (1 Corinthians 8:6) but names the Son as the actual agent or mediating cause of creation (John 1:3; Colossians 1:16; Hebrews 1:2).

2. *The danger of materialism.* A love of money and riches can lead to sure destruction. The apostle Paul stated that "those who desire to be rich fall into temptation, into a snare, into many senseless and harmful desires that plunge people into ruin and destruction" (1 Timothy 6:9). Jesus warned His followers, "Take care, and be on your guard against all covetousness, for one's life does not consist in the abundance of his possessions" (Luke 12:15). He urged His followers to have an eternal perspective, laying up treasures in heaven instead of on earth (Matthew 6:19-20).

DIGGING DEEPER WITH CROSS-REFERENCES

Self-deception—Psalm 36:2; Isaiah 44:20; Galatians 6:3; James 1:22, 26; 1 John 1:8

Christ's example in being zealous—Isaiah 59:17; Luke 2:49; John 2:17; 4:34; 9:4; Acts 10:38

Fellowship with Christ—Matthew 18:20; 1 Corinthians 1:9; 1 John 1:3

LIFE LESSONS

1. *Being fervent for God.* Scripture reveals that people can be cold toward God (Matthew 24:12), warm toward God (Luke 24:32), and lukewarm toward God (Revelation 3:16). God desires that we be "fervent in spirit" (Romans 12:11). This ought to be our daily goal.

2. *Divine discipline motivated by love.* Revelation 3:19 reveals that even though Christians may have significant problems in their lives, Christ nevertheless loves them. In fact, Christ loves them so much that He will not idly stand by, allowing them to remain in sin. That's why He brings divine discipline. His discipline is designed to woo us to repentance and restored fellowship with Him (see Hebrews 12:5-11).

QUESTIONS FOR REFLECTION AND DISCUSSION

1. Has your attitude toward money ever been a hindrance to your spiritual life? Do you ever feel as if you need to "keep up with the Joneses"? What problems does that cause?

2. On a spectrum that runs from cold to hot, where would you place your own spiritual life?

3. God is the Creator (Revelation 3:14). What implications does this have for your sense of obligation to Him?

Day 7

GOD'S MAJESTIC THRONE IN HEAVEN

REVELATION 4

SCRIPTURE READING AND INSIGHTS

Begin by reading Revelation 4 in your favorite Bible. As you read, keep in mind that just as we eat food for physical nourishment, so we need the Word of God for spiritual nourishment (1 Corinthians 3:2; Hebrews 5:12; 1 Peter 2:2).

In the previous four lessons, we focused attention on seven churches in Asia Minor. In this chapter, we switch locations as we zero in on God's majestic throne in heaven. With your Bible still accessible, consider the following insights on the biblical text, verse by verse.

Revelation 4:1

A door standing open in heaven! (4:1): John was granted a visionary entrance into the heavenly domain to witness the awesome things of heaven and receive knowledge of the end times.

"Come up here, and I will show you what must take place after this" (4:1): John was transported to heaven in the Spirit. Once there, he was given revelation about the future, including the tribulation period (Revelation 4–18), the second coming (19), the millennial kingdom (20), and the eternal state (21–22).

Revelation 4:2-4

I was in the Spirit (4:2): This refers to a state of spiritual ecstasy in which John received a vision of the future. The Lord supernaturally "pulled back the veil" so John could see things to come (see Acts 10:11). Apparently, John's physical body remained on the island of Patmos while this vision took place.

A throne stood in heaven, with one seated on the throne (4:2): This points to God's absolute sovereignty (Proverbs 19:21; 21:30; Ecclesiastes 7:13; Isaiah 14:24; 46:10; Lamentations 3:37; 1 Timothy 6:15).

He who sat there had the appearance of jasper and carnelian (4:3): Human language is inadequate to describe the actual glory of God and His throne room. John thus uses jewels to portray the matchless beauty of what he beheld.

Jasper is a glittering precious stone of various colors that was placed in the high priest's breastplate (Exodus 28:20). The walls of the new Jerusalem are built with this precious stone (Revelation 21:18-19). Sardius, or carnelian, is a fiery-bright, ruby-like jewel. God's appearance is characterized by the brilliance of these wondrous jewels. The sight must be even more glorious because God is clothed "with light as with a garment" (Psalm 104:2).

Around the throne was a rainbow that had the appearance of an emerald (4:3): An emerald is a light green jewel, and this light green hue permeates the multicolored rainbow surrounding God's throne (see Ezekiel 1:28).

Around the throne were twenty-four thrones, and seated on the thrones were twenty-four elders (4:4): The identity of the 24 elders has prompted much debate. Some suggest they are angelic beings—perhaps a heavenly ruling council (see Jeremiah 23:18, 22). However, they seem to be glorified, crowned, and enthroned—characteristics that seem more in keeping with redeemed human beings. Scripture elsewhere reveals that believers will be judged (1 Corinthians 3:1-10; 2 Corinthians 5:10) and then rewarded with crowns (2 Timothy 4:8; James 1:12; 1 Peter 5:4; Revelation 2:10), unlike angels.

It makes good sense to view the 24 elders as representatives of the church. This would coincide with the pretribulational view of the rapture, which holds that the church will be raptured and taken to heaven before the tribulation.

Why the number 24? First Chronicles 24:3-5 tells us there were 24 courses of priests in the Old Testament temple, and Revelation 1:6 refers to God's people as "a kingdom, priests" (compare with 1 Peter 2:9).

Revelation 4:5-11

From the throne came flashes of lightning, and rumblings and peals of thunder

(4:5): Lightning and thunder point to the awesome majesty and glory of God. They also indicate that God's fiery and awesome judgments are about to be unleashed on the world (see Revelation 8:5; 11:19; 16:18).

Before the throne were burning seven torches of fire, which are the seven spirits of God (4:5): This is apparently a metaphorical reference to the Holy Spirit in His fullness (see Isaiah 11:2). The number seven denotes completeness or fullness.

Before the throne there was as it were a sea of glass, like crystal (4:6): The floor of God's throne room appears as a glistening sea, like crystal. This brings to mind Exodus 24:9-10 (NIV): "Moses...saw the God of Israel. Under his feet was something like a pavement made of lapis lazuli, as bright blue as the sky" (see also Ezekiel 1:22). Some suggest that the crystal sea may be indicative of God's holiness.

Around the throne...are four living creatures, full of eyes in front and behind (4:6): These angels are apparently cherubim (Ezekiel 1:18). Some believe there may be a connection with angels called "watchers" (Daniel 4:13).

The etymology of the word "cherubim" is not known for certain, though some have suggested that the word means "to guard." They guarded the entrance to Eden (Genesis 3:24). In Revelation 4:6, they are apparently guardians of God's holiness.

The first living creature like a lion (4:7): The creature is mighty and powerful.

The second living creature like an ox (4:7): Just as an ox is engaged in faithful and patient service to its owner, so this living creature is engaged in humble service to God.

The third living creature with the face of a man (4:7): Scripture often portrays men as intelligent and rational beings (Isaiah 1:18), so this creature is similarly intelligent and rational.

The fourth living creature like an eagle (4:7): Just as an eagle can fly swiftly and is considered the greatest of all birds, so this creature is a great being who is swift in service to God.

Each of them with six wings (4:8): The wings of the angels are often mentioned in Scripture (for example, Exodus 25:20; Isaiah 6:1-5; Ezekiel 1:6). Other Bible verses don't mention wings on angels (for example, Hebrews 13:2).

"Holy, holy, holy" (4:8): God is the absolute holy One of the universe. The threefold affirmation echoes Isaiah 6:3 and indicates the totality of God's holiness. It may also relate to the Trinity. God is absolutely righteous (Leviticus

19:2), majestic in holiness (Exodus 15:11), and separate from all that is morally imperfect (see Exodus 15:11; 1 Samuel 2:2; Psalms 99:9; 111:9; Revelation 15:4).

"The Lord God Almighty" (4:8): Some 56 times Scripture describes God as Almighty (Revelation 19:6). God is abundant in strength (Psalm 147:5) and has incomparably great power (2 Chronicles 20:6; Ephesians 1:19-21). No one can hold back His hand (Daniel 4:35), and no one can thwart Him (Isaiah 14:27). Nothing is too difficult for Him (Genesis 18:14; Jeremiah 32:17, 27).

"Who was and is and is to come!" (4:8): God is eternal. He is from everlasting to everlasting (Deuteronomy 33:27; Psalm 90:2) and abides forever (Psalm 102:27; Isaiah 57:15). He is the King eternal (1 Timothy 1:17) who alone is immortal (6:16).

Glory and honor and thanks to him (4:9): This is the first of many hymns of praise in the book of Revelation (see also Revelation 4:8, 11; 5:9-13; 7:12-17; 11:15-18; 12:10-12; 15:3-4; 16:5-7; 18:2-8; 19:2-6).

Seated on the throne (4:9): The fact that God is on a throne indicates His absolute sovereignty (Proverbs 19:21; 21:30; Ecclesiastes 7:13; Isaiah 14:24; 46:10; Lamentations 3:37; 1 Timothy 6:15).

Who lives forever and ever (4:9): God is eternal (Deuteronomy 33:27; Psalms 90:2; 102:12, 27; Isaiah 57:15; 1 Timothy 1:17; 6:16).

The twenty-four elders fall down before him who is seated on the throne and worship him (4:10): The Hebrew (Old Testament) word for worship, *shaha*, means "to bow down" or "to prostrate oneself" (see Genesis 22:5; 42:6). Likewise, the Greek (New Testament) word for worship, *proskuneo*, means "to prostrate oneself" (see Matthew 2:2, 8, 11). In Old English, "worship" was rendered "worthship," pointing to the worthiness of the God we worship. Such worship is the creature's proper response to the divine Creator (Psalm 95:6).

> "The Ancient of Days took his seat; his clothing was white as snow, and the hair of his head like pure wool; his throne was fiery flames; its wheels were burning fire. A stream of fire issued and came out from before him; a thousand thousands served him, and ten thousand times ten thousand stood before him" (Daniel 7:9-10).

They cast their crowns before the throne (4:10): All believers will one day stand before the judgment seat of Christ (Romans 14:8-10), where He will examine each believer's earthly actions. This judgment has nothing to do with whether the Christian will remain saved. Those who have placed their faith in Christ *are* saved, and nothing threatens that (see Romans 8:30; Ephesians 4:30). Instead, this judgment determines only the reception or loss of rewards, based on how one lives as a Christian.

Scripture often describes these rewards as crowns that we wear (see 1 Corinthians 9:25; 2 Timothy 4:8; 1 Peter 5:4; James 1:12; Revelation 2:10). This verse pictures believers casting their crowns before the throne of God in an act of worship and adoration. Clearly the crowns (as rewards) are bestowed on us not for our own glory but ultimately for the glory of God (compare 1 Corinthians 6:20).

"Worthy are you, our Lord and God, to receive glory and honor and power" (4:11): Rich Mullins reminded us, "Our God is an awesome God." Unlike the false pagan deities of ancient times, the true God is worthy of worship and praise.

"You created all things" (4:11): Scripture consistently points to God as the Creator of all things. He said in Isaiah 44:24, "I am the Lord, who made all things, who alone stretched out the heavens, who spread out the earth by myself." Other Scriptures reveal that all three persons of the Trinity were involved—the Father (1 Corinthians 8:6), the Son (John 1:3; Colossians 1:16; Hebrews 1:2), and the Holy Spirit (Job 26:13; 33:4; Psalm 104:30).

Because God is our Creator, a worshipful response is appropriate. "Oh come, let us worship and bow down; let us kneel before the Lord, our Maker! For he is our God, and we are the people of his pasture, and the sheep of his hand" (Psalm 95:6-7).

MAJOR THEMES

1. *The tribulation period.* Our passage describes a scene in heaven just before the tribulation period begins on earth. The tribulation will be a definite period of time at the end of the age that will be characterized by great travail (Matthew 24:29-35). This period will last seven years (Daniel 9:24, 27). It will be characterized by...

    - wrath (Zephaniah 1:15, 18)

- judgment (Revelation 14:7)
- indignation (Isaiah 26:20-21)
- trial (Revelation 3:10)
- trouble (Jeremiah 30:7)
- destruction (Joel 1:15)
- darkness (Amos 5:18)
- desolation (Daniel 9:27)
- overturning (Isaiah 24:1-4)
- punishment (Isaiah 24:20-21)

2. *The source of the tribulation.* Scripture reveals that this is a time of satanic wrath and especially divine wrath. It is the "day of the wrath of the LORD" (Zephaniah 1:18; see also Isaiah 26:21; Revelation 6:16-17). Satan's wrath is evident in Revelation 12:4, 13, 17.

DIGGING DEEPER WITH CROSS-REFERENCES

Heaven opened—Matthew 3:16; Acts 7:56; 10:11; Revelation 19:11

Throne of God—Psalm 45:6; Isaiah 66:1; Revelation 20:11

Worship of God—Exodus 20:3-5; 1 Samuel 15:22-23; Psalms 29:2; 95:6; 100:2; Isaiah 29:13; Hebrews 12:28; Revelation 14:7

LIFE LESSONS

1. *Be holy.* Revelation 4:8 tells us that God is "Holy, holy, holy." First Peter 1:16 quotes Leviticus 11:44: "You shall be holy, for I am holy." You and I are called to be set apart from sin and set apart to God on a daily basis.

2. *A continual attitude of worship.* Revelation 4:8 reveals that the angelic creatures do not rest in their worship and praise of God. In Western culture we tend to worship God only on Sunday. Why not do it daily? One way we can do this is by daily giving ourselves to God. The apostle Paul encourages us, "I appeal to you therefore, brothers, by the mercies

of God, to present your bodies as a living sacrifice, holy and acceptable to God, which is your spiritual worship" (Romans 12:1).

QUESTIONS FOR REFLECTION AND DISCUSSION

1. Are you satisfied with your worship life?

2. Is thanksgiving a regular feature of your prayer life?

3. Self-examination can be uncomfortable, but it can also be a helpful spiritual exercise. Does a particular sin in your life often trip you up as you seek to be holy before God?

DAY 8

HE WHO IS WORTHY: JESUS CHRIST

REVELATION 5

SCRIPTURE READING AND INSIGHTS

Begin by reading Revelation 5 in your favorite Bible. As you read, keep in mind that just as we eat food for physical nourishment, so we need the Word of God for spiritual nourishment (1 Corinthians 3:2; Hebrews 5:12; 1 Peter 2:2).

In yesterday's reading, we focused attention on God's glorious throne in heaven. Now let's find out more about Jesus Christ, the only one worthy to open the sealed scroll. With your Bible still accessible, consider the following insights on the biblical text, verse by verse.

Revelation 5:1-4

I saw in the right hand of him who was seated on the throne (5:1): The throne points to God's absolute sovereignty (Proverbs 21:30; Ecclesiastes 7:13; Isaiah 14:24; 46:10; 1 Timothy 6:15). This sovereign One, God the Father, is in possession of the scroll.

A scroll written within and on the back, sealed with seven seals (5:1): People often used long strips of papyrus to write on in the first century. These sheets of papyrus were glued side by side to make the scrolls longer, though rarely would a scroll have more than 20 sheets or exceed 30 feet. After the writing was complete, the bulky scroll was rolled up and sealed to protect its contents.

People often wrote on both sides of the papyrus. The important details of the document were on the inside of the scroll. A summary of the inner contents was written on the outside. Important documents were often sealed seven times at the edge of each roll within the scroll.

I saw a mighty angel proclaiming with a loud voice (5:2): The name of the angel is not given. It may have been Gabriel, whose name means "mighty one of God" (see Daniel 8:16). Gabriel gave Daniel special revelations from God regarding the coming Messiah (Daniel 8:16; 9:21). More than 500 years later, he appeared to Mary with the news that she, a virgin, would give birth to the promised Messiah.

"Who is worthy to open the scroll and break its seals?" (5:2): This scroll contains the seven seal judgments to be unleashed during the tribulation period. No created being—human or angelic—was found worthy to open it.

No one in heaven or on earth or under the earth was able to open the scroll (5:3): This is a biblical way of indicating that no creature in the universe was qualified to open the scroll.

I began to weep loudly because no one was found worthy (5:4): The Greek word translated "weep" literally means "kept on shedding many tears." John wept in sorrow because God's sovereign plan would apparently remain hidden and postponed because no one had sufficient authority to open the scroll.

Revelation 5:5-7

One of the elders (5:5): The elder is not identified, but his identity is unimportant, for the center of attention is Jesus Christ.

"Weep no more" (5:5): John did not need to weep any further. God's sovereign plan would not remain hidden or postponed. Jesus is worthy to open the scroll, and once opened, the revelations would continue.

"Behold, the Lion of the tribe of Judah" (5:5): The tribe of Judah is the kingly tribe (Genesis 49:9). The term "lion" symbolizes dignity, nobility, sovereignty, strength, courage, fierceness, and victory. This term points to the Messiah, who is from the kingly tribe of Judah and who possesses all these attributes.

"The Root of David" (5:5): Jesus, the Messiah, is the promised One who descended from David's line and fulfills the Davidic covenant (2 Samuel 7:12-16; Isaiah 11:1, 10; see also Matthew 1:1).

"Has conquered" (5:5): Jesus Christ conquered Satan, sin, and death, so

He is worthy to reveal and implement God's purposes for the future, which this scroll represents.

I saw a Lamb standing, as though it had been slain (5:6): The term "Lamb" refers to Christ's first coming and His death on the cross. Christ is called a Lamb some 27 times in this book. The phrase "as though it had been slain" indicates that the resurrected Christ still bears the scars of His crucifixion on His hands and feet (see Luke 24:40; John 20:20, 27).

With seven horns (5:6): Animals use horns as weapons (see Genesis 22:13; Psalm 69:31), so horns became symbols of power and might. By extension, they signified dominion, representing kingdoms and kings, as in the books of Daniel and Revelation (see Daniel 7:8; Revelation 13:1, 11; 17:3-16). In the Bible, the number seven indicates completeness or perfection. Christ's seven horns therefore symbolize His complete dominion and omnipotence.

With seven eyes (5:6): Christ, the omnipotent One, sees everything.

Which are the seven spirits of God sent out into all the earth (5:6): The "seven spirits of God" apparently points to the Holy Spirit (see Revelation 1:4; 4:5). That the Holy Spirit is sent out into all the earth may be a metaphor for His omnipresence (see Psalm 139:2-9).

He went and took the scroll from the right hand of him who was seated on the throne (5:7): This Lamb-Lion was found worthy, so the scroll was given to Him. This brings to mind Daniel 7:13-14: "With the clouds of heaven there came one like a son of man, and he came to the Ancient of Days and was presented before him. And to him was given dominion and glory and a kingdom, that all peoples, nations, and languages should serve him." How awesome it is to ponder such heavenly scenes involving the Father and the Son.

Revelation 5:8-10

The four living creatures and the twenty-four elders fell down before the Lamb (5:8): Worship is the proper response of a creature to his Creator (Psalms 95:6-7; 100:3).

Each holding a harp (5:8): Harps were often used in worship settings in biblical times. David the psalmist was a gifted harpist (1 Samuel 16:18-23). The psalmist proclaimed, "On the harp I will praise You, O God, my God" (Psalm 43:4 NKJV; see also 71:22; 150:3-5). The 24 elders do the same.

And golden bowls full of incense, which are the prayers of the saints (5:8): Incense was burned on the incense altar morning and evening while the priest tended the lamp (Exodus 37:25-26). The altar was inside the tabernacle, in front of the veil that separated the Most Holy Place from the rest of the worship area (Exodus 40:26-27). As the fumes of the incense drifted into the Most Holy Place, it metaphorically entered God's nostrils. In the Bible, incense often represents the prayers of God's people (Psalm 141:2). These facts would seem to indicate, then, that each elder (representative of the redeemed church) brought prayers before God.

They sang a new song (5:9): The new song celebrates and anticipates the final and glorious redemption that God will soon bring about, and the saints will possess (Revelation 21–22).

"Worthy are you" (5:9): The Lamb of God is worthy because He shed His blood—of inestimable value—for the sins of the world (John 3:16-17). We were "ransomed…not with perishable things such as silver or gold, but with the precious blood of Christ" (1 Peter 1:18-19).

"You were slain…you ransomed people" (5:9): Christ ransomed us from sin by His substitutionary death on the cross. "Substitutionary" means He took the penalty instead of us. At the Last Supper, Jesus said, "This is my body which is given for you" (Luke 22:19). Paul exults that "God demonstrates His own love toward us, in that while we were still sinners, Christ died for us" (Romans 5:8 NKJV; see also Galatians 3:13; 1 Timothy 2:6).

"From every tribe and language and people and nation" (5:9): God's redeemed are from all the races of humanity. God loves the whole world (John 3:16) and desires all to come to repentance and be saved (2 Peter 3:9), though obviously not all will accept Him. He desires that the message of redemption be taken to the whole world (Matthew 28:18-20).

"You have made them a kingdom and priests" (5:10): All Christians become a part of God's kingdom. They submit to Christ's rule. As priests, Christians have the privilege of entering directly into God's presence and serving Him forever (see 1 Peter 2:5-10).

"They shall reign on the earth" (5:10): Faithful believers will participate in the millennial rule of Christ—that 1,000-year period in which Christ will reign on earth following the second coming (Revelation 20:6; see also 1 Corinthians 6:2-3; 2 Timothy 2:12; Revelation 3:21).

Revelation 5:11-14

I heard...the voice of many angels, numbering myriads of myriads and thousands of thousands (5:11): The word "myriad" means "vast number," "innumerable." Daniel 7:10, speaking of God, says that "ten thousand times ten thousand stood before him" (that's a hundred million). Job 25:3 understandably asks, "Is there any number to his armies?" (see also Psalm 68:17; Daniel 7:10; Luke 2:13).

"Worthy is the Lamb who was slain" (5:12): The Lamb is worthy to receive "power and wealth and wisdom and might and honor and glory and blessing!" Each of these seven qualities belong intrinsically to Christ. The word "and" is inserted between each quality to emphasize the fact that Christ possesses the fullness of each distinct quality.

I heard every creature in heaven and on earth and under the earth and in the sea (5:13): Every creature in heaven and on earth joins in praise to God. This reminds us of Psalms 148 and 150, where we behold all of creation bringing praise and worship to God.

"Amen" (5:14): This is an expression of approval and agreement.

The elders fell down and worshiped (5:14): Note that Jesus was worshiped as God many times according to the Gospel accounts, and He always accepted such worship as perfectly appropriate (Matthew 2:11; 8:2; 9:18; 15:25; 28:9, 17; John 9:38; 20:28; Hebrews 1:6). Of course, only God is to be worshiped (see Exodus 34:14; Deuteronomy 6:13).

MAJOR THEMES

1. *The Lamb—a type of Christ.* A "type" is an Old Testament institution, event, person, object, or ceremony that has reality and purpose in biblical history, but which also, by divine design, foreshadows something yet to be revealed. The Passover lamb in the Old Testament (Exodus 12:21) was a type of Christ, who is the Lamb of God (John 1:29, 36).

2. *The Passover.* The sacrificial lamb had to be unblemished (Exodus 12:5; Leviticus 4:3, 23, 32). At the time of the sacrifice, a hand would be laid on the unblemished sacrificial animal to symbolize a transfer of guilt (Leviticus 4:4, 24, 33). Notice that the sacrificial lamb did not thereby

actually become sinful by nature; rather, sin was imputed to the animal, and the animal became a sacrificial substitute. In like manner, Christ the Lamb of God was utterly unblemished (1 Peter 1:19), but our sin was imputed to Him, and He was our sacrificial substitute on the cross of Calvary (see 2 Corinthians 5:21).

DIGGING DEEPER WITH CROSS-REFERENCES

Strong angels—Psalm 103:20; 2 Thessalonians 1:7

Worship and singing—Exodus 15:1-21; Judges 5:1-12; Psalms 33:3; 40:3; Isaiah 12:5-6; 27:2; 30:29; 42:10-11; 44:23; Ephesians 5:19; Colossians 3:16

Universal worship—Psalm 22:27-28; Isaiah 45:22-23; 66:23; Romans 14:11; Philippians 2:9-11

LIFE LESSONS

1. *Five components of prayer.*

    - thanksgiving (Psalms 95:2; 100:4; Ephesians 5:20; Colossians 3:15)
    - praise (Psalms 34:1; 103:1-5, 20-22; Hebrews 13:15)
    - worship (Exodus 20:3-5; Deuteronomy 5:7; Psalm 95:6; Hebrews 12:28; Revelation 14:7)
    - confession (Proverbs 28:13; 1 John 1:9)
    - requests to God for specific things (Matthew 6:11; Philippians 4:6-7)

2. *Principles of answered prayer.*

    - All our prayers are subject to the sovereign will of God (1 John 5:14).
    - Prayer should be continual (1 Thessalonians 5:17).
    - Sin is a hindrance to answered prayer (Psalm 66:18).
    - Living righteously is a great benefit to prayer being answered (Proverbs 15:29).
    - We should pray in faith (Mark 11:22-24).
    - We should pray in Jesus' name (John 14:13-14).

QUESTIONS FOR REFLECTION AND DISCUSSION

1. Can you think of any recent answers to prayer or spiritual experiences with God that move you to exult, "Worthy are You, O Lord"?

2. Are you hesitant to be expressive in your worship and praise of God? Do you want to be more expressive?

3. Have you thanked Jesus lately for ransoming you from sin?

DAY 9

THE FIRST FOUR SEAL JUDGMENTS

REVELATION 6:1-8

SCRIPTURE READING AND INSIGHTS

Begin by reading Revelation 6:1-8 in your favorite Bible. As you read, remember that storing God's Word in your heart can help you to avoid sinning (Psalm 119:9, 11).

In the previous lesson, we learned that Jesus Christ is the only one who is worthy to open the sealed scroll containing the seven seal judgments. Now let's examine the first four of those judgments. With your Bible still accessible, consider the following insights on the biblical text, verse by verse.

Revelation 6:1-2

I watched when the Lamb opened one of the seven seals (6:1): The Lord Jesus Christ, who died as the Lamb of God on the cross for the sins of humankind, is alone worthy to open the seven seals.

The book of Revelation reveals that human suffering will steadily escalate during the tribulation period. As Jesus Christ breaks each of the seven seals, a new divine judgment is unleashed on the earth.

In Jesus' Olivet Discourse (Matthew 24–25), He speaks of things that will occur during the first half of the tribulation period. More than a few Bible expositors have noticed parallels between these events and the seal judgments.

The Olivet Discourse (Matthew 24)	The Seven Seals (Revelation 6)
the rise of false Christs (verses 4-5)	the first seal: the antichrist (verses 1-2)
wars and rumors of wars (verse 6)	the second seal: the sword (verses 3-4)
famines (verse 7)	the third seal: inflation and famine (verses 5-6)
earthquakes (verse 7)	the sixth seal: an earthquake and more (verses 12-14)

I heard one of the four living creatures say with a voice like thunder, "Come!" (6:1): Each time one of the first four seals on the scroll is broken by the sovereign Lord Jesus Christ, one of the four living creatures (cherubim) summons a rider on a horse to engage in its activities on earth. These are the four horsemen of the apocalypse.

Behold, a white horse (6:2): In Scripture, horses sometimes represent God's activity on earth. They are metaphors for the forces God uses to accomplish His sovereign purposes (see Zechariah 1:7-17).

In Revelation 6, a person rides a white horse. Some have speculated that perhaps the rider is Jesus Christ because Jesus rides a white horse in Revelation 19:11. However, the contexts are entirely different. In Revelation 19 Christ returns to the earth as a conqueror at the end of the tribulation. Revelation 6 deals with a rider on a horse at the beginning of the tribulation in association with three other horses and their riders, all associated with judgment. The rider of the white horse in Revelation 6:2 is apparently the antichrist (Daniel 9:26).

Its rider had a bow, and a crown was given to him (6:2): The crown suggests that this individual is a ruler. The Greek word for "crown" (*stephanos*) is the same word used of the laurel wreaths given to winning athletes. Because the crown was given to him, some take this verse to mean that the world's inhabitants will make the antichrist their leader and subsequently submit to his leadership.

A bow without an arrow may indicate that the antichrist's world government will be established without initial warfare. (Peace will not be removed from the earth until the second seal is opened—verse 3.) Perhaps the antichrist is counting on the peace covenant he will make with Israel, which will begin the tribulation period (Daniel 9:24-27).

The antichrist's government apparently begins with a time of peace, but it is short-lived, for destruction will follow. This seems to be parallel to Paul's words in 1 Thessalonians 5:3: "While people are saying, 'There is peace and security,' then sudden destruction will come upon them as labor pains come upon a pregnant woman, and they will not escape."

> "There shall be a time of trouble, such as never has been since there was a nation till that time" (Daniel 12:1).

He came out conquering, and to conquer (6:2): World dominion is the ultimate goal of the antichrist (see Revelation 13).

Revelation 6:3-4

He opened the second seal (6:3): The Lamb of God, Jesus Christ, is the only one worthy to open the seal. When He does so, one of the four living creatures summons a rider on another horse.

Out came another horse, bright red (6:4): Red represents bloodshed, killing with the sword, and war (see Matthew 24:6-7). The rider carries a large sword.

Its rider was permitted to take peace from the earth (6:4): Many world leaders will no doubt be seeking to bring about peace in the world, but such efforts will be utterly frustrated, for peace will be taken from the entire earth. As bad as this will be, however, it represents only the initial birth pangs of what is yet to come upon the earth (see Matthew 24:8; Mark 13:7-8; Luke 21:9). Of course, history tells us that war also brings economic instability and food shortages. These things will soon come upon the earth.

Some Bible expositors believe that just as God permitted Satan to inflict pain and suffering on Job (see Job 1–3), so God permits the antichrist to inflict war on the earth. We must not forget that God is sovereign and remains in control on the throne in heaven even if things on earth seem tumultuous (Isaiah 46:9-11).

Revelation 6:5-6

He opened the third seal (6:5): Again, the Lamb of God, Jesus Christ, is the only one worthy to open the seal, and another one of the four living creatures summons a rider on another horse.

Behold, a black horse (6:5): Black days of famine now fall on the earth. Black is an appropriate color, for it points to the lamentation and sorrow that naturally accompany extreme deprivation. Lamentations 4:8-9 illustrates this:

> Now their face is blacker than soot; they are not recognized in the streets; their skin has shriveled on their bones; it has become as dry as wood. Happier were the victims of the sword than the victims of hunger, who wasted away, pierced by lack of the fruits of the field.

Its rider had a pair of scales in his hand (6:5): This apparently symbolizes famine (with subsequent death), as the prices for food are extravagantly high (see Lamentations 5:8-10). Such a famine would not be unexpected following a global war.

This is in keeping with Jesus' words about the end times in the Olivet Discourse. He affirmed that the first three birth pangs of the end times will be false messiahs, war, and famine (Matthew 24:5-7). Much of the famine at this point in the tribulation will be due to the outbreak of war (the second horseman). Even more intense famine awaits those who refuse to take the mark of the beast (Revelation 13:18). These people will not be permitted to buy or sell, which means they will have much less food than everyone else.

I heard what seemed to be a voice (6:6): The voice in the midst of the four living creatures is not identified. It is likely that of God the Father, the ultimate source of all these judgments.

Saying, "A quart of wheat for a denarius, and three quarts of barley for a denarius, and do not harm the oil and wine" (6:6): A Roman denarius was worth about 15 cents, which was the daily wage of laborers in the first century. (Fifteen cents had a lot more buying power then than it does today!) This verse indicates that prices will be so escalated in that future day of judgment that a person will have to spend an entire day's wages just to buy either a quart of wheat or three quarts of barley.

A quart of wheat would make for one good meal. Three quarts of barley would provide three meals, but nothing would be left over for oil or wine. Foods that are considered bare necessities nowadays will become luxuries during that future day of judgment. Many people will understandably die from starvation during the tribulation period.

He opened the fourth seal (6:7): The Lamb of God, Jesus Christ, is the only one worthy to open the seal. When He does so, another of the four living creatures summons another horse.

Behold, a pale horse (6:8): This fourth horse is pale—literally, yellowish-green, the sickening color of a corpse.

Its rider's name was Death, and Hades followed him (6:8): The death symbolized here is the natural consequence of the three previous judgments. War and starvation will produce many dead bodies. This leads to an escalation in plagues and illnesses around the globe. Wild beasts feed on the dead, spreading disease even further.

Note that Hades is a biblical term for the place of the dead—a New Testament counterpart to the Old Testament Sheol. The word is fitting here because of the prevalence of death due to the judgments of God. Death and Hades are companions—death claims the body, and Hades claims the soul.

They were given authority over a fourth of the earth, to kill (6:8): The death toll will be catastrophic—a fourth of earth's population. In today's figures, about 1.7 billion people will die.

MAJOR THEMES

1. *God and judgment.* Our God of love, grace, and mercy is also a God of judgment when people will not repent of their sin. Judgment fell on the Jews for rejecting Christ (Matthew 21:43), on Ananias and Sapphira for lying to God (Acts 5), on Herod for self-exalting pride (Acts 12:21-23), and on Christians in Corinth for irreverence regarding the Lord's Supper (1 Corinthians 11:29-32; 1 John 5:16). Christians will one day stand before the judgment seat of Christ (1 Corinthians 3:12-15; 2 Corinthians 5:10). Unbelievers will be judged at the great white throne judgment (Revelation 20:11-15).

2. *Famine.* In biblical times, threats to the food supply were common even in Palestine, the land of milk and honey (Exodus 13:5). An enemy might invade and destroy all the crops. Famine almost always follows wars and extensive battle campaigns. The book of Joel speaks of a devastating swarm of locusts that ripped through Judah, resulting in famine. Joel saw in this catastrophe a foretaste of the future day of judgment coming upon the world (Joel 1:15–2:11).

DIGGING DEEPER WITH CROSS-REFERENCES

War as a judgment from God—Leviticus 26:25, 33; Deuteronomy 28:22; Isaiah 1:20; Jeremiah 5:17; 6:25; 25:9; Ezekiel 5:17; 6:3; 21:12; 32:11

The death of the wicked—Numbers 16:30; 1 Samuel 25:38; Job 27:8; Psalms 37:9-10; 78:50; Proverbs 2:22; 10:25, 27; Luke 12:20; 16:22

LIFE LESSONS

1. *Don't worry, trust God.* Our sovereign God remains on the throne, bringing about His eternal purposes, even when the world around us seems tumultuous. Our study this week is a bit fearful. As an antidote to fear, meditate on these Bible verses, which speak of God's absolute control of all things: Deuteronomy 10:14; 1 Chronicles 29:12; 2 Chronicles 20:6; Job 42:2; Psalms 33:8-11; 47:2; 103:19; Isaiah 46:10; Ephesians 1:20-22; John 14:1-3.

2. *Deliverance from the wrath to come.* Many prophecy scholars believe that the rapture of the church will take place before the tribulation period—before all the judgments we've examined in this chapter. It is good to remember that Jesus "delivers us from the wrath to come" (1 Thessalonians 1:10), for "God has not destined us for wrath, but to obtain salvation through our Lord Jesus Christ" (5:9).

QUESTIONS FOR REFLECTION AND DISCUSSION

1. Does the wrath that will one day come upon the unbelieving world motivate you in regard to evangelism and apologetics?

2. How can we maintain a sense of peace, knowing what will one day come upon the world? How does the sovereignty of God help us answer this question?

3. What comfort do you find in Jesus' words in John 14:1-3?

DAY 10

THE FIFTH AND SIXTH SEAL JUDGMENTS

REVELATION 6:9-17

SCRIPTURE READING AND INSIGHTS

Begin by reading Revelation 6:9-17 in your favorite Bible. As you read, remember that storing God's Word in your heart can help you avoid sin (Psalm 119:9, 11).

In yesterday's reading, we examined the first four seal judgments. Now let's learn about the fifth and sixth seal judgments. With your Bible still accessible, consider the following insights on the biblical text, verse by verse.

Revelation 6:9-11

He opened the fifth seal (6:9): The Lamb of God, Jesus Christ, is the only one worthy to open the seal.

I saw under the altar the souls of those who had been slain (6:9): These believers were put to death by the forces of the antichrist for the very same reasons John had been exiled to live on Patmos: "the word of God and the testimony of Jesus" (Revelation 1:9).

The souls of these believers were in heaven while their dead bodies were yet on earth. The state of existence between physical death and the future resurrection is called the "intermediate state." It is a disembodied state. One's physical body is in the grave, but the spirit or soul is either in heaven with Christ or in a place of great suffering apart from Christ (see Luke 16:19-31;

2 Corinthians 5:8; Philippians 1:21-23). One's destiny depends wholly upon whether one has trusted in Christ for salvation (Acts 16:31).

Human beings have both a material part and an immaterial part. The material part is the body. The immaterial part is the soul or spirit (these terms are used interchangeably in Scripture). At the moment of death, the soul or spirit departs or separates from the material body (Genesis 35:18; Ecclesiastes 12:7; Luke 23:46; Acts 7:59). This is what happened to the martyrs of Revelation 6. One day in the future, all believers will be resurrected. Their spirits will be reunited with glorious new bodies that will never die (see 1 Thessalonians 4:13-17).

They cried out with a loud voice (6:10): These martyrs had a strong sense of urgency and emotion.

"O Sovereign Lord, holy and true" (6:10): These believers recognized that God is the sovereign Ruler of the universe. He is "the blessed and only Sovereign, the King of kings and Lord of lords" (1 Timothy 6:15; see also Proverbs 21:30; Ecclesiastes 7:13; Lamentations 3:37).

In Revelation 3:7, God is called "the holy one, the true one." God is holy in that He is utterly righteous and set apart from all sin. He does not just *act* holy; He *is* holy. Likewise, God doesn't just *communicate* that which is true; He *is* true.

"How long before you will judge and avenge our blood?" (6:10): This verse raises two interesting realities to ponder—people are still conscious following the moment of death, and people still have a sense of time in the afterlife.

As for consciousness in the afterlife, Scripture reveals that following the moment of death, unbelievers are in conscious woe (see Mark 9:43-48; Luke 16:22-23; Revelation 19:20). Believers are in conscious bliss (2 Corinthians 5:8; Philippians 1:23).

Regarding the sense of time in heaven, the fact that the martyrs asked God, "How long...?" indicates that they were aware of the passing of time in heaven. Revelation provides other indications of time in heaven. God's people "serve him day and night in his temple" (7:15). The tree of life yields its fruit "each month" (22:2).

God, of course, is a timeless being. To Him, events are not a "succession of moments." Because God transcends time, because He is above time, He can see the past, present, and future as a single intuitive act. However, simply because God is beyond time does not mean that He cannot act within time. From a biblical perspective, God is eternal, but He can do temporal things.

They were each given a white robe (6:11): Each of the martyrs is given the white robe of the overcomer (Revelation 3:5). Some believe the robes are metaphorical, for how can souls wear robes? Others suggest that perhaps believers are given temporary bodies in heaven until that future day of resurrection when believers will receive their permanent, glorious resurrection bodies (Revelation 20:4).

Rest a little longer (6:11): God informs the martyrs that He will deal with their murderers soon enough. He will avenge their deaths in His time (see Revelation 19:2). God elsewhere affirms, "Vengeance is mine" (Deuteronomy 32:35; Romans 12:19).

Meanwhile, these martyrs are to wait a little while longer and rest. Some expositors suggest that God is instructing them to rest from their desire for vengeance. Others suggest God desires them to simply rest in peace (see Revelation 14:13). Perhaps both senses are intended.

Until the number of their fellow servants and their brothers should be complete, who were to be killed as they themselves had been (6:11): God, in His sovereignty, has apparently predetermined a precise number of martyrs to be killed before He destroys those killing His children (see Revelation 11:7; 12:11; 14:13; 20:4-5).

Let's not forget that God is sovereign over life and death. Job 14:5 says of man, "His days are determined, and the number of his months is with you, and you have appointed his limits that he cannot pass" (see also Psalm 139:16; Acts 17:26). In view of God's sovereignty over life and death, these martyrs in Revelation 6 seem to have died by divine appointment, not by human accidents.

Revelation 6:12-14

He opened the sixth seal (6:12): The Lamb of God, Jesus Christ, is the only one worthy to open the seal.

There was a great earthquake (6:12): Scripture reveals there will be an increase in earthquakes in the end times. Jesus affirmed that "nation will rise against nation, and kingdom against kingdom, and there will be famines and earthquakes in various places" (Matthew 24:7; see also Mark 13:8; Luke 21:11). However, the earthquake associated with the sixth seal will be so severe that all the earth's faults will begin to fracture simultaneously with devastating worldwide effects.

The sun became black as sackcloth, the full moon became like blood (6:12): With the earth being shaken to its core, many volcanic eruptions will likely spew huge amounts of ash and debris into the atmosphere. This may be what causes the sun to darken and the moon to appear red (see Joel 2:31).

Others suggest the possibility that a darkened sun and reddened moon could result from nuclear explosions. Revelation 8:7 reveals that "a third of the earth was burned up, and a third of the trees were burned up, and all green grass was burned up." Revelation 16:2 says that people around the world will break out with loathsome sores—perhaps due to radiation poisoning. Some believe Jesus alluded to nuclear weaponry when He spoke of "people fainting with fear and with foreboding of what is coming on the world. For the powers of the heavens will be shaken" (Luke 21:26). If nuclear weapons are, in fact, detonated during the tribulation, enough dust and debris would fill the atmosphere to dim the light of the sun and moon.

The stars of the sky fell to the earth (6:13): This apparently refers to asteroids or meteor showers. There will be many cosmic disturbances during the tribulation period.

The sky vanished like a scroll that is being rolled up (6:14): The earth's atmosphere will be catastrophically affected by all these judgments (compare Isaiah 34:4). Perhaps the terminology indicates simply that people will no longer be able to see the sky (with all the dust and debris), thus causing great fear on earth.

Every mountain and island was removed from its place (6:14): Another result of the global earthquake, with all the earth's faults fracturing simultaneously, will be that mountains and islands would move, apparently because of the shifting of the earth's plates. The actual landscape of the earth will change.

Revelation 6:15-17

The kings of the earth (6:15): Regardless of how strong or weak one is, how rich or poor, whether one has high authority or no authority, virtually everyone on the planet will be stunned with fear as a result of these horrific judgments.

Hid themselves in the caves and among the rocks of the mountains (6:15): Some expositors take this literally, saying people will take refuge in caves and mountains. Others say that the caves and mountains are powerful metaphors for people's desperate search for escape. The mountains will have shifted, and many will be destroyed as a result of the great earthquake.

Calling to the mountains and rocks, "Fall on us" (6:16): For the first time, those who dwell on the earth recognize with sobering clarity that they are experiencing the wrath of the Lamb, the sovereign Lord Jesus. The Lamb had provided a way of escape (salvation by trusting in Him—John 3:16-17), but these unbelievers have impenitently turned their faces against Him. Earth's inhabitants therefore desire to be put out of their misery.

"The great day of their wrath has come" (6:17): The wrath of God the Father (Him who is seated on the throne) and God the Son (the Lamb) is now being unleashed.

"Who can stand?" (6:17): Only those who have availed themselves of the grace of God and trusted in Jesus for salvation will be able to stand as God deals with the earth in this final period of great distress. There will be martyrs, but those who are saved are ultimately victorious.

In view of these horrific judgments, the prospect of the church being raptured prior to this time of divine wrath becomes all the more plausible and understandable (1 Thessalonians 1:10; 5:9). This gives added meaning to the rapture being described as a "blessed hope" (Titus 2:13).

MAJOR THEMES

1. *Tribulation saints.* Scripture reveals that even though the church will be raptured prior to the tribulation period (1 Thessalonians 1:10; 4:13-17; 5:9; Revelation 3:10), many people will become believers during this time (see Matthew 25:31-46). There will be many conversions (Revelation 7:9-10), and many will become martyrs (Revelation 6:9-11).

2. *Martyrdom during the tribulation.* The tribulation martyrs will include not only those mentioned in Revelation 6:9-11 but also the great multitude

mentioned in Revelation 7:9-17 and the two prophetic witnesses of Revelation 11. These two, however, will be raised from the dead after three days and then ascend into heaven (verses 8-12). In Revelation 2:13, Christ made special mention of one of His faithful martyrs—Antipas. Christian martyrs need not fear, however, for each will receive the crown of life (Revelation 2:10).

DIGGING DEEPER WITH CROSS-REFERENCES

Cosmic disturbances in the end times—Isaiah 13:10; 24:23; Ezekiel 32:7; Joel 2:10, 31; 3:15; Amos 5:20; 8:9; Zephaniah 1:15; Acts 2:20

How long, O Lord?—Psalms 74:9-10; 79:5; 94:3-4; Habakkuk 1:2

The wrath of God in Revelation—Revelation 11:18; 14:10; 16:19; 19:15

LIFE LESSONS

1. *Be aware of your mortality.* None of us knows when we will die. The Old Testament patriarch Isaac once said, "Behold, I am old; I do not know the day of my death" (Genesis 27:2). Ecclesiastes 9:12 affirms, "Man does not know his time. Like fish that are taken in an evil net, and like birds that are caught in a snare, so the children of man are snared at an evil time." In Proverbs 27:1 we are urged, "Do not boast about tomorrow, for you do not know what a day may bring." The psalmist prayed, "O LORD, make me know my end and what is the measure of my days; let me know how fleeting I am!" (Psalm 39:4).

2. *It is better to kneel in repentance than to stand in judgment.* Judgment always comes when repentance does not (see Isaiah 55:6-7; Ezekiel 18:32; Luke 13:3; Acts 3:19; 2 Peter 3:9).

QUESTIONS FOR REFLECTION AND DISCUSSION

1. If it ever came to it, would you give your life as a martyr rather than deny Jesus Christ?

2. When you are mistreated by others, do you trust God to bring about justice in His own timing, or are you tempted to return evil for evil?

3. If indeed you trust God to judge, are you able to identify any negative feelings you have toward others and release those feelings so they don't eat you up?

DAY 11

THE 144,000 JEWISH EVANGELISTS

REVELATION 7:1-8

SCRIPTURE READING AND INSIGHTS

Begin by reading Revelation 7:1-8 in your favorite Bible. As you read, remember that the Word of God teaches us, trains us, and corrects us (2 Timothy 3:15-17).

In the previous lesson, we examined the fifth and sixth seal judgments. Today we switch scenery as we focus our attention on 144,000 Jewish believers who will be witnesses for Jesus Christ all over the earth. With your Bible still accessible, consider the following insights on the biblical text, verse by verse.

Revelation 7:1

After this (7:1): That is, after the events associated with the sixth seal judgment—the great earthquake, the sun becoming black as sackcloth, and the full moon becoming like blood (6:12-17).

I saw four angels standing at the four corners of the earth (7:1): Four of God's angels will be strategically positioned around the earth—north, south, east, and west.

Holding back the four winds of the earth (7:1): These four angels will temporarily nullify the earth's winds that come from the north, south, east, and west. Elsewhere in the book of Revelation, God's angels are associated with fire (14:18) and water (16:5). In the present case, nullifying the winds seems to metaphorically represent a lull before the storm of judgment resumes.

Revelation 7:2-3

I saw another angel ascending from the rising of the sun (7:2): The east often has significance in Scripture. Genesis 2:8 tells us that "the LORD God planted a garden in Eden, in the east, and there he put the man whom he had formed." Ezekiel 43:2 tells us that "the glory of the God of Israel was coming from the east." Matthew 2:1-2 tells us that "after Jesus was born in Bethlehem of Judea in the days of Herod the king, behold, wise men from the east came to Jerusalem...to worship him."

With the seal of the living God (7:2): In ancient times, a seal was a symbol of ownership (2 Corinthians 1:22) and protection (Ephesians 1:14; 4:30).

He called with a loud voice to the four angels who had been given power to harm earth and sea (7:2): The angel's loud voice indicates urgency and importance.

"Do not harm the earth or the sea or the trees, until we have sealed the servants of our God on their foreheads" (7:3): The judgments are placed on temporary hold—between the sixth seal judgment (6:12-17) and the seventh seal judgment (8:1)—until God's 144,000 Jewish witnesses become "sealed" with supernatural protection.

These Jewish believers belong to God, and by His sovereign authority He protects them during their time of service during the tribulation period (Revelation 14:1-4; see also 2 Corinthians 1:22; Ephesians 1:13; 4:30; Revelation 13:16-18).

The seal that God's Jewish servants receive seems to be a counterpart to the mark of the beast on all who follow the antichrist (see Revelation 13:17; 14:11; 16:2; 19:20).

Revelation 7:4-8

The number of the sealed, 144,000, sealed from every tribe of the sons of Israel (7:4): Some modern Christians have taken this as metaphorically referring to the church. However, the context indicates that the verse is referring to 144,000 Jewish men—12,000 from each tribe—who live during the future tribulation period (see 14:4). The fact that specific tribes are mentioned along with specific numbers for those tribes removes all possibility that this is a figure of speech. Nowhere else in the Bible does a reference to the 12 tribes of Israel mean anything but the 12 tribes of Israel.

God had originally chosen the Jews to be His witnesses, to share the good news of God with all other people around the world (see Isaiah 42:6; 43:10). The Jews failed at this task, particularly when they didn't recognize Jesus as the divine Messiah. During the future tribulation, these 144,000 Jews who believe in Jesus the divine Messiah will finally fulfill this mandate from God and become His witnesses all around the world.

These 144,000 Jewish evangelists seem to emerge on the scene in the early part of the tribulation period (that is, after the rapture). They must engage in the work of evangelism early in the tribulation because some of their hearers will believe and become the martyrs of Revelation 6:9-11 in the first half of the tribulation.

These Jews probably become believers in Jesus in a way that is similar to what the apostle Paul, himself a Jew, experienced. Recall that Paul had a Damascus Road encounter with the risen Christ (see Acts 9:1-9). Interestingly, in 1 Corinthians 15:8, when the apostle Paul refers to his conversion, he describes himself as "one untimely born." Paul may have been alluding to his 144,000 Jewish tribulation brethren, who would be spiritually "born" in a way similar to him even though Paul was spiritually born far before them. These Jewish witnesses, like Paul, will be mighty witnesses for Jesus Christ.

Many believe these 144,000 have a connection to the judgment of the nations (Matthew 25:31-46), which will take place following the second coming of Christ. The nations are comprised of the sheep and the goats, representing the saved and the lost among the Gentiles. According to Matthew 25:32, they are intermingled and require separation by a special judgment.

They will be judged according to their treatment of Christ's "brothers" (Matthew 25:40). Who are these brothers? They are likely the 144,000 Jews mentioned in Revelation 7, Christ's Jewish brothers who bear witness to Him during the tribulation.

These Jewish witnesses will struggle to buy food because they refused to receive the mark of the beast (Revelation 13:16-17). Only true believers in the Lord will be willing to jeopardize their lives by extending hospitality to the messengers. These "sheep" (believers) who treat the brothers (the 144,000) well will enter into Christ's millennial kingdom. The goats (unbelievers), by contrast, go into eternal punishment.

Parenthetical note on the 12 tribes. The tribes of Israel are listed in verses 5-8. Many readers wonder why the Old Testament tribes of Dan and Ephraim are omitted. Note that the Old Testament has no fewer than 20 lists of the tribes, and these lists include from 10 to 13 tribes, though the number 12 is predominant (see Genesis 49; Deuteronomy 33; Ezekiel 48). Revelation 7 and 14 maintain this number.

Most scholars today agree that Dan's tribe was omitted because it was guilty of idolatry on many occasions and, as a result, was largely obliterated (Leviticus 24:11; Judges 18:1, 30; see also 1 Kings 12:28-29). To engage in unrepentant idolatry is to be cut off from God's blessing. There was also an early tradition that the antichrist would come from the tribe of Dan.

Ephraim's tribe was also involved in idolatry and paganized worship (Judges 17; Hosea 4:17) and was omitted from the list in Revelation 7. The readjustment of the list to include Joseph and Levi to complete the 12 thus makes good sense.

There is another reason Levi is included here. Levi is usually not included in lists of the tribes because it was the priestly tribe and therefore did not inherit land. But the priestly functions of the tribe of Levi ceased with the coming of Christ, the ultimate high priest. Indeed, the Levitical priesthood was fulfilled in the person of Christ (Hebrews 7–10). The priestly services of the tribe of Levi were no longer needed, so there was no further reason to keep this tribe distinct and separate from the others. Therefore, they were properly included in the tribal listing in the book of Revelation.

12,000 from the tribe of Judah (7:5): Judah was the fourth of Jacob's 12 sons. His mother was Leah (see Genesis 29:35; 37:26; 44:14; 49:8-10; Numbers 1:27; Judges 1:8; 2 Samuel 2:4).

12,000 from the tribe of Reuben (7:5): Reuben was the eldest son of Jacob and Leah (Genesis 29:32).

12,000 from the tribe of Gad (7:5): Gad was Jacob's seventh son. His mother was Zilpah, Leah's handmaid (Genesis 30:11-13; 46:16-18).

12,000 from the tribe of Asher (7:6): Asher was Jacob's eighth son. His mother was also Zilpah (Genesis 30:13; 35:26; 46:17; Exodus 1:4).

12,000 from the tribe of Naphtali (7:6): Naphtali was the fifth son of Jacob. His mother was Bilhah, Rachel's handmaid (Genesis 30:8).

12,000 from the tribe of Manasseh (7:6): Manasseh was Joseph's first son, who was born in Egypt (Genesis 41:51; 48:1).

12,000 from the tribe of Simeon (7:7): Simeon was Jacob's second son. His mother was Leah (Genesis 29:33).

12,000 from the tribe of Levi (7:7): Levi was the third son of Jacob by Leah (Genesis 29:34). His tribe served in the temple.

12,000 from the tribe of Issachar (7:7): Issachar was Jacob's ninth son. His mother was Leah (Genesis 30:18).

12,000 from the tribe of Zebulun (7:8): Zebulun was Jacob's tenth son, Leah's sixth (Genesis 30:20).

12,000 from the tribe of Joseph (7:8): Joseph was Jacob's eleventh son and Rachel's first. His name means "May God give increase" (Genesis 37:31-35; 39:1-6, 20; 41:37-57).

12,000 from the tribe of Benjamin were sealed (7:8): Benjamin was Jacob's twelfth son and Rachel's second (Genesis 35:18).

MAJOR THEMES

1. *The remnant.* God has had His faithful remnant in all ages. For example, though the time of Elijah was characterized by great apostasy, 1 Kings 19:18 indicates that God had 7,000 people who were yet faithful to Him (see also Isaiah 1:9; 4:3; 11:16; 37:4; Jeremiah 6:9; 23:3; 31:7; Ezekiel 14:22; Micah 2:12; Zephaniah 2:9; Romans 9:27; 11:5). During the tribulation period, the faithful remnant of Jews will include the 144,000 Jewish witnesses (Revelation 7) as well as God's two prophetic witnesses (Revelation 11).

2. *God protects His people.* God has a long history of protecting His people from judgment. Enoch was transferred to heaven and Noah and his family were in the ark before the judgment of the flood. Lot was taken out of Sodom before judgment fell on the city. The firstborn among the Hebrews in Egypt were sheltered by the blood of the Paschal Lamb before judgment fell. The spies were safe and Rahab was secured before judgment fell on Jericho. Likewise, God keeps His 144,000 Jewish servants safe, but this time He does so by "sealing" them.

DIGGING DEEPER WITH CROSS-REFERENCES

The living God—Joshua 3:10; 1 Samuel 17:26; Psalms 42:2; 84:2; Isaiah 37:17; Jeremiah 23:36; Daniel 6:26; Matthew 26:63; Acts 14:15; 1 Thessalonians 1:9; Hebrews 10:31

Servants of God—1 Kings 18:36; 1 Chronicles 6:49; Ezra 5:11; Daniel 3:28; 6:20; Romans 1:9; 2 Timothy 1:3; James 1:1; 1 Peter 2:16

LIFE LESSONS

1. *God seals His people.* Just as the 144,000 Jewish believers receive God's seal, so believers today are sealed by the Holy Spirit for the day of redemption (Ephesians 1:13; 4:30). This seal guarantees that you and I will be "delivered" into eternal life on the "day of redemption." Our salvation is secure, so we can now live in joyful thankfulness day to day (Psalm 100:4; Philippians 4:6).

2. *We are Christ's witnesses.* Just as the 144,000 will be God's witnesses during the future tribulation period, so you and I are called to be witnesses for Jesus Christ today (see Matthew 28:19-20). Let's let our light shine (Matthew 5:14-16)!

QUESTIONS FOR REFLECTION AND DISCUSSION

1. What have you learned about the sovereignty of God in today's passage? Does this bring comfort to you? Why or why not?

2. God is a living God. What does that mean to you personally?

3. Can you think of any opportunities you might have this month to be a witness of Christ?

DAY 12

THE GREAT MULTITUDE OF BELIEVERS

REVELATION 7:9-17

SCRIPTURE READING AND INSIGHTS

Begin by reading Revelation 7:9-17 in your favorite Bible. As you read, remember that the Word of God teaches us, trains us, and corrects us (2 Timothy 3:15-17).

In yesterday's reading, we focused attention on the role of the 144,000 Jewish witnesses of Jesus Christ. Now let's find out about the many people who become believers in Christ during the future time of judgment on the earth. With your Bible still accessible, consider the following insights on the biblical text, verse by verse.

Revelation 7:9-10

A great multitude that no one could number, from every nation, from all tribes and peoples and languages (7:9): Many will become believers during the tribulation period (see Matthew 25:31-46).

Many may become convinced of the truth of Christianity after witnessing millions of Christians supernaturally vanish off the planet at the rapture. (Bibles and Christian books will be left behind to explain the event.) Many will no doubt become believers as a result of the ministry of the 144,000 Jewish evangelists introduced in Revelation 7. Perhaps many become believers as a result of the miraculous ministry of the two witnesses of Revelation 11, prophets whose powers are apparently similar to those of Moses and Elijah.

Matthew 24:14 tells us that during the tribulation period, "this gospel of the kingdom will be proclaimed throughout the whole world as a testimony." Even though persecution and affliction will be widespread, and even though many will have hearts hardened against God, God in His mercy will nevertheless have His witnesses on earth who are committed to spreading His message about Jesus Christ and the coming kingdom.

In the Gospels, John the Baptist and Jesus often preached that the kingdom of God was near. God's witnesses will do the same during the tribulation period. Jesus will be presented as the divine Messiah, the King who will rule in the soon-coming millennial kingdom. The gospel of the kingdom is the good news that Christ is coming to set up His kingdom on earth and that those who receive Him by faith during the tribulation will enjoy the blessings of His millennial rule.

Standing before the throne and before the Lamb (7:9): This great multitude of believers is now pictured in heaven. They have either died or have been martyred during the tribulation. Such martyrdom is not unexpected, for in His Olivet Discourse, Jesus warned of a tribulation "such as has not been from the beginning of the world until now, no, and never will be" (Matthew 24:21). These believers' physical bodies remain buried or destroyed on earth, but their spirits or souls are with God in heaven.

The Greek word for "before" (*enopion*) in verse 9 is used a number of times in Revelation to speak of those who are in the actual physical presence of God's throne (see Revelation 5:8; 7:11; 14:3). They had previously been before the forces of antichrist, and now they are before God. How awesome!

This multitude of believers will be comprised of many different ethnic groups from around the world. God's love knows no boundaries. People from every nation will come to know the Lord on that day.

Clothed in white robes (7:9): Revelation 3:5, 18 reveals that the white robes are the garments of overcoming believers. These white garments point to their righteous triumph (Revelation 6:11; 7:13; 19:8, 14).

With palm branches in their hands (7:9): Palm branches in Bible times were associated with celebrations (see John 12:13). Certainly this great multitude has reason to celebrate, for their suffering is over, and they now enjoy the very presence of God. Never again will they be subject to persecution or death. In the presence of God are eternal pleasures (Psalm 16:11).

Crying out with a loud voice, "Salvation belongs to our God who sits on the throne, and to the Lamb" (7:10): In this loud acclamation of praise, the theme of worship is the salvation of the saints. All recognize that this awesome salvation comes from God on the throne and the Lamb of God, Jesus Christ. Though these believers had no doubt been sorrowful during their sufferings on earth, they are now joyful in heaven, loudly singing praises to the Father and to the Lamb. Their worship is exuberant and unrestrained.

Revelation 7:11-12

And all the angels...worshiped God (7:11): All the angels—myriads upon myriads of them (Revelation 5:11)—surround God's throne and are apparently intermingled with the 24 elders and the four living creatures. The 24 elders (Revelation 4:4) represent the church, which was raptured to heaven prior to the beginning of the tribulation period. The four living creatures are apparently cherubim, for they are "full of eyes" (Ezekiel 1:18). Overcome with the majesty and glory of God, they collectively fall before God's throne and worship Him.

"Amen! Blessing and glory and wisdom and thanksgiving and honor and power and might" (7:12): This is a wondrous doxology in the book of Revelation. God surely deserves blessing, for He brings matchless blessing to others (Revelation 5:12-13). Glory is due Him because He is the God of glory, who does glorious things in rescuing His people and bringing them to heaven (Revelation 1:6; 4:11; 5:12-13; 19:1). Wisdom is ascribed to God, for He is infinitely wise in His plan of redemption (Revelation 5:12). Thanksgiving is an expression of great gratitude for what God has done for the redeemed (Revelation 4:9). Honor is certainly what God deserves, for He not only planned this great salvation but also brought it about in a way that honors His character (Revelation 4:11; 5:12-13). Power and might are ascribed to Him because He is the omnipotent One, who overcomes all lesser powers in bringing about His plan of redemption. Satan, the antichrist, and the false prophet are no match for God (see Revelation 4:11; 5:12; 19:1).

The word "Amen" carries the idea of truthfulness, meaning that all that has just been affirmed of God is absolutely true.

Revelation 7:13-17

One of the elders addressed me, saying, "Who are these?" (7:13): One of the 24 elders asked John a question that anticipated the very question that was no doubt in John's own mind. A clarification of their identity immediately follows.

"These are the ones coming out of the great tribulation" (7:14): Why weren't these believers caught up at the rapture? The answer is simple: They had not yet become believers. Only those who are believers prior to the tribulation are caught up in the rapture. These individuals will become believers during the tribulation, and once they die, they will go to be with the Lord in heaven.

"They have washed their robes and made them white in the blood of the Lamb" (7:14): This metaphoric language has in view the cleansing nature of salvation (Titus 2:11-14). The blood of the Lamb is Jesus' blood sacrifice at the cross (see Romans 3:24-25; 5:9; Revelation 1:5; 5:9).

"They are before the throne" (7:15): God's throne is the centerpiece in the book of Revelation. As we have seen, God's throne points to His absolute sovereignty over the affairs of humankind.

"Serve him day and night in his temple" (7:15): "Serve" indicates priestly activity on behalf of the Lord (Revelation 1:6; 5:10). The service is perpetual and ongoing.

"He who sits on the throne will shelter them with his presence" (7:15): God's presence among them will be intimate and unfettered. His very presence will shelter them from every form of evil and suffering. They will never again experience hunger, thirst, or scorching heat—a promise that implies that this is precisely what they had suffered while they were on earth.

"They shall hunger no more, neither thirst anymore; the sun shall not strike them" (7:16): In our present life on earth, there are times when we go hungry and thirsty. There are times when our needs are not met. In the eternal state, however, God will abundantly meet every need. These verses promise that these believers will never again suffer any kind of want.

"The Lamb...will be their shepherd" (7:17): In Psalm 23 David said of his shepherd, "He leads me beside still waters." In remarkably similar language, John writes, "The Lamb in the midst of the throne will be their shepherd, and he will guide them to springs of living water." This description has led

many to believe that Christ may be the shepherd who led His people beside still waters in Old Testament times.

Later in the book of Revelation, Jesus makes this declaration: "It is done! I am the Alpha and the Omega, the beginning and the end. To the thirsty I will give from the spring of the water of life without payment" (Revelation 21:6). This must have brought back memories for John, for he well remembered the words from his own Gospel about the woman at Jacob's well to whom Jesus offered the gift of living water (John 4:10). The offer John had just heard from the Alpha and Omega was the same now at the end of God's revelation in Jesus Christ as it had been at the very beginning.

"God will wipe away every tear from their eyes" (7:17): God is not only a sovereign Judge but also a compassionate and loving parent to the redeemed. He will tenderly wipe away the tears of these believers due to their suffering (see Revelation 21:4). A truly blessed existence lies ahead for all of the redeemed.

MAJOR THEMES

1. *Christ the shepherd.* Jesus is the good shepherd, for He cares for and watches over His sheep (believers) (John 10:1-16). Jesus is the great shepherd, for He brought us peace with God through His blood (Hebrews 13:20). Jesus is the chief shepherd who will one day come again (1 Peter 5:4). Jesus is also the caring shepherd who brings His people to living water (Revelation 7:17).

2. *Living water.* John had earlier recorded Jesus' promise: "Whoever drinks of the water that I will give him will never be thirsty again. The water that I will give him will become in him a spring of water welling up to eternal life" (John 4:14). Jesus also promised, "Whoever believes in me, as the Scripture has said, 'Out of his heart will flow rivers of living water'" (John 7:38; see also Jeremiah 2:13; 17:13).

DIGGING DEEPER WITH CROSS-REFERENCES

Glory of God—Exodus 24:17; 40:34; 1 Kings 8:11; Psalm 19:1-4; Isaiah 48:11; Ezekiel 10:4; Luke 2:9; Acts 7:55; 2 Corinthians 3:18

Wisdom of God—Job 12:13; Psalm 104:24; Proverbs 3:19; Romans 11:33; 16:27; James 3:17

LIFE LESSONS

1. *The Great Commission.* The book of Revelation informs us that God's redeemed will be from every nation, from all tribes and peoples and languages (Revelation 7:9). This will be in fulfillment of Christ's Great Commission (which you and I can help fulfill): "Go therefore and make disciples of all nations, baptizing them in the name of the Father and of the Son and of the Holy Spirit, teaching them to observe all that I have commanded you. And behold, I am with you always, to the end of the age" (Matthew 28:19-20).

2. *No more tears.* Every believer can receive comfort from knowing that God will one day banish all sorrow. Isaiah 25:8 promises that God "will swallow up death forever; and the Lord God will wipe away tears from all faces." Isaiah 35:10 promises, "Sorrow and sighing shall flee away." Isaiah 60:20 adds, "Your days of mourning shall be ended." Jeremiah 31:12 promises that His people "shall languish no more." These verses find their ultimate fulfillment in the book of Revelation (7:17; 21:4). Even today, God heals our sorrowing hearts (Psalm 147:3).

QUESTIONS FOR REFLECTION AND DISCUSSION

1. The redeemed will come from every nation on the earth. What does that tell you about the heart of God?

2. Do you ever fall on your knees before God in worship, praise, or prayer (Revelation 7:11)?

3. Does pondering the afterlife affect your outlook? How?

DAY 13

THE SEVENTH SEAL JUDGMENT

REVELATION 8:1-6

SCRIPTURE READING AND INSIGHTS

Begin by reading Revelation 8:1-6 in your favorite Bible. As you read, never forget that you can trust everything that is recorded in the Word of God (Matthew 5:18; John 10:35).

In yesterday's reading, we focused attention on the great company of people who become believers in Christ during the tribulation period. Today we shift our attention back to the seventh seal judgment. This last seal judgment constitutes a whole new series of judgments to be unleashed on the earth. With your Bible still accessible, consider the following insights on the biblical text, verse by verse.

Revelation 8:1-2

The Lamb opened (8:1): The Lamb of God—the Lord Jesus Christ, who died on the cross for the sins of humankind (see 2 Corinthians 5:19-21)—He alone is worthy to open the seventh seal.

The seventh seal (8:1): Once the Lamb of God breaks the seventh seal, the seven trumpet judgments are unleashed on the earth. In other words, the seventh seal judgment constitutes a whole new series of judgments—the trumpet judgments. We will see later that the seven bowl judgments proceed out of the seventh trumpet judgment.

Silence in heaven (8:1): After the seal is opened, heaven is silent for about half an hour. Scholars offer various opinions about this. Many believe (myself included) that all of heaven becomes soberly aware of what now lies ahead for the earth and its inhabitants. All of heaven becomes awestruck at what they learn. One might consider this time of silence to be the lull before a very bad storm.

The seal judgments were bad enough, but now the trumpet judgments are about to be unleashed. All in heaven recognize that the first four trumpet judgments will bring about a destruction of earth's ecology (Revelation 8:6-12). The last three will devastate earth's inhabitants (Revelation 9). Therefore a sobering silence falls on the halls of heaven. Charles Swindoll offers this sobering observation:

> Until this moment in John's visions, there have been sounds of enormous volume—all creatures in antiphonal worship, angelic hosts belting out hallelujahs, a cacophony of earthly calamities, and a reverberating celebration of praise among the redeemed. Yet when Christ broke the seventh and final seal and a distinct group of seven unidentified angels were handed seven trumpets, all that explosion of noise turned to silence...When God prepares to intensify His wrath, every creature is reduced to open-mouthed silence.[1]

My friend Skip Heitzig puts it this way:

> All of the exaltation stops, all of the alleluias cease; all the music is put on pause. No one says a word. This is a silence of awe, a stillness of solemn anticipation as the citizens of heaven gaze upon the opened scroll and see the calamities to come upon the earth. They know what is about to happen.[2]

A look through Scripture reveals that silent moments before the Lord are common, especially when judgment is about to fall. "From the heavens you uttered judgment; the earth feared and was still" (Psalm 76:8). "Be silent before the Lord GOD! For the day of the LORD is near" (Zephaniah 1:7). "Be silent, all flesh, before the LORD, for he has roused himself from his holy dwelling" (Zechariah 2:13). "The LORD is in his holy temple; let all the earth keep silence before him" (Habakkuk 2:20).

Other scholars take a different approach to the silence in heaven. They believe it may relate to the respectful silence of those who witness temple ceremonies. Ed Hindson explains it this way:

> The imagery that follows, including the half hour of silence, follows the liturgy of the Jewish temple services. After the sacrificial lamb was slain, the altar of incense was prepared. Two of the priests would go into the holy place and take the burnt coals and ashes from the golden altar and relight the lamps of the golden lampstand. One priest filled the golden censer with incense while the other placed burning coals from the altar into a golden bowl. Deep silence fell over the temple during this solemn ceremony.[3]

Either way, the silence is short-lived—about a half hour.

I saw the seven angels...and seven trumpets (8:2): God Himself is likely the One who gives the seven angels the seven trumpets during this 30 minutes of silence. After all, we often find angels around the throne of God (see Revelation 1:4; 3:1; 8:6; 15:1).

Trumpets in Bible times were sometimes used to sound an alarm or a call to arms, much like bugles were still used on battlefields centuries later. Here, the trumpets let people know that serious things are about to happen.

It is not precisely clear who the seven angels are. Some identify them with the pastors of the seven churches mentioned in Revelation 2–3. But human pastors have no power to inflict judgment, so this view seems unlikely.

Others relate the seven angels to the seven archangels of Jewish tradition—Uriel, Raphael, Raguel, Michael, Sarakiel, Gabriel, and Phanuel (these angels are named in the Jewish Book of Jubilees, Tobit, and 1 Enoch). Scripture, however, only delineates one archangel, and he is named Michael (1 Thessalonians 4:16; Jude 9).

It seems best to conclude that these are simply seven other angels who have great authority. We know they have great authority because they stand before God (Revelation 8:2).

This brings to mind the angel who told Zechariah and Elizabeth they would have a son, John the Baptist. Zechariah responded in disbelief: "How shall I know this? For I am an old man, and my wife is advanced in years" (Luke 1:18). The angel appealed to his commission: "I am Gabriel, who stands in the presence of God, and I was sent to speak to you and to bring you this good news" (verse 19).

The angels of the seven trumpet judgments also stand before God. Some theologians conclude that these angels must be preeminent, perhaps in the same league as Gabriel.

Revelation 8:3-4

Another angel came and stood at the altar with a golden censer (8:3): Another angel appears on the scene and engages in priest-like activities. A censer is a golden pan suspended by a chain. Priests used censers to transport fiery coals from the brazen altar to the altar of incense.

In our text, the angel stands before the golden incense altar in heaven. He receives more incense to add to the prayers of the saints already there. Some expositors interpret this to mean that the prayers of those who become believers during the tribulation period are now joined with the prayers of the rest of God's people. They collectively beseech God to bring about justice on earth, put an end to evildoers, and inaugurate God's glorious kingdom.

The smoke of the incense, with the prayers of the saints, rose before God (8:4): The angel offered the incense on the coals of the golden incense altar. As incense is thrown on the altar, the smoke represents the prayers of God's people mingling together and rising into God's holy presence. Scholars have been careful to point out that even though an angel is engaged in this activity, only Jesus Christ is the true mediator between God and man (1 Timothy 2:5).

Revelation 8:5-6

The angel took the censer and filled it with fire...and threw it on the earth (8:5): After the angel took the censer and filled it with fire, he threw this fire (representing judgment) on the earth. The result was massive thunder, lightning, and an earthquake. These are mere foreshocks of the seven trumpet judgments to come. These judgments appear to be thrown on the earth in response to the prayers of God's people.

Note that God's judgment of evildoers in answer to the prayers of His people is not unique to the book of Revelation. Exodus 3:7-10 shows that God brought judgment against the Egyptians in direct response to the prayers of His people: "I have surely seen the affliction of my people in Egypt and have heard their cry...Come, I will send you [Moses] to Pharaoh that you may bring my people, the children of Israel, out of Egypt."

The seven angels who had the seven trumpets prepared to blow them (8:6): In response to the prayers of God's people, the seven trumpet judgments are about to be unleashed on the earth. The judgments escalate in horror and intensity throughout the tribulation period.

Scripture reveals that God is a God of patience. He says, "I have no pleasure in the death of anyone" (Ezekiel 18:32). He urges, "I have no pleasure in the death of the wicked, but that the wicked turn from his way and live" (Ezekiel 33:11). The wicked of the tribulation period, however, harden themselves against God. Judgment in this case is inevitable.

MAJOR THEMES

1. *Angels execute judgments.* Angels not only announce God's impending judgments but also execute them. In Acts 12, an angel of God put Herod to death because Herod was a pretender to the divine throne and chose not to give God glory (Acts 12:22-23). Likewise, in Revelation 8, the angels of God unleash the seven trumpet judgments that are poured out on humankind (see also Revelation 16:1).

2. *Similarities to the Exodus judgments.* Some Bible expositors have noted the similarity of the trumpet judgments to the Exodus judgments. For example, the trumpet judgments include hail and fire falling on the earth, the sea turning to blood, and a variety of cosmic disturbances—all of which God inflicted upon the Egyptians. Moreover, the general attitude of people during the tribulation will be much like that of Pharaoh, who pridefully and defiantly asked, "Who is the Lord, that I should obey his voice?" (Exodus 5:2).

3. *Trumpets.* In the Old Testament, trumpets gathered the Lord's people (Numbers 10:7-8), assembled the Lord's army (Numbers 10:9), and announced

a new king (1 Kings 1:34-39). Trumpets also play a major role in Bible prophecy. John was summoned up into heaven by a trumpet (Revelation 4:1). The rapture of the church will be accompanied by a trumpet blast (1 Corinthians 15:52; 1 Thessalonians 4:16). Now, in Revelation 8–9, we encounter the trumpet judgments.

DIGGING DEEPER WITH CROSS-REFERENCES

"Another angel" in Revelation—Revelation 7:2; 8:3; 10:1; 14:6, 8-9, 15-18; 18:1

Earthquakes in Revelation—Revelation 6:12; 8:5; 11:13, 19; 16:18

God answers prayer—Psalms 50:15; 91:15; 99:6; 118:5; 138:3; Isaiah 30:19; 58:9; 65:24; Jeremiah 29:12; Daniel 9:21-23; 10:12; Matthew 7:7

Fire and God's judgment—Exodus 9:23-24; Leviticus 10:1-2; Numbers 11:1; 16:35; 2 Kings 1:10; Psalm 97:3; Isaiah 47:14; 66:16

LIFE LESSONS

1. *Silence before God.* Sometimes it is good to be silent before God. In Psalm 62:1 the psalmist says, "For God alone my soul waits in silence; from him comes my salvation." Later he exhorts himself, "For God alone, O my soul, wait in silence, for my hope is from him" (verse 5; see also Psalm 37:34). In Lamentations 3:26 we are told, "It is good that one should wait quietly for the salvation of the LORD."

2. *Angels.* In this portion of the book of Revelation, the angels do scary things related to judgment, but let's keep all this in perspective. Remember the good things angels do on our behalf. Angels are celestial guardians of God's people (2 Kings 6:17; Psalm 91:9-11). God sometimes uses angels to answer the prayers of God's people (Acts 12:5-10), escort believers into heaven following the moment of death (Luke 16:22), and minister to us in a variety of ways (Hebrews 1:14).

QUESTIONS FOR REFLECTION AND DISCUSSION

1. Your prayers are always heard directly by God in heaven. How does knowing that make you feel?

2. Do you ever feel moved to silence as you contemplate the things of God?

3. Are you thankful for the ministry of angels in your life, even though you may never perceive their actual presence or activities? Do you think you've ever been rescued by an angel?

DAY 14

THE FIRST FOUR TRUMPET JUDGMENTS

REVELATION 8:7-13

SCRIPTURE READING AND INSIGHTS

Begin by reading Revelation 8:7-13 in your favorite Bible. As you read, never forget that you can trust everything that is recorded in the Word of God (Matthew 5:18; John 10:35).

In the previous lesson, we witnessed an announcement of the seventh seal judgment, which actually constitutes seven new trumpet judgments. Now let's find out the details of the first four trumpet judgments. With your Bible still accessible, consider the following insights on the biblical text, verse by verse.

Revelation 8:7

The first angel blew his trumpet, and there followed hail and fire, mixed with blood (8:7): The seal judgments were bad, but the trumpet judgments are even worse. They are so bad that when heaven's inhabitants become aware of them, they are silent for 30 minutes.

In the first trumpet judgment, hail and fire, mixed with blood, fall upon the earth. This reminds us of God's plague on the Egyptians at the hand of Moses (Exodus 9:18-26).

It is not clear how hail and fire could be mixed with blood. But remember that this will be a supernatural judgment, so it is entirely possible. Joel 2:30 prophesied a judgment of "blood and fire and columns of smoke" in the end times.

This judgment sounds very much like catastrophic volcanic activity—something that could result from the powerful earthquake mentioned just earlier (Revelation 8:5). Volcanic lava spewing into the atmosphere could look like hail and fire falling on the earth. It could mix with other dust and debris (and perhaps even birds) in the atmosphere, producing blood or a blood-like residue.

A third of the earth was burned up...(8:7): A third of the earth and trees will be incinerated, as will all of the grass. This would seem to imply that much of the earth's crops will also be destroyed, depleting food supplies on an already starving planet.

Volcanoes erupting around the world could account for a third of the trees burning up. We have seen that as a result of God's judgments, the earth's plates will shift and some mountains will be flattened. Massive global volcanic activity will likely result.

Some modern prophecy scholars suggest the possibility that nuclear detonations could play a role in this judgment. This could easily explain how a third of the earth could be burned in a short time. Other Scripture verses might substantiate this, such as Revelation 16:2, which tells us that people around the world will break out with loathsome and malignant sores. Could this be a result of radiation poisoning following the detonation of nuclear weapons? As well, some believe Jesus Himself may have alluded to nuclear weaponry: "There will be...people fainting with fear and with foreboding of what is coming on the world. For the powers of the heavens will be shaken" (Luke 21:25-26). At any rate, the technology now exists for a third of the earth to be burned up, causing mass casualties.

Revelation 8:8-9

The second angel blew his trumpet, and something like a great mountain, burning with fire, was thrown into the sea (8:8): As a result of this, a third of the sea turns bloody. Some suggest this might be a massive island volcano that explodes, hurling what appears to be a fiery mountain into the sea. Others see this fiery mountain as something that falls from the heavens onto the earth—an asteroid. Still others suggest this refers to a large fiery nuclear missile plunging into the sea and detonating.

The waters could turn bloody because of the blood of dead sea creatures. Or this could refer to a "red tide," in which billions of dead microorganisms contaminate the water and make it appear red. Or this could be much like an extension of the first plague in Egypt, where God supernaturally turned the waters of the Nile River into blood (Exodus 7:17-21).

A third of the living creatures in the sea died (8:9): This not only fouls (and possibly bloodies) the waters but also further cuts into the food supply. The effect on the world economy will be devastating.

A third of the ships were destroyed (8:9): A giant asteroid striking the ocean would create such a gigantic tidal wave that a third of the earth's ships could easily be destroyed. At present, tens of thousands of ships transport industrial goods across the seas. The shipping industry will be in chaos once this judgment strikes, for a third of the ships will no longer be available for service. This too will have a catastrophic effect on the world economy.

Revelation 8:10-11

The third angel blew his trumpet, and a great star fell...on a third of the rivers (8:10): Many prophecy scholars believe this will be a "deep impact" of a massive meteor or asteroid. It looks like a star because it bursts into flames in the earth's atmosphere.

It turns a third of the waters bitter, and many people die. It may contaminate this large volume of water by the residue that results from the meteor disintegrating as it races through earth's atmosphere. Or the debris may plummet into the headwaters of some of the world's major rivers and underground water sources, thereby spreading the poisonous water to many people on earth.

The name of the star is Wormwood (8:11): Wormwood is a woody herb common to Palestine that has a strong, bitter taste (see Deuteronomy 29:18; Proverbs 5:4; Jeremiah 9:15; Lamentations 3:15). The plant is used in the book of Revelation as a symbol of bitterness. This wormwood-like asteroid will render a third of the earth's waters unfit for human consumption.

Today's top scientists are saying that the question is not *if* such a celestial body will strike the earth, but *when*. Mathematical probabilities render this an eventual certainty. And when it happens, it will likely involve a significant celestial body striking the earth at a minimum of 130,000 miles per hour. The sad reality is that this event will in fact happen during the tribulation period, and the result will be truly catastrophic. Many will die.

Revelation 8:12

The fourth angel blew his trumpet, and a third of the sun was struck (8:12): The severe cosmic disturbances continue. The diminishing of sunlight, moonlight, and starlight may be due to thousands of tons of dust from the large meteor or asteroid strike associated with the third trumpet judgment. Volcanoes will also be spewing debris into the atmosphere.

Of course, our text does not demand such natural explanations for the diminishing of light from these stellar bodies. God Himself could supernaturally cause the heavenly bodies to dim.

Whatever the case, all of this will lower the global temperature, and with a third of the trees already having been destroyed, there will be much less firewood to keep people warm. Moreover, plant life will suffer, thereby further reducing the food supply. And things will continue to go from bad to worse.

Revelation 8:13

I heard an eagle crying… "Woe, woe, woe" (8:13): This may be the eagle-like angelic creature mentioned in Revelation 4:7-8. Three trumpet judgments remain, so the angel proclaims, "Woe, woe, woe." The first four trumpet judgments have been bad enough, but the last three will be unimaginably worse.

MAJOR THEMES

1. *Earth: a center of divine activity.* The first four trumpet judgments assault the earth's environment—a tragedy in view of the important role the earth has in the Bible. Relatively speaking, the earth is but an astronomical atom among the whirling constellations, only a tiny speck of dust among the ocean of stars and planets in the universe. But the earth is nevertheless the center of God's work of salvation in the universe. Here God created man and appeared to people throughout biblical times. Here Jesus became incarnate and died for the sins of man, and to the earth the Lord Jesus will come again. He will then create the new heavens and new earth (Revelation 21:1-2; 22:3).

2. *Woe.* The word "woe" in the book of Revelation should be understood against its Old Testament backdrop. Old Testament prophets used the Hebrew word for "woe" to point to impending doom, grief, and sorrow. It warns of a dire threat in the face of present or coming danger. Isaiah uses the word "woe" 22 times—more than any other book of the Bible. Jesus pronounced severe woes on the scribes and Pharisees (see Luke 11:42-44). Revelation uses the word to describe God's judgments during the tribulation period.

3. *Those who dwell on the earth.* The book of Revelation often refers to "those who dwell on the earth" (see 3:10; 6:10; 8:13; 11:10; 13:14). This term communicates not only geographical location but also personal character. In other words, their character is earthly instead of heavenly. They are worldlings who reject the things of God.

DIGGING DEEPER WITH CROSS-REFERENCES

Eagles—Exodus 19:4; Proverbs 23:5; 30:19; Isaiah 40:31; Lamentations 4:19; Ezekiel 1:10; Revelation 4:7; 12:14

A loud voice—Deuteronomy 5:22; 1 Samuel 28:12; 2 Samuel 19:4; 2 Chronicles 15:14; Matthew 27:46, 50; Luke 19:37; Revelation 1:10; 5:2, 12; 6:10; 7:2, 10; 8:13; 10:3; 11:12; 12:10; 14:2, 7, 9, 15, 18; 16:1, 17; 19:1, 17; 21:3

Hail—Exodus 9:23; Joshua 10:11; Psalm 18:13; Isaiah 28:2; Ezekiel 13:11; Revelation 8:7

LIFE LESSONS

1. *Repent early.* God often intensifies judgment and discipline in order to move people to repentance. Some people become hardened against God to the point of no return, as seems to be the case with many on earth during the future tribulation. But others respond by turning to God. Even in the case of Christians, God may escalate His discipline to move us to repent. David took almost a full year to repent of his sin with Bathsheba. God had to discipline him severely. When he finally did repent, he beseeched God, "Let the bones that you have broken rejoice" (Psalm 51:8; see also

Psalm 32:3-4; Hebrews 12:5-11). The lesson: Repenting promptly is always in our best interest.

2. *Avoid worldliness.* Christians should not have a worldly character, focused only on the things of this earth like "those who dwell on the earth" in the book of Revelation. One of the best ways for us to avoid worldliness is to regularly feed on the Word of God and allow it to do its transforming work in our lives. As the apostle Paul put it, "Do not be conformed to this world, but be transformed by the renewal of your mind" (Romans 12:2).

QUESTIONS FOR REFLECTION AND DISCUSSION

1. Do you ever struggle with worldliness? Do you ever feel that you have been contaminated by the things of this world?
2. Consider the influences on your life. Do you ever feel contaminated by the books you read? By the TV shows you watch? By the movies you go to? By the music you listen to?

DAY 15

THE FIFTH AND SIXTH TRUMPET JUDGMENTS

REVELATION 9

SCRIPTURE READING AND INSIGHTS

Begin by reading Revelation 9 in your favorite Bible. As you read, trust God to open your eyes so you can discover wondrous things from His Word (Psalm 119:18).

In yesterday's reading, we learned about the first four trumpet judgments. Now let's examine the details of the fifth and sixth trumpet judgments. With your Bible still accessible, consider the following insights on the biblical text, verse by verse.

Revelation 9:1-12

The fifth angel blew his trumpet (9:1): The fifth trumpet judgment—the worst so far—is now unleashed.

I saw a star fallen from heaven to earth (9:1): Angels are sometimes associated with the stars in Scripture (see Job 38:7; Psalm 148:1-3; Revelation 12:3-4, 7-9). Many Bible expositors believe the star (or angel) in verse 1 is "the angel of the bottomless pit" mentioned in verse 11. We know that the "star" is not a literal star, for it is called "he" in verses 1-2.

Some suggest that this verse may refer to Satan (compare with Isaiah 14:12-15). Jesus once commented to His disciples, "I saw Satan fall like lightning from heaven" (Luke 10:18).

He was given the key to the shaft of the bottomless pit (9:1): The bottomless pit is the abyss, or the abode of imprisoned demons and disobedient spirits. It is the place to which Jesus sent demons when He expelled them from people, a place they clearly dreaded (Luke 8:31). The term is translated seven times as "the bottomless pit" (Revelation 9:1-2, 11; 11:7; 17:8; 20:1, 3) and two times as "the abyss" (Luke 8:31; Romans 10:7). The angel, whatever his identity, was given the keys to the abyss.

He opened the shaft...from the shaft rose smoke...the sun and the air were darkened (9:2): Hideous demons are released from the bottomless pit. Smoke is a graphic visual description of a huge locust swarm. The "smoke" arises out of the abyss, so the swarm is undoubtedly demonic. This metaphor points to an unimaginably large company of fallen angels exiting the bottomless pit.

From the smoke came locusts on the earth (9:3): A devastating swarm of locusts can rip through the land like a black cloud, devouring crops almost instantly. Locusts are therefore an apt metaphor for the desolation the demonic spirits will inflict on the world.

They were given power like the power of scorpions (9:3): Scorpion bites can be agonizing and cause people to foam at the mouth and grind their teeth in pain. These demonic spirits will inflict torturous wounds that could be physical, spiritual, or both.

They were told not to harm the grass of the earth or any green plant or any tree (9:4): Satan and demonic spirits are "on a leash." They cannot go beyond what God will allow them (as Job 1–2 demonstrates). The demonic spirits are not permitted to harm the grass, green plants, or trees.

Only those people who do not have the seal of God (9:4): The 144,000 Jewish evangelists will be kept safe from the torment of these spirits. The converts of the 144,000 will also likely be exempt. It seems likely that all who have trusted in the Lord for salvation will be sealed in some special way and protected from torment.

They were allowed to torment them for five months (9:5): The life cycle of locusts is typically from May to September—five months. The hideous locust-like demonic spirits will relentlessly torment people during this time, but they will not be permitted to kill them.

People will seek death (9:6): People will long for death rather than repent before a holy God. We are not told how their death wishes are frustrated, but God is sovereign over life and death, so no one can die before God's appointed time (Job 14:5; Acts 17:26; Psalms 31:15; 139:16).

The locusts were like horses prepared for battle (9:7): To describe these evil spirits, John is forced to use the term "like" nine times.

On their heads were what looked like crowns of gold (9:7): These demonic spirits evidently have a higher rank or level of authority than other demonic spirits.

Their faces were like human faces (9:7): The locusts have some humanlike characteristics—perhaps rationality and intelligence.

Their hair like women's hair, and their teeth like lions' teeth (9:8): Locusts are elsewhere described as having bristles like hair (see Jeremiah 51:27). Insects also often have long antennae for navigation. Like lions, these evil spirits will be fierce predators. Just as an unarmed human is no match for a lion, so people will not be able to escape the torment of these demonic spirits.

They had breastplates (9:9): Iron breastplates are designed to protect one's organs. The metaphor indicates that these fallen angels are invulnerable.

The noise of their wings (9:9): People jolt out of the way at the sound of a locust (a fear reflex). But when people sense the presence of these tormenting spirits, they won't be able to escape.

They have tails and stings like scorpions (9:10): Scorpions carry an agonizing sting, but they aren't generally lethal. These demonic spirits will cause similar agony for five months.

They have as king over them the angel of the bottomless pit...Abaddon...Apollyon (9:11): Abaddon and Apollyon both mean "destruction." This angel-king is characterized by destruction.

Scripture reveals that there are ranks among the fallen angels (Ephesians 6:12). Their ranks include principalities, powers, rulers of the darkness of this world, and spiritual wickedness in high places. All fallen angels, regardless of their individual ranks, follow their malevolent commander in chief—Satan. Many expositors believe that Apollyon may be among Satan's most notable subordinate commanders. Others suggest that Satan himself is the angel of the bottomless pit and is therefore the destroying angel. Jesus, speaking of Satan, once said, "The thief comes only to steal and kill and destroy" (John 10:10). Satan's natural tendency is to destroy.

The first woe has passed (9:12): The "first woe" is the first of the last three trumpet judgments. Two more remain—the sixth (9:13-21; 11:14) and seventh trumpets (11:15-19).

Revelation 9:13-21

The sixth angel blew his trumpet (9:13): The sixth trumpet judgment is now unleashed. The horror increases.

I heard a voice from the four horns of the golden altar (9:13): Each corner of the golden altar had small protrusions, or horns (Exodus 30:2). In Old Testament times, people went to the golden altar to obtain mercy. Here, a metaphorical voice calls out for vengeance. Perhaps the voice is that of the Lamb, Jesus Christ.

"Release the four angels who are bound at the great river Euphrates" (9:14): The Euphrates was one of four rivers that flowed through the Garden of Eden (see Genesis 2:14). It is the longest river in Western Asia (almost 1,800 miles), and many ancient cities, including Ur and Babylon, were located on it. This region has given birth to many pagan and idolatrous religions.

In the sixth trumpet judgment, the fallen angels bound at the Euphrates are released. We know that these four angels are fallen, for no holy angel of God is ever bound as these angels are.

The four angels...were released to kill a third of mankind (9:15): Adding this to the one-fourth who were killed as a result of the fourth seal judgment, about half of the earth's population is killed.

The number of mounted troops was twice ten thousand times ten thousand (9:16): This is 200 million—an incalculably large army.

The horses...and those who rode them (9:17): Through the years, many people have assumed this must refer to the army of China, which has long claimed to be able to mount an army of 200 million. Contextually, however, this does not seem to make sense. We have seen that these 200 million are led by four fallen angels. Besides, the description of these "mounted troops" on strange horses appears to be anything but human in verse 17. Note also that the horses themselves and their killing power seem to be the primary focus of attention in these verses, not the riders. Apparently, these are demonic spirits led by four fallen angels, and they murder millions of people (verses 15, 18).

By these three plagues a third of mankind was killed (9:18): A biblical plague is a disease or epidemic that God causes or allows for the purpose of judgment. The end times will bring a massive outbreak of plagues (see Revelation 6:8; 9:20; 11:6; 15:1, 6, 8; 16:9, 21; 18:4, 8; 21:9; 22:18). The three plagues mentioned in Revelation 9:18—fire, smoke, and sulfur—will kill a third of humankind.

The power of the horses (9:19): These are apparently not natural horses, but fallen angels who are instruments of divine judgment. They supernaturally wound people of the earth.

The rest of mankind...did not repent (9:20): Amazingly, the rest of humankind who are still alive refuse to repent of their evil acts. The hearts of these people are hardened against God. This reminds us of Pharaoh, who refused to repent despite the plagues brought by Moses (see Exodus 7:22; 9:7).

These hardened humans refuse to cease their worship of demons and their idolatry. The rapture of the church will have taken place prior to the tribulation period, so false religion, spirit worship, and idolatry will rapidly escalate. Satan, of course, has always wanted to be worshiped (Isaiah 14:12-15; Matthew 4:8-10).

Nor did they repent of their murders or their sorceries or their sexual immorality or their thefts (9:21): One would think that after witnessing such unbelievable horror and suffering, any person would be moved to repentance. But these tribulation rebels refuse, falling ever deeper into sin and occultism, thereby justifying God's judgments.

MAJOR THEMES

1. *Violation of some of God's Ten Commandments.* During the tribulation, people will break a number of God's Ten Commandments. By making and then worshiping pagan idols, they will break God's first and second commandments. In murdering other people, they will violate God's sixth commandment. In engaging in theft, they will break the eighth commandment. By their sexual immorality, they will break God's seventh commandment. These will be evil times.

2. *Some angels are confined.* There are two broad classes of demons. One

group is free to actively oppose God and His people (Ephesians 2:1-3). The other is confined (see Luke 8:31; 2 Peter 2:4; Jude 6; Revelation 9:1-3, 11). The confined fallen angels are apparently being punished for some sin other than the original rebellion against God (Isaiah 14:12-17; Ezekiel 28:11-19). Some theologians believe these angels are guilty of the heinous unnatural sin mentioned in Genesis 6:2-4.

DIGGING DEEPER WITH CROSS-REFERENCES

Murder—Genesis 9:5-6; Exodus 20:13; Numbers 35:16, 30-31; Deuteronomy 5:17; Psalm 5:6; Matthew 15:19; 1 John 3:15

Sexual immorality—Acts 15:20; 1 Corinthians 5:9-10; 10:8; Galatians 5:19; Colossians 3:5; 1 Thessalonians 4:3; 2 Peter 2:14; Jude 7

Suicide—1 Samuel 31:4-6; 2 Samuel 17:23; Matthew 27:3-10; Acts 1:18-19; John 8:22

LIFE LESSONS

1. *Avoid idolatry.* Idolatry involves worshiping other things in place of God. It can take many forms: the desire to be rich, materialism, the pursuit of fame, sexual immorality, and more. The New Testament consistently urges Christians to beware of idolatry (1 Corinthians 5:11; 10:7, 14; 2 Corinthians 6:16; Galatians 5:20; Colossians 3:5; 1 John 5:21).

2. *Avoid occultism.* Some Christians today flirt with whitewashed occultism. Though God condemns mediums and psychics (Leviticus 20:27; Deuteronomy 18:11), today there are so-called Christian psychics. God condemns witchcraft (1 Samuel 15:23), but we see so-called Christian witches. Moreover, many Christians read astrology columns (see Isaiah 47:13; Jeremiah 10:2; Daniel 4:7). Christians beware: Avoid all forms of occultism.

QUESTIONS FOR REFLECTION AND DISCUSSION

1. What is your attitude toward the Ten Commandments? How do you relate the Ten Commandments to the New Testament teaching that we live under grace and not the law (Ephesians 2:15)?

2. Do you enjoy watching television shows featuring psychics? Do you read the astrology columns in newspapers?

3. Do you prioritize anything in your life higher than God?

DAY 16

THE MESSAGE OF THE LITTLE SCROLL

REVELATION 10

SCRIPTURE READING AND INSIGHTS

Begin by reading Revelation 10 in your favorite Bible. As you read, trust God to open your eyes so you can discover wondrous things from His Word (Psalm 119:18).

In the previous lesson, we examined the fifth and sixth trumpet judgments. Now, in a brief interlude, we read of a little scroll that is both sweet and sour to John—sweet because it contains God's Word but sour because of the promises of judgment. With your Bible still accessible, consider the following insights on the biblical text, verse by verse.

Revelation 10:1-4

I saw another mighty angel (10:1): We now have an interlude between the sixth and seventh trumpet judgments. During this interlude, God's people are assured that God is absolutely sovereign over the affairs of earth and that victory is soon to come.

This angel is characterized as a mighty angel. This reminds us of the "mighty angel" mentioned in Revelation 5:2. Scripture reveals that all angels excel in strength (Psalm 103:20), but apparently some angels are more powerful than others (Daniel 10:12-14).

This mighty angel is apparently a high-ranking angel characterized by splendor, brightness, and strength (compare Revelation 5:2; 8:3; 18:1). God's angels can appear so glorious that people may be tempted to worship them (Revelation 22:8-9).

Wrapped in a cloud (10:1): Clouds are often biblical metaphors for the glory of God (Exodus 13:21; 40:28-34; Job 37:15-16; Matthew 26:64; Revelation 14:14). Perhaps this angel is often in the presence of the God of glory and continues to emanate God's glory as he engages in his assigned duties. Recall that after Moses had been with God on the mountain, "the skin of his face shone because he had been talking with God" (Exodus 34:29).

With a rainbow over his head (10:1): In the Noahic covenant, the rainbow was a sign that God would never again destroy the entire world with a flood. The rainbow is thus a potent reminder that even in the midst of woe and judgment, God is also a God of mercy (Habakkuk 3:2).

His face was like the sun, and his legs like pillars of fire (10:1): When an angel appeared to shepherds in a field to announce the birth of Jesus, "the glory of the Lord shone around them, and they were filled with great fear" (Luke 2:9). Angels are often so glorious that humans are terrified when they show up. When Daniel saw an angel he was left without strength (Daniel 10:8). Zechariah was gripped with fear when an angel appeared to him (Luke 1:12). The Roman soldiers trembled with fear and became as dead men when an angel appeared and rolled back the stone blocking Jesus' tomb (Matthew 28:2-4).

Some Bible interpreters believe this angel might be an appearance of the Lord Jesus Christ. After all, in an earlier vision, Jesus' face shines like the sun, and his feet are like burnished bronze (Revelation 1:15-16). However, Christ is never called an angel anywhere in the New Testament. Further, the angel is introduced as "another angel," indicating that this angel is in the same class as other angels in Revelation. Further, this angel is mighty but not Almighty, which God (Jesus) is throughout Scripture (for example, see Revelation 19:6). In the book of Revelation, Jesus is not a mighty angel but is rather the King of kings and Lord of lords (Revelation 19). Scripture consistently reveals that the next time Christ comes to the earth will be at the second coming and not before.

Moreover, Jesus was physically resurrected from the dead, and even today in heaven, Jesus retains His permanent glorified (human) resurrection body.

When Christ comes again at the second coming, He will come as the Son of Man (Matthew 26:64; see also Acts 1:11).

All things considered, it seems best to interpret the angel's glory as a reflection of God's glory, much as the moon brightly reflects the light of the sun at night.

He had a little scroll (10:2): We aren't told what was written on the scroll, but it probably represented the Word of God. Another possibility is that it contains the angel's written orders for the mission he was about to fulfill.

He set his right foot on the sea, and his left foot on the land (10:2): Standing with one foot on the sea and the other on the land conveys the image of taking possession. The angel is God's representative, so his action represents God's absolute sovereignty over this planet. This is a direct challenge to Satan, who has long engaged in the role of "god of this world" (2 Corinthians 4:4; see also John 12:31).

When he called out, the seven thunders sounded (10:3): The seven thunders indicate that more powerful storms of judgment are impending. God's voice is often compared to or associated with thunder (Job 26:14; 37:5; Psalm 29; John 12:28-29).

I heard a voice... "Seal up what the seven thunders have said" (10:4): We do not know what the seven thunders uttered, because a heavenly voice—perhaps that of Jesus Himself—commanded John to seal up what he had heard (compare with Daniel 12:4, 9). The message is to remain concealed until God's appointed time (Revelation 22:10; Daniel 8:26-27).

Revelation 10:5-7

The angel...raised his right hand to heaven (10:5): A person raises a hand when taking an oath or making a solemn vow. The angel is portrayed as taking an oath with his hand raised toward God. The oath apparently affirms the solemnity and certainty of the words.

Swore...there would be no more delay (10:6): Only by the authority of the sovereign and mighty eternal Creator can the angel make the declaration about how and when "the mystery of God" will be fulfilled and finished (verse 7).

The phrase "no more delay" indicates that when the seventh angel sounds the seventh trumpet (11:15), the seven bowl judgments will begin (chapter 16).

Following this, the tribulation period will rapidly come to a close, and the Lord Jesus will gloriously return again to set up His kingdom (chapters 19–20).

That "there would be no more delay" is good news for the tribulation martyrs who asked the Lord when they would be vindicated (Revelation 6:10-11). These words also indicate that the question long ago asked of Christ by the disciples on the Mount of Olives is now being answered: "Tell us, when will these things be, and what will be the sign of your coming and of the end of the age?" (Matthew 24:3). The age would soon close. The prayer of all Christians, "Your kingdom come" (Matthew 6:10), is about to be answered.

In the past God delayed judgment so that human beings would have sufficient time to repent and turn to Him for salvation. "The Lord is not slow to fulfill his promise as some count slowness, but is patient toward you, not wishing that any should perish, but that all should reach repentance" (2 Peter 3:9). Now, however, time is running out. God's final judgment is about to fall.

The mystery of God would be fulfilled (10:7): Prophecy expositors have many opinions on the "mystery of God." Some relate it to past prophetic announcements of the glorious return of the Son of God and the establishment of His righteous kingdom. Others suggest it has to do with God's plan to punish evildoers. Still others suggest it involves prophecy relating to the middle and second half of the tribulation period. Still others say it relates more generally to the final consummation of all things. Still others interpret it as relating to why God allows bad things to happen on the earth. In view of such diversity of opinion, it is unwise to be dogmatic on this mystery. It's a mystery!

Revelation 10:8-11

The voice...spoke... "Go, take the scroll" (10:8): The command comes from either God or the Lord Jesus Christ. John obeys without hesitation.

He said to me, "Take and eat it" (10:9): The Bible often uses the language of ingesting in a figurative sense. We are urged, "Oh, taste and see that the Lord is good" (Psalm 34:8). Jeremiah affirmed of God's Word, "Your words were found, and I ate them, and your words became to me a joy and the delight of my heart" (Jeremiah 15:16). The apostle Peter instructed young believers, "Like newborn infants, long for the pure spiritual milk" (1 Peter 2:2). The writer of Hebrews speaks of "solid food" for mature Christians (5:14). The apostle Paul informed the immature Corinthian Christians, "I fed you with milk, not solid food" (1 Corinthians 3:1-2).

John obeyed the angel's instruction to eat the scroll, and it was sweet as honey in his mouth. The symbolism indicates that God's Word was sweet to John, for it abounds with the glorious promises of God. The Word of God speaks of victory in the end for God's people. For this reason, God's Word is more to be desired "than gold, even much fine gold; sweeter also than honey and drippings of the honeycomb" (Psalm 19:9-10).

However, the scroll quickly soured in John's stomach. The Word of God is bitter to unbelievers because it promises woe and judgment. Scripture promises doom, not victory, for those who reject God. So this passage of the Word of God is both sweet and bitter.

I took the little scroll...and ate it (10:10): As instructed by the angel, John took the scroll and ate it. Just as promised, it was both delightful and bothersome.

I was told, "You must again prophesy" (10:11): John's work was not yet complete. He was called to sound a warning about the approaching bitter judgment in the seventh trumpet, which constitutes the seven bowl judgments.

MAJOR THEMES

1. *Mystery (Revelation 10:7)*. A biblical mystery is a truth that cannot be discerned simply by human investigation, but requires special revelation from God. Generally, this word refers to a truth that was unknown to people living in Old Testament times but was revealed to humankind by God in the New Testament (Matthew 13:17; Colossians 1:26).

2. *God's servants the prophets (Revelation 10:7)*. The Hebrew word for prophet, *nabi*, refers to people who are taken over by the power of God and who speak God's words to the people. Often their words were directed at specific situations or problems that needed to be dealt with. In other cases, they spoke of the future. They typically prefaced their words with "Thus saith the Lord," thereby indicating that their words were not their own but came from God. These prophets were called into service directly by God, some even before birth (Jeremiah 1:5; Luke 1:13-16).

DIGGING DEEPER WITH CROSS-REFERENCES

Seal up—Isaiah 8:16; Daniel 8:26; 12:4; Revelation 10:4; 22:10

Him who lives forever—Revelation 4:9-10; 10:6; 15:7

God the Creator—Genesis 1; Exodus 20:11; Psalm 33:6, 9; Isaiah 44:24; Jeremiah 32:17; John 1:3; 1 Corinthians 8:6; Colossians 1:16; Hebrews 1:2; 11:3

LIFE LESSONS

1. *A burden for the lost.* Our passage speaks of the bitter circumstances of unbelievers during the tribulation period. This reality ought to give you and me a burden for the lost. The more people we can reach for Christ prior to the tribulation, the more people will participate in the rapture and thereby escape this approaching bitterness. Christ's Great Commission thus takes on new significance: "Go therefore and make disciples of all nations" (Matthew 28:19-20).

2. *A sense of urgency.* Our passage refers to God having "no more delay" as His prophetic plan moves toward its culmination. You and I ought not delay in our commitment to God, for life is all too short. James 4:14 tells us that we are like "a mist that appears for a little time and then vanishes." The psalmist expresses a similar sentiment: "Behold, you have made my days a few handbreadths, and my lifetime is as nothing before you. Surely all mankind stands as a mere breath!" (Psalm 39:5). It is wise for each of us to give our time to God while there is yet time to give.

QUESTIONS FOR REFLECTION AND DISCUSSION

1. Do you have a burden for the lost? If yes, what are you doing about it?

2. Do you yearn for God to have "no more delay" in bringing history to its close so we can dwell with Jesus face to face in the new heavens and new earth?

DAY 17

THE MINISTRY OF THE TWO PROPHETIC WITNESSES

REVELATION 11:1-6

SCRIPTURE READING AND INSIGHTS

Begin by reading Revelation 11:1-6 in your favorite Bible. As you read, allow the Word of God to bring revival to your soul (Psalm 119:25, 93, 107).

In yesterday's reading, we briefly focused attention on the little scroll that was both sweet and sour to John—sweet because it contained God's Word but sour because of promises of judgment. Now we zero in on God's two prophetic witnesses who emerge during the tribulation period. With your Bible still accessible, consider the following insights on the biblical text, verse by verse.

Revelation 11:1-2

I was given a measuring rod... "Measure the temple of God..." (11:1): In Bible times, the measuring rod was a bamboo-like reed that was light and rigid (see Ezekiel 40:3, 5).

Bible expositors have offered several interpretations of what the measuring symbolizes. Some say the act of measuring the temple indicates that God is making a claim for it—that He owns it (compare Revelation 21:15). Despite how the Gentiles (the evil forces of the antichrist) are oppressing the city, God says, "It's all mine!"

Other expositors suggest that the temple and worshipers are measured to ascertain their character. In this view, the temple and the Jews have been measured and found to be apostate, in need of revival and restoration. Eventually, the Jews will be restored to their Messiah when they call out for deliverance from the antichrist at Armageddon. (More on this later in the book.)

"Do not measure the court outside the temple" (11:2): Gentiles were prohibited from entering the inner court of the temple (a prohibition enforced by the death penalty), but they were permitted access to the outer court. God's instruction that John was not to bother measuring the outer court (with its Gentiles) symbolizes God's rejection of the unbelieving Gentiles for their oppression of the Jews, God's covenant people, for 42 months (three and a half years).

"It is given over to the nations" (11:2): The holy city had been oppressed by Assyria, Babylon, Medo-Persia, Greece, and Rome. During the tribulation period, the holy city will be oppressed by the antichrist and his forces. The antichrist will proclaim himself to be God and set up an image of himself in the Jewish temple, thereby defiling it (2 Thessalonians 2:4).

As the holy city is being trampled by Gentile forces—apparently during the last three and a half years of the tribulation period—God shelters the Jews in the wilderness from these evil forces. These Jews will exit Jerusalem right at the midpoint of the tribulation period, when the antichrist exalts himself as God (see Matthew 24:20-22).

Revelation 11:3-6

"I will grant authority to my two witnesses" (11:3): During the tribulation period, God will raise up two mighty witnesses who will testify to the true God, His judgment, and His salvation with astounding power. In the Old Testament two witnesses were required to confirm testimony (Deuteronomy 17:6). These two witnesses will confirm God's truth to those living in tribulation times.

The time frame of these two witnesses—1,260 days—equals three and a half years. This period is elsewhere defined as 42 months (Revelation 11:2) and "a time, and times, and half a time" (12:14). A "time" is one year, "times" is two years, and "half a time" is half of a year.

It is not clear from Revelation 11 whether this is the first or last three and a half years of the tribulation. It may be best to conclude that the two witnesses do their miraculous work during the first three and a half years, for the antichrist's execution of them seems to fit best with other events that will transpire at the midpoint of the tribulation, such as the antichrist's exaltation of himself to godhood. Moreover, the resurrection of the two witnesses—after being dead for three days—would make a bigger impact on the world at the midpoint of the tribulation than at the end, just prior to the glorious second coming of Christ.

Clothed in sackcloth (11:3): These witnesses will wear clothing made of goat or camel hair, garments that symbolically express mourning (see Genesis 37:34). The mourning is over the wretched spiritual condition and lack of repentance in the world.

These are the two olive trees and the two lampstands (11:4): The imagery here is taken from Zechariah 3–4. Bible expositors have offered several interpretations. One understanding is that lamps in biblical days were typically fueled by olive oil. The reference to olive trees and lampstands is believed to symbolize the light of spiritual revival. The preaching of the two witnesses will bring this light of revival during the dark days of the tribulation.

Other Bible expositors relate this imagery to the Holy Spirit. Zechariah 4:2-14 focuses on Joshua the high priest and Zerubbabel the governor. Both of these individuals were empowered by the Holy Spirit, something symbolized by the olive oil. It is thus inferred that the two witnesses of Revelation 11 will likewise be empowered by the Holy Spirit during their ministry and will shine as lights, just like a lamp.

If anyone would harm them, fire pours from their mouth and consumes their foes (11:5): Prior to their execution by the antichrist, the two witnesses are sustained by the supernatural protection of God. Similarly, Jesus was providentially protected during His ministry. Once Jesus' ministry was over, He was put to death on the cross. Until that time, Jesus continually affirmed that His time had not yet come (see, for example, John 7:6-8). Likewise, only when the ministry of these two witnesses is complete will they finally be executed by the forces of the antichrist. And, like Jesus, they will be resurrected and ascend into heaven.

Anyone who tries to harm either of the two prophetic witnesses will come to a fiery end. Their ministry is unstoppable for three and a half years, until "they have finished their testimony" (Revelation 11:7).

In the Bible, fire can point to the wrath of God. Scripture tells us that God's "wrath is poured out like fire" (Nahum 1:6). God said, "My wrath [will] go forth like fire, and burn with none to quench it, because of the evil of your deeds" (Jeremiah 4:4). Those who stand against God's two prophets will come face to face with God's wrath.

They have the power to shut the sky...they have power over the waters...and to strike the earth with every kind of plague (11:6): In both testaments, God uses miracles to authenticate His messengers (Acts 2:43; Romans 15:18-19; 2 Corinthians 12:12). During the tribulation period, when the world is overrun by supernatural demonic activity, false religion, murder, sexual perversion, and unrestrained wickedness, these two witnesses will perform supernatural signs that will mark them as true prophets of God.

Some expositors believe the two witnesses will be Moses and Elijah. These are some of their reasons:

1. In the tribulation period, God deals with the Jews, just as He did in the first 69 weeks of Daniel. Moses and Elijah are two of the most influential figures in Jewish history. Their appearance during the tribulation period would thus make good sense.

2. Both the Old Testament and Jewish tradition expected Moses (Deuteronomy 18:15, 18) and Elijah (Malachi 4:5) to return in the future.

3. Moses and Elijah appeared on the Mount of Transfiguration with Jesus. This shows their centrality. Therefore, we might expect them to appear during the tribulation.

4. The miracles portrayed in Revelation 11 are similar to those performed by Moses and Elijah (see Exodus 7–11; 1 Kings 17; Malachi 4:5).

5. Both Moses and Elijah left the earth in unusual ways. Elijah never died, but rather was transported to heaven in a fiery chariot (2 Kings 2:11-12). God supernaturally buried Moses' body in an unknown location (Deuteronomy 34:5-6; Jude 9).

These are some of the reasons why some Bible expositors suggest that in the tribulation period, God will send two of His mightiest servants: Moses, the great deliverer and spiritual legislator of Israel, and Elijah, a prince among Old Testament prophets. These individuals rescued Israel from bondage and idolatry in the past, and they may appear again during the tribulation period to warn Israel against succumbing to the false religion of the antichrist and the false prophet.

Other Bible expositors have suggested that perhaps the two witnesses will be Enoch and Elijah. After all, Enoch and Elijah were both upright men who were raptured to heaven. Neither one of them experienced death. Both of them were prophets—Enoch a Gentile and Elijah an Israelite. The Church Fathers unanimously held to this view during the first 300 years of church history. God may ordain Elijah to speak to the Jews and Enoch to speak to the Gentiles during the tribulation.

Still other expositors say that these two witnesses will not be biblical personalities of the past. They reason that the text would surely identify famous Old Testament personalities if they were indeed coming back. They conclude that the two witnesses will likely be new prophets that God specially raises up for ministry during the tribulation (see Matthew 11:14).

MAJOR THEMES

1. *Previous Jewish temples.* The first Jewish temple was built by Solomon, son of David, in Jerusalem in about 960 BC (1 Kings 6–7; 2 Chronicles 3–4). It was the heart and center of Jewish worship for the kingdom of Judah. It was destroyed by Nebuchadnezzar and the Babylonians in 587 BC. The second temple was a smaller, leaner temple built after the Babylonian exile, completed in 515 BC, and not nearly as magnificent as Solomon's temple (see Ezra 3:12). It lasted some 500 years. The third temple was built by King Herod the Great, who believed this would endear the Jews (his subjects) to him. It was completed in AD 64 but destroyed in AD 70 along with the rest of Jerusalem by Titus and his Roman army.

2. *Authority.* God gave His two witnesses authority (Revelation 11:3). The term "authority" surfaces often in Revelation.

- Jesus received authority from the Father (2:27; 12:10).
- Jesus will give authority to overcomers in the millennial kingdom (2:26).
- Death and Hades will be given authority over a fourth of the earth (6:8).
- Satan, the dragon, gives authority to the antichrist (13:2, 4).
- The antichrist exercises authority for three and a half years (13:5).
- He is given authority over "every tribe and people and language and nation" (13:7).
- The false prophet is also given authority (13:12).
- Angels have authority during the tribulation period (14:18; 18:1).
- Kings of the earth have authority for a short time (17:12).

DIGGING DEEPER WITH CROSS-REFERENCES

Gentile oppression of the Jews—2 Kings 25:8-10; Psalm 79:1; Isaiah 63:18; Lamentations 1:10

Two witnesses—Deuteronomy 17:6; 19:15; Matthew 18:16; John 8:17; Hebrews 10:28

Sackcloth—Genesis 37:34; 2 Samuel 3:31; 2 Kings 6:30; 19:1; Esther 4:1; Isaiah 22:12; Jeremiah 6:26; Matthew 11:21

LIFE LESSONS

1. *Spiritual drought.* Just as a physical drought can ravage the land, a spiritual drought can parch people's souls. In Psalm 63:1, the psalmist affirms, "My soul thirsts for you…in a dry and weary land where there is no water." Psalm 68:6 affirms that "the rebellious dwell in a parched land." Isaiah 1:30 indicates that those who are disobedient to God are "like a garden without water." Returning to the Lord in repentance is the only solution to spiritual drought (Isaiah 41:17).

2. *God's Word can seem both bitter and sweet.* God's Word can seem bitter when we disobey its teachings. "Oh, that my ways were steadfast in obeying your decrees! Then I would not be put to shame when I consider all your commands" (Psalm 119:5-6 NIV). The good news is that Scripture is also especially sweet because it can revive our souls and fill us with joy (see Psalm 119:11, 28; Romans 12:12; Ephesians 4:22-23; Colossians 3:16; 2 Timothy 3:15-17).

QUESTIONS FOR REFLECTION AND DISCUSSION

1. Do you ever feel as if you are suffering a spiritual drought? What steps can you take today to help satisfy your spiritual thirst?

2. Self-examination is healthy. Ask yourself, "Am I in complete submission to the authority of God in all areas of my life? Am I holding anything back?"

3. Are you in need of revival from God's Word? I recommend Psalm 119.

DAY 18

THE DEATH, RESURRECTION, AND ASCENSION OF THE TWO WITNESSES

REVELATION 11:7-14

SCRIPTURE READING AND INSIGHTS

Begin by reading Revelation 11:7-14 in your favorite Bible. As you read, allow the Word of God to bring revival to your soul (Psalm 119:25, 93, 107).

In the previous lesson, we were introduced to God's two mighty prophetic witnesses. In today's reading, we find out about their death, resurrection, and ascension into heaven. With your Bible still accessible, consider the following insights on the biblical text, verse by verse.

Revelation 11:7-10

When they have finished their testimony (11:7): We have seen that during the tribulation period, God will raise up two mighty witnesses who will testify to Him with astounding power. The miracles they perform are reminiscent of Moses (Exodus 7–11) and Elijah (1 Kings 17; Malachi 4:5). These prophetic witnesses apparently emerge on the scene at the beginning of the tribulation period. They continue to minister for 1,260 days, or three and a half years.

Only when "they have finished their testimony" are they permitted to be killed. God's obedient servants are immortal until their work is done. Once they are finished, they will be executed by the antichrist.

The word "finished" in this verse is the same word used by Jesus on the cross when He said, "It is finished" (John 19:30). Christ died in Jerusalem after He had finished His work of redemption. The two witnesses die in Jerusalem after they have completed their work of redemptive ministry.

The beast that rises from the bottomless pit will make war on them (11:7): The fact that the beast, or antichrist, ascends out of the bottomless pit (the habitation of demons) may point to the antichrist's apparent death and resurrection (Revelation 13:3-4). Some suggest that while the antichrist's wounded body appears dead, his spirit visits the bottomless pit and later ascends out of the bottomless pit to rejoin his "resurrected" body. (More on this hypothesis later.)

Once the two witnesses complete their ministry, God will withdraw His providential protection from them. At this point, the antichrist will kill them, something that many had already lost their lives attempting to do. The witnesses will not die prematurely. It all goes according to God's divine timing.

Their dead bodies will lie in the street of the great city (11:8): The bodies of the witnesses lie lifeless in Jerusalem. Jerusalem is referred to as "the great city," something true only from a human perspective. God looks not at externals but at spiritual realities. From a spiritual perspective, Jerusalem is anything but great at this time.

Sodom and Egypt (11:8): Jerusalem is figuratively called "Sodom and Egypt" because of the people's apostasy and rejection of God. Sodom was brimming with perverted sex, and Egypt was known for its persecution of God's people. Both cities were rebellious against God. The description of Jerusalem as no better than Sodom and Egypt indicates that this once holy city is now in the same league as those known for their hatred of the true God and His Word.

For three and a half days...gaze at their dead bodies (11:9): It is apparently by television and the Internet that "the peoples and tribes and languages and nations" will gaze at the dead witnesses for three and a half days. Our modern technology has set the stage for the things we read about in the tribulation period and may indicate that we are living in the end times.

Refusing to bury a corpse was a way of showing contempt (see Acts 14:19). The Old Testament prohibits this practice (Deuteronomy 21:22-23). By leaving the dead bodies in the street, the people of the world render the greatest possible insult to God's spokesmen. This was considered among the greatest indignities that could be perpetrated on someone (see Psalm 79:2-3). It is equivalent to people spitting on the corpses.

Even though our text does not say so, the antichrist will no doubt receive glory from people around the globe for putting the witnesses to death. He will be their hero, their deliverer.

Those who dwell on the earth will rejoice (11:10): In the book of Revelation, "those who dwell on the earth" refers to unbelievers. The phrase carries the idea of earth dwellers or worldlings—those characterized by the anti-God world system.

These worldlings will essentially have a satanic Christmas celebration when the witnesses are put to death. They exchange presents, apparently because they do not have to listen to these convicting messages from God any longer. Biblical history seems to indicate that the only prophets people love are dead ones. This is the only instance of rejoicing during the tribulation period recorded in the book of Revelation.

Revelation 11:11-14

A breath of life from God entered them (11:11): The Christmas celebration quickly gives way to fear as people witness a mighty act of God. The lifeless corpses suddenly stand up in full view of television and Internet feeds. Clips of this event will no doubt be replayed over and over on various media and go viral on the Internet. The resurrection and ascension of God's two witnesses will be huge exclamation points to their prophetic words throughout their three-and-a-half-year ministry.

The term "breath" recalls the ancient prophecy of the dry bones, in which God promised, "I will cause breath to enter you, and you shall live" (Ezekiel 37:5). This refers to the rebirth of the nation of Israel, which was fulfilled in 1948. Likewise, in terms of the two witnesses, "a breath of life from God entered them," and they are resurrected from the dead. God is a master of bringing new life!

Then they heard a loud voice from heaven saying to them, "Come up here!" (11:12): The loud voice is authoritative. "Come up here" is a sovereign directive to ascend into heaven, which the two witnesses promptly do. The apostle John was commanded, "Come up here," in Revelation 4:1 so he could receive God's great prophetic revelation of the future.

The witnesses go up to heaven in a cloud, perhaps a cloud of God's glory. This recalls how Christ Himself, following His resurrection, ascended into the clouds (Acts 1:9). This is also similar to the rapture, in which the dead in Christ rise first, and then living believers on earth "will be caught up together with them in the clouds to meet the Lord in the air" (1 Thessalonians 4:17).

The enemies of the two witnesses will see it all and will likely hate them all the more as a result of their victorious resurrection and ascension. The whole world will surmise that the antichrist's murderous activities have been overruled by heaven.

There was a great earthquake (11:13): Following this ascension, the city of Jerusalem—where the murder takes place and the bodies are publicly displayed—will receive a sudden judgment. Jerusalem will suffer an immense earthquake that will destroy one-tenth of the city and kill 7,000 inhabitants.

The rest were terrified and gave glory to the God of heaven (11:13): After witnessing this, many will give glory to God. This does not mean that all these people will become believers, but at the very least many will acknowledge God's hand in these events. Apparently, many (but not all) will just be giving lip service to God. Soon enough many of these same people will be cursing Him. "People gnawed their tongues in anguish and cursed the God of heaven for their pain and sores. They did not repent of their deeds" (Revelation 16:10-11).

Some scholars suggest that God's resurrection of the two prophetic witnesses and the verbal witness of God's 144,000 Jewish evangelists will expose millions of souls to the truth about God. How wonderful to contemplate that despite the horrific efforts of the antichrist and the false prophet to promote false religion, God will give a powerful testimony of Himself during the tribulation.

Let's not forget that God takes no pleasure in the death of the wicked (Ezekiel 18:32; 33:11) but rather desires that all people be saved (see 2 Peter 3:9). Despite the hardness of heart of many people during those days, many others will nevertheless turn to the Lord and be saved. We know this to be true, for by the time the Lord comes again at the second coming, Christ will invite all believers who have survived the woes of the tribulation period into His millennial kingdom (see Matthew 25:31-46).

The second woe has passed (11:14): But things are about to get even worse!

MAJOR THEMES

1. *Jerusalem.* Jerusalem has often been referred to as the holy city. It is famous for being the scene of Jesus' arrest, trial, crucifixion, and resurrection. The city itself rests in the Judean hills at about 2,640 feet above sea level. During Jesus' time, the city was probably home to about a quarter of a million people. The Jews believed no city could possibly compare with Jerusalem. It was the geographical heart of the Jewish religion. Jesus Himself made a number of visits there (Luke 2:22-51; 10:38-42; 13:34). How sad to see Jerusalem so morally and spiritually degraded in the end times.

2. *Burial customs.* Funerals in biblical times were performed quickly because the hot climate rapidly caused decay and odor. When people died, they were immediately bathed and then wrapped in strips of linen. Sometimes a gummy combination of spices was applied to the wrappings of the body. It was then carried by stretcher to the place of burial, whether in the ground or in a cave. In some cases, entire families might be buried in a large cave. Eventually, because some areas lacked space in caves, bones would later be removed from a cave and stored in a wooden or stone chest.

DIGGING DEEPER WITH CROSS-REFERENCES

Testimony—1 Chronicles 16:8-9; Psalms 9:11; 26:7; 119:172; 145:12; Isaiah 12:4; Jeremiah 51:10; Matthew 5:15; 10:32; John 15:27; Acts 1:8; Romans 10:9; 2 Timothy 1:8; Hebrews 2:12; 1 Peter 3:15

War on the saints—Daniel 7:25; Revelation 6:9-11; 7:9-14; 13:7, 10; 20:4-5

Bottomless pit—Revelation 9:1-2, 11; 11:7; 17:8; 20:1

LIFE LESSONS

1. *Giving a testimony.* Like the two witnesses, we ought always to be willing to give our testimony to others. We should never hesitate to speak about how Jesus has changed our lives forever (see 1 John 1:3). Giving a personal testimony of what the Lord Jesus has done in your life is a very important

component of any witnessing encounter (see 1 Chronicles 16:8-9; Matthew 10:32; Mark 5:19-20; John 4:28-30, 39; 2 Timothy 1:8; 1 Peter 3:15). Talk about the full assurance you have that your sins are forgiven and the joyful expectation of spending all eternity with Jesus. Remember, you may not be an expert on every verse in the Bible, but you are an expert on what Jesus has done in your life!

2. *Standing strong in the face of persecution.* We may not die for our faith, as will the two witnesses, but we will all likely encounter persecution for our faith. The wicked despise the godly (Proverbs 29:27), and the godly will suffer persecution (2 Timothy 3:12). We should not be surprised if the world hates us (1 John 3:13). However, as Jesus indicated, those who are persecuted for righteousness are blessed (Matthew 5:10-11). We ought to rejoice in being counted worthy to suffer (Acts 5:41). We ought also to pray for those who persecute us (Matthew 5:44).

QUESTIONS FOR REFLECTION AND DISCUSSION

1. Are you comfortable or uncomfortable in giving your testimony to others? If you need help becoming a stronger witness for Jesus, I recommend my friends at EvanTell (www.evantell.org).

2. Can you think of a time when someone mocked you or spoke condescendingly of you for being a Christian? How did you respond? Do you have a thick skin or a thin skin when it comes to standing for Jesus?

DAY 19

THE SEVENTH TRUMPET JUDGMENT

REVELATION 11:15-19

SCRIPTURE READING AND INSIGHTS

Begin by reading Revelation 11:15-19 in your favorite Bible. As you read, never forget that God urges you to quickly obey His Word in all things (Psalm 119:60).

In yesterday's reading, we focused on the death, resurrection, and ascension of God's two prophetic witnesses. Now we shift our attention back to the seventh trumpet judgment. This last trumpet judgment constitutes a whole new series of judgments to be unleashed on the earth. With your Bible still accessible, consider the following insights on the biblical text, verse by verse.

Revelation 11:15

The seventh angel blew his trumpet, and there were loud voices in heaven (11:15): We often read of a loud voice in heaven (Revelation 1:10; 5:2, 12; 6:10; 7:2, 10; 8:13; 10:3; 11:12; 12:10; 14:7, 9, 15, 18; 16:1, 17; 19:1, 17; 21:3). On this occasion, however, we read of loud voices (plural). They likely belong to the whole host of heaven.

The seventh trumpet includes the seven bowl judgments, which are God's final judgments to be unleashed on the earth. They include all the events that lead up to Christ's second coming (chapter 19) and the establishment of His kingdom on earth (chapter 20). Things are rushing toward a culmination at this point.

"The kingdom of the world has become the kingdom of our Lord" (11:15): The loud voices proclaim that the long-awaited kingdom of Jesus Christ will soon commence (see Revelation 20:1-10; see also Psalm 2:2; Isaiah 9:6-7; Ezekiel 21:26-27; Daniel 2:35, 44; 4:3; 6:26; 7:14, 26-27; Zechariah 14:9). This will take place after the judgments associated with the seventh trumpet have run their course.

The term "Lord" refers to the Father, the first person of the Trinity. The phrase "and of his Christ" refers to Jesus, the second person of the Trinity.

This verse points forward to Jesus' establishment of the millennial kingdom, over which He will rule for 1,000 years. Following His second coming, Christ will set up this kingdom and will assume the throne of David, as promised in the Davidic covenant (2 Samuel 7:12-14).

The world has long been a part of Satan's kingdom. He is portrayed as "the ruler of this world" (John 12:31; 14:30; 16:11) and "god of this world" (2 Corinthians 4:4). As well, ungodly human governments have long been under Satan's relentless influence (Psalm 2:2; Acts 4:26). Such evil governments will soon come to an end. Christ will set up the long-promised messianic kingdom (Isaiah 2:2-3; Daniel 2:44; 7:13-14, 18, 22, 27; Luke 1:31-33).

Revelation 11:16-18

The twenty-four elders...fell on their faces and worshiped God (11:16): To review, the 24 elders are glorified, crowned, and enthroned—traits that seem to indicate that they are redeemed human beings. Scripture elsewhere reveals that believers will be judged (1 Corinthians 3:1-10; 2 Corinthians 5:10) and then rewarded with crowns (for example, 2 Timothy 4:8; James 1:12; 1 Peter 5:4; Revelation 2:10). Apparently then, the 24 elders symbolize the church in heaven.

When they hear the announcement of the soon establishment of Christ's kingdom, the elders—representing the church—fall prostrate before God and worship Him. What a contrast this is to the rebellious defiance of God on earth.

"We give thanks to you, Lord God Almighty" (11:17): The elders express thanks to God for this wonderful reign. God is addressed in majestic terms. "Lord" points to His sovereignty; "Almighty," His omnipotence.

God is also called the One "who is and who was," referring to God's eternal nature. As Psalm 90:2 puts it, "Before the mountains were brought forth, or ever you had formed the earth and the world, from everlasting to everlasting you are God." God's endless existence points to His endless rule over all things. That rule is now about to be enforced *in toto*. Until now, God has permitted hostile rulers, culminating with the antichrist. But soon all evil rule will be put to an end, and Christ will rule over all.

The 24 elders address God: "You have taken your great power and begun to reign." Does this mean that Christ's reign begins at this very moment? Some expositors think so, but their affirmation is more likely an anticipation of Christ's nearing millennial rule. The event is viewed as so absolutely certain that it is spoken of as having already begun. Christ does not claim His royal rights until He returns at the second coming, but the actual victory has already been won.

We might call this a "past tense of certainty," indicating that this rule is as good as done. We find this literary device elsewhere in Scripture. In Romans 8:30, believers are said to be justified and glorified. Our future glorification is so certain that it is spoken of as having already happened.

"The nations raged, but your wrath came" (11:18): The elders speak of the raging response of unbelieving Gentiles on earth (compare with Psalm 2:1, 5, 12). God has given them plenty of opportunities to repent and turn to Him, but they continue to harden their hearts against Him. God in His righteousness and justice pours out His wrath against such rebellion (Romans 2:5, 8).

The demonic rage of these Gentiles culminates when they attempt to fight against Christ at the second coming. Revelation 16:14 tells us that demonic spirits will "go abroad to the kings of the whole world, to assemble them for battle on the great day of God the Almighty." Revelation 19:19 informs us, "I saw the beast and the kings of the earth with their armies gathered to make war against him who was sitting on the horse and against his army." Of course, this action is utterly futile, for Christ will slay them in an instant. (More on this later.)

"And the time for the dead to be judged, and for rewarding your servants, the prophets and saints" (11:18): The elders again speak as if future events are already present realities. The dead are as good as judged, and the saints are as good as rewarded. This is anticipatory language. These events have not yet occurred but will surely occur soon.

Notice that two groups of believers are mentioned—the prophets and saints. More specifically, the verse refers to both Old and New Testament prophets as well as saints, a term that embraces all other believers.

"Those who fear your name, both small and great" (11:18): "Fear" means reverence for God. "Both small and great" recognizes that not all saints are the same: Some are fervent and completely committed to Christ while others may be more timid in their faith. But all are saved and will be rewarded.

"Destroying the destroyers of the earth" (11:18): The elders also recognize God's judgment against those who, because of their rank and unrepentant rebellion, experience judgments that destroy the earth itself. These destroyers include Babylon, the antichrist, the false prophet, the forces of the antichrist, and Satan.

Revelation 11:19

God's temple in heaven was opened (11:19): Recall that at the beginning of Revelation 11, John witnesses the temple of God on earth being measured. Now we find the temple in heaven being opened to John. Some believe that this opening of the temple symbolizes believers in heaven enjoying intimate fellowship with God.

The ark of his covenant was seen within his temple (11:19): Many Bible expositors see the ark to be an emblem of God's atonement, His faithfulness, and His presence among the Israelites. We last saw God's Ark of the Covenant in 2 Chronicles 35:3, when it was placed in Solomon's temple. The Ark's present whereabouts are unknown, though many Christian archeologists continue to look for it. Multiple theories have emerged as to what has happened to it, including these three:

1. It was destroyed when Nebuchadnezzar burned the temple in 586 BC.
2. It was destroyed during the Babylonian captivity (see 1 Kings 14:26; 2 Kings 25:9; 2 Chronicles 33:7; Jeremiah 3:16).
3. Jeremiah hid it in a cave at Mount Sinai (see 2 Maccabees 2:4-8).

All this is probably a moot point, however, for many Bible expositors believe that Revelation 11 refers to a heavenly counterpart to the earthly Ark of the Covenant. Hebrews 9:24 tells us, "For Christ has entered, not into holy places made with hands, which are copies of the true things, but into heaven itself, now to appear in the presence of God on our behalf" (see also Hebrews 10:20).

In any event, the fact that the ark is mentioned here indicates that God will soon faithfully fulfill His covenant promises to Israel (represented by the ark). A remnant of Israel will soon come to faith in Jesus and will come into full possession of the ancient land promises in the millennial kingdom.

There were flashes of lightning, rumblings, peals of thunder, an earthquake, and heavy hail (11:19): Notice that this verse addresses both heaven and earth. Lightning, rumblings, and peals of thunder emanate from God's throne in heaven, and an earthquake and heavy hail inflict further damage on earth. As John witnesses glory in heaven, he witnesses destruction on earth.

MAJOR THEMES

1. *Jesus the King.* Genesis 49:10 includes a prophecy that the Messiah would come from the tribe of Judah and reign as King. The Davidic covenant in 2 Samuel 7:16 promised a Messiah who would reign on an eternal throne. Daniel 7:13-14 tells us that the Messiah-King will have an everlasting dominion. In the New Testament, an angel appeared to Mary and informed her she would give birth to a son who would "reign over the house of Jacob forever, and of his kingdom there will be no end" (Luke 1:32-33). At the second coming, Jesus will be revealed as the King of kings and Lord of lords (Revelation 19:16).

2. *The Ark of the Covenant.* Scripture indicates that the ark symbolized God's presence (1 Samuel 4:3-22). It was kept in the Most Holy Place, the innermost shrine of the tabernacle and the temple (Exodus 26:33). The lid of the ark held great significance. It was known as the mercy seat or atonement cover. On the annual Day of Atonement, the high priest sprinkled the blood of a sacrificial animal on it to symbolize the nation's repentance for the sins committed the previous year. Israel's guilt was transferred to the animal (Leviticus 23:27; Numbers 29:7).

DIGGING DEEPER WITH CROSS-REFERENCES

God rewards Old Testament saints—Daniel 12:1-3; see also 1 Corinthians 3:8; 4:5; Revelation 22:12

God rewards church-age saints—Romans 14:10-13; 1 Corinthians 15:51-52; 2 Corinthians 5:9-11; 1 Thessalonians 4:13-18

God rewards tribulation saints—Revelation 20:4

LIFE LESSONS

1. *The fear of God.* Christians are called to live in reverent fear of God (1 Samuel 12:14, 24; 2 Chronicles 19:9; Acts 10:35; 1 Peter 1:17; 2:17). Fear of the Lord motivates one to be obedient to God (Deuteronomy 5:29; Ecclesiastes 12:13), to serve Him (Deuteronomy 6:13), and to avoid evil (Proverbs 3:7; 8:13; 16:6). Fear of the Lord is true wisdom (Job 28:28; Psalm 111:10) and the beginning of knowledge (Proverbs 1:7). God blesses those who fear Him (Psalm 115:13). Fear of the Lord leads to riches, honor, and long life (Proverbs 22:4). God shows mercy to those who fear Him (Luke 1:50).

> "People are to tremble and fear before the God of Daniel, for he is the living God" (Daniel 6:26).

2. *Forfeiting rewards.* Spend a few minutes meditating on the following Bible passages: Romans 14:10-13; 1 Corinthians 15:51-52; 2 Corinthians 5:9-11; 1 Thessalonians 4:13-18. Did you know Scripture reveals that some Christians will forfeit their rewards because of unrepentant sin or a failure to obey God? Some Christians will even experience a sense of shame at the judgment (see 2 John 8). We ought to follow the resolution of Jonathan Edwards (1703–1758): "Resolved, never to do anything, which I should be afraid to do, if it were the last hour of my life."

QUESTIONS FOR REFLECTION AND DISCUSSION

1. Does your lifestyle at home and at work or school consistently show that you revere the Lord?
2. Does the possibility of losing a reward at the judgment seat of Christ motivate you or scare you?
3. Would you like to make any resolutions?

DAY 20

THE OUTBREAK OF WAR

REVELATION 12

SCRIPTURE READING AND INSIGHTS

Begin by reading Revelation 12 in your favorite Bible. As you read, never forget that God urges you to quickly obey His Word in all things (Psalm 119:60).

In yesterday's reading, we were introduced to the seventh trumpet judgment, which actually constitutes seven new bowl judgments. These judgments will be unleashed on the earth just a little later in Revelation. In today's reading, we focus attention on a preliminary event: Satan's ousting from heaven and his great persecution of Israel. With your Bible still accessible, consider the following insights on the biblical text, verse by verse.

Revelation 12:1-2

A great sign appeared in heaven: A woman (12:1): The woman represents Israel, the wife of God (Isaiah 54:5-6; Jeremiah 3:6-8; 31:32; Ezekiel 16:32; Hosea 2:16). The moon alludes to God's covenant relationship with Israel. New moons are associated with covenant worship (1 Chronicles 23:31; 2 Chronicles 2:4; 8:13). The 12 stars represent the 12 tribes of Israel.

She was pregnant and was crying out in birth pains (12:2): This likely refers to the harsh experience of the Jewish nation throughout the centuries as it awaits the eventual "birth" (or appearance) of its Messiah.

Revelation 12:3-6

Behold, a great red dragon (12:3): This is Satan. Red may imply bloodshed, for Satan has always been a murderer (John 8:44).

Seven heads and ten horns, and on his heads seven diadems (12:3): From similar descriptions in Daniel 7:7-8, 24 and Revelation 13:1, we infer that this points to Satan's control over world empires during the tribulation period, apparently through the antichrist.

The ten horns apparently represent the ten kings of Daniel 7:7 and Revelation 13:1, over whom the antichrist—empowered by Satan—will gain authority. The ten countries headed by the ten kings will form the nucleus of the world empire that the antichrist (and thus Satan) will control. The seven heads and seven crowns apparently refer to the principal rulers of the empire.

Satan, the dragon, is also called a serpent (Genesis 3:1; Revelation 12:9). The serpent is characterized by treachery, deceitfulness, venom, and murder.

His tail swept down a third of the stars of heaven (12:4): The first five verses of Revelation 12 appear to contain a mini-history of Satan. Verse 4 refers to the fall of the angels who followed Satan. (The word "stars" is sometimes used of angels in the Bible—Job 38:7.) Lucifer apparently convinced a third of the angelic realm to join him in his rebellion against God.

So that...he might devour it (12:4): Satan desired to kill the promised Messiah at birth. Under the providence of God, Satan was unsuccessful. Some expositors believe the mention of the dragon seeking to devour the child alludes to Herod's massacre of male children—an attempt to kill Jesus Christ as a child (Matthew 2:13-18). The image of Satan devouring people reminds us of 1 Peter 5:8.

She gave birth to a male child (12:5): The male child is Jesus, born as a Jew (Matthew 1:1; 2 Timothy 2:8; see also Romans 1:3; 9:4-5).

Caught up to God and to his throne (12:5): Jesus ascended to heaven following His resurrection (Acts 1:9; 2:33; Hebrews 1:1-3; 12:2).

The woman fled into the wilderness (12:6): In the middle of the tribulation, the antichrist will break his covenant with Israel and exalt himself as a deity, even putting up an image of himself in the Jewish temple (2 Thessalonians 2:4). Christ, in His Olivet Discourse, warns of how quickly the Jews will have to flee for their lives (Matthew 24:16-31). Many will apparently flee to the deserts and mountains, perhaps in the area of Bozrah or Petra, about 80 miles south of Jerusalem. Others suggest Moab, Ammon, and Edom to the east.

The Lord will take care of this remnant of Jews in the wilderness for 1,260 days, or three and a half years. This is the last half of the tribulation period.

Revelation 12:7-9

War arose in heaven (12:7): War now erupts in heaven between God's holy angels and the evil angels. Michael the archangel leads God's angels, and Satan leads the fallen angels.

Michael the archangel is called a chief prince (Daniel 10:13) and "the great prince" (Daniel 12:1). He appears to be specially related to Israel as its guardian. His name means "Who is like God?" It speaks of his unwavering devotion to God, in stark contrast to Satan, who wanted to take God's place (see Isaiah 14:14).

He was defeated, and there was no longer any place for them in heaven (12:8): Satan and his fallen angels are no match for God's heavenly hosts, under the leadership of the archangel Michael. Though Satan previously had access to heaven (as in the book of Job), that access now permanently ends.

The great dragon was thrown down (12:9): The great dragon is "that ancient serpent" who tempted Adam and Eve in the Garden of Eden (Genesis 3:1). He is called the devil (Matthew 4:1), a title meaning "adversary" or "slanderer." The name Satan also carries the idea of "adversary."

Satan is "the deceiver of the whole world." He is the "father of lies" (John 8:44) and blinds people to the truth (2 Corinthians 4:4). He spreads deception through false prophets (Matthew 24:11) and especially through the antichrist (2 Thessalonians 2:9-11).

Revelation 12:10-12

I heard a loud voice in heaven (12:10): The loud voice may be a burst of praise from all the tribulation martyrs in heaven. They exult in God's salvation and His exercise of authority in overcoming Satan.

"The accuser of our brothers has been thrown down, who accuses them day and night" (12:10): Accusing God's people is Satan's continuous, ongoing work. He does this in two ways. First, he accuses believers before the throne of God (Job 1:6; 2:1; Zechariah 3:1; Romans 8:33). Second, he accuses believers to their own consciences, causing excessive guilt in order to bring depression and defeat.

"They have conquered him by the blood of the Lamb" (12:11): No accusation of Satan against believers in Jesus can stand. Their sins have been forgiven because of the shed blood of the Lamb (Romans 8:33-39).

"The word of their testimony" (12:11): These individuals openly witnessed about Jesus during the tribulation period. They did not back down from witnessing in the face of death threats. They would rather give up their lives than deny Jesus.

"Therefore, rejoice, O heavens...But woe to you, O earth" (12:12): Notice the contrast between the rejoicing and the woe in this verse. Satan's access to heaven is removed, and he will no longer be able to stand before the throne of God and accuse Christians. For this, there is rejoicing in heaven. On earth, however, Satan is filled with fury because he knows his time is short. Only half of the tribulation period is now left, so Satan knows his time is limited to a mere 1,260 days, the last three and a half years of the tribulation period. This brings woe to the earth.

Revelation 12:13-17

The dragon...pursued the woman (12:13): Once Satan is ousted from heaven and is thrown down to earth, he seeks to persecute the Jews, from whose lineage the Messiah was born. Part of this persecution will no doubt be carried out through the antichrist (Daniel 9:27; Matthew 24:15; 2 Thessalonians 2:4).

Scripture reveals that Jesus will not return until the Jewish people are endangered at Armageddon and the Jewish leaders cry out for deliverance from Him, their divine Messiah (see Zechariah 12:10). In his perverted thinking, Satan may reason that if he can destroy the Jews, he can prevent the second coming of Christ and save himself from defeat.

The woman was given the two wings of the great eagle (12:14): Wings often represent protection and deliverance in the Bible (see Psalm 91:4; Isaiah 40:31). For example, after God delivered the Jews from Egyptian bondage, He affirmed, "You yourselves have seen what I did to the Egyptians, and how I bore you on eagles' wings and brought you to myself" (Exodus 19:4). Therefore, the "two wings" in this verse point to God's supernatural delivering power (see Matthew 24:16; Mark 13:14; Luke 21:21).

God will preserve a remnant of Jews through this persecution, but this should not be taken to mean that all Jews will survive. Zechariah prophesies,

"In the whole land, declares the LORD, two thirds shall be cut off and perish, and one third shall be left alive" (13:8). Many will die, but a remnant will survive the onslaught.

She is to be nourished for a time, and times, and half a time (12:14): God preserves the Jews throughout the last three and a half years of the tribulation period (see Daniel 7:25; 12:7).

The serpent poured water like a river out of his mouth (12:15): Some Bible expositors take this to mean that Satan will cause a flood in an attempt to dislodge and destroy the Jews. Others take the flood metaphorically, suggesting that a satanically driven army will rapidly advance against the Jews like a flood. It may also refer more broadly to an outpouring of hatred and anti-Semitism.

The earth came to the help of the woman (12:16): Whichever of the above interpretations is correct, the earth comes to the aid of the Jews, under God's providence. If the flood is literal water, perhaps God causes the earth to open up and swallow the water. If the flood is a rapidly advancing army (or militant anti-Semites), perhaps such people will be destroyed by an earthquake that causes the ground to open up (see Matthew 24:7; Revelation 6:12; 8:5; 11:13, 19; 16:18).

Recall that God promised the Jews in Isaiah 54:17, "No weapon that is fashioned against you shall succeed." Not even water, literal or metaphorical.

The dragon became furious with the woman and went off to make war on the rest of her offspring (12:17): In view of his failure to destroy the Jews, an infuriated Satan now resorts to war against a related group—believers in Jesus Christ. These are the spiritual offspring of the woman, or Israel (see Galatians 3:29). Satan wars against the saints.

MAJOR THEMES

1. *Symbolic women in the book of Revelation*. The woman in our passage symbolizes Israel. Other symbolic women include the great prostitute, or apostate religion (Revelation 17:3-6); Jezebel, or paganism (2:20); and the bride of the Lamb, or the church (19:7).

2. *Horn*. Animals used horns as weapons (Genesis 22:13; Psalm 69:31), so horns eventually came to be seen as symbols of power and might. They

became emblems of dominion, representing kingdoms and kings (Daniel 7–8; Revelation 12:13; 13:1, 11; 17:3-16).

DIGGING DEEPER WITH CROSS-REFERENCES

Israel as a mother giving birth—Isaiah 26:17-18; 54:1; 66:7-12; Hosea 13:13; Micah 4:10; 5:2-3; Matthew 24:8

Christ's ascension—Mark 16:19; Luke 24:51; John 6:62; 20:17; Acts 1:9; Ephesians 4:8; Hebrews 4:14; 9:24; 1 Peter 3:22

The blood of the Lamb—Matthew 26:28; Mark 14:24; John 6:53; Acts 20:28; Romans 5:9; 1 Corinthians 11:25; 1 John 1:7; Revelation 1:5; 5:9

LIFE LESSONS

1. *Christ our advocate.* Satan is our accuser, but Jesus is our advocate: "We have an advocate with the Father, Jesus Christ the righteous" (1 John 2:1). The word "advocate" means defense attorney. When Satan accuses us before the divine Judge (the Father), Jesus, our defense attorney, steps up to the Father and reveals that our slate has been wiped clean by His blood sacrifice. We are therefore innocent of the crimes we have committed.

2. *Faithful unto death.* Revelation 12:11 speaks of believers who were so bold in their faith that they "loved not their lives even unto death." Recall the Lord's instructions to the Christians at Smyrna: "Do not fear what you are about to suffer. Behold, the devil is about to throw some of you into prison, that you may be tested...Be faithful unto death, and I will give you the crown of life" (Revelation 2:10). Never fear—eternal life awaits all Christians.

QUESTIONS FOR REFLECTION AND DISCUSSION

1. Has Satan ever neutralized your spiritual life by inflicting relentless guilt on your conscience for your perceived weaknesses and failures?

2. Do you live every day with the confidence that Christ is your advocate and defender?

DAY 21

THE RISE OF THE ANTICHRIST

REVELATION 13:1-4

SCRIPTURE READING AND INSIGHTS

Begin by reading Revelation 13:1-4 in your favorite Bible. As you read, ask God to help you understand His Word (Psalm 119:73).

In the previous lesson, we focused on Satan's ousting from heaven and his subsequent persecution of the Jews. In today's reading, we witness the rise of the antichrist, who will come into great power during the tribulation period. With your Bible still accessible, consider the following insights on the biblical text, verse by verse.

Revelation 13:1

I saw a beast rising out of the sea (13:1): Revelation pictures the antichrist as a beast 32 times. The image points to the brutal, bloody, uncontrolled, and wild character of this diabolical dictator. It also contrasts the antichrist with Christ, who is most commonly called the Lamb. The Lamb saves sinners, but the beast persecutes and executes the saints. The Lamb is gentle, whereas the beast is ferocious. The Lamb is loving, but the beast is heartless and cruel.

This beast rises out of the sea. The sea refers to the Gentile nations (17:15), indicating that the antichrist will be a Gentile. "Anti" can mean "instead of" or "against" or "opposed to." So "antichrist" can mean "instead of Christ," "against Christ," or "opposed to Christ." The antichrist is the "man of lawlessness," the "son of destruction," who will lead the world into rebellion against God (2 Thessalonians 2:3, 8-10; Revelation 11:7) and deceive multitudes (Revelation 19:20).

With ten horns and seven heads (13:1): We have seen that because animals use horns as weapons (Genesis 22:13; Psalm 69:31), horns eventually became symbols of power and then of dominion, representing kingdoms and kings. Comparing this text with Daniel 7:16-24, we conclude that the antichrist will rise up from ten kingdoms that will constitute a revived Roman Empire, the final form of Gentile world power before Christ returns.

> "The other horn...made war with the saints and prevailed over them" (Daniel 7:20-21).

Some Bible expositors say the seven heads are the principal rulers of the antichrist's revived Roman Empire. Others suggest that the seven heads may be successive world empires—Egypt, Assyria, Babylon, Medo-Persia, Greece, Rome, and the antichrist's revived Roman Empire. Still others say the seven heads represent seven mountains (Revelation 17:9). A mountain can symbolize a kingdom (see Daniel 2:34-35, 44-45). This may be a veiled reference to Rome, which was built on seven hills (Revelation 17:18). All these views support the idea that the antichrist's kingdom will be a revived Roman Empire.

With ten diadems on its horns (13:1): The ten diadems, or crowns, point to the dominion of the antichrist's kingdom, which will eventually embrace the entire globe.

And blasphemous names on its heads (13:1): These point to the antichrist's character—he will have a mouth full of blasphemy (verses 5-6) and will exalt himself above all that is called God or that is worshiped (2 Thessalonians 2:4).

Revelation 13:2

The beast that I saw was like a leopard (13:2): Much of the imagery in this verse is from Daniel 7. The leopard was known for its swiftness, cunning, and agility (see Daniel 7:6). The imagery in Daniel represents Greece under Alexander the Great, which had a swift, cunning, and agile army. Such will be the case with the antichrist as he comes into world dominion.

Its feet were like a bear's (13:2): The bear in Daniel's account refers to Medo-Persia (Daniel 7:5), well known for its strength and fierceness in battle (Isaiah 13:17-18). Such strength and fierceness will certainly characterize the antichrist and his forces.

Its mouth was like a lion's (13:2): The lion in Daniel's account refers to Babylon (Daniel 7:4), with lion-like qualities of power and strength. Babylon was known for its ability to move quickly (like a lion). Such qualities will characterize the antichrist.

A comparison of Revelation 13:2 with Daniel 7 reveals that the final world empire of the antichrist—a revived Roman Empire—will be rooted in all the previous empires. It will unite in a single kingdom the evil and power that characterized all the previous kingdoms.

To it the dragon gave his power and his throne and great authority (13:2): The ultimate source of the antichrist's power is Satan.

Revelation 13:3

Seemed to have a mortal wound (13:3): Some Bible expositors believe this mortal wound refers to the pagan Roman Empire, which died in the past but will be revived in the end times. Others say a historical character of the past, such as Nero, Judas Iscariot, Mussolini, Hitler, or Stalin, will come back to life and fulfill the role of the antichrist in the end times.

Others say the antichrist will be killed and then resurrected. Still others say that perhaps the antichrist will be severely wounded, and Satan will supernaturally heal this wound. Perhaps he will simply appear to be killed, though he really is not, and through satanic trickery will appear to be resurrected.

The revived Roman Empire view seems unfeasible because verse 12 specifically refers to "the first beast, whose mortal wound was healed." The "first beast" is the antichrist. Then, in verse 14, we find a parallel reference to "the beast that was wounded by the sword and yet lived." This verse is interpreted most naturally as referring to a person—not a reincarnation of a past person, but a unique anti-God person of the future.

It is unlikely that the antichrist will actually be resurrected, but he may give the appearance of having been resurrected. Satan has supernatural abilities (John 12:31; 2 Corinthians 4:4; Ephesians 2:2), but he is not powerful enough to resurrect people from the dead. Only God can create life (Genesis 1:1, 21; Deuteronomy 32:39); the devil cannot (see Exodus 8:19).

The devil has great power to deceive people (Revelation 12:9). He is a master magician and a super scientist. With his vast knowledge of God, man, and the universe, he is able to perform counterfeit miracles (2 Thessalonians 2:9).

Some theologians believe Satan may be able to perform limited "grade-B" miracles. But only God can perform "grade-A" miracles. Only God can fully control and supersede the natural laws He Himself created.

Satan will likely engage in a grade-B miracle to heal the wounded (but not dead) antichrist, or engage in some kind of masterful deception, or perhaps a combination of both. In any event, the antichrist will appear to be resurrected from the dead. Second Corinthians 4:4 informs us that Satan can blind people's minds. If Satan pulls off some kind of counterfeit resurrection, he may blind people's minds so that they accept this as an indication of the antichrist's power and deity and subsequently worship him.

If the antichrist only appears to be dead but is not genuinely dead, a scenario suggested by Bible scholar Walter Price becomes viable:

> The apostle Paul was stoned in Lystra, and the citizens "dragged him out of the city, supposing that he was dead" (Acts 14:19). While in an unconscious state, Paul "was caught up into Paradise, and heard unspeakable words, which it is not lawful for a man to utter" (2 Cor. 12:4)...At the same time he was thought to be dead, his spirit was caught up into the third heaven and there received a profound revelation from God. This same thing, in reverse, will happen to the Antichrist. The Antichrist...will be no more dead than was the apostle Paul. But just as the citizens of Lystra thought Paul was dead, so the Antichrist will be thought dead.[1]

Just as Paul's spirit departed from his body and was taken to heaven, where he received further revelations, so the antichrist's spirit may depart from his body and be taken into the abyss, where Satan will offer the world's kingdoms to him.

The antichrist's spirit will then return from the abyss (Revelation 11:7), re-enter what appears to be a dead body, and thereby give the appearance of a resurrection from the dead. Mark Hitchcock suggests that while his spirit is in the abyss, the "Antichrist probably receives his orders and strategy from Satan, literally selling his soul to the devil, and then comes back to earth with hellish ferocity to establish his world domination over a completely awestruck earth."[2]

The whole earth marveled as they followed the beast (13:3): This event will no doubt make headlines around the world. Internet videos of the event will go viral. Television reports of the event will be shown around the clock.

Revelation 13:4

They worshiped the dragon (13:4): During Christ's three-year ministry, Satan tried to persuade Him to fall down and worship him (Matthew 4:9). Before that, Lucifer (Satan's original name) sought to place himself on God's throne (see Isaiah 14:12-17; Ezekiel 28:11-19). Satan will finally have what he has yearned for—worship.

They worshiped the beast... "Who is like the beast?" (13:4): This contrasts with believers, who say to God, "Who is like you, O LORD?" (Exodus 15:11).

THE TRIBULATION PERIOD		
TOPIC	**DANIEL**	**REVELATION**
Time of Trouble	Daniel 12:1	Revelation 16:18
Persecution	Daniel 3:8; 6:16	Revelation 12:13; 17:6
Time, Times, and Half a Time	Daniel 12:7	Revelation 12:14
Idolatry	Daniel 3:7	Revelation 13:4
Sudden Destruction	Daniel 5:30	Revelation 18:10, 19

MAJOR THEMES

1. *The genius of the antichrist.* Scripture reveals that the antichrist will be a genius in intellect (Daniel 8:23), commerce (Daniel 11:43; Revelation 13:16-17), war (Revelation 6:2; 13:2), speech (Daniel 11:36), and politics (Revelation 17:11-12).

2. *The antichrist mimics Christ.* Christ is God (John 1:1-2; 10:36), and the antichrist will claim to be God (2 Thessalonians 2:4). Christ did miracles (Matthew 9:32-33; Mark 6:2); the antichrist will mimic such miracles (Matthew 24:24; 2 Thessalonians 2:9). Christ is crowned with many crowns (Revelation 19:12); the antichrist is crowned with ten crowns (Revelation 13:1). Christ rides a white horse (Revelation 19:11) as does the antichrist (Revelation 6:2). Christ was resurrected (Matthew 28:6); the antichrist will appear to be resurrected (Revelation 13:3, 14). Christ is a member of the holy Trinity—Father, Son, and Holy Spirit (2 Corinthians 13:14), but the antichrist is a member of an unholy trinity—Satan, the antichrist, and the false prophet (Revelation 13).

DIGGING DEEPER WITH CROSS-REFERENCES

Blasphemy—Exodus 20:7; Leviticus 19:12; 22:32; Deuteronomy 5:11; Matthew 12:31-32; 2 Thessalonians 2:4

Satanic power—Job 1:12; Luke 4:6; Acts 26:18; Ephesians 6:12; 2 Thessalonians 2:9

The worship of evil spirits (such as Satan)—Leviticus 17:7; Deuteronomy 32:17; 2 Chronicles 11:15; Psalm 106:37; 1 Corinthians 10:20; Revelation 9:20

LIFE LESSONS

1. *Who is like the Lord?* People will worship both the devil and the antichrist, saying, "Who is like the beast?" (Revelation 13:4). We, however, proclaim with the Scriptures, "Who is like you, O Lord?" (Exodus 15:11). The Lord declares, "There is none who can deliver from my hand" (Isaiah 43:13). The true God is incomparably great.

2. *Test all things.* We ought to consistently test all doctrines and religious ideas against Scripture. Even today, the spirit of antichrist is at work promoting heretical doctrine (see 1 John 4:1-3; 2 John 7). Scripture often warns against being deceived by false doctrine (Matthew 7:15-16; 24:4, 11; Acts 20:28-30; 2 Corinthians 11:2-3; 2 Timothy 4:3-4). We protect ourselves by testing all teachings against Scripture (Acts 17:11; 1 Thessalonians 5:21).

QUESTIONS FOR REFLECTION AND DISCUSSION

1. Have you ever been awestruck at how the Lord came through for you, such that you were moved to ask, "Who is like you, O Lord" (Exodus 15:11)?

2. Do you think you could ever be deceived by false doctrine? Why or why not? (See Acts 17:11; 1 Thessalonians 5:21.)

DAY 22

THE BLASPHEMY OF THE ANTICHRIST

REVELATION 13:5-10

SCRIPTURE READING AND INSIGHTS

Begin by reading Revelation 13:5-10 in your favorite Bible. As you read, ask God to help you understand His Word (Psalm 119:73).

In yesterday's reading, we were introduced to the person of the antichrist. Now let's find out more about his blasphemous, self-exalting nature. With your Bible still accessible, consider the following insights on the biblical text, verse by verse.

Revelation 13:5-6

The beast was given a mouth uttering haughty and blasphemous words (13:5): The root meaning of the Greek word for blasphemy can range from showing a lack of reverence for God to a more extreme attitude of contempt for either God or something considered sacred (see Leviticus 24:16; Matthew 26:65; Mark 2:7). It can involve speaking evil against God (Psalm 74:18; Isaiah 52:5; Romans 2:24; Revelation 13:1, 6; 16:9, 11, 21) or showing contempt for the true God by making claims of divinity for oneself (see Mark 14:64; John 10:33). The antichrist will engage in all these aspects of blasphemy.

When the antichrist first comes into power, he will appear to be a dynamic, charismatic leader who can solve the problems of the world. At the midpoint of the tribulation period, however, he will deify himself. He will set up an image of himself in the Jewish temple, thereby committing the "abomination of desolation" (Matthew 24:15).

In the book of Daniel, the phrase "the abomination that makes desolate" (11:31; 12:11; see also 9:27) conveys a sense of outrage or horror at witnessing a barbaric act of idolatry in God's holy temple. Such acts utterly profane and desecrate the temple.

> "He shall make a strong covenant with many for one week, and for half of the week he shall put an end to sacrifice and offering. And on the wing of abominations shall come one who makes desolate, until the decreed end is poured out on the desolator" (Daniel 9:27-28).

Daniel 11:36 confirms that the antichrist "shall exalt himself and magnify himself above every god." We also read in 2 Thessalonians 2:4 that the antichrist ultimately "opposes and exalts himself against every so-called god or object of worship, so that he takes his seat in the temple of God, proclaiming himself to be God." There is no greater blasphemy than this. The antichrist truly is anti-Christ, putting himself in Christ's place.

> "The king shall do as he wills. He shall exalt himself and magnify himself above every god, and shall speak astonishing things against the God of gods" (Daniel 11:36).

The antichrist—the world dictator—will then demand that the world worship and pay idolatrous homage to him. Any who refuse will be persecuted, and many will be martyred. The false prophet, who is the antichrist's first lieutenant, will see to this.

It was allowed to exercise authority for forty-two months (13:5): Just as Satan is on a leash (Job 1–2), answerable to our sovereign God, so the antichrist is on a leash as well. God has set well-defined parameters regarding what the antichrist will be permitted to do and say. God will grant authority to the antichrist to act as he desires during the great tribulation, the last three and a half years of the tribulation.

It opened its mouth to utter blasphemies against God (13:6): The blasphemous words of the antichrist are in keeping with his blasphemous nature (2 Thessalonians 2:3-4). Recall that in the Old Testament, Satan himself blasphemed God: "I will set my throne on high...I will make myself like the Most High" (Isaiah 14:13-14). The antichrist, energized by Satan, now utters blasphemies, claiming to be God and demanding to be worshiped.

Notice the specific objects of the antichrist's blasphemy in Revelation 13:6. First is God's name. In biblical times, a person's name represented everything that person was. It pointed to his or her very nature. It included the very attributes of a person. For the antichrist to blaspheme God's name means that he is blaspheming God's very identity and His nature.

The antichrist also blasphemes God's dwelling, or heaven (see Hebrews 9:23-24).

"Those who dwell in heaven" includes both the holy angels and the glorified saints (believers who were caught up in the rapture and then taken to heaven prior to the tribulation period). This will be the antichrist's way of saying to God, "I disdain everything about You."

Revelation 13:7-8

It was allowed to make war on the saints (13:7): The antichrist will be permitted to persecute God's people during the tribulation period. Recall that in Revelation 6:11, martyrs in heaven are informed that there will be still more martyrs: "They were each given a white robe and told to rest a little longer, until the number of their fellow servants and their brothers should be complete, who were to be killed as they themselves had been." Revelation 13:5-7 appears to refer to some of these new martyrs.

On the one hand, Israel—which gave birth to the divine Messiah, Jesus Christ—will come under heavy persecution by the antichrist. This will take place in the middle of the tribulation when the antichrist moves into Jerusalem and sets up an image of himself in the Jewish temple, proclaiming himself to be God (see Daniel 9:27; see also Matthew 24:16-22).

On the other hand, Christians will also be persecuted. Daniel 7:25 prophetically affirms that the antichrist "shall wear out the saints of the Most High...and they shall be given into his hand for a time, times, and half a time." The phrase "time, times, and half a time" refers to the last three and a half years of the seven-year period of the antichrist's power. This is the same as the "42 months" mentioned in Revelation 13:5.

> "He shall speak words against the Most High, and shall wear out the saints of the Most High...they shall be given into his hand for a time, times, and half a time" (Daniel 7:25).

Authority was given it over every tribe and people and language and nation (13:7): The antichrist now exercises global dominion. He is not only a political leader but also the central religious object of worship (2 Thessalonians 2:4). He thus exercises both political and religious authority—an all-encompassing global authority over all peoples.

Even today, we witness a movement toward globalism in many different areas, including economics, banking, commerce and trade, business, management, manufacturing, environmentalism, population control, education, religion, agriculture, information technologies, the entertainment industry, the publishing industry, science and medicine, and even government. Revelation 13 tells us that the antichrist will ultimately lead a global anti-God union. It will be a political union, an economic union, and a religious union.

When one considers the multiple cascading problems now facing humanity—including the Middle East conflict, terrorism, overpopulation, starvation, pollution, national and international crime, cyber warfare, and economic instability—it is entirely feasible that increasing numbers of people will come to believe that ultimately such problems can be solved only on a global level. They may think that the only hope for human survival is a strong and effective world government.

The technology that makes possible a world government—including instant global media through television and radio, cyberspace, and supercomputers—is now in place. Technology has "greased the skids" for the emergence of globalism in our day. Without such technology, a true globalism would be impossible.

All who dwell on earth will worship it (13:8): Just as all in heaven worship Him who sits on the throne and the Lamb (Revelation 4–5), so all who are on earth will worship the antichrist, empowered by the devil.

Everyone whose name has not been written before the foundation of the world (13:8): The names of the redeemed were written in the book of life in eternity past, before the world even began. As Ephesians 1:4 puts it, "He chose us in him before the foundation of the world."

In the book of life (13:8): Paul speaks of believers as those "whose names are in the book of life" (Philippians 4:3). Revelation mentions the book of life six times (3:5; 13:8; 17:8; 20:12, 15; 21:27). It contains the names of all those belonging to God.

Of the Lamb who was slain (13:8): The book of life belongs specifically to the Lamb of God, Jesus Christ (Revelation 21:27). Those not recorded in the Lamb's book of life will worship the antichrist.

Revelation 13:9-10

If anyone has an ear, let him hear (13:9): This phrase is similar to the instruction given to the seven churches in Revelation 2–3. However, it is shorter, for the churches were told, "Let him hear what the Spirit says to the churches." Perhaps reference to the churches is omitted here because the church was raptured prior to the tribulation period (see Revelation 3:10).

If anyone is to be taken captive, to captivity he goes (13:10): This passage speaks of God's perfect justice. Those who are sovereignly destined for captivity (such as the antichrist, the false prophet, and the forces of the antichrist) will indeed one day end up as captives forever in the lake of fire. Perfect justice will be rendered.

Here is a call for the endurance and faith of the saints (13:10): The assurance that God will punish evildoers helps to sustain the faith of those who are persecuted during these difficult days (see 1 Peter 2:19-24). As the saints patiently endure, they can rest assured that vengeance is God's (Romans 12:19).

MAJOR THEMES

1. *God's sovereign allowance.* We often witness God's sovereign allowance of prophetic events, as in Revelation 13:5. Revelation 6:4 tells us that the rider of the red horse "was permitted to take peace from the earth," and in verse 8, the rider of the pale horse was "given authority over a fourth of the earth, to kill with sword and with famine." Revelation 7:2 refers to "four angels who had been given power to harm earth and sea." Revelation 9:5 tells us that demonic spirits "were allowed to torment" earth dwellers for five months.

2. *Satan, the antichrist, and godhood.* The antichrist takes on the character of the one who energizes him (Satan). Just as Lucifer (Satan) aspired to make himself like God in Isaiah 14:13-14, so the antichrist proclaims himself to be God (2 Thessalonians 2:4). Just as Lucifer was judged for his pretense to godhood (Ezekiel 28:17), so will the antichrist (Revelation 19:20).

3. *Satan, the antichrist, and murder.* Jesus speaks of the devil's character in John 8:44: "He was a murderer from the beginning." The devil empowers the antichrist, who shares his murderous nature (see Revelation 13:7).

DIGGING DEEPER WITH CROSS-REFERENCES

War on the saints—Daniel 7:23-25; 8:25; Matthew 24:15-22; Revelation 6:9-11; 11:7; 17:14

The book of life—Revelation 3:5; 17:8; 20:12, 15; 21:27

Christ the Lamb—Isaiah 53:7; John 1:29; 1 Corinthians 5:7; 1 Peter 1:19; Revelation 7:9

LIFE LESSONS

1. *Obey God.* In every age, God appeals to all who will "hear"—that is, those who receive His message and act on it (see Matthew 11:15; 13:9, 43; Mark 4:9, 23; Luke 8:8; 14:35). As James put it, "Be doers of the word, and not hearers only, deceiving yourselves" (James 1:22). Obedience to God's Word is non-negotiable.

2. *Satan's attack against Christians.* Satan will attack God's people during the tribulation period, and he spiritually attacks Christians today. God gives us instructions on overcoming this diabolical enemy. He provides spiritual armor for our defense (Ephesians 6:11-18). We are told, "Resist the devil, and he will flee from you" (James 4:7). We are to "stand firm" against the devil (Ephesians 6:13-14). We should be aware of Satan's strategies (2 Corinthians 2:11; 1 Peter 5:8). We must depend on the Holy Spirit, all the while remembering John's comforting words: "He who is in you is greater than he who is in the world" (1 John 4:4). As well, God has assigned His angels to watch over us (Psalm 91:9-11).

QUESTIONS FOR REFLECTION AND DISCUSSION

1. Your name was written in God's book of life before the world was even created. How does this make you feel? Does it give you a sense of security in your salvation?

2. Do you suffer any guilt or shame in your life? Did you know there is a close connection between these emotions and a failure to obey God's Word? Faithfulness to God's Word is the key to emotional stability.

DAY 23

THE RISE OF THE FALSE PROPHET

REVELATION 13:11-14

SCRIPTURE READING AND INSIGHTS

Begin by reading Revelation 13:11-14 in your favorite Bible. As you read, remember that God's Word is the true source of hope (Psalm 119:81).

In the previous two readings, we learned much about the antichrist. Now let's find out about his first lieutenant—the false prophet. With your Bible still accessible, consider the following insights on the biblical text, verse by verse.

Revelation 13:11

I saw another beast rising out of the earth (13:11): Many false prophets will emerge on the religious landscape in the end times (Matthew 24:4-5, 24). Such prophets are mouthpieces of Satan, spreading doctrines of demons (1 Timothy 4:1). We are about to see that during the tribulation period, a supreme false prophet will emerge who will be the antichrist's "right-hand man."

The antichrist will primarily be a military and political leader, and the false prophet will primarily be a religious leader. In fact, we might say that a diabolical trinity will emerge during the tribulation period—the antichrist (the first beast), the false prophet (the second beast), and Satan (the dragon), each with a distinctive role.

Today's passage in Revelation reveals that the false prophet will control religious affairs on earth and will be motivated by Satan (verse 11). He will promote the worship of the antichrist (verse 12) and will execute those who refuse (verse 15). He will control commerce to enforce worship of the antichrist (verse 17). He will perform apparent signs and miracles (verse 13) and will promote deception and false doctrine (verse 14).

Verse 11 describes the false prophet as "another beast." The Greek word for "another" is *allos*, meaning "another of the same kind." Together, this beastly duo will wreak havoc on the earth for seven years.

The second beast rising "out of the earth" is a subject of much discussion. Some expositors suggest that the antichrist will be a Gentile who emerges out of the "sea" of nations (verse 1), but the false prophet will be a Jew. My friend David Reagan explains:

> Just as the sea is used symbolically in prophecy to refer to the Gentile nations, the land (or earth) is used to refer to Israel. This does not mean the False Prophet will be an Orthodox Jew. It only means that he will be of Jewish heritage. Religiously, he will be an apostate Jew who will head up the One World Religion of the Antichrist."[1]

Other Bible expositors, including my former mentor John F. Walvoord, say this is reading too much into the word "earth."

> While the first beast was a Gentile, since he came from the entire human race as symbolized by "the sea" (v. 1), the second beast was a creature of the earth. Some have taken this as a specific reference to the Promised Land and have argued that he was therefore a Jew. There is no support for this in the context as the word for "earth" is the general word referring to the entire world...Actually his nationality and geographic origin are not indicated.[2]

Still other Bible expositors believe that the phrase "rising out of the earth" could relate to rising out of the abyss that lies below the earth. The abyss is the bottomless pit, the abode of demons. It is suggested that perhaps the false prophet will be energized by a powerful demon from below.

In view of the diversity of opinions, it is wise not to be overly dogmatic on the issue.

It had two horns like a lamb (13:11): The antichrist will have ten horns (Revelation 13:1). Horns indicate dominion, so we can infer that the false prophet will have less authority than the antichrist. He will be like a lamb in the sense that he will be more meek and gentle in his dealings with others. Notice that this is the only verse in Revelation where the term "lamb" does not refer to Jesus Christ.

It spoke like a dragon (13:11): True prophets are inspired by the Holy Spirit, but the false prophet is inspired by the *un*holy spirit—the dragon, or Satan.

We can infer from Scripture that the false prophet will be a gifted communicator—particularly adept at inspiring commitment to the false world religion and to the antichrist. John Phillips explains:

> The role of the False Prophet will be to make the new religion appealing and palatable to men…The dynamic appeal of the False Prophet will lie in his skill in combining political expediency with religious passion, self-interest with benevolent philanthropy, lofty sentiment with blatant sophistry, moral platitude with unbridled self-indulgence. His arguments will be subtle, convincing, and appealing. His oratory will be hypnotic, for he will be able to move the masses to tears or whip them into a frenzy. He will control the communication media of the world and will skillfully organize mass publicity to promote his ends. He will be the master of every promotional device and public-relations gimmick. He will manage the truth with guile beyond words, bending it, twisting it, and distorting it. Public opinion will be his to command. He will mold world thought and shape human opinion like so much potter's clay. His deadly appeal will lie in the fact that what he says will sound so right, so sensible, so exactly what unregenerate men have always wanted to hear.[3]

Revelation 13:12

It exercises all the authority of the first beast in its presence (13:12): The source of authority for both the false prophet and the antichrist is Satan. Both are empowered by this diabolical spirit. And the authority of the false prophet is a delegated authority—that is, he speaks on behalf of the antichrist.

Makes the earth and its inhabitants worship the first beast (13:12): This is the goal of the false prophet. In his efforts to move the entire world to worship the antichrist, this second beast will be the epitome of a false prophet because he will point to a god other than the Creator.

People will worship the antichrist because they will believe he was raised from the dead, just as Jesus Christ was. We have seen that Satan may engage in a limited grade-B miracle to heal a wounded (but not dead) antichrist, or he may engage in some kind of masterful deception or perhaps a combination of both. Whatever the case, the antichrist will appear to have been resurrected, and people will therefore worship him.

Revelation 13:13-14

It performs great signs (13:13): We have seen that Satan, the energizer of the antichrist and the false prophet, cannot perform grade-A miracles the way God does. He can only perform grade-B miracles, but those are nonetheless impressive. He empowers the false prophet to perform these kinds of miracles (see Exodus 7:11; 2 Timothy 3:8). People will be mesmerized into worshiping Satan's substitute for Christ, the antichrist (see Daniel 9:27; 11:31; 12:11; Matthew 24:15).

The word "performs" is in the present tense in the Greek. This indicates the false prophet will engage in one miraculous sign after another. People will be impressed.

The miracles are "great." The Greek word indicates that which is outstanding, significant, important, or prominent. The signs performed by the false prophet will seem similar to those of prophets like Elijah (1 Kings 18:38; 2 Kings 1:10-15) and God's two prophetic witnesses (Revelation 11:5).

By the signs...it deceives those who dwell on earth (13:14): These miraculous signs are designed to deceive people. The Greek word for "deceive" (*planaw*) literally means "to lead astray, cause to wander, mislead." The word is often used in the Bible in connection with false teachers who lead people into false forms of worship (2 Thessalonians 2:9-12).

Of course, Satan is a master deceiver. His deception is rooted in his character. John 8:44 affirms, "When he lies, he speaks out of his own character, for he is a liar and the father of lies." The word "father" is used here metaphorically of the originator of a family or company of persons animated by a deceitful character. Satan was the first and greatest liar. All who follow his lead—including the false prophet—are deceivers as well.

Telling them to make an image for the beast that was wounded by the sword and yet lived (13:14): The deception will be so enormous that humans willingly make an image for the beast. The image of the antichrist will be placed in the Jewish temple at the midpoint of the tribulation period (see Matthew 24:15).

The apostle Paul earlier revealed that the antichrist himself will sit in God's temple (see 2 Thessalonians 2:4) and receive worship that properly belongs only to God. Some suggest that when the antichrist is not present in the temple, an image of him will be placed there to provide an object of worship in his absence (see Revelation 14:9, 11; 16:2; 19:20; 20:4).

MAJOR THEMES

1. *The significance of signs.* The Greek word translated "sign," *semeion*, carries the idea of "a miracle with a message." A sign is a miracle that attests to something. Jesus' signs (miracles) attested that He was who He claimed to be (John 2:11; 4:54; 6:2; 12:18). The apostles' signs (miracles) attested that they were genuine messengers of God (Hebrews 2:3-4). The unspoken assumption is this: Where miracles are, there God is. The false prophet's signs are deceptive. They seem to support the antichrist's claim to deity. However, these are "false signs and wonders" (2 Thessalonians 2:9).

2. *Satan, the arch-deceiver of humanity.* Satan has long sought to bring about the ruin of humankind through deception. He does this in many ways. He distorts the Scriptures (Genesis 3:4-5; Matthew 4:6). He schemes to outwit humans (2 Corinthians 2:11). He masks himself by appearing as an angel of light (2 Corinthians 11:14). He is a master "deceiver of the whole world" (Revelation 12:9).

DIGGING DEEPER WITH CROSS-REFERENCES

Fire from heaven—Genesis 19:24-25; Exodus 9:23-24; 2 Kings 1:9-12; Luke 9:51-55; Revelation 8:1-9; 11:5

Earth and its inhabitants—Psalm 33:14; Isaiah 26:9, 21; 40:22; Jeremiah 25:29-30; 46:8; Lamentations 4:12; Daniel 4:35; Zephaniah 1:18; Micah 7:13

LIFE LESSONS

1. *Submission to the lordship of Christ.* During the tribulation period, most of the world will submit to the authority of the antichrist and the false prophet (Revelation 13:12). You and I are always to submit to the authority and lordship of Jesus Christ. Jesus has complete authority in heaven and earth (Matthew 28:18; John 3:35). He is the Creator and Sustainer of the universe (Colossians 1:16-17) and is thus sovereign over it (Hebrews 1:3). He calls you and me to always obey Him (John 10:27; 14:15; 15:14).
2. *Christians can be deceived.* Revelation 13:14 says that those who dwell on the earth will be deceived. Did you know that God's people can be deceived as well? Ezekiel 34:1-7 affirms that God's sheep can be led astray by wicked shepherds. Jesus warned His followers to beware of false prophets who may appear to be good on the outside but on the inside are dangerous (Matthew 7:15-16). Why would Jesus warn His followers to beware if they could not possibly be deceived? (See also Acts 20:28-30; 2 Corinthians 11:2-3; Ephesians 4:14; 2 Timothy 4:3-4.) Christians who are not grounded in biblical truth are especially vulnerable.

QUESTIONS FOR REFLECTION AND DISCUSSION

1. Why is consistent submission to the authority and lordship of Christ so critically important?
2. How much time do you spend each week reading and meditating on the Word of God? How does that compare with other activities, such as watching TV?

DAY 24

THE FALSE PROPHET'S EXALTATION OF THE ANTICHRIST

REVELATION 13:15-18

SCRIPTURE READING AND INSIGHTS

Begin by reading Revelation 13:15-18 in your favorite Bible. As you read, remember that God's Word is the true source of hope (Psalm 119:81).

In yesterday's reading, we were introduced to the false prophet. Now let's find out about his global mission to exalt the antichrist. With your Bible still accessible, consider the following insights on the biblical text, verse by verse.

Revelation 13:15

It was allowed to give breath to the image of the beast (13:15): Some Bible expositors believe the antichrist's image will breathe and speak mechanically, like some robots today. Others say that some kind of hologram may be employed. Satan certainly has great intelligence and could likely accomplish this sort of thing. Still others see something more supernatural going on here. J. Hampton Keathley offers this explanation:

> We are told that the false prophet is able to give breath to the image. This gives it the appearance of life. However, it isn't *real* life but only breath. Since breath or breathing is one of the signs of life, men think the image lives, but John is careful not to say that

> he gives life to the image. Only God can do that. It is something miraculous, but also deceptive and false...Then we are told the image of the beast, through this imparted breath, speaks. This is to be a further confirmation of the miraculous nature of the beast's image. Some might see this as the result of some product of our modern electronic robot-type of technology. But such would hardly convince people of anything spectacular. Evidently it will go far beyond that.[1]

Christian scholars may differ on the specifics, but the apparent animation of the image sets it apart from typical Old Testament idols. "The idols of the nations are silver and gold, the work of human hands. They have mouths, but do not speak; they have eyes, but do not see" (Psalm 135:15-16). "Woe to him who says to a wooden thing, Awake; to a silent stone, Arise! Can this teach? Behold, it is overlaid with gold and silver, and there is no breath at all in it" (Habakkuk 2:19).

That the image of the beast might even speak and cause those who would not worship the image of the beast to be slain (13:15): The ultimate goal of the false prophet's supernatural acts is to induce people around the world to worship the antichrist. Because the antichrist puts himself in the place of Christ, the antichrist seeks worship, just as Jesus was worshiped many times during His three-year ministry on earth (Matthew 2:11; 28:9, 17; John 9:38; 20:28).

Exodus 34:14 instructs us, "You shall worship no other god, for the LORD, whose name is Jealous, is a jealous God." When the antichrist demands worship, he places himself in the position of deity. Those who refuse to worship him are slain.

Revelation 13:16-17

It causes all...to be marked on the right hand or the forehead (13:16): Followers of both the antichrist and Christ will have identifying marks during the tribulation period. Christ's 144,000 Jewish witnesses will be supernaturally marked on their foreheads (Revelation 14:1). It would seem that the antichrist's "mark of the beast" is a parody of God's sealing of these 144,000 witnesses.

Receiving the mark of the beast is a serious business, for Revelation 14:9-11 affirms that those who do so will be on the receiving end of God's wrath and will be tormented with fire forever and ever. Even before they die, however, they also suffer painful sores (Revelation 16:2). Such words are sobering. All who express loyalty to the antichrist and his cause will suffer the wrath of our holy and just God (see Psalm 75:8; Isaiah 51:17; Jeremiah 25:15-16).

In contrast, Revelation 20:4 reveals that believers in the Lord Jesus will choose death instead of receiving the mark of the beast. They will be rewarded for their loyalty.

No one can buy or sell unless he has the mark (13:17): This mark will be a commerce passport during the second half of the tribulation period. It will indicate that one is religiously orthodox—as defined by the antichrist and the false prophet. The mark will identify the submissive followers of the beast and worshipers of his image. Those without the mark are labeled as traitors.

A cashless economic system seems to be the means by which the antichrist will control who can buy or sell. After all, if the world economy were still cash-based, people anywhere who possessed cash could still buy and sell. Only in a cashless world with a centralized electronic transaction system would such control be possible.

Someone once said that prophetic events cast their shadows before them. Today the technology is now in place—with supercomputers, the Internet, online banking, and the like—to make possible the economic control of the world. The stage has thus been set for the future dominion of the antichrist.

Even today, certain aspects of our society are already cashless. For example, airlines sell sandwiches during flights, but you can't use cash to buy them. Toll roads use smart technologies to automatically charge credit cards or bank accounts to avoid time-consuming transactions at tollbooths. Paychecks are deposited electronically.

Economists tell us that the amount of real cash in circulation today is about half that used in the 1970s. Why so? Because more and more people are using cashless options, such as credit cards and debit cards. That is the wave of the future. Even checks today are often read by check scanners that instantly transfer money from the payer's bank account to the payee's account.

Presently, more than 70 percent of all consumer payments are electronic, and the writing of checks continues to plummet. More than 2 billion credit cards are used in the United States alone. The nature of how we pay for things is changing drastically. Some financial experts are saying that in the next few years, we may have to pay a surcharge to pay for items with cash.

Technology makes a cashless society convenient and quick. Small chips could soon be injected or implanted beneath the surface of the skin—in the fatty part of one's palm, for example—so that wherever a person goes, the information stored in that chip is accessible. Financial data stored on such a chip would make it easy to just wave one's hand to pay for a bus fare, a toll fare, or a product in a store. Such chips are now being tested at the university level in England.

So, for example, bank transactions and purchases could be electronically enabled for people who submit to receiving the mark of the beast—and disallowed for those who don't.

It is important to differentiate between this technology and the mark of the beast, for the technology itself is not the mark. The mark itself will identify allegiance to the antichrist, but that is separate and distinct from the technology that enables him to enforce his economic system. This mark will be *on* people, not *in* them (like some kind of microchip). It will be on the right hand or forehead and will be clearly visible (perhaps like a tattoo), not hidden beneath the skin. But a microchip might indeed be inserted beneath people's skin as a means of enforcing the mark.

Revelation 13:18

This calls for wisdom (13:18): John says wisdom is required to figure out the number of the beast (Revelation 17:9; see also Daniel 9:22; 12:10). Those in the tribulation period who are able to figure out the beast's number will be able to recognize him for who he really is.

His number is 666 (13:18): Bible interpreters have offered many suggestions as to the meaning of 666. Some believe that inasmuch as seven is the number of perfection, and 777 reflects the Trinity, perhaps 666 points to a being who aspires to perfect deity (like the Trinity) but never attains it. (In reality, the antichrist is just a man, though influenced and possibly indwelt by Satan.)

Others suggest that perhaps the number refers to a specific man—such as the Roman emperor Nero. It has been suggested that if Nero's name were translated into the Hebrew language, the numerical value of its letters is 666. Some suggest that the antichrist will be a man similar to Nero of old. Of course, all this is highly speculative. Scripture does not clearly define what is meant by 666. Interpreting this verse therefore involves some guesswork.

One thing is certain. In some way that is presently unknown to us, this number will be a crucial part of the antichrist's identification. Receiving the mark of the beast is apparently an unpardonable sin (Revelation 14:9-10). The decision to receive the mark is an irreversible decision. Once made, there is no turning back.

Receiving this mark signifies approval of the antichrist as a leader and agreement with his purpose. No one accidentally takes this mark. One must volitionally choose to do so with all the facts on the table. It will be a deliberate choice with eternal consequences. Those who choose to receive the mark will do so with the full knowledge of what they have done.

MAJOR THEMES

1. *Marks of preservation.* Ezekiel 9:4 speaks of putting a mark on the foreheads of people who are dismayed by abominations. This mark on the forehead was one of preservation, just as blood on the doorposts spared the Israelites from death during the tenth plague in Egypt (see Exodus 12:21-29). In the case of the antichrist, the mark of the beast will be a mark of preservation in the sense that those who receive it will be preserved from famine and martyrdom.

2. *Marks of ownership.* In biblical times, soldiers, slaves, and even temple devotees were commonly branded. Such devotees would have a tattoo indicating ownership by a certain god (compare Isaiah 44:5). The antichrist's brand, which will be visible on the hand or forehead, will mark people as possessions of the antichrist.

DIGGING DEEPER WITH CROSS-REFERENCES

Breath—Genesis 2:7; Psalm 135:17; Jeremiah 10:14; 51:17; Habakkuk 2:19

Mark—Revelation 14:9-11; 15:2; 19:20; 20:4

LIFE LESSONS

1. *Trust God for provision.* Those living during the future tribulation period will not be able to obtain daily needs without submitting to the antichrist and receiving his mark. Today, you and I as Christians trust our sovereign God for daily provisions (Psalms 33:19; 34:10; Proverbs 30:8; Matthew 6:11; John 6:31).

2. *Pursue wisdom.* Those living during the tribulation period will need wisdom to figure out the number of the beast (Revelation 13:18). Actually, God desires that we all have wisdom on all matters. The Hebrew word for wisdom (*hokmah*) was commonly used to describe the skill of craftsmen, sailors, singers, administrators, and counselors. *Hokmah* points to the experience and efficiency of these various workers in using their skills. Similarly, a person who possesses *hokmah* in his spiritual life is one who is both knowledgeable and experienced in following God's way. Biblical wisdom involves skill in the art of godly living. Want wisdom? Read the book of Proverbs.

QUESTIONS FOR REFLECTION AND DISCUSSION

1. Have you expressed thanks to God lately for providing for your food and shelter? Thanksgiving should be a regular component of all our prayers (Psalm 100:4; Ephesians 5:20; Colossians 3:15).

2. Do you possess the kind of wisdom described in the Bible? Have you considered reading through the book of Proverbs three or four times a year (in addition to your other Scripture reading)?

DAY 25

ANNOUNCEMENTS FROM HEAVEN

REVELATION 14

SCRIPTURE READING AND INSIGHTS

Begin by reading Revelation 14 in your favorite Bible. As you read, remember that great spiritual wisdom comes from studying God's Word (Psalm 119:98-104).

In the previous lesson, we saw that the false prophet will exalt the antichrist around the world. In today's reading, we pause for a glimpse of a glorious scene that will take place following the second coming of Christ. With your Bible still accessible, consider the following insights on the biblical text, verse by verse.

Revelation 14:1-5

On Mount Zion stood the Lamb, and with him 144,000 (14:1): These introductory verses provide a preview of what will take place following the second coming. Christ's second coming does not occur until chapter 19. However, in his panoramic vision, John sees it here as if it were taking place now. The description of an event as if it were already happening is a Hebrew literary device that indicates assurance that it will happen.

John here witnesses Jesus, the Lamb of God, standing on Mount Zion with the 144,000 Jewish witnesses who evangelized the earth. This is apparently the literal Mount Zion in earthly Jerusalem. Mount Zion typically refers to the hill in Jerusalem where the Jewish temple was built.

These Jewish witnesses will have had the protective seal of God on them throughout the tribulation (Revelation 7:3-4) so they could not be killed. This means they will still be alive on earth at the end of the tribulation. Following the second coming, they are invited directly into Christ's earthly millennial kingdom (compare with Matthew 25:34).

I heard a voice from heaven (14:2): The identity of the voice is not clear. Some suggest it could be that of Christ (see Revelation 1:15). Others suggest it could be the tribulation martyrs (Revelation 6; 7:9-10). Still others suggest it could be either one angel (Revelation 6:1) or many angels (Revelation 5:11-12; 7:11-12; 19:6). All things considered, I opt for the tribulation martyrs, for verse 3 indicates that they sing a redemptive song, which is quite fitting for redeemed humans.

They were singing a new song (14:3): The new song celebrates God's mercies and victories. It anticipates God's final and glorious redemption, which the saints will soon fully possess (Revelation 21–22).

No one could learn that song except the 144,000 (14:3): Perhaps this is because they alone went through half of the tribulation. They could fully appreciate what the song expressed. That they learn the song implies that someone teaches it to them. Perhaps the martyrs who sing the song in heaven end up teaching it to the 144,000 on earth. (They will all be together soon enough.)

These who have not defiled themselves with women...who follow the Lamb (14:4): As celibates, these men were able to focus their full attention on serving Christ (see Matthew 19:12; 1 Corinthians 7:26-38).

Firstfruits for God and the Lamb (14:4): These 144,000 may be the first of many who will enter directly into Christ's millennial kingdom in their mortal bodies (not yet resurrected). Or perhaps they are like "firstfruit sacrifices" to God, blameless and perfect—the cream of the crop.

In their mouth no lie was found (14:5): These witnesses had told the truth in a tribulation environment filled with deception (Revelation 12:9; 13:14; 19:20).

Revelation 14:6-13

Then I saw another angel directly overhead with an eternal gospel to proclaim (14:6): John shifts to a new scene in his panoramic vision. He sees an angel that flies "directly overhead" so that all people everywhere can hear him. The gospel is eternal in that it has eternal consequences, and it is gospel because it is good news.

"Fear God...worship him" (14:7): The message reveals that God's final series of catastrophic judgments are ready to fall on humankind. The angel calls on its hearers to fear God—to show reverence to Him (see Ecclesiastes 12:13; Luke 12:5). Those who truly fear God seek to obey God and honor Him in the way they live. Fearing God and worshiping Him is the proper response of a creature before his Creator (Nehemiah 9:6; Psalms 33:6-9; 146:6).

Another angel... "Fallen, fallen is Babylon the great" (14:8): The prophetic message from this angel anticipates the fall of Babylon that will be fully described in Revelation 17–18. The repetition of "fallen" points to the certainty and completeness of the coming judgment.

Many have taken the term "Babylon" to metaphorically refer to various cities—from Rome to New York—but it is best to take this as a literal Babylon on the Euphrates River. This is in keeping with the way other geographical references in Revelation refer to real places (Revelation 1:9; 2:1, 8, 12, 18; 3:1, 7, 14).

Though Babylon is a literal city, it is also a symbol for ungodliness and immorality. Babylon was a literal city that represented anti-God values. In the end times, the rebuilt city will represent the entire worldwide political, economic, and religious kingdom of the antichrist. Our present verse personifies Babylon as a temptress who seduces people to partake of her sin and fornication.

Another angel... "If anyone worships the beast and its image and receives a mark on his forehead or on his hand, he also will drink the wine of God's wrath" (14:9-10): This angel pronounces doom and torment on those who receive the mark of the beast, and he urges believers to remain faithful and not give in to receiving the mark (see Matthew 10:28).

The Greek word for "torment" in this verse is *basanizo*, meaning "to vex with grievous pain," or torture. The same word is used to describe the pains of childbirth (Revelation 12:2), palsy (Matthew 8:6), and suffering in Hades (Luke 16:23, 28).

The smoke of their torment goes up forever (14:11): The torment is never-ending. The endless smoke points to endless suffering. The punishment in the lake of fire will be eternal (Matthew 25:46; Romans 2:3-9; 2 Thessalonians 1:6-9).

The words translated "forever and ever" literally mean "to the ages of the ages." The plural forms reinforce the idea of never-ending duration. This same emphatic construction is used of the eternality of God in Revelation 4:10 and 10:6. The physical torment of the wicked is endless.

Here is a call for the endurance of the saints (14:12): Those who are loyal to the antichrist will be on the receiving end of endless torment, so true believers are called to patiently endure and not give in to the antichrist. Submitting to the antichrist for temporal relief will ultimately end in eternal suffering. It's not an even trade.

I heard a voice from heaven... "Blessed are the dead who die in the Lord from now on" (14:13): The voice John heard is likely that of Jesus Christ (see Revelation 1:10-11; 10:4, 8; 11:12; 14:2; 18:4; 21:3). The primary message is that great blessing awaits all martyrs.

Though the Lord Jesus likely speaks the initial words of blessing here, the Holy Spirit also speaks. He affirms that those who die in the Lord will enjoy serene rest (see Hebrews 4:10). This is in notable contrast to the lack of rest of unbelievers, who are tormented forever.

Revelation 14:14-16

A white cloud, and seated on the cloud one like a son of man (14:14): The white cloud John sees is likely a cloud of glory (Daniel 7:13-14; Matthew 24:30; 26:64; Acts 1:9-11). The one like a son of man is the Lord Jesus Christ. "Son of Man" is a common messianic title for Christ (Daniel 7:13-14; Matthew 8:20; 24:30; 26:64; John 5:27).

With a golden crown on his head, and a sharp sickle in his hand (14:14): The crown signifies that Christ will be victorious over the antichrist and his forces. The sickle represents swift and devastating judgment.

Another angel...calling... "Put in your sickle, and reap" (14:15): Christ is not in submission to an angel. After all, Christ Himself created the angels (Colossians 1:16), and they worship Him (Hebrews 1:6). Recognizing that the earth had yielded a large crop of unbelievers, the angel merely affirmed that this crop was now ready to be "harvested" (punished).

He who sat on the cloud swung his sickle (14:16): Just as a sickle easily cuts wheat, so Jesus' sickle easily cuts down the enemies of God.

Revelation 14:17-20

The angel swung his sickle across the earth and gathered the grape harvest (14:19): The judgment spoken of here will apparently take place at the end of the tribulation period. Like some of the preceding verses, this verse is a proleptic description of the coming judgment. That is, it represents something as existing before it actually does.

The winepress was trodden...blood flowed (14:20): In biblical days, grapes were squeezed to get the grape juice out, which was then used to make wine. This squeezing took place by putting the grapes into small vats with special floors that were angled toward container jars. Hired workers would literally stomp on the grapes with their bare feet, causing the juice to flow into the jars. This treading upon grapes became a common metaphor for judgment. Instead of grape juice flowing, however, the blood of unbelievers would flow.

Scripture reveals that the final battle in the campaign of Armageddon will take place near Jerusalem, in the Valley of Jehoshaphat. In this final battle, the carnage will be so horrific that the blood will rise to the height of the horses' bridles (about four and a half feet). The distance (1,600 stadia) is about 160 miles.

MAJOR THEMES

1. *Harvest and judgment.* The term "harvest" is sometimes used in the Old Testament to point to divine judgment. "Put in the sickle, for the harvest is ripe. Go in, tread, for the winepress is full. The vats overflow, for their evil is great" (Joel 3:13). Jesus referred to grain harvests in the same way (Matthew 13:30, 39).

2. *Believers will endure.* Revelation 14:12 speaks of the endurance of the saints. Other verses speak of the endurance of Christians today. For example, "If God is for us, who can be against us?...In all these things we are more than conquerors through him who loved us" (Romans 8:31, 37). "I give them eternal life, and they will never perish" (John 10:28). "Everyone who has been born of God overcomes the world. And this is the victory that has overcome the world—our faith" (1 John 5:4).

DIGGING DEEPER WITH CROSS-REFERENCES

Mount Zion—2 Samuel 5:7; Psalm 48:1-2; Isaiah 2:3; 24:23; Joel 2:32; Obadiah 17, 21; Micah 4:1-2, 7

Singing a new song—Psalms 33:3; 40:3; 96:1; 98:1; 144:9; 149:1; Isaiah 42:10

Eternal torment in the lake of fire—Matthew 25:41; 2 Thessalonians 1:8-9; Revelation 19:20; 20:10; 21:8

LIFE LESSONS

1. *Follow Jesus.* Like the 144,000, you and I are called to follow the Lamb, regardless of the cost. "If anyone would come after me, let him deny himself and take up his cross and follow me" (Matthew 16:24). Jesus affirmed, "My sheep hear my voice, and I know them, and they follow me" (John 10:27). He stated, "If anyone serves me, he must follow me" (John 12:26). Jesus calls for a life of no compromise.

2. *No deceit.* The 144,000 Jewish evangelists were said to have no deceit. God desires that you and I avoid deceit as well. The Lord detests deceivers (Psalm 5:6). We should keep our lips from telling lies (1 Peter 3:10). God desires truth (Psalm 51:6), so we ought to always speak the truth (Psalm 120:2; Proverbs 12:17; 14:25; Zechariah 8:16).

QUESTIONS FOR REFLECTION AND DISCUSSION

1. If you were ever accused of being a Christian, would there be enough evidence to convict you?

2. Why do you think God puts such a high priority (in both testaments) on living without deceit?

DAY 26

PRELUDE TO THE BOWL JUDGMENTS

REVELATION 15

SCRIPTURE READING AND INSIGHTS

Begin by reading Revelation 15 in your favorite Bible. As you read, remember that great spiritual wisdom comes from studying God's Word (Psalm 119:98-104).

On day 19, we were introduced to the seventh trumpet judgment, which constitutes the seven bowl judgments. In today's reading, we read of the prelude to the unleashing of these judgments—tribulation martyrs in heaven worshiping and praising God. With your Bible still accessible, consider the following insights on the biblical text, verse by verse.

Revelation 15:1-4

I saw another sign in heaven, great and amazing (15:1): This signifies that God's final series of judgments are about to be unleashed. These "great and amazing" judgments represent the climax of God's holy wrath poured out on God-rejecting humankind, the antichrist, and the false prophet.

Seven angels with seven plagues (15:1): God used angels in the unleashing of the seal and trumpet judgments, and now He does so again in the unleashing of the bowl judgments. The angels are doing the bidding of God (see Psalm 103:20). Bible expositors have noticed similarities between the bowl judgments and the plagues that God inflicted on the Egyptians at the hand of Moses. Just as God severely judged the ancient Egyptians, so God now severely judges the God-rejecting inhabitants of the earth.

The last, for with them the wrath of God is finished (15:1): The last judgments are the worst of all. These bowl judgments are apparently unleashed at the end of the seven-year tribulation period. They unfold rapidly, with each new judgment worse than the former.

I saw what appeared to be a sea of glass mingled with fire (15:2): We saw in Revelation 4:6 that "before the throne there was as it were a sea of glass, like crystal." When Moses and the elders of Israel saw the Lord, "there was under his feet as it were a pavement of sapphire stone, like the very heaven for clearness" (Exodus 24:10).

The fire may indicate that judgment is about to be unleashed on the earth from the throne room of heaven. It could also refer to the fire of God's holiness, which calls for wrath against sin.

Those who had conquered the beast and its image and the number of its name, standing beside the sea of glass (15:2): These are the ones who conquered the antichrist and its image in the Jewish temple and its mark. These are tribulation martyrs who refused to go along with the antichrist and his diabolical agenda. They have "loved not their lives even unto death" (Revelation 12:11).

Harps of God in their hands (15:2): Harps are used in worship. Because of God's awesome deliverance for these martyrs, their response is worshipful (compare Revelation 5:8).

They sing the song of Moses (15:3): Moses' song of victory seems particularly appropriate for these tribulation martyrs.

> I will sing to the Lord, for he has triumphed gloriously...The Lord is my strength and my song, and he has become my salvation; this is my God, and I will praise him...I will exalt him...In the greatness of your majesty you overthrow your adversaries...Who is like you, O Lord, among the gods? Who is like you, majestic in holiness, awesome in glorious deeds, doing wonders? (Exodus 15:1-11).

Moses brought deliverance to God's people in Old Testament times, and Jesus brings a much greater deliverance to God's people during the tribulation period.

The song of the Lamb (15:3): The song of the Lamb is not recorded elsewhere in Scripture. The song's lyrics seem to be recorded in verses 3-4: "Great and amazing are your deeds, O Lord God the Almighty! Just and true are your ways, O King of the nations!" Notice that the absolute deity of Jesus Christ is affirmed in this song. He is the Almighty, as He amply demonstrates in overcoming the antichrist and his forces on earth.

"Who will not fear, O Lord, and glorify your name?" (15:4): The tribulation martyrs continue to sing. This brings to mind the incomparability of Yahweh in the Old Testament. In the midst of various polytheistic nations and their many gods, Yahweh was often shown to be incomparably great. One of the ways the Old Testament demonstrates this is with a rhetorical question, such as the one we just saw in Exodus 15:11: "Who is like you, O LORD, among the gods? Who is like you, majestic in holiness, awesome in glorious deeds, doing wonders?"

"You alone are holy" (15:4): The tribulation martyrs sing of the holiness of Christ. Jesus is the holy (Luke 1:35) and righteous One (Acts 3:14). He had no sin (2 Corinthians 5:21; Hebrews 4:15) and was holy and blameless (Hebrews 7:26-28) and utterly unblemished (Hebrews 9:14; 1 Peter 1:18-19).

"All nations will come and worship you" (15:4): This will ultimately be fulfilled in Christ's millennial kingdom, which follows the second coming. Christ will physically rule on the throne of David in Jerusalem, and all the nations will come and worship Him.

Revelation 15:5-8

After this I looked, and the sanctuary of the tent of witness in heaven was opened, and out of the sanctuary came the seven angels with the seven plagues (15:5-6): This sanctuary of the tent of witness is apparently the Most Holy Place, in which the Ark of the Covenant was kept. Once the sanctuary was open, the angels who initiate the horrific bowl judgments, under God's directive, were permitted to exit.

Clothed in pure, bright linen (15:6): This points to holiness and righteousness. Scripture consistently reveals that God's angels are holy. Angels are sometimes called "holy ones" (Job 5:1; 15:15; Psalm 89:7; Daniel 4:13, 17, 23; 8:13; Jude 14). The word "holy" literally means "set apart." The title "holy ones" is appropriate because God's angels are set apart from sin to God's service. Their service here involves judgment against an unbelieving, unrepentant world.

With golden sashes around their chests (15:6): Scholars have different views as to what this may symbolize. Some suggest it may point to the majesty and glory of these angels. Some relate it to purity. Others relate it to the punitive nature of the angels' mission. In any event, the angels are about to engage in their task.

One of the four living creatures gave to the seven angels seven golden bowls full of the wrath of God (15:7): The four living creatures are apparently cherubim (Revelation 4:6), for they are full of eyes (Ezekiel 1:18). Many believe the word "cherubim" came from a word meaning "to guard." Certainly this meaning fits well with their function of guarding the entrance to Eden (Genesis 3:24). It also fits with the cherubim embroidered on the temple veil that barred entrance into the Most Holy Place (Exodus 26:31; 2 Chronicles 3:14).

Here, as a guardian of God's holiness, one cherub gives the seven bowls to the seven angels who will unleash judgments on an unholy world. These bowl judgments are full of the wrath of our eternal God, appropriate for a God-rejecting and unrepentant world.

The sanctuary was filled with smoke (15:8): Smoke often appears when God is present. For example, Exodus 19:18 tells us that "Mount Sinai was wrapped in smoke because the LORD had descended on it in fire." Some expositors relate this smoke to the cloud of glory that often surrounds God. Exodus 40:34 tells us that "the cloud covered the tent of meeting, and the glory of the LORD filled the tabernacle." First Kings 8:10 reveals that "when the priests came out of the Holy Place, a cloud filled the house of the LORD." Second Chronicles 5:13-14 tells us that the house of the Lord "was filled with a cloud, so that the priests could not stand to minister because of the cloud, for the glory of the LORD filled the house of God" (see also Isaiah 6:4; Ezekiel 11:23; 44:4).

No one could enter the sanctuary until the seven plagues of the seven angels were finished (15:8): This is not said of the earlier seal and trumpet judgments, so we can assume that this display of God's awesome glory within the sanctuary points to the climactic nature of the bowl judgments.

MAJOR THEMES

1. *God's eternality.* The eternal nature of God is a common theme in Scripture ("who lives forever and ever"—Revelation 15:7). God is from everlasting to everlasting (Psalm 90:2). He is the Alpha and the Omega (Revelation 1:8) and the "King of the ages, immortal" (1 Timothy 1:17), who abides forever (Psalm 102:27; Isaiah 57:15).

2. *Yahweh's incomparability.* Moses often expressed God's incomparability by negation: "There is no one like the LORD our God" (Exodus 8:10). He also used rhetorical questions: "Who is like you, O LORD, among the gods?" (Exodus 15:11). The implied answer is, no one in all the universe. This was particularly significant in view of Moses' experience with Egypt, which was brimming with false gods. During the tribulation period, God's incomparability will be shown in contrast to the false god of the antichrist (Revelation 15:3-4).

DIGGING DEEPER WITH CROSS-REFERENCES

"I saw," "I looked"—Revelation 13:1, 11; 14:1, 6, 14; 15:2, 5

Tribulation martyrs—Revelation 6:9-11; 7:9-17; 12:11; 14:1-5, 13

Universal worship of Jesus during the millennial kingdom—Psalms 2:8-9; 24:1-10; 66:1-4; 72:8-11; 86:9; Isaiah 2:2-4; 9:6-7; 66:18-23; Jeremiah 10:7; Daniel 7:14; Zephaniah 2:11; Zechariah 14:9

LIFE LESSONS

1. *Deliverance from wrath.* We have focused heavily on the wrath of God in this section of Revelation. But remember that God's church—that's you, me, and all believers in Jesus—are not appointed to this wrath. First Thessalonians 1:10 instructs us to "wait for his [God the Father's] Son from heaven...Jesus who delivers us from the wrath to come." In 1 Thessalonians 5:9 we read, "For God has not destined us for wrath, but to obtain salvation through our Lord Jesus Christ." These verses point to the rapture of the church.

2. *Music and worship.* In our passage we read of harps and singing (Revelation 15:2-3). Musical instruments have long played a pivotal role in the worship of God. Many of the psalms were originally designed for musical accompaniment. Psalm 4 was to be accompanied with stringed instruments. Psalm 5 was to be accompanied by flutes. The psalmist proclaims, "I will praise you with the lyre, O God, my God" (Psalm 43:4). He exults: "I will also praise you with the harp for your faithfulness, O my God; I will sing praises to you with the lyre, O Holy One of Israel" (Psalm 71:22). Indeed, "Praise him with trumpet sound; praise him with lute and harp! Praise him with tambourine and dance; praise him with strings and pipe! Praise him with sounding cymbals; praise him with loud clashing cymbals!" (Psalm 150:3-5). We ought to rejoice at the variety of musical instruments now available for worship.

QUESTIONS FOR REFLECTION AND DISCUSSION

1. Are you living in joyful anticipation as you await the rapture of the church, which could take place at any time? Do you feel you are morally and spiritually prepared?

2. Do you prefer traditional hymns or contemporary Christian music? Do you appreciate both? What do you think are the strengths and weaknesses of each?

DAY 27

THE FIRST FOUR BOWL JUDGMENTS

REVELATION 16:1-9

SCRIPTURE READING AND INSIGHTS

Begin by reading Revelation 16:1-9 in your favorite Bible. As you read, remember that reading Scripture can strengthen your faith in God (Romans 10:17).

In yesterday's reading, we focused on a prelude to the seven bowl judgments in which the tribulation martyrs in heaven worship and praise God. Now, let's find out what happens on earth when the first four bowl judgments are unleashed. With your Bible still accessible, consider the following insights on the biblical text, verse by verse.

Revelation 16:1-2

I heard a loud voice... "Go and pour out on the earth the seven bowls" (16:1): To review, human suffering will steadily escalate throughout the tribulation period. First are the seal judgments, involving bloodshed, famine, death, economic upheaval, a great earthquake, and cosmic disturbances (Revelation 6). Then come the trumpet judgments, involving hail and fire mixed with blood, the sea turning to blood, water turning bitter, further cosmic disturbances, affliction by demonic scorpions, and the death of a third of humankind (Revelation 8:6–9:21). Then come the increasingly worse bowl judgments, which are introduced in Revelation 16.

We have seen that the seven bowl judgments constitute the seventh trumpet judgment, just as the trumpet judgments constitute the seventh seal judgment. The bowl judgments are the last and most severe of God's judgments to be unleashed on the earth.

The first four bowl judgments target people and lead to increasing misery. The last three judgments are international and lead to the war campaign of Armageddon.

The "loud voice from the temple" was apparently that of God Himself. Recall that in Revelation 15:8, God is in the heavenly temple, and no other heavenly being is permitted to enter it "until the seven plagues of the seven angels were finished." That the voice is loud indicates that the revelation to follow was both important and urgent.

Notice that God instructs the seven angels at the same time. This would seem to indicate that the judgments will fall upon the earth rapidly.

The first angel went and poured out his bowl (16:2): The first angel's bowl brings harmful and painful sores on people loyal to the antichrist. The Greek word for "sores" carries the idea of skin ulcers on the surface of the body. Some expositors wonder whether this could come about as a result of some kind of germ warfare or even radiation poisoning from nuclear weapons. (We have seen that in Revelation 8:7 we are told that "a third of the earth was burned up, and a third of the trees were burned up, and all green grass was burned up.")

Revelation 16:3

The second angel poured out his bowl (16:3): When the second angel poured out his bowl, the sea became like blood, leading to the death and extinction of sea creatures. One will recall that in the second trumpet judgment, the waters were turned into blood, but only one-third of the sea creatures died (Revelation 8:8-9). In the present judgment, all life in the sea is destroyed.

Some Bible commentators view this verse symbolically, referring to the "sea of humanity" dying. However, nothing in the context of this passage indicates that it is symbolic. It would appear that the real sea will become "like the blood of a corpse." This, of course, brings to mind God's first judgment against the Egyptians (Exodus 7:17-21).

Revelation 16:4-7

The third angel poured out his bowl (16:4): Now the rivers and springs of water became blood, like the sea. This is particularly devastating because there will be no remaining fresh water sources. When God turned the Nile into blood, the people "could not drink the water of the Nile" (Exodus 7:24). Psalm 78:44 puts it this way: "He turned their rivers to blood, so that they could not drink of their streams." People can live for a time without food, but they can't live long without water. This will greatly increase the suffering of people during the tribulation.

I heard the angel... "Just are you, O Holy One... you brought these judgments" (16:5): An angel now proclaims the justice of God in the light of these judgments against a Christ-rejecting world. This particular angel is called "the angel in charge of the waters." Scripture sometimes relates angels to various elements of nature. For example, "He makes his messengers winds, his ministers a flaming fire" (Psalm 104:4; see Hebrews 1:7). Revelation 7:1 tells us that four of God's angels hold back the four winds of the earth. Revelation 14:18 mentions an angel who has authority over fire. So it is not surprising to read of an angel of the waters, who apparently has authority over the sea and bodies of fresh water.

The theme of God's justice runs like a thread through the pages of Scripture. Justice is the foundation of God's throne (Psalm 89:14). God always deals justly with the earth (Genesis 18:25). He always judges with righteousness (Psalm 98:9). He stands against injustice (see Deuteronomy 32:4; Job 34:12). This means that as bad as these bowl judgments are, they are just judgments against an unbelieving world. The earth's inhabitants are ripe for such judgment.

"They have shed the blood of saints and prophets" (16:6): The angel continues his affirmation of God's justice in inflicting these judgments. He reveals that being forced to drink blood is an appropriate judgment for these rank unbelievers. After all, they were responsible for shedding the blood of God's people and God's prophets. The punishment thus perfectly fits the crime (see Isaiah 49:26). They took the lives of others, so their own lives were now being forfeited in judgment.

I heard the altar saying... "True and just are your judgments" (16:7): As if to echo a hearty "amen" to the words just spoken by the angel, John hears words from the altar. These words were apparently spoken by the tribulation martyrs—those "under the altar" (Revelation 6:9). They were among those whose blood was spilled by the evildoers still on earth. These same martyrs earlier asked God, "O Sovereign Lord, holy and true, how long before you will judge and avenge our blood on those who dwell on the earth?" (Revelation 6:10). The wait is over. Judgment is now falling.

The proclamation "true and just are your judgments" echoes what we were told earlier in Revelation: "O Lord God the Almighty! Just and true are your ways" (Revelation 15:3). Later in Revelation, we find a reaffirmation that God's "judgments are true and just" (19:2). These judgments are horrible, but they are truly just.

Revelation 16:8-9

The fourth angel poured out his bowl (16:8): Somehow, when the fourth angel pours out his bowl on the sun, the intensity of the sun's heat is greatly increased so that it scorches people (compare Isaiah 24:6; 42:25; Malachi 4:1). Another possibility is that with all the other judgments that have affected the environment during the tribulation period, the ozone layer may become so depleted and thin that the sun's rays become more intense. The combination of no fresh water to drink and a scorching-hot sun will lead to immense misery.

This seems to be quite the opposite of the fourth trumpet judgment, in which the sun was darkened (Revelation 8:12). The earth was created to be an ideal environment for humankind, but during the tribulation period it will become a hellish place.

They were scorched...they cursed the name of God...they did not repent (16:9): Instead of repenting and turning to God, the people who are scorched on the earth will curse God's name. Just as Pharaoh's heart became increasingly hardened as judgments fell against Egypt (Exodus 7:13-14, 22; 8:15, 19, 32; 9:7, 34-35; 13:15), so the people of the tribulation will become increasingly calloused against God (see Psalm 95:8; Ephesians 4:18).

MAJOR THEMES

1. *Painful sores.* The painful sores of Revelation 16:1-2 are reminiscent of God's judgments in Old Testament times. During the Exodus account, for example, we read of "boils breaking out in sores on man and beast throughout all the land of Egypt" (Exodus 9:9). The Lord later warned His people of the dangers of disobedience: "The LORD will strike you with the boils of Egypt, and with tumors and scabs and itch, of which you cannot be healed" (Deuteronomy 28:27). Indeed, "The LORD will strike you on the knees and on the legs with grievous boils of which you cannot be healed, from the sole of your foot to the crown of your head" (Deuteronomy 28:35). The righteous Job suffered from such a malady at the hand of Satan: "Satan went out from the presence of the LORD and struck Job with loathsome sores from the sole of his foot to the crown of his head" (Job 2:7).

2. *Just judgments.* Have you noticed that people in the Bible often seem to receive punishments from God that perfectly fit their crimes? Pharaoh tried to arrange for all the Hebrew boys to be drowned, but instead Pharaoh's army drowned (see Exodus 1:22; 14:28). The evil Haman conspired to have Mordecai the Jew hanged, but instead he himself was hanged on the very gallows he had built for Mordecai (Esther 7:10; 9:6-10). Judgment was pronounced against the evil Joab, and the Lord brought "back his bloody deeds on his own head" (1 Kings 2:32). Adonibezek once said, "As I have done, so God has repaid me" (Judges 1:7).

DIGGING DEEPER WITH CROSS-REFERENCES

Holy One—2 Kings 19:22; Job 6:10; Psalms 16:10; 71:22; 78:41; Proverbs 9:10; 30:3; Isaiah 1:4; 5:19; 40:25; 43:3, 15; Luke 4:34; Acts 2:27; Revelation 3:7

Pour out—Psalm 69:24; Jeremiah 6:11; 10:25; Ezekiel 7:8; 14:19; 20:8, 13, 21; 21:31; Hosea 5:10

LIFE LESSONS

1. *Calloused hearts.* Even Christians can have calloused or hardened hearts. Psalm 95:8 exhorts God's people, "Do not harden your hearts." Picking up

on this theme, Hebrews 3:8 warns, "Do not harden your hearts as in the rebellion, on the day of testing in the wilderness" (see verse 15). Hebrews 4:7 urges again: "Today, if you hear his voice, do not harden your hearts." Just as calloused skin is insensitive, so a calloused heart is insensitive to the things of God. That is a bad place to be in. The best way to avoid a calloused heart is to have regular exposure to God's Word (Psalm 119), be obedient to God (John 14:21; 1 John 5:3), and repent immediately whenever you fall into sin (Acts 3:19). Keep your heart sensitive to the things of God.

2. *Repentance brings relief.* In our text, the people of the earth refused to repent in the face of God's judgments. The truth is, repentance can bring relief from God's judgments and discipline. In Jeremiah 18:7-8 God Himself promises, "If at any time I declare concerning a nation or a kingdom, that I will pluck up and break down and destroy it, and if that nation, concerning which I have spoken, turns from its evil, I will relent of the disaster that I intended to do to it." However, if no repentance comes, continued judgment is righteous and just. Do you want to shorten God's disciplines in your life (Hebrews 12:5-11)? If so, develop a lifestyle of repentance.

QUESTIONS FOR REFLECTION AND DISCUSSION

1. Do you ever feel as though you may be insensitive to the things of God? If so, what have you learned in this study that can help you rectify this?

2. Would you say you are a quick responder when repentance is called for? Or do you have a tendency to lag for a while until God brings discipline?

DAY 28

THE FIFTH, SIXTH, AND SEVENTH BOWL JUDGMENTS

REVELATION 16:10-21

SCRIPTURE READING AND INSIGHTS

Begin by reading Revelation 16:10-21 in your favorite Bible. As you read, remember that reading Scripture can strengthen your faith in God (Romans 10:17).

In the previous lesson, we learned about the first four bowl judgments. Now let's zero in on the fifth, sixth, and seventh bowl judgments. With your Bible still accessible, consider the following insights on the biblical text, verse by verse.

Revelation 16:10-11

The fifth angel poured out his bowl on the throne of the beast (16:10): The "throne of the beast" is the antichrist's dominion on earth.

Its kingdom was plunged into darkness (16:10): Darkness is associated with God's judgment in Isaiah 60:2; Joel 2:2; Mark 13:24-25.

People gnawed their tongues...cursed God...did not repent (16:10-11): The fresh water supply has been destroyed, the sun has become more intense, and now people affiliated with the antichrist's kingdom gnaw their tongues and curse God. This is a picture of relentless misery. But despite the horror of these woes from the hand of God, people's hearts continue to harden, and they refuse to repent. They choose to continue their loyalty to the antichrist instead of turning to the one true God of heaven, who can bring relief. Their minds continue to be blinded by the power of Satan (2 Corinthians 4:4).

And yet there is always time to repent and turn to God. The gospel of the kingdom will be preached even in the midst of this pervasive rejection of God (Matthew 24:14).

Revelation 16:12-16

The sixth angel poured out his bowl on the great river Euphrates (16:12): The Euphrates River—the longest river in Western Asia at almost 1,800 miles—begins in modern-day Turkey, heads toward the Mediterranean Sea, turns south and flows for more than 1,000 miles before eventually converging with the Tigris River, which then flows into the Persian Gulf. Many ancient cities, including Ur and Babylon, were on this river.

To prepare the way for the kings from the east (16:12): Here, at the unleashing of the sixth bowl judgment near the end of the tribulation period, the allied armies of the antichrist will gather for the final destruction of the Jews. The Euphrates River will be dried up, thereby making it easier for the kings of the east to assemble.

"Kings from the east" is more literally "kings from the rising of the sun." Who are these kings? A survey of 100 prophecy books reveals more than 50 different interpretations as to who they are. Some suggest they are the seven kings of Daniel 7 who have submitted to the authority of the antichrist. But prophecy scholar John F. Walvoord offers a different interpretation.

> The simplest and best explanation…is that this refers to kings or rulers from the Orient or East who will participate in the final world war. In the light of the context of this passage indicating the near approach of the second coming of Christ and the contemporary world situation in which the Orient today contains a large portion of the world's population with tremendous military potential, any interpretation other than a literal one does not make sense.[1]

This is what makes the Euphrates River so strategic. The river is the primary water boundary between the Holy Land and Asia to the east. For this reason, theologian Charles Ryrie observes that "the armies of the nations of the Orient will be aided in their march toward Armageddon by the supernatural drying up of the Euphrates River."[2] (Compare with Isaiah 11:15.)

As for their motivation, these kings will be aware that their suffering is due to the God of Israel. In their perverted thinking, they may resolve that moving against the Jews (whom they view as God's people) will constitute a vengeful attack against God Himself.

I saw...three unclean spirits like frogs (16:13): The goal of the invading coalition will be to once and for all destroy the Jewish people. The entire satanic trinity—Satan (the dragon), the antichrist (the first beast), and the false prophet (the second beast)—will be involved. Demons (the three unclean spirits) who emerge at the behest of the satanic trinity (from their mouths) will summon the kings of the earth.

Why were these demons said to be like frogs? Frogs were ritually unclean (Leviticus 11:9-12, 41). Many viewed them as vile, plague-inducing creatures. The demons are thus frog-like in the sense that they are vile and unclean.

They are demonic spirits, performing signs, who go abroad to the kings of the whole world (16:14): The signs performed by these demonic spirits are grade-B miracles (2 Thessalonians 2:9; see also Revelation 13:13-14). The unclean spirits will apparently need this limited miraculous power to cause the kings to journey to Palestine, for they will be thirsty (no fresh water), scorched (from the sun), and covered with sores (16:2). The journey will be painful, but the demons will use their miraculous powers to induce them to make the trek.

Battle on the great day of God the Almighty (16:14): This is another way of referring to the campaign of Armageddon.

"Behold, I am coming like a thief" (16:15): In the midst of judgment and chaos, we find a parenthetical call to surviving believers in Jesus to remain watchful and alert. After all, Christ will come when people least expect Him.

"Keeping his garments on, that he may not go about naked and be seen exposed" (16:15): The backdrop to this odd statement is that in biblical times, a guard who was caught sleeping on the job was stripped of his clothing, leaving him naked so his disgrace would be evident to all around him. First-century readers would have understood this as a way of saying, "Be watchful and alert!" The one who does so will be blessed.

They assembled them at the place that in Hebrew is called Armageddon (16:16): The word "Armageddon" literally means "Mount of Megiddo" and refers to a location about 60 miles north of Jerusalem. This is the location of Barak's battle with the Canaanites (Judges 4) and Gideon's battle with the Midianites (Judges 7). This will be the site for the final horrific battles of humankind just prior to the second coming.

As we will see in the coming pages, a number of stages will comprise the campaign of Armageddon. It is therefore not one battle or a single event. Armageddon will involve an extended, escalating conflict, and it will be increasingly catastrophic.

Revelation 16:17-21

The seventh angel poured out his bowl...a loud voice (16:17): The loud voice is no doubt from God Himself. Recall that no other heavenly being (aside from God) was permitted to enter the heavenly temple "until the seven plagues of the seven angels were finished" (15:8).

The loud voice of God proclaims, "It is done!" This bowl judgment will at last complete God's wrath on the world. The original Greek carries the idea, "It is now done and will remain done." God's wrath will now be truly over.

There were flashes of lightning...and a great earthquake (16:18): This earthquake will be more severe than all previous earthquakes (see Haggai 2:6; Hebrews 12:26-27; Revelation 6:12; 8:5; 11:13, 19). This final earthquake is much like an exclamation point on the previous destructive judgments.

The great city was split into three parts (16:19): Scholars debate whether the great city is Jerusalem or Babylon. Some note that in Revelation 11:8, Jerusalem is "the great city that symbolically is called Sodom and Egypt, where their Lord was crucified." If the great city is Jerusalem, this verse would coincide with Zechariah 14:4, which predicts that an earthquake will change its topography.

Other scholars say that the context in verse 19 seems to infer that the great city is Babylon. The latter part of the verse actually singles out Babylon as the prime target of God's wrath. The destruction of Babylon will be explained in detail in Revelation 17–18. God will act on His earlier promise that Babylon would fall and that the cup of His wrath would be poured out on it (Revelation 14:8, 10).

Every island fled away (16:20): The landscape will change dramatically toward the end of the tribulation. This change in topography is apparently to prepare the earth for the millennial kingdom. As we read in Isaiah 40:4, "Every valley shall be lifted up, and every mountain and hill be made low; the uneven ground shall become level, and the rough places a plain."

Great hailstones...fell from heaven (16:21): With each hailstone weighing about a hundred pounds, the damage will be unfathomable. Very little will be left standing following the great earthquake and the apocalyptic hailstorm. Amazingly, despite the destruction, people will still refuse to repent.

MAJOR THEMES

1. *Unclean spirits.* This is a common designation of demons in the New Testament (see Matthew 12:43; Mark 1:23). Luke 8:29 equates the two terms.

2. *Spirits are often not named.* Spirits are often identified in Scripture simply by their character. Our text refers to "unclean spirits." Scripture also refers to "evil spirits" (Luke 7:21; Acts 19:13) and "deceitful spirits" (1 Timothy 4:1). The Holy Spirit is also identified by His completely different character—holiness (John 14:26).

DIGGING DEEPER WITH CROSS-REFERENCES

Always be ready—1 Thessalonians 5:2-4; 2 Peter 3:10; see also 1 John 2:28

Cursing God—1 Kings 21:10, 13; Job 1:5; 2:9

Give God glory—Joshua 7:19; Isaiah 24:15; Jeremiah 13:16; Acts 12:23; Revelation 14:7

LIFE LESSONS

1. *Don't be unprepared.* God's people are called to be alert and watchful as the end times unfold. First Thessalonians 5:2 warns, "You yourselves are fully aware that the day of the Lord will come like a thief in the night." Verse 4 affirms, "You are not in darkness, brothers, for that day to surprise you like a thief." Second Peter 3:10 likewise affirms, "The day of the Lord will come like a thief." The rapture is imminent (Philippians 4:5), and

we don't know the day it will occur. We ought always to be prepared by living righteously every moment.

2. *It is done.* In Revelation 16:17 we read, "It is done!" God's wrath against an unbelieving world is finally over. This reminds us of the wrath of God being poured out on Jesus for our sins at the cross of Calvary. Once Christ's saving work was complete, He uttered those famous words, "It is finished" (John 19:30), which can also be translated "paid in full." Jesus took our individual certificates of debt, listing all our sins, and nailed them to the cross. Our sins have been paid in full so we can be saved (see Colossians 2:14).

QUESTIONS FOR REFLECTION AND DISCUSSION

1. If the rapture were to happen in the next hour, would you be morally and spiritually prepared?

2. What steps can you take so that when He comes for us, you will not be ashamed? (See Luke 9:26; Philippians 1:20; 1 John 2:28.)

3. Your certificate of debt, listing all your sins for your entire life, was nailed to Christ's cross, and your debt was paid in full. How does this make you feel?

DAY 29

THE FALL OF RELIGIOUS BABYLON

REVELATION 17

SCRIPTURE READING AND INSIGHTS

Begin by reading Revelation 17 in your favorite Bible. As you read, keep in mind that God desires you not only to hear His Word but also to do it (James 1:22).

In yesterday's reading, we witnessed the conclusion of the seven bowl judgments. In today's reading, we see the utter destruction of religious Babylon—the false religious system that will engulf the earth during the tribulation period. With your Bible still accessible, consider the following insights on the biblical text, verse by verse.

Revelation 17:1-6

One of the seven angels...said to me, "Come, I will show you the judgment of the great prostitute" (17:1-2): John wrote the book of Revelation in the order in which the truth was revealed to him. However, the events described are not necessarily all in chronological order. This is the case with Revelation 17, which depicts a scene from the first half of the tribulation.

Revelation 17 focuses on religious Babylon. Verses 1-7 provide a description of religious Babylon. Verses 8-18 interpret the description.

The term "Babylon" in Revelation 17–18 refers to both a literal city along the Euphrates River and a religious/commercial system. It is similar to the term Wall Street, which refers both to a literal street as well as a commercial system.

Why does Babylon represent false religion? In ancient times, the Babylonians believed in many false gods and goddesses and were deeply entrenched in paganism, idolatry, and divination. With such a history, it is not surprising that the false religious system of the tribulation period is identified with Babylon.

Verse 1 refers to a great prostitute. Prostitution is a common and graphic scriptural metaphor for unfaithfulness to God (see Jeremiah 3:6-9; Ezekiel 20:30). The great prostitute here symbolizes the apostate religious system of Babylon—probably apostate Christendom, embracing all those who were left behind at the rapture.

"Who is seated on many waters, with whom the kings of the earth have committed sexual immorality" (17:1-2): This symbolizes the false religion's control over various peoples, multitudes, nations, and languages. The fornication described here refers not to actual sexual sin but rather to idolatry, which is unfaithfulness to the true God (see Revelation 14:8).

"The dwellers on earth have become drunk" (17:2): Just as wine can intoxicate people, so people around the globe will become intoxicated by this false religion. Wine has a controlling influence on people, and this false religion will control people worldwide.

This false religious system will apparently emerge into prominence during the first half of the tribulation period. But now, our text informs us, this religious system comes under judgment.

A woman sitting on a scarlet beast that was full of blasphemous names (17:3): The woman is the great prostitute mentioned in verses 1-2. This great prostitute (or blasphemous religion) sits on, or controls, the scarlet beast, who is the antichrist. The color scarlet points to the splendor of the antichrist. The beast's blasphemous names indicate its blasphemous character (see Psalm 74:18; Isaiah 52:5; Romans 2:24; Revelation 13:1, 6; 16:9, 11, 21).

The woman was arrayed...holding in her hand a golden cup full of abominations (17:4): This imagery indicates that this false religious system will be wealthy and will have a glorious outer appearance. Note that in ancient times, prostitutes often dressed extravagantly to seduce men. This false religious system will be adorned so as to lure the people of the world into its religious web. This religious system will be outwardly attractive.

The woman has a golden cup, which on the outside is appealing. Regardless of how beautiful a cup looks on the outside, however, if it contains poison, it is deadly. This false religion will appear good on the outside, but on the inside it will be poisonous (see Deuteronomy 18:9; 29:17; 32:16; Jeremiah 51:7).

On her forehead was written... "Babylon the great, mother of prostitutes" (17:5): Prostitutes in ancient Rome typically wore a headband with their name on it (see Jeremiah 3:3).

I saw the woman, drunk with the blood of the saints (17:6): The woman—the false religious system—is drunk with the blood of the saints and Christian martyrs. This includes the blood of God's two prophetic witnesses (11:10) and all who refuse to receive the mark of the beast (13:15).

Revelation 17:7-18

The angel said... "I will tell you the mystery of the woman" (17:7): Recognizing that John was baffled by what he saw, the angel will provide more information about both the beast (verses 7-14) and the woman (see verses 15-18).

"The beast that you saw was, and is not, and is about to rise" (17:8): The antichrist was alive prior to his mortal wound. Then he was apparently mortally wounded, and now he "is about to rise from the bottomless pit" (see Revelation 13:3-4, 12-14). How will the antichrist arise from the bottomless pit? As noted previously, while his body lies apparently mortally wounded, his spirit departs the body and goes to the abyss for a time, perhaps being further instructed by Satan. When the antichrist's physical wound is healed, his spirit ascends out of the bottomless pit and reunites with the supposedly resurrected body.

In this scenario, the antichrist will appear to be physically dead but will not really be dead. Once revived, people will assume that he was resurrected. Having encountered Satan in the bottomless pit, he is invigorated to carry out his anti-God purpose (see chapter 20).

"And go to destruction" (17:8): Fresh from the abyss, and empowered by Satan, the antichrist will now take a destructive path in the final years of the tribulation period that will ultimately lead to eternal destruction in the lake of fire (see 2 Thessalonians 2:3; Revelation 19:20).

"The dwellers on earth whose names have not been written in the book of life"

(17:8): These earth dwellers are characterized by the things of the earth. We might call them worldlings or worldly people. The book of life records the names of all who are redeemed, who will inherit heaven (Revelation 3:5; 13:8; 20:12, 15; 21:27; see also Luke 10:20; Philippians 4:3). The names of the worldlings are not in this book.

"Will marvel to see the beast, because it was and is not and is to come" (17:8): These worldlings marvel that the beast was alive, and then supposedly died, and then appeared to come to life again.

"The seven heads are seven mountains on which the woman is seated" (17:9): The seven mountains symbolize the seven kingdoms and their kings, as explained in the next verse. Mountains often symbolize kingdoms in Scripture (Psalms 30:7; 68:15-16; Isaiah 2:2; 41:15; Jeremiah 51:25; Daniel 2:35, 44-45; Habakkuk 3:6, 10; Zechariah 4:7).

These seven kingdoms are Egypt, Assyria, Babylon, Medo-Persia, Greece, Rome, and that of the antichrist. False paganized religion influenced all these empires—the woman was seated on them all.

"They are also seven kings" (17:10): The seven heads are identified as seven rulers over seven kingdoms—five of which have fallen, one still exists, and one is yet to come. At the time of John's writing, the Egyptian, Assyrian, Babylonian, Medo-Persian, and Greek Empires had fallen. Rome still existed in his day. The antichrist's kingdom was yet to come.

He must remain only a little while (17:10): He will be "allowed to exercise authority for forty-two months" (Revelation 13:5)—the last half of the tribulation period.

"The beast...is an eighth but it belongs to the seven" (17:11): The antichrist is both the seventh and the eighth king. He is the seventh king prior to his mortal wound. He is the eighth king after his so-called resurrection. This eighth king "goes to destruction."

"The ten horns that you saw" (17:12): These ten kings who don't yet have power will receive delegated authority under the antichrist during the tribulation. They will rule "for one hour"—a short time, as we might expect because the reign of the antichrist will also be short-lived (Revelation 13:5).

"These are of one mind" (17:13): These kings will be unanimously committed to serving under the antichrist.

"They will make war on the Lamb" (17:14): In making war against Jesus Christ, they follow the lead of the antichrist, who has always been against Jesus Christ. This war against the Lamb will be waged at Armageddon. It will be a futile endeavor, for the Lamb is the Lord of lords and King of kings. He is sovereign over all things (see 1 Timothy 6:15; Revelation 19:16; see also Deuteronomy 10:17; Psalm 136:3). None can defeat Him.

"The waters that you saw" (17:15): Water was a common symbol for people (Psalms 18:4, 16; 124:4; Isaiah 8:7; Jeremiah 47:2). This imagery indicates that this single religious system will influence the entire world.

"The ten horns that you saw, they and the beast will hate the prostitute" (17:16): The antichrist will utilize the false religious system (the prostitute) to initially bring unity to the peoples of the world. Once he has accomplished this purpose, he no longer needs the false religion. He will hate it and dispose of it with the help of his ten lieutenants.

By the middle of the tribulation period, the antichrist now intends to be the sole object of worship. (See Daniel 9:27; 11:26-38; Matthew 24:15; 2 Thessalonians 2:4; and Revelation 13:8, 15.)

"God has put it into their hearts to carry out his purpose" (17:17): Even though the antichrist and his ten lieutenants destroy the false religious system, God is actually bringing about His sovereign purposes through them. God will allow the antichrist to come into world dominion—but only for a short time.

"The woman that you saw" (17:18): As noted previously, just as Wall Street is a literal place as well as an economic system, so Babylon refers to both a real city and a false religious system. The woman personifies this false religious system.

MAJOR THEMES

1. *God's eternal purpose.* Human history in all its details, even the most minute, is but the outworking of the eternal purposes of God. What has happened in the past, what is happening today, and what will happen in the future are all evidence of the unfolding of a purposeful plan devised by the wondrous personal God of the Bible (Ephesians 3:11; 2 Timothy 1:9).

2. *God is sovereign over evil.* God sovereignly uses the forces of evil to accomplish

His supreme purposes. For example, He allows demonic spirits to gather the kings of the world to assemble for Armageddon (Revelation 16:13-16). He causes wicked armies to engage in friendly fire against each other and destroy themselves (see Judges 7:22; 1 Samuel 14:20; 2 Chronicles 20:23; Ezekiel 38:21). God's methods are inscrutable. In the end, evil will be defeated and all will be perfect (Revelation 21–22).

DIGGING DEEPER WITH CROSS-REFERENCES

In the Spirit—Revelation 1:10; 4:2; 21:10

Prostitution: a symbol of idolatry—Isaiah 23:15-17; Jeremiah 2:20-31; 13:27; Ezekiel 16:17-19; Hosea 2:5; 4:15; 5:3; 6:10; 9:1; Nahum 3:4

LIFE LESSONS

1. *You can trust Bible prophecy.* Revelation 17:17 affirms that the words of God will be fulfilled. Bible prophecy is trustworthy! The precedent has already been set. We have seen that more than 100 Old Testament prophecies were literally fulfilled in the first coming of Jesus (for example, Genesis 12:3; 49:10; Isaiah 7:14; 40:3; 53; Zechariah 12:10; Daniel 9:24-25; Micah 5:2). Likewise, all the prophecies dealing with the end times will be literally fulfilled.

2. *Called and chosen and faithful.* These three attributes describe believers in Revelation 17:14. You and I were called and chosen by God before the foundation of the world (1 Peter 1:20). We are also called to be faithful (Proverbs 3:3; Matthew 25:23; Romans 12:12; Revelation 2:10).

QUESTIONS FOR REFLECTION AND DISCUSSION

1. We live in an age of prophetic agnosticism. Many seem unsure about Bible prophecy. In view of what you have learned in our study, do you trust Bible prophecy?

2. Many things in our culture can distract us from God. What steps can you take to beef up your spiritual defenses to ensure faithfulness to God in the face of such distractions?

DAY 30

THE FALL OF COMMERCIAL BABYLON, PART 1

REVELATION 18:1-8

SCRIPTURE READING AND INSIGHTS

Begin by reading Revelation 18:1-8 in your favorite Bible. As you read, keep in mind that God desires you not only to hear His Word but also to do it (James 1:22).

In yesterday's reading, we witnessed the destruction of religious Babylon. Now let's find out about the destruction of commercial Babylon—the antichrist's economic headquarters. With your Bible still accessible, consider the following insights on the biblical text, verse by verse.

Revelation 18:1-3

I saw another angel coming down (18:1): This portion of Revelation presents an interesting irony. While the antichrist is preparing his armies to attack Israel (the initial stages of the campaign of Armageddon), God judges and destroys the antichrist's economic headquarters in Babylon along the Euphrates River (see Isaiah 13:19; Jeremiah 50:11-27, 40).

This destruction will come on Babylon as a direct, decisive judgment from the hand of God. Indeed, God will settle the score for Babylon's long history of standing against His people of Israel. Just as Babylon showed no mercy to its oppression against Israel in the past, so God will now show no mercy to Babylon during the tribulation. This judgment will apparently occur at the very end of the seven-year tribulation period.

In Revelation 18:1, the angel is said to have great authority, so we can surmise that an important judgment is about to be unleashed.

The earth was made bright with his glory (18:1): This does not necessarily mean that the angel has intrinsic glory. More likely, having just come from God's presence in heaven, the angel still shines forth with the radiating glory of God. This is similar to what happened to Moses when receiving the two stone tablets of the law. On that occasion, "Moses did not know that the skin of his face shone because he had been talking with God" (Exodus 34:29).

"Fallen, fallen is Babylon the great" (18:2): The dual occurrence of the word "fallen" apparently indicates both the woeful condition of commercial/political Babylon as well as the certainty of judgment (compare Isaiah 21:9; Jeremiah 51:8).

This is another proleptic announcement—a description of a future action as if it had already occurred. It emphasizes that God's triumph over evil Babylon is an accomplished fact even though its execution is yet future (in the seventh bowl judgment).

Religious Babylon is apparently destroyed about halfway through the tribulation period (Revelation 17), but the destruction of economic/political Babylon is apparently at the end of the seven-year period (Revelation 18). Revelation 18:2 describes the city of Babylon as it will be once God finally judges it at the end of the tribulation (see also Isaiah 13:21; 47:7-9; Jeremiah 50–51).

"She has become a dwelling place for demons, a haunt for every unclean spirit, a haunt for every unclean bird, a haunt for every unclean and detestable beast" (18:2): This demonstrates how horrific God's judgment will be. Babylon will become utterly desolate.

"All nations have drunk the wine of the passion of her sexual immorality" (18:3): The words of this verse are quite similar to those in Revelation 17:2. The earlier verse, however, dealt with religious Babylon (a false religious system), whereas our present verse deals with economic/political Babylon. Just as religious Babylon entices the people of the world into committing spiritual fornication (Revelation 17:2, 4), so commercial/political Babylon will entice the unbelieving world into anti-God materialism. In both cases, people will be utterly unfaithful to God.

The imagery seems to indicate that the anti-God political, economic, and commercial system of Babylon will influence everyone on earth—"all nations" and "the kings of the earth." The influence of Babylon will be universal. It will have an octopus-like reach around the world.

"The merchants of the earth have grown rich" (18:3): Because of the commercial success of this city, merchants around the world will become wealthy. Anti-God materialism will be rampant. The city and all that it represents will be ripe for judgment.

Revelation 18:4-8

Another voice... "Come out of her, my people" (18:4): John then hears another voice from heaven—perhaps an angel who speaks for God—urging the faithful to dissociate themselves from Babylon. Otherwise, sin may result, and they may end up being on the receiving end of the plagues that will shortly fall on Babylon (see Isaiah 52:11; 2 Corinthians 6:14-17; 1 John 2:15-17).

If they separate, the implication is that they will receive God's protection (compare Matthew 24:16; Revelation 12:14). Both Isaiah and Jeremiah called the people of God to leave Babylon (see Isaiah 48:20; Jeremiah 50:8; 51:6-9, 45).

Prophecy scholars Thomas Ice and Timothy Demy provide this helpful explanation of how Jews are able to make it out of Babylon before judgment falls on the city:

> When Babylon is destroyed, the Antichrist will not be present in the city. He will be told of its destruction by messengers (Jeremiah 50:43; 51:31, 32)...The attack will be swift, but there will be some warning or opportunity for Jews who are living in Babylon to flee from the city (Jeremiah 50:6-8, 28; 51:5, 6). Even in these last days, God will preserve a remnant of His people. These refugees are to go to Jerusalem and tell them of the city's destruction and their escape (Jeremiah 51:10, 45, 50; Revelation 18:4, 5).[1]

"Her sins are heaped high as heaven" (18:5): Here is the reason God's people must quickly exit Babylon. Babylon's sins are almost immeasurable. "God has remembered her iniquities"—His patience has now been exhausted. Judgment is about to fall. A righteous and holy God must judge such unrepentant evil.

"Pay her back...repay her double" (18:6): Here we find an echo of the *lex talionis*, the law of retaliation. As Matthew 7:2 puts it, "With the judgment you pronounce you will be judged, and with the measure you use it will be measured to you." Galatians 6:7 tells us, "Whatever one sows, that will he also reap."

Babylon had sown evil and is now about to reap evil. Babylon will now receive the payment that it had paid out to others. It will now be on the receiving end of what it had dished out to others (such as the Jews throughout biblical history).

In fact, Babylon will be repaid double. This was a common judicial requirement in Old Testament law (see Exodus 22:4, 7, 9; Isaiah 40:2; 61:7; Jeremiah 16:18; 17:18; Zechariah 9:12). Babylon's judgment would be thorough, even overflowing.

Such a judgment might seem harsh at first glance. One must keep in mind, however, that all the people associated with economic/political Babylon had fallen into such deep wickedness, with no repentance in view, that they were essentially beyond the point of no return in their moral choices. They seemed irrevocably committed to the person and program of the antichrist. They had permanently crossed the line, declaring allegiance to the antichrist and against God. Judgment was thus unavoidable.

"Give her a like measure of torment and mourning, since in her heart she says, 'I sit as a queen'" (18:7): What irony we see in this verse. Though Babylon had been proud, she will now be humbled. Though Babylon enjoyed glory and luxury, she will now be brought low in torment and mourning. Though Babylon had pretended to be a queen, she will now be brought low by the royal King of kings. Babylon had seemed superior in every way, but its moral inferiority will now be judged.

One cannot help but notice that the description of Babylon in this verse bears at least some resemblance to the Laodicean church. Christ said to this church: "You say, I am rich, I have prospered, and I need nothing, not realizing that you are wretched, pitiable, poor, blind, and naked" (Revelation 3:17). Self-delusion is a wretched state.

"Her plagues will come in a single day" (18:8): The people of God must make haste to separate themselves from the evil system of Babylon, for judgment will come suddenly in one day. There will be death and mourning and famine and fire. The collapse of the city will be stunning.

"Mighty is the Lord God who has judged her" (18:8): Babylon had thought itself to be mighty, but the Lord God is truly mighty.

MAJOR THEMES

1. *Sin: missing the target.* A key meaning of sin in the Bible is "to miss the target." Sin is failure to live up to God's standards. All of us miss the target. No one person is capable of fulfilling all of God's laws at all times (Romans 3:23). Some people may be more righteous than others, but all of us fall short of God's infinitely perfect standards. When we sin, God desires repentance and confession (see 1 John 1:9). When people such as those associated with Babylon go deeper and deeper into sin, with no repentance in sight, they become ripe for judgment (see Psalms 9:7; 96:13; Ecclesiastes 3:17; Romans 2:1-5; 1 Thessalonians 5:2-3; 2 Peter 3:7).

2. *God's holiness and human sin.* Human sin shows up in the light of God's holiness (Romans 3:23). This is illustrated in the life of Isaiah. He was a relatively righteous man, but when he saw God in His infinite holiness, his own personal sin came into clear focus: "Woe is me! For I am lost; for I am a man of unclean lips, and I dwell in the midst of a people of unclean lips" (Isaiah 6:5). When we measure ourselves against other human beings, we may come out looking okay. But other human beings are not our moral measuring stick—God is. And as we measure ourselves against God in His infinite holiness and righteousness, our sin shows up in all of its ugliness. God's judgment falls on unrepentant people in the tribulation period because their sin represents a calloused disregard for God in His holiness. They do not even care that they fall short of God's righteous standards.

DIGGING DEEPER WITH CROSS-REFERENCES

Flee from evil Babylon—Genesis 19:12; Numbers 16:26; Isaiah 48:20; 52:11; Jeremiah 50:8; 51:6-9, 45

Materialism and riches—Proverbs 15:27; Ecclesiastes 5:10; Jeremiah 17:11; Matthew 6:19-21; 1 Timothy 6:10; James 5:3

LIFE LESSONS

1. *God forgets our sins.* Revelation 18:5 says that God remembers the sins of the Babylonians. But in the new covenant, God says of those who turn to Him, "I will forgive their iniquity, and I will remember their sin no more" (Jeremiah 31:34). In Hebrews 8:12 God promises, "I will be merciful toward their iniquities, and I will remember their sins no more." Psalm 103:12 proclaims, "As far as the east is from the west, so far does he remove our transgressions from us." It is a wondrous thing to be forgiven of our sins such that God no longer remembers them!

2. *Come out and be separate.* Christians today are called to separate themselves from that which is ungodly. The apostle Paul urges Timothy, "Do not... take part in the sins of others; keep yourself pure" (1 Timothy 5:22). To the Ephesians he writes, "Take no part in the unfruitful works of darkness, but instead expose them" (Ephesians 5:11). And he writes this to the church in Corinth:

    > Do not be unequally yoked with unbelievers. For what partnership has righteousness with lawlessness? Or what fellowship has light with darkness? What accord has Christ with Belial? Or what portion does a believer share with an unbeliever? (2 Corinthians 6:14-15).

QUESTIONS FOR REFLECTION AND DISCUSSION

1. God has not only forgiven your sins but also forgotten them—all based on the work of Christ on the cross. Do you find that spiritually motivating? How does it affect your level of joy in life?

2. In view of the enticements of Western society, do you sometimes find it difficult to "come out and be separate"? In what ways?

3. Do you ever struggle with materialism?

DAY 31

THE FALL OF COMMERCIAL BABYLON, PART 2

REVELATION 18:9-24

SCRIPTURE READING AND INSIGHTS

Begin by reading Revelation 18:9-24 in your favorite Bible. As you read, stop and meditate on any verses that speak to your heart (Psalm 1:1-3; Joshua 1:8).

In the previous lesson, we saw the destruction of commercial Babylon. Now let's find out how this destruction affects the people of the earth. With your Bible still accessible, consider the following insights on the biblical text, verse by verse.

Revelation 18:9-20

The kings of the earth, who committed sexual immorality and lived in luxury with her, will weep and wail (18:9): The rulers of the earth, with their vested interest in the economic growth of their countries, will grieve and wail—literally, loudly lament—when they witness the collapse of the economic system that had enabled them to live so luxuriously. The collapse of Babylon will indicate to the rulers of the world that the sumptuous empire of the antichrist is utterly doomed. This is devastating news for them, for the antichrist is the source of their own power and wealth.

The "sexual immorality" of these leaders is not to be taken literally but is rather a graphic metaphor indicating that these leaders were intimately connected—prostituting themselves—with the anti-God Babylonian system (see

Ezekiel 26:16; 27:30-35). They will witness the smoke of Babylon burning, perhaps indicating that the primary instrument of judgment against Babylon will be fire (perhaps caused by nuclear detonations).

"You great city, you mighty city" (18:10): The world leaders will recognize that Babylon had been great and mighty, but more mighty than the city will be the mighty divine Judge—God Almighty—who brings the city to ruin. No wonder the world leaders will be in fear.

"In a single hour your judgment has come" (18:10): Babylon will fall rapidly. This means that world leaders, watching from a distance (perhaps via live television and Internet feeds), will have no time to prepare for the calamity or make economic adjustments in order to save their own countries.

The merchants of the earth weep and mourn for her, since no one buys their cargo anymore (18:11): First we are told that world rulers will lament over the fall of Babylon. Now merchants join their lament. Business and government are so intertwined that what affects one affects the other.

Recall from Revelation 13 that no one on earth could buy or sell without having received the mark of the beast. In the chapters that follow in the book of Revelation, it becomes increasingly clear that economic Babylon, as a global system, became the heart and center of economic operations for the antichrist. Now, with the collapse of economic Babylon, the merchants of the earth are no longer able to buy or sell their goods. This means that they themselves become economically ruined.

There is an obvious irony here. Formerly the economic system of the antichrist was such that no one could buy or sell without having received the mark of the beast. Now, however, the economic system itself collapses, and all who are affiliated with this system can no longer buy or sell.

Cargo (18:12-13): The listing of multiple commercial products in verses 12-13 indicates that prior to the fall of economic Babylon, global trade will be extensive. These commercial products include precious metals and gems, clothing, furnishings, spices, food, animals, and even people.

Apparently slavery will continue into the end times. As horrible as it is to think about it, slavery even exists in our own day. In certain parts of the world, for example, young girls are abducted and forced into sexual servitude.

"The fruit for which your soul longed has gone" (18:14): These trade merchants

will lose all the luxurious possessions that their eyes of avarice had longed for. Gone forever will be their culinary delicacies and their splendorous clothing. These items are "never to be found again." The Greek contains two double negatives, indicating the absolute certainty and finality of their loss of these items of wealth.

The merchants... will stand far off (18:15): These individuals will be in stunned disbelief at what has happened to Babylon. They are mentally and emotionally unprepared for this catastrophic turn of events, for it happens so very quickly.

"Fine linen, in purple and scarlet, adorned with gold, with jewels, and with pearls!" (18:16): Notice how Babylon as an economic system is described much like Babylon as a religious system was: "The woman was arrayed in purple and scarlet, and adorned with gold and jewels and pearls" (17:4). These words point to the "prostitute" dressing in such a way as to entice people into joining with her. Economic Babylon will likewise entice people to join her in all of her splendor. But now Babylon has fallen, its splendor is gone, and its economy is collapsing.

"In a single hour all this wealth has been laid waste" (18:17): The sudden nature of Babylon's fall is reiterated. Babylon is devastated. The consequences will be far worse than the collapse of the stock market in 1929. This event will catastrophically and permanently devastate the global economy and world trade.

Four categories of sea people are affected by this dire turn of events: shipmasters, seafaring men, sailors, and all whose trade is on the sea (such as fishermen and pearl divers). These individuals mourn over what has happened to Babylon. Perhaps the shipmasters, seafaring men, and sailors mourn because they are all involved in the transport and distribution of the merchandise of those affiliated with economic Babylon. Perhaps those "whose trade is on the sea" (such as fishermen and pearl divers) mourn because, like everything else, their goods will no longer be purchased, so they too will fall to economic ruin.

They threw dust on their heads (18:19): In Old Testament times, putting dust on one's head was a common means of expressing great grief. For example, when Job's friends beheld Job's suffering, they put dust on their heads (see Job 2:12). Those who made their living on or in the sea are brimming with grief over the sudden, fatal demise of Babylon. Babylon had been flattened—laid waste—"in a single hour."

"Rejoice over her, O heaven...God has given judgment for you against her" (18:20): Here we witness a change of scenery from earth's perspective to heaven's perspective. In contrast to the grief-ridden earth dwellers, God's people in heaven will respond with exuberant joy when economic Babylon collapses. It is interesting to observe that heaven also rejoiced when ancient Babylon fell (Jeremiah 51:48-49). The times may change, but heaven always rejoices when sin is overthrown. God's people rejoice that God's righteousness and justice prevail.

Notice in our verse that there are three categories of the redeemed in heaven—saints, apostles, and prophets. The word "saints" refers to all believers. All who have become born again are saints (see Philippians 1:1). God's apostles and prophets are in a special category of saints, for they were the instruments of God's revelation to humankind. All of these believers collectively rejoice at the collapse of economic Babylon. God had earlier pronounced His verdict, and now His verdict is executed against Babylon.

Revelation 18:21-24

A mighty angel took up a stone...and threw it into the sea, saying, "So will Babylon the great city be thrown down with violence" (18:21-22): This graphically symbolizes the demise of Babylon in judgment (see Exodus 15:5; Nehemiah 9:11; Jeremiah 51:63-64; Matthew 18:6). In Bible times, millstones were huge, weighing thousands of pounds. They were used to grind grain. When such large and weighty stones are thrown into the sea, they can never be recovered. Similarly, once Babylon falls in judgment, it will never rise again. Babylon's destruction will be permanent.

Our text includes images that emphasize how completely Babylon is destroyed. Musicians, craftsmen, mills, lamps, bridegrooms...all are gone. The constant hum of a busy city will now be replaced with a deathly silence.

Such judgment against Babylon is justified, for all the nations of the earth had been seduced by its economic system. The seduction is rooted in materialism, the philosophy that wealth and luxury provide meaning in life. God is left entirely out of the picture. Now the city that represents materialism will be materially destroyed.

"In her was found the blood of prophets and of saints" (18:24): Our passage

closes with the reason for God's judgment and destruction of Babylon: This city was responsible for slaying God's prophets and His saints. God's people had been martyred because of their testimonies for Jesus. Those associated with Babylon will shed the blood of God's witnesses, and now their own blood will be shed in response. God brings about His justice. Vengeance is His (Romans 12:19-21). Economic Babylon falls, and the second coming is imminent.

MAJOR THEMES

1. *Expressing grief.* In Bible times, people expressed grief by putting dust on their heads. Joshua and the elders, in fear of the people being destroyed by the Amorites, put "dust on their heads" (Joshua 7:6). When the Israelites were defeated in battle by the Philistines, a man put "dirt on his head," made his way to Shiloh, and informed the high priest Eli that his two sons had been killed (1 Samuel 4:12; see also 2 Samuel 1:2; 13:19; 15:32; Job 2:12; Lamentations 2:10). Some of those who witness the fall of Babylon during the tribulation period will do the same.

2. *Sudden destruction.* We often find sudden destruction falling on the wicked in the Bible. Proverbs 6:15 warns, "Therefore calamity will come upon him suddenly; in a moment he will be broken beyond healing." Proverbs 24:22 warns that disaster "will arise suddenly." Isaiah 47:11 warns that "ruin shall come upon you suddenly, of which you know nothing." God affirms in Jeremiah 15:8, "I have made anguish and terror fall upon them suddenly." In 1 Thessalonians 5:3, the apostle Paul warns, "While people are saying, 'There is peace and security,' then sudden destruction will come upon them as labor pains come upon a pregnant woman, and they will not escape."

DIGGING DEEPER WITH CROSS-REFERENCES

Great city—Revelation 11:8; 14:8; 16:19; 17:18

Rising smoke—Genesis 19:28; Isaiah 34:10

"Saints" in the book of Revelation—Revelation 5:8; 8:3-4; 11:18; 13:7, 10; 14:12; 16:6; 17:6; 19:8; 20:9

LIFE LESSONS

1. *Wealth and luxury.* Scripture reveals that wealth is fleeting. We are told that "riches do not last forever" (Proverbs 27:24). All people die, and at death they "leave their wealth to others" (Psalm 49:10). King Solomon lamented, "I hated all my toil in which I toil under the sun, seeing that I must leave it to the man who will come after me" (Ecclesiastes 2:18). The apostle Paul affirms that "we brought nothing into the world, and we cannot take anything out of the world" (1 Timothy 6:7). Such factors ought to influence the way we think about wealth and luxury.

2. *Your citizenship.* The earth dwellers who live during the tribulation period will be "citizens of Babylon" even though they may not live in the actual city. They will be citizens there because they live according to its anti-God and materialistic values. You and I, even though we live in different cities on earth, are citizens of heaven. The apostle Paul said, "Our citizenship is in heaven, and from it we await a Savior, the Lord Jesus Christ" (Philippians 3:20). Paul also said that we are "fellow citizens with the saints and members of the household of God" (Ephesians 2:19). We are pilgrims passing through on earth, on our way to another country, another land, another city (Hebrews 11:16). And we are to behave here below as citizens of that city above.

QUESTIONS FOR REFLECTION AND DISCUSSION

1. What is your attitude toward wealth and the possession of material things?

2. Can you possess wealth without wealth possessing you? If you suddenly lost your wealth, how would it affect you?

3. Do you live more like a citizen of earth or like a citizen of heaven?

DAY 32

SHOUTS OF HALLELUJAH AND THE MARRIAGE SUPPER OF THE LAMB

REVELATION 19:1-10

SCRIPTURE READING AND INSIGHTS

Begin by reading Revelation 19:1-10 in your favorite Bible. As you read, stop and meditate on any verses that speak to your heart (Psalm 1:1-3; Joshua 1:8).

In the previous two readings, we witnessed the destruction of commercial Babylon and its effect on the entire earth. In today's reading, we focus on an outbreak of praise in heaven. With your Bible still accessible, consider the following insights on the biblical text, verse by verse.

Revelation 19:1-3

After this I heard... a great multitude in heaven, crying out, "Hallelujah" (19:1): The phrase "after this" tells us that what now takes place follows the destruction of Babylon, just prior to the second coming of Christ.

John hears a "loud voice" of a great multitude offering praise in heaven (see Revelation 7:9-10). The imminent second coming of Christ may be among the reasons for this eruption of praise.

"His judgments are true and just" (19:2): This is another reason for the outbreak of praise in heaven. God's people yearn for God's holy and true judgments against sin and rebellion. Recall that in Revelation 6:10 the souls of the martyrs who were under God's altar cried out with a loud voice, "O Sovereign

Lord, holy and true, how long before you will judge and avenge our blood on those who dwell on the earth?" Now that God has brought about this just judgment, praise erupts in heaven.

Once more they cried out, "Hallelujah!" (19:3): The multitude exclaims again, for Babylon has been justly destroyed. The rising smoke represents the effects of the fire that will destroy Babylon (Revelation 17:16; 18:8-9, 18). This smoke "goes up forever and ever," symbolizing that Babylon's destruction will be permanent. One of the more sobering aspects of Scripture is that the enemies of God will be punished forever and ever.

Revelation 19:4-5

The twenty-four elders and the four living creatures fell down and worshiped God (19:4): Recall that the 24 elders apparently represent the church. The four living creatures are apparently cherubim. Both groups now fall down and worship God on the throne. Cherubim often seem to be associated with worship in the book of Revelation (4:8, 11; 5:9-12, 14; 11:16-18).

From the throne came a voice saying, "Praise our God" (19:5): This is apparently the voice of an angel that calls out, inviting all who serve God—regardless of their rank, position, or heavenly status ("small or great")—to participate in praising God (compare with Psalms 113:1; 115:13).

Revelation 19:6-8

The voice of a great multitude, like the roar of many waters and like the sound of mighty peals of thunder (19:6): The proclamation sounds like Niagara Falls or a Texas thunderstorm.

"Hallelujah! For the Lord our God the Almighty reigns" (19:6): The term "Almighty" is a common title for God in the book of Revelation (1:8; 4:8; 11:17; 15:3; 16:7, 14; 21:22).

The acclamation that God reigns should not be taken to mean that He has just started to reign. The verse simply means that God is now about to actively and sovereignly overthrow the thrones of earthly kings, the antichrist, and Satan. God's sovereign kingship is about to kick into high gear. God's will is now going to be done on earth as it has been in heaven!

Of course, a new aspect of God's reign will soon be established on earth.

During Christ's millennial reign, He will rule from the actual throne of David in Jerusalem, in fulfillment of the Davidic covenant (2 Samuel 7:12-13). The whole planet will become a theocracy.

"Let us rejoice and exult...the marriage of the Lamb has come" (19:7): Heaven's inhabitants are now invited to rejoice and exult over the imminent marriage of the Lamb. Scripture often refers to the relationship between Christ and the church as a marriage (see Matthew 9:15; 22:2-14; 25:1-13; Mark 2:19-20; Luke 5:34-35; 14:15-24; John 3:29). The church is pictured as a virgin bride awaiting the coming of her heavenly Bridegroom (2 Corinthians 11:2; Ephesians 5:22-33). While she waits, she keeps herself faithful and pure, unstained from the world.

The wedding metaphor plays out in three parts. First, the Hebrew bride is betrothed to the bridegroom. This is certainly true of the church's relationship to Jesus Christ. When individuals come to salvation today, they become part of the church, the bride of Christ, betrothed to Christ the Bridegroom.

In the second part of the wedding metaphor, the Hebrew bridegroom comes to claim his bride. Jesus the Bridegroom will come to claim His bride at the rapture, at which time He will take His bride to heaven, the Father's house, where He has prepared a place for them to live (John 14:1-3). The marriage of Christ and the church will take place in heaven sometime after the church has been raptured, prior to the second coming. (I will discuss the third part of the wedding metaphor shortly.)

"It was granted her to clothe herself with fine linen" (19:8): Arnold Fruchtenbaum suggests that the marriage ceremony takes place after the judgment seat of Christ, for the bride is portrayed as wearing white linen.

> The marriage...must take place after the judgment seat of Messiah... for the bride is viewed as being dressed in white linen...Thus, following the rapture of the church in which the Bridegroom brings the bride with Him to His home, and following the judgment seat of Messiah which results in the bride having the white linen garments, the wedding ceremony takes place.[1]

The brightness of the fine linen indicates divine glory. Its purity indicates that all remnants of sin are now gone. The bride is utterly pure. Believers in their glorified bodies will no longer have a sin nature, so the church will be dressed appropriately in "fine linen, bright and pure." The garment will be positively dazzling.

"The fine linen is the righteous deeds of the saints" (19:8): This does not refer to the imputed righteousness of Christ that is given to Christians at the moment of conversion (Romans 3:28; 5:1-2; Galatians 2:16). Rather, it refers to the acts that grow out of that imputed righteousness (Ephesians 2:10; 2 Corinthians 5:10; James 2:17-18). That is, believers on earth will engage in external righteous acts that reflect an inner transformation. The white garments thus signify that the church faithfully and habitually does righteous works in dependence on the Holy Spirit (see Galatians 5:22-23) and thus is worthy of reward at the judgment seat of Christ.

Revelation 19:9-10

"Blessed are those invited to the marriage supper of the Lamb" (19:9): The third part of the Hebrew wedding metaphor is the marriage supper, which was a feast that lasted several days. The marriage supper of the Lamb—yet future from the vantage point of this verse—apparently takes place on earth after the tribulation period but before the millennial kingdom. (Daniel 12:11 reveals that there will be a 75-day interim period between the end of the tribulation period and the beginning of the millennial kingdom.)

The guests at the marriage supper of the Lamb are blessed. What a wondrous privilege it will be. The guests will include all believers who were saved prior to the day of Pentecost (the day the church was born). Like the church (the bride of Christ), these believers will be given glorified resurrection bodies and will participate in Christ's millennial rule. Also included among the guests are those who become believers during the tribulation and were not killed. They will enter into Christ's millennial kingdom in their mortal bodies. (These will be given resurrection bodies following the millennial kingdom.)

"These are the true words of God" (19:9): Biblical prophecy is trustworthy! Whatever is recorded in the pages of the Bible will surely come to pass. The Bible is the Word of God, so what the Bible says, God says.

"Worship God" (19:10): John was so overwhelmed by the glorious angel that spoke to him, his natural inclination was to bow down and worship him. The

angel promptly instructed John not to worship him. To worship any person or object other than God is a form of idolatry (Exodus 20:3-5). The angel told John to worship God alone.

Angels are indeed glorious and awesome-looking creatures, far more so than anything humans are accustomed to seeing on earth. When Daniel saw the angel, he was left without strength (Daniel 10:8). Zechariah was gripped with fear when an angel appeared to him while he was in the temple (Luke 1:12). The shepherds in the field were very afraid when an angel appeared to them (Luke 2:9). The Roman soldiers trembled with fear and became as dead men when an angel appeared and rolled back the stone blocking Jesus' tomb (Matthew 28:2-4).

Angelic appearances in biblical times were so awesome and so glorious that people naturally responded with fear, trembling, and sometimes even worship. However, Scripture consistently emphasizes that humans are never to worship God's angels.

Apparently the church at Colossae had fallen into this error, because when the apostle Paul wrote to them, he included a prohibition against the worship of angels (Colossians 2:18). God's holy angels themselves refuse worship and affirm that God alone is worthy of such honor (see Revelation 22:8-9). Of course, God explicitly commands that only He is to be worshiped.

The testimony of Jesus is the spirit of prophecy (19:10): The verse indicates that the very nature and purpose of prophecy is to testify of Jesus Christ and to bring glory to Him. The Bible is a Jesus book. The entire Old Testament prophetically anticipates Jesus Christ. The four Gospels speak of the actual manifestation of Jesus Christ. The epistles speak of how the church is to live in view of Jesus Christ. The book of Revelation prophesies the second coming and reign of Jesus Christ. The Spirit of Christ is involved in the actual proclamation of prophecy (see 1 Peter 1:12).

MAJOR THEMES

1. *Praise.* Like the redeemed humans and angels in heaven, we should always have praise for God on our lips (Psalm 34:1). We should praise God in the depths of our heart (Psalm 103:1-5, 20-22) and continually "offer up a sacrifice of praise to God" (Hebrews 13:15). One means of praising God is through spiritual songs (Psalm 69:30).

2. *Worship*. We ought to always bow down in worship before the Lord our Maker (Psalm 95:6). We are to "worship him who made the heaven and earth, the sea and the springs of water" (Revelation 14:7). We should worship Him with "reverence and awe" (Hebrews 12:28) and worship Him alone (Deuteronomy 5:7).

DIGGING DEEPER WITH CROSS-REFERENCES

Praise in the book of Revelation—Revelation 4:8, 11; 5:9-14; 7:10-17; 11:15-18; 15:3-4; 16:5-7

God's judgments and believers' petitions—Revelation 5:8; 6:9-11; 8:3-5; 14:18; 16:7; 19:2

The bride purifies herself—Matthew 25:14-23; 2 Corinthians 7:1; 1 John 3:3; Jude 21

LIFE LESSONS

1. *Betrothed to Christ*. Today, the church is betrothed, or engaged, to Jesus Christ. Just as betrothed brides in Bible times kept themselves pure and faithful until the marriage ceremony, so you and I as members of the church ought to seek purity and faithfulness as we await our divine Bridegroom from heaven (see Titus 2:11-14; see John 14:1-6; 1 Thessalonians 4:13-18).

2. *Hallelujah*. "Hallelujah" literally means "praise Yahweh." It is an exclamation of exuberant praise to the one true God (see the first verse of Psalms 106; 111; 112; 113; 117; 135; 146). The word often occurs in contexts where God delivers His people from their enemies, when God is meting out justice, and when God judges rebellion. Its appearance in the book of Revelation is thus appropriate.

QUESTIONS FOR REFLECTION AND DISCUSSION

1. Is your lifestyle befitting a bride who is awaiting the soon appearance of her Bridegroom?

2. Is the word "hallelujah" a part of your daily vocabulary? If not, what's holding you back?

DAY 33

THE SECOND COMING OF CHRIST

REVELATION 19:11-16

SCRIPTURE READING AND INSIGHTS

Begin by reading Revelation 19:11-16 in your favorite Bible. As you read, notice how the Word of God is purifying your life (John 17:17-18).

In yesterday's reading, we witnessed an outbreak of praise in heaven, perhaps due to the anticipation of Christ's second coming. Now let's zero in on this glorious appearance of Christ. With your Bible still accessible, consider the following insights on the biblical text, verse by verse.

Revelation 19:11

I saw heaven opened (19:11): At His first coming, Jesus came as the Lamb of God to take away the sins of the world. Now, at His second coming, He comes as King of kings and Lord of lords.

John's words recall Jesus' baptism, when "the heavens were opened, and the Holy Spirit descended on him in bodily form" (Luke 3:21-22). Just as the heavens opened for the coming of the Holy Spirit on Jesus, so now the heavens open for the second coming of Jesus.

Behold, a white horse (19:11): In biblical times, generals in the Roman army rode white horses. Christ on a white horse will be the glorious Commander in Chief of the armies of heaven. This signifies His coming triumph over the forces of wickedness in the world, the details of which follow. This is in notable contrast to the lowly colt Jesus rode during His first coming (see Zechariah 9:9).

The one sitting on it is called Faithful and True (19:11): Names and titles in biblical times revealed a person's character, and Christ's character is here revealed as faithful and true in all things. Perhaps Jesus is called Faithful and True in this context because He is returning to earth in glory just as He promised He would (Matthew 24:27-31).

> "Behold, with the clouds of heaven there came one like a son of man...To him was given dominion and glory and a kingdom, that all peoples, nations, and languages should serve him; his dominion is an everlasting dominion, which shall not pass away, and his kingdom one that shall not be destroyed" (Daniel 7:13-14).

Note the obvious contrast between Christ and the antichrist. The antichrist is unfaithful (he breaks the covenant he made with Israel). He is also false (he consistently disseminates falsehood and deception).

In righteousness he judges and makes war (19:11): Unlike the antichrist, who will rule and judge the world in unrighteousness, Jesus Christ will rule and judge in righteousness (see Revelation 20:11-15).

Christ will be Victor. All who oppose Him in this war will be instantly slain. This war will be an expression of God's holy wrath against the antichrist and unrepentant sinners. In Revelation 13:4, the whole earth asked who could possibly fight against the beast. Christ will definitively answer that question at His second coming.

Revelation 19:12

His eyes are like a flame of fire (19:12): This description points not only to Christ's absolute holiness but also to His penetrating scrutiny in seeing all things as they truly are (see Revelation 1:14). At the second coming, no one will be able to escape His omniscient gaze.

On his head are many diadems (19:12): The many diadems, or crowns, represent total sovereignty and royal kingship. No one will be able to challenge Christ's kingly authority.

He has a name written that no one knows but himself (19:12): Perhaps this will be the same name that Christ will write on the overcomers (see Revelation 2:17; 3:12).

Revelation 19:13

He is clothed in a robe dipped in blood (19:13): Some Bible expositors suggest that the blood may speak of Christ's redemptive death on the cross. Others say the blood is likely that of the enemies Christ slays at the close of Armageddon (verse 15). Still others deny this, for Christ's enemies are not slain at this moment (Christ hasn't yet arrived on earth from the perspective of this verse). Some thus conclude that perhaps the blood relates to Christ's previous battles against sin, Satan, death, and God's enemies.

The name by which he is called is The Word of God (19:13): This recalls John 1:1: "In the beginning was the Word, and the Word was with God, and the Word was God." The Greek noun for "Word" in John 1:1 is *logos*. In John's theology, Christ the Logos is the preexistent, eternal being—God. The Logos is the Creator of the universe (John 1:3).

In the Old Testament, God's Word is an active and effective agent for accomplishing God's will (see Isaiah 55:11).

Another aspect of the Jewish understanding of "the Word" is evident in the Jewish Targums (simplified paraphrases of the Old Testament Scriptures). Here the Jews, out of reverence for God, sometimes substituted the phrase the "Word of God" in place of the word "God." The Jews were fearful of breaking the third commandment about taking God's name in vain (Exodus 20:7). So, for example, where our Bible says, "Then Moses brought the people out of the camp to meet God" (Exodus 19:17), the Targum reads, "to meet the Word of God."

When we come to John's Gospel, the Word is a divine person who has come into the world to reveal another person (the Father—see John 1:14, 18). For John, the Logos is a living being—the second person of the Trinity, the source of all life, and nothing less than God Himself (John 1:1).

Revelation 19:14

The armies of heaven, arrayed in fine linen, white and pure, were following him (19:14): We know that one of the armies is made up of redeemed human beings because of the "fine linen, white and pure." These are the very words used to describe the wedding gown of the bride of Christ, which is the church (verse 8). Some Bible expositors believe that Christ's human army will also include Old Testament saints (Jude 14; Daniel 12:1-2) and tribulation martyrs (Revelation 7:13).

The other army that accompanies Christ is angelic. Matthew 16:27 says, "The Son of Man is going to come with his angels in the glory of his Father." Matthew 25:31 affirms, "When the Son of Man comes in his glory, and all the angels with him, then he will sit on his glorious throne" (see also 2 Thessalonians 1:7).

Note that Christ does not need the help of these armies in battle. Christ alone—omnipotent God, King of kings and Lord of lords—engages in battle against all the enemies of God. Rather, the heavenly armies accompany Christ to participate in the events that *follow* the second coming, including the establishment of Christ's millennial kingdom (see 1 Corinthians 6:2; 2 Timothy 2:12; Revelation 20:4).

Revelation 19:15

From his mouth comes a sharp sword with which to strike down the nations (19:15): The sharp sword is a symbol of Christ's omnipotent power to execute His enemies (compare Isaiah 11:4). Because the sword comes out of His mouth, Christ likely accomplishes His victory over His enemies by the power of His spoken word, just as He created the universe by His spoken word (Psalm 33:6; Colossians 1:16; John 1:1-3).

Christ strikes down the nations (the forces of the antichrist) at Armageddon because they attacked Israel (Joel 3:2; Zechariah 12:2-3). At the end of the tribulation, the Israelites will be acutely aware that the forces of the antichrist have gathered to destroy them. In this dire situation, they will finally see that Jesus really is the promised Messiah. Their spiritual blindness will be removed, and the Jewish remnant will experience national regeneration. This will be in fulfillment of Joel 2:28-29, which promises a spiritual awakening of the Jewish remnant. This will also be a fulfillment of the apostle Paul's prophecy of the Jews in Romans 11:25-27.

As the forces of the antichrist advance, the Israelites will plead for their newly found Messiah to return and deliver them (Zechariah 12:10; Matthew 23:37-39), at which point their deliverance will surely come (see Romans 10:13-14). As we see in the next verse, Jesus subsequently comes and strikes down the hostile nations.

He will tread the winepress of the fury of the wrath of God the Almighty (19:15): Treading on grapes is a common metaphor for judgment. Instead of grape juice flowing, however, the blood of unbelievers will flow when Christ slays them.

Revelation 19:16

He has a name written, King of kings and Lord of lords (19:16): This title means that Jesus is the One who is absolutely supreme and sovereign over all earthly rulers and angelic powers (1 Timothy 6:15; see also Deuteronomy 10:17; Psalm 136:3). The long-awaited messianic King has now finally arrived.

MAJOR THEMES

1. *Christ the King.* The kingship of Jesus Christ is a common theme in Scripture. Genesis 49:10 prophesied that the Messiah would come from the tribe of Judah and reign as a king. The Davidic covenant in 2 Samuel 7:16 promised a Messiah who would have a dynasty and a people over whom He would rule, and an eternal throne (see also Luke 1:32-33). In Psalm 2:6, God the Father announces the installation of God the Son as King in Jerusalem. Psalm 110 affirms that the Messiah will subjugate His enemies and rule over them. Daniel 7:13-14 tells us that the Messiah-King will have an everlasting dominion.

2. *Angelic armies.* In Scripture, angels are often collectively called God's heavenly host. Micaiah the prophet, for example, said, "I saw the Lord sitting on his throne, and all the host of heaven standing on his right hand and on his left" (2 Chronicles 18:18). The term "host" has a distinctive military ring to it. The angels may be viewed as a celestial military force that accomplishes God's will. The Bible often calls God Himself "Lord

of hosts"—the sovereign commander of the great heavenly army (see 1 Samuel 17:45; Psalm 89:6, 8).

DIGGING DEEPER WITH CROSS-REFERENCES

Christ's wondrous names—Isaiah 9:6; Luke 1:31; Philippians 2:9-11

Christ judges in righteousness—Matthew 25:31-46; John 5:25-30; Acts 17:31; Revelation 20:11-15

Rod of iron—Psalm 2:9; Revelation 2:27; 12:5

LIFE LESSONS

1. *Christ is Faithful and True (Revelation 19:11).* We've seen before that Christ is Faithful and True, but the book of Revelation keeps reaffirming this, so we will as well. Because Christ is Faithful and True, you can trust all the prophecies, promises, and spiritual truths in the Bible. You can also trust that He'll save you—just as He promised!

2. *Jesus is King of kings and Lord of lords (Revelation 19:16).* Christ sovereignly oversees all that comes into our lives. Regardless of what we may encounter, and regardless of whether we understand why certain things happen in life, the knowledge that our sovereign King of kings is in control anchors us in the midst of life's storms.

3. *Jesus' eyes are like a flame of fire.* Jesus is all-seeing and all-knowing (Revelation 19:12). Therefore, He already knows everything about us. He won't suddenly discover something He didn't know before that will cause Him to change His mind about us being in His family (see John 13:18-19, 38). What a wonderful Savior!

QUESTIONS FOR REFLECTION AND DISCUSSION

1. Christ is Faithful and True. What does that mean to you personally? Does it give you confidence in your salvation?

2. Are you facing any difficult circumstances that you would like to completely and unreservedly entrust to our sovereign King of kings?

3. Christ knows everything about you—including all your sins of yesterday, today, and all the tomorrows in the future—and still loves you. How does that make you feel?

DAY 34

THE CAMPAIGN OF ARMAGEDDON

REVELATION 19:17-21

SCRIPTURE READING AND INSIGHTS

Begin by reading Revelation 19:17-21 in your favorite Bible. As you read, notice how the Word of God is purifying your life (John 17:17-18).

In the previous lesson, we focused on the glorious appearance of Jesus Christ. Now let's find out about how Christ will conquer the armies that gather to wage war against Him. With your Bible still accessible, consider the following insights on the biblical text, verse by verse.

Revelation 19:17-18

"Come, gather for the great supper of God" (19:17): The main battle of Armageddon is now about to occur. An angel, therefore, invites birds to gather for a hearty feast. The angel is "standing in the sun," where birds could easily see him. He cries out with a loud voice so birds everywhere will hear him.

Jesus prophesied about Armageddon and mentioned that birds would have a feast on the battlefield: "Wherever the corpse is, there the vultures will gather" (Matthew 24:28; Luke 17:37). The scene is gruesome.

"To eat the flesh of kings, the flesh of captains, the flesh of mighty men" (19:18): The casualties of this judgment will be massive and broad. All who have resisted Jesus Christ will be targets of this judgment, regardless of their status in the world. Everyone will be included—free and slave, small and great.

Here we find another application of the *lex talionis*, or law of retaliation—that is, an "eye for an eye." Recall that the bodies of God's two prophetic witnesses were not buried (Revelation 11:9-10). Likewise, those executed at Armageddon will not be buried, and the birds will have a feast.

Revelation 19:19-21

I saw the beast and the kings of the earth with their armies gathered to make war (19:19): The antichrist will not give up without a fight. A multinational anti-God force, comprised of the armies of the beast and the kings of the earth, will gather to engage in battle against Christ as they see Him coming in glory.

This brings up a question related to the actual duration of Christ's second coming. If the antichrist and his forces have sufficient time to gather and unite in preparation to fight Christ, this seems to imply that the second coming will not be an instantaneous event.

Revelation 1:7 says, "Behold, he is coming with the clouds, and every eye will see him, even those who pierced him, and all the tribes of the earth will wail on account of him." Matthew 24:30 likewise tells us, "Then will appear in heaven the sign of the Son of Man, and then all the tribes of the earth will mourn, and they will see the Son of Man coming on the clouds of heaven with power and great glory."

If every eye will witness the second coming, the whole world may be able to see a majestic military processional en route from heaven to earth. As they witness this glorious entourage, they gather forces to do battle against Christ. If this processional takes a day or longer, then as the earth revolves, people all over the world will be able to witness the event firsthand. Of course, there will also be live television and Internet feeds.

The beast was captured, and with it the false prophet... These two were thrown alive into the lake of fire (19:20): The battle will instantly be over. None can thwart the King of kings. The Lord Jesus will promptly cast the antichrist and the false prophet alive into the lake of fire. Their punishment is just, for this diabolical duo will have deceived multitudes of people.

> "His dominion shall be taken away, to be consumed and destroyed" (Daniel 7:26).

The Scriptures assure us that the lake of fire (hell) is a real place. But hell was not part of God's original creation, which He called good. Hell was created later to accommodate the banishment of Satan and his fallen angels, who rebelled against God (Matthew 25:41). Human beings who reject Christ will join Satan and his fallen angels in this infernal place of suffering. The Scriptures use a variety of words to describe the horrors of hell:

- the fiery furnace (Matthew 13:42)
- unquenchable fire (Mark 9:47-48)
- the lake of fire (Revelation 20:15)
- eternal fire (Matthew 18:8)
- eternal punishment (Matthew 25:46)
- destruction (Matthew 7:13)
- eternal destruction (2 Thessalonians 1:8-9)
- the place of weeping and gnashing of teeth (Matthew 13:42)
- the second death (Revelation 20:14)

The antichrist and false prophet will be consigned to this place before Christ's millennial kingdom.

Scripture describes degrees of punishment in hell. Christ's justice is perfect, and this requires that extremely evil persons (such as the antichrist and the false prophet) will experience much greater punishment than, for example, a non-Christian moralist. Theologians generally appeal to the following verses in support of the idea that there are degrees of punishment in hell: Matthew 10:15; 16:27; Luke 12:47-48; Revelation 20:12-13; 22:12. The suffering of the antichrist and the false prophet will be eternal (see Matthew 25:46; Revelation 14:11; 20:10).

The rest were slain by the sword (19:21): God's judgment is universal and comprehensive. All the rest of Christ's enemies will die in an instant as Christ speaks the word of judgment. The antichrist and the false prophet are cast into the lake of fire, but wicked humans are cast into Hades, a temporary abode of punishment where people await the great white throne judgment, after which they will be consigned to the lake of fire for all eternity (see 2 Peter 2:9). (More on this later in the book.)

C.S. Lewis once said that in the end, there are two groups of people. One group of people says to God, "Thy will be done." These are people who recognize that they are sinners, and they trust in Christ for salvation. The other group of people are those to whom God says, "Thy will be done." These are people who have refused to turn to Christ for salvation, thus ensuring their own destiny in hell forever.

A 75-Day Interim Period

Though the book of Revelation does not directly speak of it, other prophetic verses describe a 75-day interval between the end of the tribulation period and the beginning of the millennial kingdom. During this brief interim, a number of significant events transpire.

For example, the image of the antichrist that had caused the abomination of desolation at the midpoint of the tribulation will be removed from the temple after 30 days. Daniel 12:11 tells us, "From the time that the regular burnt offering is taken away and the abomination that makes desolate is set up, there shall be 1,290 days." The last half of the tribulation lasts only 1,260 days (or three and a half years). So the abomination that causes desolation is removed from the Jewish temple 30 days after the tribulation ends.

An additional 45 days must also be added to the prophetic timetable. Daniel 12:12 states, "Blessed is he who waits and arrives at the 1,335 days." (The 1,335 days minus the 1,290 days means another 45 days are added into the mix.) Apparently the judgment of the nations, recorded in Matthew 25:31-46, takes place during this time. The Jewish survivors of the tribulation period will also be judged (Ezekiel 20).

Many theologians also believe that Old Testament saints will be resurrected from the dead during this interim period. "Your dead shall live; their bodies shall rise. You who dwell in the dust, awake and sing for joy! For your dew is a dew of light, and the earth will give birth to the dead" (Isaiah 26:19). "Many of those who sleep in the dust of the earth shall awake, some to everlasting life, and some to shame and everlasting contempt" (Daniel 12:2).

Finally, tribulation saints who died are resurrected from the dead. "I saw the souls of those who had been beheaded for the testimony of Jesus and for the word of God, and who had not worshiped the beast or its image and had not received its mark on their foreheads or their hands. They came to life and reigned with Christ for a thousand years" (Revelation 20:4).

The governmental structure of the coming millennial kingdom may also be set up during the extra 45 days. We have just read that the saints will reign with Christ in the millennial kingdom (see also 2 Timothy 2:12). After believers and unbelievers are separated and the unbelievers are removed in judgment, some time will be required to appoint saints to various government positions and inform them of their various responsibilities.

The marriage feast of Christ—featuring the divine Bridegroom, Jesus Christ, and His bride, the church—may also take place at the close of the 75-day period. If so, it will be the highlight of those two and a half months. The invitation to the marriage feast, mentioned in Revelation 19:9, immediately precedes the second coming of Christ: "Blessed are those who are invited to the marriage supper of the Lamb." It would make good sense that the marriage feast would take place shortly thereafter.

Following the 75-day interval, Christ will set up His millennial kingdom (Isaiah 2:2-4; Ezekiel 37:1-14; 40–48; Micah 4:1-7; Revelation 20). (More on this in the next chapter.)

MAJOR THEMES

1. *Death of the body.* The term "flesh" in Revelation is used of the bodies of both humans and animals. Humans are made up of both a material part (the physical body) and an immaterial part (the soul or spirit). When human beings physically die, their immaterial part departs from the material body. The souls or spirits of Christians go directly to heaven (2 Corinthians 5:8; Philippians 1:21-23). The souls or spirits of unbelievers go to a place of temporary punishment, where they await the great white throne judgment (see Luke 16:19-31; 2 Peter 2:9; Revelation 20:11-15).

2. *Birds feasting on the dead.* The Bible often graphically depicts judgment in terms of birds feasting on the dead. Deuteronomy 28:26 says, "Your dead body shall be food for all birds of the air and for the beasts of the

earth, and there shall be no one to frighten them away" (compare with Psalm 79:2). Isaiah 18:6 says, "They shall all of them be left to the birds of prey of the mountains and to the beasts of the earth." Jeremiah 7:33 says, "The dead bodies of this people will be food for the birds of the air, and for the beasts of the earth, and none will frighten them away" (see also Jeremiah 16:4; 19:7; 34:20).

DIGGING DEEPER WITH CROSS-REFERENCES

Eternal punishment—Matthew 13:40-42; 25:41; Mark 9:43-48; Luke 3:17; 12:47-48; Revelation 14:10-11

Fire and brimstone—Revelation 14:10; 20:10; 21:8; see also Genesis 19:24; Psalm 11:6; Isaiah 30:33; Ezekiel 38:22; Luke 17:29

LIFE LESSONS

1. *The blessings of the second coming.* The judgment aspect of the second coming is a bit overwhelming. It's easy to lose sight of the greater significance of the blessings of the second coming for believers. Here are two: Christ will set up His own kingdom of perfect righteousness on earth, and you and I as resurrected believers will be with Christ not only during the millennial kingdom but throughout all eternity. How awesome it will be!

2. *Avoid prophetic apathy.* Some Christians seem to pay little attention to the second coming. One reason for this is that there are many Christians who like to argue about the finer points of biblical prophecy, such as whether the rapture will happen before or after the tribulation period. For these Christians, prophecy has become a hot potato to be avoided. This is a tragic attitude because a significant part of the Bible is prophetic. A better policy is to regularly study Bible prophecy and become convinced in your own mind of what Scripture really teaches. On debated finer points, we simply agree to disagree in an agreeable way.

QUESTIONS FOR REFLECTION AND DISCUSSION

1. Do you look forward to the second coming of Christ? Why or why not?
2. Do you ever feel tempted to pay less attention to matters related to end-times biblical prophecy because some Christians get a little too animated on the issue?
3. Has your study of biblical prophecy bolstered your faith in God and your confidence in the Bible? If so, how?

DAY 35

CHRIST'S MILLENNIAL KINGDOM

REVELATION 20:1-6

SCRIPTURE READING AND INSIGHTS

Begin by reading Revelation 20:1-6 in your favorite Bible. As you read, notice how the Word of God is purifying your life (John 17:17-18).

In yesterday's reading, we focused on Christ's victory over the armies that gather to fight Him. In today's reading, we zero in on Christ's establishment of His millennial kingdom on earth. With your Bible still accessible, consider the following insights on the biblical text, verse by verse.

Revelation 20:1-3

I saw an angel coming down from heaven, holding in his hand the key to the bottomless pit and a great chain (20:1): The bottomless pit serves as the place of imprisonment for demonic spirits (Luke 8:31; 2 Peter 2:4).

He seized the dragon, that ancient serpent, who is the devil and Satan, and bound him for a thousand years (20:2): "Dragon" is an apt metaphor that points to the ferocity and cruelty of this evil spirit being. "Serpent" is apparently an allusion to Satan's first appearance in the Garden of Eden, where he deceived Eve (Genesis 3; 2 Corinthians 11:3; 1 Timothy 2:14).

"Devil" (see Matthew 4:1) carries the ideas of "adversary" and "slanderer." The devil was and is the adversary of Christ; he is the adversary of all who follow Christ. The word "Satan" also carries the idea of "adversary."

The devil—along with all demonic spirits—will be bound in the bottomless pit for 1,000 years during Christ's millennial kingdom. ("Millennium" comes from two Latin words—*mille*, which means "thousand," and *annum*, which means "year.") This quarantine will effectively remove a powerful, destructive, and deceptive force from all areas of human life and thought during Christ's kingdom.

Christ's millennial kingdom will be wondrous. During this time, righteousness will flourish (Isaiah 11:3-5), peace will be universal (Isaiah 2:4), and the fruitfulness and productivity of the earth will be greatly increased (Isaiah 35:1-2).

KINGDOM OF GOD/CHRIST		
TOPIC	**DANIEL**	**REVELATION**
Second Coming	Daniel 7:13	Revelation 19:11-16
Christ the Conqueror	Daniel 2:34	Revelation 3:21; 5:5; 17:14
Christ's Dominion	Daniel 7:14	Revelation 11:15
God's Reign and Kingdom	Daniel 2:44	Revelation 11:17; 12:10; 19:6
Christ's Kingdom Established	Daniel 7:27	Revelation 11:15
Possessing the Kingdom	Daniel 7:22	Revelation 1:6; 3:21

The millennial kingdom is one of those doctrines that Christians seemingly love to debate. There are three primary theological views—premillennialism, amillennialism, and postmillennialism (see "Major Themes" below). I hold to premillennialism, the view that following the second coming, Christ will institute a kingdom of perfect peace and righteousness on earth that will last 1,000 years. This view is based on a literal interpretation of prophecy.

The imprisonment of Satan and his host of fallen angels will greatly change the religious landscape during the millennial kingdom. Gone will be their deception, their destructive influence, their temptations to sin and rebel against

God, their continued stance against the purposes of God, and the guilt they inflict on the consciences of Christians.

> "The God of heaven will set up a kingdom that shall never be destroyed" (Daniel 2:44).
>
> "His kingdom is an everlasting kingdom, and his dominion endures from generation to generation" (Daniel 4:3).
>
> "His dominion is an everlasting dominion, and his kingdom endures from generation to generation" (Daniel 4:34).
>
> "The saints of the Most High shall receive the kingdom and possess the kingdom forever, forever and ever" (Daniel 7:18).

Threw him into the pit, and shut it and sealed it over him, so that he might not deceive the nations any longer (20:3): After the angel casts Satan into the bottomless pit, he seals it to prevent escape. He thereby ensures that Satan will be unable to deceive people during Christ's millennial kingdom.

After that he must be released for a little while (20:3): Satan is released after the millennial kingdom to allow him one last attempt to lead some of earth's people astray. But who are these people?

Scripture reveals that only believers will enter the millennial kingdom in their mortal bodies (for example, Matthew 25:34), but some of their descendants will not be believers. These are the people Satan will seek to gather against God in one final rebellion.

Christ will quickly and decisively crush this rebellion. Following the millennial kingdom, the great white throne judgment—which is the judgment of the wicked—will take place, and the lake of fire will be populated (Revelation 20:11-15). Those who participate in Satan's rebellion will be among the inhabitants of the lake of fire. (More on this in the next chapter.)

Revelation 20:4-6

I saw thrones (20:4): Many have wondered who occupies these thrones because we are not told. There are two popular views. One is that they are the 12 disciples. Luke 22:30 refers to the disciples sitting "on thrones judging the twelve tribes of Israel." The other popular view is that they represent the church. First Corinthians 6:2 tells us that the saints will judge the world. As well, 2 Timothy 2:12 affirms, "If we endure, we will also reign with him." Both of these views are viable.

I saw the souls of those who had been beheaded for the testimony of Jesus and for the word of God (20:4): The souls who had been beheaded are the martyrs of the tribulation period (see Revelation 6:9; 18:24; 19:2).

They came to life and reigned with Christ for a thousand years (20:4): The idea of reigning with Christ is confirmed throughout the book of Revelation. For example, Revelation 5:10 reveals that believers have been made "a kingdom and priests to our God, and they shall reign on the earth." Revelation 20:6 adds this: "Blessed and holy is the one who shares in the first resurrection! Over such the second death has no power, but they will be priests of God and of Christ, and they will reign with him for a thousand years." Finally, Revelation 22:5 tells us, "They will reign forever and ever." The saints' privilege of reigning with Christ continues even beyond the millennial kingdom.

The rest of the dead did not come to life until the thousand years were ended (20:5): This refers to the resurrection of the wicked dead, who will be raised to face Christ at the great white throne judgment following the millennial kingdom (discussed in verses 11-15). This will be a somber event.

This is the first resurrection (20:5): We can easily get confused by this verse, so some explanation is in order.

The original Hebrew and Greek manuscripts of the Bible did not have chapter and verse numbers. People inserted these later to make for easier navigation in the Bible. In the great majority of cases, the chapter and verse divisions are very helpful. In very few instances, such as Revelation 20:5, they can be misleading.

> "Many of those who sleep in the dust of the earth shall awake, some to everlasting life, and some to shame and everlasting contempt" (Daniel 12:2).

Bible expositors are in essential agreement that the last part of verse 5—"This is the first resurrection"—fits into the flow of verses 4 and 6. But the first half of verse 5 is a parenthetical truth. The resurrection of the wicked dead is *not* part of the first resurrection. Rather, the first resurrection involves the resurrection of the righteous, as other verses on the first resurrection make clear.

Scripture mentions two types of resurrections. The first is appropriately called the "first resurrection," as in this verse. This is also called the "resurrection of life" (John 5:29), the "resurrection of the just" (Luke 14:14), and the "better life" (Hebrews 11:35).

The second resurrection is the last resurrection (Revelation 20:5a, 11-15). It is appropriately called the resurrection of judgment (John 5:29; see also Daniel 12:2; Acts 24:15).

To be even more specific, the term "the first resurrection" refers to *all* the resurrections of the righteous even though they are widely separated in time. There is one resurrection of the righteous at the rapture (before the tribulation—1 Thessalonians 4:13-17), another during the tribulation (the two witnesses—Revelation 11:3, 11), another at the end of the tribulation (the martyred dead—Revelation 20:4-5), and apparently another at the end of the 1,000-year millennial kingdom (not recorded in Scripture). They are all "first" in the sense of being before the second (final) resurrection, in which the wicked dead are raised. Accordingly, the term "first resurrection" applies to all the resurrections of the saints, regardless of when they occur, including the resurrection of Christ Himself (the "firstfruits"—see 1 Corinthians 15:23).

The second resurrection, or last resurrection, is an awful spectacle. All the unsaved of all time will be resurrected at the end of Christ's millennial kingdom, judged at the great white throne judgment, and then cast alive into the lake of fire (Revelation 20:11-15). People will be given resurrection bodies that will last forever, but these bodies will be subject to pain and suffering. They will exist eternally in the lake of fire.

Blessed and holy is the one who shares in the first resurrection! (20:6): Those who share in the first resurrection are blessed because they will have unfettered access to the presence of God forever. They will dwell with God (and Christ) face to face. Can there be any higher privilege and blessing than for the creature to dwell face to face with his Creator?

Those who share in the first resurrection are also called holy because they are set apart from all sin. In the glorified state, the sin nature is obliterated, for "we shall be like him" (1 John 3:2). Christ "will transform our lowly body to be like his glorious body" (Philippians 3:21).

Over such the second death has no power (20:6): The first death is physical death—that is, the separation of the spirit or soul from the body (for example, see Genesis 35:18). Virtually all people—except those Christians alive on earth when the rapture occurs—will experience the first death (1 Corinthians 15:50-55; 1 Thessalonians 4:13-17).

The "second death," which is for unbelievers only, entails eternal separation from God in the lake of fire, or eternal hell. "Their portion will be in the lake that burns with fire and sulfur, which is the second death" (Revelation 21:8). The lake of fire will be populated immediately following the great white throne judgment, which is the judgment of the wicked dead (Revelation 20:11-15).

They will be priests of God and of Christ (20:6): Priests do not need go-betweens to relate to God. Priests have direct access to God. Those who participate in the first resurrection (that's you and me) will have direct access to God forever and ever.

MAJOR THEMES

1. *Premillennialism.* This view teaches that following the second coming, Christ will institute a kingdom of perfect peace and righteousness on earth that will last for 1,000 years. After this reign of true peace, the eternal state begins (Revelation 20:1-7; see also Isaiah 65:17-25; Ezekiel 37:21-28; Zechariah 8:1-17). I subscribe to this view because it takes a literal approach, recognizing that Old Testament prophecies of Christ's first coming were also literally fulfilled.

2. *Amillennialism.* This is a spiritualized view that teaches that when Christ comes, the eternal state will begin with no prior literal 1,000-year reign on earth. The 1,000-year reign is understood metaphorically as Christ's present spiritual reign from heaven over a long time.

3. *Postmillennialism.* This is another spiritualized view. It teaches that through the church's progressive influence, the world will eventually be "Christianized"

before Christ returns. Following this return, the eternal state will begin (there will be no 1,000-year kingdom). A practical problem for this view is that the world seems to be getting progressively worse instead of being "Christianized."

DIGGING DEEPER WITH CROSS-REFERENCES

The Old Testament basis for the millennial kingdom—Psalm 2:6-9; Isaiah 65:18-23; Jeremiah 31:12-14, 31-37; Ezekiel 34:25-29; 37:1-13; 40–48; Daniel 2:35; 7:13-14; Joel 2:21-27; Amos 9:13-14; Micah 4:1-7; Zephaniah 3:9-20

The work of Satan—Genesis 3:1-5; John 8:44; Acts 5:3; 1 Corinthians 7:5; 2 Corinthians 11:14; 1 Timothy 3:6; 1 Peter 5:8; Revelation 12:10

LIFE LESSONS

1. *Satan is on a leash.* Our passage graphically illustrates how God puts boundaries around Satan and his host of fallen angels. Satan is not free to do anything he wants to you. All Satan's activities have divinely imposed parameters beyond which he cannot go (see this in Job 1:12 and 2:6). We ought all to be thankful for this protective ministry of God (compare Psalm 91:1-12).

2. *Our wondrous resurrection bodies.* In 1 Corinthians 15:42-43 the apostle Paul describes the resurrection: "What is sown is perishable; what is raised is imperishable. It is sown in dishonor; it is raised in glory. It is sown in weakness; it is raised in power." Our present bodies will wear out, but our resurrection bodies will be glorious, never again subject to aging, decay, death, or burial. How awesome!

QUESTIONS FOR REFLECTION AND DISCUSSION

1. Do you worry about attacks from the devil and demons? We should definitely have a healthy respect for the powers of darkness (2 Corinthians 2:11), resist them (James 4:7), and wear our spiritual armor (Ephesians 6:10-18). But let's keep our eyes focused on Jesus (Hebrews 12:2).

2. Do you struggle with any bodily ailments? As each year passes, do you become increasingly aware of the frailty of the human body? Rejoice! We've got a fantastic body upgrade coming!

DAY 36

SATAN'S FINAL REBELLION AND THE GREAT WHITE THRONE

REVELATION 20:7-15

SCRIPTURE READING AND INSIGHTS

Begin by reading Revelation 20:7-15 in your favorite Bible. As you read, notice how the Word of God is purifying your life (John 17:17-18).

In the previous lesson, we focused on Christ's establishment of His glorious millennial kingdom on earth. In today's lesson, we read of His final defeat of Satan after the millennial kingdom. With your Bible still accessible, consider the following insights on the biblical text, verse by verse.

Revelation 20:7-10

When the thousand years are ended, Satan will be released (20:7): We have seen that the bottomless pit serves as a prison for demonic spirits (Luke 8:31; 2 Peter 2:4). The devil and all demonic spirits will be bound here for the 1,000 years of Christ's millennial kingdom (Revelation 20:1-3). This quarantine will effectively remove a powerful, destructive, and deceptive force from all areas of human life and thought during Christ's kingdom.

At the end of the 1,000 years, Satan will be loosed from the bottomless pit. He will have one last opportunity to deceive the nations. God's purpose seems to be to prove once and for all that the heart of every human being is desperately wicked. Even in the best of environments (Christ's kingdom), the fallen human heart still has a great propensity to sin.

To deceive the nations...to gather them for battle; their number is like the sand of the sea (20:8): Believers who survive the tribulation will physically enter into Christ's millennial kingdom (Matthew 25:31-46; Ezekiel 20:34-38). Longevity will characterize the millennial kingdom (see Isaiah 65:20), but both Jews and Gentiles will continue to age and die. Married couples among both groups will also continue to have children throughout the millennium. Apparently, some of the children of the saints (and grandchildren, great-grandchildren, and so forth) will not be believers. They are nevertheless permitted to live in Christ's kingdom so long as they do not rebel. When Satan is released at the end of the millennium, he will lead many of these unbelievers in a massive rebellion against Christ. This will represent Satan's last stand.

Gog and Magog (20:8): These terms relate to a military coalition made up of Russia, Iran, Sudan, Turkey, and a number of other Muslim nations who will attack Israel, either prior to the tribulation period or at the very beginning of it (see Ezekiel 38–39). God will destroy these invaders. In this verse, John apparently uses Gog and Magog as a metaphor for evil invaders, much like we today use Wall Street as a metaphor for the stock market. In other words, Satan and his human rebels will launch a Gog-and-Magog-like invasion against Christ and His people.

Surrounded the camp of the saints and the beloved city (20:9): Jerusalem will be the headquarters of Christ's government throughout the millennium (Isaiah 2:1-5). This beloved city—with believers camped around and about—will be the target city of this satanic revolt.

Fire came down from heaven and consumed them (20:9): The revolt is a suicide mission. Christ quickly and decisively crushes this rebellion.

The devil...was thrown into the lake of fire (20:10): All three persons of the satanic trinity—Satan, the antichrist, and the false prophet—suffer the same dire destiny. The antichrist and the false prophet had been thrown into the lake of fire after the tribulation period and before the millennial kingdom (Revelation 19:20). Now Satan joins them. All three will burn for all eternity. Demons too will be judged and cast into the lake of fire (see Matthew 25:41).

On page 555 I listed some of the Bible's other descriptive names for the lake of fire.

Revelation 20:11-15

I saw a great white throne and him who was seated on it (20:11): Thrones are mentioned almost 50 times in Revelation (see, for example, Revelation 4:2-3, 9; 5:1, 7, 13; 6:16; 7:10, 15). The throne of Revelation 20:11 is a judgment throne, where Jesus Christ sits as Judge of the wicked dead.

In his vision, John witnessed the earth and sky flee from the presence of the divine Judge. John saw a universe contaminated by sin and Satan vanish out of existence. Peter described this in more detail in 2 Peter 3:10-13.

> The heavens will pass away with a roar, and the heavenly bodies will be burned up and dissolved, and the earth and the works that are done on it will be exposed...The heavens will be set on fire and dissolved, and the heavenly bodies will melt as they burn! But according to his promise we are waiting for new heavens and a new earth in which righteousness dwells.

The dead were judged (20:12): All the wicked dead, both great and small, are forcefully brought before the divine tribunal. A strong sense of dread will be pervasive.

Books were opened (20:12): These books detail the lives of the unsaved. These books will provide the evidence to substantiate the divine verdict of a destiny in the lake of fire. Their works that will be judged will include their actions (Matthew 16:27), their words (Matthew 12:37), and even their thoughts and motives (Luke 8:17; Romans 2:16). These books will also be used to determine degrees of eternal suffering in the lake of fire (see Matthew 10:14-15; 11:22; Mark 12:38-40; Luke 12:47-48; Hebrews 10:29).

The book of life will also be there. As noted previously, this book contains the names of all of God's redeemed (see Philippians 4:3; Revelation 21:27). No unsaved person's name will be in the Lamb's book of life (Luke 10:20).

Those who participate in the great white throne judgment will be resurrected in order to face judgment (see John 5:28-29). They stand before this throne of judgment in much the same way that a criminal stands in a court of law as the judge reads a sentence. Warren Wiersbe notes some significant differences from a normal court scene: "There will be a Judge but no jury, a prosecution but no defense, a sentence but no appeal. No one will be able to defend himself or accuse God of unrighteousness."[1]

These individuals appear at this judgment because they are already unsaved. This judgment will not separate believers from unbelievers, for all who will experience it will have already made the choice during their lifetimes to reject God. They have a horrible destiny ahead:

- weeping and gnashing of teeth (Matthew 13:41-42)
- condemnation (Matthew 12:36-37)
- destruction (Philippians 1:28)
- eternal punishment (Matthew 25:46)
- separation from God's presence (2 Thessalonians 1:8-9)
- trouble and distress (Romans 2:9)

The sea gave up the dead who were in it, Death and Hades gave up the dead who were in them (20:13): Virtually every possible location and place will yield the bodies and souls of the unrighteous dead—the sea, Death, and Hades. Each of the wicked will receive a resurrection body capable of suffering forever (John 5:28-29).

Hades is a New Testament term that refers to the temporary place of the dead (Luke 16:19-31). The spirits or souls of the wicked dead are held captive there (2 Peter 2:9). On that future day, wicked evildoers will be raised from the dead—their spirits being reunited with resurrection bodies—and they will be judged at the great white throne judgment. Following this, their permanent place of suffering will be the lake of fire.

Death and Hades were thrown into the lake of fire (20:14): The apostle Paul affirmed that "the last enemy to be destroyed is death" (1 Corinthians 15:26). Finally, after all this time during which death has reigned supreme, this last enemy is destroyed. Death and Hades (the abode of death) are tossed into the lake of fire. This is the "second death."

We saw that the first death is physical death, or the separation of the spirit or soul from the body (Genesis 35:18). Virtually everyone will experience the first death. The exceptions are those Christians who are alive on earth at the rapture of the church and those who are alive at the end of the millennial kingdom. These two groups will instantly receive glorified bodies (1 Corinthians 15:50-55; 1 Thessalonians 4:13-17).

The term "second death" refers to eternal separation from God in the lake of fire, which is eternal hell. No believer will experience the second death.

If anyone's name was not found written in the book of life (20:15): When Christ opens the book of life, no name of anyone present at the great white throne judgment is in it. Their names do not appear in the book of life because they have rejected the source of life—Jesus Christ. And because they rejected the source of life, they are cast into the lake of fire, which constitutes the second death.

MAJOR THEMES

1. *Fallen angels.* Some fallen angels are already confined, awaiting future judgment. Jude 6 affirms, "The angels who did not stay within their own position of authority, but left their proper dwelling, he has kept in eternal chains under gloomy darkness until the judgment of the great day." Peter writes, "God did not spare angels when they sinned, but cast them into hell and committed them to chains of gloomy darkness to be kept until the judgment" (2 Peter 2:4). Other demonic spirits remain free to continue their attacks on Christians (for example, Matthew 12:43; Mark 1:23, 26; 3:30; 5:2, 8; 7:25; 9:25; Luke 4:33; 8:29; 9:42; 11:24).

2. *The last of Satan's six judgments.* The Bible notes six distinct judgments against Satan:

    - cast out of heaven (Ezekiel 28:16)
    - cursed in the Garden of Eden (Genesis 3:14-15)
    - defeated at the cross (John 12:31; Colossians 2:15; Hebrews 2:14)
    - cast out of heaven in the middle of the tribulation (Revelation 12:13)

- confined in the abyss during the millennial kingdom (Revelation 20:2)
- cast into the lake of fire after the millennial kingdom (Matthew 25:41; Revelation 20:10)

DIGGING DEEPER WITH CROSS-REFERENCES

Fire of judgment—Genesis 19:24; Exodus 9:23-24; Leviticus 9:24; 10:2; Numbers 11:1; 16:35; 26:10; 1 Kings 18:38; 2 Kings 1:10-14; Psalm 11:6

The judgment of the wicked—Psalm 62:12; Proverbs 24:12; Matthew 16:27; Romans 2:6; Revelation 2:23

LIFE LESSONS

1. *No infants at the great white throne.* Many Christian parents who have lost infants and young children in death ask for assurance that they are saved. I am firmly convinced they are saved. Infants and young children are not morally responsible and therefore cannot possibly be called before the great white throne judgment (Deuteronomy 1:39; Isaiah 7:15-16; Romans 9:11). Jesus expressed great love for little children (see Matthew 18:3). David certainly knew he would be with his dead child in heaven (2 Samuel 12:22-23).

2. *The depths of human sin.* The rebellion at the end of Christ's millennial kingdom demonstrates the depth of human sin. You and I are thoroughly contaminated. Jesus often spoke of sin in metaphors that illustrate the havoc sin can wreak. He described sin as blindness (Matthew 23:16-26), sickness (Matthew 9:12), bondage (John 8:34), and darkness (John 8:12; 12:35-46). Jesus also taught that both inner thoughts and external acts render a person guilty (Matthew 5:28; Mark 7:21-23). We can be delivered from the power of sin by depending on the Holy Spirit (see Galatians 5:16-25) and being rooted in Jesus (John 15:1-11).

QUESTIONS FOR REFLECTION AND DISCUSSION

1. Have you or someone you know lost an infant or young child in death? Have you thought much about Scriptures that may relate to their salvation? Meditate for a few moments on Matthew 18:1-10.

2. Many spiritual leaders have commented that the more mature they become as Christians, the more they become aware of the depth of sin in their lives (see Romans 7:15-20). Have you noticed the same thing? Have you noticed that the closer you get to God and His light, the more clearly you notice the darkness? Truly, none of us could be saved apart from God's grace (Ephesians 2:8-9).

DAY 37

THE DESCENT OF THE NEW JERUSALEM

REVELATION 21:1-8

SCRIPTURE READING AND INSIGHTS

Begin by reading Revelation 21:1-8 in your favorite Bible. As you read, keep in mind that the Word of God brings spiritual maturity (1 Corinthians 3:1-2; Hebrews 5:12-14).

In yesterday's reading, we focused on Christ's final victory over Satan after the millennial kingdom. In today's reading, we zero in on God's creation of a new heaven and a new earth. The new Jerusalem—a heavenly city—will come down to rest on the new earth. With your Bible still accessible, consider the following insights on the biblical text, verse by verse.

Revelation 21:1

I saw a new heaven and a new earth (21:1): Notice that the Bible begins in paradise, but it is quickly lost. The Bible ends with paradise restored! In the Garden of Eden, Adam and Eve sinned against God. God subsequently cursed the earth (Genesis 3:17-18; Romans 8:20-22). So before the eternal kingdom can appear, God must deal with this cursed earth.

Satan has also long carried out his evil schemes on earth (see Ephesians 2:2), so the earth must be purged of all stains resulting from his extended presence. In short, the earth—along with the first and second heavens (the earth's atmosphere and the stellar universe)—must be renewed. The old must make room for the new.

The Scriptures often speak of the passing of the old heavens and earth (Psalm 102:25-26; Isaiah 51:6; Matthew 24:35). Indeed, the present earth and heavens (earth's atmosphere and the stellar universe) will be destroyed by fire in preparation for the new heavens and new earth (2 Peter 3:7-13).

After the universe is cleansed, God will create a new heaven and a new earth. All vestiges of the curse and Satan's presence will be utterly and forever removed. There will be no more curse, no more germs, and no more sickness, sorrow, tears, or death.

Scripture reveals that even while Christians are on the new earth, they will also be in heaven. The new earth will be subsumed in the heavenly existence. Peter speaks of this glorious future reality in 2 Peter 3:13. Heaven and earth will unite in a glory that exceeds the imaginative capabilities of the finite human brain (see Isaiah 65:17).

There will be geological changes in the new earth, for there will be no more sea (Revelation 21:1). Our present environment is water-based (our blood, for example, is 90 percent water). The environment in the new heavens and new earth, by contrast, will not be water-based. It will rather be based on a different life principle, a life principle that certainly includes the "water of life" (Revelation 22:1, 17). Glorified humanity will inhabit a glorified earth, re-created and adapted to eternal conditions.

Revelation 21:2

I saw the holy city, new Jerusalem, coming down out of heaven (21:2): The new Jerusalem—the eternal city that you and I will one day inhabit—is a holy city, for it will contain no sin or unrighteousness of any kind.

The new Jerusalem is portrayed as a real city, not some kind of ethereal twilight zone. This is important because you and I will have real, physically resurrected bodies. As real persons with real bodies, we would naturally live forever in a real city—the new Jerusalem.

John witnessed the city coming down out of heaven. This means the city is being constructed (perhaps even now by Jesus Christ—see John 14:1-3) in heaven. Eventually the new Jerusalem will come down and rest on the new earth. (More on this in the next chapter.)

Prepared as a bride (21:2): This metaphorical bride of Christ, the new

Jerusalem, will include two previous brides of Christ: redeemed Israelites who had lived in Old Testament times (Isaiah 62:5; Jeremiah 2:2; 3:20; Ezekiel 16:8; Hosea 2:19-20) and the New Testament church (2 Corinthians 11:2; Revelation 19:7). The habitat is identified according to its inhabitants.

Revelation 21:3-4

"Behold, the dwelling place of God is with man" (21:3): God will now live directly with redeemed humankind (compare Leviticus 26:11-12; Deuteronomy 12:5). Here at last we find unfettered companionship between the Creator and His creation.

He will wipe away every tear from their eyes, and death shall be no more (21:4): The Old Testament promises that in the heavenly state, death will be swallowed up forever (Isaiah 25:8). This is in contrast to the ancient Hebrew belief that death has a nasty habit of swallowing up the living. Paul speaks of this same reality as it relates to the future resurrection: "When the perishable puts on the imperishable, and the mortal puts on immortality, then shall come to pass the saying that is written: 'Death is swallowed up in victory'" (1 Corinthians 15:54).

There will be no more disease, no more weakness, no more decay, no more coffins, no more funerals, and no more graves. There will be no reason for tears. Life in the eternal city will be painless, tearless, and deathless.

It is not that we will be sad in heaven and need to be cheered. We will not start crying and then need to have our crying eased. Rather, tears will be utterly foreign to the whole setting. It will be a time of rejoicing in the grace of God. There will be nothing to cry about!

Bible expositor Albert Barnes reflects on the absolute absence of mourning in heaven: "How innumerable are the sources of sorrow here; how constant is it on the earth…How different, therefore, will heaven be when we shall have the assurance that henceforward grief shall be at an end!"[1]

Revelation 21:5-7

"Behold, I am making all things new" (21:5): There are two primary views as to how everything will be made new.

The replacement view holds that the universe will be annihilated and replaced with a brand-new, second universe created *ex nihilo* ("out of nothing"). It will be an entirely different and entirely new earth and universe. In favor of this view is Peter's affirmation that the present heavens and earth will be destroyed by fire (2 Peter 3:10-13).

On the other hand, according to the renewal view (my personal view), the new heavens and new earth will be our present universe, but it will be purified by fire of all evil, sin, suffering, and death. The Greek word for "new" in Revelation 21 does not mean "new in origin," but rather "new in quality." Our future cosmos will stand in continuity with the present cosmos, but it will be utterly renewed and renovated. It will be gloriously rejuvenated.

This means that a resurrected people will live in a resurrected universe! John Piper put it this way: "What happens to our bodies and what happens to the creation go together. And what happens to our bodies is not annihilation but redemption...Our bodies will be redeemed, restored, made new, not thrown away. And so it is with the heavens and the earth."[2]

"Write this down, for these words are trustworthy and true" (21:5): God's revelation about the future can be trusted because God always faithfully speaks the truth (see Revelation 3:14; 19:11).

"It is done" (21:6): This is a statement of divine finality. It represents a promise from God Almighty that what He has created for humankind's eternal state will indeed last forever and ever. It is an accomplished fact.

"I am the Alpha and the Omega, the beginning and the end" (21:6): God restates His name, as if to put an exclamation point on the reality that "it is done." As we have seen, this name expresses eternality and omnipotence.

"To the thirsty I will give from the spring of the water of life without payment" (21:6): Jesus gives the water of life, which eternally satisfies (see Revelation 7:17; 22:1, 17; see also Isaiah 55:1-2; John 4:13-14; 7:37-38). This water cannot be earned. It is a grace-gift, given without payment.

"The one who conquers...I will be his God and he will be my son" (21:7): The one who conquers or overcomes seems to be the one who places saving faith in Jesus Christ. "Everyone who has been born of God overcomes the world. And this is the victory that has overcome the world—our faith. Who is it that overcomes the world except the one who believes that Jesus is the Son of God?" (1 John 5:4-5).

The one who overcomes—or trusts in Christ for salvation—is fortunate indeed, for he or she will dwell with God in a parent-child relationship. This will be the heritage or the inheritance of the believer as a child of God (see 1 Peter 1:4).

Revelation 21:8

As for the cowardly, the faithless, the detestable...their portion will be in the lake that burns with fire and sulfur (21:8): In the midst of all this glorious news for believers is a somber warning for unbelievers. Indeed, their inheritance will be an eternity in the lake of fire. This is the second death—eternal separation from God.

MAJOR THEMES

1. *God dwelling among us.* In the Garden of Eden, God walked with Adam and Eve. Once sin entered the world, God dwelt among the Israelites by means of the tabernacle (Exodus 40:34) and later the temple (2 Samuel 22:7). In New Testament times, God "tabernacled" among us in the person of Jesus (John 1:14). Today, Christians are the temple of the Holy Spirit (1 Corinthians 3:16; 6:19). In the new Jerusalem, God will dwell with His people face to face (Revelation 22:4).

2. *A better country.* Heaven is not only called a city but also "a better country" (Hebrews 11:13-16). And what a glorious country it is, as eighteenth-century Bible expositor John Gill wrote:

   > [The heavenly country] is full of light and glory; having the delightful breezes of divine love, and the comfortable gales of the blessed Spirit...Many are the liberties and privileges here enjoyed; here is a freedom from a body subject to diseases and death, from a body of sin and death, from Satan's temptations, from all doubts, fears, and unbelief, and from all sorrows and afflictions.[3]

DIGGING DEEPER WITH CROSS-REFERENCES

Adopted into God's eternal family—Romans 8:14, 29; Galatians 3:26; 4:5; Ephesians 1:5; 2:19; 3:6; Philippians 2:15; Hebrews 12:6-9; 1 John 3:1

Christians' inheritance in heaven—Matthew 5:5; 19:29; 25:34; Hebrews 1:14; 9:15; 1 Peter 1:4

LIFE LESSONS

1. *How can we be happy in heaven when people are suffering in hell?* Some theologians believe God may purge our memories so that we do not retain memories of those in hell. In Isaiah 65:17-19, God speaks of the new heavens and a new earth: "Behold, I create new heavens and a new earth, and the former things shall not be remembered or come into mind...no more shall be heard in it the sound of weeping and the cry of distress."

2. *Recognition in heaven.* Scripture reveals that we will recognize our Christian loved ones in the new Jerusalem. The Thessalonian Christians were concerned about their Christian loved ones who had died. Paul responds that they will be reunited in heaven, implying that they'll recognize each other (1 Thessalonians 4:13-17). David knew he'd be reunited with his deceased son in heaven and had no doubt about recognizing him (2 Samuel 12:23). Lazarus, Abraham, and the rich man all recognized each other in the afterlife (Luke 16:19-31).

QUESTIONS FOR REFLECTION AND DISCUSSION

1. Think about being reunited with some of your Christian loved ones who are now in heaven. Does this put wind in your spiritual sails?

2. You have been adopted into God's eternal family, and you have a family inheritance awaiting you in heaven. What do those things mean to you personally?

DAY 38

A DESCRIPTION OF THE NEW JERUSALEM

REVELATION 21:9-27

SCRIPTURE READING AND INSIGHTS

Begin by reading Revelation 21:9-27 in your favorite Bible. As you read, keep in mind that the Word of God brings spiritual maturity (1 Corinthians 3:1-2; Hebrews 5:12-14).

In the previous lesson, we focused on God's creation of a new heaven and a new earth. Now let's discover more about the new Jerusalem, the glorious heavenly city that will rest on the new earth. With your Bible still accessible, consider the following insights on the biblical text, verse by verse.

Revelation 21:9-21

"Come, I will show you the Bride, the wife of the Lamb" (21:9): In this context, the bride is the new Jerusalem.

The holy city Jerusalem coming down out of heaven (21:10): As John was carried away in the spirit to a high mountain (a perfect vantage point), he witnessed firsthand the eternal city—the new Jerusalem—coming down out of heaven from God.

Physically resurrected believers will live in this physical city (1 Corinthians 15:35-53). Jesus in John 14:1-3 describes this eternal abode using such words as "house," "rooms," and "a place," thereby indicating physicality. Today's passage describes the new Jerusalem as having walls, gates, foundations, a street, river, trees, and more.

Having the glory of God (21:11): John's words no doubt represent a human attempt to describe the utterly indescribable. George Marsden, author of *Jonathan Edwards: A Life*, explained Edwards's view:

> However wonderful it might be to imagine these things, earthly images are not really adequate...These biblical images, he explained, are "very faint shadows" that represent the joys of heaven humans are intended to enjoy.[1]

The heavenly city will be far more wondrous than we can possibly imagine.

The city is designed to reflect and manifest the incredible glory of God (it is "clear as crystal"). The transparency within the city distributes the glory of God throughout the city without hindrance. The human imagination is incapable of fathoming the immeasurably resplendent glory of God that will be perpetually manifest in the eternal city. This is especially so when one considers that all manner of precious stones will be built into the eternal city. This is a scene of indescribable beauty with the glory of God shining through a variety of multicolored stones. No wonder heaven is described as the paradise of God (2 Corinthians 12:3; Revelation 2:7).

Twelve gates...twelve angels...twelve tribes (21:12): Angels are positioned at each of the 12 gates, not only as guardians but also to minister to the heirs of salvation (Hebrews 1:14). The names of the 12 tribes of Israel are written on the gates, perhaps to remind us that "salvation is of the Jews" (John 4:22).

Twelve foundations...twelve apostles (21:14): Perhaps the names of the apostles appear on the foundations of the city in order to remind us that the church was built on these men of God (Ephesians 2:20). (What was John's reaction when he saw his own name inscribed on one of the foundations?)

Perhaps the inclusion of the names of the 12 tribes of Israel and the 12 apostles indicates that Jewish and Gentile believers will both be in God's eternal family. The heavenly city includes the redeemed—both Jew and Gentile—of all ages.

The one who spoke with me had a measuring rod of gold...He measured the city with his rod (21:15-16): The heavenly city measures 12,000 stadia on each side, meaning that the city is approximately 1,400 miles by 1,400 miles by 1,400 miles. Though some interpret these big numbers symbolically, I think the dimensions are intended to be interpreted literally.

The eternal city is so huge that it would measure approximately the distance from Canada to Mexico, or from the Atlantic Ocean to the Rockies. The city is tall enough to reach about one-twentieth of the way from the earth to the moon. If the city has stories, each being 12 feet high, then the city would have more than 500,000 stories.

The eternal city could either be cube-shaped or pyramid-shaped—and there are good Christian scholars on both sides of the debate. Some prefer to consider it shaped like a pyramid, for this would explain how the river of the water of life could flow down its sides as pictured in Revelation 22:1-2.

Others prefer to consider it shaped as a cube. After all, the Most Holy Place in Solomon's temple was cube-shaped (1 Kings 6:20). The eternal city could be likened to an eternal Most Holy Place.

Every kind of jewel (21:18-21): The mention of beautiful, diverse, multicolored jewels is an attempt to describe the indescribable, to depict that which is perfect with imperfect language, to portray that which is infinite and eternal with language that is finite and temporal. Such beautiful jewels provide only a faint analogy of the awesome beauty of heaven.

The colors of these various jewels include white, gold, blood red, bright red, orange-red, blue, sky blue, greenish blue, sea green, yellow green, apple green, and purple. All these jewels are transparent, so God's glory shining throughout the city will be an awesome thing to behold. The entire city will glisten.

Revelation 21:22-27

I saw no temple in the city, for its temple is the Lord (21:22): The temple in the eternal state is not a building but is rather God Himself (compare John 2:19, 21). This communicates the idea that one need not go to a specific place or location to encounter the Lord. Rather, the presence of God will permeate the entire new heaven and new earth (see Revelation 21:3). God's presence will be limitless. Fellowship with God will be unbroken.

The city has no need of sun or moon to shine on it, for the glory of God gives it light, and its lamp is the Lamb (21:23): This is in keeping with the prophecy in Isaiah 60:19: "The sun shall be no more your light by day, nor for brightness shall the moon give you light; but the LORD will be your everlasting light, and your God will be your glory." Dr. Lehman Strauss's comments on the Lamb's glory are worthy of meditation:

> In that city which Christ has prepared for His own there will be no created light, simply because Christ Himself, who is the uncreated light (John 8:12), will be there...The created lights of God and of men are as darkness when compared with our Blessed Lord. The light He defuses throughout eternity is the unclouded, undimmed glory of His own Holy presence. In consequence of the fullness of that light, there shall be no night.[2]

Related to this, Colossians 1:12 refers to heaven as "the inheritance of the saints in light." Christ, of course, is the light of the world (John 8:12). The eternal kingdom thus takes on the character of the King.

By its light will the nations walk (21:24): The nations are the redeemed people from every nation, tribe, and people. All races of humanity blend into God's eternal family on the new earth. There will be no racial divisions among human beings!

The kings of the earth will bring their glory into it (21:24): All these kings will be believers. They have glory only by the grace of God, who sovereignly institutes kings (Romans 13:1).

Its gates will never be shut by day—and there will be no night there (21:25): In ancient times, city gates were closed at night for protection against invaders. Gates were part of the city's security. In the eternal city, however, there will never be any external threat to those who dwell within. Satan, demons, and unbelievers will be in eternal quarantine in hell. Besides, God Himself will dwell within the city. Who would dare attack it?

They will bring into it the glory and the honor of the nations (21:26): In Jewish worship in biblical times, Gentiles were not allowed to enter into the holy precincts. Recall the riotous stir some Jews caused by accusing the apostle Paul of bringing a Gentile into the temple (Acts 21:28-29). Gentiles were considered unclean. But no believing Gentiles will be unwelcome in the holy precincts of heaven!

Nothing unclean will ever enter it (21:27): The city will be characterized by absolute perfection. No more sin. No more Satan. No more demons. No more antichrist. No more false prophet. The environment of heaven will be righteous, pure, and clean.

Only those whose names are written in the Lamb's book of life are within the city. All others—the wicked dead of all ages, along with Satan and all fallen angels—are eternally quarantined in the lake of fire.

What a remarkable city! Because you and I are so accustomed to living in a fallen world that has been viciously marred by sin and corruption, we cannot imagine life in a heavenly habitat (see 1 Corinthians 2:9). From birth to death, we are confronted with imperfection on every level. But in the eternal city, we will experience nothing but perfection.

MAJOR THEMES

1. *The number 12.* The number 12 surfaces often in Revelation 21–22. There are 12 gates, angels, tribes, foundations, apostles, pearls, fruits, and months. As well, the side of the city measured 12,000 stadia. The wall measured 144 cubits (12 times 12).

2. *The perfection of heaven.* Heaven will be perfect in every way, as A.T. Pierson notes:

> There shall be no more curse—perfect restoration. The throne of God and of the Lamb shall be in it—perfect administration. His servants shall serve him—perfect subordination. And they shall see his face—perfect transformation. And his name shall be on their foreheads—perfect identification. And there shall be no night there; and they need no candle, neither light of the sun; for the Lord giveth them light—perfect illumination. And they shall reign forever and ever—perfect exultation.[3]

DIGGING DEEPER WITH CROSS-REFERENCES

The glory of God—Exodus 24:17; 40:34; 1 Kings 8:11; Psalms 8:1; 19:1; Ezekiel 10:4; Luke 2:9; Acts 7:55; 2 Corinthians 3:18

Unclean—Leviticus 11; 22:8; Deuteronomy 14:3-20; Judges 13:4, 14; Acts 10:14, 28

LIFE LESSONS

1. *A top-down perspective.* Gary R. Habermas and J.P. Moreland speak of the necessity of maintaining a top-down perspective (see Matthew 6:19-34): "The God of the universe invites us to view life and death from his eternal vantage point. And if we do, we will see how readily it can revolutionize our lives."[4] The more we keep our eyes focused on the realities of heaven, the better our perspective on temporal, earthly things (Colossians 3:1-2).

2. *Living clean.* Our text tells us that nothing unclean will enter into the eternal city, the new Jerusalem. Today, we ought to allow nothing unclean to enter our lives. We ought to be pure. As James 4:8 puts it, "Cleanse your hands, you sinners, and purify your hearts, you double-minded" (see also 1 Peter 1:22; 1 John 3:3).

QUESTIONS FOR REFLECTION AND DISCUSSION

1. Do you make a habit of maintaining a top-down perspective? How might this practice help you to keep earthly problems and difficult circumstances in perspective?

2. Is any part of your present lifestyle interfering with clean living?

DAY 39

THE DELIGHTS OF THE NEW JERUSALEM

REVELATION 22:1-5

SCRIPTURE READING AND INSIGHTS

Begin by reading Revelation 22:1-5 in your favorite Bible. As you read, remember that the Word of God can help you be spiritually fruitful (Psalm 1:1-3).

In the previous two readings, we were introduced to the new Jerusalem, God's heavenly city that will rest on the new earth. Now let's find out more about the wondrous delights of the new Jerusalem. With your Bible still accessible, consider the following insights on the biblical text, verse by verse.

Revelation 22:1-2

The river of the water of life (22:1): This pure river of life, though it may be a real and material river, is likely also symbolic of the abundance of spiritual life that will characterize those who are living in the eternal city. The stream seems to symbolize the perpetual outflow of spiritual blessing to the redeemed of all ages, now basking in the full glow of eternal life. What spiritual blessedness the eternal state will bring.

From the throne of God and of the Lamb (22:1): God Himself is the source of this wondrous water and the wondrous blessing that accompanies it. Notice that the Lamb and God the Father are on the throne. This is as it should be, for Christ is absolute deity (John 1:1; 8:58; 10:30; 20:28) as well as King of kings and Lord of lords (Revelation 17:14; 19:16).

The tree of life with its twelve kinds of fruit (22:2): The tree of life is first seen bestowing continuing life in the Garden of Eden (see Genesis 2:9; 3:22-24). When Adam and Eve sinned, death entered the universe, and God assigned cherubim to guard the tree of life so that Adam and Eve could no longer partake of it.

This, of course, was an act of God's grace. How awful it would have been for Adam and Eve to eat of the tree of life and live forever in a state of fallenness and sin. Death was a blessing in disguise, for it limited the time God allowed His fallen creatures to suffer in a state of sin.

In any event, paradise was lost. In the book of Revelation, however, paradise is restored, and we again witness the tree of life in the glorious eternal state. The leaves on the tree are for the healing of nations. This should not be taken to mean that sickness and disease will be a part of the eternal state (see 21:4). The Greek word for healing (*therapeia*) carries the idea of "health-giving." It is from this Greek word that we get the English words "therapy" and "therapeutic." The leaves on the tree promote health and have a therapeutic effect.

Revelation 22:3-5

No longer will there be anything accursed (22:3): In the Garden of Eden, Adam and Eve sinned against God, thereby bringing a curse on all humanity (see Genesis 3:16-19). All such curses will be gone forever in the eternal state. Never again will God have to judge sin. All will forever be well and blessed.

The throne of God and of the Lamb will be in it, and his servants will worship him (22:3): There will be unbroken and unfettered fellowship between redeemed humans and God.

Notice that even though verse 3 speaks of both God the Father and God the Son, the singular pronoun "him" is used. This points to the essential oneness of the Trinity (see Matthew 28:19; 2 Corinthians 13:14). As Jesus said in John 10:30, "I and the Father are one."

They will see his face (22:4): The apostle Paul affirmed, "Now we see in a mirror dimly, but then face to face. Now I know in part; then I shall know fully, even as I have been fully known" (1 Corinthians 13:12). The psalmist wrote, "As for me, I shall behold your face in righteousness" (Psalm 17:15). John affirmed, "We know that when he appears we shall be like him, because we shall see him as he is" (1 John 3:2).

Can there be anything more sublime and more utterly satisfying for the Christian than to enjoy the sheer delight of unbroken fellowship with God and immediate and unobstructed access to the divine glory? (See John 14:3; 2 Corinthians 5:6-8; Philippians 1:23; 1 Thessalonians 4:17.) We will gaze on His countenance and behold His resplendent beauty forever.

God "who alone has immortality, who dwells in unapproachable light" (1 Timothy 6:16) will reside intimately among His own. "They will be his people, and God himself will be with them" (Revelation 21:3). No wonder the psalmist exults, "In your presence there is fullness of joy; at your right hand are pleasures forevermore" (Psalm 16:11).

In the afterlife, fellowship with the Lord will no longer be intermittent and blighted by sin and defeat. Instead, there will be continuous fellowship. The sin problem will no longer exist. When we enter into glory we will no longer have the sin nature within us (Philippians 3:21; 1 John 3:2). Sin will be banished from our very being. All things will be made new!

To fellowship with God is the essence of heavenly life, the fount and source of all blessing. We may be confident that the crowning wonder of our experience in the eternal city will be the perpetual and endless exploration of the unutterable beauty, majesty, love, holiness, power, joy, and grace of God Himself.

When our beloved Christ was born on earth, He was called Immanuel, which means "God with us" (see Matthew 1:23). Throughout the entire eternal state, Jesus will be with us in the closest possible sense, face to face. In the old hymn "Face to Face with Christ, My Savior," we read words worthy of meditation:

> Face to face with Christ, my Savior,
> Face to face—what will it be—
> When with rapture I behold Him,
> Jesus Christ who died for me?
>
> Face to face—O blissful moment!
> Face to face—to see and know;
> Face to face with my Redeemer,
> Jesus Christ who loves me so.

Face to face I shall behold Him,
Far beyond the starry sky.
Face to face in all His glory,
I shall see Him by and by.

Some theologians speak of "beatific vision" when addressing the wondrous reality that we will be in the direct presence of God throughout the rest of eternity. The term comes from three Latin words that carry the meaning, "a happy-making sight."

The idea is that seeing God brings perpetual happiness and joy. Randy Alcorn says that "our primary joy in Heaven will be knowing and seeing God."[1] Barry Morrow suggests that "this contemplation of God will not be a static, boring experience of simply staring at God but rather a dynamic, unending exploration of God and His attributes."[2] Because God's attributes are perfect, one could spend an eternity contemplating them.

One further fact is worthy of mention here. In biblical times, no human could see God's face and live (Exodus 33:20-23). In heaven, however, Christians will have new resurrection bodies that will enable us to live directly in God's presence. The apostle Paul affirmed, "This perishable body must put on the imperishable, and this mortal body must put on immortality" (1 Corinthians 15:53). Once that happens, we can live with God face to face.

Believers will also have God's name on their foreheads (Revelation 22:4). This seems to be in obvious contrast to unbelievers who will receive the mark of the beast during the tribulation period (Revelation 13:16-17). This also represents the fulfillment of God's promise to the faithful believers at the church of Philadelphia: "I will write on him the name of my God" (Revelation 3:12).

Night will be no more (22:5): This is obvious because the glory of God will light up the eternal city (compare with Isaiah 60:19). Night cannot fall where God's glory is perpetually present.

They will reign forever and ever (22:5): God's faithful believers will be involved in some capacity in the heavenly government. Perhaps one aspect of this will involve judging the angels somehow. "Do you not know that the saints will judge the world?...Do you not know that we are to judge angels?" (1 Corinthians 6:2-3).

This is noteworthy because humanity at present is lower than the angels (see Psalm 8:5). The situation will be reversed in the eternal state. Angels will be lower than redeemed human beings in heaven.

Finally, the purposes of God are fulfilled. God's plan of salvation, conceived in eternity past, is now brought into full fruition, as Wilbur Smith exults:

> All the glorious purposes of God, ordained from the foundation of the world, have now been attained. The rebellion of angels and mankind is finally subdued, as the King of kings assumes his rightful sovereignty. Absolute and unchangeable holiness characterizes all within the universal kingdom of God. The redeemed, made so by the blood of the Lamb, are in resurrection and eternal glory. Life is everywhere—and death will never intrude again. The earth and the heavens both are renewed. Light, beauty, holiness, joy, the presence of God, the worship of God, service to Christ, likeness to Christ—all are now abiding realities.[3]

My friends, any way you look at it, the eternal city—the new Jerusalem—is going to be absolutely wonderful, far more so than any human mind could possibly fathom or even begin to imagine. Christians are merely pilgrims en route to the final frontier of the new Jerusalem, just passing through this brief dot of time on earth.

MAJOR THEMES

1. *Serving God and Christ in heaven.* Scripture indicates that we will be busy in our service to God (Revelation 1:5-6), but this service will be invigorating and fulfilling, not toilsome or draining. It will not be tedious, but joyous, fully meeting our hearts' every desire. We will find immeasurable satisfaction in serving God. There will be no time demands, no frustrations, no fear of failure, and no exhaustion.

2. *Jesus and the water of life.* We noted previously that Jesus gives the water of life, which eternally satisfies (see John 4:13-14; 7:37-38; compare with Isaiah 55:1-2). This is likely the backdrop to the affirmation that the

river of the water of life flows from the throne of God and of the Lamb (Revelation 22:1). God is the source!

DIGGING DEEPER WITH CROSS-REFERENCES

God's throne—Psalms 9:7; 45:6; 47:8; 93:2; 103:19; Isaiah 6:1; 66:1; Hebrews 1:8

Worship of God—Exodus 20:3-5; Deuteronomy 5:7; Psalms 29:2; 95:6; 100:2; Hebrews 12:28

LIFE LESSONS

1. *Jesus' parable in Luke 19:11-27.* Our faithfulness in serving Christ during our mortal state here on earth will in part determine our service in the eternal state. In Jesus' parable of the ten minas, the master affirmed to one of the servants, "Because you have been faithful in a very little, you shall have authority over ten cities." The idea seems to be that if we are faithful in this life, Christ will entrust us with greater responsibility as we serve Him in the next life.

2. *The throne of grace.* Our passage speaks of the throne of God and of the Lamb (Revelation 22:3). The truth is, however, we don't have to wait until we get to heaven to approach God's throne. We can approach it today by faith. As Hebrews 4:16 exhorts us, "Let us then with confidence draw near to the throne of grace, that we may receive mercy and find grace to help in time of need." Do you have a need? God's throne of grace is available to you now!

QUESTIONS FOR REFLECTION AND DISCUSSION

1. Scripture reveals that if we are faithful in this life, Christ will entrust us with more in serving Him in the next life. What is your reaction to this truth?

2. God's throne is a "throne of grace" (Hebrews 4:16). What does that mean to you?

3. How do you need God's favor today? Go to the throne!

DAY 40

JOHN'S EPILOGUE

REVELATION 22:6-21

SCRIPTURE READING AND INSIGHTS

Begin by reading Revelation 22:6-21 in your favorite Bible. As you read, remember that the Word of God can help you be spiritually fruitful (Psalm 1:1-3).

In the previous three readings, we discovered a great deal about the new Jerusalem. As John brings the book of Revelation to a close, he instills in us an eternal perspective. With your Bible still accessible, consider the following insights on the biblical text, verse by verse.

Revelation 22:6-11

"These words are trustworthy and true" (22:6): This is because they come from the One who is Faithful and True (Revelation 19:11). The trustworthy and true revelations contained in this book are intended to inform God's servants—believers in the Lord Jesus Christ—about what will take place in the future. This knowledge comforts us in our present tribulations.

"Behold, I am coming soon" (22:7): Jesus says this once in 3:11 and three times in this chapter (see verses 12, 20). Almost 2,000 years have transpired since Jesus said this. Scholars offer two primary suggestions as to what He might have meant.

Some suggest that from a human perspective, Jesus' return may not have come soon, but from the divine perspective, it will. We have been in the last days since the incarnation of Christ (Hebrews 1:2; James 5:3). Moreover, James 5:9 affirms that "the Judge is standing at the door." Romans 13:12 exhorts us that "the night is far gone; the day is at hand." First Peter 4:7 warns, "The end of all things is at hand." In view of such verses, Christ is coming soon from the divine perspective.

Other scholars suggest that perhaps Jesus meant He is coming soon from the perspective of the events described in the book of Revelation. In other words, from the vantage point of those living during the time of the tribulation period itself, Christ is coming soon.

Still others say that the main idea in these words is that the coming of Christ is imminent. This being the case, we must all be ready, for we do not know precisely when Christ will come.

Why has God seemingly delayed? Second Peter 3:9 affirms, "The Lord is not slow to fulfill his promise as some count slowness, but is patient toward you, not wishing that any should perish, but that all should reach repentance." God's delay is to allow people plenty of time to turn to Him. Of course, the time will come when the delay will end, after which there will be no further opportunity to turn to Him.

"Blessed is the one who keeps the words of the prophecy of this book" (22:7): We keep the sayings of the prophecy in the book of Revelation by protecting its contents from alteration and by being obedient to what we learn.

I fell down to worship at the feet of the angel (22:8): Angels are such awesomely glorious creatures that humans who see them are fearful and may even be tempted to worship them (compare Daniel 10:8; Matthew 28:2-4; Luke 1:12; 2:9). John's response to the angel was inappropriate but understandable.

"You must not do that... Worship God" (22:9): To worship any person or object other than God is idolatry (Exodus 20:3-6). The apostle Paul explicitly condemned the worship of angels in Colossians 2:18.

"Do not seal up the words of the prophecy of this book, for the time is near" (22:10): The prophecies of Daniel were sealed because the time was not yet ready (Daniel 8:26; 12:4-10). Earlier in Revelation John had been commanded to seal up (or not write down) the utterances of the seven thunders (Revelation 10:4). Now, however, John is not to seal up the words of the prophecy because the time of fulfillment is potentially drawing near.

> "You, Daniel, shut up the words and seal the book, until the time of the end...Go your way, Daniel, for the words are shut up and sealed until the time of the end" (Daniel 12:4, 9).

"Let the evildoer still do evil...and the righteous still do right" (22:11): Following the second coming of Christ, people's destinies will be sealed. One's decision for or against Christ will become set in stone. Evil people will continue in their evil, just as the righteous will continue in their righteousness and the holy in their holiness.

Revelation 22:12-17

"Behold, I am coming soon" (22:12): The imminence of Christ's coming is emphasized. We do not know precisely when Christ is coming again, so we must always be ready (see Titus 2:13-14) and be busy doing good works, for which we will be rewarded. Our salvation is not rooted in good works, but the rewards we will receive from the Lord are rooted in good works.

"To repay each one for what he has done" (22:12): Believers will face Christ at His judgment seat (Romans 14:8-10; 1 Corinthians 3:11-15). Unbelievers, however, will face Christ at the great white throne judgment (Revelation 20:11-15).

"I am the Alpha and the Omega" (22:13): Christ is again called the Alpha and Omega. These words were intended to comfort and encourage Christians as they await their King. When used of God (or Christ), the first and last letters of the Greek alphabet express eternality and omnipotence.

The phrase "the first and the last" is used of God Almighty in the Old Testament (see Isaiah 44:6; 48:12). Christ's use of this title of Himself in this verse was undoubtedly intended to demonstrate His equality with God. And this is precisely what brings comfort and encouragement to Christ's followers. Christ wanted them to be absolutely assured that He is the all-powerful Sovereign, who will be victorious.

Blessed are those who wash their robes, so that they may have the right to the tree of life (22:14): Those who wash their robes are blessed because they have been cleansed by the blood of the Lamb (Hebrews 9:14; 1 Peter 1:18-19), so their sins have been forgiven. The redeemed will thus have access to the tree of life and will live forever in the new creation.

Outside are the dogs…and everyone who loves and practices falsehood (22:15): The term "dogs" was sometimes used as a metaphor for people of low character. Such people, along with sorcerers (who practice the magic arts), the sexually immoral (fornicators and adulterers), murderers (such as those who martyred God's people), and idolaters will be outside heaven. They will dwell forever in the lake of fire.

"I, Jesus, have sent my angel to testify" (22:16): This recalls Revelation 1:1, where we are told that Jesus' revelation was made known to John through an angel.

The apostle Paul affirmed that through Christ "all things were created… whether thrones or dominions or rulers or authorities—all things were created through him and for him" (Colossians 1:16). These are different orders of angels (see Romans 8:38; Ephesians 1:21; 3:10; 6:12; Colossians 2:15). All these angels—like all else in creation—were brought into being for Christ. All creation is intended to serve His will and to contribute to His glory. The angel mentioned in Revelation 1:1 and throughout chapter 22 is merely one of many angels at Christ's disposal.

"I am the root and the descendant of David, the bright morning star" (22:16): Christ is the root (or source) of David because Christ is the eternal Creator of all things (Colossians 1:16; John 1:3). At the same time, Christ is the offspring of David because He physically descended from David's line (2 Samuel 7:12-14).

The term "morning star" in this verse has a messianic sense related to Numbers 24:17: "A star shall come out of Jacob." The star had become a symbol of the coming messianic king, who was Jesus. The phrase "morning star" communicates that a spiritual dawn is right around the corner. The cold dark night of spiritual lethargy is nearly over with the coming of Jesus, the morning star.

Let the one who is thirsty come (22:17): The Holy Spirit and the bride (the church) extend an invitation to all who will listen. Those who hear the invitation are encouraged to extend the invitation to still others. Spread the word that salvation is entirely by grace. All who desire to have their thirsty souls satisfied are invited to come to Christ for the water of life.

Revelation 22:18-19

If anyone adds...if anyone takes away (22:18-19): Changing God's Word is a serious crime (see Deuteronomy 4:2; 12:32; Proverbs 30:6). It was customary in biblical times for writers to attach this type of warning at the end of their books. This served to dissuade copyists from tampering with what was written.

Of course, Scripture is much more important than a human book, for Scripture contains the Word of God. This is why such severe penalties are promised against those who add to or take away from God's Word.

Revelation 22:20-21

He who testifies to these things says, "Surely I am coming soon" (22:20): Jesus is the faithful and true witness (Revelation 3:14; 19:11). A witness is one who testifies. Jesus testifies that His coming is imminent!

Come, Lord Jesus! (22:20): This phrase is rooted in the Aramaic term *maranatha*, which was a common greeting among New Testament saints. Believers often used the term because they greatly anticipated the soon coming of the Lord. Notice that as soon as the Lord affirms He is coming soon, the natural response is, "Amen. Come, Lord Jesus!" Christ's coming is the hope of the ages.

The grace of the Lord Jesus be with you all. Amen. (22:21): The book of Revelation begins and ends with a reference to the grace of God (see Revelation 1:4). The implication is clear: Any and all are urged to turn to Christ for the free gift of salvation.

MAJOR THEMES

1. *Grace.* The water of life is without price (Revelation 22:17). God gives it freely by His grace. The word "grace" literally means "unmerited favor." "Unmerited" means that this favor cannot be earned. The apostle Paul wrote, "The free gift of God is eternal life in Christ Jesus our Lord" (Romans 6:23; see also Ephesians 2:8-9; Hebrews 4:16).

2. *Anticipating the second coming.* In 2 Timothy 4:8, the apostle Paul said, "There is laid up for me the crown of righteousness, which the Lord, the righteous judge, will award to me on that Day, and not only to me but also to all who have loved his appearing." Presently we are "eagerly waiting

for him" (Hebrews 9:28). We are "waiting for our blessed hope, the appearing of the glory of our great God and Savior Jesus Christ" (Titus 2:13). I can't wait!

DIGGING DEEPER WITH CROSS-REFERENCES

The churches—Revelation 2–3

Plagues in the book of Revelation—Revelation 9:18, 20; 11:6; 15:1, 6, 8; 16:9, 21; 18:4, 8; 21:9

LIFE LESSONS

1. *Never predict dates.* It is unwise for Christians to predict dates regarding end-time events.

    - People who have predicted dates have been wrong every time.
    - Predicting dates may lead to harmful decisions, such as not saving for the future.
    - Failed predictions may damage one's faith in the Bible.
    - After failed predictions, prophecy might not motivate purity in daily life.
    - The timing of end-time events is in God's hands, not ours (Acts 1:7).

2. *Jesus' parable in Mark 13:33-37: Always be ready.* This parable indicates that we ought always to be ready:

    > Be on guard, keep awake. For you do not know when the time will come. It is like a man going on a journey, when he leaves home and puts his servants in charge, each with his work, and commands the doorkeeper to stay awake. Therefore stay awake—for you do not know when the master of the house will come, in the evening, or at midnight, or when the rooster crows, or in the morning—lest he come suddenly and find you asleep. And what I say to you I say to all: Stay awake.

QUESTIONS FOR REFLECTION AND DISCUSSION

1. Have you ever been influenced by radio or TV preachers who have predicted or implied dates regarding end-time matters?

2. What lesson do you learn from Christ's parable in Mark 13:33-37?

POSTSCRIPT

The Bible begins in paradise, but within a few chapters, paradise is lost, and pain, suffering, and death enter the human race (Genesis 1–3). The Bible ends with paradise restored. Pain, suffering, and death will be a thing of the past for the redeemed (Revelation 21–22). In the meantime, we continue our sojourn on this fallen earth with the Bible in hand. This divine book informs us of what the future will look like.

As we close our journey through the book of Revelation, let's remember that our life on earth is ever so short. Theologian John Wenham once commented that "not only is it certain that this life will end, but it is certain that from the perspective of eternity it will be seen to have passed in a flash."[1] Christian writer Philip Yancey says our time on earth amounts to a mere "dot in eternity."[2]

This dot in eternity is quickly passing away. It will soon be over. Our destiny in heaven, by contrast, is an eternal destiny. We will live forever in a pain-free and death-free environment. A realization of our glorious future gives us much-needed strength today. This was true of the original recipients of the book of Revelation. It is just as true for us.

Consider the Puritans! They set an example for us. The Puritans saw themselves as "God's pilgrims, traveling home through rough country; God's warriors, battling the world, the flesh, and the devil; and God's servants, under orders to worship, fellowship, and do all the good they could as they went along."[3] We should have the same kind of attitude. John strategically engineered the book of Revelation to help Christians foster such an attitude.

I close with one of my favorite passages: "If then you have been raised with Christ, seek the things that are above, where Christ is, seated at the right hand of God. Set your minds on things that are above, not on things that are on earth" (Colossians 3:1-2). The original Greek of this passage is intense: "Diligently, actively, single-mindedly pursue the things above." It is also a present tense in the original Greek, carrying the idea, "perpetually keep on seeking the things above...Make it an ongoing process."

Let's remember that "our citizenship is in heaven, and from it we await a Savior, the Lord Jesus Christ" (Philippians 3:20). Meanwhile, we are "strangers and exiles on the earth" (Hebrews 11:13). We are pilgrims en route to a better country, a heavenly one (verse 16).

As we make our way to the heavenly country, may the book of Revelation be a continual source of spiritual strength and encouragement!

BIBLIOGRAPHY

Barnhouse, Donald Grey. *Revelation: An Expository Commentary*. Grand Rapids: Zondervan, 1971.

Brown, Colin, ed. *The New International Dictionary of New Testament Theology*. Grand Rapids: Zondervan, 1979.

Brown, Francis, S.R. Driver, and Charles A. Briggs. *The Brown-Driver-Briggs Hebrew and English Lexicon*. Peabody: Hendrickson, 1994.

Bruce, F.F., ed. *The International Bible Commentary*. Grand Rapids: Zondervan, 1979.

Dyer, Charles. *The Rise of Babylon: Sign of the End Times*. Chicago: Moody, 2003.

Feinberg, Charles. *A Commentary on Revelation*. Winona Lake: BMH Books, 1985.

Fruchtenbaum, Arnold. *The Footsteps of the Messiah*. San Antonio: Ariel, 2004.

Gaebelein, Frank E., ed. *The Expositor's Bible Commentary*. Grand Rapids: Zondervan, 1978.

Geisler, Norman. *A Popular Survey of the Old Testament*. Grand Rapids: Baker, 1978.

———. *Systematic Theology*, vol. 4: *Church/Last Things*. Saint Paul: Bethany House, 2005.

Hays, J. Daniel, J. Scott Duvall, and C. Marvin Pate. *Dictionary of Biblical Prophecy and End Times*. Grand Rapids: Zondervan, 2007.

Heitzig, Skip. *You Can Understand the Book of Revelation*. Eugene: Harvest House, 2011.

Helyer, Larry, and Richard Wagner. *The Book of Revelation for Dummies*. Hoboken: Wylie, 2008.

Hengstenberg, E.W., and Theodore Meyer. *Christology of the Old Testament*. Grand Rapids: Kregel, 1970.

Hindson, Ed. *Book of Revelation: Unlocking the Future*. Chattanooga: AMG, 2002.

Hitchcock, Mark. *The Coming Islamic Invasion of Israel*. Sisters: Multnomah, 2002.

———. *The Complete Book of Bible Prophecy*. Wheaton: Tyndale House, 1999.

———. *Iran: The Coming Crisis*. Sisters: Multnomah, 2006.

———. *Is America in Bible Prophecy?* Sisters: Multnomah, 2002.

———. *The Second Coming of Babylon*. Sisters: Multnomah, 2003.

Hoyt, Herman. *The End Times*. Chicago: Moody, 1969.

Ice, Thomas, and Timothy Demy. *Prophecy Watch*. Eugene: Harvest House, 1998.

———. *When the Trumpet Sounds*. Eugene: Harvest House, 1995.

Ice, Thomas, and Randall Price. *Ready to Rebuild: The Imminent Plan to Rebuild the Last Days Temple*. Eugene: Harvest House, 1992.

Ironside, H.A. *Revelation*. Grand Rapids: Kregel, 1978.

Keil, C.F., and Franz Delitzsch. *Biblical Commentary on the Old Testament*. Grand Rapids: Eerdmans, 1954.

LaHaye, Tim. *The Beginning of the End*. Wheaton: Tyndale, 1991.

———. *The Coming Peace in the Middle East*. Grand Rapids: Zondervan, 1984.

———. *Revelation Illustrated and Made Plain*. Grand Rapids: Zondervan, 1975.

LaHaye, Tim, ed. *Prophecy Study Bible*. Chattanooga: AMG, 2001.

LaHaye, Tim, and Ed Hindson, eds. *The Popular Bible Prophecy Commentary*. Eugene: Harvest House, 2006.

———. *The Popular Encyclopedia of Bible Prophecy.* Eugene: Harvest House, 2004.

LaHaye, Tim, and Thomas Ice. *Charting the End Times.* Eugene: Harvest House, 2001.

LaHaye, Tim, and Jerry Jenkins. *Are We Living in the End Times?* Wheaton: Tyndale, 1999.

Lindsey, Hal. *There's a New World Coming: A Prophetic Odyssey.* Santa Ana: Vision House, 1973.

MacArthur, John. *Daniel: God's Control Over Rulers and Nations.* MacArthur Bible Studies, vol. 5. Nashville: W Publishing Group, 2000.

MacDonald, W., and A. Farstad. *Believer's Bible Commentary.* Nashville: Thomas Nelson, 1997.

Newell, William. *Revelation Chapter-by-Chapter.* Grand Rapids: Kregel, 1994.

Pentecost, J. Dwight. *Things to Come.* Grand Rapids: Zondervan, 1964.

Pfeiffer, Charles F., and Everett F. Harrison, eds. *The Wycliffe Bible Commentary.* Chicago: Moody, 1974.

Phillips, John: *Exploring Revelation.* Grand Rapids: Kregel, 1974.

Pink, Arthur W. *The Antichrist: A Study of Satan's Christ.* Blacksburg: Wilder, 2008.

Price, Randall. *Jerusalem in Prophecy.* Eugene: Harvest House, 1998.

Price, Walter K. *The Coming Antichrist.* Neptune: Loizeaux Brothers, 1985.

Reid, T.R. *The United States of Europe: The New Superpower and the End of American Supremacy.* New York: Penguin, 2004.

Reymond, Robert L. *Jesus, Divine Messiah: The Old Testament Witness.* Scotland, UK: Christian Focus, 1990.

Rhodes, Ron. *The Coming Oil Storm: The Imminent End of Oil…and Its Strategic Global Role in End-Times Prophecy.* Eugene: Harvest House, 2010.

———. *Five Views on the Rapture: What You Need to Know.* Eugene: Harvest House, 2011.

———. *Is America in Bible Prophecy?: What You Need to Know*. Eugene: Harvest House, 2011.

———. *The Middle East Conflict: What You Need to Know*. Eugene: Harvest House, 2009.

———. *Northern Storm Rising: Russia, Iran, and the Emerging End-Times Military Coalition Against Israel*. Eugene: Harvest House, 2008.

———. *The Popular Dictionary of Bible Prophecy*. Eugene: Harvest House, 2010.

———. *The Topical Handbook of Bible Prophecy*. Eugene: Harvest House, 2010.

———. *Unmasking the Antichrist*. Eugene: Harvest House, 2012.

Rosenberg, Joel. *Epicenter: Why Current Rumblings in the Middle East Will Change Your Future*. Carol Stream: Tyndale House, 2006.

Ryrie, Charles. *Ryrie Study Bible*. Chicago: Moody, 2011.

Stedman, Ray. *God's Final Word: Understanding Revelation*. Grand Rapids: Discovery House, 1991.

Swindoll, Charles. *Insights on Revelation*. Grand Rapids: Zondervan, 2011.

Tenney, Merrill C., ed. *The Zondervan Pictorial Encyclopedia of the Bible*. Grand Rapids: Zondervan, 1978.

Unger, Merrill. *Beyond the Crystal Ball: What Occult Practices Cannot Tell You About Future Events*. Chicago: Moody, 1973.

———. *Unger's Guide to the Bible*. Wheaton: Tyndale House, 1974.

Walvoord, John F. *Daniel*. Revised and edited by Philip E. Rawley and Charles H. Dyer. Chicago: Moody Publishers, 2012.

———. *End Times*. Nashville: Word, 1998.

———. *The Millennial Kingdom*. Grand Rapids: Zondervan, 1975.

———. *The Prophecy Knowledge Handbook*. Wheaton: Victor, 1990.

———. *The Return of the Lord*. Grand Rapids: Zondervan, 1979.

Walvoord, John F., and John E. Walvoord. *Armageddon, Oil, and the Middle East Crisis*. Grand Rapids: Zondervan, 1975.

Whitcomb, John C. *Daniel: Everyman's Bible Commentary*. Chicago: Moody, 1985.

Wiersbe, Warren. *Be Resolute (Daniel): Determining to Go God's Direction*. The BE Series Commentary. Colorado Springs: David C. Cook, 2008.

———. *Be Victorious*. Colorado Springs: David C. Cook, 1985.

NOTES

INTRODUCTION: THE PROPHETIC CONNECTION BETWEEN DANIEL AND REVELATION

1. See Irenaeus of Lyons, *Against Heresies* (*Adversus Haereses*), book 5, chapters 25–30, written circa AD 180; Hippolytus of Rome, *Commentary on Daniel*, written circa AD 202–211, chapters 2–4, 11–12; Hippolytus of Rome, *Treatise on Christ and the Antichrist*, written circa AD 200–211, chapters 19–28; Jerome, *Commentary on Daniel* (*Commentarius in Danielem*), written circa AD 407, preface, chapters 7–12; Victorinus of Pettau, *Commentary on the Apocalypse* (*Commentarius in Apocalypsin*), written circa AD 270–303, chapters 4–20, particularly chapters 7, 13, and 17; Augustine of Hippo, *The City of God* (*De Civitate Dei*), written between AD 413–426, book 18, chapters 23–54 and book 20, chapters 5–24; Bede the Venerable, *Exposition of the Apocalypse* (*Expositio Apocalypseos*), written circa AD 703–709, chapters 7, 11–13, 17–19; Joachim of Fiore, *Exposition of the Apocalypse* (*Expositio in Apocalypsim*), written circa AD 1183–1195; Joachim of Fiore, *The Book of Figures* (*Liber Figurarum*), written circa AD 1200–1202; Martin Luther, *Preface to the Prophet Daniel* (*Praefatio in Prophetam Danielem*), written AD 1530; Martin Luther, *Preface to the Revelation of St. John* (*Praefatio in Apocalypsim S. Joannis*), written AD 1522, revised in 1530 and 1546; Philip Melanchthon, *Annotations on the Book of Daniel* (*Annotationes in Librum Danielem*), written AD 1543; Philip Melanchthon, *Loci Communes Theologici* (*Loci Communes*), first published AD 1521, with revisions in later editions; John Knox, *Selected Writings of John Knox*, various writings from the 1550s and 1560s; Jonathan Edwards, *Notes on the Apocalypse*, written circa AD 1739–1757, published posthumously; Jonathan Edwards, *A History of the Work of Redemption*, written AD 1739, published 1774.

DANIEL—DAY 8: DANIEL REVEALS THE MEANING OF THE DREAM TO NEBUCHADNEZZAR

1. John F. Walvoord, *Daniel* (Chicago: Moody, 2012), Kindle edition, location 1512.

DANIEL—DAY 14: NEBUCHADNEZZAR REVEALS HIS SECOND DREAM TO DANIEL

1. Earnest C. Lucas, "Daniel," in John H. Walton, ed., *Zondervan Illustrated Bible Backgrounds Commentary*, vol. 4 (Grand Rapids: Zondervan, 2009), at Daniel 4:11.

DANIEL—DAY 15: DANIEL INTERPRETS THE SECOND DREAM

1. Michael Green, ed., *1,500 Illustrations for Biblical Preaching* (Grand Rapids: Baker Books, 1991), 350.

DANIEL—DAY 23: THE GOD OF DANIEL IS EXALTED

1. R.T. France, *The Living God* (Downers Grove: InterVarsity Press, 1972), 25.

DANIEL—DAY 38: PROPHECIES CONCERNING THE TIME OF THE END

1. Louis Berkhof, *Systematic Theology* (Grand Rapids: Eerdmans, 1982), 147.

BRIDGING DANIEL AND REVELATION

1. Bernard Ramm, *Protestant Bible Interpretation* (Grand Rapids: Baker, 1978), 105.

REVELATION—DAY 13: THE SEVENTH SEAL JUDGMENT

1. Charles Swindoll, *Insights on Revelation* (Grand Rapids: Zondervan, 2011), 127.
2. Skip Heitzig, *You Can Understand the Book of Revelation* (Eugene: Harvest House, 2011), 90.
3. Ed Hindson, *The Book of Revelation: Unlocking the Future* (Chattanooga: AMG, 2002), 99.

REVELATION—DAY 21: THE RISE OF THE ANTICHRIST

1. Walter K. Price, *The Coming Antichrist* (Neptune, NJ: Loizeaux Brothers, 1985), 145.
2. Mark Hitchcock, *The Complete Book of Bible Prophecy* (Wheaton: Tyndale House, 1999), 199-200.

REVELATION—DAY 23: THE RISE OF THE FALSE PROPHET

1. David Reagan, "The Rise and Fall of the Antichrist," Rapture Ready, https://www.raptureready.com/2014/09/07/the-rise-and-fall-of-the-antichrist-by-dr-david-r-reagan/.
2. John F. Walvoord, "Revelation," in *The Bible Knowledge Commentary.*
3. John Phillips, *Exploring Revelation* (Grand Rapids: Kregel, 1987), 171.

REVELATION—DAY 24: THE FALSE PROPHET'S EXALTATION OF THE ANTICHRIST

1. J. Hampton Keathley III, "The Beast and the False Prophet (Rev. 13:1-18)," Bible.org, bible.org/seriespage/beast-and-false-prophet-rev-131-18.

REVELATION—DAY 28: THE FIFTH, SIXTH, AND SEVENTH BOWL JUDGMENTS

1. John F. Walvoord, "Revelation," in The Bible Knowledge Commentary.
2. Charles Ryrie, *The Ryrie Study Bible* (Chicago: Moody Press, 2011).

REVELATION—DAY 30: THE FALL OF COMMERCIAL BABYLON, PART 1

1. Thomas Ice and Timothy Demy, *Prophecy Watch* (Eugene: Harvest House, 1998), 191.

REVELATION—DAY 32: SHOUTS OF HALLELUJAH AND THE MARRIAGE SUPPER OF THE LAMB

1. Arnold Fruchtenbaum, *The Footsteps of the Messiah* (Tustin: Ariel Ministries, 2003), 597.

REVELATION—DAY 36: SATAN'S FINAL REBELLION AND THE GREAT WHITE THRONE

1. Warren Wiersbe, *Be Victorious: Revelation* (Colorado Springs: David C. Cook, 2008), 176.

REVELATION—DAY 37: THE DESCENT OF THE NEW JERUSALEM

1. Albert Barnes, "Revelation," in *Notes on the New Testament* (Grand Rapids: Baker, 1996), 444-445.
2. Cited in Randy Alcorn, *Heaven* (Wheaton: Tyndale, 2004), 125.
3. John Gill, "Hebrews 11:13-16" in The Online Bible.

REVELATION—DAY 38: A DESCRIPTION OF THE NEW JERUSALEM

1. George Marsden, *Jonathan Edwards: A Life* (New Haven: Yale, 2003), 98.
2. Cited in Tim LaHaye, *Revelation: Illustrated and Made Plain* (Grand Rapids: Zondervan, 1975), 315.
3. Cited in John F. Walvoord, *The Revelation of Jesus Christ* (Chicago: Moody, 1966), 332.
4. Gary R. Habermas and J.P. Moreland, *Immortality: The Other Side of Death* (Nashville: Thomas Nelson, 1992), 185.

REVELATION—DAY 39: THE DELIGHTS OF THE NEW JERUSALEM

1. Randy Alcorn, *Heaven* (Wheaton: Tyndale, 2004), 169-170.
2. Barry Morrow, *Heaven Observed: Glimpses of Transcendence in Everyday Life* (Colorado Springs: NavPress, 2001), 324.
3. Cited in "Revelation," *Wycliffe Bible Commentary* (Chicago: Moody, 1960), 1,524.

POSTSCRIPT

1. John Wenham, *The Enigma of Evil: Can We Believe in the Goodness of God?* (Grand Rapids: Zondervan, 1985), 55.
2. Philip Yancey, *Where Is God When It Hurts?* (Grand Rapids: Zondervan, 1977), 176.
3. J.I. Packer, ed., *Alive to God: Studies in Spirituality* (Downers Grove: InterVarsity, 1992), 163.

SCRIPTURE COPYRIGHT NOTIFICATIONS

OTHER GREAT HARVEST HOUSE BOOKS BY RON RHODES

Basic Bible Prophecy

40 Days Through Genesis

40 Days Through Daniel

40 Days Through Revelation

40 Days Through Bible Prophecy

The Big Book of Bible Answers

Commonly Misunderstood Bible Verses

Find It Fast in the Bible

A Popular Survey of Apologetics for Today

The Popular Dictionary of Bible Prophecy

Understanding the Bible from A to Z

8 Great Debates of Bible Prophecy

Bible Prophecy Under Siege

Cyber Meltdown

New Babylon Rising

End Times Super Trends

Jesus and the End Times

The End Times in Chronological Order

The Complete Reference Guide to Bible Prophecy

Northern Storm Rising

Unmasking the Antichrist

Spiritual Warfare in the End Times

Israel on High Alert

Secret Life of Angels

What Happens After Life?

Why Do Bad Things Happen If God Is Good?

Wonder of Heaven

Reasoning from the Scriptures with the Jehovah's Witnesses

Reasoning from the Scriptures with Mormons